Mark Bittman

THE FOOD MATTERS COOK BOOK

500 Revolutionary Recipes for Better Living

Simon & Schuster
New York London Toronto Sydney

Simon & Schuster
1230 Avenue of the Americas
New York, NY 10020

First Simon & Schuster hardcover edition October 2010

SIMON & SCHUSTER and colophon are registered trademarks of Simon & Schuster, Inc.

For information about special discounts for bulk purchases, please contact Simon & Schuster Special Sales at 1-866-506-1949 or business@simonandschuster.com.

The Simon & Schuster Speakers Bureau can bring authors to your live event. For more information or to book an event contact the Simon & Schuster Speakers Bureau at 1-866-248-3049 or visit our website at www.simonspeakers.com.

Designed by Davina Mock-Maniscalco

Manufactured in the United States of America

10 9 8 7 6 5 4 3 2 1

Library of Congress Cataloging-in-Publication Data

Bittman, Mark.
  The food matters cookbook / by Mark Bittman.
       p. cm

    1. Food. 2. Nutrition. 3. Health. 4. Cooking. 5. Cookbooks. I. Title.
TX353.B614 2010
   641.3—dc22   2010028623

ISBN 978-1-4391-2023-1
ISBN 978-1-4391-4123-6 (ebook)

For my mom and dad

Contents

Introduction

As of this writing, I've been eating like *Food Matters*—the title of this book's predecessor, a book that encourages us to concentrate on eating more plants and fewer animal products and processed foods—for three years. During that period I've met scores if not hundreds of people who have either come to similar diets on their own (it's not that complicated, after all) or read *Food Matters*. The result of my own and just about everyone else's experiences, as well as most of the research studies that have been published since then, have confirmed the conclusion I reached in the first place: If you swap the basic proportions in your diet—increasing unprocessed fruits, vegetables, legumes, nuts, and whole grains—you'll wind up losing weight and improving your overall health while also improving more difficult-to-measure situations like global warming, the environment in general, and animal welfare.

For me, it's been astonishingly easy to remain on a diet that relies on far fewer animal products and processed foods than the typically "American" one. And this has been true even though I'm a journalist and author making his living from cooking, eating, and writing about the same. At no time has my new way of eating made my job—or my life—more difficult. If anything it's easier, since I pay better attention to what goes into my mouth and fully appreciate all sorts of food, now more than ever.

Obviously, I'm not alone in touting a plant-heavy diet. The publication of

Food Matters in January 2009 came at the beginning of the seemingly endless discussion about national health care. But in the course of that debate, more and more people—including outspoken people in the big insurance companies, Big Pharma, and even Big Food—were seeing the link between our diet and major health issues like obesity, diabetes, and heart disease. And now that these links are accepted by the mainstream, so finally, the implications—and the costs—of the typical American diet are getting the attention they deserve.

Food and diet have become integral in food policy discussions, as they relate to issues as wide-ranging as global warming, other environmental issues, and childhood obesity. But it's not only activists and advocates who are influencing the dialogue. Anyone who purchases food—which is to say everyone—has the opportunity to advance the changes advocated in *Food Matters*. I've come to call this "personal food policy," because collectively our choices can stand up to the legislators, lobbyists, and special interest groups that continue to shape the way our food is raised, produced, packaged, shipped, and marketed.

For a variety of reasons, most Americans are more aware of what they're eating than ever before, and many sincerely want to eat better, though they might not know exactly how to do it. I hear this over and over again, and it's not hard to believe, given the often confusing and conflicting information floating around. We're certainly not getting much help from our supermarket shelves or favorite restaurants, where we still have to pass up undeniably tempting and convenient junk to get at the real food.

For a more detailed summary of what "Eating Like Food Matters" means, read on. If none of this is new to you, skip to Part II, page 13—there I discuss the practicalities and principles of the Food Matters kitchen. Part III (beginning on page 35) includes more than 500 recipes and variations that demonstrate just how easy and delicious it can be to become a less-meatarian and begin eating a plant-heavy diet.

PART I: EATING LIKE FOOD MATTERS

Food Policy, Made Personal

When I began work on *Food Matters* in 2007, I had been writing about food for nearly thirty years. So I was in the press box while the American diet underwent huge changes, few of them for the better. Restaurants were booming and people were cooking less and less, while waistlines—and the health problems that accompany excess weight—were growing exponentially.

Yet despite my awareness, my own health had become a problem: I was 57, and 35 pounds overweight. My blood sugar was up, my cholesterol was up, I had sleep apnea, and I had just had knee surgery. My doctor unironically told me to become a vegan. I reminded him that I was a food writer and asked him if he was out of his mind. He reminded me that I was a smart guy and that this was serious. "Figure something out," he said.

I could have seen this coming; I'd just spent a couple of years working on *How to Cook Everything Vegetarian*, in part because I saw the writing on the wall. I knew a plant-heavy diet was a healthier diet; I was just unwilling to make the change. Still, when my marching orders came down, at least I knew a lot about cooking without meat.

And there were further incentives: As if on cue, across my (virtual) desk came a paper from the United Nations called *Livestock's Long Shadow*, a damning report about the connection between industrial livestock and global warming, which I can sum up very easily: The more animals we raise industrially, the more greenhouse gases we are producing. This study estimated that about 70 percent of all the land on earth is devoted to livestock production and generates 18 percent of our annual greenhouse gas emissions. More recently, analysts at an environmental organization called Worldwatch have reported that livestock and their by-products actually may account for as much as 50 percent of global greenhouse gas emissions. In the United States we eat almost 10 billion chickens, pigs, cows, and turkeys each year. And that's just us!

So I put all this together—the state of Americans' eating habits, my own health crisis, the fate of the planet if we don't reduce the number of animals raised and slaughtered—and I came up with a personal action plan: I follow a strict vegan diet until dinnertime—eating only whole grains, beans, vegetables, fruit, nuts, and seeds. After that I eat whatever I want. That's my way; your way may be different. The critical thing is simply to shift the proportions of what you eat and make your diet as plant-heavy as you can.

Because what you *are* eating is just as important as what you're not. When you reduce the amount of animal products—and processed food, but more on that in a minute—you wind up eating a lot more plants: Beans. Whole Grains. Fruits. Vegetables. These are precisely the ingredients that will improve both your health and the health of the planet. All you have to do is change the proportion of some foods you eat in favor of others. It's that simple.

Turning the Tables on Animal Consumption

Americans consume 200 pounds of meat per year (that's about 8 ounces a day, twice the global average), 237 pounds of dairy, and 32 pounds of eggs. That's more than 469 pounds of animal products per capita, over a pound a day. Industrialized production of livestock—factory farming—is the only way to raise enough animals to produce enough animal products for us to eat at this rate.

But factory farming is just that, a way to produce animals the same way we produce widgets, as quickly and efficiently as possible with little or no thought to how they're treated for their brief life spans. I won't get into details here, but industrialized meat production is so colossally inhumane that watching how most livestock is raised and slaughtered in this country would horrify even the most die-hard carnivores. Even if you believe animals were put on earth to be eaten, you probably don't believe they should be tortured. Nor should the workers who raise them, yet the industrial accident rates in meatpacking plants are among the highest of any industry, the wages are among the lowest, and the working conditions among the worst.

But I didn't set out to write *Food Matters* as an animal rights activist, a union organizer, or a vegetarian (remember, I still eat meat). So although I believe that animals' and workers' rights are valid issues, they're far from the only reasons we should reduce our consumption of meat. Equally important are the personal health consequences of overeating meat and the environmental issues I mentioned above.

There are other reasons too: Raising animals to produce food is incredibly inefficient. Consider some numbers: It requires 2.2 calories of fossil fuel to grow 1 calorie of corn, but it takes 40 calories of fossil fuel—in the form of land use, chemical fertilizers (largely petroleum-based), pesticides, machinery, transport, drugs, water, and so on—to produce 1 calorie of beef. At the rate we're going—we currently raise 60 billion animals each year for food, 10 for every one of us on the planet—we will need to double meat production by the year 2050 just to sustain current consumption levels.

How does this translate to what we have for lunch? Like this: If each of us ate the equivalent of three fewer cheeseburgers a week, it would have the same impact on the environment as getting rid of all the SUVs in the country. And if all the land in the United States that's used to raise food for animals each year was instead used to feed humans, we could end world hunger.

Our current consumption of animals is simply not sustainable: It requires more land than exists and taxes the earth's resources beyond what's available. More than twenty years ago, we reached a point known as "ecological overshoot," and now the stress we're putting on the planet—to feed our consumption and absorb our waste—requires 1.3 planet Earths to accommodate it. In other words, our planet needs a year and four months to regenerate the resources we're gobbling up each year. (If the entire world lived the average American lifestyle we would need over 4.5 planet Earths.) And since that obviously isn't possible, we're at the breaking point. The only viable solution is to reduce demand for the foods that take the most resources to raise.

The Story of Junk

The news would be bad enough if meat were our only problem. But, unfortunately, processed food—often a brew of ultrarefined carbohydrates (white flour, sugar, high-fructose corn syrup, and so on) and fats (oils, hydrogenated vegetable shortening or "trans fat," and super-refined animal products) based almost entirely on corn and soybean products (remember, animals are mostly fed corn and soy)—are also a significant part of the typical American diet. These largely empty calories not only have little benefit for human health, they're destructive. And like livestock production, the processing and packaging of junk foods are incredibly energy inefficient. How inefficient? Producing a single can of calorie-free diet soda (which has no caloric or nutritional value) consumes 2,200 calories of energy.

Almost one-third of our total caloric intake comes from nutrient-poor foods like sweets, salty snacks, and fruit drinks. Soda alone accounts for a whopping 7 percent of our total daily caloric intake, with doughnuts, cheeseburgers, pizza, and potato chips not far behind. Incredibly, less than 6 percent of our calories come from unprocessed fruits and vegetables—perhaps the healthiest food group of all. And though manufacturers are in the process of rejigging junk food to reduce or eliminate trans fat (the solid form of vegetable oil that's worse for your heart than butter or lard) their products are still loaded with gratuitous oil and chemicals.

And as our overconsumption of processed foods is exported, so are our ailments: heart disease, stroke, diabetes, and certain cancers are now showing up like never before in places that embrace the American way of eating. The common denominator among these health issues is obesity, which has reached epidemic proportions around the globe; over 1 billion adults are currently considered overweight. (Meanwhile, 1 billion people also go hungry every day.)

Change is in the air: Many public health officials, researchers, legislators, nutritionists, and, yes, even food writers are beginning to compare obesity to smoking and advocating similar policies to combat its impact on public health. Though the United States isn't making the biggest strides—other countries are far ahead on this—there is a growing movement to do something: a soda tax, mandatory labeling on fast-food menus, improved school lunch programs and nutritional education, restricted junk food advertising to children. Everything is now on the table, and it's about time.

In *Food Matters* I outlined how advertising, government supports, and other marketing tools have fueled our overconsumption of processed food and animal products, both here and abroad, for years. It's actually a fascinating history, and if you're interested in learning more about how we got to where we are, I urge you to read those chapters. For our purposes here, I'm more interested in getting you cooking. But before we can do that, let's talk a little more about "sane eating."

An Introduction to Sane Eating

By some calculations, at least 70 percent of the calories Americans eat come from food that is either animal based or highly processed. That leaves less than 30 percent that comes from what we used to call natural or whole foods—meaning fruits, vegetables, whole grains, and legumes. Frankly I think these numbers are conservative; the USDA shows that Americans get about 5 percent of their daily calories from fresh fruit and vegetables. But for argument's sake let's use these numbers.

Think of a seesaw, the heavy side loaded down with animal products and junk, the light side with the food that's actually good for us. Sane eating— eating like food matters—means that we flip this seesaw in the other direction, loading the heavy side with plant foods while minimizing meat, poultry, fish, dairy, and processed foods. In a perfect world the seesaw would instantly invert and we'd all be getting 70 percent of our calories from plants, or even more.

Oddly enough, the beneficial ratio of plant-to-animal foods is similar to the way our ancestors ate, and people still cook and eat that way throughout parts of Asia, Africa, Europe, and Latin America—places where meat and processed foods are too rare or too expensive to dominate the diet. But here in the United States, the combination of government support and industrialized production artificially lowers the price of animal products and processed foods.

Of course, these cheap products still come at a cost: We wind up paying for the cost of obesity and other dietary diseases in our health care system, and there will be huge environmental costs that are only now being recognized. And the price tag is significant. Obesity-related diseases cost the American taxpayers an estimated $840 billion annually. Other costs remain incalculable, but they're equally huge.

Environmental damage, for example, involves every aspect of food production from land clearing to raising and slaughtering livestock, and from transporting and packing to consumption and waste disposal. One expert I've interviewed estimates that producing a single burger gobbles up as much as 50 feet of tropical rainforest, degrades up to 2,500 gallons of water, and loses as much as 300 pounds of topsoil. These numbers are staggering, but they raise some vital questions. How can we possibly put a cost on the loss of such a diverse range of plant species? What if the cure for cancer is in the section of rainforest destroyed by our burger consumption? The discussion quickly becomes philosophical and complex, but we need to raise the issue. If, as some scientists claim, a single burger costs up to $200 in terms of total environmental degradation, but we're only paying $2 for it at the drive-through, how do we reconcile this discrepancy? If the real costs were clearer, wouldn't our consumption patterns change?

Well, they can, and it's easier than you might realize. Rethinking the seesaw might at first feel as extreme as trading in your car for a bicycle, and difficult to maintain over the long term. But small, gradual, incremental change makes it easy and is much more likely to stick. And it's small change that I propose when I talk about sane eating. You might start by eating one less meat-based meal a week or go entirely meatless one day a week. If you also swap your daily vending machine snack for an apple or carrot sticks, that's real progress; build from there.

Sane eating is flexible: You can structure the day strictly to eat "vegan before six," as I do: Avoid all animal and processed foods (except for maybe some milk on your cereal or sugar in your coffee) until dinnertime; then eat whatever you'd like. Or you might substantially reduce the amount of meat, fish, poultry, and dairy you eat at every meal—down to an ounce or two per sitting. Others have great success eating a vegetarian or vegan diet on weekdays and splurging on the weekend. A friend of mine allows himself five meat splurges a month. For some people, eating a big meal at noon works best. You can come up with whatever plan works for you, and change and adjust as needed.

The point is to look at each snack, each meal, each day, and ultimately each month and year, as an opportunity to flip the seesaw, using the basic *Food Matters* principles for sane eating:

1. Eat fewer animal products than average.

The average American eats a half pound of meat each and every day, but no one (least of all me) is suggesting you become a vegetarian: Just aim for less, a pound or two a week. Start thinking about fish, poultry, meat, eggs, and dairy the way traditional cultures do: as a garnish, seasoning, or treat—almost as a condiment. When used as a flavoring ingredient rather than as the focus of the meal, a little meat goes a long way. But don't drive yourself crazy; cream in your coffee or milk on your cereal is totally fine, though experimenting with dairy alternatives is a fine idea too (see page 32).

2. Eat all the plants you can manage.

Breakfast, lunch, dinner, and snacks—turn first to fruits and vegetables. Salads, cooked vegetables, raw vegetables, whole fruits, nuts, seeds . . . eat them with abandon. You really can't go overboard, because when you satisfy your hunger with plants, you're automatically reducing the amount of animal and junk foods and tipping the seesaw in the right direction.

3. Make legumes and whole grains part of your life.

This means every day. These foods are the workhorses of sane eating. Both are loaded with fiber, and beans especially provide a lot of protein. You don't want to gorge on them as you do other plants, but any time you eat beans instead of meat or whole grains instead of white bread, rice, and pasta, you're doing yourself a favor. (This book is loaded with good recipes for cooking beans and grains, so you'll never tire of them.)

4. Avoid processed foods.

You know what they are—foods where most of the calories come from fat or sugar, or those with more than five ingredients, one or more of which you can't pronounce. None of these is going to be as good for you as a piece of fruit or a handful of nuts or other real food. A candy bar or a Pop-Tart won't kill you; it's the continual eating of these kinds of things that will. Save your splurges! (And see Rule 5.)

Many so-called convenience foods are neither convenient nor satisfying. By the time you wait in line at the takeout counter, you could have cooked a bowl of pasta or thrown together a stir-fry. How much time do you waste going back and forth to the vending machine at work? A simple grab bag of nuts, apples, and maybe a few whole grain crackers can easily fuel your entire afternoon.

5. Everything else is a treat—and you can have treats daily.
Sane eating is about moderation, not deprivation, so feel free to eat the foods you'd miss, just in smaller portions and less frequently. Drink wine or beer with dinner or eat a decadent dessert now and then. As long as you're making real changes in the way you eat most of the time, an indulgence every day is well deserved. I'm also confident that as your diet changes, so will the sorts of foods you crave.

Thinking Like Food Matters

Sane eating will naturally change the way you think about putting meals together, no matter where you are. You'll begin to gravitate toward vegetables automatically, and then make room for a little meat on your plate. You might still be making pork chops, but since you'll have just a pound of them in the fridge—you bought a smaller package than you used to—you'll be even more interested in how to season the cabbage and sweet potatoes you're cooking with them.

Since you're changing the way you eat, you'll probably change the way you cook—more imaginatively and creatively. You might find yourself cooking vegetables for breakfast. You'll buy one chicken and use it for two meals instead of one, or serve eight people instead of four. You might add cooked grains to hamburgers, using half as much beef. This line of thinking will soon become second nature.

You'll also pay more attention to labels. Ignore the claims on the package, which are usually misinformation for marketing purposes; just focus on what the product actually contains. If you follow Rule 4 on page 9 ("Avoid processed foods") and keep loading up on fruits and vegetables, you won't give a hoot about whether the carton in your hand is vitamin fortified.

Snacking, eating out, and eating while traveling can be a bit more challenging, but mostly because of how we've been trained to eat, not because finding real food is particularly difficult. I frequently share fish or meat entrées with my dining companions and order vegetable soup, salads, and side dishes. Whenever possible I pack a bag of food and bring it with me, or buy decent snacks or light meals from the produce section of supermarkets: apples, carrots, nuts, whole grain crackers, premade hummus . . . even decent chocolate once in a while.

But I'm not perfect, and you won't be either. That's part of what makes sane eating so appealing: its flexibility and forgiveness. We do what we can, knowing that adjusting our food choices as individuals will have a cumulative effect on all the plants, animals, and humans that share our planet. It's the aggregate of all our small changes that will bring about bigger ones.

PART II: COOKING LIKE FOOD MATTERS

Debunking Some Myths

Cooking is easy. Cooking like food matters is really, really easy. There are no special techniques or equipment. (In fact in most cases you only need one pot or pan.) And the recipes—which are flagged with icons that alert you to those that are particularly fast or can be made ahead—contain common ingredients that can be found in any supermarket. (Though if you want to expand your options, I'll tell you how.) All you'll be doing is cooking with more vegetables. Ordinary vegetables, for that matter.

Whenever I speak in public, someone asks me if they must buy organic, locally raised food to eat like food matters. The answer is an unequivocal *No.* By reducing your consumption of animal products and junk food and increasing the amount of fresh produce in your diet, you'll be eating in a way that's better for you and for the planet. Period. That is the critical step and, fortunately, the easiest one. You can buy everything you need to eat sanely in any supermarket.

But since changing my diet, my awareness of what I'm eating has increased dramatically. And this will happen to you too, especially if you're simultaneously cooking more. You might also see your food choices as a way to "vote with your mouth," in an effort to change our food system. And since you're eating less meat, fish, and poultry, you'll probably have a little extra money in your grocery budget. So maybe you'll start spending more on higher quality food.

Here's the main point: Whatever the degree of your enthusiasm (or advocacy), anyone can cook like food matters. In fact, you could skip directly to the recipes on page 35 and begin now. But if you want to know more about specific ingredients, stocking your pantry, making simple substitutions, generally cooking with more plants, and using the recipes here, read on.

What Ingredients Matter

To cook delicious, fresh, and nourishing food, you're going to have to start with good ingredients—real ingredients. That doesn't necessarily mean expensive ingredients—fancy techniques and equipment are not my style, nor are they particularly useful for cooking like food matters—but it does mean unprocessed food.

Processed ingredients dominate supermarkets, but real ones are easy enough to find. There's a wide variety of shelf-stable staples at supermarkets—grains, beans, spices, produce, of course, and more. There is way more than even a few years ago, and farmers' markets—often the best option—are increasingly widespread.

The recipes in this book all give specific instructions for which items to buy or substitute in any given dish. But here's some general information about how to shop for good ingredients, category by category:

Produce

The more you buy fresh produce, the better you'll get at judging freshness and quality. Start taking some time to look for obvious flaws, rotten spots, mold, or discoloration. Though visual beauty doesn't necessarily translate to flavor (as anyone who's ever bought a ruby-red but wooden-tasting tomato knows), damaged produce rots faster.

Whenever possible, find out where your produce was grown. (As of 2009, most supermarket foods must be labeled with the country of origin.) Even if produce that travels long distances can be less expensive (and even more energy efficient, though that's a topic of debate), it will almost never be as fresh as something grown nearby. I also try to eat fruits and vegetables when they're in season, which helps minimize how much imported produce I buy. Learn to be flexible: whenever something on your shopping list doesn't look fresh or isn't in season, be willing to change your plans; with a few tips for easy substitutions (see page 18), swapping ingredients in recipes is easy.

If you're concerned about consuming pesticides—and who isn't?—you may want to buy organic produce at least some of the time. Produce being sold as "pesticide free," especially from someone you know and trust, is another option, though this distinction isn't regulated. It's especially worthwhile to buy organic when it comes to fruits and vegetables with thin, edible, or no skins, like apples, berries, leafy greens, and potatoes. (Conventional bananas, avocados, onions, and shell beans are less likely to contain traces of pesticides. To see how the most popular fruits and veggies rank for pesticide residue, see http://www.foodnews.org/fulllist.php.) But, again, the important thing is to buy more vegetables. I still believe that in most cases, local, fresh produce trumps industrially grown organic, in large part because buying local usually means encouraging sustainable agriculture and supporting growers within your community. And buying industrially produced organic products— especially processed junk food—is still buying industrially produced food.

In winter it often makes sense to buy frozen vegetables, especially peas, "fresh" shell beans like favas and limas, Brussels sprouts, okra, and corn, all of which retain much of their flavor and texture when frozen. I also buy canned tomatoes for cooking during that part of the year when fresh are not in season.

When you eat like food matters, you go through loads of fruits and vegetables, so keep them handy. A bowl of fruit is a start of course, but you might also set aside a little time every day or two to prepare vegetables for snacking. If, for example, your refrigerator is stocked with a spinner full of salad greens, a container of celery and carrot sticks, and a bowl of steamed broccoli or roasted sweet potatoes, I guarantee you'll eat them.

The Case for Gardening

Gardening is hotter than it has been since World War II, when 40 percent of America's vegetables were grown in our backyards. Today, about a third of all Americans are growing some of their own produce or herbs. When the Obamas planted a vegetable garden on the White House lawn in the spring of 2009, it served to confirm what was happening—a full-blown, homegrown renaissance.

Most people say they garden for "better-tasting food," and that's as good a reason as any. And if you grow food instead of grass, you're using land productively; you can even restore nutrients to it instead of relying on artificial fertilizers.

Anyone with a little time and a little space—even a spare ten square feet or a windowsill for potted herbs—can garden (www.garden.org is a good place to start, but there are literally hundreds of reputable resources). If you can't garden at home, you might consider a community garden, or a cooperative agreement with a neighbor or two.

Substituting Seasonal Produce

Cooking with the seasons allows you to focus on what's available locally and regionally and helps minimize the use of long-hauled fruits and vegetables. This chart—which you can read left to right or vice versa—is half inspirational and half practical, with ideas for exchanging ingredients within a season, or back and forth between seasons. For example, if you want to make a corn recipe in January, I suggest using frozen; but in the dead of winter, you have plenty of options if a recipe calls for cabbage.

Season	Vegetable or Fruit	Easy Substitutions
Winter	Beets	Turnips or rutabagas
	Cauliflower	Broccoli, broccoflower, Romanesco, or broccoli rabe
	Brussels sprouts	Cabbage
	Fennel	Celery
	Oranges	Grapefruit, pomelos, clementines, tangelos, or tangerines
	Cooking greens like kale, chard, escarole, mustard, beet greens, or bok choy	All interchangeable; cooking time will vary depending on the thickness of their leaves and stems; or use cabbage
	Leeks	Onions, shallots, or scallions
	Jícama	Radishes, especially daikon; kohlrabi
	Pineapple	Oranges

Season	Vegetable or Fruit	Easy Substitutions
Spring	Asparagus	Green beans, snap peas, or broccoli rabe
	Lettuce and salad greens like arugula, mesclun, iceberg, romaine, spinach, and so on	Raw, they're all virtually interchangeable
	Tender greens for cooking, like spinach or arugula	Watercress or Napa cabbage
	Rhubarb	Cranberries or tart cherries
	Fava beans	Lima beans or edamame (frozen are fine)
	Snap or snow peas, or fresh peas	Frozen shelled peas
Summer	Mango	Papaya or cantaloupe
	Basil	Cilantro, mint, chives, or parsley
	Peaches	Apricots, plums, or nectarines
	Cherries	Currants, raspberries, blueberries, or grapes; for tart cherries, try cranberries
	Cucumber	Celery, kohlrabi, or water chestnuts
	Corn	Frozen corn
	Tomatoes	Canned tomatoes
	Apricots or plums	Dried apricots or plums
	Bell peppers	Mild cabbage like Napa or Savoy, or frozen bell peppers
Fall	Shallots	Any onion, especially red, or the white part of leeks
	Eggplant	Zucchini or summer squash
	Apples	Pears
	Parsnips	Carrots
	Sweet potatoes	Carrots, parsnips, or winter squash

Beef, Pork, and Lamb

Almost *all* supermarket meat is industrially raised—the animals are confined, fed an unnatural diet, then slaughtered and packaged in factories. That said, there are other options, though none is perfect.

Again, don't think "organic" is an automatic solution: These animals may or may not be treated well or spend much time outdoors (for example, see "Poultry," below). And, of course, eating 5 pounds a week of organic meat and poultry isn't going to help reduce the environmental or moral impact of raising animals for food.

If you want meat from well-treated animals that are fed what they were born to eat and drugged only when they're sick, you can find it. It's expensive, it's not sold everywhere (and it may taste different from what you're used to!), but it's out there. And increasingly, both in cities and out, you can buy such meat from local farmers, which is really the best of all worlds. Visit farmers' markets, local food stores as opposed to chains, and co-ops, and talk to your friends. Since you're going to be eating a lot less meat, paying more for it may not be so painful, and it will raise the overall quality of what you're putting in your body.

No matter what kind of meat, poultry, or fish you buy, cooking with less takes a little practice. Since meat is so often sold in large quantities, the simplest thing is to buy what looks good, then divide it up when you get home and freeze what you don't need for another time. (If you're dealing with a butcher or fishmonger, just ask for smaller portions.) A kitchen scale is a handy tool until you get used to visualizing what 8 or 12 ounces of meat looks like.

In this book, the recipes that call for beef, pork, or lamb usually suggest the most full-flavored cut that is appropriate to the cooking technique. If more than one cut is an option, I'll say so; if not, stick to the recipe for best results.

Poultry

The pitfalls of the USDA's labeling guidelines are most evident with chicken. (See the paragraphs that follow.) I avoid mass-produced supermarket birds, since, even more than beef and pork, they're a product of factories and an even worse eating experience. Recently, several major chicken producers have reduced or in some cases eliminated the routine use of antibiotics with their birds, though this change does not translate into better conditions for the chickens—or a better-tasting final product.

So-called natural labels don't guarantee humane conditions or a lack of prophylactic drugs, so you've got to look for (and try to verify) whatever claims are made on the label. A "premium" distinction means nothing—some premium brands produce decently raised, decently flavored birds, but others are little more than factory farm chickens with a heftier price tag.

Kosher and organic chickens are at least produced according to well-defined rules. Birds labeled with the USDA organic seal must live free of cages, have access to the outdoors (usually quite limited), not receive antibiotics or other drugs, and eat only organic, non-GMO (genetically modified organism) feed. Kosher chickens generally start with better breeds than conventional chickens, have been slaughtered according to religious law (which may or may not be somewhat less horrific, depending on the company), and are presalted, which helps boost both flavor and texture.

"Free-range" chicken can be a bit of a scam—the terms "free range" and "free roaming" are regulated by the USDA, but all they mean is that the birds had some access to the outdoors. They might still spend most of their life in a tiny cage.

Again, your best bet is usually a locally raised chicken, available at farmers' markets, specialty stores, and even some regular markets. Though more expensive—sometimes incredibly so, I'm sorry to say—at least you can find out how the bird was raised. And the price will remind you that meat is a treat and something that cannot be taken for granted.

For what it's worth, ducks and turkeys are subject to the same labeling distinctions as chickens. Supermarket turkeys—and chickens and ducks and geese for that matter—are bred to grow abnormally large breasts and are, therefore, nothing like the birds that used to grace our holiday tables. But as with chickens, there are other options available.

Seafood

Eating fish is no longer the simple pleasure it was for millennia. Although wild fish is by far the healthiest animal product you can eat, there's simply not enough of it to go around; we must see it as a treat, so I advocate choosing seafood that's not only safe (uncontaminated with lead, mercury, or other pollutants) but also sustainable.

Farmed seafood may become a viable alternative to wild fish, but the impact aquaculture has on the environment and safety is not what we'd want it to be. And most of it still tastes bland at best and muddy at worst. (One notable exception is the time-honored tradition of farming mollusks, like clams and oysters; this is not only sustainable but also yields a good product.)

Fish is a fast-changing field, so it's worth an occasional visit to the websites of the Blue Ocean Institute *http://www.blueocean.org/home*, Monterey Bay Aquarium *http://www.montereybayaquarium.org/cr/seafoodwatch.aspx*, and Environmental Defense Fund *http://www.edf.org/page.cfm?tagID=17694*. But the specifics you need to make truly informed decisions are difficult to come by. For one thing, the species susceptible to overfishing change constantly. For another, we're at the mercy of supermarket labels, restaurant chefs, and fishmongers to tell us the truth. And they may not even know what they're really buying or selling.

The seafood recipes here represent a new approach for me. In most cases, the ingredients list (for example) "sturdy" or "firm" thick white fish fillets or steaks, in which case I'm suggesting you choose something sustainable—and, ideally, local—that will stand up to turning in a pan or on a grill. What I'm saying is that the name of the fish is less important than either the qualities the recipe needs or the practicality of finding the fish. If I call for "cod," there's both a chance of your not finding it or of it being overfished, or imported from 10,000 miles away. If I call for "thick white fillets," you have a better shot.

When recipes call for specific seafood like shrimp, crab, clams or mussels, scallops, mackerel, or in rare cases salmon or tuna, it's best to choose American-caught or -raised over their foreign counterparts, which tend to be less well monitored and regulated.

Fish and shellfish have a short shelf life, so check out as many fish counters as it takes to find one that's spotlessly clean and sells the best-cared-for seafood. Though superfresh is ideal, whether the fish is "fresh" or frozen matters less than how it looks and smells *now*. Trust your nostrils; good fish has little or no smell other than that of seawater, and firm, unblemished, non-gaping flesh. Try to avoid prewrapped fish; it might look nice, but you can't really know how fresh it is until you smell it.

Once you get seafood home, the best way to store it is in a pan packed with ice. If that's not possible, keep it in the coldest part of the refrigerator (usually at the back of the top-to-middle shelves) and cook it as soon as you can.

Substituting Seafood, Poultry, Meat, and Dairy

Although beef and pork have many differences, they—and other meats, fish, and poultry—are (to beginning cooks at least) surprisingly interchangeable in recipes. Just use your judgment when seasoning, so you don't overpower mild or subtle flavors. That said, here are some suggestions for making simple swaps:

Foods	Easy Substitutions
Shrimp	Scallops, squid, or crawfish
Lump crab meat	Cooked lobster or shrimp
Mussels	Clams or oysters
Tuna	Mackerel, swordfish, or sardines
Salmon	Trout, char
Boneless chicken breasts	Boneless chicken thighs (they generally take a little longer to cook); pork, turkey, or veal cutlets
Chicken (cutlets, boneless parts, or cut up for stir-fry)	Pork (chops, tenderloin medallions, or cut-up shoulder), or turkey
Ground beef	Ground pork, turkey, chicken, lamb, or shrimp
Short ribs	Lamb shanks, beef brisket, or bone-in chicken or turkey legs
Beef roasts	Lamb shoulder, pork shoulder, or boneless chicken thighs
Boneless or bone-in pork shoulder	Boneless or bone-in fresh ham, beef chuck, or lamb shoulder; or beef chuck or brisket
Butterflied leg of lamb	Flank steak or tri-tip
Bone-in leg of lamb	Pork rib roast
Sour cream	Yogurt (drained if possible)
Parmesan cheese	Pecorino Romano, grana Padano, dry Jack, Manchego, or Asiago
Heavy cream	Half-and-half (unless you're whipping it)
Crème fraîche	Heavy cream, lightly whipped

Eggs and Dairy

Organic standards are the same for laying hens as for chickens raised for meat, and many of the same misleading claims are made about eggs. But neither "free range" nor "cage free" tell you much about how the hens were treated. Other popular egg labels include "omega-3" (the hens were fed an omega-3 rich diet to increase the amount of supposedly beneficial fat in their eggs—a marketing ploy) and "vegetarian" (the chickens weren't fed animal products; this isn't nationally regulated). There are also a few third-party egg labeling groups interested in animal welfare; "Certified Humane," "Free Farmed," and "Animal Care Certified" all refer to the chickens' living conditions regarding air, water, food, noise, stress, and living space.

Note that egg grade, as determined by the USDA, is based on appearance, shape, and quality of an egg. AA and A are nearly identical; B eggs are lower grade but are generally sold to industrial kitchens, not individual consumers. The USDA also judges eggs based on size; extra-large and large are the most common and fairly interchangeable. I assume you're using large eggs in the recipes here.

It boils down to this: If you can, buy eggs from a local farmer whom you trust.

When it comes to dairy products, though, local is not necessarily better; real Parmesan cheese, for instance, comes only from Italy. But there are many burgeoning cheesemaking regions in the United States, and fresh dairy products from small, independent dairies are widely available at farmers' markets. Sometimes local milk isn't homogenized, so the cream rises to the top; this is great if you want to make your own yogurt or cheese.

You can also buy national brands of organic milk at most supermarkets, but be skeptical. On many large-scale organic dairy operations, cows are confined in feedlots no different from those on conventional dairy operations, and organic milk might actually be reconstituted from powdered milk shipped from across the globe.

I use primarily whole milk and yogurt, which give you the best flavor and texture, though you can substitute reduced-fat (2 percent) or low-fat (1 percent) milk if you feel it necessary. (Fat-free, skim, and nonfat—which all mean the same thing—tend to be insipid and watery.) In baking recipes I sometimes call for buttermilk, which is a thick, cultured liquid that's easy enough to find in supermarkets. Yogurt is a perfect substitute, or you can sour milk by adding 1 tablespoon white vinegar to 1 cup regular milk and letting it sit for a few minutes.

Cream and half-and-half are valuable ingredients in the Food Matters kitchen, since a tiny amount can make a huge difference in flavor and texture. Look for brands that aren't ultrapasteurized and don't have any additives or emulsifiers. Butter is another irreplaceably rich ingredient that you'll often want in small quantities; buy unsalted (also called sweet) butter—since salt acts as a preservative, unsalted butter tends to be fresher. (This also means that you get to control the amount of salt you add to recipes.) Many European-style, higher fat butters are now available; they tend to be of good quality. (You can freeze butter if you like.)

The Basic Food Matters Pantry

When I say basic, I mean basic—these are the handful of ingredients you should always keep around for quick, easy, Food Matters meals. As your repertoire and interests expand, you'll want to start adding unfamiliar foods (see The Advanced Food Matters Pantry, below). In general, it pays to buy items in bulk when possible; they tend to be cheaper and are often of better quality than their prepackaged counterparts (they also require less packaging). That said, here goes:

Grains. Buy an assortment of whole and ground grains. My short list: short- and long-grain brown rice, medium- or coarse-ground cornmeal (which can serve as grits and polenta), rolled and/or steel-cut oats, bulgur, and whole wheat flour. Whole grains, because of their natural oils, tend to go rancid faster than those that are processed and milled to remove their fattier outer layers. So if you won't go through them quickly, store them in the freezer. (For more about specific grains, see the sidebar on page 268.)

Beans. I cook my own beans 90 percent of the time (there's no need to soak them), though canned—more expensive and not quite as good—are undeniably handy. I store both and recommend you do too. (It's worth noting that there's concern about the safety of bisphenol A or BPA, the plastic used to line most canned foods—see the "Canned tomatoes" entry on page 27.) When you cook your own, beans become a convenient pantry item since after cooking, they can be refrigerated for days or frozen for months. Cannellini or other white beans and chickpeas are good ones to start with (if you like red beans or black beans, by all means start there), as are lentils, which cook in a half hour, sometimes less.

Dried pasta and noodles. The best dried pasta comes from Italy (why wouldn't it?). I use both semolina (white) and whole wheat pasta but now reserve regular pasta for treats. Buy whatever shapes you like; it's nice to have some variety. Asian noodles are also extremely useful; I like soba, since it's either all or part whole grain, and brown-rice fettuccine is starting to win me over, but thin white rice noodles are also great to have on hand.

Extra virgin olive oil. Your go-to fat for cooking, roasting, pan-frying, and drizzling. Don't worry about country of origin or price, unless you're an aficionado with a big budget. Since it goes rancid in sunlight or near heat within a month or so after opening, keep only what you'll use in a couple of weeks on the counter; store the bulk of it in a dark cupboard or in the refrigerator. (It will become cloudy and thick when chilled but will revert to its normal texture and color at room temperature.)

Other oils. For high-heat cooking and most deep-frying, or when a dish calls for non-Mediterranean flavors, you'll want something other than olive oil. My recipes call for "vegetable oil," meaning you can use any neutral-flavored oil, like grapeseed, sunflower, safflower, corn, or peanut, which is best for Asian dishes. (I don't like the taste of canola oil.) Look for minimally processed, high-quality, cold-pressed oil whenever possible.

Long-keeping vegetables and fruits. There are vegetables you'll use almost daily, especially those known as "aromatics": onions, garlic, shallots, carrots, and celery. Others—cabbage, root vegetables, potatoes, of course, and winter squash—also store well. It's not a bad idea to keep a few frozen vegetables on hand, too—spinach, peas, and corn are good, providing they are not processed with any chemicals (most are not). Citrus and apples keep in the refrigerator for weeks, which makes them infinitely handy.

Dried fruit, nuts, and seeds. Excellent both for snacking and for cooking. Because of their high fat content, nuts and seeds go bad quickly, so store them in the fridge or freezer if you're not planning to use them within a couple of weeks. I include unsweetened coconut and nut butters in this category, too, especially peanut butter and tahini, both of which can become the foundation for excellent sauces. Dried fruits (including but not limited to raisins) add a nice touch to pilafs, bean dishes, and desserts.

Fish, meat, poultry, and dairy. There is obviously a place for animal products in the Food Matters pantry. These are the most important:

>   **Eggs:** Possibly the most useful of all animal products.
>
>   **Parmesan cheese:** An expensive investment but not bad per serving (it lasts forever) and grated over almost any salad or pasta dish, just killer. It absolutely must be genuine Parmigiano-Reggiano; don't waste your money on anything else.
>
>   **Bacon:** Keep a hunk in the freezer or fridge and use it an ounce at a time for seasoning. Prosciutto, guanciale, and other cured and/or smoked meats serve much the same purpose.
>
>   **Butter:** As an occasional alternative to olive oil in cooking or flavoring, a real pleasure. Often just a tablespoon makes an impact.
>
>   **Canned tuna and anchovies:** Preferably packed in olive oil.

Canned tomatoes. In most parts of the country, good fresh tomatoes are a summer luxury; luckily, canned and boxed are a truly decent (not to mention easy and inexpensive) substitute. Diced tomatoes make life a little easier, though I usually buy whole canned (preferably plum) tomatoes, which are more versatile, and chop them myself when necessary. (Stay away from crushed or puréed, which are too watery.) Tomato paste—especially from a tube—is also a boon. Always look for canned tomatoes with few or no additives and seasonings. And because there is growing concern about the safety of the plastic coating used to line the inside of most cans (known as BPA or bisphenol A), you might want to seek out processed tomatoes that are packed in boxes or jars, or look for cans that are labeled BPA-free.

Salt and black pepper. With good ingredients and simple cooking, these gain importance. Invest in a grinder and buy whole black peppercorns; the difference is huge. For salt, kosher (which is not iodized like table salt) has a pure flavor I love (I like the feel of it for cooking, too). Sea salt is marginally better than mined salt. Trendy, expensive salts are unnecessary.

Fresh herbs. If you were to buy a bunch of every type of herb you see whenever you went to the store, you'd be wasting your money—and a lot of herbs, since it's impossible to use that much. Instead, buy a couple at a time—the ones that look best—and use them until you need more; many are interchangeable anyway. Parsley is the most useful (and best in winter), but basil, mint, dill, rosemary, thyme, and cilantro are also great to have around. Rinse the entire bunch and put them in a cup or vase of water—like flowers—then cover with a plastic bag for even longer keeping, and refrigerate.

Spices, chiles, and dried herbs. For the most part, these are inexpensive, last a long time (I figure a year, but many keep them around longer), and don't take up much room, so buy as big an assortment as you can. Primary spices (for me; you may feel differently): cardamom, cumin, fennel seeds, pimentón (smoky Spanish paprika), cinnamon, coriander, ground ginger, nutmeg. Dried herbs are trickier, because other than sage, thyme, rosemary, oregano, and tarragon, they're generally way inferior to fresh. It pays to have a variety of chiles on hand, too: hot (like Thai), mild (like pasilla), and perhaps smoked (like chipotle). For blends, you'll want curry and chili powders. Ethnic markets and online specialists (like Penzeys, www.penzeys.com) are great resources for all these items.

Vinegar. If you buy only one vinegar, make it sherry vinegar, which is the most versatile and most flavorful and the best buy for the money. Keep in mind that genuine sherry vinegar has "vinagre de Jerez" somewhere on its label. My next choice is rice vinegar, which is low in acid and extremely useful for Asian-style dishes. If you like acidity as a seasoning or eat a lot of salads, good balsamic, red wine, and white wine vinegars are also handy. And when vinegar appears in a recipe here, feel free to add more to taste.

Soy sauce. Look for brands that contain no more than soy, wheat, salt, water, and bacteria, and avoid those that contain textured vegetable protein (TVP) or caramel coloring.

Other condiments. Good-quality coarse and/or smooth mustards; ketchup if you're a fan (I am); mayonnaise (you can make your own, of course). Barbecue sauce, hot sauce, salsas, pickles, relishes—these are all optional but, unless they're loaded with sugar, completely fine.

Sweeteners. Sugar is fine, in moderation, but it's a little one-dimensional; maple syrup and honey deliver both flavor and sweetness. (See Refined Sugars and Other Sweeteners, page 554.)

Baking soda, baking powder, instant yeast, and white flour. Requisite for most baking, obviously.

A Quick Guide to Changing the Seasonings in Virtually Any Recipe

You know you're becoming an intuitive cook when you start changing recipes, and one of the easiest ways to do that is with basic flavorings. Here are the basics:

Herbs: Fresh herbs will always have a brighter flavor than dried. Use stronger herbs like rosemary, thyme, tarragon, sage, and oregano more sparingly than their tamer cousins (parsley, basil, cilantro, mint, dill, chives). As a rule of thumb: In dishes that serve four, it is rare that you'll need more than a tablespoon of the strong herbs (a teaspoon of fresh tarragon is usually enough for most dishes) and one-quarter to one-half cup of the mild ones. For dried, use even less.

Aromatics: Garlic, onions, shallots, scallions, and fresh ginger can be swapped for one another or used in combination. Increase or decrease the quantity to your taste: For some people, a clove of garlic is garlicky enough for a whole dish; for others, ten cloves aren't enough.

Spices and chiles: If you're new to improvising, spice blends (like curry and chili powders or other specialized blends) add the most bang for the buck and are easier (and less risky) than experimenting with combining single spices. Fresh hot chiles, dried and smoked chiles, and canned chiles can all be switched for one another, added to almost any dish, or omitted from any dish if you don't like things too fiery.

Sweeteners: Hardly compulsory, but a teaspoon or more of sugar, honey, molasses, or some chopped dried fruit can complement and enhance many savory dishes.

Nuts and seeds: Consider virtually all nuts and seeds interchangeable—and remember that almost all varieties taste better if you toast them first. (Heat them gently in a dry skillet, shaking occasionally, until fragrant.) Adding nuts to a dish as a garnish adds another layer of texture and flavor, as well as a little bit of protein.

Acids: Many dishes—especially those high in fat—benefit from a little acidity to counterbalance the richness. Just be careful not to overdo it. Balsamic vinegar, sherry vinegar, red wine vinegar, and lemon juice are used often in European dishes; rice vinegar and lime juice are more common in Asian recipes; orange juice can be used in either.

Fats: Oils and butter have their own unique flavors (see pages 26 and 27), so when in doubt, go with a neutral-tasting vegetable oil. Melted butter, of course, adds creaminess (don't use butter in dishes that are going to be served cold, or it'll congeal). Cream and coconut milk are also good substitutes—in small doses—for oils and butter.

Salty additions: Cheese, cured meats, olives, capers, anchovies, and soy or fish sauce can add a nice hit of saltiness (as well as a rich texture); when replacing one with another, remember that a little goes a long way.

The Advanced Food Matters Pantry

If you have the room, the money, and the curiosity, you'll soon want to add to your pantry; most of these foods keep for long periods of time, so it's easy enough to give yourself more options, all without frequent shopping. My kitchen has most of these things in it most of the time:

More grains and beans. Some of my personal favorites: quinoa (perennially underappreciated, and really fantastic), farro, hominy (with all the flavor you love in corn tortillas), and whole wheat couscous (actually a pasta, but used as if it were a grain). For beans, try pintos, black beans, or black-eyed peas; frozen favas, lima beans, edamame, or other fresh shell beans. Red lentils and yellow and green split peas are great for dals and soups. Check out, too, the pretty, flavorful (and generally expensive) so-called heirloom beans, which are available at natural food stores or by mail order.

Dried mushrooms. Soak them in boiling water until they're soft (anywhere from 10 to 30 minutes, depending on how dehydrated they are) and you've got two super-flavorful ingredients: the mushrooms themselves and the soaking liquid. Porcini (cèpes) and shiitakes are the most versatile. Buy the first in bulk and the second in Asian stores; do not buy little tiny (overpriced) packages at the supermarket.

Bread crumbs. It's easy to make these yourself—just put stale bread in a food processor and crush—but if you must buy, panko (Japanese bread crumbs) are best. (Some are even made with whole wheat flour now.)

Capers. Packed in vinegar or salt, their briny flavor and subtle crunch are incomparable. Especially valuable for people who don't like or won't eat anchovies.

Miso. Few single ingredients are more complex than miso paste, which is made from fermented soybeans, rice or barley, and salt. Stir it into soups for instant complexity, or just add water for a quick sauce, marinade, or dressing. White, red, and brown are virtually interchangeable as long as you keep in mind that darker miso is stronger in flavor.

Sesame oil. Made of roasted sesame seeds and sold in Asian markets and many supermarkets. Adds a smooth, fragrant finish to stir-fries and other Asian dishes.

Sea greens (seaweed). Flavorful and high in protein, vitamins, and minerals. Hijiki, kombu (kelp), and nori (laver) are particularly fun to use in salads and stir-fries. Soak in hot water until pliable (from 5 minutes for the thin types to 20 minutes or more for kombu and other thick leaves).

Coconut milk. Unsweetened coconut milk (even the "light" or reduced-fat kind if you're worried about extra calories) adds flavorful creaminess to all sorts of dishes, but especially curries.

Tofu. Refrigerated bricks come packed in their own liquid and will keep for a few weeks. Bulk (unpackaged) tofu must be kept in water in the fridge; change the water every day or two and use it as soon as you can. (If it starts to smell sour, cut a slice from every side before using.) Some tofu is sold in shelf-stable boxes, doesn't need to be refrigerated, and keeps for months. Pressed tofu also keeps a long time.

Interesting Asian seasonings. Fermented black beans, nam pla (fish sauce), hoisin sauce, tamarind paste, curry paste, mirin, and sake are all worth your consideration if you want to make a lot of Asian dishes. If you start getting enthusiastic about spices, buy them whole: they're cheaper and keep longer and have better flavor than ground. Toast lightly in a dry skillet (see page 29), then grind them in small quantities in a (clean) coffee grinder or with a mortar and pestle.

Other flours. If you're a regular baker or someone who wants to explore the world of sweet and savory baking, you'll want brown-rice flour, masa harina, buckwheat flour, whole wheat pastry flour, chickpea flour, and maybe more. (See page 518 for some specific descriptions.)

Wine. If you drink it, you already have it; a splash in place of water or stock is rarely a bad idea.

Making Meals Vegan

If you were a full-time vegan, you probably wouldn't be reading this book. But maybe you're interested in taking even more animal foods out of your diet. The recipes here are a good place to start, since the focus is always on vegetables, grains, or beans and the substitutions are relatively easy.

Where vegan dishes often disappoint is not flavor but texture. It's tough to mimic the cooking characteristics of eggs, butter, cream, and meat. But as long as you pay attention to include foods that deliver some crunch, chew, heft, and creaminess, you can cook very well without using any animal products at all.

Commercial meat substitutes—those patties, burgers, "riblets," and sausage links made of processed soy protein, industrial seasonings, and who knows what else—always taste like, well, fake meat. In my world, they're a small step above junk food, and I come down—as always—on the side of real food.

But tofu and tempeh, and to a lesser degree, seitan (a sliceable food made from concentrated wheat gluten), can serve as good stand-ins for animal products. You can stir-fry strips of firm or pressed tofu or seitan, for example, just as you would chicken, pork, or shrimp, and crumbled tempeh is a fair approximation, texture-wise, of ground beef. Beans, of course, when mashed and mixed with vegetables or grains and spices, make excellent burgers.

There are decent vegan substitutes for other animal foods, too, but they're nowhere near perfect. (Eggs are nearly impossible to replace, and without them or butter you'll never be able to duplicate the magic of most baked foods; but you can get some surprisingly good results, as you'll see with the desserts on pages 571 and 579. Here's a quick rundown of direct substitutions for vegan cooking:

Instead of . . .	Use . . .
Milk	For sweetness: nut milk For neutrality: oat milk or rice milk For creaminess: soy milk For thickness and richness: coconut milk
Butter	Vegetable or olive oil, frozen or refrigerated until solid and opaque

Instead of . . .	Use . . .
Honey	Maple syrup Brown sugar warmed in a little water
Eggs (in baking; per egg)	2 tablespoons water mixed with 1 tablespoon vegetable oil and 1 teaspoon cornstarch 3 tablespoons silken tofu

Cheese	For richness and flavor contrast: ground nuts or
	    toasted bread crumbs
	For creaminess: silken tofu or crumbled firm
	    tofu

A Word About Technique

Cooking is cooking. I don't use any techniques that everyone else doesn't use (in fact, I probably use fewer and I tend to use simple, visual terms like "cook" and "bubble" instead of "sauté" and "simmer"), but you'll be amazed how efficiently meals come together when you free yourself from the American convention of putting meat at the center of the plate with a starch and a vegetable on the side.

I do increasing amounts of one-pot cooking, building dishes by, for example, searing a little meat or poultry in a skillet, then removing it once it's brown, adding some aromatic vegetables to the fat and cooking them until they're fragrant, then tossing in more vegetables, grains, beans, spices, liquid, and so on—finally, I add back the meat and heat it through a minute. This fluid style combines various techniques, saves time, and results in full-flavored, nice-looking dishes that don't take a lot of work. Other dishes come together in a roasting pan, under the broiler, on the grill, or even on the plate.

I'm also keen on serving dishes at room temperature, since many plant foods don't need to be piping hot to be thoroughly enjoyable. (The recipe directions indicate which dishes work best this way and how long ahead of time they can be made.) This takes the pressure off of timing everything to be ready simultaneously and makes the cooking experience more enjoyable.

Using *The Food Matters Cookbook*

The Food Matters Cookbook is a little unusual; it contains nine chapters, none of which focus on meat, poultry, fish, eggs, or dairy. But this is by no means a vegetarian cookbook. Rather, it's a cookbook that—like the entire Food Matters concept—encourages you to think about food proportions differently, by considering grains, vegetables, and legumes as the center of your meal and animal products as garnishes, flavor enhancements, treats, and treasures. This means setting aside preconceived notions of a square meal consisting of a serving each of meat, starch, and vegetables. Instead, you'll find all these components integrated in (I hope) interesting, novel, and appealing ways.

With the exception of desserts and other dishes that take extra time to make but store well (like some bean dishes, for example), the recipes in this book generally serve four. This estimate is based on the assumption that you're serving the dish as the main focus of a meal, with perhaps one or two simple sides—like plain steamed vegetables or a salad—and that the people you're serving are hungry. If you're serving a dish as a snack or appetizer, or alongside several other equally hearty dishes, any recipe might easily stretch to feed six to eight.

To build feasts around these recipes, serve a soup or appetizer first, and add cooked vegetables or salads on the side (there are recipes here for those, too, of course). Or cook several dishes from different chapters and put them all out at once. This is an especially nice way to entertain since (as I mentioned above) so much of the food here can be served at room temperature.

Onward. Remember the seesaw!

Key to the Icons.

- **F** **Fast.** If you have even a little experience, you can make these dishes in 30 minutes or less.
- **M** **Make-Ahead.** You can prepare the dish, either in full or to a certain point, and store it (usually in the fridge) before finishing or serving it, or serve it warm or at room temperature.
- **P** **Pantry Staple.** These are the simple grain, bean, vegetable, and condiment preparations that I consider basic and essential. I suggest that you make pantry staples frequently and in large quantities, so that you'll have them at your fingertips when you need them. (For lists that sort recipes by their icon, see pages 589–603.)

PART III: THE RECIPES

Appetizers and Snacks

Why deny it? When you eat more plant foods and fewer animal products, you're probably going to eat more often—so snacking takes on increased importance. This is a good thing: Most current research indicates that eating several small meals is better for your metabolism, energy level, and weight management than piling it on your plate three times a day.

This chapter, then, takes on more significance than the typical appetizer chapter, with plenty of satisfying tidbits that mimic the sweetness, saltiness, and crunch of the things you might crave from packages, but without their downsides. These are recipes you can make days ahead of time, grab fast, pack up to go, whatever works.

But it's important to note the other—even easier—snacks that take almost no work at all. It's cliché, I know, but fruit, nuts, celery and carrot sticks, peanut butter on a whole grain cracker, last night's leftover vegetables, more fruit—these are foods that often get me through the day.

In any case, the dishes here are mostly foods you can bring to your mouth with fingers, toothpicks, or skewers. All are designed to work for both everyday eating and casual celebrations. In other words, there is nothing too fancy or time consuming, and since all of the more substantial recipes make between four and eight servings, you can eat them alone as a light meal, part of a multicourse feast or buffet, or as a tasty little something before dinner.

Seasoned Popcorn

Makes: 4 to 8 servings   Time: About 10 minutes

Real hot popcorn is one of nature's ultimate convenience foods. I can't say this strongly enough: There's no reason to use microwavable packages, no matter how "natural" they claim to be. Any popcorn can be microwaved, as you'll see below.

Toss the popcorn with extra ingredients while it's still warm and the seasonings will stick pretty well, even without adding any more fat. You can even cook popcorn in olive oil as long as you lower the heat as needed to keep it from burning; the flavor is delicious.

> 2 to 3 tablespoons vegetable oil
>
> ½ cup popping corn
>
> 2 to 4 tablespoons butter or olive oil, optional
>
> Salt (and other seasonings from the list that follows if you like)

1. Put the vegetable oil in a large, deep pan (6 quarts or so). Turn the heat to medium, add 3 kernels of corn, and cover.

2. When the kernels pop, remove the lid and add the remaining corn. Cover and shake the pot, holding the lid on. Cook, shaking the pot occasionally, until the popping sound stops after about 5 minutes. Meanwhile, melt the butter or gently warm the olive oil if you're using it.

3. Turn the popcorn into a large bowl; drizzle with butter or olive oil if you like, and sprinkle with salt while tossing the popcorn. Serve immediately.

Microwave Popcorn (Makes 2 to 4 servings). In a small glass container, or a brown paper lunch bag, combine ¼ cup popping corn with ¼ teaspoon salt and fold the top of the bag over a couple of times. Microwave on high for 2 to 3 minutes, until there are 4 or 5 seconds between pops. Open the bag or container carefully, because steam will have built up. Toss with your seasonings and a drizzle of butter or olive oil or serve as is.

Garlic Popcorn. Use the optional butter or oil and as you melt or heat it, add a tablespoon minced garlic and cook until soft and turning golden. Strain the garlic bits out as you pour the butter over the popcorn—or not.

A Dozen Ways to Spike Your Popcorn

Toss any of these with just-cooked popcorn, alone or in combination. Since some are more potent than others, start with a light sprinkle and taste as you go.

Chopped fresh herbs
Black pepper
Chili powder
Curry powder, or garam or chaat masala
Old Bay seasoning
Five-spice powder
Toasted sesame seeds
Cayenne or red chile flakes
Grated Parmesan cheese
Brown sugar
Finely ground nuts or shredded, unsweetened coconut
Chopped dried fruit

Gorp, Your Way

Makes: 4 cups   Time: 10 minutes

The classic hiker's snack is an acronym for "good old raisins and peanuts," but you can jazz it up a bit to make an always appealing afternoon pick-me-up (I keep a batch at my desk) or a predinner nosh with drinks.

Toasting the nuts before tossing them with the other ingredients helps intensify their flavor, but if that's too much bother, just throw everything in a jar or bag, shake, and away you go. Sub any nut and dried fruit here and be sure to check out the ideas below. You might also play with the proportions—I, for example, like more peanuts than raisins.

2 cups peanuts, salted or not

2 cups raisins

Salt, optional

1. Toast the peanuts in a large dry skillet over low heat, shaking the pan until the nuts are fragrant and just beginning to brown, about 5 minutes.

2. Combine the warm peanuts with the raisins and salt to taste in a bowl and serve, or store, tightly covered, for a couple weeks.

Chile-Cherry Gorp. In Step 2, add a tablespoon or so chili powder (with or without a pinch of ground dried chiles or cayenne pepper) and toss with dried cherries instead of raisins.

Cinnamon-Cocoa Gorp. Especially good with hazelnuts instead of peanuts. In Step 2, add 1 teaspoon cinnamon and 1 teaspoon unsweetened cocoa powder. For even more chocolatiness, add 1 cup semisweet chocolate chips (wait a few minutes for the peanuts to cool to prevent the chocolate from melting).

Spanish Gorp. A special party treat, best eaten within a couple of hours. Substitute almonds for the peanuts and chopped apricots or dates (or a combination) for the raisins. In Step 2, add about ½ cup each cubed smoked chorizo and Manchego cheese, along with 1 teaspoon pimentón (or regular paprika) and 1 teaspoon grated orange zest. Toss immediately.

Coconut-Curry Gorp. Golden raisins are nice here. Use pistachios instead of peanuts and add 1 cup unsweetened coconut (ribbons are better than flakes) to the skillet in Step 1. Add 1 tablespoon curry powder to the warm nut mixture just before tossing with the raisins.

Sesame-Ginger Gorp. In Step 1, add 2 tablespoons sesame seeds to the peanuts after they've warmed for a couple minutes. Add 2 tablespoons chopped crystallized ginger and 1 tablespoon soy sauce along with the raisins in Step 2 (go easy on the salt).

Seaweed Gorp. Walnuts are good here. In Step 1, when the nuts are just about toasted, add ½ cup shredded nori (or arame or dulse). Proceed with the recipe.

Breakfast Gorp. Add 2 cups granola (for homemade, see page 276) with the fruit in Step 2.

Tropical Gorp. Substitute pecans for the peanuts. Substitute chopped dried bananas for the raisins and add chopped dried mango, pineapple, or papaya, or unsweetened coconut ribbons, alone or in combination.

(F) Fast   (M) Make-Ahead   (P) Pantry Staple

Crispy Rice Treats

Makes: About 3 dozen bite-size balls · Time: 15 minutes

Like its white rice counterpart, crispy brown rice—what Snap, Crackle, and Pop would make if they were health nuts rather than marketing stooges—is both a ready-to-eat cereal and a useful ingredient. (You can buy it under several brand names at natural food stores and some supermarkets.) You'll never miss the marshmallows in this sweet, savory, spicy, and nutty snack.

> 2 cups crispy brown rice
>
> 1 cup peanut, almond, or cashew butter
>
> ¼ cup honey or maple syrup
>
> ½ cup chopped peanuts, almonds, or cashews
>
> ½ cup chopped dried apricots
>
> 1 tablespoon curry powder
>
> Salt and black pepper
>
> ½ cup shredded, unsweetened coconut, toasted if you like

Combine the crispy brown rice, nut butter, sweetener, nuts, fruit, curry powder, and a sprinkling of salt and pepper in a large bowl. Using wet hands, form into walnut-size balls and roll them in the shredded coconut. Serve immediately, or store in a tightly covered container at room temperature for up to several days.

Crispy Tahini Rice Balls. Omit the nuts and coconut. Substitute tahini for the peanut butter and dates for the apricots. Roll the balls in sesame seeds instead of the coconut.

Fruit and Cereal Bites

You can turn your favorite ready-to-eat whole grain cereal into something halfway between a bonbon and an energy bar with little effort and just a few extra ingredients. Any dried fruit will do here; dates and dried plums are particularly sweet and smooth.

> 1½ cups dried fruit (see the headnote)
>
> 2 tablespoons vegetable oil
>
> 2 tablespoons honey, optional
>
> Fruit juice or water as needed
>
> 1 cup ready-to-eat breakfast cereal, like granola (for homemade, see page 276), crumbled shredded wheat, or any whole grain flakes or "nuts"
>
> Shredded, unsweetened coconut, finely ground nuts, or cocoa for rolling, optional

1. Put the dried fruit, oil, and honey if you're using it in a food processor and purée until smooth, adding fruit juice a little at a time to keep the machine running. You'll need to stop once or twice to scrape down the sides of the bowl. (Add small amounts of water or fruit juice if the fruit is dried out and is not processing.) Fold in the cereal until evenly distributed.

2. Take a heaping tablespoon of the mixture and roll it into a ball. Then, if you like, roll the ball around in the coconut, nuts, or cocoa. Put the balls between layers of waxed paper in a tightly covered container and refrigerate until set, about 45 minutes. Eat immediately, or store in the fridge for up to several days. You can also wrap the balls individually in wax paper, like candies.

Fruit and Cereal Bars. Line an 8- or 9-inch square or round pan with foil. Follow the recipe through Step 1. Spread the mixture in the pan, pushing it into the corners and evening the top. If you like, dust the top with coconut, nuts, or cocoa. Refrigerate until set, then cut into squares.

Radishes with Olive Oil and Sea Salt

Makes: 4 to 8 servings   Time: 20 minutes

It's hard to argue with radishes dipped in butter and sea salt, unless, of course, you'd rather skip the butter. Try this classic snack with extra virgin olive oil for a delicious spin on the original. And to expand this recipe into full-blown crudités, see the sidebar on page 44.

> ½ cup olive oil
>
> 2 tablespoons coarse sea salt
>
> 1 pound assorted radishes

1. Pour the oil into one or more ramekins or small bowls, season it with a little salt, and put some more salt nearby in another small bowl or plate.

2. Leave the radishes whole or halve or quarter them as you like. Refrigerate them in a bowl of ice water until ready to serve, up to several hours. Serve the radishes alongside the olive oil and salt for dipping and sprinkling.

Daikon with Sesame Oil and Sea Salt. Use daikon radishes, peeled and sliced crosswise into coins. Substitute sesame oil for the olive oil.

Reverse Antipasto

In America, at least, antipasto is pretty heavy on cured meats and all sorts of hard and soft cheeses. Antipasto, Food Matters style is a little different and, in fact, more like what you'd find in Italy. You may still want one or two kinds of meat and cheese; see if you can find good-quality sopressata, prosciutto, bocconcini (fresh mozzarella balls), or pecorino; keep the amounts moderate, though, so they take up about a quarter of your serving platter. Fill another quarter of your plate with good olives, dried fruit, spiced nuts, sweet or hot pickles, and roasted garlic (for homemade, see page 421).

For the rest of the platter, go wild with vegetables: fennel, artichoke hearts, bell peppers, zucchini, broccoli, cauliflower, carrots, asparagus, mushrooms. To marinate them, bring 1 cup red wine vinegar, ¾ cup olive oil, 1 quart water, a little garlic, 2 tablespoons salt, and the herbs of your choice to a boil. Add the vegetables of your choice and let them cool to room temperature before refrigerating them for up to a month.

How to Prep, Store, and Serve Crudités

Some vegetables—not all, but some—are really terrific raw; others need cooking, even if you're going to serve them cold. My rules of thumb: cucumber, cherry tomatoes, radishes, celery, summer squash, jícama, and carrots—all good as is. Beets, turnips, and other root vegetables—only good raw if thinly sliced or young, small, and not woody. Potatoes and sweet potatoes must be cooked until completely tender but not mushy. Cook everything else for a few seconds—until that fleeting moment when the color turns quite vibrant—and shock it in a bowl of ice water to cool it back down quickly.

Before cooking, cut the vegetables into coins, spears, or pieces (or in the case of cauliflower and broccoli, break them into florets) that are big enough to be dipped but not so big that you're left with a big piece of vegetable in your hand once you've taken a bite out of it. You can prepare most crudités—except the foods that discolor when you cut them—up to a day ahead of time; refrigerate them. Store raw vegetables in cold water (drain them and pat them dry before serving); put cooked vegetables in ziplock bags or airtight containers. When serving, it's nice to have at least a few different kinds of vegetables set out on plates or in bowls or glassware; or you can always simply put them on a large platter around a bowl of dip.

Once you get the vegetables situated, here are a few candidates for dips:

Puréed White Beans with Tons of Fresh Herbs (page 355)
Hummus Served Hot (page 356)
Easiest Dal with Extra Flavor (page 361)
The olive salad from More-or-Less Muffuletta (page 505), puréed
Any-Herb Pesto (page 197)
The tapenade from Fennel and Orange Salad with Green Olive Tapenade
  (page 151)
The chutney from Chickpea Salad with Cashew Chutney (page 174)
The anchovy-caper vinaigrette from Mediterranean Cobb Salad (page 149)
The miso dressing from Soba Salad with Walnuts, Sea Greens, and Miso Dress-
  ing (page 168)
Either of the two eggless mayonnaises (page 188–189)
Creamy Carrot and Chickpea Soup (page 116), puréed

Ⓕ Fast   Ⓜ Make-Ahead   Ⓟ Pantry Staple

Beet Tartare

Makes: 4 to 8 servings   Time: 30 minutes

I first learned about beet tartare—just love the name—from Jean-Georges Vongerichten, who uses roasted beets. I've eliminated that step and use raw beets. You can serve the dish as you would traditionally serve beef tartare: with chopped hard-boiled egg, onions, cornichons, a dash of Worcestershire sauce, or even a crumbling of strong blue cheese, like Stilton or Roquefort.

You can have a bit of fun with color here: make one batch with golden beets and another with red—serve them side by side for a spectacular presentation.

> 2 pounds red or yellow beets (about 4 large), peeled
>
> ¼ cup chopped red onion
>
> 1 tablespoon olive oil, or more as needed
>
> 1 to 2 tablespoons grated horseradish, or to taste
>
> 1 tablespoon lemon juice, or more as needed
>
> 1 tablespoon chopped capers
>
> 1 tablespoon chopped fresh dill, tarragon, or chives
>
> Salt and black pepper
>
> 8 slices whole grain bread, 2 small heads endive, or crackers, for serving

1. Cut the beets into quarters and put them in a food processor; pulse the beets until they're ground up into small pieces—about the size of grains of rice—careful not to overprocess. If you don't have a food processor, grate the beets instead. If the beets release a lot of liquid, squeeze them gently with your hands or drain them on paper towels to remove some of the moisture.

2. Combine the onion, oil, horseradish, lemon juice, capers, and herbs together in a bowl large enough to hold the beets. Fold in the beets and sprinkle with salt and pepper; taste and add more lemon juice, oil, or seasoning if needed. If you like, chill quickly in the freezer or refrigerate for up to a day.

3. Toast the bread and cut each slice diagonally into 4 toast points. (Or separate and trim the endive into leaves.) Serve the tartare cold or at room temperature with the toast points, spooned into endive leaves, or in a bowl next to crackers.

Celery Root Tartare. Replace the beets with celery root.

Five Quick Salsas for Chips, Dips, and Other Stuff

Makes: About 2 cups   Time: 15 minutes

The main recipe here is for basic *pico de gallo* (you might call it *salsa fresca*), but all of these are great on top of vegetable, meat, or grain dishes—or eaten with a spoon. And given that many fruit-herb-acid combinations are delicious, they're open to endless variation.

Remember, though, that they're all best when made with perfectly ripe, seasonal fruit. (Colorful garden tomatoes are particularly gorgeous.) When out of season, you're better off using drained canned tomatoes, fresh oranges, tangerines, grapefruits, avocados, or even grated raw butternut squash.

> 2 large ripe tomatoes, chopped
>
> ½ large white or red onion or 2 medium scallions, chopped
>
> 1 teaspoon minced garlic, or to taste
>
> 1 fresh hot chile (like habanero or jalapeño), seeded and minced, or to taste
>
> ½ cup chopped fresh cilantro
>
> 2 tablespoons lime juice
>
> Salt and black pepper

1. Combine all the ingredients in a bowl, taste, and adjust the seasoning.

2. Let the mixture rest for 15 to 30 minutes if possible to allow the flavors to meld.

Peach Salsa. Use 3 medium peaches (peeled if you like) in place of the tomatoes, minced ginger instead of the garlic, and orange juice instead of the lime juice.

Green Apple–Cucumber Salsa. Substitute 2 large Granny Smith apples for the tomatoes, ½ chopped cucumber for the garlic, and lemon juice for the lime juice. Use fresh mint in place of the cilantro.

Tomatillo–Black Bean Salsa. Substitute 2 cups chopped tomatillos for the tomatoes and add 1 cup cooked or canned black beans. Let sit for at least half an hour before serving so the beans soak up the other flavors.

Corn Salsa. Fresh or dried cherries are a nice addition here. Use 2 cups corn kernels (thawed frozen are fine) instead of the tomatoes. Roast or grill the corn first if you like.

Baked Tortilla Chips, Pita Chips, and Croutons

Makes: 4 to 8 servings   Time: About 30 minutes

A hot oven, a little olive oil, and a few minutes in the kitchen work wonders on slightly stale bread and tortillas, turning them into crisp, tasty chips or croutons. And when you make your own, you control the oil and seasonings, so the results are infinitely fresher and better for you than the ones that come from a factory.

A hand-pumped spray bottle is useful for distributing a small amount of oil evenly, but dabbing with a brush or drizzling from a spoon also works well. Some people find that all they need to do is grease the baking sheet and leave it at that.

> For Tortilla Chips: 8 small corn tortillas, each cut into 6 or 8 wedges
>
> For Pita Chips: 2 or 3 whole wheat pitas, each cut into 6 or 8 wedges and split into 2 thin layers
>
> For Croutons: 1 baguette, preferably whole grain, cut into ½-inch slices or cubes
>
> Olive oil as needed
>
> Salt
>
> Black pepper, optional

1. Heat the oven to 450°F. Put the pieces of tortilla, pita, or bread on 1 or 2 rimmed baking sheets in a single but crowded layer. Bake, undisturbed, until they begin to turn golden, about 15 minutes. Drizzle, brush, or spray with oil.

2. Turn the pieces over, coat the opposite side with a thin layer of oil, and continue baking until they're golden and crisp, anywhere from 5 to 15 minutes more. While they're still hot, sprinkle with salt and pepper—or other seasoning (see the list below). Serve immediately with dip, soup, or salad, or store in an airtight container for up to a week.

Herbed Tortilla Chips, Pita Chips, or Croutons. In Step 2, sprinkle ¼ cup chopped fresh parsley, dill, or chervil on the slices after turning them over and coating them with olive oil.

Simple Seasonings for Tortilla Chips, Pita Chips, and Croutons

Sprinkle the hot chips or croutons with any of the following seasonings as soon as they come out of the oven. The exact amount is a matter of taste (and the strength of your ingredients), but a good rule of thumb is to start with a teaspoon and go from there.

Chili powder
Curry powder or garam masala
Cumin, coriander, cardamom, or caraway seeds
Poppy or sesame seeds
Grated Parmesan cheese
Turbinado sugar

Ⓕ Fast Ⓜ Make-Ahead Ⓟ Pantry Staple

Crisp Vegetable or Fruit Chips

Makes: 4 to 8 servings   Time: About 1 hour, largely unattended

Chips you make from scratch are phenomenal, gorgeous in their imperfection, and way more flavorful than anything from a bag. Here the slices are dried and crisped in a not-too-hot oven, so there's not much fussing and turning. (For soft oven-dried fruit, see page 422.) Season these simply with salt and pepper or dust them with ground spices like cumin, chiles, or curry blends.

The best fruits and vegetables for chips are apples, green bananas, boniato, beets, cassava, carrots, kohlrabi, malanga, parsnips, pineapple, peaches, pears, green plantains, potatoes, pumpkin, rutabagas, sunchokes, sweet potatoes and yams, taro, turnips, and winter squash.

> 3 to 4 tablespoons olive or vegetable oil
>
> 1 pound almost any root vegetable or fruit (see the headnote), trimmed and peeled as needed
>
> Salt, black pepper, or other seasonings (see the headnote)

1. Heat the oven to 325°F. Lightly grease a couple of baking sheets with a very thin film of the oil. (For extra-crisp chips, heat the pans in the oven while you prepare the vegetables, then carefully spread the slices out directly on the hot pans.)

2. Cut the vegetable or fruit into slices about ⅛ inch thick. (A mandoline makes this task easier.) Gently toss the slices in the oil and spread them out on the baking sheets, close but not overlapping.

3. Roast the slices until they're beginning to brown on the bottom, 20 to 30 minutes. Flip, sprinkle with salt and pepper or other seasonings, and continue roasting until they're browned and crisp, another 10 to 20 minutes. (Apples, bananas, plantains, and other sugary fruits and vegetables have a tendency to burn, so keep an eye on them.) They crisp as they cool, so serve them at room temperature.

Roasted Red Pepper and Walnut "Pesto"

Makes: 4 to 8 servings   Time: About 5 minutes with roasted peppers

Coarsely ground walnuts add a nice crunch and some richness while balancing the sweetness of the roasted red bell peppers, making a purée you can use in dozens of ways, just as you would Any-Herb Pesto (page 197)—as a pasta sauce, over vegetables, as a spread or dip, or post-grilling.

For an even richer flavor and creamier texture, see the first variation.

> 2 garlic cloves
>
> 1 cup walnuts
>
> 8 roasted red bell peppers (for homemade, see page 417)
>
> 1 cup fresh basil, optional
>
> ½ cup olive oil
>
> Salt and black pepper

1. Pulse the garlic in a food processor until finely chopped. Add the walnuts and pulse 2 or 3 more times to break up any large pieces.

2. Add the roasted red peppers and basil and process, streaming in the oil as you go, until all the ingredients are well combined and as coarse or as smooth as you want them. Sprinkle with salt and pepper and serve immediately with crudités, crostini, or vegetable chips, or spread on sandwiches; or cover and refrigerate for a day or so or freeze.

Cheesy Roasted Red Pepper and Walnut "Pesto." In Step 2, add ½ cup crumbled goat cheese or feta or grated Parmesan.

Roasted Red Pepper and White Bean Dip. Substitute 2 cups cooked (or canned) and drained cannellini beans for half the roasted red peppers and proceed with the recipe.

Bruschetta, Rethought

Makes: 4 to 8 servings   Time: About 20 minutes

Bruschetta is more than an excellent vehicle for tomatoes and dips—it can serve as a base for salad, any vegetable preparation or bean dish, and more. Choose a good European-style loaf—something crusty with a coarse crumb—so that there will be as much contrast between the interior and exterior as possible. (Though the difference is slight, to make something more akin to crostini—what we might call a toast point or crouton—just slice the bread thinner, in smaller pieces.)

> 8 thick slices rustic bread, preferably whole grain
>
> 1 or more garlic cloves, halved or crushed, optional
>
> ¼ cup olive oil, or more as needed
>
> Salt and black pepper

1. Prepare a grill or turn on the broiler; the heat should be medium-high and the rack about 4 inches from the fire. Grill or broil the bread until lightly browned on both sides, ideally with some grill marks or light charring.

2. While the bread is still hot, rub the slices with the garlic, if using, on one or both sides. Put the bread on a plate, then drizzle or brush it with oil and sprinkle with salt and pepper. Serve warm with any of the toppings below.

Some Dishes for Topping Bruschetta

Tomato Carpaccio (page 145)

Raw Butternut Salad with Cranberry Dressing (page 155)

Lentil Salad with Peas and Green Beans (page 172)

Fava Bean, Asparagus, and Lemon Salad (page 175)

Chopped Cauliflower Salad, North African Style (page 167)

Italian-American Antipasto Salad with Tomato Vinaigrette (page 180)

Cannellini with Shredded Brussels Sprouts and Sausage (page 394)

Garlicky Chard with Olives and Pine Nuts (page 425)

Caramelized Leeks with Gently Cooked Scallops (page 453)

The sauce from Pasta with Artichokes (page 204)

Updated Tea Sandwiches

Tea sandwiches may be old-fashioned, but they're easy to modernize and not at all gimmicky. (The classic is plain cucumber and butter—you don't get much less gimmicky than that.) Consider these as a springboard to your own combinations.

In general, the bread is fine-crumbed and sliced thin, the fillings are fresh, and there's little or no lag between making and serving. All of this makes homemade whole wheat sandwich bread perfect, but really any loaf with a dense texture, relatively soft crust, and fine crumb is good.

Seasonal vegetables are almost universally well suited for small sandwiches—even leftover roasted or grilled vegetables or salads. Just make sure the ingredients are drained of any dressing or marinade and chopped up a bit, which makes the sandwiches easier to cut and eat.

You can, of course, add a little cheese or meat to many tea sandwiches. Try blending crumbled feta or blue cheese or grated Parmesan in with the pesto-like spreads. Or before closing the sandwiches, sprinkle the fillings with crumbled bacon or add a thin shard of prosciutto, roast beef or pork, or shredded grilled chicken.

Cucumber-Wasabi Tea Sandwiches

Makes: 4 to 8 servings   Time: 10 minutes

2 tablespoons mayonnaise (for homemade, see page 188)

½ teaspoon wasabi powder, or more to taste

8 thin slices sandwich bread, preferably whole wheat

1 medium cucumber, peeled, seeded, and very thinly sliced

1 cup chopped watercress

Salt and black pepper

Combine the mayonnaise and wasabi in a small bowl. Spread a thin layer of this mixture on each of the bread slices. Top half the bread slices with the cucumber and watercress. Sprinkle with salt and pepper, close the sandwiches, cut each into quarters on the diagonal, and serve.

Ⓕ Fast   Ⓜ Make-Ahead   Ⓟ Pantry Staple

Gingered Pea Tea Sandwiches

Makes: 4 to 8 servings   Time: 10 minutes

2 cups fresh or thawed frozen peas

2 tablespoons softened butter or olive oil, or more as needed

1 tablespoon minced ginger

½ cup chopped fresh mint

Salt and black pepper

8 thin slices sandwich bread, preferably whole wheat

1. Mash the peas with the butter or oil and ginger until the mixture is pasty but not smooth; add a little more butter or oil if necessary to make the peas spreadable. (You can make the filling ahead to this point, cover, and refrigerate for up to a day; return to room temperature before proceeding.) Add the mint and sprinkle with salt and pepper.

2. Smear about ¼ cup of the filling on 4 of the bread slices and top to make sandwiches. Cut each into quarters on the diagonal and serve.

Pumpkin-Apple Tea Sandwiches

Makes: 4 to 8 servings   Time: 10 minutes with cooked or canned pumpkin

½ cup mashed or puréed cooked pumpkin or winter squash (good-quality canned is okay)

2 green apples, cored and thinly sliced

8 thin slices sandwich bread, preferably multigrain

½ teaspoon coriander or cinnamon

Salt and black pepper

Spread a thin layer of the pumpkin or squash on each of the bread slices. Top half the bread slices with the apple. Season with the spice and a little salt and pepper, close the sandwiches, cut each into quarters on the diagonal, and serve.

Egg and Olive Tea Sandwiches

Makes: 4 to 8 servings   Time: 10 minutes with already cooked eggs

¼ cup mayonnaise (for homemade, see page 188)

½ cup good-quality green olives, pitted and chopped

1 cup chopped spinach

8 thin slices sandwich bread, preferably whole wheat

2 tablespoons Dijon mustard

2 hard-boiled eggs, thinly sliced

Salt and black pepper

1. Combine the mayonnaise, olives, and spinach in a small bowl. Spread a thin layer of the mixture on half of the bread slices; smear the rest of the slices with the mustard.

2. Put the hard-boiled egg on top of the mustard, sprinkle with salt and pepper, and close the sandwiches, pressing down slightly to seal. Cut each sandwich into quarters on the diagonal and serve.

 Ⓕ Fast   Ⓜ Make-Ahead   Ⓟ Pantry Staple

Radish-Walnut Tea Sandwiches

Makes: 4 to 8 servings   Time: 20 minutes

> ½ pound radishes
>
> 1 cup arugula
>
> ½ cup walnuts
>
> Grated zest of 1 orange
>
> 2 tablespoons olive oil, or more as needed
>
> Salt and black pepper
>
> 8 thin slices bread, preferably whole wheat baguette

1. Pulse the radishes in a food processor until they're chopped up a bit but not puréed; remove, scraping what you can out of the bowl.

2. Combine the arugula, walnuts, and orange zest in the processor and, with the machine on, drizzle in the oil, adding enough to make a paste. Taste and season with salt and pepper. Spread a thin layer of the walnut mixture on each of the bread slices. Top half the slices with the radishes, close the sandwiches, cut each into small sandwiches on the diagonal (or into quarters if you're using sandwich bread), and serve.

Pear "Crostini" with Spiced Pecans and Blue Cheese

Makes: 4 to 8 servings   Time: 20 minutes

Where folks go wrong with this classic combo is to assume that more cheese is better. The opposite is actually true: Too much blue cheese is overpowering. Just be sure to use pears that are ripe but still firm, not mealy. (And try this with ricotta salata, Parmesan, or Manchego.) Add lightly toasted seasoned nuts and the result is an irresistible "crostini"—without the bread.

    1 tablespoon vegetable oil

    ½ cup (about 4 ounces) chopped pecans or walnuts

    ¼ teaspoon cayenne

    Salt and black pepper

    2 ounces blue cheese

    1 tablespoon chopped fresh sage or 1 teaspoon dried, optional

    2 pears, cored and cut into ¼-inch slices

1. Heat the oven to 450°F; grease a rimmed baking sheet with the oil. Spread the nuts evenly on the pan and roast for 10 minutes, tossing once or twice with a spatula. Remove the nuts from the oven, toss with the cayenne and some salt and pepper, and let cool a bit.

2. While the nuts are still warm, fold them into the cheese. Add the sage if you're using it and stir with a fork until the nuts are evenly distributed. Taste and adjust the seasoning if necessary. Top each pear slice with a small bit of the blue cheese mixture and serve.

Fig "Crostini." Substitute 12 fresh figs, halved lengthwise, for the pears.

Ⓕ Fast   Ⓜ Make-Ahead   Ⓟ Pantry Staple

Cheese-Nut Balls

Makes: 4 to 8 servings   Time: 10 minutes

The common cheese ball comprises terrifying quantities of processed cheese with a meager coating of chopped nuts. Here, I've put the nuts on the inside with just enough Parmesan and Gorgonzola to give it pep. When you're using real cheese, you can use less of it and still have more flavor. (The tofu variation is pretty nice too.)

Cheese balls take well to additions, like olives, fresh chiles, cranberries, dried fruit, roasted peppers or garlic (for homemade, see pages 417 and 421), caramelized onions, sautéed spinach or mushrooms, or almost any leftover cooked vegetable. And feel free to try different nut and cheese combinations too.

> 2 cups almonds or hazelnuts
>
> Juice of ½ lemon
>
> ¼ teaspoon cayenne, optional
>
> Salt and black pepper
>
> ¼ cup grated Parmesan cheese
>
> 2 ounces Gorgonzola cheese, crumbled
>
> Salt and black pepper
>
> ½ cup chopped fresh parsley or chives

1. Put the nuts in a food processor and pulse until very finely chopped and almost paste-like. Add the lemon juice, cayenne, Parmesan, Gorgonzola, a pinch of salt and pepper, and ½ cup water. Process until the mixture is creamy and spreadable; add a tablespoon or 2 more water if it seems too thick.

2. Shape the mixture into 1 large or 2 medium balls. Roll the balls in the chopped herb and flatten them into a disk shape (it's easier to cut into). Wrap in plastic and refrigerate to set up firmly if you like. Serve with crackers, bread, or crudités.

Tofu-Nut Balls. Add 2 tablespoons olive or nut oil and 2 tablespoons miso along with the lemon juice and cayenne, and don't add any water. Use 6 ounces drained firm tofu instead of the Parmesan and Gorgonzola.

Quick-Pickled Watermelon with Feta

Makes: 4 to 8 servings   Time: About 1 hour

Pickled watermelon is one of the great old-fashioned treats of summer, and you can make it fast and fresh, with almost no forethought. An hour of marinating leaves the fruit (even the rind) pliable but still crunchy. Toss in a little feta at the last minute for a creamy counterpoint to the sweet and sour melon.

> About 1 pound watermelon
>
> Salt
>
> 1 tablespoon honey
>
> 2 teaspoons sherry or white wine vinegar
>
> 1 tablespoon chopped fresh mint
>
> About 4 ounces feta cheese, rinsed and cut into cubes

1. Seed the watermelon and cut it into bite-size cubes or thin slices (you can leave the rind on, or remove it as you like), put it in a colander, and sprinkle with 2 teaspoons salt. Toss a few times, taking care not to break up the melon too much. Let the watermelon sit for 30 to 45 minutes, tossing once or twice. Rinse, then drain for 5 minutes more.

2. Stir the honey, vinegar, and mint together in a large bowl. Add the melon and feta and toss gently. Serve immediately in soup spoons or with toothpicks.

Quick-Pickled Corn on the Cob. Omit the feta. Substitute 4 or 5 ears shucked corn for the watermelon; cut each crosswise into slices ½ inch wide. Use lime juice instead of the vinegar and chopped cilantro instead of the mint, and add a pinch of chili powder. Proceed with the recipe and serve with plenty of napkins.

Quick-Pickled Green Tomatoes with Mozzarella. Substitute 1 pound sliced green tomatoes for the watermelon and ½ cup cubed fresh mozzarella for the feta. Don't rinse the cheese; when you toss it with the tomatoes in Step 2, add 1 tablespoon minced garlic and a pinch red chile flakes.

Quick-Pickled Lima Beans with Parmesan. Instead of the watermelon, use 2 cups cooked large lima beans; you want them to be tender but not falling apart. Substitute ½ cup crumbled Parmesan cheese for the feta (don't rinse it) and 1 tablespoon chopped fresh rosemary for the mint.

Ⓕ Fast   Ⓜ Make-Ahead   Ⓟ Pantry Staple

Cucumber Cups with Melon Gazpacho

Makes: 4 to 8 servings   Time: About 30 minutes

Hollowed-out cucumbers make functional and delicious vessels for cold soups, salads, and dips (or even for an ice-cold shot of tequila or gin). So they're ideal for gazpacho—and lots of other things too (see below).

> 2 large cucumbers, peeled if the skins are thick or bitter
>
> 1 cantaloupe or other melon, about 2 pounds, flesh seeded, removed from the rind, and cut into large chunks
>
> 2 tablespoons lemon juice, or to taste
>
> Salt and black pepper
>
> ½ cup chopped fresh basil or mint
>
> 2 tablespoons olive oil

1. Cut each cucumber crosswise into equal pieces about 2 inches long. With a spoon or melon baller, scoop out most of the seeds to make a little cup, being careful not to pierce through the sides or the bottom. Put the cucumbers in a bowl of ice water until ready to fill.

2. Put the melon and lemon juice in a food processor with a sprinkling of salt and pepper. You can make it chunky or smooth, depending on whether you turn the machine on and leave it on or just pulse a few times. Add a few tablespoons water at a time, just enough to keep the machine working, and blend or pulse until smooth or chunky. (You can make the gazpacho ahead if you like; cover and refrigerate for up to several hours.)

3. Just before serving, taste the gazpacho and add more salt, pepper, or lemon as needed. Drain the cucumber cups and fill with the gazpacho. Garnish with a light sprinkle of basil or mint and a few drops of olive oil and serve.

Cucumber Cups with Tomato-Melon Gazpacho. Substitute 1 pound chopped tomatoes (squeeze the seeds out if you like) for 1 pound of the melon.

Cucumber Cups with Bloody Mary Gazpacho. Substitute 2 pounds chopped tomatoes for the melon. In Step 2, add a garlic clove, prepared horseradish to taste, a small fresh hot red chile (or a dash of hot sauce), a splash of Worcestershire sauce, and vodka instead of the water. Garnish each cup with a slice of celery.

Cucumber Cups with Fruit Gazpacho. Substitute berries, seedless grapes, pineapple, or peeled plums for the melon.

Many More Fillings for Cucumber Cups

Sesame Noodles with Spinach and Salmon (page 239)

Upside-Down Tuna Salad (page 502)

Hummus Served Hot (page 356)

Any of the Five Quick Salsas for Chips, Dips, and Other Stuff (page 46)

Sushi Rice with Daikon and Sesame Seeds (page 292) with a cube of avocado

The purée from Gingered Pea Tea Sandwiches (page 53)

Apple Slaw (page 154)

Quinoa Tabbouleh (page 164)

Black Bean and Corn Salad (page 171)

Ⓕ Fast   Ⓜ Make-Ahead   Ⓟ Pantry Staple

Crisp Marinated Brussels Sprouts

Makes: 4 to 8 servings   Time: Less than 1 hour, including marinating

Bright green and slightly crunchy, these make a perfectly piquant finger food, one that doesn't depend on bacon or cheese for flavor and texture (though you can add a crumble of either to the vinaigrette). Try the same boil-shock-and-dress method with broccoli or cauliflower florets, asparagus spears, carrot coins, whole green beans, or even strips of cabbage.

Salt

1 pound Brussels sprouts

¼ cup olive oil

2 tablespoons sherry or wine vinegar, or more to taste

2 teaspoons Dijon mustard

1 medium shallot or small red onion, chopped

Black pepper

1. Bring a large pot of water to a boil and salt it. Trim the hard edges of the stems and remove any loose leaves from the Brussels sprouts. Leave whole or cut in half. Set up a large bowl of water with lots of ice cubes.

2. Drop the Brussels sprouts into the boiling water and cook until they are crisp-tender, 3 to 5 minutes. You should be able to pierce one easily with a sharp knife, but they should still have a little crunch. Drain the vegetables and plunge into the bowl of ice water until cool; drain again.

3. While the sprouts are draining, whisk together the oil, vinegar, mustard, shallot, and some pepper in a large bowl. Taste and adjust the seasoning, adding more vinegar a teaspoon or 2 at a time until the balance tastes right to you. Toss the Brussels sprouts with the vinaigrette, cover, and chill in the fridge for at least 30 minutes or up to a day. Serve with toothpicks.

Crisp Horseradish Brussels Sprouts. Substitute prepared or grated fresh horseradish to taste for the Dijon mustard in the vinaigrette.

Crisp Black-Olive Brussels Sprouts. Substitute ½ cup chopped black olives for the mustard and 1 tablespoon minced garlic for the shallot.

Roasted Carrot Spears with Scallion-Ginger Glaze

Makes: 4 to 8 servings   Time: 45 minutes

The standby, taken-for-granted carrot takes on a brilliant, unfamiliar guise when combined with a sharp scallion-ginger sauce. Use sweet, whole baby carrots—the slender ones sold with their greens still attached, not the tiny cut nubbins—if they're available. But big carrots—cut lengthwise into spears—are fine here too.

About 1 pound carrots

4 tablespoons vegetable oil

2 tablespoons minced ginger

¼ cup chopped scallions

1 tablespoon minced garlic

½ teaspoon salt

1. Heat the oven to 400°F. Unless you're using baby carrots, cut the carrots into spears about 3 inches long and ½ inch wide. Toss them with 2 tablespoons of the vegetable oil on a baking sheet and roast them, shaking the pan or turning them occasionally, until tender and browned, 30 to 40 minutes.

2. Meanwhile, mix the ginger, scallions, garlic, and ½ teaspoon salt together in a heatproof bowl. Put the remaining 2 tablespoons oil in a small saucepan or skillet over high heat until smoking. Carefully pour the oil over the ginger-scallion mixture and mix well, mashing a bit with the back of your spoon. (The mixture can be stored in the refrigerator for up to 3 days if you're not using it immediately.)

3. Remove the carrots from the oven and toss them with the ginger-scallion mixture. Serve warm.

Roasted Carrot Spears with Scallion-Chile Glaze. Add 1 minced fresh hot chile to taste to the ginger-scallion mixture in Step 2.

Roasted Parsnip Spears with Shallot Glaze. Use ¼ cup chopped shallots instead of the ginger, scallions, and garlic; substitute parsnips for the carrots and olive oil for the vegetable oil.

Ⓕ Fast   Ⓜ Make-Ahead   Ⓟ Pantry Staple

Fried Chickpeas

Makes: 4 to 8 servings   Time: 25 minutes with cooked or canned chickpeas

These addictively crunchy morsels are a mind-blowing alternative to roasted nuts and take seasoning just as well. Home-cooked chickpeas will always have the best flavor and texture, but you can use canned in a pinch. Either way, be sure to drain the chickpeas as thoroughly as possible and dry them gently with a clean towel before frying them or they won't get as crisp.

> 3 tablespoons olive oil
>
> 2 cups cooked or canned chickpeas, as dry as possible
>
> Salt and black pepper
>
> ¼ cup chopped fresh parsley, optional

1. Put the oil in a skillet large enough to hold the chickpeas in one layer over medium-high heat. When it's hot, add the chickpeas and sprinkle with salt and pepper.

2. Cook, shaking the pan occasionally, until the chickpeas are browned, 15 to 20 minutes. Serve hot or at room temperature, seasoned with more salt and garnished with parsley if you like.

Roasted Chickpeas. Heat the oven to 400°F. Combine the chickpeas and oil in an ovenproof skillet or roasting pan and roast for 15 to 20 minutes, shaking the pan occasionally.

Seasonings for Fried or Roasted Chickpeas

Toss them with a tablespoon of any of the following before serving:

Cumin (ground or seeds)
Curry powder or garam masala
Chili powder or ground dried chiles
Toasted ground nuts or seeds
Chopped fresh herbs like thyme, rosemary, or sage
Five-spice powder
Lemon juice

Lentil "Caviar" with All the Trimmings

Makes: 4 to 8 servings   Time: 45 minutes, plus time to chill   Ⓜ

Small, dark lentils (like the famed Le Puy variety from France) are often called "poor man's caviar" for their small size and shiny appearance. With this sea green glaze, they even take on a briny flavor.

8 ounces (about 1½ cups) dried Le Puy or other dark green or black lentils, washed and picked over

2 tablespoons vegetable oil

1 large shallot or small onion, chopped

¼ cup crumbled dried dulse, arame, or hijiki

1 cup sake, brewed green tea, or water

2 tablespoons mirin or honey

Salt and black pepper

8 slices whole grain bread, or crackers, for serving

½ cup capers or chopped cornichons, for garnish, optional

½ cup chopped red onion, for garnish, optional

2 hard-boiled eggs, chopped, for garnish, optional

½ cup mayonnaise (for homemade, see page 188), sour cream, or crème fraîche, for garnish, optional

1. Put the lentils in a medium pot and cover with cold water by 2 to 3 inches. Bring the water to a boil, then reduce the heat so that the lentils bubble gently. Partially cover and cook, stirring occasionally, checking the lentils for doneness every 10 to 15 minutes. (This is a good time to hard-boil the eggs if you haven't already.) When the lentils are tender but not falling apart, drain them.

2. Put the oil in a deep skillet over medium-high heat. When it's hot, add the shallot and sea greens and cook, stirring constantly, for 3 to 5 minutes. Stir in the sake and mirin. Sprinkle with a little salt and pepper and let the mixture bubble away until it reduces and thickens to a thin syrup, 5 to 7 minutes; strain.

3. Pour the glaze over the lentils and toss gently to coat; taste and adjust the seasoning. Chill for at least 30 minutes or up to a few days. Toast the bread if you're using it and cut each slice diagonally into 4 toast points. Serve with the toast points or crackers, along with any garnishes you like.

Ⓕ Fast   Ⓜ Make-Ahead   Ⓟ Pantry Staple

Spicy-Sweet Green Beans

Makes: 4 to 8 servings   Time: 20 minutes

An exotic finger food or side dish, this Asian-inspired take on green beans has an appealing variety of tastes and textures happening all at once: the crunch of almonds, the spiciness of chiles, the sweetness of honey, and the complex flavor of soy. Use the same technique with Mediterranean ingredients for an equally addictive variation. Or try thin asparagus spears.

Salt

1 pound green beans

1/2 cup whole almonds

3 garlic cloves

1 or 2 dried hot red chiles, or to taste

3 tablespoons olive oil

1/3 cup chopped shallots

2 tablespoons honey

3 tablespoons soy sauce

Black pepper

1. Bring a large pot of water to a boil and salt it. Add the beans and cook until crisp-tender, about 2 minutes, depending on the size of the beans. Shock the beans in a bowl of ice water to stop the cooking and drain again (this can be done up to a day ahead of time).

2. Put the almonds, garlic, and chiles in a food processor and process; while the machine is running, add a tablespoon or 2 of the oil to get the mixture moving. Continue to process until you have a thick paste.

3. Put the remaining olive oil in a large skillet and cook the shallots over medium heat, stirring occasionally, until they're just soft, about 3 minutes. Add the almond paste and continue cooking for another couple of minutes, then add the honey and soy sauce. Cook for another minute or 2 over high heat, stirring constantly, before adding the green beans. Toss to coat the beans well in the almond-shallot mixture and cook just until the beans are warmed through; if the paste becomes too thick, add a tablespoon or 2 of water to thin it out. Sprinkle with salt and pepper and serve hot or at room temperature.

Garlicky Green Beans. Use pine nuts instead of the almonds, omit the chiles, and proceed through Step 2. In Step 3, add ½ cup good-quality chopped black olives along with the pine nut paste, and instead of the soy sauce, use 2 to 3 tablespoons balsamic vinegar with the honey. Garnish with Parmesan cheese.

Olives, Cucumbers, and Tuna, Mediterranean Style

Makes: 8 or more servings   Time: About 15 minutes

Fresh tuna and olives are a classic combination in *salade niçoise*, but they're also great with crunchy cucumbers and dressed with olive oil, garlic, parsley, and lots of lemon. Note the canned tuna, a real from-the-pantry option; if you're going to use fresh tuna, make sure it's sushi-grade and sustainably harvested (see page 22). Serve with toothpicks, crackers, or toasted bread; it also makes a nice topping for a bed of greens.

    8 ounces olives: green, black, or a mixture, preferably imported

    4 ounces oil-packed canned tuna, drained

    2 cups peeled, seeded, and cubed cucumber

    2 tablespoons olive oil, or to taste

    2 garlic cloves, crushed

    ¼ cup chopped fresh parsley

    1 teaspoon grated lemon zest, or to taste

    2 tablespoons chopped lemon sections, optional

    Lemon juice to taste

    1 teaspoon red chile flakes, optional

Pit the olives if you like by crushing them with the flat side of a knife and removing the pits. Mix all the ingredients and transfer to a serving bowl. Serve immediately.

Marinated Cherry Tomatoes and Olives. Omit the tuna (or not). Substitute 2 cups halved cherry tomatoes for the cucumbers.

Ⓕ Fast   Ⓜ Make-Ahead   Ⓟ Pantry Staple

Oven-Dried Cherry Tomatoes
with Soy Glaze

Makes: 4 to 8 servings   Time: About 1 hour, largely unattended, plus time to soak wooden skewers

As unexpected and impressive a presentation of cherry tomatoes as you can imagine. The tomatoes end up with a pleasing, jammy texture, somewhere between fresh and fully dried. (Keep an eye on them to keep them from becoming too leathery in the oven.)

Do try the last variation, which uses jalapeños as a main ingredient.

2 pints cherry tomatoes, cut in half lengthwise

2 tablespoons soy sauce, or to taste

¼ teaspoon sugar

2 teaspoons sesame oil

Salt and black pepper

2 tablespoons chopped fresh chives or scallions, optional

1. If you're using wooden skewers, soak them in water for 20 to 30 minutes (see page 69). Heat the oven to 300°F. Thread the tomatoes onto metal or wooden skewers and place the skewers on 2 rimmed baking sheets. Put them in the oven and forget about them for 30 minutes. Turn the skewers over and bake for another 30 minutes or so (depending on their size), until the tomatoes are still soft but somewhat shriveled. Remove from the oven and let cool while you make the glaze.

2. Combine the soy sauce, sugar, sesame oil, and a sprinkling of salt and pepper in a small saucepan and cook over medium heat until thick and syrupy.

3. When the tomatoes have cooled a bit, put them on a plate and drizzle them with the glaze. Garnish with the chives or scallions if you like and serve warm or at room temperature.

Oven-Dried Cherry Tomatoes with Balsamic Glaze. Use good balsamic vinegar instead of soy sauce and olive oil instead of sesame oil. Garnish with chopped fresh rosemary or thyme.

Tomato-Jalapeño Skewers with Maple Glaze. Substitute 1 pint jalapeño peppers, halved lengthwise and seeded, for 1 pint of the cherry tomatoes (you can mix the peppers and the tomatoes together on the skewers). In the glaze, use 2 tablespoons maple syrup in place of the soy sauce and omit the sugar.

Skewered Panzanella

Makes: 4 to 8 servings   Time: 30 minutes, plus time to soak wooden skewers

This veggie-heavy spin on classic panzanella puts bread salad in kebab form so you can toast it on a grill or under a broiler. It's so chunky that you may need a knife and fork to eat it, but to make it an out-of-hand hors d'oeuvre, simply cut the pieces smaller, make more skewers, and cook them for less time. Day-old bread—the heartier, the better—is a good option here. For a mini meal on a stick, try the variations with mozzarella and prosciutto.

    4 thick slices bread, preferably whole grain, cut into large cubes

    2 small red onions, quartered and separated into small pieces

    12 button mushrooms, halved

    1 red bell pepper, cut into chunks

    4 tomatoes, quartered

    4 tablespoons olive oil

    Salt and black pepper

    ½ cup chopped fresh basil

    1 tablespoon sherry or red wine vinegar

1. If you're using wooden skewers, soak them in water for 20 to 30 minutes (see page 69). Prepare a grill or turn on the broiler; the heat should be medium-high and the rack about 4 inches from the fire. Thread the bread and vegetables, alternating ingredients, tightly on the skewers.

2. Brush the skewers with 2 tablespoons of the oil. Sprinkle each with salt and pepper. Grill or broil, turning occasionally, until the vegetables are slightly tender and begin to char and the bread is crisp, 5 to 10 minutes.

Ⓕ Fast   Ⓜ Make-Ahead   Ⓟ Pantry Staple

3. Mix the remaining 2 tablespoons oil with the basil and vinegar and add some more salt and pepper if you like. When the skewers are done, brush or drizzle with the dressing (just to moisten them) and serve.

Mozzarella Panzanella on a Stick. Substitute zucchini cubes for the mushrooms. In Step 2, when the bread and vegetables are just about ready, sprinkle each skewer with a tablespoon or so grated mozzarella and grill or broil until the cheese melts, just another minute or 2. Drizzle with the dressing and serve.

Prosciutto Panzanella on a Stick. In Step 1, halve 6 thin slices prosciutto lengthwise, fold each like an accordion into "chunks," and thread on the skewers along with the bread and vegetables.

More About Skewers

Wood or bamboo skewers are disposable and inexpensive, especially if you buy them in large quantities. The only trick to using wooden and bamboo skewers is that you have to first soak them in water for 20 to 30 minutes or they will scorch.

Metal skewers are another option. They are durable, reusable, and don't require any preparation before using. But they get hot on the grill or in the oven, which means you (and your guests) have to handle them with care.

Chipotle-Glazed Squash Skewers

Makes: 4 to 8 servings   Time: About 1 hour, plus time to soak wooden skewers

Sweet, starchy winter squash takes well to the smoky heat of chipotle chiles, especially when you concentrate the flavors by roasting slowly. Use any winter squash here, or even sweet potatoes—in either case, these kebabs are drop-dead gorgeous.

1½ pounds butternut or other winter squash, peeled, seeded, and cut into
  1-inch cubes

¼ cup olive oil, plus some for greasing the pan

1 or 2 canned chipotle chiles, chopped, with 2 tablespoons adobo sauce

1 tablespoon minced garlic

1 tablespoon honey

Salt and black pepper

Lime wedges, optional

Chopped fresh cilantro, optional

1. If you're using wooden skewers, soak them in water for 20 to 30 minutes (see page 69). Heat the oven to 300°F. Grease a large rimmed baking sheet or roasting pan with oil. Thread the squash tightly on 8 to 12 wooden or metal skewers and put them in the roasting pan.

2. Combine the ¼ cup oil, 1 chipotle chile, the adobo sauce, garlic, honey, and some salt and pepper in a small bowl. (A mortar and pestle is ideal here.) Taste and add another chile if you like.

3. Brush the glaze evenly over the squash skewers and roast for 45 to 60 minutes, turning once or twice and basting with any pan juices. When the squash is tender and deeply colored, remove the skewers from the oven. Serve hot or at room temperature with lime wedges and cilantro if you like.

Miso Squash Skewers. Substitute peanut oil for the olive oil, ¼ cup any miso for the chipotles and adobo, 1 tablespoon rice vinegar for the garlic, and 2 tablespoons mirin for the honey.

Ⓕ Fast   Ⓜ Make-Ahead   Ⓟ Pantry Staple

Sweet Potato, Ginger, and Chicken Teriyaki Skewers

Makes: 4 to 8 servings   Time: About 45 minutes, plus time to soak wooden skewers

Roasting small pieces of sweet potatoes brings out their natural sweetness in an irresistible way. Add something else to the skewers—a bit of chicken and a sweet-and-salty teriyaki glaze, for example—and the results are wonderful. I like to eat the pieces of ginger, too, but be warned that they are fairly spicy. Broccoli florets, zucchini, carrot, parsnip, and eggplant would work here too, but sweet potatoes are really the best.

  Salt

  1 large knob ginger, peeled and sliced

  ¼ cup soy sauce

  ¼ cup mirin or honey

  2 large sweet potatoes, peeled (if you like) and cut into ¾-inch cubes

  2 boneless, skinless chicken thighs, cut into ¾-inch pieces

  Black pepper

  Chopped scallion or cilantro, for garnish

1. If you're using wooden skewers, soak them in water for 20 to 30 minutes (see page 69). Heat the oven to 375°F.

2. Bring a small saucepan of water to a boil and salt it. Blanch the sliced ginger in the boiling water until it begins to soften, 3 to 5 minutes. Remove the ginger with a small strainer or a slotted spoon and put it in a bowl of ice water. Combine the soy sauce and mirin.

3. Thread the sweet potatoes, ginger, and chicken pieces, alternating ingredients, on wood or metal skewers. Sprinkle with salt and pepper. Put the skewers in a roasting pan or on a rimmed baking sheet. Roast, brushing occasionally with the teriyaki sauce and turning once or twice, until the sweet potatoes are golden and tender and the chicken is cooked through, 20 to 30 minutes. Serve the skewers garnished with chopped scallion or cilantro and a final drizzle of teriyaki sauce.

Grilled or Broiled Pineapple Skewers with Ham and Honey-Chile Glaze

Makes: 4 to 8 servings   Time: 30 minutes, plus time to soak wooden skewers

When I was a kid, ham was often decorated with pineapple rings (canned, of course) and with the coveted maraschino cherries too. But if you turn the concept on its head and skewer it, you've got a contemporary winner.

¼ cup olive oil

1 red onion, cut into chunks, about 1 tablespoon of it chopped

1 tablespoon minced fresh hot chile (like jalapeño or Thai), or red chile flakes to taste

1 tablespoon honey

Salt and black pepper

1 pineapple, cubed

1 cup cubed cooked ham

2 red bell peppers, cut into chunks

1. If you're using wooden skewers, soak them in water for 20 to 30 minutes (see page 69). Prepare a grill or turn on the broiler; the heat should be medium-high and the rack about 4 inches from the fire.

2. Put the oil in a small saucepan over medium-high heat. When it's hot, add the chopped onion and chile and cook, stirring occasionally, until they soften (turn the heat down if they start to color), a minute or 2. Stir in the honey and 2 tablespoons water and sprinkle with salt and pepper. Maintain the heat so it bubbles gently for a minute or 2, making sure not to burn the honey.

3. Thread the pineapple, ham, peppers, and onion, alternating ingredients, on wood or metal skewers. Sprinkle the kebabs with salt and pepper. Grill or broil, brushing occasionally with the honey-chile glaze, until the ham and pineapple are lightly charred, 5 to 10 minutes. Serve drizzled with a little of the glaze.

Spice-Rubbed Pineapple-Ham Skewers. Omit the sauce ingredients. Before grilling or broiling, sprinkle the kebabs with chili powder, pimentón (smoked paprika), or curry powder.

Grilled or Broiled Melon-Prosciutto Skewers. Use a medium cantaloupe, cassava, or honeydew melon instead of the pineapple and skip the ham. Instead wrap a thin slice of prosciutto around the skewer before grilling.

Mexican Street Corn

Makes: 4 to 8 servings   Time: 30 minutes, plus time to soak wooden skewers

Vendors selling seasoned corn from carts and stands are common in Mexico and have popped up around the United States too. But you can easily make these yourself at home and even experiment with other flavor combinations. (See the variations for some ideas.) It's traditional to simply brush the spicy mayo on the corn and call it a day, but a final roll in something crunchy is a nice way to gild the lily.

4 ears fresh corn, shucked

¼ cup mayonnaise (for homemade, see page 188)

2 tablespoons olive oil

1 tablespoon chili powder

Grated zest and juice of 1 lime

Salt and black pepper

½ cup chopped fresh cilantro, optional

2 cups tortilla chips (for homemade, see page 47) or cubed whole grain
    bread, optional

2 ounces queso fresco or cotija cheese, optional

1. If you're using wooden skewers, soak them in water for 20 to 30 minutes (see page 69). Prepare a grill to medium-high heat and put the rack about 4 inches from the fire. Or turn the oven to 500°F. Spear each ear of corn lengthwise with a wooden or metal skewer. Grill or roast the corn, turning occasionally, until some of the kernels char a bit and others are lightly browned, 10 to 20 minutes.

2. Meanwhile, combine the mayonnaise, olive oil, chili powder, lime zest and juice, and a sprinkling of salt and pepper in a small bowl. If you're making the final topping, pulse the remaining ingredients in a food processor until coarse and crumbly and spread the mixture out on a plate.

3. When the corn is done, remove the ears from the heat and smear them evenly with the mayonnaise mixture. Then roll them in the crumb mixture if you like and serve immediately.

Indian-Style Street Corn. Omit the cilantro, chips or bread, and cheese. In Step 2, for the smearing sauce, substitute ⅓ cup coconut milk mixed with 1 tablespoon curry powder for the mayonnaise, olive oil, and chili powder; roll the sauced corn in 1 cup toasted shredded unsweetened coconut instead of the crumb mixture.

Italian Street Corn. Omit the mayonnaise, olive oil, chili powder, cilantro, chips, and cheese. In Step 2, for the smearing sauce, use ⅓ cup pesto (for homemade, see page 197); for the crumb mixture, just use the cubed bread and pulse as directed.

Thai Street Corn. Omit the cilantro, chips or bread, and cheese. In Step 2, for the smearing sauce, substitute ⅓ cup coconut milk mixed with 1 teaspoon (or more) chile paste or minced fresh Thai or jalapeño chile, 2 teaspoons sugar, and 1 tablespoon nam pla (fish sauce). Instead of the crumb mixture, roll the ears in 1 cup chopped peanuts.

Ⓕ Fast Ⓜ Make-Ahead Ⓟ Pantry Staple

Greek "Nachos" with Feta Drizzle

Makes: 4 to 8 servings   Time: 30 minutes

A summertime salad you eat with pita chips. For an all-veggie version, replace the pita with any crisp root vegetable chips (for homemade, see page 49); for a bigger dish, top with a little sliced grilled or roasted chicken or browned ground lamb. In wintertime, substitute roasted vegetables like eggplant and squash for the tomatoes and cucumber.

4 pitas, split and cut into wedges

¼ cup olive oil, plus more as needed

Salt

4 ounces feta cheese

½ cup yogurt, preferably Greek or whole milk

½ cup chopped fresh mint

Grated zest and juice of 1 lemon

Black pepper

2 or 3 ripe tomatoes, chopped

1 cucumber, peeled, seeded, and chopped

½ cup kalamata olives, pitted and halved

1 small red onion, halved and thinly sliced

1. Heat the oven to 350°F. Arrange the pita wedges in one layer on baking sheets and brush or drizzle with oil if you like. Bake, turning as needed, until they begin to color, about 10 minutes. Sprinkle with salt, turn off the oven, and put the chips back in the oven to keep warm.

2. Combine the feta, yogurt, ¼ cup oil, mint, and lemon zest and juice in a food processor; sprinkle with salt and pepper. Process until smooth (or use a fork to combine the ingredients in a bowl).

3. Put the chips on a serving plate (or use the baking sheets). Top with the tomatoes, cucumber, olives, and red onion and drizzle with the feta-yogurt sauce.

Spinach Frico

Makes: 4 to 8 servings   Time: 20 minutes

"Frico" sounds so much fancier than "cheese crisp," but that's essentially what its most basic form is: hard shredded cheese cooked in oil until crunchy. (Montasio is traditional, but Parmesan works just fine.) With spinach, fricos become more flavorful, more attractive, and, obviously, more vegetable oriented. Snapped into bite-size pieces, fricos make a flavorful garnish for salads, soups, and even bean, grain, and vegetable main dishes.

If you already have cooked spinach or any other cooked vegetable on hand, so much the better: Chop whatever you have in fairly small pieces and put a cup of it in the olive oil along with the Parmesan. Your frico will be done in 10 minutes instead of 20.

2 tablespoons olive oil

2 cups spinach leaves, chopped

Black pepper

2 cups grated Parmesan cheese

1. Put the oil in a large skillet over medium-high heat. When it's hot, add the spinach and cook, stirring, until the leaves have wilted and all of their liquid has evaporated, 4 to 5 minutes. Sprinkle with a good amount of black pepper and the Parmesan and stir.

2. Use a rubber spatula to distribute the spinach and cheese evenly over the bottom of the pan. Cook until the cheese is melted and golden brown on the bottom, about 2 minutes.

3. Use the spatula to slide the crisp onto a plate; put another plate on top of the crisp. Put one hand firmly in the center of the bottom plate and the other hand the same way on the top plate; flip the crisp over. Use the spatula to slide it back into the pan and continue cooking until the cheese is golden brown, 1 to 2 minutes. Serve whole as an appetizer or broken into smaller pieces as a garnish.

Spinach-Herb Frico. Reduce the chopped spinach to 1 cup and add 1 cup chopped fresh parsley or mint in Step 1 along with the Parmesan.

Broccoli-Romano Frico. Substitute 1½ cups chopped broccoli or broccoli rabe for the spinach; sauté it in the oil until tender-crisp. Use Pecorino Romano instead of Parmesan.

Chard-Manchego Frico. Substitute 2 cups chopped chard leaves (save the stems for another use) for the spinach and Manchego cheese for the Parmesan.

Mini Potato-Parmesan Röstis

Makes: 4 substantial to 12 snack-size servings   Time: 45 minutes

Röstis (sometimes considered the national dish of Switzerland) are not at all unlike hash browns. They're traditionally shaped into a large cake, fried, and served at breakfast, but this version bakes them in muffin tins to turn them into individual hors d'oeuvres—very cool. The potato mixture is prone to sticking, so if your muffin tin isn't nonstick, use a baking sheet instead and give the röstis plenty of time to cool on the sheet before you remove them with a spatula.

   ¼ cup olive oil, plus extra for greasing the pan and your hands

   1½ pounds waxy potatoes (like new or red potatoes), peeled if you like

   1 onion

   1 tablespoon coarsely chopped fresh rosemary or thyme, or 1 teaspoon
      dried

   ½ cup grated Parmesan cheese

   1 tablespoon whole wheat flour

   Salt and black pepper

1. Heat the oven to 350°F. Grease a 12-cup nonstick muffin tin or a large baking sheet with some oil. Grate the potatoes and onion in a food processor or by hand, then squeeze them dry with paper towels. Put them in a large bowl and add the herb, Parmesan, flour, and ¼ cup oil. Sprinkle with salt and pepper and toss until everything is well combined.

2. Distribute the potato mixture among the muffin cups, then press down firmly. Or use your hands to press the potato mixture into 12 mounds and distribute them evenly on the baking sheet. Bake until crisp and golden, about 30 minutes. Let cool for 10 minutes before removing from the pan. Serve warm or at room temperature.

Mini Apple-Cheddar Röstis. Substitute peeled apples for the potatoes and grated cheddar for the Parmesan; the röstis will need only 20 to 25 minutes in the oven.

Baked Fries with Dried Tomato Ketchup

Makes: 4 to 8 servings   Time: 1 hour

Far be it from me to avoid ketchup and fries, and this novel version won't disappoint—in fact, these give their deep-fried cousins a run for the money. The homemade ketchup is so rich you might want to keep a jar in the fridge for dipping cut vegetables or spreading on sandwiches. Ditto the pesto variation.

> 1 cup boiling water
>
> 1 cup dried tomatoes
>
> 4 tablespoons olive oil, or more as needed
>
> 2 garlic cloves, smashed
>
> 1 teaspoon balsamic or sherry vinegar, or to taste
>
> Salt and black pepper
>
> 4 large russet or other baking potatoes

1. Pour the boiling water over the tomatoes and keep them submerged until they soften, about 20 minutes; drain, reserving the soaking liquid.

2. Meanwhile, put 2 tablespoons of the oil in a small saucepan over medium-low heat. Add the garlic and cook until very soft, about 5 minutes. Let cool slightly, then put in a food processor with the tomatoes and vinegar. Purée until smooth, adding the reserved liquid a little at a time to reach the consistency of ketchup. Taste and add some salt and pepper, and more vin-

Ⓕ Fast Ⓜ Make-Ahead Ⓟ Pantry Staple

egar if you like. (The ketchup can be made and refrigerated up to several days ahead.)

3. Heat the oven to 400°F and put 2 large baking sheets inside to heat. Scrub the potatoes but do not peel them. Cut them into ¼-inch-thick disks or sticks and put them in a large bowl. Pat them dry if they feel watery, then toss the potatoes with the remaining 2 tablespoons oil (or enough to coat them lightly). Sprinkle with salt and pepper.

4. Carefully remove the hot baking sheets from the oven and spread the potatoes on them in a single layer; return the pans to the oven. Cook for 30 minutes, then use a spatula to flip and cook until crisp and golden on both sides, another 15 minutes. Sprinkle with more salt if you like, then serve with the ketchup.

Baked Fries with Tomato "Pesto." Omit the balsamic vinegar. In Step 2, add 2 tablespoons pine nuts, ¼ cup grated Parmesan cheese, and 1 cup fresh basil to the food processor, adding enough of the reserved tomato liquid to make a thin paste; add a little more oil too if you like. Proceed with the recipe.

Cumin Sweet Potato Chips with Tomatillo Pico

Makes: 4 to 8 servings   Time: 30 minutes

Here, sweet potatoes are sliced thin, baked until crisp, then dusted with cumin and served with a bowl of tomatillo *pico de gallo*, a roughly chopped raw salsa. (You could also serve these with any of the salsas on page 46.) Plantains are a wonderful substitute for sweet potatoes here; see the variation.

1 pound sweet potatoes, peeled

2 tablespoons olive oil, plus more for greasing the pan

Salt

1 teaspoon cumin

1 pound fresh tomatillos, husked, cored, and chopped

½ large white onion or 3 or 4 scallions, chopped

1 teaspoon minced garlic, or to taste

Minced fresh hot chile (like jalapeño, Thai, or less of habanero), red chile flakes, or cayenne, to taste

½ cup chopped fresh cilantro or parsley

Juice of 2 limes

Black pepper

1. Heat the oven to 400°F. Slice the sweet potatoes about ⅛ inch thick, using a mandoline, food processor, or sharp knife, then toss them with the 2 tablespoons oil. Grease a couple of baking sheets with some more oil. Spread the sweet potato slices out in a single layer (it's okay if they're close) and sprinkle with salt. Bake, turning as needed, until they're crisp and lightly browned, 10 to 15 minutes total. Remove the chips from the oven and immediately sprinkle the tops with the cumin; transfer them to wire racks to cool.

2. Meanwhile, combine the tomatillos, onion, garlic, chile, cilantro, and lime juice in a serving bowl. Sprinkle with salt and pepper, then taste and adjust the seasoning. If possible, let the flavors develop for a few minutes before serving with the chips.

(F) Fast   (M) Make-Ahead   (P) Pantry Staple

Chili-Dusted Plantain Chips with Tomatillo Pico. Peel and thinly slice 3 medium green plantains instead of the sweet potatoes. Bake as above, dust the chips with chili powder instead of the cumin, and serve with the tomatillo pico.

Polenta Cakes with Garlicky Mushrooms

Makes: 4 to 8 servings   Time: 3 hours, mostly unattended

I like a mix of different mushrooms here—shiitake, chanterelle, oyster, and cremini combine beautifully—but everyday button mushrooms are fine, especially if you combine them with a few reconstituted dried porcini (see page 30). In any case, the mushrooms are so rich and meaty that even the staunchest carnivore will love these crisp little cakes. Try other toppings too or any of the Five Quick Salsas for Chips, Dips, and Other Stuff on page 46.

   1 cup coarse cornmeal

   Salt

   ½ cup milk, preferably whole (or use water)

   Black pepper

   2 tablespoons olive oil, plus more as needed

   1 pound mushrooms, preferably an assortment (see the headnote), sliced

   1 tablespoon chopped fresh thyme

   ¼ cup dry white wine

   1 tablespoon minced garlic, or more to taste

1. Put the cornmeal and a large pinch of salt in a medium saucepan; slowly whisk in 2½ cups water and the milk to make a lump-free slurry. Set the pot over medium-high heat and bring almost to a boil. Reduce the heat to low and bubble gently, whisking frequently, until thick, 10 to 15 minutes. If the mixture becomes too thick, whisk in a bit more water; you want the consistency to be like thick oatmeal. Taste for seasoning and add salt if necessary and plenty of black pepper.

2. Grease a large baking sheet with some of the oil. While the polenta is still hot, pour it onto the sheet and use a spatula to spread it out evenly at least ½ inch thick. Brush the top lightly with oil, cover with plastic wrap, and refrigerate the polenta until it sets up, about 2 hours (or up to a day).

3. Heat the oven to 375°F. Grease a clean large baking sheet with some of the oil. When the polenta is set, cut it into at least 12 squares or diamonds or use a round cookie cutter to make disks. Put the cakes on the baking sheet, brush with a bit more oil, and bake until they're warmed through and the edges begin to brown (the outside should be nice and toasted while the inside should stay soft), 20 to 30 minutes.

4. Meanwhile, put the 2 tablespoons oil in a large skillet over medium-high heat. When it's hot, add the mushrooms and thyme and sprinkle with salt and pepper. Cook, stirring occasionally, until the mushrooms are tender and dried out a bit, about 10 minutes. Add the wine and let it bubble away for a couple of minutes; turn the heat to medium-low and add the garlic. Continue cooking until most of the wine has cooked off. Taste and adjust the seasonings. Serve a spoonful of mushrooms on top of each polenta cake.

Ⓕ Fast   Ⓜ Make-Ahead   Ⓟ Pantry Staple

Beet "Sandwiches"

Makes: 4 to 8 servings　　Time: About 45 minutes　

A fine model for all sorts of colorful finger sandwiches based on baked vegetable chips; change the nuts, greens, and cheese as you like.

You don't need a pastry bag here: You can either put the mixture in a ziplock plastic bag, cut off a corner, and squeeze out the filling, or just use two teaspoons to place the filling—like you were handling cookie dough.

> 1 pound beets (about 2 large), peeled
>
> 2 tablespoons olive oil, plus more as needed
>
> Salt
>
> 4 ounces fresh goat cheese, optional
>
> 1½ cups shelled pistachios
>
> 1 bunch watercress, baby spinach, or arugula (about 2 cups leaves)
>
> Black pepper

1. Heat the oven to 400°F. Slice the beets about ⅛ inch thick, using a mandoline, food processor, or sharp knife. Grease a couple of baking sheets with some of the oil. Spread the beet slices out in a single layer (it's okay if they're close) and sprinkle with salt. Bake, turning as needed, until they're crisp and lightly browned, 10 to 15 minutes total. Remove them from the pans and cool on wire racks.

2. Combine the goat cheese if you're using it with the pistachios and greens in a food processor. Sprinkle with salt and pepper and, with the machine running, drizzle in the 2 tablespoons oil. If the mixture doesn't come together, add more oil until the filling is smooth and fluffy. Taste and adjust the seasoning; then cover and refrigerate it until you are ready to assemble the sandwiches (or up to a few hours ahead).

3. Transfer the goat cheese mixture to a pastry bag (or use one of the alternatives mentioned in the headnote). Squeeze dabs of the filling onto a beet chip, then top with another and press gently. Repeat until either the chips or the filling run out, then serve.

Stuffed Semi-Dried Tomatoes

Makes: 4 to 8 servings   Time: About 1 hour

Tasty and colorful, these roasted plum tomatoes, stuffed with pesto, are year-round staples in southern France and much of Italy. You can use almost any stuffing you like here, or hollow out (for example) zucchini and treat them the same way.

 ½ cup olive oil, plus more as needed

 1 pound Roma (plum) tomatoes, halved lengthwise and seeded

 2 loosely packed cups fresh basil

 Salt

 ½ garlic clove, or to taste

 2 tablespoons pine nuts or chopped walnuts

 ½ cup grated Parmesan, Pecorino Romano, or other hard cheese

1. Heat the oven to 325°F. Grease a large rimmed baking sheet or roasting pan with some of the oil. Put the tomatoes facedown on the baking sheet (it's okay if they're a little close) and drizzle with a little more oil. Roast (there's no need to turn) until dry and beginning to shrivel a bit, about 30 minutes. (You can make the tomatoes up to a day ahead. Cover tightly and refrigerate but bring back to room temperature before proceeding.) Turn on the broiler; the heat should be medium-high and the rack about 4 inches from the fire.

2. Combine the basil with a pinch of salt, the garlic, nuts, and about ¼ cup of the remaining oil in a food processor or blender. Process, stopping to scrape down the sides of the bowl if necessary, adding the rest of the oil gradually. (You can make the pesto ahead, too. Store in the refrigerator for a week or 2 or in the freezer for several months.) Stir in the cheese by hand just before assembling.

3. Spoon a little pesto into each tomato cup and broil just long enough for the filling to bubble and brown a bit, just a minute or 2 (so watch them). Serve hot.

Ⓕ Fast   Ⓜ Make-Ahead   Ⓟ Pantry Staple

Panisses (Chickpea Fries)

For a time, these were My New Favorite Thing, and you may have the same reaction. They're based on the concept that any batter, porridge, or dough can be chilled, cut into shapes, and fried. When done right—either with chickpea flour or either of the grain-based variations—they're velvety on the inside, crisp on the outside, and ten times more interesting than French fries. This recipe includes a sea salt topping with Spanish flavors, but you can also serve these fries with flavored mayonnaise (for homemade, see page 188), ketchup, salsa (for homemade, see page 46), chutney, pesto (for homemade, see page 197) . . . or any other condiment you can think of.

> 2 cups chickpea flour (besan)
>
> Salt and black pepper
>
> 6 tablespoons olive oil
>
> 1 tablespoon coarse sea salt
>
> ½ teaspoon pimentón (smoked paprika)
>
> ½ teaspoon grated lemon or lime zest

1. Bring a quart of water to a boil in a medium saucepan. Whisk in the chickpea flour, reduce the heat to medium-high, and cook, stirring constantly, until the mixture is thick and smooth, about 10 minutes. Stir in a sprinkling of the regular salt, a little pepper, and 2 tablespoons of the oil. Pour the chickpea flour mixture onto a greased rimmed baking sheet, cover with plastic wrap, and refrigerate for at least 1 hour (leaving it in the refrigerator overnight is fine too).

2. Meanwhile, combine ½ teaspoon black pepper, the sea salt, pimentón, and lemon zest in a small bowl.

3. When the batter is firm, cut it into sticks about ½ inch by 2 to 3 inches. Put the remaining 4 tablespoons oil in a large skillet over medium-high heat. Fry the panisses in the oil until golden and crisp on both sides. (You may have to work in batches, depending on the size of your skillet.) Drain the cooked panisses on paper towels. Serve immediately or at room temperature sprinkled with the salt mixture.

Polenta Fries. Nice served with All-Purpose Tomato Sauce (page 194) for dipping. Substitute 1 cup polenta and 3 cups water for the chickpea flour and water in the main recipe.

Oat Fries. Substitute rolled oats for the chickpea flour, pulsing them first in a food processor to grind them into a coarse meal. Cook in the water for 15 minutes instead of 10.

Crisp-Crusted Portobellos with Lemon Chutney

Makes: 4 to 6 servings   Time: About 1 hour

Breaded, fried mushrooms have been a bar-and-grill staple since the 1970s, and when they're good, they are really good. This pan-fried version is a consistent winner, thanks in large part to the bread crumbs, which should be either homemade or panko, the super-crunchy Japanese bread crumbs that make for impeccably crisp coatings (and are now available in whole wheat). I like to serve these with a quick lemon chutney, which contributes a salty sourness that fresh lemons just don't have.

2 lemons

1 small red onion, chopped

¼ cup brown sugar

¼ cup sherry vinegar

Salt

About 12 ounces portobello or cremini (baby portobello) mushrooms

⅔ cup whole wheat flour, for dredging

2 cups bread crumbs, preferably whole grain and homemade, or panko, for dredging

2 eggs

Black pepper

Olive oil, for frying

 Fast   Make-Ahead   Ⓟ Pantry Staple

1. Trim the ends of the lemons, then cut them in half and remove the seeds. Chop the lemons up and put them in a saucepan along with as much of their juice as possible. Add the onion, brown sugar, vinegar, a large pinch of salt, and ½ cup water and bring to a boil. Lower the heat a bit and cook, stirring occasionally, until the mixture is syrupy and the lemon peels have softened, 15 to 20 minutes. Remove from the heat and cool.

2. Heat the oven to 200°F. Clean and trim the mushrooms so that only the caps remain. If you're using large portobellos, cut them into strips. Set out the flour and bread crumbs on plates or shallow bowls next to each other on your counter. Beat the eggs in a shallow bowl, add 2 tablespoons water, and season generously with salt and pepper. Have a stack of parchment or wax paper ready.

3. Dredge the mushrooms, one at a time, in the flour, then dip in the egg, then dredge in the bread crumbs. Stack the breaded mushrooms between layers of wax paper on a plate, then refrigerate the stack for at least 10 minutes or up to 3 hours.

4. Put about ¼ inch oil in a deep pan on the stove and turn the heat to medium-high; when the oil is ready (about 350°F), a pinch of flour will sizzle in it. Start to put the mushrooms in the pan, being careful not to overcrowd them. Cook the mushrooms in batches, turning when the first side gets brown, until they are evenly crisp and golden. The total cooking time should be 5 minutes or less. As each piece is done, first put it on paper towels to drain briefly, then transfer to an ovenproof platter and put the platter in the oven. Add more oil to the pan as necessary and continue until all the mushrooms are done. Serve hot with the chutney on the side.

Crisp-Crusted Baby Artichokes. Use 1½ pounds baby artichokes (or high-quality marinated artichoke hearts) in place of the mushrooms. If they're very large, cut them in half. Drain the artichokes well and pat them dry before dredging them or the flour, egg, and bread crumbs won't stick.

Crisp-Crusted Baked Portobellos. Aside from cutting down on the amount of fat in the recipe, baking the mushrooms in the oven requires less attention than frying; however, they won't get quite as brown and crisp as their stovetop siblings. Heat the oven to 400°F. At the beginning of Step 4, put the breaded slices about 1 inch apart on one or more greased baking sheets. Bake until golden, 15 to 20 minutes.

Sweet Potato and Corn Fritters with Thai Dipping Sauce

Makes: 4 to 8 servings   Time: 30 minutes

Crazy good, crazy simple—and not to mention pretty—these pan-fried fritters are best with peak summer corn, but frozen works all right too. Or, since fresh sweet potatoes are available all year, you can just skip the corn and increase their quantity to 3 cups.

¼ cup lime juice

1 tablespoon nam pla (fish sauce) or soy sauce, or to taste

½ teaspoon minced garlic

1 teaspoon minced ginger

Pinch of red chile flakes

Pinch of sugar, optional

2 cups grated sweet potato, squeezed dry if necessary

1 cup corn kernels (frozen are fine)

1 fresh hot chile (like Thai), minced

4 scallions, chopped

3 tablespoons chopped fresh cilantro

1 egg or 2 egg whites, lightly beaten

⅓ cup whole wheat or all-purpose flour

Salt and black pepper

Vegetable oil, for frying

1. Combine the lime juice, fish sauce, garlic, ginger, chile flakes, and sugar if you're using it in a small bowl with 1 tablespoon water.

2. Heat the oven to 275°F. Put the sweet potato, corn, chile, scallions, cilantro, egg, and flour in a bowl and mix well; sprinkle with salt and pepper. (You can do this ahead of time and refrigerate the batter for a couple of hours before cooking.)

3. Put about ⅛ inch oil in a large skillet over medium-high heat. When it's hot, drop spoonfuls of the sweet potato mixture into the oil and spread

Ⓕ Fast   Ⓜ Make-Ahead   Ⓟ Pantry Staple

them out a bit. (Work in batches to prevent overcrowding and transfer the finished fritters to the oven until all are finished.) Cook, turning once, until golden on both sides and cooked through, about 5 minutes. Serve hot or at room temperature with the dipping sauce.

Sweet Potato Fritters with Walnut-Sage Dipping Sauce. For the sauce, put ¼ cup walnuts and 2 or 3 roughly chopped sage leaves in a food processor and process until the nuts are coarsely ground. With the machine running, add ¼ cup olive oil through the feed tube and continue processing until you have a smooth sauce. Transfer the sauce to a small pan and warm it over medium heat. Sprinkle with salt and pepper and keep warm. For the fritters, use 3 cups grated sweet potato, omit the corn, and use olive or vegetable oil. Proceed with the recipe.

Fancier Fritters

When dropped fritters aren't quite elegant enough for the occasion, you can dust your hands with flour and shape the fritter batter into small patties, cylinders, or other shapes. Cook immediately or refrigerate, loosely covered, for up to a couple hours before cooking.

To make croquettes—which are essentially breaded fritters—set up 3 bowls: one with flour, one with an egg beaten with a splash of milk, and another with bread crumbs (preferably made from whole grain bread). Carefully dredge each shaped fritter in the flour, then the egg mixture, and finally the bread crumbs. Fry until crisp and golden as described in the fritter recipes here on pages 88 to 90.

Zucchini Cornmeal Fritters with Yogurt Dill Sauce

Makes: 4 to 8 servings   Time: 30 minutes

Zucchini and dill complement each other beautifully, so there's dill in the dipping sauce here as well as in the batter. The cornmeal ensures a nice crispy crust; for a bit more chew, try the variation made with whole grains.

> ½ cup plain yogurt, preferably whole milk
>
> 1 tablespoon lemon juice, or to taste
>
> 3 tablespoons chopped fresh dill, or 1 teaspoon dried
>
> Salt and black pepper
>
> 3 medium zucchini, grated (3 packed cups)
>
> ½ small onion, chopped
>
> 1 egg or 2 egg whites, lightly beaten
>
> ⅓ cup cornmeal (fine or medium grind)
>
> Olive oil, for frying

1. Heat the oven to 275°F. Combine the yogurt, lemon juice, and 2 tablespoons of the chopped dill (or ½ teaspoon dried). Sprinkle with salt and pepper, then taste and add more salt or lemon.

2. Squeeze the zucchini dry with your hands or a towel and put it in a large bowl. Add the onion, remaining 1 tablespoon fresh (or ½ teaspoon dried) dill, egg, and cornmeal; mix well and sprinkle with salt and pepper. (You can prepare the batter ahead of time to this point and refrigerate for up to a couple hours before cooking.)

3. Put about ¼ inch oil in a large skillet over medium-high heat. When it's hot, drop spoonfuls of the zucchini mixture into the oil and spread them out a bit. (Work in batches to prevent overcrowding and transfer the finished fritters to the oven until all are finished.) Cook, turning once, until golden on both sides and cooked through, about 5 minutes. Serve hot or at room temperature with the yogurt sauce.

Ⓕ Fast   Ⓜ Make-Ahead   Ⓟ Pantry Staple

Hummus Pancakes with Mediterranean Spice Mix

Makes: 4 to 8 servings   Time: About 30 minutes with cooked or canned chickpeas

These taste a lot like falafel—but they're smoother, more delicate, and don't require any soaking or deep-frying. The spice mix here is fantastic, but the pancakes also go great with Green Apple-Cucumber Salsa (page 46), Chimi-churri (page 460), or a dollop of yogurt. You can also make pancakes from any bean; check out the variations below for some ideas.

> 2 teaspoons cumin
>
> 1 teaspoon paprika
>
> 1 teaspoon chili powder
>
> 1 teaspoon coriander
>
> 2 cups cooked or canned chickpeas, drained, liquid reserved
>
> ½ cup tahini
>
> Juice of 1 lemon
>
> 1 egg
>
> 2 tablespoons olive oil, plus more for cooking the pancakes
>
> 1 tablespoon minced garlic
>
> Salt and black pepper
>
> ½ cup whole wheat flour, more or less

1. Put a large skillet or griddle over medium-high heat. Heat the oven to 200°F. Combine 1 teaspoon of the cumin with the paprika, chili powder, and coriander in a small bowl.

2. Combine the chickpeas, tahini, lemon juice, egg, oil, garlic, remaining 1 teaspoon cumin, and a little salt and pepper in a food processor or blender and process until very smooth; you may need to add a bit of liquid from the chickpeas (or water) to get the mixture moving. Transfer to a bowl and fold in the flour, a little at a time (you might not need all of it), until the mixture drops easily from a large spoon.

3. Start cooking when a drop of water dances on the surface of the skillet or griddle. Work in batches, greasing the surface with a little oil before adding more batter to the pan. Spoon on the batter to form 3- to 4-inch pancakes. Cook until the edges of the pancakes look set, then turn and cook the other side until golden, about 3 minutes per side. Keep the finished pancakes in the oven if you like while you cook the others. Serve hot or at room temperature sprinkled with the spice mixture and a little more salt.

White Bean Pancakes with Orange Pepper. Use white beans and the juice of ½ orange instead of the lemon juice. Replace the cumin in the pancake batter with 1 tablespoon chopped fresh parsley. In place of the spice mixture, garnish the pancakes with 1 teaspoon black pepper mixed with the grated zest of 1 orange.

Pinto Bean Pancakes with Mole Powder. Use pinto beans, lime juice instead of lemon juice, and pumpkin seeds instead of tahini. Garnish with a mix of 1 teaspoon cocoa powder, 1 teaspoon ground ancho chile (or chili powder), and 1 teaspoon cinnamon.

Lentil Pancakes with Pimentón. Use brown lentils, the juice of ½ orange instead of lemon juice, almond butter instead of tahini, and pimentón instead of cumin in the batter. Dust with a little more pimentón if you like.

Spinach-Bulgur Patties with Skordalia

Makes: 4 to 8 servings   Time: 1½ hours

Skordalia is a thick, garlicky dip with the creaminess of mayonnaise but no eggs. Make it from almonds or any other nut, and it's a wonderful accompaniment for these tender but robustly flavored Spinach-Bulgur Patties, which combine several traditional Mediterranean ingredients into one delicious dish. For the patties, try any sturdy green—kale, chard, or collards.

>   5 tablespoons olive oil, plus more for frying the patties
>
>   1 tablespoon minced garlic
>
>   About 8 ounces (1 pound before trimming) spinach leaves, chopped
>
>   1 cup bulgur

4 to 4½ cups vegetable or chicken stock (for homemade, see pages 135 to 140) or water

Salt and black pepper

1 thick slice day-old bread, preferably whole wheat

1 cup whole, skin-on almonds (not raw)

3 garlic cloves, or to taste

¼ teaspoon cayenne or 1 teaspoon not-too-hot ground dried chile, or to taste

1 tablespoon lemon juice, or to taste

1. Put 3 tablespoons of the oil in a pot over medium heat. When it's hot, add the minced garlic and cook, stirring often, until fragrant, about 2 minutes. Add the spinach and stir until wilted, about 3 minutes. Add the bulgur, 2½ cups of the stock, salt, and pepper and bring to a boil. Turn the heat down to low, cover, and cook until the grain is starchy and thick like porridge, 45 to 60 minutes. Add another ½ cup stock if the grain becomes too dry. Let the bulgur-spinach mixture cool to room temperature.

2. Meanwhile, make the skordalia. Put the bread in a food processor and saturate it with some of the remaining stock. Wait a couple minutes, then add the remaining 2 tablespoons oil, the almonds, 3 garlic cloves, and cayenne. Process the mixture until the almonds are ground. With the machine running, pour in enough of the remaining stock to form a creamy sauce. Add the lemon juice and some salt and pepper and pulse one last time.

3. When the bulgur-spinach mixture is cool, put a thin film of oil in a skillet over medium heat until it shimmers. Form the bulgur mixture into 1-inch balls and flatten the balls into patties. Working in batches to avoid overcrowding, fry the patties until crisp and golden, 3 to 5 minutes per side. Drain the patties on paper towels and serve warm or at room temperature with the skordalia.

Baked Mushroom-Sesame Rice Balls

Makes: 4 to 8 servings   Time: 2½ hours, largely unattended

This spin on *onigiri*, Japanese sticky white rice balls, combines the earthiness of brown rice and mushrooms with the crunch of a sesame seed crust. The key is cooking the rice until it releases all of its starch, then chilling it in the fridge so you can easily roll it into balls before baking.

If you have any sheets of nori (seaweed) lying around, you can cut them into strips and wrap them around the rice balls before or after baking.

  1½ cups short grain brown rice

  Salt

  Boiling water, as needed

  2 tablespoons vegetable oil, plus more for greasing the pans

  8 ounces fresh shiitake or button mushrooms, chopped

  Black pepper

  1 cup sesame seeds or finely chopped nuts, plus more as needed

  Soy sauce, for passing at the table

1. Put the rice in a large pot along with a big pinch of salt. Add enough water to cover by about 1½ inches. Bring to a boil, then adjust the heat so the mixture bubbles gently.

2. Cook, stirring occasionally and adding more boiling water if the rice begins to stick to the bottom, until the grains are very tender and burst, about an hour.

3. Meanwhile, put the oil in a large skillet over medium-high heat. When it's hot, add the mushrooms, sprinkle with salt and pepper, and cook, stirring occasionally, until dry, lightly browned, and almost crisp, 10 to 15 minutes. When the rice is starchy and very thick, stir in the mushrooms, transfer to a bowl, and let cool in the fridge, at least 45 minutes and up to 24 hours.

4. When you are ready to bake the rice balls, heat the oven to 375°F and grease two large baking sheets. Pour the sesame seeds into a shallow bowl. Roll the rice mixture into 1½-inch balls, dip each ball into the sesame seeds to coat it completely, and put the balls 2 inches apart on the prepared pans.

Ⓕ Fast   Ⓜ Make-Ahead   Ⓟ Pantry Staple

Bake the rice balls, turning them as needed, until crisp and golden, 25 to 30 minutes. Serve immediately, passing soy sauce at the table.

Tabbouleh-Stuffed Chard Leaves

Makes: 4 to 8 servings   Time: About 1 hour

A new take on Greek dolmades, grape leaves which are usually stuffed with rice and meat or lentils. This version is easy enough to be part of any Mediterranean-style spread, since the herb-based stuffing comes together in minutes and requires no cooking.

If chard is unavailable (or tired looking), use kale, cabbage, or large spinach leaves (you'll need more of these though). Or, to save even more time, use grape leaves, sold in jars in most supermarkets. Green Barley Pilaf (page 297), Farro or Wheat Berries with Grapes and Rosemary (page 309), and Chickpea Tagine with Chicken and Bulgur (page 388) also make good fillings for this recipe.

These are delicious alone, but Fresh Tomato Sauce (page 195) makes a really nice accompaniment for dipping.

½ cup bulgur

Salt

⅓ cup olive oil, or more as needed

¼ cup lemon juice, or to taste

12 to 16 whole chard leaves, any size

2 cups chopped fresh parsley

1 cup roughly chopped fresh mint

½ cup chopped scallions or red onion

Black pepper

Lemon wedges

1. Soak the bulgur in hot water to cover until tender, 15 to 30 minutes. Bring a large pot of water to a boil and salt it. Have a large bowl of ice water handy. Drain the bulgur, then squeeze out as much of the water as possible. Toss with the oil and lemon juice and season to taste.

2. Put half of the chard in the boiling water and count to 20 or so. When they're just pliable, carefully fish the leaves out and immediately plunge in the ice water. Repeat with the remaining leaves. When cool, drain. Carefully remove the toughest part of each chard stem by cutting close along either side of it (scissors are good for this), chop them, and add them to the bowl of bulgur.

3. Add the parsley, mint, and scallions to the bulgur and toss gently. Sprinkle with salt and pepper; taste and adjust the seasoning if necessary.

4. On a clean towel, lay one of the leaves in front of you and bring together the cut center of the leaf so the sides overlap a bit, closing the gap. Put a couple tablespoons of the tabbouleh on top of that seam (more if the leaves are large) and roll the leaf about a third of the way up; fold in both ends to enclose the filling like you would a burrito and then roll up the entire leaf. Put each stuffed leaf, seam side down, on a serving plate. Repeat with the remaining leaves and serve with lemon wedges.

Summer Rolls with Peanut Sauce

Makes: 4 to 8 servings   Time: About 1 hour

I've made summer rolls with Vietnamese grandmothers and been laughed at for my technique, but believe me—they were fine. Since they're nothing more than salad wrapped in moistened rice paper, there's only one technique to master, and it's not that difficult. The components, which might include a fair share of leftovers, can all be made ahead.

It takes a little practice to soak the rice paper for just the right amount of time (too short and it won't be pliable enough, too long and it'll fall apart), so you might want to have a few extra sheets on hand. What you use inside hardly matters, but don't overstuff them or they'll be difficult to roll up. After one or two, I promise you, you'll get it right.

 ½ cup roasted peanuts

 ½ cup coconut milk

 2 tablespoons lime juice

(F) Fast (M) Make-Ahead (P) Pantry Staple

1 tablespoon brown sugar

1 tablespoon soy sauce

1 tablespoon minced garlic

Salt and black pepper

1 head butter lettuce, 8 leaves left whole and the rest torn

1 cup shredded Napa cabbage

½ cup chopped fresh cilantro or mint

½ cup chopped fresh basil, preferably Thai

½ cup grated, shredded, or julienned carrot

½ cup chopped or slivered cucumber

2 scallions, cut lengthwise into slivers

8 ounces cooked shrimp, fish, chicken, pork, or tofu, chopped up or sliced into slivers, optional

Hot water as needed

8 sheets rice paper, 8 to 10 inches in diameter

1. Process the peanuts, coconut milk, lime juice, brown sugar, soy sauce, and garlic in a food processor until fairly smooth; taste and add salt and pepper as you like. (You can make the dipping sauce up to a day ahead; cover and refrigerate until ready to serve.)

2. Prepare the other ingredients and set them out on your work surface. Set out a bowl of hot water (110° to 120°F) and a clean kitchen towel.

3. Put a sheet of rice paper in the water and let it soak for about 10 seconds, just until soft (don't let it become too soft; it will continue to soften as you work). Lay it on the towel. (You can soak them all and stack them between layers of towels if you like; they'll keep in the refrigerator that way for up to several hours.)

4. Lay a lettuce leaf toward the bottom third of one rice paper and top with a small amount of each filling ingredient (using no more than ½ cup per roll). Roll up the rice paper to enclose the filling, then tuck in the sides as you would a burrito; keep it fairly tight and continue rolling, then press the seam to seal. Serve whole or cut in half with the dipping sauce on the side.

Soups

One of the simplest ways to get a meal on the table is to make a pot of soup, and this collection of substantial recipes will help you do just that. The great thing about most soups is that you can make them ahead of time and reheat later, over the course of days if you like. At any time, add bread or a salad and you've got a meal.

Stock is an important component of good-tasting soup, but it's not essential; plain water is almost always an option. When you have fresh vegetables, grains, beans, and seasonings—with or without meat, poultry, or seafood—you will get flavorful soup (far better than anything from a box or can) even if water is your only liquid. (Remember that stock is simply water with flavors added.)

Will your soup be more luxurious and deeply flavored if you use homemade stock? You bet. That's why I've included stock recipes at the end of the chapter for anyone who wants to make them. (I would say at this point I make stock twice a year. While I'm never sorry I've made it, it's gone before I know it, and then I live without it again.)

How about stock from a can or carton? I *never* use it anymore. Though there are some better-quality canned stocks, most add unwanted flavors and mask the true taste of the other ingredients. (And the added expense is undeniable and often significant.)

In general, when you're making soup, there's no need to fuss over how your vegetables are cut or worry about timing their additions perfectly. Just let the mixture bubble gently for a bit to thicken and evolve. (Usually this can happen while you're doing something else.) Clean-Out-the-Fridge Vegetable Soup and the tomato-based soups that follow are perfect examples, which is why they kick off this chapter. The ingredients do the work of developing both texture and taste.

A word about portions: The recipes are all designed to serve four people 1½ cups of substantial soup. If soup is all you're eating, you might want more—up to 8 cups—so double the recipe and plan to have leftovers. For an appetizer or first course, 1 cup is probably enough for a serving, so you might consider that each recipe yields six servings or so.

Ⓕ Fast   Ⓜ Make-Ahead   Ⓟ Pantry Staple

Clean-Out-the-Fridge Vegetable Soup

Makes: 4 servings   Time: 45 to 60 minutes

A blueprint for building soup out of just about any vegetable you have handy. Start by cooking some aromatics in olive oil, add tomatoes for body and balance, and finish with various flavor boosters—you can't go wrong. A little Parmesan or meat (see the variation) are nice options, and depending on which vegetables you're using, a couple tablespoons of heavy cream might be nice. If you have some stock, by all means use it, but water works just fine.

> 4 tablespoons olive oil
>
> 1 onion, 3 scallions, or 1 leek (trimmed and well rinsed), chopped
>
> 2 carrots, 2 parsnips, or 2 turnips, roughly chopped
>
> 2 zucchini, 2 yellow squash, or 2 small bell peppers, roughly chopped
>
> 1 cup corn kernels (frozen are fine), fresh or frozen beans (like lima, fava, or edamame), or fresh or frozen peas
>
> 8 ounces spinach, cabbage, broccoli, or other leafy green or cruciferous vegetable, chopped
>
> Salt and black pepper
>
> 1 cup cored, chopped tomatoes (canned are fine; include their juice)
>
> ½ cup chopped fresh basil, plus more for garnish
>
> ½ cup grated Parmesan cheese, for serving, optional

1. Put 3 tablespoons of the oil in a large pot or Dutch oven over medium-high heat. When it's hot, add the onion and carrots. Cook, stirring, until the onion softens and the vegetables begin to color, 10 minutes or so.

2. Add the zucchini, corn, and spinach; sprinkle with salt and pepper. Cook, stirring, for a minute or 2, then add the tomatoes and 6 cups water. Bring to a boil, then adjust the heat so the mixture bubbles gently. Cook, stirring every now and then, until the vegetables are soft and the tomatoes have broken up, about 15 minutes. (The soup can be made up to this point a day or 2 ahead; gently reheat before proceeding.)

3. Add the ½ cup basil and adjust the heat once again so that the mixture bubbles gently. Cook until all the vegetables are very tender, 5 to 15 minutes longer. Taste and adjust the seasoning and drizzle with the remaining 1 tablespoon oil. Serve, passing basil and cheese at the table if you like.

Clean-Out-the-Fridge Vegetable Soup with Ground Beef or Sausage. Before adding the onion and carrots, brown 8 ounces crumbled ground beef or sausage in the olive oil. Remove the meat and proceed with the recipe. Stir the beef or sausage back into the soup along with the basil in Step 3.

Tomato-Bulgur Soup

Makes: 4 servings   Time: 30 minutes

There's no faster, surer way to enrich soup than by stirring in a handful of grains; they absorb the surrounding flavors and release starch to make the broth thick and creamy. Bulgur is ideal because it cooks in a flash, but you can use whatever you've got, including already cooked grains (leftovers are perfect) or ground grains like cornmeal. Depending on which you choose, the cooking time may decrease or increase from a little to (rarely) a lot, and you might need to add more liquid.

2 tablespoons olive oil

1 large onion, halved and sliced

1 large celery stalk, chopped

1 tablespoon minced garlic

Salt and black pepper

½ cup white wine

3 cups chopped tomatoes (canned are fine; include their juice)

1 tablespoon chopped fresh thyme, or 1 teaspoon dried

5 to 6 cups vegetable stock (for homemade, see pages 135 to 138) or water, or more as needed

¾ cup bulgur

¼ cup chopped fresh parsley, for garnish, optional

½ cup grated Parmesan cheese, for garnish, optional

  Ⓕ Fast   Ⓜ Make-Ahead   Ⓟ Pantry Staple

1. Put the oil in a large pot or Dutch oven over medium heat. When it's hot, add the onion, celery, and garlic. Sprinkle with salt and pepper and cook, stirring, until the onion begins to soften and turn golden, 5 to 10 minutes. Add the white wine and cook, stirring to loosen the bits of vegetable that have stuck to the bottom of the pan, for about 1 minute.

2. Add the tomatoes and thyme and cook, stirring occasionally, until the tomatoes break up, 10 to 15 minutes. Stir in the stock and bulgur, bring to a boil, and reduce the heat so the mixture gently bubbles. Cover and cook, stirring once or twice, until the bulgur is tender, about 10 minutes. If the mixture is too thick, add a little more stock or water. (You can make the soup up to this point and refrigerate for several days or freeze for months. Gently reheat before proceeding.) Taste and adjust the seasoning. Garnish with the parsley and Parmesan if you're using them, and serve.

Tuscan Tomato-Farro Soup with Seafood. Use farro instead of bulgur; it will need to cook for 20 to 25 minutes. When the grain is tender, add 8 ounces chopped shelled shrimp, squid, or scallops and cook until the seafood is opaque but still tender, about 2 minutes. Squeeze lemon juice into the pot if you like, garnish with parsley, and serve (omit the Parmesan).

Unfussy Tomatoes

There was a time when I peeled and seeded fresh tomatoes before cooking them, but now I rarely bother. The most I ever do is cut them in half and squeeze out some of the seeds—sometimes over a strainer if I want to catch the juice. Yes, the results are less elegant, but the flavor is better and the workload lighter. If you don't like big pieces of tomato skin in your soup or sauce, just chop the tomatoes in smaller pieces or pulse them in a food processor.

The other option is to use canned tomatoes. When I'm not in a hurry, I use whole peeled tomatoes, pluck out the cores, and squish or chop them up a bit right in the measuring cup. Diced tomatoes are fine too. Every recipe in this book specifies whether to drain canned tomatoes or reserve their juice.

Provençal Soup

Makes: 4 servings   Time: 45 to 60 minutes, largely unattended

Here are all the flavors of ratatouille, the sturdy, classic vegetable stew of southern France. To make an even more substantial soup, check out the variations.

¼ cup olive oil, plus a little more for garnish

1 large onion, chopped

4 to 6 garlic cloves, smashed or chopped

Salt and black pepper

1 medium or 2 small eggplants, cut into small cubes

1 large or 3 small zucchini, chopped

2 red bell peppers, chopped

3 cups chopped tomatoes (canned are fine; include their juice)

3 cups chicken or vegetable stock (for homemade, see pages 135 to 140) or water, or more as needed

½ cup black olives, pitted and chopped

½ cup chopped fresh basil, plus more for garnish

¼ cup grated Parmesan cheese, for garnish, optional

1. Put the oil in a large pot or Dutch oven over medium heat. When it's hot, add the onion and garlic, sprinkle with salt and pepper, and cook, stirring, until the onion begins to soften and turn golden, 3 to 5 minutes.

2. Add the eggplant, zucchini, bell peppers, tomatoes, and stock. Bring to a boil, then reduce the heat to medium-low. Cook, stirring occasionally, until the tomatoes have broken up and the eggplant and zucchini are super tender, about 45 minutes. (The soup can be made up to this point and refrigerated for several days or frozen for months; gently reheat before proceeding.) Stir in the olives and basil in the last 5 minutes of cooking. Serve garnished with a drizzle of olive oil, more basil, and the Parmesan if you like.

Provençal Soup with Anchovies. Add 4 or 5 oil-packed anchovies to the pan along with the onion and garlic in Step 1 and mash them roughly with a spoon before adding the other vegetables.

Provençal Soup with Lamb. Sear 8 ounces chopped lamb leg or shoulder (or use lamb sausage) in the oil before adding the onion and garlic in Step 1.

Tomato and Bread Soup
with Fennel and Fish

Makes: 4 servings   Time: 40 minutes

When you cross two classic Mediterranean soups—bouillabaisse and *pappa al pomodoro*, made from little more than bread and tomatoes—you get a flavorful blend that's simple enough for a weeknight but satisfying enough for dinner anytime, especially if you use a good whole grain bread.

¼ cup olive oil, plus more for garnish

Two 4-ounce fillets any firm white fish

1 large onion, halved and sliced

2 fennel bulbs, cored and thinly sliced

1 tablespoon minced garlic, or to taste

Salt and black pepper

3 cups chopped tomatoes (canned are fine; drain and reserve their juice)

1 to 2 cups vegetable stock (for homemade, see pages 135 to 138), water, or
    the liquid from the tomatoes if you're using canned (or a combination)

½ loaf (or more) day-old rustic bread, preferably whole wheat, cut into cubes

¼ cup torn fresh basil, optional

1. Put the oil in a large pot or Dutch oven over medium-high heat. A minute later, add the fish fillets, raise the heat to high, and cook for 1 to 3 minutes on each side, until the fillets are opaque and seared on the outside but still nearly raw on the inside. Remove the fish from the pot and reduce the heat to medium.

2. Add the onion, fennel, and garlic to the pan. Sprinkle with salt and pepper and cook, stirring, until everything is fragrant and the onion and fennel soften and turn golden, 5 to 10 minutes.

3. Add the tomatoes and cook, stirring occasionally, until the pieces break up, 10 to 15 minutes. Cut the fish into bite-size pieces and add it along with the stock and bread to the tomato mixture. Bring to a gentle boil, bubble for another minute, and take the pot off the heat. Cover and let it sit until the bread is saturated with the soup, about 10 minutes.

4. Stir in the basil if you're using it, then taste and adjust the seasoning. Divide the soup among bowls, top with a drizzle of oil and more black pepper, and serve.

Watermelon and Tomato Gazpacho with Feta

Makes: 4 servings   Time: 20 minutes, plus time to chill (optional)

The combination of cool watermelon and tomatoes with feta is as good as it gets in the summer, and just about as easy. One simple variation: use peaches instead of the watermelon *or* the tomatoes—it's great either way.

> 1 garlic clove
>
> 1 small watermelon, or a section of a larger one, about 3 pounds, flesh removed from the rind, seeded, and cut into large chunks
>
> 2 ripe tomatoes, cored and cut into wedges
>
> 2 tablespoons lemon juice, or to taste
>
> Salt and black pepper
>
> 4 ounces crumbled feta cheese
>
> ¼ cup olive oil
>
> ½ cup chopped fresh basil or mint, for garnish

1. Put the garlic in a food processor and pulse a few times to chop it. Add the watermelon, tomatoes, and lemon juice, with a sprinkling of salt and pepper. You have two choices here: chunky or smooth. It all depends on whether you turn the machine on and leave it on, or just pulse a few times. Add a few ice cubes, one at a time, just enough to keep the machine working, and blend or pulse until smooth or chunky. Put the gazpacho in the fridge to chill a bit if you like, up to several hours.

2. Just before serving, taste the gazpacho and add more salt, pepper, or lemon juice as needed (remember you'll be adding feta, which is usually salty). Pour the gazpacho into 4 bowls, top with the feta, drizzle with a few drops of olive oil, garnish with the herb, and serve.

Ⓕ Fast   Ⓜ Make-Ahead   Ⓟ Pantry Staple

Curried Tomato Soup
with Hard-Boiled Eggs

Makes: 4 servings   Time: 40 minutes

This hearty vegetable soup is based on *makhani*, a spicy Indian tomato sauce that's hot, slightly sweet, and frequently used for braising hard-boiled eggs. The difference here is that I add lots of chopped vegetables and some coconut milk, turning the sauce into a thick soup with a sublimely silky texture. Don't let the long ingredient list put you off; the soup comes together rather quickly.

¼ cup vegetable oil

1 onion, chopped

1 tablespoon minced garlic

1 tablespoon minced ginger

1 tablespoon minced fresh hot chile (like jalapeño or Thai)

2 tablespoons curry powder

1 teaspoon cumin

Pinch of sugar

2 all-purpose potatoes, peeled and chopped

1 carrot, chopped

Salt and black pepper

3 cups vegetable stock (for homemade, see pages 135 to 138) or water

1 cup coconut milk

3 cups chopped tomatoes (canned are fine; include their juice)

1 small cauliflower, cored and roughly chopped

4 hard-boiled eggs, roughly chopped, for garnish

¼ cup chopped fresh cilantro, for garnish

1. Put the oil in a large pot or Dutch oven over medium-high heat. When it's hot, add the onion, garlic, ginger, and chile. Cook, stirring occasionally, until softened, 3 to 5 minutes. Stir in the curry powder, cumin, and sugar. Cook and stir until the spices become fragrant, a minute or 2 more.

2. Add the potatoes and carrot and sprinkle with salt and pepper. Cook, stirring, for a minute or 2, then add the vegetable stock, coconut milk, and tomatoes with their liquid. Bring to a boil, then lower the heat so the mixture bubbles gently. Cook, stirring once in a while, until the potatoes and carrots are fairly soft, 15 to 20 minutes.

3. Add the cauliflower and adjust the heat so that the mixture bubbles gently. Cook until all the vegetables are very tender, about 15 minutes more. (The soup can be made up to this point in advance and refrigerated for several days or frozen for months; gently reheat before proceeding.) Serve garnished with the hard-boiled eggs and cilantro.

Curried Tomato Soup with Poached Eggs. Instead of garnishing each bowl with chopped hard-boiled eggs, during the last 5 minutes of cooking in Step 3, carefully crack 4 eggs into the gently bubbling soup and cover the pot. Start checking the eggs after about 3 minutes; cook until the whites are firmed up a bit or longer if you prefer. To serve, spoon some soup and an egg in each bowl and garnish with cilantro.

(F) Fast (M) Make-Ahead (P) Pantry Staple

Vegetable-Lentil Soup with Fragrant Broth

Makes: 4 servings   Time: 1½ hours, largely unattended

Onion and garlic, cooked until they nearly melt together, give this soup a base with incredible aroma and a touch of sweetness. Common brown lentils are best here, but you can also use red lentils or yellow or green split peas, all of which cook faster. This soup is on the brothy side, so if you like it thicker, add another ¼ cup lentils.

    2 tablespoons olive oil, plus more for drizzling

    1 onion, chopped

    1 tablespoon minced garlic

    Salt and black pepper

    2 cups chopped tomatoes (canned are fine; include their juice)

    3 carrots, chopped

    3 celery stalks, chopped

    ½ cup dried lentils, rinsed and picked over

    6 cups vegetable stock (for homemade, see pages 135 to 138) or water

    Several sprigs fresh thyme, or several pinches dried

1. Put the oil in a large pot or Dutch oven over medium-high heat. When it's hot, add the onion and cook, stirring occasionally, until softened, 3 to 5 minutes. Add the garlic and cook for another minute, sprinkling with salt and pepper. Turn the heat down to medium-low and cook, stirring occasionally, until the vegetables are golden and beginning to melt together, about 20 minutes.

2. Turn the heat back up to medium-high and stir in the tomatoes, carrots, celery, and lentils. Add the stock and thyme, then bring to a boil. Turn the heat down to medium-low so that the soup bubbles gently.

3. Cook, stirring occasionally, until the lentils and vegetables are tender, 20 to 30 minutes; add water as necessary to keep the mixture brothy. Fish out the thyme sprigs, then taste and adjust the seasoning. (The soup can be made up to this point in advance and refrigerated for several days or frozen for months; gently reheat before proceeding.) Serve each bowl of soup with a drizzle of olive oil on top.

Roasted Asparagus and White Bean Soup with Parmesan

Makes: 4 servings   Time: About 45 minutes with cooked or canned beans

The combination of tender white beans and crisp roasted asparagus gives this soup incredible texture and big-time flavor. It's a nice first course for entertaining, since you can prepare both components up to a day ahead of time and then heat them together just before serving. For extra elegance, purée the beans (see the first variation). If you cooked the beans from scratch, use the cooking water as some or all of the liquid here.

 4 tablespoons olive oil, plus more for garnish

 2 whole leeks, trimmed, well rinsed, and thinly sliced

 1 tablespoon minced garlic

 1 tablespoon chopped fresh rosemary, or 1 teaspoon dried

 Salt and black pepper

 ½ cup dry white wine

 2 baking potatoes, peeled and chopped

 3 cups cooked or canned white beans, drained, liquid reserved

 6 cups vegetable or chicken stock (for homemade, see pages 135 to 140),
    bean-cooking liquid, or water, plus more as needed

 About 1½ pounds asparagus, peeled if thick

 One 2-ounce piece Parmesan cheese

1. Heat the oven to 450°F. Put 2 tablespoons of the oil in a large pot or Dutch oven over medium-high heat. When it's hot, add the leeks and cook, stirring occasionally, until softened a bit and beginning to color, 3 to 5 minutes. Add the garlic and rosemary and cook for another minute. Sprinkle with salt and pepper, add the white wine, and stir to loosen the bits of vegetable that have stuck to the bottom of the pan.

2. Add the potatoes, about half of the beans, and the stock. Bring to a boil, then lower the heat so that the mixture bubbles steadily. Cover partially and cook, stirring infrequently, until the potatoes are disintegrating, 20 to 30 minutes; add more liquid as necessary so the mixture remains soupy.

Ⓕ Fast   Ⓜ Make-Ahead   Ⓟ Pantry Staple

3. Meanwhile (or ahead of time), put the asparagus in a shallow roasting pan, drizzle with the remaining 2 tablespoons oil, and sprinkle with salt. Roast, turning the spears once or twice, just until the thick part of the stalks can be pierced with a knife, 10 to 15 minutes. Remove from the oven to cool a bit. Meanwhile, use a vegetable peeler to shave slices from the piece of cheese.

4. When the soup is ready, mash the potatoes and beans a bit. Chop the asparagus and add it to the pot along with the remaining beans to warm through. Taste and adjust the seasoning. Serve each bowl with some shaved cheese on top.

Puréed Asparagus and White Bean Soup. After you add the chopped roasted asparagus in Step 4, carefully purée the soup in batches in a food processor or blender or with an immersion blender; or simply mash with a potato masher. If you prefer, purée only the beans and broth and add the chopped asparagus just before serving.

Cabbage and White Bean Soup with Sausage. Before adding the leeks to the oil in Step 1, fry 8 ounces of crumbled Italian sausage in the oil. Substitute 1 small head cabbage for the asparagus. Instead of roasting it, slice the cabbage into ribbons and stir it into the pot along with the potatoes in Step 2.

Two-Pea Soup with Frizzled Ham

Makes: 4 servings   Time: About 1 hour

Split pea soup with ham is a classic, and a perennial favorite, but that doesn't mean you can't update it. This version is considerably fresher than the norm, with the addition of fresh (or frozen) peas, and ham doing double-duty as both seasoning and garnish. (If you happen to have a ham bone, by all means toss that in there, too—but in Step 2 increase the cooking time until the meat falls off the bone.)

3 tablespoons olive oil

8 ounces smoked ham or prosciutto, chopped

2 onions, chopped

2 carrots, chopped

2 tablespoons minced garlic

Salt and black pepper

8 cups vegetable or chicken stock (for homemade, see pages 135 to 140) or water, plus more as needed

1½ cups dried split peas, washed and picked over

2 cups fresh or frozen peas

¼ cup chopped fresh mint

1. Put 2 tablespoons of the olive oil in a large pot or Dutch oven over medium-high heat; when it's hot, add the ham and cook until it begins to crisp and release from the pan, 3 to 5 minutes. Stir to turn the pieces, and continue to cook and stir until they are quite crisp, about 10 minutes total. Remove with a slotted spoon and drain on towels. Lower the heat to medium.

2. Add the remaining oil to the pot, along with the onions, carrots, and garlic. Sprinkle with salt and pepper and cook, stirring occasionally, until the vegetables soften and begin to turn golden, 5 to 7 minutes. Add the stock and the split peas. Bring to a boil, then turn the heat down so the mixture bubbles gently but steadily. Cook, stirring occasionally, until the split peas are tender, at least 30 minutes and up to 1 hour; add more liquid as necessary so the mixture remains soupy.

Ⓕ Fast   Ⓜ Make-Ahead   Ⓟ Pantry Staple

3. When the split peas are tender and the soup is thickened, stir the green peas and mint into the pot. Cook until they are heated through and turn bright green, no more than 5 minutes; taste and adjust the seasoning and serve with bits of the frizzled ham on top.

Red Bean Soup with Hearty Greens

Makes: 4 servings   Time: About 1½ hours

Once the pot is bubbling you can walk away from this easily assembled soup, at least for the first 30 minutes or so. The ham hock is optional, but it really does add a lot of flavor, as well as nice bits to chew on—so unless you're a vegetarian, do include it (or a small piece of smoked ham if you can't find a hock).

1 cup dried red kidney beans, rinsed, picked over, and soaked if you have time

1 onion, chopped

1 carrot, chopped

1 celery stalk, chopped

2 bay leaves

1 smoked ham hock, optional

2 bunches collard greens or kale (about 2 pounds), chopped

1 tablespoon minced garlic, optional

Salt and black pepper

1. Put the beans in a large pot or Dutch oven. Add 6 cups water, the onion, carrot, celery, bay leaves, and ham hock if you're using it. Bring to a boil over medium-high heat, then turn the heat down so the mixture bubbles gently but steadily. Cook, stirring infrequently, until the beans are very soft and the meat is falling off the bone, anywhere from 45 to 90 minutes; add more liquid as necessary so the mixture remains soupy.

2. Remove the hock from the pot and let it cool slightly. Pull all of the meat off the bone and return it to the pot. (You can make the soup ahead to this point and refrigerate it for a few days or freeze it for weeks; gently reheat before proceeding.) Remove the bay leaves and add the greens, along with the garlic if you're using it. Cover and cook until the greens are tender, about 10 minutes. Taste, add salt and pepper, and serve.

Pasta and Beans with Escarole. Don't make this in advance or the pasta will become mushy. When you add the ingredients to the pot in Step 1, add 2 cups chopped tomatoes (or use canned and include some of the liquid). Substitute escarole for the collards or kale. Add ½ cup uncooked small pasta, like shells or elbows, or larger pasta broken into bits, a few minutes after adding the escarole. Cook, checking after 5 minutes or so, until the escarole is tender and the pasta is tender but not mushy. Garnish each bowl with a drizzle of olive oil.

No Time for Dried Beans? Use Canned.

Most of the bean soups in this chapter start with dried beans, since they create a rich, thick "stock" as they cook. Canned beans are undeniably faster so, of course, they're an option when you're in a hurry. Here's how to adjust the recipe: Use 2 cans—about 3 cups—canned beans for each cup of dried beans. (I drain and rinse them. If you like to use their canning water for some of the liquid called for in the recipe, go right ahead; just be careful not to oversalt the soup.) Then follow the directions, but hold back on the canned beans until the last step so they don't turn to mush.

Ⓕ Fast   Ⓜ Make-Ahead   Ⓟ Pantry Staple

Black Bean and Rice Soup with Carrot Relish

Makes: 4 to 6 servings   Time: About 2 hours, largely unattended

A quickly pickled carrot relish adds punch to a classic black bean soup that includes brown rice for texture and flavor. Add some corn tortillas or chips and you've got a meal—including the salad—right in the bowl.

2 tablespoons olive oil

4 ounces fresh or smoked chorizo, chopped

1 onion, chopped

1 red bell pepper, chopped

1 tablespoon minced garlic

1 cup dried black beans, rinsed, picked over, and soaked if you have time

4 carrots, grated

Salt

1 fresh hot chile (like jalapeño or Thai), minced

1 teaspoon cumin

Juice of 2 limes

½ cup brown rice

Black pepper

¼ cup chopped fresh cilantro

1. Put the oil in a large pot or Dutch oven over medium heat. When it's hot, add the chorizo, onion, bell pepper, and garlic and cook, stirring occasionally, until the chorizo is nicely browned and the vegetables begin to soften, 5 to 10 minutes.

2. Add the beans and cover with 2 quarts water. Bring to a boil, then turn the heat down to low so that the mixture bubbles gently. Partially cover and cook, stirring infrequently.

3. Meanwhile, put the carrots in a colander. Add ½ teaspoon salt and toss well. Let them sit in the sink or over a bowl for 30 minutes, tossing occasionally. Rinse off the salt with cold water, squeeze the carrots a bit to dry them, and toss with the chile, cumin, and lime juice. Refrigerate until the soup is ready.

4. When the beans are about half done—softening but not yet tender in the middle, anywhere from 45 to 60 minutes or more—stir the rice into the pot along with a good amount of salt and pepper. Return the soup to a boil, then turn the heat down so that the mixture bubbles gently. Cover and cook until the rice and beans are tender, about 40 minutes; check occasionally to make sure there is enough liquid and add a little more water if necessary. (The soup and relish can be made several hours ahead to this point. Cover and refrigerate and gently reheat the soup before proceeding.) Taste and adjust the seasoning and stir the cilantro into the relish. Serve each bowl of soup with a mound of relish on top.

Creamy Carrot and Chickpea Soup

Makes: 4 servings   Time: 1 to 2 hours, largely unattended

Chickpeas require quite a bit of cooking time (which can be shortened if you soak them first), but since chickpea broth is one of the most delicious liquids you can make, it's worth it. I like to purée this Spanish-style soup, which makes it so smooth and rich you'll swear there's cream in it, but you can skip that step and serve it rustic style.

¼ cup olive oil

2 onions, chopped

1 pound carrots, chopped

2 tablespoons minced garlic

Salt and black pepper

2 teaspoons cumin

2 teaspoons pimentón (smoked paprika)

6 cups vegetable or chicken stock (for homemade, see pages 135 to 140)
    or water, plus more as needed

1 cup dried chickpeas, rinsed, picked over, and soaked if you have time

Ⓕ Fast   Ⓜ Make-Ahead   Ⓟ Pantry Staple

1 cup orange juice

¼ cup chopped almonds, for garnish

Chopped fresh parsley, for garnish

1. Put the oil in a large pot or Dutch oven over medium heat; a minute later, add the onions, carrots, and garlic and sprinkle with salt and pepper. Cook, stirring occasionally and adjusting the heat as needed to keep the vegetables from burning, until the onions and carrots have colored, 10 to 15 minutes. Add the cumin and paprika and cook, stirring, for another 30 seconds or so.

2. Add the stock and chickpeas. Bring to a boil, then turn the heat down so the mixture bubbles gently but steadily. Cook, stirring occasionally, until the chickpeas are very soft, at least 1 hour; add more liquid as necessary so the mixture remains soupy.

3. When the chickpeas are very tender, add the orange juice, then taste and adjust the seasoning. Carefully purée the soup in batches in a blender or in the pot with an immersion blender. (You can make the soup ahead to this point. Refrigerate for up to 2 days or freeze for months; gently reheat it before proceeding.) Serve garnished with the almonds and parsley.

Corn and Sweet Potato Chowder with Chipotle

Makes: 4 servings   Time: About 1 hour

In late summer, when markets are overflowing with fresh, sweet corn, chowder is just the thing to make. I like to add just a half cup of cream for luxury; the cornmeal also helps thicken things up, while adding extra corny flavor. Make this soup as spicy or mild as you like by adjusting how many chipotle chiles you use. One adds just enough smokiness and not too much heat; 3 or 4 will have smoke streaming out of your ears, especially if you include some of the adobo sauce.

Kernels from 6 ears fresh corn, cobs reserved

Salt

¼ cup olive oil

½ cup chopped scallions

2 canned chipotle chiles, minced, with some of their adobo sauce

¼ cup cornmeal (fine or medium grind) or masa harina

Black pepper

½ cup half-and-half or cream

2 large sweet potatoes, peeled if you like and chopped

Chopped fresh parsley or cilantro, for garnish, optional

1. Put the corn cobs and 6 cups water in a pot over medium-high heat and salt it. Cover the pot and bring to a boil. Lower the heat so the water bubbles gently and cook for about 15 minutes. Let the cobs steep until you're ready to make the soup, then remove them and save the broth.

2. Put the oil in a large pot or Dutch oven over medium-high heat. When it's hot, add the scallions and chipotles with some of their adobo sauce (you can always add more later); cook, stirring occasionally, until the scallions are soft, about 1 minute. Turn the heat down to medium-low and stir in the cornmeal and some pepper. Cook, stirring constantly with a whisk or a wooden spoon, until the mixture starts to turn golden, 5 to 10 minutes. Add the half-and-half and reserved broth and turn the heat up to medium-high.

(F) Fast   (M) Make-Ahead   (P) Pantry Staple

Stir or whisk constantly until the cornmeal is dissolved and the soup starts to thicken, about 2 minutes.

3. Stir in the corn kernels and sweet potatoes and bring to a boil. Cover the pot and lower the heat so that the soup bubbles gently. Cook, stirring occasionally, until the corn and sweet potatoes are tender and the soup has thickened, 10 to 15 minutes. Taste and adjust the seasoning. Garnish with the herb if you like and serve.

Soup and the Slow Cooker

The slow cooker was designed to make soup (or stock): Load it up with all the ingredients, turn it to low, then walk away for 8 to 12 hours. You'll end up with a perfectly fine soup, if one with more or less universally soft textures. If you take a little extra time to cook the onions, garlic, or other aromatics and seasonings—or brown any meat—before adding them to the pot and starting to simmer, the soup's flavor will be more fully developed.

Roasted Butternut Chowder with Apples and Bacon

Makes: 4 servings   Time: About 1½ hours

Roasting the squash, onion, and apples, then simmering them until they break apart, leaves you with a thick, rich soup that you'll turn to every fall. Try the mixed root vegetable variation, too; it's just as good. And to sweeten the pot, add a pinch of nutmeg or allspice just before serving.

> 1 butternut squash (about 1½ pounds), peeled, seeded, and cut into cubes
>
> 1 large onion, chopped
>
> 2 large apples, peeled, cored, and chopped
>
> 4 bacon slices, or one ½-inch-thick strip slab bacon, chopped
>
> 2 tablespoons minced garlic
>
> Salt and black pepper
>
> 3 tablespoons olive oil
>
> 1 tablespoon chopped fresh sage, or 1 teaspoon dried
>
> ½ cup dry white wine or water
>
> 6 cups vegetable or chicken stock (for homemade, see pages 135 to 140) or water

1. Heat the oven to 400°F. Spread the squash, onion, apples, bacon, and garlic in a deep roasting pan or on a baking sheet. Sprinkle with salt and pepper and drizzle with the oil. Roast, stirring every now and then, until the squash, onion, and apples are tender and browned and the bacon is crisp, about 45 minutes.

2. Remove the roasting pan from the oven. Stir in the sage and white wine and scrape up all the browned bits from the bottom. If you're using a roasting pan that can be used on the stovetop, position the pan over 2 burners and put both on medium heat. Otherwise, transfer the contents of the pan to a large pot or Dutch oven and set it over medium heat.

3. Add the stock and cook until the squash, onion, and apples break apart and thicken and flavor the broth, about 25 minutes. You can help the process along by breaking the mixture up a bit with a spoon. Taste, adjust the seasoning, and serve.

Roasted Root Vegetable Chowder. Substitute any combination of celery root, turnips, parsnips, and rutabagas for the butternut squash.

Potato Chowder with Dried Tomatoes and Clams

Makes: 4 servings   Time: 30 minutes

I've never been a huge fan of Manhattan clam chowder, because the tomatoes water down the clamminess of the broth. But dried tomatoes solve this problem, and the resulting soup is a terrific balance of sweet, tart, and briny flavors. If you like chowder with more tomatoes, simply throw in 3 cups chopped tomatoes (peeled, cored, and seeded—or not) instead of the dried ones in Step 2 and cut the amount of water you add to about 4 cups. You want this chowder to be soupy but not too thin.

Be sure to scrub the clams well. There is no sand in their interiors (do not use "steamers" or there will be), but the shells may be sandy.

> 2 tablespoons olive oil
>
> 1 large leek, trimmed, well rinsed, and chopped
>
> 1 large carrot, chopped
>
> 1 tablespoon minced garlic
>
> 1 tablespoon chopped fresh rosemary, or 1 teaspoon dried
>
> Salt and black pepper
>
> ½ cup dry white wine
>
> 2 large waxy or all-purpose potatoes, peeled and roughly chopped
>
> 2 pounds littleneck or other hard-shell clams, well scrubbed, those with broken shells discarded
>
> ½ cup chopped dried tomatoes
>
> 2 lemons: 1 halved, 1 quartered
>
> Chopped fresh parsley, for garnish

1. Put the oil in a large pot or Dutch oven over medium heat. When it's hot, add the leek, carrot, garlic, and rosemary. Sprinkle with salt and pepper and cook, stirring, until the vegetables soften and begin to turn golden, 5 to 10 minutes. Add the wine and cook, stirring to loosen the bits of vegetable that have stuck to the bottom of the pan, for about a minute.

2. Add the potatoes and 6 cups water. Bring the soup to a gentle boil and cook until the potatoes are almost tender, 5 to 10 minutes. Mash the mixture a few times with a fork or potato masher to thicken it just a bit. Add the clams and dried tomatoes, cover, and reduce the heat to maintain a steady simmer. Cook, undisturbed, for 5 minutes, then lift the lid to check the clams' progress. If the majority of shells haven't opened, cover again and give the clams a couple more minutes.

3. When all the clams are open (if any don't, you can open them with a butter knife), turn off the heat, squeeze the juice from the halved lemon into the pot, and stir. Remove the clams from the shells if you like and return them to the pot. Taste and adjust the seasoning. Serve with the lemon wedges and garnished with the parsley.

Potato Chowder with Parsnips and Lobster. Omit the rosemary, clams, and tomatoes. To begin, bring 6 cups water to a boil in a large pot. Add a 2-pound lobster, cover, return to a boil, and cook for 10 to 12 minutes. Reserve the lobster cooking water to use in the soup. When the lobster is cool enough to handle, crack open its shell, extract as much meat as you can, and chop it roughly. Proceed with the recipe from Step 1, using 2 or 3 parsnips instead of the carrot and the reserved lobster broth instead of the water. In Step 2, cook the potatoes until completely tender before stirring in the reserved chopped lobster meat. Garnish with a pinch of chopped tarragon if you like.

(F) Fast   (M) Make-Ahead   (P) Pantry Staple

Cold Cucumber and Avocado Chowder with Shrimp

Makes: 4 servings   Time: 30 minutes, plus time to chill

You can't beat this cold summer soup, which is really more like a chopped salad that you eat with a spoon. No matter what you call it—or what seafood you use—the dish is light and fresh, with incredibly bright flavors. If you have time, refrigerate the purée for even longer (up to an hour or so) before serving.

3 cucumbers, peeled, seeded, and chopped

Salt

2 avocados, skin and pits removed, 1 of them chopped

2 large oranges, 1 of them peeled, seeded, and chopped or cut into segments

8 ounces shrimp, peeled, or use squid or scallops (see page 22)

2 tablespoons olive oil

Black pepper

½ cup chopped scallions

Chopped fresh mint or dill, for garnish

Lime wedges

1. Prepare a grill or turn on the broiler; the heat should be medium-high and the rack about 4 inches from the fire. Put the chopped cucumbers in a strainer and sprinkle them with a large pinch of salt. Let them sit for 5 minutes.

2. Meanwhile, put the whole avocado and the juice of 1 orange in a blender or food processor and purée until smooth, adding a little water if necessary to get the machine started. Refrigerate the purée.

3. Toss the shrimp with the oil and sprinkle with salt and pepper. Grill or broil, turning once, for 2 to 3 minutes per side. When cool enough to handle, roughly chop the shrimp and put them in a large bowl. Rinse the cucumbers and add to the shrimp along with the chopped orange, chopped avocado, and scallions. Divide the mixture among serving bowls, drizzle each with the avocado and orange purée, garnish with the herb, and serve with lime wedges.

Tortilla Soup with Lots of Garnishes

Makes: 4 servings   Time: About 1 hour

Some tortilla soups are based on a complicated broth, but I've saved the frills for the toppings. Consider all of the garnishes optional—you can enjoy tortilla soup with just a few chopped scallions and crumbled tortillas on top—but try this at least once brimming precariously with fresh veggies, salsa (for homemade, see page 46), and chips.

2 tablespoons olive oil

8 ounces bone-in chicken thighs or beef chuck steak (or use brisket, shank, even sirloin; cut it into chunks)

Salt and black pepper

2 large onions, halved and sliced

1 tablespoon minced garlic

2 small corn tortillas, roughly chopped

1 dried hot chile (like the hot chipotle or milder ancho)

1 tablespoon fresh oregano, or 1 teaspoon dried

2 limes, 1 of them juiced, the other cut into wedges

1 cup crumbled tortilla chips (for homemade, see page 47), for garnish

2 medium tomatoes, cored and chopped, for garnish

½ cup chopped scallions, for garnish

1 cup shredded cabbage, for garnish

1 cup chopped fresh cilantro, for garnish

2 avocados, skin and pits removed, sliced, for garnish

1 cup thinly sliced radishes, for garnish

¼ cup sour cream, for garnish

2 or more fresh hot chiles (like serrano, Fresno, or jalapeño), chopped, for garnish

1. Put the oil in a large pot or Dutch oven over medium-high heat. When it's hot, add the chicken or beef and sprinkle with salt and pepper. Sear the pieces, rotating and turning them as necessary, until they're well

      Fast    Make-Ahead   P Pantry Staple

browned, 3 to 5 minutes total. As the pieces are done, remove them from the pot.

2. Pour off all but 2 tablespoons of the fat and reduce the heat to medium. Add the onions and garlic and cook, stirring occasionally, until they soften and begin to turn golden, 5 to 10 minutes. Add the tortillas, dried chile, and oregano along with more salt and pepper. Cook until the mixture starts to come together like a paste, another 3 to 5 minutes. Return the chicken or beef to the pan, add 6 cups water, and bring to a boil. Adjust the heat so that the liquid bubbles gently but steadily, cover, and cook until the meat is cooked through, 15 to 20 minutes. (Meanwhile, prepare the garnishes.)

3. When the soup has thickened and the meat is tender, remove as much meat as you can from the bones and return the meat to the pot along with the lime juice. (You can prepare the soup up to this point a day or 2 in advance; gently reheat before proceeding.) Taste and adjust the seasoning. Serve (leaving the chile behind in the pot) with the garnishes in bowls at the table.

Green Gumbo with Potatoes and Zucchini

Makes: 6 to 8 servings   Time: About 1 hour

Gumbo z'herbes (or gumbo vert) is a Creole stew usually served during Lent. I've added potato and zucchini and have even been known to toss in some peeled shrimp or sliced andouille sausage as it simmers. Use whatever—and how many—greens you like (traditionally, seven different kinds bring good luck). Dandelions add a particularly wonderful bitterness that complements this gumbo's distinctive spices. Serve each bowlful with a scoop of brown rice in the center.

¼ cup olive oil

2 tablespoons butter

⅓ cup whole wheat flour

1 onion, chopped

1 green bell pepper, chopped

2 celery stalks, chopped

2 tablespoons minced garlic

Salt and black pepper

6 cups vegetable or chicken stock (for homemade, see pages 135 to 140) or water

1 tablespoon fresh thyme, or 1 teaspoon dried

1 tablespoon fresh oregano, or 1 teaspoon dried

2 bay leaves

Cayenne to taste

½ teaspoon pimentón (smoked paprika), or to taste

1 bunch dandelion or other dark leafy greens (about 1 pound), chopped

1 large all-purpose or waxy potato, peeled and chopped

2 zucchini, chopped

Chopped fresh parsley, for garnish

1. Put the oil and butter in a large pot or Dutch oven over medium-low heat. When the butter is melted, add the flour and cook, stirring almost constantly, until the roux darkens to the color of black tea and becomes fragrant, 15 to 20 minutes. As it cooks adjust the heat as necessary to keep

Ⓕ Fast   Ⓜ Make-Ahead   Ⓟ Pantry Staple

the mixture from burning. Add the onion, bell pepper, celery, and garlic and raise the heat to medium. Sprinkle with salt and pepper and cook, stirring frequently, until the vegetables have softened, another 10 minutes or so.

2. Stir in the stock, thyme, oregano, bay leaves, cayenne, paprika, dandelion greens, potato, and zucchini. Cover and bring to a boil, then reduce the heat so the soup bubbles steadily. Cook until the vegetables are very tender, about 30 minutes. (You can make the soup up to this point a day or 2 ahead; gently reheat before proceeding.) Remove the bay leaves. Taste and adjust the seasoning. Serve garnished with the parsley.

Miso Soup with Bok Choy, Soba, and Broiled Fish

Makes: **4 servings**   Time: **About 30 minutes**

The complex flavor of miso is instantly recognizable but subtle enough to let other ingredients shine through, as it does in this fantastic vegetable soup. (Remember: the darker the miso, the more intense the taste.) You can add sea greens to this recipe too: Soak a handful of arame or hijiki in boiling water for 10 minutes or so to soften; then drain and stir it into the miso along with the bok choy in Step 4.

Salt

8 ounces soba noodles

8 ounces salmon, mackerel, or other fish fillets, preferably wild (see page 22)

1 tablespoon vegetable oil

1 teaspoon five-spice or chili powder

Black pepper

⅓ cup any miso

1 pound bok choy, stems separated and chopped, leaves cut into ribbons

2 tablespoons sesame seeds, toasted if you like

¼ cup chopped scallions

1. Bring a large pot of water to a boil and salt it. Heat the broiler until very hot with the oven rack as close to the heat source as possible. Put a sturdy pan on the rack and let it heat while you cook the noodles.

2. Add the soba to the boiling water and cook until tender but not mushy, 3 to 5 minutes. Drain, reserving 2 cups of the cooking liquid, and rinse the noodles with cold water until cool. Put 1 quart clean water in the pot with the reserved liquid and set it to boil again (without salt).

3. Brush the fish fillets lightly with the vegetable oil and sprinkle with the five-spice powder and a little salt and pepper. Put the fish in the hot pan, skin side (or former skin side if it's been skinned) down. Broil for 5 to 10 minutes without turning; the fish is done when you can insert a thin-bladed knife without resistance. Remove the pan from the broiler and break the fillets into flakes.

4. When the water in the pot is almost boiling, put the miso in a small bowl, ladle in a cup or so of the heated water, and whisk until smooth. When the water boils, add the bok choy stems to the pot and let them cook for about a minute. Add the ribbons and continue cooking, adjusting the heat so the soup bubbles steadily, until the bok choy get silky, 3 to 5 minutes more. Turn the heat down to low, pour the miso mixture into the pot along with the noodles, and heat just long enough to warm everything, only a minute or 2. Taste and adjust the seasoning. Serve the soup immediately, garnished with the flaked fish, sesame seeds, and scallions.

Miso Soup with Bok Choy, Soba, and Broiled Tofu. Omit the fish and cut 1 block firm tofu (about 1 pound) into slices. Season and broil them as described in Step 3 and proceed with the recipe.

Ⓕ Fast Ⓜ Make-Ahead Ⓟ Pantry Staple

Chicken Jook with Lots of Vegetables

Makes: 4 servings   Time: About 3 hours, largely unattended

This creamy Chinese rice porridge—also known as congee—is a perfect cold-weather soup, and a fine vehicle for delicious add-ins. It takes a while for the grains to break down and thicken the water, but luckily you have options: Jook cooks perfectly in a slow cooker (see the sidebar on page 119), or you can make the soup a couple days ahead and simply reheat it. It also requires virtually no attention as it simmers, so making it on the stove is not all that much work.

3 tablespoons vegetable oil

3 bone-in chicken thighs

Salt and black pepper

2 tablespoons minced garlic

2 tablespoons minced ginger

1 fresh chile (like jalapeño or Thai), minced

½ cup chopped scallions, plus more for garnish

1 cup short-grain brown rice

2 cups cabbage sliced into very thin ribbons

1 cup snow peas

1 cup bean sprouts

2 tablespoons soy sauce, plus more for serving

1 tablespoon sesame oil

½ cup chopped fresh cilantro, for garnish

1. Put the oil in a large pot or Dutch oven over medium-high heat. When it's hot, add the chicken thighs and sprinkle them with salt and pepper. Cook until they are very well browned, 5 minutes per side or longer. Remove the chicken from the pot. Add the garlic, ginger, chile, and ½ cup scallions and cook until they are soft, just a minute or 2.

2. Add the rice along with 6 cups water. Bring to a boil, then adjust the heat so it bubbles. Partially cover the pot and cook for about 1 hour, stirring occasionally to make sure the rice is not sticking to the bottom. Add the

chicken and cook for another hour or more, again stirring. The jook should have a porridge-like consistency; if it becomes very thick too quickly, turn down the heat and stir in more water. When it is done, the jook should be soupy and creamy but still have a little chew.

3. Remove the meat from the bones if you like and return the meat to the pot. Stir in the cabbage, snow peas, bean sprouts, 2 tablespoons soy sauce, and sesame oil; cook until the vegetables are just tender, another 5 minutes. Taste and adjust the seasoning. Serve, passing the cilantro, additional scallions, and additional soy sauce at the table.

Pork Jook with Lots of Vegetables. Substitute about 8 ounces pork chops for the chicken thighs.

Mushroom Stew with Beef Chunks

Makes: 4 servings   Time: 1½ hours, largely unattended

It doesn't take much beef to flavor a stew, especially when you've got fresh and dried mushrooms for added depth and oomph. And this stew is low maintenance—just put on a lid and leave it alone. If you're looking to make this vegetarian, omit the meat and add more mushrooms—the flavor will be amazing.

    1 ounce (about 1 cup) dried porcini mushrooms

    3 cups boiling water

    1 tablespoon olive oil

    8 ounces beef chuck or round, trimmed and cut into 1-inch cubes

    1 pound fresh shiitake, cremini, portobello, or button mushrooms,
        stemmed if necessary and roughly chopped

    2 leeks, trimmed, well rinsed, and chopped

    3 carrots or parsnips, chopped

    2 tablespoons minced garlic

    Salt and black pepper

    ½ cup red wine

   Ⓕ Fast Ⓜ Make-Ahead Ⓟ Pantry Staple

3 cups mushroom or beef stock (for homemade, see pages 136 or 139) or water

2 sprigs fresh thyme or rosemary, or a pinch of each dried

1 bay leaf

1 small celery root (peeled) or 2 celery stalks, chopped

¼ cup chopped fresh parsley or chives, for garnish

1. Put the dried porcinis in a bowl and cover with the boiling water. Soak until soft, 20 to 30 minutes.

2. Meanwhile, put the oil in a large pot or Dutch oven over medium-high heat. When it's hot, add the beef and brown it on one side before stirring it. Cook until deeply browned on all sides, 5 to 10 minutes total, removing pieces as they are done.

3. Pour off all but 2 tablespoons of the fat from the pan. By now the porcinis should be soft. Lift the mushrooms out of the water, leaving behind the soaking liquid and sediment. Roughly chop the porcinis and reserve the liquid. Add the chopped porcinis to the pan along with the fresh mushrooms, leeks, carrots, and garlic. Sprinkle with salt and pepper and cook, stirring occasionally, until the vegetables begin to brown, 10 to 15 minutes. Add the red wine and cook, stirring to loosen the bits of vegetable that have stuck to the bottom of the pan, for about a minute.

4. Add the stock, the reserved porcini soaking liquid (careful to leave any grit in the bottom of the bowl), and the beef along with the herb and bay leaf. Bring to a boil, then lower the heat so that the soup bubbles gently. Cover and cook undisturbed for 30 minutes. Stir in the celery root, cover, and continue cooking until the meat and vegetables are tender, another 20 to 30 minutes. Add more liquid if the mixture seems too dry.

5. Remove the herb sprigs and bay leaf, taste, and adjust the seasoning. Garnish with the parsley and serve immediately (or cover and refrigerate for up to 2 days).

Sauerkraut and Sausage Soup

Makes: 4 servings   Time: About 1¼ hours, largely unattended

Good sauerkraut (which is what you want here and every time you eat sauerkraut) comes in jars or refrigerated packages; stay away from the canned stuff or anything that contains more than cabbage and salt. Sweet caramelized onions and apples balance its tanginess. Be sure to see the variation for this recipe's spicy Korean counterpart.

   2 tablespoons vegetable oil

   2 smoked sausage links (like kielbasa or andouille), cut into 1-inch slices

   1 large onion, halved and sliced

   2 Granny Smith or other tart apples, peeled, cored, and chopped

   1 tablespoon minced garlic

   Salt and black pepper

   1 pound sauerkraut (about 2 cups), drained and rinsed

   ½ cup white wine (slightly sweet, like riesling, is traditional, but dry is fine also)

   6 cups vegetable, chicken, or beef stock (for homemade, see pages 135 to 140) or water

   2 bay leaves

   6 cloves

   6 juniper berries, optional

1. Put the oil in a large pot or Dutch oven over medium-high heat. When it's hot, add the sausage and cook, turning as needed, until they're browned on both sides, 5 to 10 minutes total; remove.

2. Add the onion to the pot and cook, stirring occasionally, until soft, 3 to 5 minutes. Add the apples and garlic, sprinkle with a little salt and lots of pepper, and continue cooking and stirring until the apples start to release their liquid, about 3 minutes more. Turn the heat down to low and cook, stirring occasionally, until the onion and apples are very tender and golden, 15 to 20 minutes.

Ⓕ Fast   Ⓜ Make-Ahead   Ⓟ Pantry Staple

3. Return the heat to medium-high and add the sauerkraut. Keep cooking and stirring until the mixture is dry and starts to stick to the bottom of the pan, 10 to 15 minutes. Add the wine, stirring to loosen the bits of vegetable that have stuck to the bottom, then add the stock.

4. Return the sausage to the soup, and add the bay leaves, cloves, and the juniper berries if you're using them. Bring to a boil, then lower the heat so that the soup bubbles gently. Cover and cook until the sauerkraut is very tender, 20 to 25 minutes. Fish out the cloves, bay leaves, and juniper berries (if you used them), then taste and adjust the seasoning. Serve. (You can make this soup up to a day in advance and refrigerate for a day or 2 or freeze for months; reheat gently before serving.)

Kimchi and Crab Soup. Doesn't sound related, but it is, closely and wonderfully. Omit the sausage, apples, and spices. Substitute good, fresh kimchi (visit a Korean store) for the sauerkraut and use 1 cup chopped scallions instead of the onion. Begin the recipe by heating the oil in the pot and cooking the scallions as described in Step 2. When the soup is finished cooking, stir 8 ounces cooked lump crab meat into the pot. Serve immediately, garnished with chopped fresh cilantro and drizzled with a few drops of soy sauce and sesame oil.

Tahini Soup with Spinach and Lamb

Makes: 4 servings   Time: About 1 hour

Searing the lamb with a mixture of spices gives this soup an incredibly fragrant broth and a deep smokiness. The tahini, stirred in with stock and tomatoes, adds silkiness and a lovely Middle Eastern flavor.

3 tablespoons olive oil

8 ounces boneless lamb shoulder, cut into chunks (buy chops if necessary)

1 tablespoon cumin

1 teaspoon coriander

½ teaspoon turmeric

½ teaspoon cinnamon

Salt and black pepper

1 large onion, chopped

2 carrots, chopped

2 celery stalks, chopped

1 tablespoon minced garlic

4 cups vegetable, chicken, or beef stock (for homemade, see pages 135 to 140) or water

½ cup tahini

2 cups chopped tomatoes (canned are fine; include their juice)

2 pounds spinach, roughly chopped

1. Put the oil in a large pot or Dutch oven over medium-high heat. Toss the lamb in a bowl with the cumin, coriander, turmeric, cinnamon, salt, and pepper. When the oil is hot, add the lamb. Cook, turning as necessary, until the lamb is deeply browned all over, about 10 minutes total.

2. Add the onion, carrots, celery, and garlic and cook, stirring occasionally, until the vegetables are lightly browned, 5 to 10 minutes.

3. Add the stock, tahini, and tomatoes, stir, and bring to a boil. Reduce the heat so the mixture gently bubbles and cook until the meat is tender, about

Ⓕ Fast   Ⓜ Make-Ahead   Ⓟ Pantry Staple

30 minutes. (You can make the soup up to this point a day or 2 ahead; gently reheat before proceeding.)

4. Add the spinach, cover, and cook for a few more minutes until it wilts. Taste and adjust the seasoning, then serve.

Peanut Soup with Cabbage and Chicken. Substitute boneless chicken thighs for the lamb. Remove them from the pot before adding the vegetables and return to the pot after adding the liquid. Add 1 tablespoon minced ginger along with the garlic in Step 2. Substitute ½ cup chunky peanut butter for the tahini, and 1 large head cabbage, sliced into thin ribbons, for the spinach. Cook until the chicken is very tender, about 45 minutes.

Quick Vegetable Stock

Makes: More than 2 quarts   Time: 20 to 40 minutes

Vegetable stock is a good friend to the modern cook, easier to make than fish, chicken, or meat stock and equally flavorful even if with less body.

Simplicity is a virtue here, but some potential additions are dried or fresh mushrooms; dried, fresh, or canned tomatoes; root vegetables like parsnips or turnips; winter squash; fresh herbs; leeks; lemon zest; cloves or other warm spices; ginger root. Avoid bell peppers or eggplant, which are too bitter. And remember that if you use cabbage, cauliflower, or broccoli, their flavors will dominate.

> 4 carrots, cut into chunks
>
> 2 medium or 1 large onion, unpeeled, quartered
>
> 2 potatoes, cut into chunks
>
> 3 celery stalks, roughly chopped
>
> 3 or 4 garlic cloves
>
> 20 or so stems parsley, with or without leaves
>
> Salt and black pepper

1. Combine everything in a stockpot with 3 quarts water, a pinch of salt, and a sprinkling of pepper. Bring to a boil and adjust the heat so the mixture bubbles steadily but gently. Cook until the vegetables are tender, about

30 minutes. (Cooking longer will improve the flavor, but a few minutes less won't hurt much either.)

2. Strain, then taste and adjust the seasoning before using. Cool before refrigerating or freezing.

Quick Shrimp or Fish Stock. Use as many or as few of the vegetables in the main recipe as you like; they add complexity but aren't essential. In Step 1, use the shells from about 1 pound shrimp or the bones and scraps from 1 pound or so raw fish (your fishmonger often has these for sale or for free). You won't need to simmer the stock as long to extract good flavor; 10 minutes or so will do the trick. Strain, then season and use, or store as above.

Mushroom Stock

Makes: About 6 cups   Time: About 1 hour

For many of the soups in this chapter you will probably want to use vegetable stock or even just plain water, but if you are making a soup with mushrooms in it—or you just want the particular flavor of mushrooms—this rich, deeply colored stock is undoubtedly the way to go. It also makes a nice broth to just eat or drink, especially the variation.

    2 tablespoons olive oil

    1 small onion or 2 shallots (or 1 leek trimmed, well rinsed), sliced

    2 carrots, chopped

    2 celery stalks, chopped

    Salt and black pepper

    1 pound button mushrooms, chopped

    1 ounce dried shiitake, porcini, or Chinese black mushrooms, or a combination

    1 bunch fresh parsley, stems and leaves

    4 sprigs fresh thyme, or a few pinches dried

    1 teaspoon whole black peppercorns

    2 bay leaves

      Fast   Make-Ahead   Ⓟ Pantry Staple

1. Put 1 tablespoon of the oil in a large pot over medium-high heat. When it's hot, add the onion and cook, stirring occasionally, until soft, 3 to 5 minutes. Add the carrots and celery and sprinkle with salt and pepper. Cook, stirring frequently, until tender, another 10 minutes or so. Remove with a slotted spoon.

2. Put the remaining 1 tablespoon oil in the pan and turn the heat to high. When the oil is hot, add the button mushrooms. Cook, stirring, until they give up their juices and begin to brown, about 10 minutes. Sprinkle with salt, then add the dried mushrooms and cooked vegetables and stir.

3. Stir in 2 quarts water along with the parsley, thyme, peppercorns, and bay leaves. Bring to a boil, then reduce the heat so that the stock bubbles steadily. Cook, stirring once or twice, until the vegetables are very soft and the stock has reduced slightly, about 30 minutes. Strain, then taste and adjust the seasoning before using. Cool before refrigerating or freezing.

Mushroom Stock with Asian Flavors. While cooking the onion in Step 1, add 3 smashed garlic cloves and a 2-inch piece of ginger or lemongrass cut into coins. Substitute cilantro for the parsley, and omit the thyme or replace it with a couple of star anise if you have them. Add 2 tablespoons soy sauce and 1 lime, halved, along with the water in Step 3.

Roasted Vegetable Stock

Makes: 3 quarts   Time: About 2 hours, largely unattended

This recipe requires more time than the preceding vegetable stock (page 135), but it produces enough for at least two separate soups and is good enough to serve straight up. Roasting amplifies the vegetables' sweetness, earthiness, grassiness, and so on; then simmering combines and mellows everything. You have some leeway about what vegetables you choose as long as you avoid those that are strong or bitter.

   ¼ cup olive oil

   1 leek, trimmed, well rinsed, and cut into chunks

   1 large onion, unpeeled, quartered

4 carrots, cut into chunks

2 celery stalks, cut into chunks

2 parsnips, cut into chunks

½ medium winter squash, peeled, seeded, and cut into chunks

2 potatoes, quartered

6 garlic cloves

1 pound mushrooms, any variety, halved or sliced

½ cup white or red wine

1 small bunch fresh parsley, stems and leaves

3 or 4 bay leaves

¼ cup soy sauce, or to taste

1 tablespoon black peppercorns

Salt and black pepper

1. Heat the oven to 450°F. Combine the oil, leek, onion, carrots, celery, parsnips, squash, potatoes, garlic, and mushrooms in a large roasting pan; toss to coat all the vegetables with oil. Put the pan in the oven and roast, shaking the pan occasionally and turning the vegetables once or twice, until everything is nicely browned, about 45 minutes.

2. Add the wine and 2 cups water to the pan and scrape up all the crisp bits from the bottom and sides. Transfer the vegetables and liquid to a stockpot; add the parsley, bay leaves, soy sauce, peppercorns, 2½ quarts water, and a large pinch of salt.

3. Bring to a boil, then partially cover and adjust the heat so the mixture bubbles gently. Cook until the vegetables are very soft, 30 to 45 minutes. Strain, pressing on the vegetables to extract as much juice as possible. Store or use right away, but in any case wait to taste and adjust the seasoning until you use the stock.

Ⓕ Fast   Ⓜ Make-Ahead   Ⓟ Pantry Staple

Chicken-Vegetable (or Meat-Vegetable) Stock

Makes: At least 2 quarts   Time: 1 to 2½ hours, largely unattended

The only differences between using chicken and meat here are the time—meat stock takes at least twice as long—and, of course, the flavor. But you don't need to pay much attention to either. For darker, richer versions of these basic stocks, or a really intensely flavored chicken-vegetable stock, see the variations.

> About 2 pounds cut-up chicken pieces or meaty beef, veal, lamb, or pork bones
>
> 1 large onion, unpeeled and roughly chopped
>
> 2 large carrots, roughly chopped
>
> 3 celery stalks, roughly chopped
>
> 2 bay leaves
>
> 1 small bunch fresh parsley, stems and leaves
>
> Pinch of salt, or to taste
>
> 1 tablespoon whole black peppercorns

1. Combine all of the ingredients in a large stockpot with 3 quarts water (or enough to cover the ingredients by a few inches) and turn the heat to high.

2. Bring just about to a boil, then partially cover and adjust the heat so the mixture bubbles gently. Cook, skimming off any foam that accumulates on the surface, until the chicken or meat is falling off the bones, about 45 minutes for the chicken or 2 hours for the meat.

3. Cool slightly, then strain, pressing on the meat and solids to extract more juice. (You can use the meat in other recipes, but it doesn't have much flavor.) Skim off as much fat as you can and use the stock immediately or refrigerate (skim off any hardened fat from the surface) and use within 3 days or freeze for several months. Wait to season the stock until you use it.

Browner Chicken or Meat Stock. Much stronger flavored. Put 3 tablespoons vegetable oil in a roasting pan or wide pot over medium-high heat. When it's hot, add the chicken or meat bones and brown well on all sides (this might take up to 20 or 30 minutes for beef or veal bones). Add the vegetables and continue cooking until they are browned. Transfer the ingredients to a large stockpot, add 3½ quarts of water, the bay leaves, parsley, salt, and peppercorns, and continue with the recipe as written.

Twice-Cooked Chicken and Vegetable Stock. This is super-delicious; halve the recipe if you need to. In a large stockpot combine 12 cups of finished chicken stock, 2 large onions, 3 large carrots, 4 celery stalks (all roughly chopped), two bay leaves, parsley sprigs, salt, and peppercorns. Bring just about to a boil, then back down to a gentle bubble. Cover partially and cook until the vegetables are very tender and the stock has reduced a bit, about 45 minutes. Cool, strain, and store as above.

Ⓕ Fast Ⓜ Make-Ahead Ⓟ Pantry Staple

Salads and Dressings

I'm not a big fan of generalizations or rules, but here's an exception: If you want to eat well, you should eat at least one salad every day, or nearly every day. There's no excuse not to: Of all categories of dishes, salads are the easiest to improvise, the fastest to make, and the one with the most options.

There is a salad for everyone, and the recipes in this chapter offer so many options you're bound to find a few for you. Once you do, stick to them, get used to them, and play with them: Assemble that assortment of cooked or raw ingredients and whip up a little dressing that ties everything together. The whole process can take as little as five minutes. (I've organized this chapter to take you from the simplest to the most complicated; if you're at all worried about time, concentrate on the first few pages to begin with.)

Once you start working in advance, the salad universe grows to enormous dimensions. The ideal system, of course, is to clean vegetables in bulk, preferably right after bringing them home. Once they're washed and trimmed, wrap them in towels and pop them into containers, keep them crisp in bowls of cold water, or cook them simply. That way there's always something ready for salad when you are.

But many people—including me—have trouble setting aside that type of time to cook in advance, which is understandable. So many of the recipes here feature just one main ingredient, or use a food processor to do the work, or are based on cooked items you might already have in the fridge.

Another challenge of salads is the dressing; so many people appear to be just plain afraid of vinaigrette. For this there is an answer: Dress salads with oil and vinegar or freshly squeezed lemon juice right in the bowl. Period. That's what I do at least half the time, and—as long as the oil and vinegar are decent—you cannot go wrong. Having said that, all of the salads here include their own dressings (often whisked together quickly in the same vessel used for serving), but you can feel free to mix and match them as you like or, again, just use oil and vinegar. And by all means, adjust the amount of vinegar and oil to taste, as you would other seasonings or condiments.

When you are making a slightly more complicated dressing, you might double or triple the recipe and keep it refrigerated to use whenever you like. For a handful of other dressings that also double as simple sauces—including a classic but not-too-intimidating vinaigrette—see the group of recipes that begins on page 186.

(F) Fast   (M) Make-Ahead   (P) Pantry Staple

Ten-Minute Green Salad

Makes: 4 servings   Time: 10 minutes

A salad of fresh greens with no more than good olive oil and vinegar or lemon juice is basic knowledge for any cook and can even be prepared a little in advance. If you like a bit more punch, try combining the salad greens with whole fresh herbs (see the variation) or substituting any raw or cooked vegetables for some or all of the greens. And check out My Favorite Vinaigrette on page 186 for more dressing ideas.

> 8 cups assorted greens, rinsed, dried, and torn into bite-size pieces
>
> 1/3 cup olive oil, or to taste
>
> 2 tablespoons sherry vinegar, balsamic vinegar, or lemon juice, or to taste
>
> Salt and black pepper

To make the salad for immediate serving: Put the greens in a bowl, pour over the olive oil and vinegar or lemon juice, and sprinkle with salt and pepper. Toss, taste and adjust the seasoning, and serve.

To make the salad up to an hour in advance: Put the vinegar or lemon juice, oil, and salt and pepper in a salad bowl and whisk with a fork until combined. Put the greens on top, cover the bowl with a towel, and refrigerate until you're ready to eat. Toss and serve.

Nicely Dressed Herb Salad. Replace some of the greens with any combination of the following chopped fresh herbs that you like: up to 1/2 cup parsley, cilantro, basil, dill, or sorrel; up to 1/4 cup chives; a few leaves of tarragon, oregano, or thyme.

A Little Bit More About Salad Greens

The recipes in this chapter suggest specific greens, but use what you like or what you have handy; they're pretty much interchangeable. There are four basic types of lettuces, and they are—in order of crispest to softest and longest keeping to shortest—iceberg, romaine, loose-leaf, and Boston. The best salads combine one or more kinds, but an all-romaine salad, for example, is a perfectly fine thing, and probably the single salad I eat most often.

Bitter greens are also good options for salad. These include radicchio, Belgian endive, escarole, dandelion, chicory, frisée, and more. All are, obviously, bitter, and most are too crunchy to eat alone as a raw salad (for most people, anyway), so cook them before dressing or combine them with milder lettuces and other greens.

By far the biggest—and arguably the best-tasting—category of salad greens is "other." This includes arugula, watercress, spinach, tender leaves of kale or beet tops, and less common types (familiar to many gardeners) like mâche, mizuna, and tatsoi. I count mesclun in this category, since it's usually a mixture of all of the above. As a general rule, the tougher or more strongly flavored the green, the smaller pieces you want.

I don't need to tell you—but I will—that if you have rinsed greens handy, you will eat more salads. So while you don't need a salad spinner to prepare salad greens, it sure helps, especially if it's the kind that doubles as a storage container for the fridge.

In any case, to prepare greens start by trimming off all the browned leaves and removing the core if there is one (you can use your hands). If you don't have a spinner, put the greens in a colander and either submerge them in a big bowl of cold water or run them under cold water while tossing. Shake or spin them to drain. If they're not dry enough, wrap them in a towel and stick them in the fridge for a while. Once rinsed and drained, lettuce will keep for up to several days in the fridge, either in the spinner, or wrapped in a towel and put in a plastic bag.

Ⓕ Fast   Ⓜ Make-Ahead   Ⓟ Pantry Staple

Tomato Carpaccio

Makes: 4 servings   Time: 10 minutes

No, it's not "real" carpaccio, but the word is perfectly descriptive here. As you might expect, big, fleshy beefsteak tomatoes are the way to go. (In any case make sure your knife is sharp.)

You can treat other shaved or super thinly sliced vegetables the same way, especially fennel, radishes, (seeded) cucumbers, kohlrabi, small turnips, beets, and parsnips.

    4 ripe beefsteak or other large tomatoes (about 3 pounds), thinly sliced

    Salt and black pepper

    4 cups arugula, watercress, mâche, or other tender, flavorful greens

    2 tablespoons olive oil, or more if you like

    Shaved Parmesan cheese, for garnish

    1 lemon, cut into wedges

1. Spread out the tomato slices to cover individual plates or a serving platter in a thin layer. Sprinkle with salt and pepper, then top with the greens and season again. Drizzle the oil over all.

2. Scatter the shaved Parmesan on top and serve with the lemon wedges.

Tomato Carpaccio with Mozzarella. Use really good fresh mozzarella and make sure it's really cold (and your knife is sharp). Slice 4 ounces mozzarella cheese as thinly as you can and layer the pieces among the tomatoes.

Classic (or Not) Caesar Salad

Makes: 4 servings   Time: 20 to 30 minutes

Once in a while I crave a traditional Caesar, with nothing more than lettuce and croutons. More often, though, I like to add vegetables, and maybe even a bit of meat or fish, to turn the salad into a meal and take advantage of that terrific dressing.

1 garlic clove, halved

1 egg or 3 tablespoons soft silken tofu

3 tablespoons lemon juice

½ cup olive oil

1 or 2 anchovies, minced (or more to taste), optional

1 to 2 teaspoons Worcestershire sauce

Salt and black pepper

1 cup cooked or canned cannellini beans, drained

1 medium zucchini or 2 small zucchini (about 1 pound), grated and
    squeezed dry in a clean towel

1 large head romaine lettuce, torn into bite-size pieces

Croutons (for homemade, see page 47)

½ cup grated Parmesan cheese or ¼ cup chopped walnuts

1. Rub the inside of a large salad bowl with the garlic clove, then discard it. Bring a small saucepan of water to a boil and cook the egg in the boiling water for 60 to 90 seconds; it will just begin to firm up. Crack it into the salad bowl (be sure to scoop out the white that clings to the shell). If you're using the tofu, just put it in the bowl.

2. Whisk the egg or tofu while gradually adding the lemon juice and then the oil. Whisk in the anchovies if you're using them, along with the Worcestershire sauce. Taste and add salt if needed and plenty of pepper. Toss well with the cannellini beans, zucchini, and lettuce; top with the croutons, Parmesan, and a sprinkling of salt and pepper. Toss again at the table and serve.

Tossed Greens with Fruit and Mustard Vinaigrette

Makes: 4 servings   Time: 30 minutes

Sweet and sharp, light but a bit more substantial than a plain green salad, yet perhaps a bit more interesting than the typical lettuce-cuke-tomatoes-carrots. Stay seasonal: stone fruit or berries in the summer; grapes, pears, or apples in fall; and either citrus, pineapple, or dried fruit through the winter—of course, a combination is good too. For a more elaborate version, see the following recipe.

About 1 pound fresh fruit (or 1 cup dried fruit), singly or in combination

1 tablespoon lemon juice

⅓ cup olive oil

1 tablespoon balsamic vinegar, or to taste

1 large shallot, thinly sliced, optional

1 to 3 teaspoons Dijon or other good-quality mustard

Salt and black pepper

8 cups mixed greens (like mesclun), torn into bite-size pieces

1. Peel and core the fruit if necessary and remove any seeds or pits. If large, cut the fruit into ½-inch chunks. Toss the fruit with the lemon juice, then cover and refrigerate while you make the dressing.

2. Put the oil, vinegar, shallot if you're using it, mustard, and a sprinkling of salt and pepper in a large bowl and whisk until well combined. Add the fruit and greens and toss until everything is well distributed and evenly coated with dressing. Serve immediately.

Tossed Greens with Fruit, Nuts, and Cheese Vinaigrette. Instead of the mustard, use ¼ cup crumbled goat, feta, or blue cheese, or grated Parmesan and whisk until the cheese thickens the dressing (just a minute or so). Toss the salad and top with ½ cup toasted pine nuts, almonds, pecans, pistachios, or hazelnuts.

Fruity Chef Salad with Mixed Herb Dressing

Makes: 4 servings   Time: 30 minutes

The fruits' juices will release when you toss the salad, combining beautifully with the dressing. Use whatever fruits and seasonings are in season (see the variation), and you'll have a spectacularly bright and ever-changing salad. For the herbs, use large amounts of parsley, chervil, basil, or mint; smaller amounts of oregano or marjoram; or just a few leaves of tarragon, thyme, sage, or rosemary.

½ cup mixed, chopped fresh herbs (see the headnote)

2 tablespoons lemon juice

⅓ cup olive oil

Salt and black pepper

2 cups seeded chopped watermelon

3 peaches, pitted and cut into wedges

3 ripe tomatoes, cut into wedges

1 avocado, skin and pit removed, cut into wedges

8 cups torn lettuce leaves or mixed greens

¼ cup crumbled feta cheese

2 to 4 cooked bacon slices or prosciutto slices, chopped, optional

1. Put the herbs, lemon juice, oil, and a sprinkling of salt and pepper in a large salad bowl and whisk until well combined.

2. Add the watermelon, peaches, tomatoes, and avocado and toss. Add the lettuce and toss again. Sprinkle the cheese and bacon or prosciutto (if you're using it) on top and serve.

Wintertime Fruity Chef Salad with Curried Dressing. You can even use shredded Napa cabbage here instead of the lettuce if you like. Instead of the herbs, whisk 1 tablespoon curry powder (or to taste) into the dressing. Use pineapple, citrus fruit, and pears or apples for the melon, peaches, and tomatoes.

Mediterranean Cobb Salad

Makes: 4 servings   Time: 30 minutes

This Mediterranean take on a classic Cobb salad relies on a caper-and-anchovy vinaigrette to make it the most flavorful you've ever tasted. A good-quality wine vinegar is important here.

⅓ cup olive oil

2 tablespoons wine vinegar, or to taste

3 anchovy fillets, with a bit of their oil (or use more capers)

1 tablespoon capers, with a bit of their brine

2 tablespoons chopped fresh parsley

Black pepper

8 cups chopped romaine lettuce

1 cup cooked or canned chickpeas or white beans, drained

2 ripe tomatoes, chopped

1 small red onion, halved and thinly sliced

½ cup chopped hard-boiled eggs, prosciutto, or cooked chicken, or crumbled Gorgonzola

1. Combine the oil, vinegar, anchovies, capers, parsley, and black pepper in a blender and turn the machine on; a creamy emulsion will form within 30 seconds. Taste and add more vinegar or pepper if necessary. (If you don't have—or don't want to use—a blender, chop the anchovies and capers and whisk all the ingredients together in a small bowl.)

2. Put the romaine in the center of a large platter, plate, or shallow bowl and spoon the other ingredients around it in rows or mounds. Just before serving, drizzle the top with the vinaigrette, toss it at the table, and serve.

Black Kale and Black Olive Salad

Makes: 4 servings   Time: 20 minutes

Raw thinly sliced black kale—also known as Tuscan or lacinato kale—is an amazingly delicious alternative to everyday salad greens. Combined with black olives and a little shaved Parmesan, its flavor is earthy and a little briny. As an added bonus, this salad is sturdy enough to make up to an hour in advance without the leaves sogging out on you. If you can't find black kale, use chard, Napa cabbage, mustard greens, or romaine lettuce.

>   1 large bunch black kale (about 1 pound), cut into thin ribbons
>
>   ½ cup black olives, pitted and chopped
>
>   ¼ cup grated Parmesan cheese
>
>   ¼ cup olive oil
>
>   2 tablespoons sherry vinegar
>
>   Salt and black pepper

1. Combine the kale, olives, and Parmesan in a large bowl. Drizzle with the oil and vinegar, sprinkle with salt (not too much) and lots of pepper, and toss.

2. Taste and adjust the seasoning if necessary. Serve immediately or refrigerate for up to an hour.

Fennel and Orange Salad with Green Olive Tapenade

Makes: 4 servings   Time: 20 minutes

The first step of this recipe produces a terrific tapenade, one that could become a staple for you. It keeps for a long time and has many uses beyond this salad—from sandwich spread or dip, to soup garnish or quick pasta sauce.

To turn this salad into a meal, simply toss everything in a big bowl with a load of crisp greens, adding more olive oil and a squeeze of orange as needed. A bit of crumbled cheese (feta or Gorgonzola are nice) or chopped prosciutto is a good addition (you might want to cut down on the tapenade to avoid making the salad too salty). Without too much more work, you can cook up some shrimp or a thinly sliced chicken breast and add that to the salad bowl as well.

1 cup green olives, pitted

1 teaspoon fresh thyme, or ¼ teaspoon dried, optional

¼ cup olive oil, or more as needed

1 large fennel bulb, cored and thinly sliced

3 navel oranges, peeled and sliced crosswise into rounds

Fennel seeds, for garnish, optional

1. In a food processor, combine the olives and thyme if you're using it with a tablespoon or so of oil. Pulse once or twice, then turn on the processor and add the remaining oil rather quickly to result in a rough purée. Thin with more oil if necessary. (You can refrigerate this for up to a month.)

2. Put the fennel and orange slices on 4 plates or a serving platter, drizzle with a little more oil, top with the olive purée, and sprinkle with a few fennel seeds if you have them. Serve.

Asparagus Salad with Black Olive Tapenade. A little more work but well worth it if you've got good asparagus. Use black olives in the tapenade. Instead of the fennel, trim about 1½ pounds asparagus. Omit the oranges. Cook the asparagus in boiling salted water until crisp-tender, just a couple of minutes. Plunge immediately into a bowl of ice water to stop the cooking and drain well. Serve the tapenade on top of the asparagus, garnished with lemon wedges.

Chopped Salad with Thai Flavors

Makes: 4 servings   Time: 30 minutes

Spicy and crunchy, this vegetable salad is essentially a chopped slaw, so feel free to shred the cabbage and carrots if you prefer. Cooked edamame or cubes of fried tofu are nice additions here, or simply toss the whole salad with noodles, adding a little more lime juice and oil if you need to.

Juice of 2 limes

¼ cup vegetable oil

1 tablespoon nam pla (fish sauce) or soy sauce

½ teaspoon sugar, optional

1 fresh hot red chile (like Thai or serrano), seeded and minced, or to taste

1 carrot, chopped

1 red or yellow bell pepper, chopped

4 cups chopped cabbage

1 cup chopped snow peas or green beans

1 bunch radishes, chopped, or about 1 cup grated jícama or daikon

1 cup bean sprouts

¼ cup peanuts, lightly crushed

Salt and black pepper

¼ cup chopped fresh basil, preferably Thai, or cilantro

¼ cup chopped fresh mint

1. Put the lime juice, oil, nam pla, sugar if you're using it, and chile in a large salad bowl and whisk until well combined.

2. Add all of the vegetables to the bowl with the dressing and toss a few times. Top with the peanuts, taste, and add salt if necessary and lots of black pepper; toss again and refrigerate until ready to serve. (It's best to let the salad chill for an hour or so to allow the flavors to mellow; you can let it sit even longer, up to 24 hours, but drain the salad before continuing.) Just before serving, toss with the herbs.

Chopped Salad with Sesame and Soy. Substitute 1 tablespoon sesame oil for 1 tablespoon of the vegetable oil, and substitute 2 tablespoons rice vinegar and 1 tablespoon soy sauce for the lime juice and fish sauce. Garnish with sesame seeds instead of peanuts and use a bunch of chopped scallions instead of (or in addition to) the herbs.

Easiest Bean or Grain Salad on the Planet

Makes: 4 servings   Time: 10 minutes with cooked or canned beans or grains

You could make bean or grain salad every day for the rest of your life without making it the same way twice. A simple dressing of olive oil, lemon juice, and parsley is a great place to start, but the possibilities are endless (see the sidebar on page 187). For basic instructions on cooking beans, see page 350; for grains, see page 271.

> Juice of 1 lemon, or to taste
>
> ¼ cup olive oil, or to taste
>
> ¼ cup chopped red onion or shallot
>
> Salt and black pepper
>
> 4 cups cooked or canned beans, drained, or cooked grains, or a combination
>
> ½ cup chopped fresh parsley

1. Put the lemon juice, oil, onion, and a sprinkling of salt and pepper in a large bowl and whisk until well combined. If you've just cooked the beans or grains, add them to the dressing while they are still hot. Toss gently until the beans or grains are coated, adding more oil or lemon juice if you like.

2. Let cool to room temperature (or refrigerate), stirring every now and then to redistribute the dressing. Stir in the parsley just before serving, then taste and adjust the seasoning if necessary.

Apple Slaw

Makes: **4 servings**   Time: **30 minutes**

A tangy honey-mustard vinaigrette pulls together all the different flavors in this mayo-free slaw. Try substituting jícama, just-ripe pear, green papaya, or even green mango for the apple. To make quick work of the chopping, use the grater disk of a food processor.

The meaty variation makes a satisfying lunch with a piece of good whole grain bread, especially the Black Rolls with Caraway on page 547.

¼ cup olive oil

1 heaping teaspoon Dijon or other good-quality mustard, or to taste

1 tablespoon lemon juice

1 tablespoon honey

2 cups cored and shredded red cabbage (about 8 ounces)

2 medium Granny Smith or other tart, crisp apples, cored and shredded or
   grated

8 radishes, chopped

1 red onion, chopped or grated

Salt and black pepper

½ cup chopped fresh parsley

1. Put the oil, mustard, lemon juice, and honey in a large bowl and whisk until well combined.

2. Add the cabbage, apples, radishes, and onion and toss until thoroughly combined. Sprinkle with salt and pepper and refrigerate until ready to serve. (It's best to let the slaw rest for an hour or so to allow the flavors to mellow. You can let it sit even longer, up to a few hours, before the apples start to discolor; just drain the slaw before continuing.) Just before serving, toss with the parsley.

Apple Slaw with Bacon or Chicken. Add ¼ cup crumbled cooked bacon or ½ cup shredded or cubed cooked chicken to the mix right before tossing for the last time.

Raw Butternut Salad
with Cranberry Dressing

Makes: 4 servings   Time: 30 minutes

Here are two familiar fall flavors combined in a surprising way. Raw winter squash is delightful—bright flavored, with a creamy-but-crisp texture. (Mid-season butternut squash is best: too early and it won't be sweet, too late and it may be woody and tough.) This dish would be right at home as part of a Thanksgiving feast, but it's so easy that it works well on weeknights. The grape dressing in the variation is perhaps a little less festive, but it's equally delicious. For something more substantial, top with toasted almonds or pecans—or even a little crumbled goat cheese. Leftovers are terrific stir-fried in a little olive oil.

½ cup fresh or frozen cranberries, picked over and rinsed

¾ cup orange juice

1 tablespoon minced ginger

3 tablespoons olive oil

1 tablespoon honey

Salt and black pepper

1 butternut squash (about 1½ pounds), peeled and seeded

1. Combine the cranberries, orange juice, and ginger in a small saucepan over medium-low heat. Cover and cook, stirring occasionally, until the berries have begun to break, 10 minutes or so. Remove the cranberries from the heat and add the oil, honey, and some salt and pepper. Stir until well combined.

2. Meanwhile, grate the butternut squash by hand or in a food processor. Transfer the squash to a large bowl, add the warm cranberry dressing, and toss to combine everything. Serve warm or at room temperature. (Or cover and refrigerate the salad for up to several hours; bring to room temperature before serving.)

Raw Butternut Salad with Grape Dressing. Substitute ½ cup seedless green or red grapes for the cranberries.

Whole Grain Panzanella

Makes: 4 servings   Time: 45 minutes

This Italian peasant dish is most often no more than stale bread, tomatoes, and olive oil, but I like adding a little something crunchy and green. It's also a good vehicle for leftover grilled vegetables—like eggplant, zucchini, or mushrooms—or for hard-boiled eggs or anchovies.

When tomatoes are not in season, try the variation.

>   8 ounces whole grain bread (4 thick slices; stale is fine)
>
>   4 celery stalks or 1 small fennel bulb, thinly sliced
>
>   ¼ cup olive oil
>
>   2 tablespoons balsamic vinegar
>
>   1½ pounds ripe tomatoes, seeded and chopped
>
>   ½ red onion, thinly sliced
>
>   Salt and black pepper
>
>   ½ cup chopped fresh basil

1. Heat the oven to 400°F. Put the bread on a baking sheet and toast, turning once or twice, until golden and dry, 10 to 20 minutes, depending on the thickness of the slices. Remove from the oven and cool.

2. Put the celery, oil, vinegar, tomatoes, and onion in a large salad bowl. Sprinkle with salt and lots of pepper and toss to coat.

3. Fill a large bowl with tap water and soak the bread for about 3 minutes. Gently squeeze the slices dry, then crumble them into the salad bowl. Toss well to combine and let sit for 15 to 20 minutes (or up to an hour). Right before serving, taste, adjust the seasoning if necessary, and toss with the basil.

Whole Grain Bread Salad with Dried Fruit. Omit the tomatoes and basil and substitute 2 medium shallots for the onion. In Step 2, toss the celery or fennel and dressing with 1 cup chopped dried fruit (figs, dates, apricots, cherries, cranberries, or raisins are all good) and 1 tablespoon chopped fresh sage. Garnish with toasted hazelnuts or almonds.

Smashed Potato Salad with Escarole

Makes: 4 servings   Time: About 45 minutes

The key to success here is to be generous with the olive oil, whose flavor takes mere potato and greens—whether escarole or any other strong-flavored green like radicchio, dandelion, endive, or chicory—from humble to sublime. This is perfect picnic food, with or without meat, cheese, or eggs (see the variations).

2 large baking or all-purpose potatoes (about 1 pound), peeled and cut into quarters

Salt

1 pound escarole or other greens (see the headnote), thick stems chopped

¼ to ½ cup olive oil

Grated zest and juice of 1 lemon

Black pepper

1. Put the potatoes in a large, deep pot and cover them with cold water. Add a large pinch of salt and bring to a boil. Cook until soft but not falling apart, 15 to 30 minutes. Remove with a slotted spoon and drain. Add the escarole to the water and cook until it wilts, a minute or 2. Rinse under cold water. Drain well, then chop.

2. Roughly crush the drained potatoes in a bowl with a fork or potato masher, leaving lots of lumps; add ¼ cup oil and the lemon zest and juice. Mash in the escarole, adding more oil and sprinkling with salt and pepper as needed. Serve immediately (or cover and refrigerate for up to 12 hours; bring to room temperature before serving).

Potato and Escarole Salad with Parmesan and Frizzled Meat. While the potatoes are cooking, put 1 tablespoon of the oil in a medium skillet over medium-high heat. When it's hot, add 4 ounces chopped prosciutto, pancetta, or bacon, or crumbled sausage and cook until the pieces are crisp and brown, 3 to 8 minutes. Remove from the heat, add the remaining dressing ingredients, stir well, and transfer to a bowl. Add the potatoes and escarole. Garnish with ¼ cup grated Parmesan before serving.

Potato and Escarole Salad with Hard-Boiled Eggs. Add 1 or 2 chopped hard-boiled eggs to the salad along with the escarole in Step 2.

Roasted Sweet Potato Salad
with Chili Dressing

Makes: 4 servings   Time: 45 minutes

Sweet roasted vegetables, cumin-scented chili powder, and cilantro are perfect together. And since the warm potatoes soak up the dressing like a sponge, this salad is fragrant through and through. If you've got a food processor, purée the dressing and cilantro together in Step 2 for a pesto-like drizzle. You can try straight ground dried chiles—like the hot chipotles or milder anchos, for example—but go easy because they will be more powerful than the chili powder.

4 medium sweet potatoes (about 1½ pounds), peeled and cut into large sticks

1 large onion, preferably red, sliced

8 tablespoons olive oil

Salt and black pepper

2 teaspoons chili powder, or to taste

Juice of 2 limes

1 cup chopped fresh cilantro

1. Heat the oven to 400°F. Put the sweet potatoes and red onion on a large baking sheet, drizzle with 2 tablespoons of the oil, toss to coat, and spread them out in a single layer. Sprinkle with salt and pepper and roast, turning occasionally, until the potatoes are crisp and brown outside and just tender inside and the onions are soft and brown, 35 to 45 minutes. Remove from the oven and keep them on the pan until ready to dress.

2. Meanwhile, whisk together the remaining 6 tablespoons olive oil, the chili powder, lime juice, and a sprinkling of salt and pepper.

3. Toss the warm vegetables with the dressing and cilantro. Taste and adjust the seasoning if necessary. Serve warm or at room temperature (or cover and refrigerate for up to a day).

Ⓕ Fast   Ⓜ Make-Ahead   Ⓟ Pantry Staple

Roasted Beet Salad
with Peanut Vinaigrette

Makes: 4 servings   Time: About 2 hours, largely unattended

Earthy, sweet beets combine well with Asian flavors; add some crunchy peanuts and you've got a sensational, colorful salad.

> 2 pounds red beets (about 4 large)
>
> 3 tablespoons vegetable oil, preferably peanut
>
> 1 tablespoon sesame oil
>
> 2 tablespoons rice vinegar
>
> 1 tablespoon soy sauce, or to taste
>
> ½ cup peanuts, chopped
>
> ½ cup chopped scallions
>
> Black pepper
>
> Salt if needed

1. Heat the oven to 400°F. Wash the beets well. While they are still wet, wrap each one in foil and put them on a baking sheet or in a roasting pan. (Alternatively, don't wrap them but bake them in a covered casserole or roasting pan.) Bake the beets, undisturbed, until a thin-bladed knife pierces all of them with little resistance, 1 to 1½ hours. (They may cook at different rates; remove each one when it is done.)

2. Meanwhile, whisk together the oils, vinegar, soy sauce, peanuts, and scallions in a large bowl; sprinkle with pepper. Once the beets are cool enough to handle, peel off their skins, cut them into wedges or cubes, and combine them with the dressing in the bowl. Taste and adjust the seasoning, adding a little salt if necessary. Serve at room temperature (or refrigerate for up to 4 hours and return to room temperature before serving).

Roasted Green Bean Salad with Pecan Vinaigrette. Omit the peanuts and dressing ingredients. Use 2 pounds green beans instead of the beets; toss them with 3 tablespoons olive oil and roast at 400°F, stirring once or twice, for 25 minutes. For the dressing, use 2 tablespoons wine or sherry vinegar, 1 tablespoon olive oil, ½ cup chopped pecans, and 1 thinly sliced shallot or small red onion.

Brown Rice Salad with Tomatoes and Peas

Makes: 4 servings   Time: About 50 minutes

Nutty-tasting brown rice stands up better than white rice to bold flavors like garlic, briny cheese or fish, and fresh herbs. I've included the cooking instructions for the rice, but if you've got about 2½ cups cooked rice handy, use it and skip to Step 2. If you go with the anchovies here, take it easy on the salt until you taste.

> ¾ cup brown rice
>
> Salt
>
> 2 cups fresh or thawed frozen peas
>
> 1 tablespoon minced garlic
>
> 1 small red onion, halved and thinly sliced
>
> 2 anchovy fillets, chopped, optional
>
> 2 cups cherry tomatoes, halved
>
> ¼ cup olive oil, or to taste
>
> 1 tablespoon sherry or red wine vinegar, or to taste
>
> Black pepper
>
> ¼ cup crumbled ricotta salata, feta, or other salty cheese
>
> 1 cup chopped fresh basil

1. Put the rice and a pinch of salt in a small saucepan with water to cover by about 1 inch. Bring to a boil, then lower the heat so the mixture bubbles gently. Cover and cook for 30 to 40 minutes, checking occasionally to make sure the water is not evaporating too quickly (you can add a little more liquid if necessary). When the liquid has been absorbed, taste and see if the rice is tender, or nearly so. If not, add about ½ cup water and continue to cook, covered.

2. When the rice is tender, turn off the heat, stir in the peas with a fork, and let the mixture sit, covered, for 15 or even 30 minutes, during which time it will become a bit drier and cool off a bit. (You can make the rice up to

Ⓕ Fast   Ⓜ Make-Ahead   Ⓟ Pantry Staple

2 days ahead; refrigerate it, of course, but bring it back to room temperature before proceeding.)

3. Put the rice and peas, garlic, red onion, anchovies if you're using them, and tomatoes in a large bowl. Add the oil and vinegar and sprinkle with salt and pepper. Use 2 big forks to combine, fluffing the rice and tossing gently to separate the grains.

4. Stir in the cheese and basil. Taste and adjust the seasoning; moisten with a little more oil and vinegar if necessary. Serve at room temperature (or refrigerate for up to a day; bring back to room temperature before serving).

Brown Rice Salad with Tuna, Tomatoes, and Peas. Add 1 small (5- to 6-ounce) can oil-packed tuna (drained) along with the vegetables in Step 3. Omit the cheese and add 1 teaspoon red chile flakes.

Couscous Salad with Dried Cranberries and Pecans

Makes: 4 servings   Time: About 30 minutes

Coriander, cayenne, and fresh sage give this salad some oomph; try the minty Indian-tinged variation for a sprightlier version. If you like, add half a cup or so of shredded smoked turkey, flaked smoked trout, or crumbled goat cheese at the end.

1 cup couscous, preferably whole wheat

Salt

2 large carrots, grated

½ cup chopped pecans

½ cup chopped dried cranberries

¼ cup chopped scallions

¼ cup olive oil, or more as needed

Grated zest and juice of 1 lemon, or more juice as needed

1 teaspoon coriander

Pinch of cayenne, or to taste

Black pepper

½ cup chopped fresh parsley

1 tablespoon chopped fresh sage, or 1 teaspoon dried

1. Put the couscous in a small pot and add 1½ cups water and a pinch of salt. Bring the water to a boil, then cover and remove from the heat. Let steep for at least 10 minutes, or up to 20.

2. Put the slightly cooled couscous in a large salad bowl along with the carrots, pecans, cranberries, scallions, oil, and lemon zest and juice and sprinkle with the spices and salt and pepper. Use 2 big forks to combine, fluffing the couscous and tossing gently to separate the grains. (The salad can be made up to this point and refrigerated for up to a day; bring to room temperature before proceeding.)

Ⓕ Fast   Ⓜ Make-Ahead   Ⓟ Pantry Staple

3. Stir in the parsley and sage. Taste and adjust the seasoning, moisten with a little more oil and lemon juice as you like, and serve.

Curried Couscous Salad with Dried Apricots and Pistachios. Use pistachios instead of pecans, dried apricots instead of cranberries, and curry powder instead of coriander and cayenne. Stir in ½ cup chopped fresh mint in Step 3 instead of the parsley and sage.

Varying Bean and Grain Salads

To change the dressing: Use a neutral oil or nut oil, or coconut milk. Instead of the lemon juice, try lime or orange juice or any kind of vinegar. (Vinegars vary in acidity, so add to taste.)

To add substantial ingredients: Toss in up to 2 cups chopped raw, grilled, or roasted vegetables or chopped tender greens. (Chopped ripe tomatoes are lovely when they're in season.) To make the salad more of a meal, toss in up to a cup of crumbled or grated cheese, or chopped cooked seafood, poultry, or meat.

To change the seasoning: Add small amounts of chopped garlic, ginger, olives, capers, or anchovies. Use fresh mint, cilantro, chives, or basil instead of parsley. Or add up to a teaspoon (or to taste) chopped thyme, sage, or rosemary, or a little more oregano or marjoram. When fresh herbs aren't available, use dried herbs to taste. Or try seasoning the salad with a pinch of curry or chili powder, or single spices like cumin, coriander, saffron, pimentón (smoked paprika), or cardamom, also to taste; mix it in with the dressing along with the salt and pepper.

Quinoa Tabbouleh

Makes: 4 servings   Time: 40 minutes

Tabbouleh is usually made with bulgur, but quinoa, the pleasantly grassy, slightly crunchy, high-protein grain from South America, puts a lively twist on it. Don't be tempted, though, to turn this herb-and-vegetable dish into a grain salad—the grain is for texture, not heft. Instead, try experimenting with different raw or cooked vegetables. I've made some suggestions here, but use what you like and what's handy, including leftovers. Some of my favorites: asparagus, peas, spinach, or eggplant, especially grilled.

½ cup quinoa, rinsed and drained

Salt

⅓ cup olive oil, or more as needed

¼ cup lemon juice, or more as needed

Black pepper

1 cup roughly chopped fresh parsley

1 cup roughly chopped fresh mint

1 cup cooked or canned white or pink beans, drained, optional

6 or 7 radishes, chopped

½ cup chopped scallions

2 ripe tomatoes, chopped

About 6 black olives, pitted and chopped, or to taste, optional

2 celery stalks (leaves included if possible), chopped

¼ cup chopped pistachios or almonds, optional

1. Put the quinoa in a small saucepan with ¾ cup water and a pinch of salt. Bring to a boil, then reduce the heat to medium-low. Cover and bubble gently until the quinoa has absorbed all of the water, 15 minutes or so. Remove from the heat and let rest, covered, for 5 minutes. Toss the warm quinoa with the oil and lemon juice and sprinkle with pepper. (You can make the quinoa up to a day in advance: Just cover and refrigerate, then bring to room temperature before proceeding.)

Ⓕ Fast   Ⓜ Make-Ahead   Ⓟ Pantry Staple

2. Just before you're ready to eat, add the remaining ingredients and toss gently. Taste and adjust the seasoning, adding more oil or lemon juice as needed, then serve.

Root Vegetable and Quinoa Salad. Perfect in the winter. Omit the tomatoes. Peel and dice 8 ounces parsnips, turnips, sweet potatoes, celery root, or carrots, toss them with 1 tablespoon olive oil, and roast on a baking sheet or in a roasting pan at 400°F for 20 minutes (or use leftover cooked root vegetables). Cool and add to the quinoa in Step 2.

Wheat Berry Salad with Zucchini and Mozzarella

Makes: 4 servings   Time: 20 minutes with cooked grains

Assuming you have some kind of cooked grains in the fridge (always a good idea), this salad comes together quickly. Wheat berries are my first choice because of their unsurpassed chewiness, but even small grains like rice, cracked wheat, quinoa, and whole wheat couscous (or even cut pasta) work just fine. Roasted bell peppers are a tasty and colorful addition, especially ones that you make yourself (see page 417). And if you've got roasted garlic handy (or feel like cooking a batch; see page 421), it's a beautiful change from the raw garlic here.

¼ cup pine nuts

3 or 4 medium zucchini (about 1½ pounds), halved lengthwise

¼ cup plus 1 tablespoon olive oil

Salt and black pepper

2 cups cooked wheat berries (see page 271)

1 teaspoon minced garlic, or to taste

½ cup fresh dill, or 1 teaspoon dried

3 tablespoons sherry or white wine vinegar

1 cup cubed mozzarella, optional

1. Toast the pine nuts in a small, dry skillet over medium heat, shaking the pan occasionally, until lightly browned. Remove from the pan.

2. Turn on the broiler; the heat should be medium-high and the rack about 4 inches from the fire. Brush the zucchini with the 1 tablespoon oil, sprinkle with salt and pepper, and broil, turning as needed, until lightly charred on both sides and beginning to soften, 5 minutes or more. When they're cool enough to handle, cut the zucchini into chunks or slices.

3. Toss together the zucchini, wheat berries, garlic, and about half of the dill in a large salad bowl. Add the vinegar and ¼ cup oil, sprinkle with salt and pepper, and toss again. Taste and adjust the seasoning if necessary. (The salad can be made ahead to this point and refrigerated for up to a day.) To serve, toss the mozzarella into the salad, along with the remaining dill.

White Bean Salad with Zucchini and Mozzarella. Substitute cooked white beans for the wheat berries.

Ⓕ Fast Ⓜ Make-Ahead Ⓟ Pantry Staple

Chopped Cauliflower Salad, North African Style

Makes: 4 servings   Time: 25 minutes

Quickly cooking the cumin, coriander, and cinnamon in the warm dressing concentrates their flavors and helps them soak into the cauliflower (the fragrance is amazing). This is one of those uncommon salads that benefits from refrigerating for a day—but it's best served at room temperature.

Salt

1 large cauliflower, cored

3 tablespoons olive oil

1 small red onion, chopped

1 tablespoon minced garlic

1 teaspoon cumin

1 teaspoon coriander

¼ teaspoon cinnamon

Black pepper

Juice of 1 lemon

Chopped fresh parsley, for garnish

1. Bring a large pot of water to a boil and salt it; set up a bowl of ice water. Add the cauliflower to the boiling water and cook until you can just barely pierce the center with a skewer or thin-bladed knife (you want it still quite crisp), 10 to 15 minutes. Remove the cauliflower, plunge it in the ice water, and let cool for a few minutes. Drain the cauliflower well and roughly chop.

2. Dump the cooking water, put the oil in the same pot, and turn the heat to medium. Add the onion and garlic and cook, stirring once or twice, until they are no longer raw. Stir in the cumin, coriander, cinnamon, and a sprinkling of salt and pepper. Stir in the lemon juice and turn off the heat.

3. Toss the cauliflower with the warm dressing in the pot. Taste, adjust the seasoning if necessary, and garnish with chopped parsley. Serve immediately. (Or wait to add the parsley, refrigerate for up to a day or 2, bring the salad back to room temperature, and toss with the parsley right before serving.)

Soba Salad with Walnuts, Sea Greens, and Miso Dressing

Makes: 4 servings   Time: 20 minutes

Cold noodles and seaweed make a refreshing yet hearty salad. If you can find yuzu—a type of citrus sold in Asian markets—grab it; usually you'll wind up with lemons and limes, which are fine. Some possible additions: leftover cooked (especially grilled) shrimp, chicken, beef, pork, or tofu.

Salt

4 to 6 ounces soba noodles

1 ounce wakame, arame, or hijiki

1 tablespoon soy sauce

1 tablespoon fresh yuzu, lemon, or lime juice

2 tablespoons white or light miso

1 tablespoon mirin or 1 teaspoon sugar, or to taste

½ cup chopped walnuts, preferably toasted

¼ cup chopped shallot, scallions, or red onion

Pinch of cayenne

1. Bring a large pot of water to a boil and salt it. Drop in the noodles and cook them until they're tender but not mushy, 3 to 5 minutes. Drain and rinse in a colander under cold running water.

2. Meanwhile, rinse the seaweed once, then soak it in water to cover by at least 3 inches. When it is tender, about 5 minutes later, drain and gently squeeze the mixture to remove excess water. Pick through the seaweed to sort out any hard bits (there may be none) and chop or cut it up (you may find it easier to use scissors than a knife) if the pieces are large.

3. In a large salad bowl, whisk together the soy sauce, citrus juice, miso, and mirin. Add the noodles, seaweed, walnuts, and shallot and toss. Taste and season with cayenne and salt as needed. Serve immediately (or refrigerate for up to 2 hours before serving).

Soba Salad with Walnuts and Spinach. Substitute 1 pound spinach leaves for the seaweed and omit Step 2. Instead heat the soy sauce, citrus juice, miso, and mirin in a large pot or skillet. When the dressing is almost (but not quite) boiling, add the spinach, cover, and remove from the heat. Let rest for 5 minutes, then toss until well coated. Add the remaining ingredients. Serve warm or at room temperature (or refrigerate for up to 2 hours before serving).

Where's the Pasta Salad?

Aha! Not a one to be had in this chapter. Here's why: Cooked pasta does not improve with age or refrigeration. So instead of setting out to make a pasta salad that you intend to serve cold, cook a recipe from the pasta chapter (beginning on page 191)—one marked with the Make-Ahead icon. Let the dish cool to room temperature, and it will be better than any cold pasta salad. If it's not acidic enough for you, toss in a squeeze of lemon juice or a splash of vinegar.

Wild Rice Salad with Smoked Anything

Makes: 4 servings   Time: About 1 hour

Wild rice goes so well with smoked foods that you can use smoked fish, smoked meat, even smoked tofu, all with great results. If you're using salmon, chunks of steaks or fillets are best, but if you can't find them, just use sliced smoked salmon instead.

1 cup wild rice

Salt

1 pound cucumbers, peeled and seeded if you like, and chopped

½ cup pecans, toasted if you like

8 ounces chopped smoked salmon, trout, whitefish, tofu, bacon (cook it first), or sausage (cook it if necessary)

¼ cup olive oil

2 tablespoons lemon juice, or to taste

½ cup fresh dill, or 1 teaspoon dried

Black pepper

1. Put the wild rice in a saucepan with 3 cups water and a large pinch of salt. Bring to a boil and reduce the heat to low. Cover and cook undisturbed for 30 minutes, then start checking every 5 minutes or so. The rice is done when it is puffed up and very tender. Add more water if necessary; if it's done and you have excess water, drain the rice. When the rice is ready, fluff it with a fork and remove it from the heat. (The rice can be made up to a day ahead and refrigerated; bring to room temperature before proceeding.)

2. While the rice cooks, toss the cucumbers with a large pinch of salt in a colander or strainer and let them sit for 20 minutes or so. Rinse, drain, and pat dry with a clean towel.

3. Combine the rice, cucumbers, pecans, smoked salmon (or whatever you're using), oil, lemon juice, and dill. Sprinkle with lots of black pepper, stir, then taste and adjust the seasoning, adding more salt or lemon juice if necessary. Serve warm or at room temperature.

Ⓕ Fast   Ⓜ Make-Ahead   Ⓟ Pantry Staple

Succotash Salad

Makes: 4 servings   Time: 30 minutes

This is the perfect use for fresh shell beans—if you can find them. But even frozen limas, favas, black-eyed peas, or edamame will give this flavor and texture you can't get with cooked dried beans. This salad also makes a nice bed for a bit of grilled sausage, a slice of bacon, or other grilled meats or fish. You must use fresh corn here; try grilling the cobs before you remove the kernels.

    2 cups fresh or frozen lima beans, fava beans, black-eyed peas,
        or edamame

    4 ears fresh corn

    1 tablespoon apple cider vinegar, or more as needed

    ¼ cup olive oil

    Salt and black pepper

    1 red bell pepper, chopped

    ½ cup chopped scallions

1. If the beans are frozen, put them in a colander and run them under cold water for a minute or 2; set them aside to drain.

2. Husk the corn. Carefully cut the kernels from the cobs with a sharp knife, slicing away from you; save as much of their juice as you can.

3. Put the vinegar, oil, and a pinch each of salt and pepper in a large bowl and whisk until well combined. Add the beans, corn kernels, bell pepper, and scallions and toss. Taste and adjust the seasoning, adding more vinegar if necessary. Serve (or cover and refrigerate for up to a day).

Black Bean and Corn Salad. Substitute 2 cups cooked black beans for the fresh or frozen beans, and the juice of 1 lime for the cider vinegar. Garnish with chopped cilantro and a crumble of queso fresco if you like.

Lentil Salad with Peas and Green Beans

Makes: 4 servings   Time: 30 minutes

I don't often use nut oils, but I like them in salads, where they can turn a simple dressing into something magnificent. Hazelnut oil will take this salad from very good to terrific. Or toast the hazelnuts to intensify their flavor.

Brown lentils are the easiest variety to find, but green, black, and Le Puy also work well here.

> Salt
>
> 1 cup brown lentils
>
> 8 ounces green beans, cut into 2-inch segments
>
> 1 cup fresh or frozen peas
>
> ¼ cup hazelnut or olive oil
>
> 2 tablespoons sherry vinegar, or to taste
>
> 1 shallot, chopped
>
> Black pepper
>
> ½ cup chopped hazelnuts, toasted if you like
>
> 4 ounces sliced or crumbled goat cheese, optional

1. Bring a large pot of water to a boil and salt it. Add the lentils, cover, and reduce the heat to medium so the water bubbles gently. When the lentils are just beginning to soften—after 7 to 10 minutes or so—add the green beans. Cook for another 5 minutes, then taste the lentils. If they're still hard, cook for a few minutes longer; if they're mostly tender, add the peas and cook for another minute.

2. When the lentils are tender but not mushy, transfer everything to a colander, rinse under cold running water, and drain well.

3. Transfer the lentils, green beans, and peas to a large salad bowl (it's okay if they're still a little warm). Add the oil, vinegar, shallot, and plenty of salt and pepper. (You can make the salad and refrigerate for up to a day ahead at this point; bring it to room temperature before proceeding.) Taste and adjust the seasoning. Serve, topped with the hazelnuts and goat cheese if you're using it.

Ⓕ Fast   Ⓜ Make-Ahead   Ⓟ Pantry Staple

Cherry Tomato–Edamame Salad

Makes: 4 servings   Time: 30 minutes   F M

Edamame and tomatoes complement each other beautifully, right down to their colors. That said, you could certainly substitute trimmed green beans or cubed firm tofu for the soybeans; just boil and cool them as described in Step 1.

The effortless and flavorful soy dressing here is probably something you'll want to make often, because it goes wonderfully with many raw and cooked vegetables, especially grated carrots or radishes. Shiso, also known as perilla, are those spade-shaped purple or green leaves that sometimes add a bright note to sushi; you can find them in many Asian markets (they're also incredibly easy to grow).

1½ cups shelled fresh or frozen edamame

2 tablespoons soy sauce, or to taste

Pinch of sugar, or to taste

2 teaspoons sesame oil

3 cups cherry or grape tomatoes, halved crosswise

Chopped fresh hot red chile (like Thai or habanero) to taste, optional

Black pepper

½ cup chopped fresh mint, Thai basil, or shiso, for garnish

1. Bring a medium saucepan of water to a boil. Add the edamame and cook until just tender, about 3 minutes. Drain in a colander and rinse under cold running water.

2. Combine the soy sauce, sugar, and oil in a large bowl. Add the edamame, tomatoes, and chile if you're using it, and sprinkle with pepper. Stir gently to coat the tomatoes and soybeans with dressing.

3. Let stand at room temperature for up to 15 minutes, stirring once or twice. Taste and add more soy sauce and black pepper if you like. Serve garnished with the herb.

Chickpea Salad with Cashew Chutney

Makes: 4 servings   Time: About 30 minutes with cooked or canned chickpeas

Big-flavored chutneys and salsas make terrific salad dressings; just thin them with a little oil and maybe a few drops of water, vinegar, or citrus juice to get the texture you want. Here, you start with spiced cashews and toss the quick chutney with chickpeas and fresh mango or apricot. When these fruits are out of season, try the same recipe with orange or tangerine segments or use about ½ cup chopped dried mango or apricots.

> 1 teaspoon cumin or coriander seeds, or a combination
>
> ½ small dried hot red chile (like Thai), or to taste
>
> ½ cup cashews (raw are fine)
>
> 1 small garlic clove
>
> Salt and black pepper
>
> 3 cups cooked or canned chickpeas, drained
>
> 1 cup chopped fresh mango or apricots
>
> Juice of 1 lime
>
> Olive oil as needed
>
> ½ cup chopped fresh cilantro
>
> ¼ cup plain yogurt, optional

1. Toast the seeds, chile, and cashews in a small, dry skillet over medium heat, shaking the pan frequently, until everything colors slightly and becomes fragrant, 3 to 5 minutes. Transfer to a blender or food processor and add the garlic and a sprinkling of salt and pepper. Process, stopping the machine to scrape down the sides if necessary, until finely ground but not as smooth as peanut butter.

2. Toss the chickpeas and fruit with the chutney in a salad bowl, adding the lime juice and a little oil if needed to help bring everything together. Stir in the cilantro and taste and adjust the seasoning. Serve immediately, drizzled with some of the yogurt if you're using it. (Or cover and refrigerate for up to a day.)

Fava Bean, Asparagus, and Lemon Salad

Makes: 4 servings   Time: 25 minutes

Thanks to quickly made "preserved" lemon and a fair amount of mint, the dressing for this salad is incredibly bright. Crisp-tender asparagus provides a nice foil, but you will get even more contrast if you roast, broil, or grill the asparagus, which doesn't take much more time.

> 2 lemons, well washed
>
> Salt and black pepper
>
> ¼ cup olive oil
>
> 1 pound asparagus, peeled if thick, cut into 2-inch pieces
>
> 1 cup shelled fava beans (frozen are fine)
>
> ½ cup chopped fresh mint

1. Chop 1 whole lemon (peel and all) and combine with the juice of the second lemon, a pinch of salt and pepper, and the oil in a large bowl. Let sit while the vegetables cook.

2. Bring a pot of water to a rolling boil. Add some salt and the asparagus and fava beans. While they are cooking, set up a bowl of water with lots of ice cubes in it. The asparagus are done when they are just tender enough to pierce with a thin-bladed knife; the favas should be completely cooked through but not mushy, 3 to 5 minutes. When everything is done, remove the asparagus and beans with a small strainer or slotted spoon, plunge in the ice water, and cool for a few minutes.

3. Drain the asparagus and favas well, then add them to the bowl with the lemon. Add the mint and toss. Taste and adjust the seasoning if necessary. Serve immediately (or refrigerate for up to a couple of hours).

Marinated Pressed Tofu with Vegetables

Makes: 4 servings   Time: 20 minutes, plus 2 hours to marinate

The thin pieces of tofu and grated vegetables soak up tons of flavor from the marinade, just as long as you leave enough time for them to sit in the fridge—figure a couple hours or so. Make sure that you either press some of the water out of regular firm tofu or buy dry pressed tofu, which is much firmer and perfect for marinating, since it doesn't have much moisture to start with.

If this seems too complicated, let me tell you that the combination of tofu, celery, and this dressing is quite fabulous.

> 8 ounces dry pressed tofu, or extra-firm or firm tofu squeezed and patted dry (see the sidebar on page 177)
>
> 2 tablespoons soy sauce
>
> 2 teaspoons minced fresh hot chile (like Thai or serrano) or chile paste, hot sauce, or chile flakes to taste
>
> ¼ cup sesame oil
>
> 2 tablespoons rice vinegar
>
> 2 medium to large carrots, grated
>
> 2 celery stalks, grated
>
> 1 large cucumber, grated or julienned
>
> 1 daikon radish, grated or julienned
>
> 1 red bell pepper, thinly sliced

1. Cut the tofu into 2-inch matchsticks. Whisk together the soy sauce, chile, sesame oil, and vinegar in a large bowl.

2. Add the tofu and remaining ingredients, toss, and marinate for at least 2 hours in the refrigerator, stirring once or twice. Toss again immediately before serving.

Ⓕ Fast   Ⓜ Make-Ahead   Ⓟ Pantry Staple

Pressing or Freezing Tofu

You'll never be able to get regular brick tofu as dry as commercially pressed tofu, but you can do a couple of quick things to change its texture and make it absorb sauces, marinades, and liquids more easily. (Only firm tofu is worth pressing; soft and silken will just fall apart because of their high water content.)

If you have no time: Wrap a brick of firm tofu in a couple layers of towels and squeeze it gently between your palms until water comes out. (You might want to do this over a sink to catch any drips.) Be careful not to press it so hard that you crack the sides of the brick or break it.

If you have 30 minutes or more: Cut the brick in half lengthwise and sandwich both halves between towels. Put a flat plate on top and put something heavy on the plate to weigh it down a bit. Use a cast-iron skillet, cans, a brick, or whatever is heavy enough to put pressure on the tofu without causing the sides to bulge and crack. Let the tofu sit for up to 2 hours or refrigerate the whole setup for up to a day. The longer it goes, the drier it will get. You might change the towel layers once or twice.

If you have a day or more: Freezing brick tofu helps dehydrate it and changes the texture from custardy to spongy and chewy, so it really soaks up surrounding flavors. After you thaw frozen tofu, give it a good squeeze with towels (see above) before using, to make sure no water remains trapped inside.

Plum Chicken Salad

Makes: 4 servings   Time: 30 minutes with leftover cooked chicken

Firm plums are perfect here, but chicken tastes good with almost any fruit, so if plums aren't available, try peaches, apples, pears, berries, or even tropical fruit. You can vary the nuts too (check out the variation).

About 8 ounces fresh plums, pitted and thinly sliced

2 tablespoons balsamic vinegar

¾ cup chopped almonds

Salt and black pepper

1 tablespoon chopped fresh oregano, or 1 teaspoon dried

¼ cup olive oil

2 celery stalks, thinly sliced

½ red onion, chopped

8 ounces roasted or grilled boneless, skinless chicken, chopped or shredded (about 2 cups)

6 cups mixed greens (like mesclun), torn into bite-size pieces

1. Toss the plums with the vinegar in a large salad bowl. Cover and refrigerate for at least 15 minutes and up to 2 hours.

2. Meanwhile, put the almonds in a dry skillet over medium heat and toast, shaking the pan frequently, until they are aromatic and beginning to darken, 3 to 5 minutes. Remove from the heat and let cool.

3. Sprinkle the plums with salt and pepper and add the oregano, oil, celery, onion, and chicken; toss to combine. Taste and adjust the seasoning if necessary. (The salad can be made ahead to this point and refrigerated for up to an hour.) To serve, divide the greens evenly among 4 plates and top each with some of the plum-chicken mixture, or add the greens to the salad bowl and toss everything together. Garnish with the toasted almonds.

Fig Chicken Salad. Substitute fresh figs, quartered, for the plums and use hazelnuts instead of almonds.

Gingered Tomato Salad with Shrimp

Makes: 4 servings   Time: 30 minutes

The flavors of ceviche inspire this quick salad, with lots of ginger as an added twist. To make a meal of it, toss the finished dish with crisp spinach or lettuce leaves while it's still warm. You can also substitute garlic for half (or all) of the ginger.

> Olive oil as needed
>
> 2 tablespoons minced ginger
>
> 8 ounces shrimp (about 1 dozen medium shrimp), peeled (see page 22)
>
> Salt and black pepper
>
> 3 tablespoons lime juice
>
> ¼ cup chopped scallions
>
> ½ cup chopped fresh cilantro, plus more for garnish
>
> 4 large ripe tomatoes, cored and cut into wedges

1. Pour enough oil in a medium skillet to cover the bottom of the pan in a thin layer; turn the heat to low. When the oil is warm, add the ginger and cook, stirring occasionally, until golden, 3 to 5 minutes.

2. Raise the heat to medium-high and add the shrimp and some salt and pepper. Stir and continue to cook, shaking the pan once or twice and turning the shrimp until they are pink all over, about 5 minutes.

3. Transfer the shrimp to a salad bowl and toss with the lime juice, scallions, cilantro, and tomatoes. Taste and adjust the seasoning. Serve warm or at room temperature, garnished with additional cilantro (or refrigerate for up to 2 hours before serving).

Chile Tomato Salad with Crab. Substitute 1 to 2 seeded and minced fresh hot chiles (like jalapeño or Thai) for the ginger. Instead of shrimp, use 8 ounces lump crab meat, chopped; cook it in the oil just long enough to heat through before tossing with the other ingredients.

Italian-American Antipasto Salad with Tomato Vinaigrette

Makes: 4 servings   Time: 30 minutes

Use this recipe as a model for any combination of raw or cooked vegetables that you like. Roasting, grilling, broiling, or even steaming some of them will add even more contrast. I like eating whole basil leaves in this salad, but for something more subtle, toss them in the blender with the tomato. If you like anchovies, add a couple of fillets to the dressing.

1 large ripe tomato, seeded and roughly chopped

⅓ cup olive oil

Salt and black pepper

1 head romaine lettuce, torn into bite-size pieces

1 cup fresh basil

1 small red onion, thinly sliced

1 carrot, chopped

1 celery stalk, chopped

1 small cucumber, chopped

1 red bell pepper, chopped, or 1 cup sliced roasted red peppers
    (for homemade, see page 417)

½ cup olives, pitted

1 or 2 pickled pepperoncini or fresh hot peppers, sliced

4 ounces fresh mozzarella, cubed

4 thick slices prosciutto or salami, chopped

1. Combine the tomato, oil, and a sprinkling of salt and pepper in a blender. Turn the machine on and blend until a creamy emulsion forms, about 30 seconds.

2. Toss together all of the remaining ingredients in a large salad bowl. Drizzle on the tomato vinaigrette and toss again. Taste and adjust the seasoning if necessary. Serve.

Crudité Salad with Tomato Vinaigrette. Substitute 2 cups parboiled and shocked vegetables (like asparagus slices, snap peas, peas, broccoli stems, or green beans) for the olives, mozzarella, and prosciutto.

Grilled Eggplant Salad with Tomato Vinaigrette. Omit the carrot, celery, cucumber, mozzarella, and prosciutto, but use the other ingredients called for. Cut about 1 pound eggplant into thick slices, brush with olive oil, and grill or broil until tender. When the slices are done cooking, roughly chop them, then toss with the romaine and tomato vinaigrette. Garnish with crumbled feta, ricotta salata, or dry pecorino if you like.

Thai Beef Salad

Makes: 4 servings   Time: 25 minutes

Skirt or flank steak are the best cuts to use for this salad (they're also among the cheapest), but feel free to use strip or rib-eye. For a switch from beef altogether, try the seafood variation or cook some chicken breast, sliced tofu, or vegetables as described in Step 1.

    8 ounces skirt or flank steak

    6 cups mixed salad greens, torn into bite-size pieces

    1 cup torn fresh mint, cilantro, or Thai basil, or a combination

    ¼ cup chopped red onion

    1 cucumber, peeled if you like, seeded, and chopped

    1 small fresh hot red chile (like Thai), or to taste, minced

    Juice of 2 limes

    1 tablespoon sesame oil

    1 tablespoon nam pla (fish sauce) or soy sauce

    ½ teaspoon sugar

1. Prepare a grill or turn on the broiler; the heat should be medium-high and the rack about 4 inches from the fire. Grill or broil the beef, turning once or twice, until medium-rare, 5 to 10 minutes total depending on the thickness; set it aside to cool slightly. (You can prepare the recipe up to this point and refrigerate for up to a day; bring the meat to room temperature before proceeding.)

2. Toss the lettuce with the herbs, onion, and cucumber. Combine all of the remaining ingredients with 1 tablespoon water (the dressing will be thin) and toss half of this mixture with the greens. Remove the greens to a platter, reserving the remaining dressing.

3. Thinly slice the beef, reserving its juice; combine the juice with the remaining dressing. Lay the slices of beef over the salad, drizzle the dressing over all, and serve.

Thai Seafood Salad. Substitute any firm white fish, shrimp, squid, or scallops for the beef. (Firm white fish fillets like halibut or cod will take about as much time to cook as the beef; shrimp, squid, and scallops will take about half as much time.)

(F) Fast   (M) Make-Ahead   (P) Pantry Staple

Puffed Rice Salad
with Chickpeas and Coconut

Makes: 4 servings   Time: 30 minutes with cooked or canned chickpeas

One of my favorite Indian snacks (or *chaat*) is called *bhelpuri*, which combines crunchy puffed rice (think bigger, less sweet Rice Krispies) with coconut, vegetables, and a kind of chickpea noodle known as *sev*. I've streamlined the recipe and tossed everything with a coconut-lime dressing.

The salad is perfect when some grains of the puffed rice (use puffed brown rice cereal, or go to an Indian market) are still crunchy, while others have softened a bit in the surrounding flavors—but don't let it sit for too long before serving or it'll get soggy. When tomatoes aren't in season, try using a not-overripe mango instead.

½ cup shredded unsweetened coconut

1 cup cooked or canned chickpeas, drained

1 carrot, chopped

1 cucumber, peeled and seeded if you like, chopped

1 red bell pepper, chopped

½ cup chopped scallions

½ cup coconut milk

3 tablespoons lime juice

2 teaspoons curry powder

Salt and black pepper

2 cups puffed brown rice cereal

1 large ripe tomato, cored and chopped

½ cup chopped fresh cilantro

1. Put the coconut in a dry skillet over medium-low heat. As soon as it becomes fragrant, stir or shake it almost constantly until lightly browned and toasted, 3 to 5 minutes. Remove from the heat and let cool.

2. Combine the chickpeas, carrot, cucumber, bell pepper, and scallions in a large salad bowl. Add the coconut milk and lime juice, sprinkle with the curry powder, salt, and pepper, and toss well. Add the toasted coconut, puffed rice, tomato, and cilantro and toss again. Let the salad rest for a couple minutes (but not more than 10). Taste and adjust the seasonings if necessary and serve.

Corn-Avocado Salad (with a Little Something Seared on Top)

Makes: 4 servings   Time: 45 minutes

I call for scallops in this stunning restaurant-style summertime salad, but you can use the same quantity of chicken breast, peeled shrimp, cleaned squid, boneless pork chop, steak, or extra-firm tofu. Just cut them into four portions if necessary and cook the pieces virtually the same way, adjusting the cooking time as needed.

4 tablespoons olive oil, plus more as needed

2 small corn tortillas, cut into strips

4 to 6 ears fresh corn, stripped of their kernels (2 to 3 cups)

1 small red onion, chopped

1 teaspoon mild chile powder (like ancho) or regular chili powder

1/2 red bell pepper, chopped

1 ripe tomato, peeled if you like, seeded, and chopped

1 avocado, skin and pit removed, chopped

Juice of 1 orange

1/2 cup chopped fresh cilantro, plus more for garnish

Salt and black pepper

8 small or 4 large scallops (about 8 ounces)

1. Put a thin film of oil in a large skillet and turn the heat to medium-high. When the oil is very hot but not yet smoking, add the tortilla strips and fry until crisp, about 5 minutes on each side. Remove the tortilla strips from the skillet and drain on paper towels.

(F) Fast   (M) Make-Ahead   (P) Pantry Staple

2. Wipe out the skillet with a paper towel, return it to high heat, and add 2 tablespoons of the oil. When the oil is hot, toss in the corn and onion. Let it sit for a minute or so, then stir or shake the pan and brown the vegetables a bit, 5 minutes or less. Transfer the corn and onion to a large salad bowl and stir in the chile powder. Add the bell pepper, tomato, avocado, orange juice, and cilantro and sprinkle with salt and pepper. Toss well, taste, and adjust the seasoning.

3. Wipe out the skillet and return it to the burner once more, this time over medium-high heat. Add the remaining 2 tablespoons oil and, 30 seconds later, the scallops. Turn them as they brown, allowing about 2 minutes per side (less for scallops under 1 inch thick, somewhat more for those well over 1 inch). Sprinkle them with salt and pepper as they cook; put them on top of the salad as they finish. Garnish with the reserved tortilla strips and additional cilantro and serve.

My Favorite Vinaigrette

Makes: About ⅔ cup   Time: 5 minutes

A simple vinaigrette is one of the most useful and versatile recipes in all of cooking. This version is about as traditional as it gets, but once you know it, there are no limits to how you can use and vary it (see the variations and sidebar that follow).

⅓ cup olive oil

2 tablespoons sherry vinegar, or more to taste

Salt and black pepper to taste

1 teaspoon Dijon mustard, or to taste

1 medium shallot (or ½ small onion, or 2 scallions) cut into chunks, optional

1. Combine everything but the shallot in a blender and turn the machine on; an emulsion will form within 30 seconds. Taste and add more vinegar a teaspoon or 2 at a time until the balance tastes right to you.

2. Add the shallot and turn the machine on and off a few times until the shallot is minced within the dressing. Taste and adjust the seasoning. Serve. (This is best served fresh but will keep a few days in a glass jar in the refrigerator; bring back to room temperature and shake briefly before using.)

My Favorite Vinaigrette Without a Blender. If you don't have a blender, mince the shallot and combine it in a bowl with the vinegar, mustard, salt, and pepper. Slowly drizzle in the oil, whisking constantly, until all of the oil is incorporated. Don't worry if your emulsion doesn't look perfectly smooth; just whisk again right before using. (You can also simply combine the ingredients in a jar and shake until smooth, about 1 minute.)

Herb Vinaigrette. Add chopped herbs to the blender or bowl (⅓ cup for milder herbs like parsley, basil, or dill, or 1 teaspoon for stronger herbs like thyme, tarragon, or rosemary).

Ⓕ Fast   Ⓜ Make-Ahead   Ⓟ Pantry Staple

More Vinaigrettes

Now that you know the standard recipe, here are some ideas to break the rules. For starters, try varying the vinegar and oil. For example, go with rice vinegar or lime juice and a neutral vegetable oil for use with Asian flavors and dishes (a few drops of sesame oil and/or soy sauce mixed in is lovely). Balsamic is nice with olive oil, as is good-quality red or white wine vinegar. Citrus juice also makes a terrific vinaigrette; you'll just need to add a little more.

Then play around with the extra ingredients. Instead of the shallot, try garlic, ginger, lemongrass, wasabi, fresh horseradish, or the white part of scallions. Peeled soft stone fruit—like peaches or plums—make slightly sweet and colorful additions, as do roasted bell peppers (for homemade, see page 417). Nuts add body and, well, nuttiness. And finally, consider the spices: Curry or chili powder, cumin or coriander, and even cinnamon or nutmeg (in small doses) are especially good with cooked vegetable or other hearty salads.

Mayonnaise *with* Eggs

File mayo under "something I can't live without." And per serving, it contains a fraction of an egg, so I hardly even consider it a treat. A couple tips: Use vegetable oil if you want a more neutral taste, and olive oil if you want something a bit stronger. Whatever oil you use, add it VERY SLOWLY to the egg yolks as you beat them.

Here's how you do it:

To make 1 cup mayonnaise by hand, put 1 egg yolk and 2 tablespoons Dijon mustard in a bowl and beat them together with a wire whisk. Begin adding 1 cup oil in dribbles as you beat, adding a little more as the previous drops disappear in the mixture. Once a thick emulsion forms, you can add the remaining oil a little faster until it is all incorporated. Add 1 tablespoon vinegar or lemon juice and a sprinkle of salt and pepper.

To make the mayo by machine, put the yolk in a blender or food processor and turn the machine on. While it's running, add the oil in a slow, steady stream. When an emulsion forms, you can add the remaining oil a little faster until it is all incorporated. Add 1 tablespoon vinegar or lemon juice and a sprinkling of salt and pepper.

Tofu Mayo

Makes: About 1 cup   Time: 10 minutes

Here is a delicious homemade vegan mayo. To make this more of a sauce, add some soy milk, water, or a little more olive oil.

    6 ounces soft silken tofu (about ¾ cup)

    2 tablespoons olive oil

    2 tablespoons lemon juice

    2 teaspoons Dijon mustard, or to taste

    1 tablespoon honey or sugar, optional

    ¼ teaspoon paprika, optional

    ¼ teaspoon salt, or to taste

 Ⓕ Fast   Ⓜ Make-Ahead   Ⓟ Pantry Staple

1. Put all the ingredients in a blender. Turn the machine to a medium speed that keeps things moving without splattering. Let it run for a minute or 2, then turn it off.

2. Scrape the sides of the container with a rubber spatula, turn the blender back on, and repeat the process two more times. Taste and add more salt if necessary. Serve immediately (or store in a jar in the refrigerator for up to several days).

Bread-and-Nut Mayo

Makes: **About 1 cup**   Time: **10 minutes**

Like the tofu mayo above, this homemade vegan mayo is going to taste much better than store-bought eggless mayonnaise or, for that matter, most store-bought "real" mayonnaise. Plus both vegan mayos keep for days, if not longer.

Bread-and-Nut Mayo is based on skordalia, the classic Greek sauce that tastes great with almost anything. Use whole wheat bread here if you like but stay away from breads with seeds or bits of grain.

> 1 small slice day-old bread, preferably whole wheat
>
> 1 tablespoon olive oil, plus more as needed
>
> ½ cup almonds, walnuts, or cashews
>
> 1 garlic clove, or to taste
>
> 1½ teaspoons lemon juice, or to taste
>
> Salt and black pepper

1. Put the bread in a bowl and wet it with a few tablespoons of water. Squeeze the bread dry, then put it in a food processor with the oil, nuts, and garlic. Process the mixture until the nuts are ground. With the machine running, slowly pour in ¼ cup water, followed by a drizzle of oil to form a creamy sauce as thick or thin as you like.

2. Add the lemon juice and some salt and pepper and process to combine. Serve immediately (or cover and refrigerate for up to 2 days).

Pasta, Noodles, and Dumplings

I have eaten pasta at least once a week for my entire adult life, but the style in which I eat it has changed. When I was young, just exploring Italian cooking, and (seemingly) invincible to weight gain, a one-pound box of pasta often served two. A few years later, as I was researching and testing recipes for my first cookbook (and old enough to put on a few pounds), I realized that a four-ounce portion was far more typical—and reasonable.

A couple years ago, though, I started drifting toward a more-sauce-less-pasta approach. Now I almost always prefer dishes that use pasta and noodles as an integral part—but not the focus—of the dish. What's important is that I realized that the best thing about pasta is usually the sauce, whether it's all-vegetable or a sauce containing dairy, fish, or meat.

Throughout much of this transition I've stuck to pasta made with traditional semolina. There's no question that whole grain pastas can be an acquired taste, and there's no reason why you have to exclude "white" noodles from your diet, just as you wouldn't avoid moderate amounts of good white bread. And that's part of the beauty of the more-sauce-less-pasta philosophy: It's the best of both worlds.

That said, I suggest trying whole grain pastas in the recipes here. If you're already familiar with them, these sauces will offer new ways to treat them; if not, then consider these dishes an informal, friendly introduction. In all cases, you can substitute standard noodles whenever you like. (You can also skip the pasta entirely and serve these sauces over grains, plain cooked beans, even toasted bread.)

As in the other chapters in the book, the easiest, fastest, and most familiar dishes appear up front, including a smattering of Asian-inspired noodles; bean, seafood, chicken, and meat additions follow. (At the end are a handful of relatively simple dumplings.) Some pasta dishes are great at room temperature and therefore qualify as salad; these have been marked with the Make-Ahead icon.

One last word about cooking pasta and other noodles: The cooking times for dried pastas vary wildly, and people's personal preferences only somewhat less so. So taste and use your judgment. The recipes give a lot of guidance and follow the linear progression of the dish: set the water to boil, make the sauce, boil the noodles, toss. If you have a lot of kitchen experience and are comfortable multitasking, you can pull the dish together even faster if you set the water to boil, begin the sauce, put the noodles in the pot, and finish the sauce while the noodles cook. Remember that the noodles will keep cooking when you toss them in the sauce, so plan on draining them just before they're done to your liking.

Ⓕ Fast   Ⓜ Make-Ahead   Ⓟ Pantry Staple

How to Choose Pasta and Asian-Style Noodles

The most common dried pasta sold in both supermarkets and specialty stores is semolina pasta, the ivory-colored noodles made from coarsely ground durum wheat and water. Most American and Italian companies now also make whole wheat pastas, which—depending on the percentage of whole grain used—have a much darker color and nuttier flavor. They also have more fiber and protein but don't release as much starch when cooked, so they come across as a little drier and less creamy.

The recipes in this chapter compensate somewhat by encouraging you to increase the moisture of the sauce and toss the pasta with the ingredients (a venerable tradition) rather than serve the noodles with the sauce on top. Of course, you can use semolina pasta in these recipes (or egg or nonwheat noodles for that matter), but the cooking times will vary. Keep an eye on them so they don't overcook.

In general, you can use whatever shape you like. The rule of thumb is to use strands for smooth sauces, and tubes and cut pasta with chunky ones, but it's the kind of rule that has a lot of exceptions, even in Italy, so don't worry much about it.

Among the most common of Asian noodles are pure-white rice noodles, ranging from the angel-hair-thin vermicelli to the wider linguine-like strands; all are often referred to as rice sticks. Though they are the least nutritious of your options, you can use them in the recipes here. (They also cook in a flash. The most common way to soften them is to submerge them in boiling water and let them soak for several minutes.) Or you can try noodles made from refined wheat (like Chinese egg noodles, ramen, and udon) or starches (like bean threads), or even those made from tofu.

But soba noodles (made from a mixture of buckwheat and white flours) and the increasingly available brown rice noodles have a little more fiber and protein and a much more interesting taste. (Note that flatter, wider varieties of brown rice noodles cook more evenly than spaghetti-shaped ones.) I also sometimes use whole wheat spaghetti or angel hair in Asian-style dishes with excellent results.

Pasta with All-Purpose Tomato Sauce

Tomato sauce—even when made from canned tomatoes—is fast (as fast as cooking pasta), easy, and good year-round on just about anything. Try it on simply cooked vegetables, chicken, or fish, or as a braising liquid for tofu, fresh beans, or vegetables. It reheats well, so use this recipe to make a big batch. Toss as much as you like with the pasta and keep the rest in the fridge for several days, or in the freezer for months.

> Salt
>
> ¼ cup olive oil
>
> 1 large onion or 2 medium onions, chopped
>
> Black pepper
>
> About 4 pounds canned whole or diced tomatoes (two 28- or 35-ounce cans), chopped, liquid reserved
>
> ½ cup chopped fresh parsley or basil, optional
>
> 8 ounces any pasta, preferably whole wheat, optional
>
> ½ cup grated Parmesan cheese, optional

1. If you are cooking pasta, bring a large pot of water to a boil and salt it. Put the oil in another large pot over medium heat. When it's hot, add the onion, sprinkle with salt and pepper, and cook, stirring occasionally, until soft, about 5 minutes.

2. Add the tomatoes. Cook, stirring occasionally, until the tomatoes break down and the mixture comes together and thickens a bit, 10 to 15 minutes. For a thinner sauce, add some or all of the reserved liquid and cook for another 5 to 10 minutes; if you want a thick sauce, save the liquid for another use. Taste the sauce, adjust the seasoning if necessary, stir in the herb if you're using it, and keep warm. (Or let cool, cover, and refrigerate for up to several days; reheat gently before serving.)

3. Cook the pasta (or not) in the boiling water until it's tender but not mushy (start tasting after 5 minutes), then drain, reserving some of the cooking liquid. Toss the pasta with at least half of the sauce, adding enough reserved cooking liquid to keep it moist. Taste and adjust the seasoning. Serve immediately, passing the Parmesan at the table if you like. (Save any leftover sauce for another use.)

Fresh Tomato Sauce. Instead of canned tomatoes, use chopped fresh Roma (plum) or any ripe meaty tomatoes. Peel and seed them if you like, but I almost never bother.

Homemade Salsa. For either the main recipe or the fresh variation above. In Step 1, after the onion cooks for about 2 minutes, add 2 or more chopped fresh jalapeño, serrano, or other fresh hot chiles (with the seeds if you like; they're hot) along with 2 tablespoons minced garlic. Instead of parsley or basil, finish Step 2 with chopped cilantro.

Garlicky Tomato Sauce. Omit the onion. Mince 4 or more garlic cloves and add them to the hot oil in Step 1. Reduce the cooking time to a minute or so, just until they begin to brown. Proceed with the recipe.

Cooking with Canned Tomatoes

As you know by now, I'm not a big fan of processed food, but canned tomatoes are one of the notable exceptions. They're undeniably convenient and preferable to fresh tomatoes any time except in the summer, when fresh are local and good.

Canned whole tomatoes generally are the best quality and, if it bothers you, you can remove the little bit of the core with your fingers as you drop them in the pot. (Use the juice if the recipe directs, or to thin too-thick sauces, or for another use—or drink it.) Diced tomatoes will save you time, but steer clear of crushed tomatoes, which are often watery. If you want crushed tomatoes, just squeeze the whole ones in your hands as you add them to the pot (it's a great stress reliever).

The recipes in this book specify the quantity of tomatoes in pounds, number of tomatoes if they must be used whole, or in cups if they are chopped. In cases where canned is an option, they're included in the ingredient line. Large cans of tomatoes range from 28 to 35 ounces—either is fine in every case. If you're using the larger size, you might want to increase the seasonings a bit after tasting, or just hold some of the tomatoes back and refrigerate or freeze them for another use.

Pasta with Broccoli Rabe and Bread Crumbs

Makes: 4 servings   Time: 30 minutes

Broccoli rabe, crisped bread crumbs, and whole wheat pasta make a satisfying one-dish meal. And this recipe is a snap to vary just by changing the pasta shape or using a different sturdy green, including chopped broccoli. If you have roasted garlic (for homemade, see page 421) on hand—lucky you—just add some to the skillet in place of (or along with) the fresh garlic. Note that the Parmesan is optional here; I never use it in dishes like this, but others do—your call.

Salt

½ cup olive oil, or more as needed

1 cup bread crumbs, preferably whole grain and homemade

1 onion, chopped

1 tablespoon minced garlic, or to taste

About 1 pound broccoli rabe, chopped

½ cup white wine or water

8 ounces any pasta, preferably whole wheat

Black pepper

½ cup grated Parmesan cheese, optional

1. Bring a large pot of water to a boil and salt it. Put half of the oil in a large skillet over medium heat. When it's hot, add the bread crumbs, sprinkle with salt, and cook until golden, 5 minutes or so. Remove with a slotted spoon.

2. Add the remaining ¼ cup oil to the pan and let it heat a bit. Add the onion, garlic, and a little salt and cook, stirring occasionally until the onion begins to soften, about 5 minutes. Add the broccoli rabe and wine. Cook, stirring occasionally, until the rabe is quite tender, about 10 minutes.

3. Meanwhile, cook the pasta in the boiling water until it's tender but not mushy (start tasting after 5 minutes), then drain it, reserving some of the cooking water. Toss the pasta in the skillet with the rabe mixture, the bread crumbs, a good sprinkling of black pepper, and some of the reserved pasta

Ⓕ Fast Ⓜ Make-Ahead Ⓟ Pantry Staple

cooking water. Stir and heat until the mixture is saucy, adding a little more pasta cooking water (or oil) if necessary. Taste and adjust the seasoning. Serve, passing the cheese at the table if you like.

Pasta with Broccoli Rabe, Anchovies, and Bread Crumbs. In Step 2, add 4 anchovies (or more, if you like) to the skillet along with the onion and garlic; wait to salt the dish until you assemble it. Mash the anchovies with a fork or potato masher as the onion cooks, then proceed with the recipe.

Pasta with Any-Herb Pesto

Makes: 4 servings   Time: 30 minutes

Traditional pesto Genovese is, of course, based on basil. But even though some purists (especially Genoans) might scoff, lots of herbs taste great puréed with oil and garlic, with or without nuts. If you want to use stronger herbs like rosemary, thyme, tarragon, marjoram, or oregano, limit yourself to a tablespoon per batch and make up the bulk with parsley, basil, dill, or another less-intense herb.

You'll probably have a few spoonfuls of the pesto left over; fortunately it's as good with cooked vegetables or grains, or as part of a sauce or dip, as it is with pasta. It freezes well, too, but hold off on adding the cheese until you thaw it.

Salt

2½ loosely packed cups fresh basil, parsley, mint, chives, dill, cilantro, or
  any combination (see the headnote)

1 small garlic clove, or to taste

2 tablespoons pine nuts or roughly chopped walnuts

½ cup olive oil, or to taste

8 ounces any pasta, preferably whole wheat

¼ cup grated Parmesan cheese, plus more for garnish, optional

Black pepper

1. Bring a large pot of water to a boil and salt it. Combine the herbs with a pinch of salt, the garlic, nuts, and about half the oil in a food processor or blender. Process, stopping to scrape down the sides of the container if necessary and adding the rest of the oil gradually. (At this point, the pesto can be refrigerated for up to 2 weeks or frozen for up to several months.)

2. Cook the pasta in the boiling water until it's tender but not mushy (start tasting after 5 minutes), then drain, reserving some of the cooking liquid. Toss the pasta with the pesto, Parmesan if you're using it, and a sprinkling of black pepper, adding cooking water as necessary to keep the mixture from drying out. Taste and adjust the seasoning. Serve immediately with a little extra Parmesan for passing at the table.

Pasta with Herb and Goat Cheese Pesto. Rich and tangy. Substitute 2 ounces crumbled goat cheese for the Parmesan.

Any-Herb Pesto with Asian Flavors. Toss this with just-cooked soba noodles or use with rice or stir-fries. For the herb, use cilantro, mint, Thai basil, or a combination. Use ginger or lemongrass instead of (or along with) the garlic. For the oil, use 2 tablespoons sesame oil combined with 6 tablespoons vegetable oil. If you're adding nuts, walnuts, pistachios, cashews, or peanuts are all good choices.

(F) Fast (M) Make-Ahead (P) Pantry Staple

Pasta with Tender Greens

Makes: 4 servings   Time: 30 minutes

Thanks to my old friend Jack Bishop for sharing this clever, ultrasimple technique, which leaves you with less cleanup than most. Tender greens cook along with the pasta, retaining their vibrant color. Use any green that you might eat in salad: spinach, arugula, watercress, pea shoots, mizuna, tatsoi, or even romaine or shredded Napa cabbage. For a heartier dish use sturdy greens or add thick slices of waxy potato. (Both take a bit longer to cook; see the variations.)

> Salt
>
> 8 ounces any pasta, preferably whole wheat
>
> About 1½ pounds tender greens (see the headnote)
>
> ¼ cup olive oil or butter, or a combination
>
> ½ cup grated Parmesan cheese, optional
>
> 1 tablespoon minced garlic
>
> Black pepper

1. Bring a large pot of water to a boil and salt it. Add the pasta. Cook the pasta until it's tender but not mushy (start tasting after 5 minutes), then add the greens and stir. As soon as the greens are tender—this could be in 10 seconds—drain, reserving some of the cooking water.

2. Return the pasta and greens to the pot, toss with the oil or butter, the cheese if you're using it, garlic, and a good amount of black pepper; add enough of the reserved cooking water just to moisten the mixture. Taste and adjust the seasoning if necessary. Serve.

Pasta with Hearty Greens. Instead of the tender greens, use chopped escarole, chard, kale, head cabbage, turnip greens, mustard greens, or beet greens. Add them to the pot when the pasta has cooked for about 5 minutes and proceed with the recipe.

Pasta with Tender or Hearty Greens and Potatoes. Cut about 1 pound waxy potatoes in half if they're small, or in thick slices if they're large. Add them to the pot of water when you set it to boil. Once it does, add the pasta and proceed with either the main recipe or the variation above.

Pasta with Caramelized Fennel and Onion

Makes: 4 servings   Time: 30 minutes

This technique for cooking fennel and onion releases their natural sweetness and makes for a wonderfully rich sauce. The variations bulk up the dish a bit, but additions can be as simple as adding a crumble of bacon or a little chopped cooked shrimp or lump crab meat to the cooking vegetables just before tossing in the pasta.

Salt

3 large or 4 medium fennel bulbs, cored and sliced

1 large onion, halved and thinly sliced

Black pepper

4 tablespoons olive oil

8 ounces any pasta, preferably whole wheat

½ cup white wine, optional

1. Bring a large pot of water to a boil and salt it. Put the fennel, onion, and a sprinkling of salt and pepper in a large, deep skillet over medium-low heat. Cover and cook, stirring every 5 minutes, until the vegetables have given up their liquid and are almost sticking to the pan. Add 3 tablespoons of the oil, raise the heat to medium-high, and cook, uncovered, until the vegetables are nicely browned, 5 to 10 minutes. Turn off the heat.

2. Cook the pasta in the boiling water until it's tender but not mushy (start tasting after 5 minutes). When it's almost done, turn the heat under the skillet to medium, add the white wine or some of the pasta cooking water to the pan, and stir to scrape up any browned bits from the bottom. Drain the pasta, reserving a little of the cooking water. Toss the pasta in the pan with the fennel and onion, adding a little of the pasta cooking water if the dish seems dry. Taste, adjust the seasoning if necessary, and drizzle with the remaining 1 tablespoon oil. Serve immediately.

Pasta with Creamy Caramelized Fennel and Onion. Add 2 tablespoons or more cream to the fennel and onion along with the white wine in Step 2.

     Ⓕ Fast   Ⓜ Make-Ahead   Ⓟ Pantry Staple

Pasta with Caramelized Fennel and Onion with Sausage. In Step 1, begin by heating 1 tablespoon of the oil in the skillet over medium-high and crumble in 8 ounces hot or sweet Italian sausage. Cook and stir, uncovered, until it is nicely browned; turn the heat to medium-low before adding the fennel and onion. Proceed with the recipe, using just 2 tablespoons of oil when you uncover the pan and raise the heat later in Step 1.

Adding Meat to Pasta Sauces

Small bits of flavorful meat are an utterly traditional way to add richness to pasta. Prosciutto, ham, bacon, pancetta, sausage, fresh whole or ground meat, or even organ meat will all do the trick. But the idea is to use it as the backbone of the sauce rather than simply to stir it in at the end. All you have to do is chop up the meat (if it isn't already) and cook it along with the aromatic vegetables (the garlic or onions and the like) or by itself in a little oil before adding the rest of the ingredients.

Pasta with Smashed Peas, Prosciutto, and Scallions

Makes: 4 servings   Time: 30 minutes

Flavoring peas with prosciutto is nothing new, but combining the result with pasta or rice is a little unusual. Roughly mashing the peas with some of the cooking water gives you a rich and rustic sauce that clings nicely to the pasta.

> Salt
>
> 2 tablespoons olive oil
>
> 4 ounces prosciutto, chopped
>
> 1 bunch scallions, white and green parts separated, all chopped
>
> Black pepper
>
> 3 cups fresh or thawed frozen peas
>
> 8 ounces any pasta, preferably whole wheat
>
> ¼ cup grated Pecorino Romano cheese, optional

1. Bring a large pot of water to a boil and salt it. Put the oil in a large, deep skillet over medium heat. When it's hot, add the prosciutto and cook until it is crisp, about 5 minutes. Add the white parts of the scallions and a sprinkling of salt and pepper and cook, stirring occasionally, a few minutes more. Stir in the peas and cook for 2 to 3 minutes, then turn off the heat.

2. Cook the pasta in the boiling water until it's tender but not mushy (start tasting after 5 minutes). When it's almost done, return the peas to medium heat, add some of the cooking water, and roughly mash the peas. Drain the pasta, reserving a little more of the cooking water. Stir enough water into the peas to make a sauce, then toss in the pasta, chopped scallion tops, and pecorino if you're using it. Taste and adjust the seasoning if necessary. Serve immediately.

Pasta with Seared Roma Tomatoes and Ricotta

Makes: 4 servings   Time: 30 minutes

It pays to really sear the tomatoes here—don't be too afraid of burning them—so their flesh becomes very dark brown and their skin nearly black. The ricotta balances their full flavor with rich creaminess. If you want more refinement, chop up the cooked tomatoes before tossing with the pasta. Canned tomatoes are fine in this recipe, though less distinctive; to keep the sauce from being too thin, drain them beforehand.

Salt

⅓ cup olive oil, plus more as needed

4 pounds ripe Roma (plum) tomatoes, cored and halved lengthwise

Black pepper

1 tablespoon minced garlic

8 ounces any pasta, preferably whole wheat

½ cup chopped fresh basil

½ cup ricotta cheese

1. Bring a large pot of water to a boil and salt it. Put the oil in a large skillet over medium-high heat. When it's hot, add as many of the tomatoes as will fit in a single layer, skin side down. Sprinkle with salt and pepper. When the skins begin to blacken, after 5 minutes or so, turn the tomatoes. Continue cooking and turning for another 5 to 10 minutes, until they're deeply colored on both sides; remove them from the skillet. Repeat with the remaining tomatoes, adding more oil to the skillet as necessary to prevent them from sticking. (If you do wind up with lots of burnt bits on the bottom of the pan, quickly rinse and dry the pan, return it to the heat, and add another tablespoon of oil before you continue.)

2. When you're done, return all the tomatoes and any accumulated juices to the pan along with the garlic. Cook, stirring frequently, for a minute or 2, then turn off the heat. (You can make the sauce ahead of time and refrigerate for up to a day; gently reheat while the pasta is cooking.)

3. Meanwhile, cook the pasta in the boiling water until it's tender but not mushy (start tasting after 5 minutes), then drain, reserving some of the cooking liquid. Turn the heat under the skillet to medium, add about ½ cup of the cooking water, and stir to loosen the bits that have stuck to the bottom of the pan. Toss the pasta, basil, and ricotta in the skillet with the tomatoes, moistening with more pasta cooking water as needed. Taste and adjust the seasoning. Serve hot or at room temperature.

Pasta with Artichokes

Makes: 4 servings   Time: 45 minutes

There have been springs in recent years when I ate artichokes almost daily, and this combination has become one of my favorites. Taking apart whole artichokes can be intimidating at first, but it requires only enthusiastic peeling and trimming—you won't go wrong—and the results are well worth it. This sublime sauce is perfect with fresh pasta if you've got it.

    Salt

    4 large or 12 baby artichokes

    Juice of ½ lemon

    8 ounces any pasta, preferably whole wheat

    1 tablespoon olive oil

    1 tablespoon butter

    1 teaspoon minced garlic

    1 tablespoon heavy cream

    Black pepper

    ½ cup chopped fresh parsley

    ½ cup grated Parmesan cheese

1. Bring a large pot of water to a boil and salt it. If you're using large artichokes, cut them into halves or quarters; remove the leaves (you can save them for another use) and the choke (the fuzzy cluster of leaves above the heart). Trim the bottom and trim and peel the stem. If the artichokes are

(F) Fast   (M) Make-Ahead   (P) Pantry Staple

small, peel off the toughest leaves and trim the bottom; there should be no choke, or it should be small enough to ignore. Thinly slice the artichokes. Remove ½ cup of the artichokes in a bowl with the lemon juice and cold water to cover.

2. Cook the pasta in the boiling water and start tasting after about 5 minutes. Meanwhile, put the oil and butter in a large skillet over medium heat. When the butter has melted, add the rest of the sliced artichokes and the garlic and cook, stirring often, for 5 minutes.

3. When the pasta is tender but not mushy, drain it, reserving some of the cooking liquid. Toss the pasta in the skillet with the artichokes, adding reserved cooking water as necessary to moisten. Drain the reserved artichokes and toss them in along with the cream, a sprinkling of black pepper, and the parsley. Taste and adjust the seasoning. Serve with Parmesan.

Pasta with Artichokes and Baby Spinach. Add 2 cups baby spinach leaves to the artichoke mixture at the end of Step 2. Stir just until wilted and proceed with Step 3.

Noodles with Spicy Vegetable Stir-Fry

Makes: 4 servings   Time: 30 minutes

These are not unlike cold sesame (or peanut) noodles, but a) they're hot and b) they contain tons of vegetables. You can add or substitute almost any vegetable for those listed—chopped tomato, cubed winter squash, peas or snow peas, green beans, parboiled broccoli—as long as you keep the total quantity about the same (your cooking times might vary a bit of course).

The same goes for different nut butters: cashew, almond, and tahini are all quite good. To spin this dish in a Southeast Asian direction, use nam pla (fish sauce) instead of soy sauce, and—if you have it—add some lemongrass along with the garlic.

Salt

2 tablespoons vegetable oil

1 large onion, halved and sliced

1 cup chopped or grated carrot

2 tablespoons minced garlic

1 fresh hot chile (like jalapeño or Thai), seeded and minced, or to taste

Grated zest of 1 lime

1½ pounds eggplant, zucchini, summer squash, or a combination, peeled as necessary and cut into chunks

8 ounces any rice, buckwheat (soba), or wheat noodles, preferably whole grain

1 cup coconut milk

⅓ cup peanut butter

1 tablespoon sugar or honey, optional

3 tablespoons soy sauce

Black pepper

½ cup chopped fresh cilantro or Thai basil

Lime wedges

Ⓕ Fast   Ⓜ Make-Ahead   Ⓟ Pantry Staple

1. Bring a large pot of water to a boil and salt it. Put the oil in a large skillet over medium-high heat. When it's hot, add the onion and carrot and cook, stirring occasionally, until softened, about 5 minutes or so. Stir in the garlic, chile, and lime zest, then add the eggplant, zucchini, or squash. Cook, stirring occasionally and adjusting the heat as necessary so the vegetable cooks quickly without burning, until softened (zucchini will cook faster than eggplant), 10 to 20 minutes.

2. Meanwhile, cook the noodles in the boiling water until tender but not mushy. Check them frequently: The time will vary from a minute or 2 for thin rice noodles, to 5 minutes for soba, or up to 12 minutes for wide brown rice noodles. When the noodles are just tender, drain them, reserving some of the cooking water.

3. Whisk together the coconut milk, peanut butter, sugar or honey if you're using it, and soy sauce. Add the coconut mixture and noodles to the skillet and toss, adding noodle cooking water if necessary to moisten. Sprinkle with pepper, taste, and adjust the seasoning if necessary. Serve hot, garnished with cilantro and lime wedges.

Vegetable Fried Noodles

Makes: 4 servings   Time: 30 minutes

Like fried rice, the combination of stir-fried vegetables and noodles is infi-nitely variable. For the vegetables, add sliced broccoli, asparagus, zucchini, lettuce, cabbage, spinach, or hearty greens at the beginning; or stir in tender greens at the end—they'll all work just fine.

To make the dish more substantial, start Step 2 by quickly cooking thin strips of pork (see the variation), beef, or chicken, or cubes of tofu, or a few shrimp in the hot oil. Remove them and proceed with the recipe, adding a little more oil if necessary.

Salt

8 ounces any rice, buckwheat (soba), or wheat noodles, preferably whole grain

1 tablespoon sesame oil

2 tablespoons vegetable oil

1 tablespoon minced garlic

1 teaspoon minced ginger

1 cup chopped scallions

2 large carrots, chopped, sliced, or julienned

3 celery stalks, chopped, sliced, or julienned

2 cups snow peas

¼ cup stock (for homemade, see pages 135 to 140) or water, or more as needed

2 tablespoons soy sauce

1 egg, beaten, optional

Black pepper

¼ cup chopped peanuts, for garnish

1. Bring a large pot of water to a boil and salt it. Cook the noodles in the boiling water until tender but not mushy. Check them frequently: The time will vary from a minute or 2 for thin rice noodles, to 5 minutes for soba, or up to 12 minutes for wide brown rice noodles. Drain the noodles and

Ⓕ Fast   Ⓜ Make-Ahead   Ⓟ Pantry Staple

quickly rinse under cold running water. Toss them with the sesame oil to prevent sticking.

2. Put the vegetable oil in a large, deep skillet over medium-high heat. When it's hot, add the garlic, ginger, and scallions. Cook, stirring, for about 15 seconds. Add the carrots, celery, snow peas, and stock and turn the heat to high. Cook, stirring frequently, until the vegetables are tender, 5 to 10 minutes. If the mixture cooks bone dry, add a couple tablespoons more liquid.

3. Stir in the soy sauce and the beaten egg if you're using it and let the egg lightly scramble in the pan. Now add the noodles, sprinkle with pepper, and toss well. Taste and adjust the seasoning. Garnish with chopped peanuts and serve.

Vegetable and Pork Fried Noodles. Start Step 2 by frying 8 ounces of thinly sliced pork shoulder or sirloin in the oil. Cook for a minute or 2, then remove it from the pan and proceed with the recipe. Stir the cooked pork back in along with the noodles in Step 3.

Teriyaki Noodles
with Asparagus and Edamame

Makes: 4 servings   Time: 30 minutes

Just by adding a little extra liquid, you can turn virtually any stir-fry into an excellent sauce for tossing with noodles, rice, or other grains. Asparagus is particularly nice here because it browns beautifully, but you can use green beans or sliced broccoli as alternatives. (I peel thick asparagus, which isn't strictly necessary, but it only takes a minute and makes it much less fibrous. Or skip the whole thing and use broccoli florets.) For a spicier sauce, add a couple dried red chiles to the skillet along with the garlic and ginger.

> 1½ pounds asparagus, peeled if thick, cut into 2-inch lengths
>
> Salt
>
> 2 tablespoons vegetable oil
>
> ½ cup chopped scallions
>
> 1 tablespoon minced ginger
>
> 1 tabespoon minced garlic
>
> 8 ounces any rice, buckwheat (soba), or wheat noodles, preferably whole grain
>
> 2 cups shelled edamame, fresh or frozen (thaw them while you assemble the dish)
>
> ¼ cup soy sauce
>
> ¼ cup mirin, or 2 tablespoons honey mixed with 2 tablespoons water

1. If the asparagus is thick, parboil it, then shock it in a bowl of ice water and drain (see page 414). If the spears are thin, don't bother.

2. Bring a large pot of water to a boil and salt it. Put a large skillet over high heat for 3 to 4 minutes. Add the oil, wait a few seconds, and add the asparagus and scallions. Cook, stirring, for a minute, then stir in the ginger and garlic. Cook until the asparagus is dry, hot, and beginning to brown and get tender, 5 to 10 minutes; remove the pan from the heat.

3. Cook the noodles in the boiling water until tender but not mushy. Check them frequently: The time will vary from a minute or 2 for thin rice noodles,

Ⓕ Fast   Ⓜ Make-Ahead   Ⓟ Pantry Staple

to 5 minutes for soba, or up to 12 minutes for wide brown rice noodles. Drain the noodles, reserving some of the cooking liquid.

4. Turn the heat under the asparagus to medium. Add the noodles, edamame, soy sauce, mirin, and about ½ cup of the reserved water to the skillet; continue to cook, stirring, until the asparagus and edamame are heated through, about 5 minutes. Taste and adjust the seasoning. Divide the noodles among 4 bowls, spooning any extra broth in the pan over all. Serve hot.

Teriyaki Noodles with Asparagus and Chicken. Omit the edamame. Before adding the asparagus and scallions to the skillet in Step 2, add 8 ounces sliced boneless, skinless chicken breast or thigh meat. Stir once, then let the chicken sit for 1 minute to brown. Cook, stirring occasionally, until the chicken is no longer pink, 3 to 5 minutes. Add the asparagus and scallions to the skillet and proceed with the recipe.

Mushroom and Pasta Frittata

Makes: 4 servings   Time: 30 minutes

In general, you wouldn't cook pasta specifically for making a frittata, but this recipe is worth the (rather negligible) extra effort. Of course, if you have left-over cooked pasta, all the better (you can skip Step 2). Instead of the mushrooms, try this dish with red bell peppers and onions.

Salt

3 tablespoons olive oil

About 1½ pounds mushrooms, preferably an assortment, sliced

Black pepper

8 ounces any long pasta, preferably whole wheat, or about 4 ounces (2 cups) cooked pasta

1 red onion, halved and thinly sliced

2 garlic cloves, thinly sliced

2 eggs

2 teaspoons chopped fresh sage, or 1 teaspoon dried

1. Bring a large pot of water to a boil and salt it if you need to cook the pasta. Put the oil in a large skillet over medium-high heat. Add the mushrooms, sprinkle with lots of salt and pepper, and stir. Cover, turn the heat down to medium-low, and cook, undisturbed, until the mushrooms have released a fair amount of liquid, 5 to 10 minutes. Remove the lid and turn up the heat until the liquid bubbles steadily. Cook, undisturbed, until the liquid boils off, about 5 more minutes.

2. Meanwhile, cook the pasta in the boiling water until tender but not mushy (start tasting after 5 minutes), then drain it well.

3. Add the onion and garlic to the skillet with the mushrooms and cook, stirring, until the mushrooms are dry, shrunken, and fairly crisp, about 5 minutes more. Reduce the heat to low and stir in the pasta. Beat the eggs with the sage and pour over all, using a spoon if necessary to distribute them evenly. Cook, undisturbed, until the eggs are barely set, 10 minutes or so. (You can set them further by putting the pan in a 350°F oven for a few minutes or running it under the broiler for a minute or 2.) Serve hot or at room temperature.

Ⓕ Fast   Ⓜ Make-Ahead   Ⓟ Pantry Staple

Pasta with Shell Beans and Red Onion

Makes: 4 servings   Time: 40 minutes

Fresh shell beans are available from midsummer into fall and are absolutely delicious—grab a bunch when you see 'em, and if they're already shucked, so much the better. Buy a ton and freeze some; out of season, they're a real treat. (Commercially frozen shell beans are a good substitute. There's no need to thaw them, and in fact they will probably take less time to cook than fresh ones.)

Salt

2 tablespoons olive oil

2 large red onions, halved and thinly sliced

1 tablespoon minced garlic

Black pepper

3 cups fresh shell beans (about 3 pounds in their pods), or use frozen

1 cup white wine, stock (for homemade, see pages 135 to 140), or water

1 tablespoon chopped fresh thyme, or 1 teaspoon dried

8 ounces any pasta, preferably whole wheat

½ cup grated Parmesan cheese

1. Bring a large pot of water to a boil and salt it. Put the oil in a large, deep skillet over medium heat. When it's hot, add the onions and garlic, sprinkle with salt and pepper, and cook, stirring, until the vegetables begin to soften, about 5 minutes. Add the shell beans, wine, and thyme. Partially cover and bubble gently until the beans are tender and the onions are starting to dissolve, 15 to 25 minutes. Keep warm over low heat.

2. When the beans are ready, cook the pasta in the boiling water until it's tender but not mushy (start tasting after 5 minutes), then drain, reserving some of the cooking liquid. Toss the pasta with the beans and onions, adding some of the reserved cooking water as you toss to keep things moist. Taste and adjust the seasoning. Sprinkle with the Parmesan, toss, and serve immediately or at room temperature.

Pasta with Puréed Red Beans and Shiitakes

Makes: 4 servings   Time: 30 minutes

The combination of shiitakes and puréed beans is delicious and memorable, but it's important to use beans with a creamy texture (lively color helps too)—so stay away from gritty beans like black-eyed peas and brown lentils.

Salt

¼ cup olive oil

1 tablespoon minced garlic

8 ounces fresh shiitake mushrooms, sliced

Black pepper

2 cups cooked or canned red kidney or pinto beans, drained, liquid reserved

8 ounces any pasta, preferably whole wheat

½ cup grated Parmesan cheese

½ cup chopped fresh parsley

1. Bring a large pot of water to a boil and salt it. Put the oil in a large skillet over medium heat. When it's hot, add the garlic and mushrooms, then sprinkle with salt and pepper. Cook, stirring occasionally, until tender, 10 to 15 minutes.

2. Purée the beans by putting them through a food mill or using an immersion blender; add as much liquid as you need to make a smooth but not watery sauce. Add the bean purée to the skillet and cook, stirring, for about 2 minutes, just to warm everything through. Remove the pan from the heat.

3. Cook the pasta in the boiling water until it's tender but not mushy (start tasting after 5 minutes). When it's almost done, return the sauce to medium heat. Drain the pasta, reserving some of the cooking liquid, and toss with the sauce, adding a little cooking liquid if it seems too thick. Taste and adjust the seasoning. Top with the Parmesan and parsley and serve.

(F) Fast   (M) Make-Ahead   (P) Pantry Staple

Ziti with Silky Cabbage, Oranges, and Chickpeas

Makes: 4 servings   Time: 45 minutes

Pasta and oranges may seem like a strange combination, but remember—tomatoes are a fruit too. And here the juice adds a background sweetness to the slow-cooked cabbage, while the fresh segments give a burst of acid at the end and combine nicely with the cheese's saltiness and the chile's heat. Hearty and bright at the same time, this dish is especially nice in winter.

2 tablespoons olive oil

1 tablespoon minced garlic

1 fresh hot chile (like serrano or Thai), minced

1 medium Savoy or other white cabbage (about 1 pound), cored and shredded

2 oranges, 1 juiced and the other peeled and cut into segments or wheels

Salt and black pepper

8 ounces ziti, preferably whole wheat

2 cups cooked or canned chickpeas, drained

½ cup grated ricotta salata cheese

2 tablespoons chopped fresh oregano, or 2 teaspoons dried

1. Put the oil in a large, deep skillet over medium heat. When it's hot, add the garlic and chile and cook, stirring, until they begin to soften, a minute or 2. Add the cabbage and orange juice and sprinkle with salt and pepper. Cook, stirring occasionally and adding a little water if necessary to keep the mixture just moist, until the cabbage is very soft, about 30 minutes.

2. When the cabbage is about halfway done, bring a large pot of water to a boil and salt it. Cook the ziti in the boiling water until it's tender but not mushy (start tasting after 5 minutes). When it's almost done, stir the chickpeas and orange segments into the pan with the cabbage. Drain the ziti, reserving some of the cooking water, and toss it with the cabbage and chickpeas, adding a little cooking water to keep the pasta moist. Stir in the ricotta salata and oregano. Taste and adjust the seasoning if necessary. Serve immediately or at room temperature.

Pasta with Fried Zucchini and Cannellini in Vinegar Sauce

Makes: 4 servings   Time: About 1 hour, largely unattended

You don't see vinegar in pasta dishes too often, but here just a little balances the richness of the vegetables and makes the dish perfect for serving at room temperature. If you're in a rush, you can skip salting the zucchini, but it does change the texture quite a bit. If you salt the zucchini, be sure to rinse them well and wait to salt the dish until after you toss it. The beans for this dish should be quite tender; it's a good place to use canned if you don't have time to start with dried.

1 pound zucchini, cut into ½ × 3-inch sticks

Salt

Olive oil as needed

1 onion, chopped

1 tablespoon minced garlic

Black pepper

2 cups cooked or canned cannellini or other white beans, drained

1 tablespoon sherry vinegar, or to taste

8 ounces any pasta, preferably whole wheat

½ cup chopped fresh mint, dill, or parsley

½ cup grated Parmesan cheese, for serving

1. Sprinkle the zucchini with salt and let it rest in a colander for 20 minutes. Rinse the zucchini and pat dry.

2. When the zucchini is ready, bring a large pot of water to a boil and salt it. Put about ½ inch oil in a large skillet over medium-high heat. When the oil is hot, put in a few pieces of zucchini; cook in batches as necessary, making sure not to crowd the pan and adding more oil as needed. Cook, turning the zucchini pieces so they brown evenly; total cooking time will be 5 minutes or a little longer. As the pieces finish, remove them to drain on paper towels. Add more zucchini to the pan and repeat until all are done.

3. Pour off all but 2 tablespoons of the oil from the pan and turn the heat to medium. Add the onion and garlic and sprinkle with pepper. Cook, stir-

Ⓕ Fast   Ⓜ Make-Ahead   Ⓟ Pantry Staple

ring occasionally, until the onion has begun to soften, about 3 minutes. Add the beans and mash with a fork or potato masher until they are more or less broken up with a few remaining chunks. Remove the pan from the heat.

4. Meanwhile, cook the pasta in the boiling water until it's tender but not mushy (start tasting after 5 minutes). Drain it, reserving about 1 cup cooking water. Toss the pasta in the skillet with the zucchini, vinegar, herb, and enough of the pasta cooking water to keep everything moist. Taste and adjust the seasoning. Serve immediately or at room temperature, passing the cheese at the table.

Provençal Tomato Sauce with Pasta

Makes: 4 servings   Time: 40 minutes

Take classic ratatouille, add enough tomatoes to make it saucy, and you have a dish that's good even at room temperature, whether served with pasta or bread or both. Since the sauce is so chunky, a cut pasta—like penne, ziti, or one of the more exotic shapes—is best.

1 medium or 2 small eggplants, cut into large cubes

Salt

6 tablespoons olive oil

Black pepper

2 small zucchini, chopped

8 ounces mushrooms, sliced

1 small onion, chopped

1 tablespoon minced garlic

1 red bell pepper, chopped

6 tomatoes, cored and chopped (canned are fine; drain their juice)

1 tablespoon chopped fresh thyme, or 1 teaspoon dried

8 ounces any cut pasta, preferably whole wheat

¼ cup crumbled feta cheese

½ cup chopped fresh basil, for garnish

1. If time allows, sprinkle the eggplant liberally with salt, let rest in a colander for 20 minutes, rinse, and pat dry. Bring a large pot of water to a boil and salt it.

2. Put 4 tablespoons of the oil in a large skillet over medium heat. When it's hot, add the eggplant, sprinkle with pepper, and cook, stirring occasionally, until soft and golden, about 10 minutes. Remove from the pan and drain on paper towels.

3. Put the remaining 2 tablespoons oil in the pan, add the zucchini and mushrooms, and sprinkle with salt and pepper. Cook, stirring occasionally, until they are tender, 10 to 15 minutes. Add the onion, garlic, and bell pepper; cook and stir until they are soft, another 5 minutes or so. Add the tomatoes and thyme and cook for another minute until the tomatoes just start to release their juice. Return the eggplant to the pan, stir, and turn off the heat. (The sauce can be made ahead to this point. Cool, cover, and refrigerate for up to a few days or freeze for up to a few months.)

4. Cook the pasta in the boiling water until it's tender but not mushy (start tasting after 5 minutes). When it's almost done, reheat the sauce over medium heat. Drain the pasta, reserving some of the cooking liquid, and toss with the sauce, adding a little cooking liquid if it seems too thick. Taste and adjust the seasoning if necessary. Scatter the feta and basil on top. Serve immediately or at room temperature.

Ⓕ Fast   Ⓜ Make-Ahead   Ⓟ Pantry Staple

Pasta with Asparagus, Bacon, and Egg

Makes: 4 servings   Time: 30 minutes

A little egg goes a long way in a pasta sauce—it adds flavor, color, sauciness, and richness, not something you can say about too many other single ingredients. That's why it appears frequently in some of the classics (think carbonara). Cook the asparagus a few minutes longer if you prefer—it's a toss-up between crunch and vibrant color when it's slightly underdone, and tenderness and fully developed flavor when it's well cooked.

Salt

2 tablespoons olive oil

4 ounces chopped bacon, pancetta, or guanciale

1½ pounds asparagus, peeled if thick, cut into 2-inch pieces

8 ounces any pasta, preferably whole wheat

2 eggs

¼ cup grated Parmesan cheese

Black pepper

1. Bring a large pot of water to a boil and salt it. Put the oil and bacon in a large skillet over medium heat. Cook, stirring occasionally, until the bacon has started to soften and brown, about 5 minutes. Stir in the asparagus and raise the heat a bit. Cook until it has softened but is still crunchy, 5 to 10 minutes depending on its size. Turn off the heat.

2. Cook the pasta in the boiling water until it's tender but not mushy (start tasting after 5 minutes). Meanwhile, warm a large bowl and beat the eggs in it. Stir in the bacon and asparagus along with any fat that the bacon has rendered.

3. When the pasta is done, drain it, reserving some of the cooking water. Immediately toss it with the egg and asparagus mixture, adding some of the cooking water if necessary. Add the cheese and plenty of black pepper, taste and adjust the seasoning, and serve.

Pasta with Rich Leek "Pesto"

Makes: 4 servings   Time: 45 minutes

It's worth noting that "pesto" means "paste" and comes from the same root as "pestle"—as in "mortar and . . ." Since pasta also comes from that root, you might describe this recipe as Rich Leek Paste Tossed with Paste. But with a thick, custardy texture that's a lot like a carbonara or cream sauce, it's much better than that, I promise. At the last minute, toss with a crumble of crisp cooked prosciutto, pancetta, or bacon for a nice addition.

If leeks aren't in your game plan, yellow onions are almost as good when caramelized and puréed.

¼ cup olive oil

4 or 5 garlic cloves, thinly sliced

About 1½ pounds leeks (2 or 3 large), trimmed, well rinsed, and chopped

Salt

1 egg

1 cup chopped fresh parsley leaves

Black pepper

8 ounces any pasta, preferably whole wheat

½ cup grated Parmesan cheese

1. Put the oil in a large skillet over medium-low heat. When it's hot, add the garlic and leeks and cook, stirring occasionally, until very soft, 20 to 30 minutes.

2. Bring a large pot of water to a boil and salt it. Transfer the leeks to a blender or food processor with the egg, parsley, and a sprinkling of salt and pepper. Process, stopping to scrape down the sides of the container if necessary. Return the purée to the skillet, off heat.

3. Cook the pasta in the boiling water until it's tender but not mushy (start tasting after 5 minutes), then drain, reserving some of the cooking liquid. Turn the heat under the leek mixture to medium, add about ¼ cup of the reserved cooking liquid to thin the pesto, and toss in the pasta along with the cheese. Add more liquid as desired and toss. Taste and adjust the seasoning, then serve.

Ⓕ Fast   Ⓜ Make-Ahead   Ⓟ Pantry Staple

Baked Rigatoni with Brussels Sprouts, Figs, and Blue Cheese

Makes: **4 servings**   Time: **45 minutes**

Many cheesy baked pastas depend on béchamel—the classic sauce made with flour, butter, and milk—for creaminess. But this is a very cool alternative that combines a variety of textures and flavors (including fruit) without diluting the taste of the cheese. Pears, apples, and cranberries would all be fine here, and if you're not keen on blue cheese, try fontina, Gruyère, or anything that melts easily.

> 2 tablespoons olive oil, plus more for greasing the pan
>
> Salt
>
> 8 ounces rigatoni, preferably whole wheat
>
> 1½ pounds Brussels sprouts, roughly chopped
>
> 4 ounces Gorgonzola or other blue cheese, crumbled
>
> 6 to 8 fresh figs, or 1 cup dried, chopped
>
> Black pepper
>
> ¼ cup chopped almonds, for garnish

1. Heat the oven to 400°F. Grease a 9 × 13-inch baking pan with a little olive oil. Bring a large pot of water to a boil and salt it. Add the pasta and cook it halfway through (start checking after 3 minutes; it should still be quite firm inside). Add the Brussels sprouts to the pot and cook, until the pasta and vegetables are just barely tender, another 3 minutes. Drain, reserving some of the cooking water, and return the pasta and Brussels sprouts to the pot.

2. Stir in the blue cheese, figs, the 2 tablespoons oil, and a splash of the cooking water. Sprinkle with salt and pepper, toss, and taste and adjust the seasoning. Turn the pasta mixture into the prepared pan.

3. Bake, checking once or twice and adding a bit more of the cooking water if the pasta looks too dry, until the mixture is bubbling, 15 to 20 minutes. Garnish with chopped almonds and serve.

Creamy Cauliflower Mac

Makes: 4 servings   Time: About 45 minutes

Vegetables are comfort food too, as proved by this recipe, which is sure to please anyone who loves mac-and-cheese. The "secret" is cauliflower's miraculous ability to turn creamy when puréed. If you don't want to wash out a blender or food processor (and don't mind some lumps), use a potato masher to purée the cauliflower in the same pot you cooked it in. The main recipe is quite saucy; for a less smooth texture, try the variation.

> 2 tablespoons olive oil, plus more for greasing the baking dish
>
> Salt
>
> 2½ cups vegetable or chicken stock (for homemade, see pages 135 to 140) or water
>
> 2 bay leaves
>
> 1 cauliflower, cored and separated into large pieces
>
> 8 ounces elbow, shell, ziti, or other cut pasta, preferably whole wheat
>
> ½ cup grated cheese (like sharp cheddar, Gruyère, or Emmental or a combination)
>
> 1 tablespoon Dijon mustard, or to taste
>
> ⅛ teaspoon nutmeg, or to taste
>
> Black pepper
>
> ¼ cup grated Parmesan cheese
>
> ½ cup or more bread crumbs, preferably whole grain and homemade, optional

1. Heat the oven to 400°F. Grease a 9-inch square baking dish with a little oil. Bring a large pot of water to a boil and salt it. Put the stock with the bay leaves in a small saucepan over medium-low heat. When small bubbles appear along the sides, about 5 minutes later, turn off the heat and let stand.

2. Cook the cauliflower in the boiling water until very tender, 20 to 25 minutes. Scoop the cauliflower out of the water with a slotted spoon and transfer it to a blender or food processor. Add the pasta to the boiling water and cook until still somewhat chalky inside and not yet edible, about 5 minutes.

Ⓕ Fast   Ⓜ Make-Ahead   Ⓟ Pantry Staple

Drain it, rinse it quickly to stop the cooking, and put it in the prepared baking dish.

3. Remove the bay leaves from the stock. Carefully process the cauliflower with 2 cups of the stock, the 2 tablespoons oil, the cheese, mustard, nutmeg, and a sprinkling of salt and pepper. (You may have to work in batches.) If the sauce seems too thick, add the remaining ½ cup stock. Taste and adjust the seasoning. Pour the sauce over the pasta, toss, and spread the mixture evenly in the dish. (You can make the dish to this point, cover, and refrigerate for up to a day; return to room temperature before proceeding.)

4. Sprinkle the top with the Parmesan and bread crumbs if you're using them. Bake until the pasta is bubbling and the crumbs turn brown, 15 to 20 minutes. Serve hot.

Less Creamy Cauliflower Mac. Cut the cored head of cauliflower in half instead of into large pieces. In Step 2, cook only half of the cauliflower until it's very tender, then transfer it to the blender or food processor as described. Chop the remaining half of the cauliflower into large pieces and add them to the boiling water along with the pasta. Proceed with the recipe.

Grilled Vegetable and Fresh Tomato Lasagna

Makes: 4 servings   Time: About 1 hour

Nicely grilled vegetables turn traditionally heavy lasagna into a fantastic—and easy—summertime party dish. (To serve eight or more, make a double recipe; it'll fit in a 9 × 13-inch baking dish or pan.) If the eggplant and zucchini are soft or seedy, you can improve their flavor and texture by sprinkling the slices with salt, putting them in a colander, and letting them sit for at least 30 minutes, preferably 60. (It isn't necessary if you don't have time, but it's worth it if you do.)

In winter, roast the vegetables in a 400°F oven and make a batch of All-Purpose Tomato Sauce (page 194) instead of using fresh tomatoes. (In fact, you can use tomato sauce any time of year for a more traditional lasagna.)

1 large eggplant, cut lengthwise into ¼-inch slices (see the headnote)

2 zucchini, cut lengthwise into ¼-inch slices (see the headnote)

3 portobello mushrooms

1 large onion, sliced into ¼-inch rounds

2 tablespoons olive oil, plus more as needed

Salt and black pepper

9 dried lasagna noodles (about 6 ounces), preferably whole wheat

4 ounces ricotta cheese (about ½ cup)

4 ounces fresh mozzarella cheese, chopped

4 tablespoons grated Parmesan cheese, or more as needed

1 cup whole basil leaves

1 tablespoon minced garlic

1 egg

4 ripe tomatoes, cut crosswise into ¼-inch slices

1. If time allows, sprinkle the eggplant and zucchini liberally with salt, let rest in a colander for 20 minutes, rinse, and pat dry. Prepare a grill to medium-high heat and put the rack about 4 inches from the fire. Brush the eggplant, zucchini, mushrooms, and onion with 2 tablespoons of the oil,

Ⓕ Fast   Ⓜ Make-Ahead   Ⓟ Pantry Staple

then sprinkle with salt and pepper. Grill, turning and brushing with more oil if they look too dry, until nicely browned on both sides, about 10 minutes total. Remove them as they finish; cut the mushrooms into slices and set all the vegetables aside.

2. Bring a large pot of water to a boil and salt it. Cook the noodles until just tender but still too hard to eat, 4 to 8 minutes. Drain the noodles carefully into a colander and lay them flat on towels until you are ready to layer them.

3. Put the ricotta, mozzarella, half of the Parmesan, the basil, garlic, egg, and a sprinkling of salt and pepper in a blender or food processor. Turn on the machine and blend or process until a thick purée is formed, 20 to 30 seconds.

4. Heat the oven to 400°F. Grease an 8- or 9-inch square baking dish with a little olive oil. Put 3 of the noodles in the bottom of the pan; if they overlap slightly, that's okay. Cover the noodles with a thin layer of the cheese purée, then with a layer of grilled vegetables, and finally with a layer of sliced fresh tomatoes. Repeat twice more, pressing everything down into the pan as you go and ending with a layer of tomatoes. Sprinkle the remaining Parmesan on top, plus a bit more if needed to cover everything evenly. (The lasagna can be assembled to this point, covered, and refrigerated for up to several hours before proceeding.) Cover with foil and bake for 15 minutes, then remove the foil and continue baking until the lasagna is bubbly, another 5 to 15 minutes. Remove it from the oven and let it rest for 5 minutes before cutting and serving.

Bowties with Arugula, Olives, Bulgur, and Fresh Tomato Wedges

Makes: 4 servings   Time: 30 minutes, largely unattended

Think of this as a Greek pasta salad; it's bright and light and has the perfect mix of Mediterranean flavors. After you finish cooking, let it sit for a bit before serving so that the bulgur and bowties soak up the flavors and the arugula wilts a little; it works equally well served warm or at room temperature.

I cook the bulgur with the pasta here, which makes things easier, but it means you must use a strainer, not a colander, to drain the water. If you don't have one, cook the bulgur separately (see page 271). And for an earthier spin, try doubling the bulgur and reducing the quantity of pasta.

Salt

2 tablespoons olive oil

1 small red onion, chopped

1 tablespoon minced garlic

1 cup mixed olives, pitted and roughly chopped

Juice of 1 lemon

4 ripe tomatoes, cored and cut into thick wedges

½ cup crumbled feta cheese, or to taste

Black pepper

¼ cup bulgur

8 ounces bowtie or other cut pasta, preferably whole wheat

3 cups torn arugula leaves

1. Bring a large pot of water to a boil and salt it. Put the oil in a large, deep skillet over medium heat. When it's hot, add the onion and garlic and cook, stirring, until they begin to soften, about 5 minutes. Stir in the olives, then add the lemon juice, tomatoes, and feta. Sprinkle with salt and pepper and cook until the tomatoes are just heated through. Turn off the heat.

2. When the water comes to a boil, add the bulgur. Let the water return to a boil, then add the pasta. Cook the bowties until tender but not mushy (start

Ⓕ Fast   Ⓜ Make-Ahead   Ⓟ Pantry Staple

tasting after 5 minutes). Reserve some of the cooking water, then drain in a strainer to trap the grains with the pasta.

3. Toss the pasta and bulgur with the tomato mixture, adding some of the cooking water if necessary. Stir in the arugula and taste and adjust the seasoning. Let the dish sit for up to 15 minutes. Stir again and serve.

Pasta with Red Peppers and Shrimp Sauce

Makes: 4 servings   Time: About 45 minutes

A quick shrimp stock makes this sauce perfect, but if you use other quick-cooking seafood like squid or scallops, use a cup of vegetable or chicken stock or, if you have neither of them, water in its place. And if you happen to have saffron around, add a pinch to the liquid as it simmers for a distinctive Mediterranean flavor and lovely color.

    8 ounces medium to large shrimp, in their shells (see page 22)

    1 cup dry white wine

    Salt and black pepper

    3 tablespoons olive oil

    6 red bell peppers, cut into strips

    1 tablespoon minced garlic

    1 fresh hot chile (like Thai or jalapeño), minced, or to taste

    8 ounces any pasta, preferably whole wheat

    1 tablespoon chopped fresh oregano or marjoram, plus a few leaves for
        garnish, or 1 teaspoon dried

1. Peel the shrimp and chop the flesh. Put the shells in a medium saucepan with 1 cup water, the wine, and a sprinkling of salt and pepper. Bubble gently for 10 minutes, then strain the liquid (discard the shells). Bring a large pot of water to a boil and salt it.

2. Put the oil in a large skillet over medium heat. When it's hot, add the peppers and cook, stirring occasionally, until they begin to brown, 5 to 10 minutes. Add the garlic and chile and cook for just a minute. Add the shrimp stock and turn the heat down to low. Cook, stirring occasionally, until the peppers are quite soft and the liquid is reduced to a cup or so, 10 to 15 minutes. Lightly mash the peppers with a fork or potato masher.

3. Meanwhile, cook the pasta in the boiling water until it's tender but not mushy (start tasting after 5 minutes); drain it, reserving some of the cooking water. Add the chopped shrimp to the skillet and cook for about a minute. Add the pasta and oregano and toss, moistening with the reserved cooking water as necessary (you probably won't need much). Serve hot, garnished with a few leaves of oregano if you have it.

Pasta with Tomatoes and Shrimp Sauce. Substitute 1½ pounds fresh Roma (plum) tomatoes, peeled if you like, seeded, and roughly chopped, for the bell peppers.

Ⓕ Fast   Ⓜ Make-Ahead   Ⓟ Pantry Staple

Paella Made with Noodles

Makes: 4 servings   Time: 30 minutes

Rice, of course, is the basis for classic paella. But this faster version combines vegetables, seafood, and noodles, broken into smaller pieces as in the Spanish cousin of paella called *fideos*. You can cook the noodles in plain water, but if you've got even a little bit of vegetable, seafood, or chicken stock lying around, this is a good time to use it.

3 tablespoons olive oil

1 onion, chopped

1 tablespoon minced garlic

8 ounces any long, thin pasta, preferably whole wheat, broken into 2-inch or shorter lengths

Salt and black pepper

1/2 teaspoon saffron threads, optional

1 teaspoon paprika

2 cups fresh or frozen peas

1 bell pepper, chopped

1/2 cup water or stock (for homemade, see pages 135 to 140), plus more as needed

8 ounces scallops, squid, clams, mussels, or shrimp, or a combination (see page 22)

1/4 cup chopped fresh parsley, for garnish

Lemon wedges

1. Put the oil in a large skillet over medium-high heat. When it's hot, add the onion and garlic and cook, stirring, until they begin to soften, 3 to 5 minutes; remove from the pan with a slotted spoon. Add the noodles to the pan, sprinkle with salt and pepper, and cook, stirring constantly, until they brown (try not to let them blacken).

2. Return the onion and garlic to the pan and add the saffron, paprika, peas, and bell pepper. Cook, stirring frequently, for 2 to 3 minutes more. Add the water and cook, stirring and adding more liquid if things start to stick, until the noodles are nearly tender and everything is just starting to dry out, about 15 minutes.

3. Stir in the seafood and cook, stirring occasionally and adding a little more water or stock if you like, until it is just cooked through (large shrimp and scallops will take about 5 minutes; small or chopped shrimp about 3 minutes; squid no more than 1 minute). Taste and adjust the seasoning. Stir in the parsley and serve with the lemon wedges.

Linguine with Cherry Tomatoes and Clams

Makes: 4 servings   Time: 30 minutes

Linguine with clams is iconic, but if you've never made it with fresh clams, you're in for a real treat. This recipe also works with mussels (or shrimp or squid; cut the cooking time in Step 2 to about 3 minutes). Don't skimp with the olive oil here; when it combines with the clam juice and wine, the sauce is pure heaven.

Salt

About ½ cup olive oil

1 tablespoon minced garlic

1 pint cherry tomatoes, halved crosswise

½ cup dry white wine or water

1½ pounds littleneck or other hard-shell clams or cockles, well scrubbed, those with broken shells discarded

2 sprigs fresh thyme, or a few pinches dried

8 ounces linguine or other long pasta, preferably whole wheat

Black pepper

½ cup chopped fresh parsley

1. Bring a large pot of water to a boil and salt it. Put ¼ cup of the oil in a large, deep skillet over medium-high heat. When it's hot, add the garlic and cook, stirring, for about a minute.

Ⓕ Fast   Ⓜ Make-Ahead   Ⓟ Pantry Staple

2. Stir in the tomatoes, wine, clams, and thyme. Raise the heat to high, cover, and cook, gently shaking the skillet or stirring the clams occasionally, until the first few of them open, about 5 minutes. Uncover and continue to cook, stirring occasionally, until almost all of the clams are open (if any don't, you can open them with a butter knife), about 3 more minutes. (If you like, remove the shells from the clams and return the clams to the skillet; I leave them whole.) If the pasta isn't ready, turn off the heat.

3. Meanwhile, cook the linguine in the boiling water until tender but not mushy (start tasting after 5 minutes), then drain, reserving some of the cooking liquid. Turn the heat under the clams to medium; add the pasta and cook for a minute or so, stirring and sprinkling with salt, pepper, and the remaining ¼ cup oil. Add a bit of the reserved cooking water if the mixture seems dry (which is unlikely). Stir in the parsley, taste and adjust the seasoning, and serve.

Dried Tomatoes and Clams with Pasta. Cut pasta like bowties or corkscrews are good here. Substitute 1 cup dried tomatoes for the cherry tomatoes. Increase the wine or water to 1 cup.

Pasta with Tomatoes, Tuna, and Capers

Makes: 4 servings   Time: 30 minutes

Tuna, tomatoes, and capers, a can't-miss combination that comes straight from the pantry, goes beautifully with pasta—or spooned over grilled bread or alongside a bed of greens. Use tuna packed in olive oil if you can find it (I hate to say it, but the European versions are best) and make sure to pour the oil right into the sauce (it has tremendous flavor).

Salt

2 tablespoons olive oil

1 onion, chopped

One 28- or 35-ounce can tomatoes, chopped; include their juice

8 ounces any pasta, preferably whole wheat

¼ cup white wine

One 6-ounce can tuna packed in olive oil

2 tablespoons capers

½ teaspoon red chile flakes

Black pepper

½ cup chopped fresh basil

1. Bring a large pot of water to a boil and salt it. Put the oil in a large, deep skillet over medium-high heat. When it's hot, add the onion and cook, stirring occasionally, until soft, 3 to 5 minutes. Add the tomatoes and their liquid and cook, stirring occasionally, until the tomatoes break down and the mixture becomes saucy, 10 to 15 minutes. Turn the heat down to low.

2. Meanwhile, cook the pasta in the boiling water until tender but not mushy (start tasting after 5 minutes), then drain, reserving some of the cooking liquid.

3. Return the sauce to medium-high heat. Add the pasta, wine, tuna with its oil, capers, and red chile flakes and cook and stir for another minute. Add a good sprinkle of black pepper along with the basil; toss well, adding a little of the cooking water if the sauce seems too thick. Taste and adjust the seasoning. Serve immediately or at room temperature.

Ma-Ma's Pasta "Milanese"

Makes: 4 servings   Time: About 1 hour, largely unattended

It's hard to argue that there's anything Milanese about this crazy but delicious recipe from Kerri Conan's maternal grandmother. Her family were Sicilians who immigrated to New Orleans via Tunisia around the turn of the century. Whether they brought this pasta with them is unknown, but the dish (which is not unlike other Sicilian pasta dishes I know) is still popular among the Italian community in Louisiana. The name, however, just doesn't match the ingredients—especially the cauliflower, sardines, and pecans—which are a better reflection of "Ma-Ma's" journey than anything you'll find in Milan.

> 2 tablespoons olive oil
>
> 1 onion, chopped
>
> 1 green bell pepper, chopped
>
> 2 celery stalks, chopped
>
> Salt and black pepper
>
> 2 tablespoons minced garlic
>
> Two 3.75-ounce cans sardines, preferably packed in olive oil
>
> ¼ cup tomato paste
>
> 1 cup red wine or water, or more as needed
>
> One 28- or 35-ounce can chopped or whole tomatoes; include their juice
>
> 1 small cauliflower, cored and roughly chopped
>
> ½ cup raisins or currants
>
> ½ cup chopped pecans or walnuts
>
> 8 ounces any pasta, preferably whole wheat (Ma-Ma used regular spaghetti or linguine)

1. Put the oil in a large pot or Dutch oven over medium heat. When it's hot, add the onion, bell pepper, and celery and sprinkle with salt and pepper. Cook, stirring occasionally, until everything is soft and the onion becomes translucent, about 5 minutes. (If you're using whole tomatoes, now is a good time to core them and break them up a bit.) Stir in the garlic, sardines with their oil, and tomato paste and cook until the mixture is fragrant and starting to stick to the bottom of the pan.

2. Stir in the wine and scrape up any bits on the bottom of the pan. Add the tomatoes and cauliflower. Sprinkle again with salt and pepper. Bring to a boil, reduce the heat so that the mixture bubbles steadily, then partially cover and cook, stirring once in a while, until the cauliflower is extremely soft and disintegrating, 20 to 30 minutes; add more wine or water if the mixture gets too thick. Stir in the raisins and nuts. (The sauce can be made ahead to this point. Cool, cover, and refrigerate for up to a few days or freeze for longer; gently reheat before proceeding.)

3. Meanwhile, bring a large pot of water to a boil and salt it. Cook the pasta until it's tender but not mushy (start tasting after 5 minutes), then drain, reserving some of the cooking liquid. Toss with the sauce, adding enough reserved liquid to keep it moist. Taste and adjust the seasoning. Serve.

Cold Noodles with Cucumber, Avocado, and Crab

Makes: 4 servings   Time: 30 minutes

Quick-pickling the cucumbers—a good basic technique that only takes a tablespoon salt and 15 minutes—gives them the exact texture and flavor you want to grace these cold noodles. While the cucumbers pickle and the water boils, you can prep the other ingredients, so the dish comes together nicely. If you wait until the last minute to add the avocado and crab, you can combine the noodles and cucumbers up to an hour before and keep them chilled or at room temperature.

    Salt

    3 medium cucumbers, peeled, seeded, and grated

    1 tablespoon minced ginger

    8 ounces rice, buckwheat (soba), or wheat noodles, preferably whole grain

    1 tablespoon sesame oil

Ⓕ Fast   Ⓜ Make-Ahead   Ⓟ Pantry Staple

1 tablespoon vegetable oil

1 avocado, skin and pit removed, chopped or sliced

8 ounces lump crab meat

½ cup chopped fresh cilantro

¼ cup chopped peanuts

Lemon wedges

Soy sauce, for serving

1. Bring a large pot of water to a boil and salt it. Put the cucumbers and ginger in a colander, sprinkle with 1 tablespoon salt, and toss well. Let the mixture sit in the sink for about 15 minutes, then rinse with cold water and set the colander aside to drain.

2. Cook the noodles in the boiling water until they're tender but not mushy. Check them frequently: The time will vary from a minute or 2 for thin rice noodles, to 5 minutes for soba, or up to 12 minutes for wide brown rice noodles. Drain the noodles, rinse with cold water, transfer to a serving bowl or platter, and toss with the oils. Top the noodles with the cucumbers, avocado, crab, cilantro, and peanuts and toss again. Serve, passing the lemon wedges and soy sauce at the table.

Crisp Noodle Cake
with Stir-Fried Greens and Shrimp

Makes: 4 servings   Time: 45 minutes

A noodle cake makes a fantastic side dish, snack, or base for a stir-fry, where it soaks up all of the savory juices. You don't need much else to call this a meal, though a beer alongside wouldn't hurt.

1½ pounds bok choy, gai lan (Chinese broccoli), tatsoi, or other Asian green

Salt

8 ounces any rice, buckwheat (soba), or wheat noodle, preferably whole grain

3 tablespoons soy sauce, plus more to taste

2 teaspoons sesame oil

4 tablespoons vegetable oil, plus more as needed

1 tablespoon minced ginger

1 tablespoon minced garlic

1 fresh hot chile (like jalapeño or Thai), seeded and minced, or to taste

Black pepper

8 ounces shrimp, peeled (see page 22)

½ cup chopped scallions

½ cup chopped peanuts, optional

1. Cut the leaves from the stems of the bok choy. Trim the stems and cut them into 1-inch pieces; cut the leaves into bite-size pieces or ribbons. Rinse everything well.

2. Bring a large pot of water to a boil and salt it. Cook the noodles until tender but not mushy. Check them frequently: The time will vary from a minute or 2 for thin rice noodles, to 5 minutes for soba, or up to 12 minutes for wide brown rice noodles. Drain them and rinse with cold water. Toss the noodles with 1 tablespoon of the soy sauce and 1 teaspoon of the sesame oil.

3. Put 3 tablespoons of the vegetable oil in a large nonstick or cast-iron skillet over medium-high heat. When it's hot, add the noodles and press down

Ⓕ Fast   Ⓜ Make-Ahead   Ⓟ Pantry Staple

a bit. Cook, pressing down occasionally, until brown and crisp on the bottom (adjust the heat so the noodles brown but do not burn). Carefully put a large dish over the skillet and flip it to turn out the cake. Add a little more oil to the pan, swirl it around, and gently slide the cake off the plate and back into the skillet, uncooked side down, all in one piece. Brown the other side, then slide it onto a platter. (At this point you can cut the cake into 4 wedges, or wait and roughly break it apart after topping.)

4. Add the remaining 1 tablespoon oil to the skillet. Add the ginger, garlic, and chile and cook, stirring, until fragrant, about 1 minute. Add the bok choy stems, sprinkle with salt and pepper, and cook, stirring occasionally, until the stems just lose their crunch, about 3 minutes.

5. Add the shrimp to the pan along with the bok choy leaves, scallions, 2 tablespoons soy sauce, 1 teaspoon sesame oil, and ½ cup water. Cook, stirring occasionally, until most of the liquid evaporates and the stems are very tender, about 5 minutes. Taste and adjust the seasoning, adding more soy sauce if necessary. Serve the stir-fry over the noodle cake, topped with peanuts if you like.

Crisp Noodle Cake with Stir-Fried Greens and Tofu. Instead of the shrimp, cut 8 ounces extra-firm tofu into cubes and dry on paper towels. Proceed with the recipe.

Noodles with Gingered Miso Carrots and Chicken

Makes: 4 servings   Time: 30 minutes

A spoonful of miso adds oomph to just about anything, but it has a special affinity for carrots. In general, the darker the miso, the more intense it tastes, but all miso must be heated gently—if you boil it, you will literally cook the flavor right out of it.

I like this with soba noodles, but you can use whole wheat spaghetti or rice noodles too. Daikon radishes or jícama are nice alternatives to carrots.

Salt

2 tablespoons vegetable oil

8 ounces boneless, skinless chicken breast or thighs, cut into chunks

Black pepper

2 tablespoons minced ginger

1 pound carrots, grated

8 ounces any rice, buckwheat (soba), or wheat noodles, preferably whole grain

½ cup miso

½ cup chopped scallions

Rice vinegar, for serving

Sesame oil, for serving

1. Bring a large pot of water to a boil and salt it. Put the oil in a large skillet over medium-high heat. When it's hot, add the chicken, sprinkle with salt and pepper, and let it sit for about a minute. Add the ginger and stir; cook, stirring occasionally, until the chicken is no longer pink, 3 to 5 minutes. Add the carrots and cook, stirring, until they start to wilt, about 2 minutes. Turn off the heat.

2. Cook the noodles in the boiling water until they're tender but not mushy. Check them frequently: The time will vary from a minute or 2 for thin rice noodles, to 5 minutes for soba, or up to 12 minutes for wide brown rice noodles. Drain, reserving some of the cooking liquid.

Ⓕ Fast   Ⓜ Make-Ahead   Ⓟ Pantry Staple

3. Turn the heat under the skillet to medium. Whisk the miso with ½ cup of the cooking water, then pour this mixture over the carrot mixture. Toss in the noodles, adding more cooking water as needed to keep the mixture moist. Taste and adjust the seasoning, then sprinkle with the scallions. Serve hot or at room temperature, passing rice vinegar and sesame oil at the table for drizzling.

Sesame Noodles with Spinach and Salmon

Makes: 4 servings   Time: 30 minutes

The flavors of *oshitashi*—Japanese spinach salad garnished with shaved dried bonito flakes—are at play here, only the fish is fresh salmon. I love the flavor and texture of seared salmon skin, but you can discard it if you prefer. (In either case, don't eat the scales!). Instead of the spinach, you might try shredded Napa cabbage.

Salt

2 tablespoons vegetable oil

8 ounces salmon fillet, preferably wild (see page 22)

Black pepper

1 tablespoon minced garlic

3 tablespoons sesame seeds

1½ pounds spinach, roughly chopped

1 tablespoon soy sauce

1 teaspoon sugar

½ teaspoon sesame oil

8 ounces buckwheat (soba) noodles or whole wheat spaghetti

1. Bring a large pot of water to a boil and salt it. Put the vegetable oil in a large, deep skillet over medium-high heat. When it's very hot, sprinkle the salmon on both sides with salt and pepper and sear it in the pan until nicely browned on both sides, about 6 minutes total. Remove from the pan and cut or flake it into bite-size pieces.

2. Reduce the heat under the skillet to medium. Add the garlic and sesame seeds and cook, stirring constantly, until the garlic begins to soften and the sesame seeds turn golden, about 30 seconds. Add the spinach and cook, stirring, for another minute or 2. Add the soy sauce, sugar, sesame oil, and a splash of water and cook until the spinach is wilted, another 2 to 3 minutes. Remove from the heat.

3. Cook the noodles in the boiling water until they're tender but not mushy (start tasting after 5 minutes), then drain, reserving some of the cooking water. Turn the heat under the spinach mixture to medium and add the noodles and reserved salmon. Toss, adding enough reserved liquid to keep things moist. Taste and adjust the seasoning if necessary. Serve immediately or at room temperature.

Sesame Spinach and Tofu with Noodles. Instead of the salmon, cut 8 ounces firm tofu into 4 thick slices and brown about 2 minutes per side. Proceed with the recipe. Serve a slice of tofu on top of each serving of noodles.

Ⓕ Fast   Ⓜ Make-Ahead   Ⓟ Pantry Staple

Pasta with Mushrooms, Chicken, and Red Wine

Makes: 4 servings   Time: 45 minutes

It's hard to go wrong with mushrooms and red wine, especially in fall and winter. For extra intensity, soak a few dried porcini mushrooms in boiling water for a few minutes until they're soft, add them along with the fresh mushrooms, and use the soaking liquid to moisten the dish instead of the pasta cooking water in Step 3. Once you try this, you'll return to this technique often when cooking mushrooms.

Salt

2 tablespoons olive oil, or more as needed

8 ounces boneless, skinless chicken thighs or breast, cut into chunks

About 1½ pounds mushrooms, preferably an assortment, sliced

1 onion, halved and thinly sliced

Black pepper

½ cup red wine

1 tablespoon chopped fresh rosemary

8 ounces any pasta, preferably whole wheat

¼ cup chopped fresh parsley, optional

½ cup grated Parmesan cheese, optional

1. Bring a large pot of water to a boil and salt it. Put the oil in a large skillet over medium-high heat. When it's hot, add the chicken and cook, stirring occasionally, until it's no longer pink, about 5 minutes. Remove the chicken from the skillet with a slotted spoon.

2. Turn the heat to medium-low and add a little more oil if the pan seems dry. Add the mushrooms and onion and sprinkle with salt and pepper. Stir once, then cover and cook, undisturbed, until the mushrooms have released a fair amount of liquid, 5 to 7 minutes. Remove the lid, turn up the heat, and cook, undisturbed, until the mushrooms just begin to stick to the skillet, 3 to 5 more minutes. Return the chicken to the pan and stir in the red wine and rosemary; turn the heat to low.

3. Meanwhile, cook the pasta in the boiling water until it's tender but not mushy (start tasting after 5 minutes), then drain, reserving about 1 cup of the cooking liquid. Toss the pasta in the skillet, adding cooking water as necessary to keep everything moist. Taste and adjust the seasoning. Serve, sprinkled with the parsley and Parmesan if you like.

Mushrooms, Chicken Livers, and Pasta with Red Wine. Substitute 4 whole chicken livers for the skinless chicken. You'll want to cook the livers until brown and crisp on both sides but still pink on the inside, only 3 to 4 minutes. Cut them into bite-size pieces once you've seared them and return them to the pan just at the very end.

One-Pot Pasta with Zucchini and Chicken

Makes: **4 servings**   Time: **About 1 hour**

Cut pasta, like ziti or penne, is an ideal ingredient in braised dishes: It releases starch, which thickens the sauce, and, of course, the noodles themselves provide a satisfying chew. The trick lies only in the timing, but don't drive yourself nuts; as long as you add the ingredients in stages, you'll maintain a variety of textures ranging from soft to crisp-tender.

2 tablespoons olive oil

8 ounces boneless, skinless chicken thighs, cut into chunks

Salt and black pepper

2 medium red onions, halved and sliced

1 tablespoon minced garlic

4 zucchini, sliced at least ½ inch thick

½ cup white wine

1 cup stock (for homemade, see pages 135 to 140) or water, plus more as needed

8 ounces any cut pasta, preferably whole wheat

¼ cup chopped fresh dill, or 1 teaspoon dried

½ cup grated Parmesan cheese, optional

(F) Fast   (M) Make-Ahead   (P) Pantry Staple

1. Put the oil in a large, deep skillet over medium-high heat. When it's hot, sprinkle the chicken with salt and pepper and add it to the pan, skin side down. Cook, turning the pieces as necessary, until the chicken is browned on both sides, about 10 minutes. Remove the chicken from the pan.

2. Turn the heat down to medium. Add the onions and garlic, sprinkle with salt and pepper, and cook, stirring occasionally, until soft, about 5 minutes. Add all but 1 cup of the zucchini and stir to coat with the oil. Add the wine, stock, pasta, and reserved chicken.

3. Bring to a boil, scraping up any bits that might be stuck to the bottom of the pan. Reduce the heat so the mixture bubbles enthusiastically and cook, stirring frequently and adding more liquid as needed to keep the mixture saucy, until the pasta just begins to get tender, no more than 10 minutes. Stir in the remaining zucchini and cook until it softens a little and the pasta is ready but not mushy, another 3 minutes. Stir in the dill, and Parmesan if you're using it. Taste, adjust the seasoning, and serve.

Pasta with Corn, Chicken, and Salsa Cruda

Makes: 4 servings   Time: 30 minutes

With pan-roasted corn, fresh tomatoes, and mild green chiles, this pasta is a natural for the summer, especially if you grill everything (see the variation). To save the step of roasting and peeling the skin from the chiles, I cut them into small pieces before cooking; it works.

Salt

2 tablespoons vegetable oil

4 medium ears fresh corn, shucked (about 2 cups kernals; frozen are fine)

2 medium poblano chiles, chopped as finely as you can manage

Black pepper

8 ounces boneless, skinless chicken breast

2 large ripe tomatoes, cored and chopped

1 small white onion, chopped

1 tablespoon minced garlic

Juice of 1 lime

½ cup chopped fresh cilantro

8 ounces any cut pasta, preferably whole wheat

¼ cup crumbled queso fresco, optional

1. Bring a large pot of water to a boil and salt it. Put 1 tablespoon of the oil in a large, deep skillet over high heat. When it's hot, add the corn and poblanos; let sit for a moment. As the vegetables brown, shake the pan to keep them cooking evenly without burning. After about 5 minutes, sprinkle with salt and pepper, then remove from the pan with a slotted spoon.

2. Put the remaining 1 tablespoon oil in the same pan, still over high heat. Add the chicken and sprinkle with salt and pepper. Cook about 3 minutes per side, until browned on the outside or no longer pink inside, then remove.

(F) Fast   (M) Make-Ahead   (P) Pantry Staple

3. In a large bowl, combine the tomatoes, onion, garlic, lime juice, cilantro, and a sprinkling of salt and pepper. Taste, adjust the seasoning if necessary, and let it sit while you cook the pasta.

4. Cook the pasta in the boiling water until it's tender but not mushy (start tasting after 5 minutes). While it's cooking, cut the chicken into bits. Drain the pasta, reserving some of the cooking liquid, and toss it with the salsa, corn mixture, chicken, and queso fresco if you're using it, adding enough reserved liquid to keep things moist. Taste and adjust the seasoning and toss again. Serve hot or at room temperature.

Pasta with Grilled Corn and Chicken, with Salsa Cruda. Prepare a grill to medium-high heat and put the rack about 4 inches from the fire. Leave the corn on the cobs and the chiles whole. Brush the vegetables and chicken with the oil and sprinkle with salt and pepper. Grill everything, turning frequently, until the corn is browned in spots, the chicken is just cooked through, and the chiles are blackened and blistered. The corn will take about 5 minutes, the chicken about 8, and the chiles up to 10. Remove as needed. Put the chiles in a brown paper bag or covered bowl to steam. When cool enough to handle, cut the kernels from the corn cobs; peel the chiles and cut them—and the chicken—into strips. (You can prepare all these ingredients to this point up to several hours ahead.) Now proceed with the recipe from Step 3.

Pasta with Fennel and Chicken, Risotto Style

Makes: 4 servings   Time: About 45 minutes

Though cooking pasta like risotto is traditional (there are ancient recipes for cooking pasta in wine), it's become trendy. (It even has a scientific-sounding name: "absorption pasta.") Still, it's efficient (especially as you don't dirty a colander) and—if you start with good-tasting liquid—really good. You can use any kind of noodle you like—orzo will even look a little like rice—but keep in mind that longer noodles require more attention than shorter ones, since they're more likely to get stuck together. A good compromise is to use spaghetti or other long pasta broken into smaller pieces.

> 2 tablespoons olive oil, plus more as needed
>
> 8 ounces boneless, skinless chicken thighs, roughly chopped
>
> 2 large or 4 small bulbs fennel (about 2 pounds), cored and chopped
>
> 1 red onion, chopped
>
> 1 tablespoon minced garlic
>
> 8 ounces any pasta, preferably whole wheat (see the headnote)
>
> Salt and black pepper
>
> ½ cup dry white wine or water
>
> 3 to 4 cups chicken or vegetable stock (for homemade, see pages 135 to 140) or water
>
> ½ cup chopped fresh parsley

1. Put the 2 tablespoons oil in a large, deep skillet over medium-high heat. When it's hot, add the chicken and cook, stirring occasionally, until lightly browned on all sides, about 5 minutes; remove.

2. Add a little more oil to the skillet and reduce the heat to medium. Add the fennel, onion, and garlic and cook, stirring occasionally, until the fennel softens, 10 to 15 minutes. Add the pasta and cook, stirring occasionally, until it is glossy and coated with oil, 2 to 3 minutes. Add a little salt and pepper, then the wine. Stir and let the liquid bubble away.

Ⓕ Fast   Ⓜ Make-Ahead   Ⓟ Pantry Staple

3. Add the stock ½ cup at a time, stirring after each addition and every minute or so. When the liquid is just about evaporated, add more. The mixture should be neither soupy nor dry. Keep the heat medium to medium-high and stir frequently.

4. Begin tasting the pasta 10 minutes after you add it. You want it to be tender but with a tiny bit of crunch; it could take as long as 20 minutes to reach this stage. When it does, stir in the chicken, parsley, and another drizzle of oil if you like. Taste, adjust the seasoning, and serve.

Black Bean Chili Mac

Makes: **4 servings**   Time: **30 minutes with cooked or canned beans**

Chili and pasta is a Cincinnati specialty, but it's hardly an acquired taste, especially prepared this way: with pork, black beans, tomatoes, and loads of spice.

Salt

2 tablespoons vegetable oil

8 ounces pork shoulder, sliced into thin strips

Black pepper

1 onion, chopped

1 tablespoon minced garlic

1 fresh hot chile (like Thai, serrano, or jalapeño), minced

1 chipotle chile (dried is best; canned is okay; use a little of its adobo if you like), minced

1 tablespoon cumin

1 tablespoon chopped fresh oregano, or 1 teaspoon dried

6 tomatoes, chopped (canned are fine; drain their juice)

8 ounces elbows, shells, or any cut pasta, preferably whole wheat

2 cups cooked or canned black beans, drained

½ cup chopped fresh cilantro

Lime wedges

1. Bring a large pot of water to a boil and salt it. Put the oil in a large, deep skillet over medium-high heat. When it's hot, sprinkle the pork with salt and pepper and add it to the pan. Cook, stirring once or twice (no more), until the pork is nicely browned, 3 to 5 minutes. Stir in the onion, garlic, chiles, cumin, and oregano and cook until the vegetables are soft, a minute or 2.

2. Add the tomatoes, bring to a boil, then reduce the heat so the mixture bubbles gently. Cook, stirring occasionally, until the tomatoes break up and the sauce thickens a bit, about 10 minutes.

3. While the sauce cooks, cook the pasta in the boiling water until it's tender but not mushy (start tasting after 5 minutes), then drain it, reserving some of the cooking liquid. Stir the beans and cilantro into the sauce. Taste and adjust the seasoning. Toss in the pasta, adding a little of the cooking water if the sauce seems too thick. Serve with lime wedges.

Pinto Chili Mac with Beef. Substitute thinly sliced beef chuck or sirloin for the pork shoulder, and pinto beans for the black beans.

Spaghetti with Seared Radicchio, Steak, and Balsamic Sauce

Makes: 4 servings   Time: 30 minutes

You want the steak to be rare here, and give it at least 5 minutes to rest before you cut into it to capture all of the meaty juices for the sauce. I recommend spaghetti here—so you can twirl a little bit of everything into one bite—but use whatever shape you like. I think this is even better at room temperature than it is hot, which makes it one great picnic or entertaining dish.

> Salt
>
> 2 tablespoons olive oil
>
> 8 ounces sirloin, skirt, or other beef steak
>
> Black pepper
>
> 1 pound radicchio, cut into ribbons

      Ⓕ Fast   Ⓜ Make-Ahead   Ⓟ Pantry Staple

1 large red onion, halved and sliced

1 tablespoon minced garlic

8 ounces spaghetti or other long, thin pasta, preferably whole wheat

2 tablespoons balsamic vinegar, or to taste

½ cup roughly chopped fresh basil

1. Bring a large pot of water to a boil and salt it. Put the oil in a large skillet over medium-high heat. When it's hot, add the steak, sprinkle it with salt and pepper, and cook for 2 to 3 minutes per side, until browned but rare. Remove it from the skillet and cover loosely with a piece of foil or a pot lid.

2. Add the radicchio, onion, and garlic to the skillet over medium heat. Cook, stirring occasionally, until the vegetables soften, about 5 minutes. Lower the heat and cover.

3. Cook the spaghetti in the boiling water until it's tender but not mushy (start tasting after 5 minutes), then drain it, reserving about 1 cup of the cooking water. Thinly slice the steak, being careful to capture all the drippings.

4. Add the vinegar to the skillet, stir, and let it bubble until it thickens slightly but doesn't evaporate, just a few seconds. Toss in the pasta, steak with its juices, basil, and a generous sprinkling of black pepper; add just enough of the pasta water to keep the mixture moist. Taste and adjust the seasoning. Serve hot or at room temperature.

Meaty Tomato Sauce,
With or Without Pasta

Makes: 4 servings (about 1 quart)   Time: At least 2 hours, largely unattended

This is red gravy, the ragu Italian-Americans (and others) have been serving for generations. Using bone-in chuck lets you extract maximum meaty flavor from a surprisingly small amount of meat. (Check out the variations for other meats.)

Like the recipe for All-Purpose Tomato Sauce on page 194, the pasta is optional here, since this sauce is just as good on top of rice, pizza dough, or grilled vegetables. Same drill: This recipe makes enough sauce to serve four with maybe a little extra; for leftovers, make more and refrigerate or freeze it for another meal.

¼ cup olive oil

1 pound bone-in beef chuck

1 large onion or 2 medium onions, chopped

1 tablespoon minced garlic, or to taste

Salt and black pepper

¼ cup tomato paste

½ cup dry red wine, stock (for homemade, see pages 135 to 140), or water

About 4 pounds canned whole tomatoes (two 28- or 35-ounce cans),
    chopped, liquid reserved

½ cup chopped fresh parsley or basil, optional

8 ounces pasta, preferably whole wheat, optional

1. Put the oil in a large pot or Dutch oven over medium-high heat. When it's hot, add the chuck and brown it well, rotating and turning as necessary, about 10 minutes. Remove the meat from the pot and set it aside.

2. Reduce the heat to medium-low. Add the onion and garlic to the pot, sprinkle with salt and pepper, and cook, stirring occasionally, until soft, about 5 minutes. Add the tomato paste and continue to cook, stirring, for 2 minutes. Add the wine and stir to scrape up any brown bits from the bottom of the pot for about a minute.

Ⓕ Fast   Ⓜ Make-Ahead   Ⓟ Pantry Staple

3. Return the meat to the pot and add the tomatoes with about 1 cup of their liquid. Cover, bring to a boil, and lower the heat so the sauce bubbles slowly. Cook for 1½ to 2 hours, stirring occasionally to break up large pieces of tomato and adding tomato liquid as necessary to prevent the sauce from becoming too dry.

4. When the chuck is falling-from-the-bone tender, remove it from the pot. When cool enough to handle, remove the meat from the bone, chop or shred it, and return it to the pot along with the herb if you're using it. Taste, adjust the seasoning, and keep warm. (Or let cool, cover, and refrigerate for up to several days or freeze for months; reheat gently before serving.)

5. If you're serving the sauce with pasta, bring a large pot of water to a boil and salt it. Cook the pasta until it's tender but not mushy (start tasting after 5 minutes), then drain, reserving some of the cooking liquid. Toss the pasta with at least half of the sauce, adding enough reserved cooking liquid to keep it moist. Taste, adjust the seasoning, and serve. (Save the leftover sauce for another use.)

Tomato-Sausage Sauce, With or Without Pasta. Substitute 8 ounces good Italian sausage, crumbled, for the chuck. Reduce the cooking time in Step 3 to 30 to 60 minutes. You never need to remove the sausage from the pot.

Tomato-Chicken Sauce, With or Without Pasta. Use 4 medium chicken thighs in place of the beef. Proceed with the recipe, reducing the cooking time to about 1 hour. Remove the chicken from the pot and remove the meat from the bones as you would the beef.

Tomato-Duck Sauce, With or Without Pasta. Use 2 duck legs (with thighs) instead of the beef. Give them the same treatment as the chicken thighs in the above variation; the simmering time should be closer to 1½ hours.

Tomato-Rib Sauce, With or Without Pasta. Use 4 pork spareribs in place of the beef.

Pasta with Roasted Eggplant and Meat Sauce

Makes: 4 servings   Time: About 1 hour, largely unattended

Roasting this nicely seasoned eggplant-and-lamb sauce from start to finish gives it an incredibly rich flavor while requiring very little attention. The result is something like an eggplant Bolognese, perfect with a little pasta but also good spooned over a split baked potato or even a roll, like a sloppy joe.

1½ pounds eggplant, cut into small cubes

8 ounces ground beef or lamb

1 onion, thinly sliced

1 tablespoon roughly chopped garlic

¼ cup olive oil

Salt and black pepper

1 bay leaf

1 tablespoon chopped fresh oregano, or 1 teaspoon dried

1 tablespoon chopped fresh thyme, or 1 teaspoon dried

3 tablespoons tomato paste

6 ripe Roma (plum) tomatoes, chopped (canned are fine; drain them first)

½ cup dry red wine or water

8 ounces any pasta, preferably whole wheat

Chopped fresh parsley, for garnish, optional

¼ cup grated Parmesan cheese, optional

1. Heat the oven to 425°F. Put the eggplant, ground meat, onion, and garlic in a large roasting pan. Drizzle with the olive oil and sprinkle with salt and pepper. Roast, stirring occasionally and breaking up the meat, until everything is nicely browned and almost crisp, about 40 minutes.

2. Add the bay leaf, oregano, and thyme, then add the tomato paste and stir to mix it with the vegetables and meat. Stir in the tomatoes and wine and scrape up any browned bits from the bottom of the pan. Continue roasting until the mixture is thickened, 10 to 15 minutes more. (The sauce can be made ahead to this point. Cool, cover, and refrigerate for up to a few days or freeze for up to a few months. Gently reheat it before proceeding.)

3. Bring a large pot of water to a boil and salt it. When the sauce is ready, cook the pasta in the boiling water until it's tender but not mushy; drain it, reserving some of the cooking water. Remove the pan from the oven. Discard the bay leaf. Add enough of the cooking water to the sauce to loosen any browned bits from the bottom of the pan and moisten the pasta. Add the pasta and toss. Stir in the parsley and Parmesan if you're using them. Serve.

Shells with Braised Escarole, White Beans, and Sausage

Makes: 4 servings   Time: About 45 minutes with cooked or canned beans

There are several braised pasta dishes in this chapter, but this one features the most classic combination: pasta, escarole, and beans (sausage is a common partner too). Adjust the soupiness by adding more stock once the pasta is done or letting most of the liquid bubble away, but make sure not to let the pan get too dry while the pasta is still cooking, or the shells will get gummy.

If you don't have escarole, cabbage, kale, chard, beet greens, radicchio, and chicory are all fine substitutes.

2 tablespoons olive oil, plus more for serving

8 ounces sweet or hot Italian sausage

1 tablespoon minced garlic

8 ounces shell pasta, preferably whole wheat

½ cup dry white wine, optional

About 4 cups chicken, beef, or vegetable stock (for homemade, see pages 135 to 140) or water

1 pound escarole, roughly chopped

2 cups cooked or canned white beans, drained

Salt and black pepper

½ cup grated Parmesan cheese, optional

1. Put the oil in a large pot over medium heat. When it's hot, remove the sausage from its casings and crumble it into the pot. Cook, stirring occasionally, until the sausage is nicely browned, crisp, and cooked through, 10 to 15 minutes; remove it from the pot with a slotted spoon.

2. Add the garlic to the same pot over low heat and cook just until fragrant, about 2 minutes. Add the pasta, and wine if you're using it or ½ cup of the stock. Stir, raise the heat a bit, and let the liquid bubble away. Begin adding stock, ½ cup or so at a time, stirring after each addition. Adjust the heat so the mixture bubbles enthusiastically and stir frequently; cook until the pasta is just beginning to soften but is only about half-done, about 5 minutes.

3. Add the escarole and enough of the remaining stock to make the mixture a little soupy, raise the heat to medium-high, and cook, stirring once or twice, until it begins to wilt, 3 to 5 minutes. By now the pasta should be tender but still with a tiny bit of crunch. Add the beans and sausage to the pan along with some salt and pepper and a little more stock if the mixture is sticking. Cook and stir until everything is hot, another minute or 2. Remove from the heat and stir in the cheese if you're using it. Taste and adjust the seasoning and serve with a drizzle of olive oil.

Pasta with Smoky Roasted Sweet Potatoes and Bacon

Makes: 4 servings   Time: About 1 hour, largely unattended

Here's a lovely from-the-oven pasta sauce, featuring sweet potatoes and smoked paprika (also known as pimentón), which is available in most specialty food stores and some supermarkets. If you'd rather use prosciutto or smoked ham instead of bacon, just add it to the roasting pan after the sweet potatoes are cooked about halfway.

> 3 sweet potatoes, peeled and cut into 1-inch cubes
>
> 4 bacon slices or 4 ounces pancetta, chopped
>
> 3 tablespoons olive oil
>
> Salt and black pepper
>
> 2 teaspoons pimentón (smoked paprika)
>
> 1 red onion, chopped
>
> 8 ounces any cut pasta, preferably whole wheat
>
> ¼ cup chopped fresh chives
>
> ¼ cup grated Manchego or Parmesan cheese

1. Heat the oven to 400°F. Put the sweet potatoes, bacon, and oil in a large roasting pan, sprinkle with salt and pepper, and toss. Roast, stirring occasionally, until the sweet potatoes and bacon are crisp, about 30 minutes.

2. Dust the sweet potatoes and bacon with the pimentón. Add the onion to the pan, stir, and roast for another 15 minutes. Meanwhile, bring a large pot of water to a boil and salt it.

3. When the sauce ingredients are almost ready, cook the pasta in the boiling water until it's tender but not mushy (start tasting after 5 minutes), then drain, reserving some of the cooking water. Remove the roasting pan from the oven, stir in about ½ cup of the cooking water, and scrape up any browned bits that are stuck to the bottom. Toss in the pasta, chives, and cheese. Taste and adjust the seasoning and toss again. Serve hot or at room temperature.

Pasta with Cumin-Scented Squash and Lamb

Makes: 4 servings   Time: 30 minutes

A food processor makes quick work of preparing the squash, but an old-fashioned box grater will do the trick too. Either way is faster than dicing it with a knife, and the shredded pieces, which cook into a whole range of creamy-to-crisp-tender textures, are what make this dish special—and fast.

Salt

2 tablespoons olive oil

8 ounces ground lamb or minced leg of lamb

1 onion, chopped

1 tablespoon minced garlic

1 teaspoon cumin seeds, or 2 teaspoons cumin

Black pepper

¼ cup tomato paste

2 pounds butternut squash, peeled, seeded, and grated (about 4 packed cups)

8 ounces any pasta, preferably whole wheat

½ cup chopped fresh parsley

¼ cup grated Parmesan cheese, optional

1. Bring a large pot of water to a boil and salt it. Put the oil in a large, deep skillet over medium-high heat. When it's hot, add the lamb and cook, stirring occasionally, until it begins to brown, about 3 minutes. Stir in the onion and continue cooking and stirring until it softens a bit, just a minute or 2. Add the garlic, lower the heat to medium, and cook, stirring once in a while, until everything crisps and darkens, about 10 minutes.

2. Stir in the cumin, pepper, and tomato paste; cook and stir until the paste starts to stick and brown, 1 to 2 minutes. Add the squash and 2 cups water and scrape up any browned bits from the bottom of the pan. Cook, stirring infrequently, until the squash is tender and most of the liquid is absorbed, 10 to 15 minutes.

Ⓕ Fast   Ⓜ Make-Ahead   Ⓟ Pantry Staple

3. Meanwhile, cook the pasta in the boiling water until it's tender but not mushy (start tasting after 5 minutes), then drain, reserving some of the cooking liquid. Toss the pasta, parsley, and Parmesan if you're using it, with the squash mixture, adding a little of the reserved cooking liquid as needed to moisten it. Taste and adjust the seasoning and toss again. Serve.

Noodles with Roots and Ribs

Makes: 4 servings   Time: About 2 hours, largely unattended

Braising root vegetables with deliciously meaty (and fatty) ribs takes a while, but it's well worth it. The idea is for most of the vegetables to break down and thicken the sauce, all the while absorbing flavor from the ribs. If you can't find what are known as "country-style" ribs, which are ultrameaty (and not really ribs at all, but chops), use 4 to 6 spareribs.

 2 tablespoons olive oil

 2 country-style pork ribs (see the headnote)

 Salt and black pepper

 2 pounds root vegetables (celery root, rutabaga, parsnip, or sweet potato,
    or a combination), peeled and cut into large chunks

 2½ cups stock (for homemade, see pages 135 to 140) or water

 ½ cup red wine, or more stock or water

 8 ounces any pasta, preferably whole wheat

 1 tablespoon chopped fresh sage, or 1 teaspoon dried

 ¼ cup chopped fresh parsley

 ¼ cup grated Parmesan cheese, optional

1. Put the oil in a large pot or Dutch oven over medium-high heat. When it's hot, add the ribs and sprinkle with salt and pepper. Cook, turning as necessary, until the ribs are deeply browned on all sides, 10 to 15 minutes total. Remove the ribs from the pan.

2. Add the vegetables and cook, stirring infrequently, until they begin to brown, about 10 minutes. Add the stock and wine if you are using it. Bring the mixture to a boil, stirring to scrape up any brown bits from the bottom of the pan. Reduce the heat so that the liquid bubbles gently and return the ribs to the pan. Cover and cook, stirring once or twice, until the meat is tender and the vegetables break down and thicken the liquid. (Start checking after about an hour but plan on their being done in about 1½ hours.)

3. When the meat is ready, remove it from the bones, chop or shred it, and return it to the pot. If the mixture looks too thick, add a little stock or water; if too thin, turn the heat up a bit, remove the cover, and let the sauce reduce, breaking up any remaining chunks of vegetables with a spoon. Taste and adjust the seasoning. Keep warm. (You can make the sauce ahead to this point. Cool, cover, and refrigerate for up to a few days or freeze for up to several months; gently reheat the sauce before proceeding.)

4. Bring a large pot of water to a boil and salt it. Cook the pasta until it's tender but not mushy (start tasting after 5 minutes), then drain, reserving some of the cooking liquid. Toss the pasta with the vegetables and meat, adding a little cooking liquid if it seems too thick. Stir in the sage and parsley, top with Parmesan if you like, and serve.

Ⓕ Fast Ⓜ Make-Ahead Ⓟ Pantry Staple

Noodles with Spicy Cabbage and Pork

Makes: 4 servings　　Time: 40 minutes

Chile oil—the real kind that has dried chiles steeping in the bottom of the jar—is one of the easiest and most elegant ways of adding heat to a recipe. But you can also use chile paste, red chile flakes, whole dried chiles, minced fresh chiles, or even hot sauce, each to a slightly different effect. Unlike in a stir-fry, the cabbage here is well cooked, resulting in a pleasantly soft texture and an unexpectedly sweet flavor.

Salt

2 tablespoons vegetable oil

8 ounces ground pork or thinly sliced pork shoulder

1 tablespoon minced garlic

1 tablespoon minced ginger

1 head Napa cabbage (1½ to 2 pounds), chopped

8 ounces rice, buckwheat (soba), or wheat noodles, preferably whole grain

3 tablespoons soy sauce

1 tablespoon sesame oil

2 teaspoons chile oil, or to taste (see the headnote)

Black pepper

¾ cup chopped fresh cilantro

Lime wedges

1. Bring a large pot of water to a boil and salt it. Put the oil in a large, deep skillet over medium-high heat and, a minute later, add the pork, sprinkle with salt, and cook, stirring occasionally (and if you're using ground pork, breaking up the meat as you cook), until the pork browns and is no longer pink, 3 to 5 minutes. Use a slotted spoon to remove the pork and lower the heat to medium-low.

2. Add the garlic and ginger to the skillet and cook, stirring occasionally, until the garlic softens, just 1 minute. Add the cabbage along with ½ cup water and cook, stirring occasionally, until the cabbage is softened and the water evaporates, about 15 minutes. Lower the heat and continue to cook, stirring once in a while, until the cabbage begins to brown, about 5 minutes more.

3. When the cabbage is almost ready, cook the noodles in the boiling water until tender but not mushy. Check them frequently: The time will vary from a minute or 2 for thin rice noodles, to 5 minutes for soba, or up to 12 minutes for wide brown rice noodles. When the noodles are done, drain them, reserving some of the cooking water. Toss the noodles in the skillet along with the pork, soy sauce, sesame oil, chile oil, and some black pepper; add some of the cooking water if the mixture seems dry. Taste and adjust the seasoning. Sprinkle with cilantro and serve with lime wedges.

Spicy Cabbage and Tofu or Tempeh with Noodles. Substitute 8 ounces thinly sliced extra-firm tofu or crumbled tempeh for the pork.

Noodles with Broccoli, Beef, and Black Tea Sauce

Makes: 4 servings   Time: 30 minutes

Black tea adds a deep, smoky flavor to this classic beef and broccoli stir-fry. If you want it even smokier (and meatless), use cubes of smoked tofu instead of the beef.

1 tablespoon black tea leaves (or use a high-quality tea bag)

1 cup boiling water

Salt

1 pound broccoli, trimmed

2 tablespoons vegetable oil

8 ounces sirloin, skirt, or other beef steak, sliced as thinly as possible

Black pepper

1 tablespoon minced garlic

1 tablespoon minced ginger

1 fresh hot chile (like Thai or serrano), minced

1 bunch scallions, white and green parts separated, all chopped

1 tablespoon soy sauce, plus more for serving, optional

8 ounces rice, buckwheat (soba), or wheat noodles, preferably whole grain

(F) Fast   (M) Make-Ahead   (P) Pantry Staple

1. Steep the tea leaves in the boiling water for at least 5 minutes, then strain the tea. Bring a large pot of water to a boil and salt it. Core the broccoli and break it into florets; slice the stems into coins about ¼ inch thick.

2. Put 1 tablespoon of the oil in a large, deep skillet over high heat. When it's hot, add the beef to the pan, sprinkle with salt and pepper, and let it sear for a minute or 2; stir and let it cook for another minute. It should be browned outside but still pink inside. Remove from the pan.

3. Add the remaining 1 tablespoon oil to the pan along with the broccoli, garlic, ginger, chile, and scallion whites; cook, stirring, until the broccoli is bright green, glossy, and beginning to brown in spots, about 5 minutes. Return the beef to the pan, stir in the tea and soy sauce, and cook until some of the tea evaporates and the sauce thickens a bit, a minute or 2 longer.

4. Meanwhile, cook the noodles in the boiling water until they're tender but not mushy. Check them frequently: The time will vary from a minute or 2 for thin rice noodles, to 5 minutes for soba, or up to 12 minutes for wide brown rice noodles. When the noodles are done, drain them, reserving some of the cooking liquid. Toss the noodles with the broccoli and beef, adding cooking liquid as necessary to keep everything moist. Taste and adjust the seasoning, garnish with the scallion greens, and serve, passing more soy sauce at the table if you like.

Whole Grain Drop Dumplings

Makes: 4 servings   Time: 30 minutes

These are a bit like large spaetzle, the free-form cross between dumplings and noodles, but with a lot more texture and, for that matter, flavor. Serve them topped with warmed All-Purpose Tomato Sauce (page 194) or lightly brown them in a mixture of olive oil and butter. Or, while they're still hot, just toss with butter or olive oil. And if you want them for dessert, lightly brown them and drizzle with maple syrup.

Salt

1 cup whole wheat flour, or more as needed

1 cup cornmeal (fine grind if possible), plus more as needed

½ cup rolled oats

¼ teaspoon baking soda

Black pepper

¼ cup milk, or more as needed

1. Bring a large pot of water to a boil and salt it. Combine the flour, cornmeal, oats, baking soda, 1 teaspoon salt, and a sprinkling of black pepper. When the water comes to a boil, carefully transfer about 1 cup boiling water from the pot to the bowl with the dry ingredients. Add the milk and stir until all of the ingredients are incorporated and a sticky, thick batter has formed; it should be somewhere between biscuit dough and pancake batter. If the batter is too wet, add some more cornmeal or flour; if it is too stiff, add some more water or milk.

2. Using a teaspoon, drop a bit of the batter into the boiling water. Work in batches so you don't crowd the pot. Let the dumplings cook for a minute or so after they float to the surface. Remove them with a slotted spoon and dress as you'd like (see the headnote).

Herbed Whole Grain Drop Dumplings. Add ½ cup chopped fresh parsley, basil, mint, or cilantro, or 2 teaspoons chopped rosemary, sage, thyme, or lavender to the dry ingredients in Step 1 before adding the water.

Ⓕ Fast   Ⓜ Make-Ahead   Ⓟ Pantry Staple

Whole Wheat Carrot Gnocchi

Makes: 4 servings   Time: 1¾ hours, partially unattended

Making gnocchi may be impressive, but it isn't difficult. And these, with their gorgeous color, hearty texture, and nutty flavor, are especially fun. As with all gnocchi, add just enough flour to hold them together during cooking. Be gentle with the dough as well, as too much kneading will make them tough.

  1 pound carrots, cut into large chunks

  Salt

  ½ cup whole wheat flour

  ½ cup all-purpose flour, plus more for shaping

  Black pepper

  Pinch of nutmeg

  2 tablespoons olive oil

  2 tablespoons butter

  ½ cup chopped fresh parsley

  ½ cup grated Parmesan cheese

1. Put the carrots in a pot with water to cover and a pinch of salt. Bring the water to a gentle bubble and cook until the carrots are quite tender, about 45 minutes. Drain well. Return the carrots to the dry pan, cover, and dry them over the lowest possible heat, for about 10 minutes. Meanwhile, combine the flours in a small bowl. Bring a small saucepan of water to a boil (for testing the dough) and salt it.

2. Use a fork, potato masher, ricer, or food mill to purée the carrots until smooth; sprinkle with salt and pepper and the nutmeg and stir. Let the mixture cool for a few minutes. Sprinkle the carrots with ¾ cup of the flour mixture and stir gently until it is just incorporated. Pinch off a piece of the dough and boil it to make sure it will hold its shape. If it does not, knead in a bit more flour and try again; repeat as necessary. (The idea is to make the dough with as little additional flour and kneading as possible.)

3. When enough flour has been added, sprinkle a little all-purpose flour on a clean, smooth work surface and roll a piece of the dough into a rope about

½ inch thick, then cut the rope into 1-inch lengths. If you like, score each piece lightly with the tines of a fork or press down on the center a bit to indent it. As each gnoccho is ready, put it on a baking sheet lined with parchment or wax paper; do not allow the gnocchi to touch one another. (If you don't have enough room, use more paper to start another layer on top of the first.)

4. Cover everything with a towel and refrigerate for at least 20 minutes or up to 2 hours. (The recipe can be made ahead to this point and frozen for up to 3 months. Put the whole baking sheet in the freezer until the gnocchi are frozen solid. Transfer them to an airtight container or bag. Do not thaw before cooking; proceed to Step 5.)

5. When you're ready to cook the gnocchi, bring a large pot of water to a boil and salt it. When it's boiling, put the oil and butter in a large skillet over medium-low heat. A few at a time, add the gnocchi to the boiling water and gently stir; adjust the heat so the mixture doesn't boil too vigorously. A minute after they rise to the surface, the gnocchi are done; remove them with a slotted spoon and transfer to the skillet. When all are done, sprinkle them with the parsley, more salt and pepper, and some gnocchi cooking water if the mixture seems too dry. Taste and adjust the seasoning. Serve, passing the cheese at the table.

Carrot Gnocchi with Sage Butter. Omit the parsley. Add several fresh sage leaves to the skillet at the beginning of Step 5 and cook until they sizzle before you begin adding the gnocchi.

Spinach-and-Noodle "Meatballs"

Makes: **4 servings**   Time: **45 minutes**

There is something undeniably fun about making a spaghetti meatball. This is one of those rare occasions where you actually want to cook the noodles until they're mushy, because you use them (and their starch) to hold these vegetable-packed balls together. Use any green you like—kale, chard, collards, broccoli rabe, dandelion greens, bok choy, and gai lan (Chinese broccoli) are all good—as is a squeeze of sriracha sauce just before you pop them into your mouth.

(F) Fast (M) Make-Ahead (P) Pantry Staple

Salt

2 pounds spinach

8 ounces rice, buckwheat (soba), or wheat noodles, preferably whole grain, broken into 1-inch pieces

1 tablespoon minced garlic

1 tablespoon minced ginger

1 fresh hot chile (like jalapeño, serrano, or Thai), minced

½ cup chopped scallions

2 tablespoons soy sauce, plus more for serving

2 teaspoons sesame oil

2 eggs, lightly beaten

¼ cup all-purpose flour, or more as needed

Black pepper

3 tablespoons vegetable oil, plus more as needed

1. Bring a large pot of water to a boil and salt it. Add the spinach and cook for just about a minute until it wilts. Scoop out the spinach with a slotted spoon, rinse it with cold water, and squeeze dry. Add the noodles to the boiling water and cook until they're extremely tender and beginning to break apart (which might take 15 minutes), then drain.

2. Chop the spinach and put it in a bowl along with the noodles, garlic, ginger, chile, scallions, the 2 tablespoons soy sauce, the sesame oil, eggs, flour, and a sprinkling of pepper. Mash the mixture with a fork or your hands until the ingredients come together. If the mixture is too loose to form into balls, add another sprinkling of flour.

3. Put the vegetable oil in a large skillet over medium-high heat. When it's hot, form a spoonful of the spinach mixture into a ball about the size of a Ping-Pong ball and add it to the pan. Continue, working in batches so they aren't too crowded and adding more oil to the pan as needed. Cook, turning as necessary, until the outsides are crisp and brown, about 5 minutes total. Transfer the balls to towels to drain and repeat with the remaining spinach mixture. Serve hot or at room temperature, passing soy sauce at the table.

Rice and Grains

In the United States, as in much of the world, rice—most commonly white rice—is the most popular and widely available grain. But in the world of grains, rice is but one of many fantastic options, and they're almost all, almost always interchangeable. (This is especially the case when a recipe calls for using them already cooked, as many of mine do.) So my goal here is to offer a wide variety of whole grains in mostly familiar dishes, helping you to quickly become as comfortable with the ones you don't know as you probably are with white rice.

White rice is a fine starting point, although these days I eat predominantly brown rice and other whole grains. This doesn't mean I've cut traditional risotto, sticky rice, or Indian-restaurant basmati out of my diet. But since recipes for those kinds of dishes are easy to find (they're certainly in my other cookbooks), here I focus on whole grains, which are minimally processed, thus delivering the most micronutrients and fiber and requiring less energy to get from field to table. (Often, you can substitute white rice in these dishes: Reduce the cooking time by about half; or in cases where brown rice is parboiled first, simply eliminate that step.)

Other personal biases might be less obvious. There's a fair amount of bulgur in this chapter, because it's fast and easy to cook (and find!) and has a distinctive and pleasantly chewy texture and nutty flavor. Cornmeal and oats are other convenient and versatile whole grains, so they're well represented too. I've included several recipes that feature quinoa, the tasty, quick-cooking grain that's high in protein and now available in most supermarkets. (Quinoa has been "the next big thing" in whole grains for at least twenty-five years; maybe its time has come. In any case, most people who try it like it, so if you haven't, you should.)

Since cooked grains keep well in the fridge for several days—and freeze almost as well as beans—I urge you to cook them plain, in bulk, and keep them handy. Out of the fridge you can reheat them in the microwave (the best method) or gently on the stove. Add them to stir-fries or other cooked dishes, or use them cold in salads. From the freezer, they work best in soups, chilies, stews, and other high-moisture dishes. (It helps to add a little extra water to precooked frozen grains when you thaw them.)

Breakfast is the natural way to get more whole grains in your diet, so I've started this chapter with all the "breakfasty" recipes, right after the two basic grain-cooking techniques. After that come vegan dishes, then vegetarian—which may contain some cheese and/or eggs—and then those that include seafood, chicken, and finally meat.

Rice and Grains: A Short Tutorial

The easiest way to explain rice—which is in a different family from most other grains—is to first divide it by the way it's processed: brown and white. Brown rice is the general term for rice that has been milled to remove the hull only; the bran and germ remain intact. (Red, black, and other fancy colored rices are also minimally processed but have a different color bran.) Strip off the bran and germ of *any* colored rice, and it turns into white rice. White rice cooks much more quickly than brown, isn't as chewy or flavorful, and has fewer nutrients. (You might also see "converted" or "instant" rice, which has been precooked; avoid these in favor of raw rice.)

Once that's settled, the different types of rice can usually be found in both brown and white forms. Again, there are two major categories: long-grain and short-grain ("medium"-grain is actually short). Generic "long-grain rice" is usually what's known as "Southern Long-Grain" and includes the most common varieties grown worldwide. Basmati is a highly aromatic long-grain rice whose kernels cook up separate and fluffy. Jasmine is a long-grain aromatic rice that's a little stickier than basmati and has a milder flavor.

Ⓕ Fast   Ⓜ Make-Ahead   Ⓟ Pantry Staple

Short-grain rices include Arborio and the other varieties used for risotto, paella, and sticky rice—the dishes where you want a little more starch and chew. Most of the specific varieties are sold only in white form. Short-grain brown rice is a little hard to find, but what you do see in the supermarket is the generic kind, which might be either short- or medium-grain. You can use either in all the recipes in this chapter that call for short-grain brown rice. Generally, short-grain brown rice cooks in 20 to 30 minutes; long-grain brown rice takes 40 to 50 minutes—sometimes more for those specialty types with especially thick outer layers.

There are hundreds of types and varieties of other grains. Although each has its own unique flavor and texture, and their cooking times vary, they're almost all virtually interchangeable in the kitchen. So if a recipe calls for a particular cooked grain and you have something else, just go right ahead and use what you have. If the dish calls for a raw grain, however, use only that or one of the other options suggested.

Corn is almost universally popular and comes in many forms. Simple dried corn products include popcorn and cornmeal in various grinds (it often doesn't matter much which grind you use, though coarse makes the best polenta). Figure 20 or so minutes for cooking. Hominy—and the meal known as grits ground from it—is processed to remove the germ and bran so it has a corny flavor that reminds you of tortillas. Grits cook like cornmeal, but dried hominy can take 2 to 4 hours to cook (a little less if you soak it first); it also comes ready-to-use in cans. Masa harina is the flour used to make tortillas and tamales.

Wheat also comes in many forms. The smallest is couscous, which is actually a pasta made from semolina or whole wheat flour. You steep it in hot water, rather than cook it. Bulgur is cracked wheat that has been steamed so it cooks fast. It comes in fine, medium, and coarse grinds. (Use the one you like or can find; in these recipes, it makes no difference.) Most recipes call for steeping it in boiling water, but I prefer cooking it like other grains, which is faster and leaves it fluffier. Cracked wheat is like bulgur, only raw, so it takes about twice as long to cook—it's also a little chewier. Wheat berries are whole kernels and can take up to 90 minutes or more to cook. Closely related spelt, Kamut, and rye (which are increasingly available) can become tender in an hour or even less. The hearty texture and flavor of these whole grains make them all worth the wait.

Rolled oats are universally loved and familiar, though not as versatile as steel-cut oats, which cook up soupy like porridge or fluffy and chewy like other grains, depending on how much water you use. Both are made from oat groats, the edible (and sort of pyramid-shaped) kernels milled from whole grain oats (these are good, too, but harder to find). Don't bother with precooked instant rolled oats. The raw oats are far superior and cook in about 10 minutes; figure another 5 minutes for steel-cut oats and about twice as long for groats. (If you find yourself perennially behind in the morning, go for "quick-cooked" but not "instant" rolled oats; these are still whole grain but are chopped up, so they cook in 3 to 5 minutes, somewhat faster than regular rolled oats.)

Buckwheat is made into a variety of products, including kasha—nutty-tasting hulled and roasted kernels—and raw groats, with their distinctive grassy and nutty flavor. Both cook in 20 to 30 minutes. Buckwheat is also the primary grain in soba noodles (see page 193).

Barley—long my favorite rice substitute, though these days I eat more quinoa—can be either whole with only the outer hull removed (in which case it's called simply "hulled barley") or "pearled," where the outer layers have been removed and the kernels are steamed for speedier cooking and creamier texture. Pearled barley is ready in about 20 minutes; hulled is more nutritious but takes twice the time to cook.

Quinoa is increasingly popular and has an herbaceous flavor, pleasant crunch, and high protein content. The small, disk-shaped kernels come in many colors (usually beige) and cook in about 15 minutes.

Wild rice isn't actually rice but a marsh grass. You can most readily find farm-grown varieties; true wild rice (which is, of course, more expensive) has a uniquely earthy flavor and never-mushy texture. Cooking times vary wildly from 45 to 60 minutes, or even more; it's ready when fully tender, but try to stop the cooking before too many grains burst.

More and more specialty grains are becoming common. Millet is one of my favorites: The small, round, bead-like yellow grains have a nutty, almost corny flavor and fluffy texture (it cooks in 20 to 30 minutes). Farro is a wheat-like berry (traditionally served in Tuscany and still popular there). It's increasingly available and has a grassy flavor and quick (20-minute) cooking time.

Ⓕ Fast Ⓜ Make-Ahead Ⓟ Pantry Staple

Batch of Grains

Makes: 6 to 8 cups (6 to 10 servings)   Time: 10 minutes to more than 1 hour, depending on the grain

This isn't even a recipe, really, just the only method for cooking grains you need. Cooking grains (beans, too, for that matter) is fraught with too many variables to make measurements valuable, or even necessary. With this technique, the absolute *worst* that can happen is that you need to add more water as the grains cook or drain off excess when they're done. No big deal. The more you cook grains freestyle like this, the more comfortable you'll get eyeballing the progress and making adjustments.

Cooked grains keep wonderfully in the refrigerator or freezer, and they reheat easily in the microwave or covered on the stovetop with a few drops of water over low heat. Or use them as is in salads and stir-fries and for baking.

> 2 cups brown rice (any size), bulgur, quinoa, barley (any type), oat groats, buckwheat groats, steel-cut oats, millet, cracked wheat, hominy, whole rye, farro, kamut, or wild rice; or 1½ cups wheat berries
>
> Salt

1. Rinse the grains in a strainer and put them in a large pot with a big pinch of salt. Add enough water to cover by about 1 inch, no more. (If you want drier grains, cover with closer to ½ inch water.) Bring to a boil, then adjust the heat so the mixture bubbles gently.

2. Cook, undisturbed, until the grains are tender and almost all of the water is absorbed. This will take as little as 5 to 10 minutes for bulgur and steel-cut oats, 20 to 25 minutes for quinoa, at least 40 minutes for long-grain brown rice, and as long as 1 hour or more for some specialty rices and other grains with their hulls intact. As the grains cook, add boiling water as necessary to keep them just submerged and to prevent them from drying out and sticking.

3. Every now and then, test a kernel. Grains are done when tender but still a little chewy. (Think al dente.) Be careful not to overcook (unless you want them mushy, in which case see Batch of Softer Grains, page 273). When they're ready, and if the water is all absorbed (one sure sign is that little holes have formed on the top), just cover the pot and remove it from the heat. If some water still remains, drain, return to the pot, cover, and remove from the heat. Either way, undisturbed, they'll stay warm for about 20 minutes. Fluff the grains with a fork. Leave plain or season using some of the ideas from the list that follows. Serve hot or at room temperature.

Couscous with Some Measuring. Put 2 cups whole wheat couscous in the pot and add 3 cups water and a pinch of salt. Bring the water to a boil, then cover and remove from the heat. Let steep for at least 10 minutes (5 minutes if using white couscous) or up to 20. Fluff with a fork and serve with any of the additions suggested below.

Baked Brown Rice or Whole Grains Without Measuring. Heat the oven to 400°F. Put the rinsed grains in an ovenproof pot or Dutch oven, add salt, then cover with cold water by 1 inch. Bake for 30 to 60 minutes, depending on the size and sturdiness of the grain. Remove from the oven and let sit for 10 minutes before tossing with any of the additions suggested below.

Terrific Additions to Any Cooked Grains

When grains are finished cooking but still hot, stir in any or many of these ingredients:

Olive oil, butter, or flavored oils, or a combination
Cooked vegetables (ideally crisp-tender), like peas, chopped greens,
   broccoli or cauliflower florets, or chopped carrots or other root vegetables
A couple spoonfuls of sauce, like All-Purpose Tomato Sauce (page 194),
   Any-Herb Pesto (page 197), or a bottled condiment like soy sauce or hot
   sauce
A sprinkling of chopped fresh herbs, like chives, parsley, cilantro, or mint;
   or a bit of rosemary, oregano, or thyme
Any cooked beans—as much or as little as you want
Dried fruit, like raisins, cranberries, cherries, or chopped dates or apricots,
   with or without chopped nuts or seeds
Cooked mushrooms, onions, garlic (especially roasted), ginger, or shallots
Cooked chopped sausage, bacon, ham, or any cooked meat or fish
Spices, like cinnamon, cloves, cardamom, mustard seeds, cumin, coriander,
   minced fresh or dried chiles, saffron, or spice blends like curry or chili powder

Ⓕ Fast   Ⓜ Make-Ahead   Ⓟ Pantry Staple

Batch of Softer Grains

Makes: 6 to 8 cups (6 to 10 servings)   Time: 30 to 90 minutes or more, depending on the grain

Cook grains long enough and the kernels soften and eventually explode, releasing more starch into the cooking water. When cooled, the kernels set up into a solid mass that keeps its shape (think of polenta) and become endlessly useful. Keep them on the dry side, and they've got the consistency of mashed potatoes, with a stiffness that makes them perfect for shaping into grain crusts and cakes (see the recipes on pages 305 and 312). Add more water to the pot, and they become a creamy, almost smooth porridge. Like Batch of Grains, this will keep for several days in the refrigerator or months in the freezer.

> 2 cups brown rice (any size), bulgur, quinoa, barley (any type), oat groats,
>   buckwheat groats, steel-cut oats, millet, cracked wheat, hominy, whole
>   rye, farro, kamut, or wild rice; or 1½ cups wheat berries
>
> Salt

1. Rinse the grains in a strainer and put them in a large pot along with a big pinch of salt. Add enough water to cover by about 1½ inches. Bring to a boil, then adjust the heat so the mixture bubbles gently.

2. Cook, stirring occasionally, until the grains are very tender and have burst; this will take anywhere from 30 minutes to over 1 hour, depending on the grain. If you want your grains on the soupy side, add more boiling water liberally as the grains cook; if you want drier grains, add just enough boiling water to keep the grains submerged. When the grains are starchy and thick, like porridge, cover and remove from the heat; you can let it sit for up to 20 minutes. Serve hot or at room temperature. If serving right away, see Terrific Additions to Any Cooked Grains (page 272) for some flavoring ideas.

Mashed Whole Grains with Garlic and Olive Oil. You can use butter instead of olive oil here. Add 1 or more cloves of garlic to the pot in Step 1. When the grains are done cooking and resting, drizzle in 2 tablespoons olive oil (or more if you like) and mash the grains with a fork or potato masher. If the grains are too thick, add up to ¼ cup warm milk, cream, or water as you mash. When the grains are fluffy and fairly smooth (and the garlic has been evenly incorporated), drizzle with a little more olive oil and serve.

Porridge, Sweet or Savory

Makes: 4 to 6 servings   Time: 15 minutes   Ⓕ Ⓜ Ⓟ

One of the most flexible recipes there is and easily adapted to just about any grain you like (except big kernels like barley or wheat berries or quick-cooking or instant oats). I'm guessing that you'll eat more whole grains for breakfast if they're interesting, so vary the ingredients you stir in at will, whether you have a sweet tooth or a salty one in the morning. There is no right or wrong way here; don't rule out anything (especially leftovers) simply because the idea doesn't seem like "normal" breakfast food. I alternate between pungent flavors like sesame oil, soy sauce, and sliced scallions, and classics like maple syrup and berries. Take a look at the ideas below and see what strikes your fancy.

If you're cooking for one or two, make a full batch anyway. Let it cool, separate it into small airtight containers, and refrigerate or freeze them. With a microwave, you can have hot porridge for breakfast every morning in a couple of minutes.

Salt

2 cups grains, like rolled oats (or other rolled grain), cracked wheat, quinoa, millet, or short-grain brown rice

1 tablespoon butter, or to taste, optional

1. Combine 4 to 4½ cups water (more water will produce creamier porridge), a pinch of salt, and the grains in a medium saucepan and turn the heat to high. When the water boils, turn the heat down so the mixture bubbles gently and cook, stirring frequently, until the water is just absorbed: about 5 minutes for rolled oats, 15 minutes for cornmeal or cracked wheat, 30 minutes for quinoa or millet, or up to 45 minutes or more for brown rice. Add water as needed to keep the porridge from sticking.

2. When the grains are very soft and the mixture is thickened, serve or cover the pan and turn off the heat; you can let it sit for up to 15 minutes. Uncover, stir, add butter as desired, and serve with any of the additions listed opposite, alone or in combination (or store, covered, in the refrigerator for up to a week or in the freezer for up to a month).

Additions for Sweet Porridge

Honey, sugar, or maple syrup

Chopped fresh, dried, or candied fruit

Chopped nuts or seeds, or a spoonful of nut butter

Vanilla extract

A splash of milk or cream

Shredded, unsweetened coconut or a splash of coconut milk

Additions for Savory Porridge

A drizzle of olive oil or sesame oil instead of butter

Salsa (for homemade, see page 46) or chopped fresh hot chiles

Grated hard cheese or crumbled soft cheese

Hard-boiled, poached, or fried eggs

A drizzle of soy sauce

Sliced raw scallions, chopped shallots, or minced garlic

Coarse salt and black pepper

Chopped or grated raw vegetables, stirred into the porridge for the last
   5 minutes of cooking

Chopped cooked vegetables, stirred into the porridge at the last minute

Chopped cooked bacon or pancetta or crumbled cooked sausage

Cooked beans, mashed up a bit or not

Spiced Breakfast Bulgur

Makes: 4 servings   Time: 25 minutes

Wheat is a classic breakfast cereal, and bulgur is the fastest-cooking wheat
there is. Simmering the grains with citrus and spices is a wonderful way to
add distinctive but not overpowering flavor. For a more assertive flavor, stir
in another pinch of ground spices just before serving.

1 orange, halved

Any one or combination of the following: 2 cinnamon sticks, 1 whole nutmeg, 2 teaspoons whole allspice berries, 2 teaspoons cardamom pods

1 cup bulgur

Salt

2 cups sliced fresh fruit (see the headnote on page 278)

1 cup nuts, toasted if you like, optional

Honey, maple syrup, or brown sugar, for serving, optional

1. Squeeze the juice from the orange into a medium saucepan and toss in
the peels along with whatever spices you're using. Add 2 cups water and
bring the mixture to a boil. Fish out the orange peels and spices with a small
strainer or slotted spoon.

2. Stir in the bulgur and a pinch of salt and adjust the heat so that the mixture bubbles gently. Cook, without stirring, until the bulgur is tender but
still a little chewy, 5 to 10 minutes; add a little water if the mixture starts
to dry out. Cover, remove from the heat, and let sit for at least 5 minutes or
up to 1 hour. Serve hot or at room temperature, topped with the fresh fruit,
nuts, and honey if you like.

Herbed Breakfast Bulgur. This is terrific with berries. Substitute a lemon
for the orange and a sprig of rosemary, thyme, lavender, or tarragon for the
spices. Proceed with the recipe.

Granola

Makes: About 9 cups   Time: 30 minutes   Ⓕ Ⓜ Ⓟ

Increasingly, store-bought granola is made from real ingredients, and that's
a good thing. But most cost a fortune compared to the homemade version,
which has other advantages: You can customize it to your taste, change it up
every time you make a new batch, and always know what you're eating. Both
granola and muesli (see the variation) are good not only as ready-to-eat cereal but also sprinkled on top of yogurt or fruit salad or stirred into pancake,
waffle, or quick-bread batter.

5 cups rolled oats (not quick-cooking or instant) or other rolled grains (like wheat, rye, or Kamut)

3 cups chopped mixed nuts (like walnuts, pecans, almonds, and cashews) and whole seeds (like sunflower seeds, pumpkin seeds, and sesame seeds)

1 cup shredded, unsweetened coconut

1 teaspoon ground spice (like cinnamon, ginger, or cardamom), or $\frac{1}{2}$ teaspoon nutmeg, cloves, or allspice

$\frac{1}{2}$ to 1 cup honey, maple syrup, or raw sugar, or to taste

1 teaspoon vanilla or almond extract, optional

Salt

1 to 1$\frac{1}{2}$ cups dried fruit, chopped if necessary (like raisins, blueberries, apricots, figs, dates, cranberries, cherries, pineapple, crystallized ginger, or banana chips)

1. Heat the oven to 350°F. In a large bowl, combine the oats, nuts and seeds, coconut, spice, sweetener, and extract if you're using it; sprinkle with a little pinch of salt. Toss well to thoroughly distribute the ingredients. Spread the mixture on a rimmed baking sheet and bake for 30 minutes or a little longer, stirring occasionally. The granola should brown evenly; the darker it gets without burning, the crunchier it will be.

2. Remove the pan from the oven and add the dried fruit. Cool in the pan on a wire rack, stirring now and then, until the granola reaches room temperature. Serve (or store in a sealed container at room temperature for up to a week).

Muesli. Faster, but not as crunchy. Omit the extract and honey or syrup. Combine the oats, nuts, seeds, coconut, spice, and fruit in a large bowl and sprinkle with salt. Toss the mixture with $\frac{1}{4}$ cup brown sugar. Serve with yogurt, fresh fruit, honey, or milk. Store as you would granola.

Fruity Breakfast Pilaf

Makes: 4 servings   Time: 45 to 60 minutes

All the things you like about rice pilaf you'll like about this slightly sweet cousin. Stone fruits (like peaches, plums, and apricots), apples, pears, cherries, berries, grapes, and pineapple, alone or in combination, are all good choices. When you top the rice with a dollop of ricotta or cottage cheese, this dish is as satisfying and impressive as pancakes or French toast—perfect for a weekend brunch. Or make a big batch and nibble on it (reheated, cold, or at room temperature) all through the workweek.

2 tablespoons butter or olive oil

1 tablespoon honey, plus more for serving

1½ cups brown rice

Salt

1 cup orange or apple juice

3 cups chopped fruit (see the headnote)

½ cup ricotta cheese, optional

½ cup chopped fresh mint, for garnish

1. Put the butter or oil in a large, deep skillet or medium saucepan over medium heat. When the butter is melted or the oil is hot, add the honey and rice. Cook, stirring, until the rice is glossy, completely coated with oil or butter, and starting to color, 3 to 5 minutes. Add a pinch of salt, then turn the heat down to low. Add the juice and 1½ cups water, stir once or twice, and cover the pan.

2. Cook until most of the liquid is absorbed and the rice is just tender, 35 to 45 minutes. Uncover, stir in the fruit, replace the lid, and remove from the heat. Let the pilaf rest for at least 5 minutes or up to 20 minutes. Taste, add more salt if necessary, and fluff with a fork. Serve, topped with the ricotta if you're using it, mint, and an extra drizzle of honey.

Wheat Berries with Berries

Makes: 4 servings   Time: 45 minutes to 2 hours

Cute name aside, the combination of wheat berries, almond milk, and fresh berries is unfussy and delicious. The result is like a cross between berry soup and rice pudding, only dairy-free—unless you choose to replace some of the almond or oat milk with dairy milk (or even a bit of half-and-half), which you certainly can do.

Wheat berries are a notoriously temperamental grain; sometimes they cook quickly, but other times they can take hours to get soft. If you want to cut down the cooking time, soak the wheat berries in water overnight and drain them before beginning the recipe.

> ³/₄ cup wheat berries
>
> 2 cups almond or oat milk
>
> ¹/₄ cup maple syrup or honey, or to taste
>
> Salt
>
> 4 cups blueberries, raspberries, blackberries, cherries (pitted if you like),
>   or strawberries, or a combination
>
> ¹/₄ cup sliced almonds

1. In a large pot, combine the wheat berries with the milk, maple syrup, and a pinch of salt. Add water if necessary to cover the wheat berries by at least 1 inch. Bring to a boil, then adjust the heat so the mixture bubbles gently.

2. Cook, stirring occasionally, until the wheat berries are tender, which may take anywhere from 35 minutes to over 2 hours. Add boiling water as necessary to keep the wheat berries covered and to keep them from drying out as they swell and become tender. Wheat berries are done when they're tender with a slight bite to them; the mixture will still be a little soupy. (You can make the grains ahead to this point and refrigerate for up to a few days; gently reheat them before proceeding.)

3. Add the berries to the wheat berry mixture and stir until they soften a bit. Serve warm, garnished with the almonds.

Homemade Cereal

Makes: 4 servings   Time: About 40 minutes, plus time to cool

All ready-to-eat cereals—except Granola (page 276)—come from a box, right? Not necessarily. Making homemade corn cereal is as easy as making crackers; all you need is a rolling pin and a baking sheet. For best results, let the cooked sheet of dough cool *thoroughly* before breaking it up.

If you have a pasta rolling machine, this is a good place to use it. If you don't, just be patient and roll the sheet of dough as thin as practically possible; it will be thicker than cornflakes but with a wonderful texture and crunch. Once the sheets have baked and cooled, you can break them into small pieces with your hands or pulse them into bits in a food processor.

    ½ cup cornmeal (fine or medium grind), plus more as needed

    1½ cups whole wheat flour, plus more as needed

    2 tablespoons sugar

    ½ teaspoon salt

    1 tablespoon vegetable oil

1. Heat the oven to 300°F. Lightly dust a baking sheet (or 2 if necessary) with cornmeal or put a baking stone in the oven. Put the cornmeal, flour, sugar, salt, and oil in a food processor. Pulse until everything is combined. Add about ¼ cup water and let the machine run for a bit; continue to add water 1 teaspoon at a time until the mixture holds together but is not sticky.

2. Roll out the dough between 2 sheets of lightly floured wax paper until ⅛ inch thick or even thinner, if possible, adding flour as needed. Use the rolling pin, a spatula, pastry blade, or peel to transfer the dough to the prepared baking sheet or stone. Bake until lightly browned and crisp, about 30 minutes. Cool the pans completely on a wire rack. Crumble the sheets into flakes of any size or pulse them into bits in a food processor. Eat right away (or store in a sealed container for up to a week).

Ⓕ Fast   Ⓜ Make-Ahead   Ⓟ Pantry Staple

Griddled Toast with Warm Fruit

Makes: 4 servings   Time: 30 minutes

This is somewhere between French toast and milk toast, but fruity—made with apple juice instead of milk. Bread with a dense, tight crumb is the way to go here. And consider using peaches, pears, plums, berries, pineapples, or bananas instead of apples in the warm fruit topping.

> 1 egg
>
> ½ cup apple juice or apple cider
>
> Dash of salt
>
> 1 teaspoon vanilla extract
>
> Butter or vegetable oil as needed
>
> 8 slices bread, preferably whole grain
>
> 2 large apples, cored and thinly sliced
>
> Honey to taste, optional

1. Heat the oven to 200°F. Put a large skillet or griddle over medium heat. Beat the egg lightly in a wide bowl and stir in the apple juice, salt, and vanilla.

2. Add a pat of butter to the skillet. When it melts, quickly dip each slice of bread in turn in the egg mixture and put them in the skillet in a single layer. (Cook in batches if there's not enough room.) Cook the slices until they're nicely browned on each side, turning and adding bits of butter as necessary, for 5 to 10 minutes total; you may find that you can raise the heat a bit. Transfer the pieces of toast to the oven as they finish.

3. When all the toast is done, add the apples to the skillet along with a little honey if you like and cook, stirring, until soft and slightly browned, about 5 minutes. Serve the apples over the toast.

Crisp and Thin Waffles
with Loads of Fresh Fruit

Makes: 4 servings   Time: 30 minutes

When you thin waffle batter before cooking, you end up with ultracrisp waffles that still have a little bit of chew—the perfect foil for juicy fresh fruit. Since you're not cooking or seasoning the fruit—try berries, cherries, peaches, nectarines, plums, mango, or pineapple—be sure it's really ripe and juicy.

Vegetable oil, for the waffle iron

2 cups whole wheat flour

½ teaspoon salt

2 tablespoons sugar

1 teaspoon baking soda

½ cup yogurt or buttermilk

1 egg

2 tablespoons melted butter

½ teaspoon vanilla extract, optional

4 cups fresh fruit, pitted and peeled as necessary, and cut into bite-size pieces (see the headnote)

1. Brush the waffle iron lightly with oil and set it to medium-high heat. Combine the dry ingredients in a large bowl. In another bowl, whisk together the yogurt, egg, and 1½ cups water. Stir in the butter and vanilla extract if you're using it. Stir the wet ingredients into the dry until almost smooth. The consistency should be like thin pancake batter; if not, add a little more water.

2. Spread a thin layer of batter onto the waffle iron; bake until the waffle is crisp, 5 to 10 minutes. Serve immediately, topped with the fruit. Repeat for more waffles.

Savory Supercrisp Waffles. Omit the sugar, increase the salt to 1 teaspoon, and omit the vanilla. Serve as you would toast: topped with beans or a stir-fry, as sandwich bread, or alongside a soup or stew.

Anadama Waffles

Makes: 4 to 6 servings   Time: 30 to 40 minutes

These substantial but fluffy waffles capture the essence of anadama bread, a traditional New England yeast loaf made with cornmeal and molasses. Applesauce contributes a little sweetness and moisture to the batter, though the apple flavor disappears in the cooked waffles, letting the cornmeal shine through. Make extra so you can keep them handy in the freezer for popping in the toaster on busy mornings.

3 tablespoons vegetable oil, plus more for the waffle iron

1⅓ cups whole wheat flour

⅓ cup cornmeal (fine or medium grind)

2 teaspoons baking powder

¾ teaspoon salt

2 large eggs, separated

½ cup milk

¾ cup applesauce

2 tablespoons molasses

1. Brush the waffle iron lightly with oil and set it to medium-high heat. Heat the oven to 200°F. Combine the flour, cornmeal, baking powder, and salt in a large bowl.

2. Beat the egg whites with an electric mixer or a whisk just until stiff peaks form. In a separate bowl, beat the yolks, milk, applesauce, molasses, and 3 tablespoons vegetable oil until foamy, about 2 minutes. Add the applesauce mixture to the dry ingredients and stir just enough to incorporate. Fold in the egg whites until the batter is evenly colored and relatively smooth.

3. Spread enough batter onto the waffle iron to barely cover it; bake until the waffle is done, 3 to 5 minutes. Serve immediately or keep warm for a few minutes on an ovenproof plate in the oven. Repeat for more waffles.

Anadama Waffles with Corn Kernels. Stir 1 cup corn kernels (frozen are fine) into the batter in Step 2.

Oatmeal Griddle Cakes

Makes: 4 to 6 servings   Time: 30 minutes with precooked oatmeal

Griddle cakes are one of my favorite ways to use leftover oatmeal (or leftover anything, really), but it's worth it to make a fresh pot for these. With rolled oats, cinnamon, and raisins, these will remind you of soft oatmeal cookies, only not as sweet. Molasses is an excellent alternative to maple syrup, but it's strong, so use it sparingly.

¼ cup whole wheat flour

¼ cup all-purpose flour

¼ cup rolled oats

1 teaspoon baking powder

1 teaspoon cinnamon

½ teaspoon salt

1 egg

½ cup milk

2 cups cooked oatmeal

½ cup raisins

Vegetable oil, for frying

Molasses or maple syrup, for serving

1. Heat the oven to 200°F. Combine the flours, oats, baking powder, cinnamon, and salt in a large bowl.

2. In a separate bowl, whisk together the egg and milk; stir in the cooked oatmeal and raisins until just incorporated. Add the oatmeal mixture to the flour mixture and stir gently; don't overmix. The mixture should be the consistency of thick pancake batter; if not, add either a little more milk or whole wheat flour as needed.

3. Put a large skillet or griddle over medium heat. When a few drops of water dance on its surface, add a thin film of vegetable oil and let it get hot. Working in batches, spoon the batter onto the griddle or skillet, making any size pancakes you like. Cook until bubbles form on the top and pop, 2 to 3 minutes; you may have to rotate the cakes to cook them evenly, depend-

    Ⓕ Fast   Ⓜ Make-Ahead   Ⓟ Pantry Staple

ing on your heat source and pan. Carefully flip the griddle cakes and cook until they're browned on the other side, a couple of minutes more. As they finish, transfer them to the oven while you cook the remaining batter. Serve drizzled with molasses or maple syrup.

Coconut Flapjacks

Makes: 4 servings   Time: 30 minutes

Coconut and its milk provide so much richness that you can make these pancakes without any eggs or dairy at all. Fresh or dried fruit is a great topping here, but I like the slight crunch of sugar crystals combined with a few drops of lime juice. Or if you want to take these the savory route, add a tablespoon curry powder to the batter.

> 2½ cups whole wheat flour
>
> 1 cup shredded, unsweetened coconut
>
> ½ teaspoon salt
>
> One 14-ounce can coconut milk (light is fine)
>
> 1¼ cups warm water, or more as needed
>
> Vegetable oil, for frying
>
> Raw (turbinado) sugar, for serving
>
> Lime wedges, optional

1. Heat the oven to 200°F. Combine the flour, coconut, and salt in a large bowl. Stir in the coconut milk and warm water. The batter should be fairly thin but not watery; add a little more water if it seems too thick.

2. Put a large skillet or griddle over medium heat. When a few drops of water dance on its surface, add a thin film of vegetable oil and let it get hot. Working in batches, spoon the batter onto the griddle or skillet, making any size pancakes you like. Cook until bubbles form on the top and pop, 2 to 3 minutes; you may have to rotate the cakes to cook them evenly, depending on your heat source and pan. Flip the flapjacks and cook until they're browned on the other side, a minute or 2 more. As they finish, transfer them to a platter in the oven while you cook the remaining batter. While they're hot, sprinkle the tops with a little sugar and serve with lime wedges.

Grains and Mushrooms, Lightly Scrambled

Makes: 4 servings   Time: 30 minutes

This dish perfectly illustrates why you should cook large batches of grains and beans (see the variation) and keep them on hand in the fridge. It makes an awesome hearty breakfast, and it's also handy to whip up for a quick lunch or supper. If anyone gives you a batch of wild mushrooms, think of this.

> 2 tablespoons olive or vegetable oil
>
> 1 pound mushrooms (any assortment), sliced
>
> Salt and black pepper
>
> 2 cups any cooked grains (see page 271)
>
> 2 eggs, beaten
>
> Soy sauce to taste
>
> ½ cup chopped scallions

1. Put the oil in a large, deep skillet or pot over medium heat. When it's hot, add the mushrooms and sprinkle with salt and pepper. Cover and reduce the heat to medium-low. Cook, undisturbed, until the mushrooms release their liquid, about 5 minutes. Remove the cover, raise the heat a bit, and continue to cook, stirring occasionally, until the mushrooms are dry and a bit crisp, 5 to 10 minutes more.

2. Add the grains and cook, stirring occasionally, until warmed through and beginning to crisp, 3 to 5 minutes. Add the eggs and gently stir until they're set, 1 to 3 minutes. Transfer the mixture to a serving platter or individual bowls, drizzle with soy sauce, sprinkle with scallions, and serve.

Scrambled Rice and Beans with Salsa. Like fried rice, Mexican style. Substitute 2 sliced onions for the mushrooms, and 1 cup cooked and drained pinto or black beans for 1 cup of the grains. Omit the soy sauce and scallions. In Step 1, cook the onions, uncovered, over medium heat until browned and beginning to crisp, 10 to 15 minutes. In Step 2, stir in the rice and beans. Proceed with the recipe, top with a spoonful of salsa (for homemade, see page 46), and serve.

Ⓕ Fast   Ⓜ Make-Ahead   Ⓟ Pantry Staple

Super-Simple Mixed Rice, a Zillion Ways

Makes: 4 servings   Time: 30 minutes

This technique gives you creamy, risotto-like rice with minimal stirring. The basic version is very flavorful, thanks to dried mushrooms, tomatoes, basil, and Parmesan, but each variation's distinctive profile transforms the main recipe into something completely different. Using the variations (and experimenting with other whole grains), you could (and probably will) make this dish forever—and no one will get tired of it.

¼ cup dried porcini mushrooms

Hot water as needed

2 tablespoons olive oil

¾ cup short-grain brown rice

1 onion, chopped

Salt and black pepper

1½ cups chopped tomatoes (canned are fine; include their juice)

2 cups cooked or canned cannellini beans, drained

½ cup chopped fresh basil or parsley, plus more for garnish

½ cup grated Parmesan cheese, optional

1. Soak the porcini in hot water to cover. Put the oil in a large pot over medium heat. When it's hot, add the rice and cook, stirring, until it's shiny and a little translucent, about 1 minute. Add the onion, sprinkle with salt and pepper, and continue to cook, stirring occasionally, until the onion is softened, about 1 minute. Add enough water to cover by about ½ inch.

2. Bring to a boil, then lower the heat so that it bubbles gently. Cook, stirring occasionally, until the rice starts to become tender, about 10 minutes. By now the porcini should be soft; chop the mushrooms roughly and pour their soaking liquid into the rice, being careful to leave some water behind to trap the sediment. Add the tomatoes and mushrooms to the rice and continue to cook, stirring occasionally, until the tomatoes break down, about another 10 minutes. Add more water if needed to keep the mixture a little soupy.

3. When the rice is tender but retains some bite on the inside, add the beans. Continue to cook, stirring occasionally, until the mixture is no longer soupy but not yet dry. Stir in the basil and the cheese if you're using it. Taste and adjust the seasoning. Serve, garnished with a little more fresh herb.

Some Easy Variations for Mixed Rice

Chile Mixed Rice. Toss a seeded chipotle or pasilla chile into the rice mixture with the onion along with 1 to 2 teaspoons minced garlic. Use black or pinto beans instead of the cannellini, and cilantro instead of the basil. Use cheddar or queso fresco in place of the Parmesan, or omit the cheese and stir in about 1 cup cooked chicken or pork if you like. (Be sure to fish out the chile before serving.)

Japanese Mixed Rice. Substitute dried shiitakes for the porcini. Instead of the olive oil, use half vegetable oil and half sesame oil. Omit the tomatoes and stir in other vegetables like bean sprouts, sliced asparagus, broccoli florets, whole snow peas, or chopped bok choy. Instead of the cannellini beans, use edamame (frozen are fine), or add a few shrimp or cubes of tofu if you like. Keep the mixture moist with water. At the very end add a splash of soy sauce instead of the cheese. Use chopped scallions, chives, or shiso instead of the basil.

Coconut Mixed Rice. Omit the porcini and use vegetable oil instead of olive oil. When you're cooking the onion with the rice, add 2 to 3 cups chopped eggplant and 1 tablespoon each minced ginger and curry powder. When you add the tomatoes, add 1 cup coconut milk. Use chickpeas instead of the cannellini and cilantro instead of the basil. Omit the cheese and sprinkle with chopped pistachios if you like.

Peanut Mixed Rice. Omit the porcini and use vegetable oil instead of olive oil. When you're cooking the onion with the rice, add 1 large sweet potato, peeled and cut into ½-inch cubes. Use any red bean in place of the cannellini. Use 2 tablespoons (or more) peanut butter instead of the Parmesan and cilantro instead of the basil. Garnish with chopped peanuts.

Edamame and Asparagus Stir-Fry with Rice

Makes: 4 servings　　　Time: 20 minutes　　

A fast, simple dish, perfect for lunch, in which the rice is stirred in almost as an afterthought at the very end. The rice remains soft, while the asparagus and edamame retain a little crunch—a nice combo. Cooked quinoa or steel-cut oats are good substitutes for the rice.

1 pound asparagus, peeled if thick, cut into 2-inch lengths

Salt

3 tablespoons vegetable oil

1 tablespoon minced garlic

1 tablespoon minced ginger

1 small dried hot red chile (like Thai), or pinch of red chile flakes, or to taste

3 cups fresh or frozen edamame, thawed if you have time

1 tablespoon soy sauce, or to taste

2 cups cooked brown rice

Chopped scallions, for garnish

1. If the asparagus stalks are thin, skip to Step 2. If they're especially thick, put them in a large skillet (try not to crowd them too much), add water to cover and a pinch of salt. Turn the heat to high, cover the skillet, and cook until the asparagus is not quite tender (you should barely be able to pierce the thickest part with a knife). Plunge the asparagus into ice water to stop the cooking.

2. Dry out the skillet and set it over high heat until very hot, 3 to 4 minutes. Add the oil, then the asparagus. Cook, stirring, for about a minute. Add the garlic, ginger, and chile. Cook until the asparagus is dry and beginning to brown, 5 to 10 minutes. Stir in the edamame, soy sauce, and a small splash of water; cook, stirring and adding just enough water to keep everything from sticking, until the asparagus and edamame are tender, about 5 minutes more.

3. Add the rice and stir until combined, then turn off the heat and fish out the chile. Taste and add a sprinkling of salt and more soy sauce if necessary. Garnish with chopped scallions and serve hot or at room temperature.

Hippie Rice

Makes: 4 servings   Time: About 45 minutes

Sadly (or not), it sometimes feels that the only remnant of hippie culture in modern life is the popularity of health food. Unfortunately, much of what goes under the name "health food" tastes good only with the help of certain psychoactive drugs (come to think of it, there's another holdover), but hippies did have a few decent ideas in the kitchen. How wrong can you go with brown rice, broccoli, sunflower seeds, and raisins? For best results, serve while wearing a tie-dyed apron and playing folk music in a VW van.

⅓ cup sunflower seeds

1 cup any long-grain brown rice

Salt

1 head broccoli (about 1 pound), cored and roughly chopped

2 tablespoons olive oil

⅓ cup raisins

½ teaspoon red chile flakes, or to taste

Lemon wedges

1. Put the sunflower seeds in a medium saucepan over medium-low heat and toast, shaking the pan often, until they begin to brown but don't burn, 5 to 10 minutes. Remove the seeds from the pan and let cool in a big serving bowl.

2. Put the rice in the pan and add water to cover by about 1 inch. Add a pinch of salt and bring to a boil over medium-high heat, then adjust the heat so the mixture bubbles gently. Cover and cook until most of the water is absorbed and the rice is just getting tender, 20 to 30 minutes.

3. Pack the broccoli into the pan on top of the rice—don't stir; just leave it on top—and add a little more liquid if the water is evaporating too quickly. Replace the lid and continue cooking, adding a small amount of water if the pan boils dry, until the rice and broccoli are both tender, 5 to 10 more minutes. Transfer the rice and broccoli to the bowl with the sunflower seeds and toss with the oil, raisins, and red chile flakes. Taste and adjust the seasoning. Serve immediately or at room temperature with the lemon wedges.

Hippie Rice with Tofu. Use a large saucepan and add 1 pound cubed tofu to the pan along with the broccoli in Step 3. Use extra-firm or firm tofu if you want the cubes to keep their shape; use silken tofu if you want it to melt into the rice.

Grilled Eggplant and Scallions with Miso Rice

Makes: 4 servings   Time: About 45 minutes

Miso and eggplant are one of my favorite combinations—especially when I can get my hands on long, thin Asian eggplants—but you could use zucchini or portobello mushrooms instead. This dish is fantastic at room temperature, so feel free to make it an hour or more ahead of time.

1½ pounds eggplant

Salt

1 cup short-grain brown rice

1 bunch scallions, with a lot of the greens remaining

4 to 6 tablespoons vegetable oil

1 tablespoon minced ginger

⅓ cup any miso

2 teaspoons sesame oil

Black pepper

Soy sauce, for serving

1. Cut large eggplants into ½-inch slices or halve the long narrow ones. Put the slices in a colander, sprinkle them liberally with salt, and let them rest while you cook the rice.

2. Put the rice in a small saucepan with water to cover by about 1 inch. Add a pinch of salt and bring to a boil over medium-high heat, then adjust the heat so the mixture bubbles gently. Cover and cook for 30 to 40 minutes, checking occasionally to make sure the water is not evaporating too quickly (add a little more liquid if necessary).

3. Meanwhile, prepare a grill or turn on the broiler; the heat should be medium-high and the rack about 4 inches from the fire. Rinse the eggplant and pat dry. Brush or rub the eggplant and scallions with the oil until well coated. Grill or broil, turning once or twice, until deeply colored and tender, 5 to 10 minutes. (You may have to remove the scallions from the heat before you remove the eggplant.)

4. When the rice is tender and all the water has been absorbed, turn off the heat. Stir the ginger, miso, sesame oil, and a sprinkling of black pepper into the rice with a fork. Taste and adjust the seasoning. Serve the grilled vegetables on top of the rice, passing soy sauce at the table for drizzling.

Roasted Eggplant and Scallions with Miso Rice. For a deeper flavor and softer texture, toss the vegetables with a little of the miso paste during the last 5 minutes of roasting. Instead of grilling or broiling, heat the oven to 400°F. Spread the eggplant and scallions on a rimmed baking sheet and roast, turning once or twice, until lightly browned and tender, about 20 minutes for the scallions and 30 to 40 minutes for the eggplant.

Sushi Rice with Daikon and Sesame Seeds

Makes: 4 servings   Time: 1 hour

A simple cold or room-temperature dish that's more like a rice bowl than a salad. Use it as the base for all sorts of leftovers that you might like to add before serving. Try cooked, sliced meat or seafood, shredded chicken, or avocado cubes.

    1 cup short-grain brown rice

    Salt

    3 tablespoons rice vinegar

    1 tablespoon sugar

1 tablespoon minced ginger

1 pound daikon radishes, grated; or use raw turnips or kohlrabi

1 cup chopped scallions

2 tablespoons sesame seeds

2 tablespoons soy sauce, plus more for serving

Sesame oil, for serving

1. Put the rice in a medium saucepan. Add water to cover by about 1 inch and a large pinch of salt. Bring to a boil, then adjust the heat so that the mixture bubbles gently. Cover and cook for 20 to 30 minutes, checking occasionally to make sure the water is not evaporating too quickly (you can add a little more liquid if necessary). When the water has been absorbed, taste and see if the rice is tender. If not, add a little more water and continue to cook, covered, until it's tender.

2. While the rice is cooking, combine the vinegar, sugar, ginger, and 1 teaspoon salt in a small saucepan over medium heat. Cook, stirring, until the sugar dissolves, less than 5 minutes, remove from the heat, and let cool a bit.

3. When the rice is done, put it in a very large bowl. Toss the hot rice vigorously with a flat wooden paddle or spoon or a rubber spatula. While you're tossing and the rice is cooling, sprinkle the rice with the vinegar mixture. (You can make the rice up to this point an hour ahead; cover it with a damp towel and let it sit.)

4. Divide the rice among 4 serving bowls, then top with the grated daikon, scallions, sesame seeds, and soy sauce. Serve, passing sesame oil and more soy sauce at the table.

Baked Curried Rice
with Apples and Coconut

Makes: 4 servings   Time: About 1 hour, largely unattended

Baked brown rice is mostly hands-off—no fussing or checking for doneness, just a relaxing, undisturbed 45 minutes in the oven. Your reward for doing next to nothing is a pot of tender, fragrant, slightly spicy grains (if you want more heat, use up to a tablespoon more curry powder). This recipe and the variation would go perfectly with any simply seasoned pot of chickpeas or other beans.

  2 tablespoons vegetable oil

  1 tablespoon curry powder

  1 tablespoon minced ginger

  1 cup brown basmati rice

  Salt and black pepper

  One 14-ounce can coconut milk

  ¼ cup shredded, unsweetened coconut

  2 tart apples, cored and chopped

  ½ cup chopped fresh cilantro

  ¼ cup yogurt, optional

1. Heat the oven to 350°F. Put the oil in a large ovenproof saucepan over medium heat. A minute later, add the curry powder and ginger and cook, stirring, for about a minute. Add the rice and some salt and pepper; cook, stirring, until the rice is glossy and translucent, just a minute or 2.

2. Measure 1¾ cups of the coconut milk; stir it into the rice mixture. Bring to a boil, then cover tightly and transfer to the oven. Bake, undisturbed, for 45 minutes.

3. Meanwhile, put the shredded coconut in a small skillet over medium heat and toast, shaking the pan and stirring often, until it begins to brown, 5 to 10 minutes. Remove the rice from the oven, uncover, and use a fork to stir in the shredded coconut, apples, and cilantro. Replace the lid and let it rest for 10 minutes. Taste and adjust the seasoning and fluff again. Serve immediately or at room temperature, topped with yogurt if you like.

Ⓕ Fast   Ⓜ Make-Ahead   Ⓟ Pantry Staple

Baked Curried Mango Rice. Omit the shredded coconut and apples. Peel, pit, and chop 2 mangoes and stir them in after you take the rice out of the oven in Step 3.

Rice Pilaf with Apricots, Chickpeas, and Almonds

Makes: 4 servings   Time: About 1 hour, largely unattended

Both the main recipe and the superquick couscous variation benefit from resting off the heat after cooking, so this pilaf is easy to time with a slew of other dishes for buffets or holidays. The recipe is also a good place to use millet: Its cornlike flavor and grainy texture team nicely with the apricots and orange, and it cooks a little faster than brown rice.

½ cup slivered or chopped almonds

2 tablespoons olive oil, plus more for serving

1 small red onion, chopped

1 tablespoon minced garlic

1 tablespoon pimentón (smoked paprika)

Salt and black pepper

1 cup brown basmati rice

Juice of 1 orange

½ cup white wine

½ cup chopped dried apricots, or 1 cup chopped fresh apricots

1 cup cooked or canned chickpeas, drained

½ cup chopped fresh parsley

1. Put the almonds in a large, deep skillet or medium saucepan over medium heat. Toast, shaking the pan and stirring often, until they begin to brown but don't burn, 5 to 10 minutes. Remove the almonds from the pan.

2. Add 2 tablespoons oil to the skillet. When it's hot, add the onion and garlic. Cook, stirring, until the onion softens and begins to turn golden, 5 to

10 minutes. Add the paprika, salt, and pepper and continue to stir until fragrant, just another minute.

3. Add the rice and stir until it's glossy, completely coated with oil, and starting to color lightly, 3 to 5 minutes. Add the orange juice, wine, and 1½ cups water. Bring to a boil, then reduce the heat so it bubbles steadily. Cover the pan and cook until almost all of the liquid is absorbed and the rice is just tender, 40 to 50 minutes.

4. Stir in the apricots, chickpeas, and parsley; cover and remove from the heat. Let the pilaf rest for at least 10 minutes or up to 30 minutes. Taste and adjust the seasoning. Add the reserved almonds and a little more oil if you like, and fluff with a fork. Serve hot or at room temperature.

Couscous Pilaf with Apricots, Chickpeas, and Almonds. Ready in half the time. Substitute whole wheat couscous for the rice and reduce the amount of water to 1 cup. In Step 3, after stirring the couscous in the oil, add everything but the parsley to the skillet. Bring the mixture a boil, then cover and remove it from the heat. Let steep until the water is absorbed, 15 to 20 minutes. Add the almonds and parsley, fluff with a fork, and serve.

Swapping Brown Rice for White Rice in Any Recipe

Since brown rice cooks more slowly and absorbs more water than white rice, simply using brown instead of white rice in your go-to recipes usually won't work. So try this easy, foolproof technique: Bring a large pot of salted water to a boil and stir in the same quantity and type (short- or long-grain) of rice directed in the recipe—only brown, not white. Let the rice bubble and cook like pasta, for 10 to 15 minutes, then drain it. Use the parcooked brown rice immediately, let it sit in the strainer for up to an hour or so, or refrigerate for up to a couple days.

 Ⓕ Fast Ⓜ Make-Ahead Ⓟ Pantry Staple

Green Barley Pilaf

Makes: 4 servings   Time: 45 minutes with pearled barley, or 90 minutes with
                     hulled barley

Pilaf is a classic side dish, but you can easily turn it into a big main course. Here, lay some scallops or boneless chicken breasts on top for the last 10 minutes of cooking, or stir in some shrimp or squid before the resting time. Last-minute additions might include chopped nuts or chopped olives. Try the variation alongside tacos and refried beans.

> 2 tablespoons olive oil, plus more for serving
>
> 1 onion, chopped
>
> 1 tablespoon minced garlic
>
> 1 cup pearled or hulled barley
>
> 3 cups vegetable stock (for homemade, see pages 135 to 138) or water, or more as needed
>
> Salt and black pepper
>
> 1 pound spinach, roughly chopped

1. Put the oil in a deep skillet or large saucepan over medium-high heat. When it's hot, add the onion and garlic and cook, stirring, until softened, 3 to 5 minutes.

2. Add the barley and cook, stirring, until glossy, about 1 minute. Add the liquid and a good sprinkling of salt and pepper and bring to a boil.

3. Turn the heat down to low, cover, and cook until the grains are tender and the water is almost entirely absorbed, 15 to 25 minutes for pearled barley or 30 to 45 minutes (or more) for hulled. (Add a little more liquid if the grains are not ready but begin to look dry.) Uncover, remove from the heat, and stir in the spinach. Replace the lid and let rest off the heat for at least 10 minutes or up to 20 minutes. Combine and fluff the grains and spinach with a fork. Taste and adjust the seasoning. Serve hot or at room temperature, with a drizzle of olive oil if you like.

Green Barley Pilaf with Chile and Lime. In Step 1 as you cook the onion and garlic, add a dried chile or a minced fresh hot chile and the grated zest of 1 lime to the skillet. Stir in the juice of 2 limes just before serving.

Bulgur Chili with Beans and Loads of Veggies

Makes: 6 to 8 servings   Time: 1 hour, largely unattended

You'll find more chilies in the Beans chapter, but this one is here because its terrific texture comes from bulgur. It's a hearty stew, vegetable heavy with plenty of possibilities—zucchini, squash, eggplant, sweet potato, carrot, celery root, parsnip, celery, leafy greens, green beans, cauliflower, and corn kernels (frozen are fine) are all good choices. If you don't want too much heat, skip the dried chiles and proceed directly to Step 2.

Since this keeps and reheats so well, the ingredients here make a big batch. Serve it to a crowd, plan to eat it over a few days, or freeze what's left.

2 (or more) dried hot chiles (like chipotle), optional

Boiling water as needed

2 tablespoons olive oil

1 onion, chopped

1 red bell pepper, chopped

2 tablespoons minced garlic

3 tablespoons tomato paste

2 tablespoons chili powder

Salt and black pepper

3 cups chopped vegetables, alone or in combination (see the headnote)

3 cups chopped tomatoes (canned are fine; include their juice)

6 cups vegetable or chicken stock (for homemade, see pages 135 to 140) or water, plus more as needed

1 cup bulgur

2 cups cooked or canned kidney or pinto beans, drained

½ cup chopped fresh cilantro or scallions, for garnish

1. Put the chiles in a small bowl and add boiling water to cover. Let them soak until they're soft and pliable, 15 to 20 minutes. Drain, discard the stems, seeds, and veins, then chop finely.

(F) Fast   (M) Make-Ahead   (P) Pantry Staple

2. Put the oil in a large pot or Dutch oven over medium-high heat. When it's hot, add the onion, bell pepper, and garlic. Cook, stirring occasionally, until the onion is softened, 3 to 5 minutes. Stir in the tomato paste, the chiles (if you're using them), and chili powder. Sprinkle with salt and pepper and cook until fragrant, another minute or 2.

3. Add the vegetables, tomatoes, and stock. Bring to a boil, then turn the heat down so the mixture bubbles steadily. Cook, stirring occasionally, until the vegetables are tender and the mixture is thickened, 15 to 20 minutes.

4. Add the bulgur and cook, stirring occasionally and adjusting the heat so the chili keeps bubbling, until the bulgur plumps and becomes tender, 10 to 15 minutes. Add the beans and a little more liquid if the mixture looks dry. Cook until the beans heat through, 2 to 3 minutes. Taste and adjust the seasoning. Serve, garnished with cilantro or scallions if you like.

Bulgur Chili with Meat and Loads of Veggies. Omit the beans (or include them for an even heartier chili). At the beginning of Step 2, before adding the onion, bell pepper, and garlic to the hot oil, add 8 ounces hand-chopped or ground beef, pork, lamb, turkey, or chicken and cook, stirring, until the meat is no longer pink and begins to crisp, 5 to 10 minutes. Add the onion, pepper, and garlic to the pot and proceed with the recipe.

Red Bean Paella with Tomatoes

Makes: 4 servings   Time: About 45 minutes

Paella—real, legit paella—can be and *is* made with almost any ingredient that complements baked rice. Here's a juicy and rather lovely vegetarian paella that features beans and tomatoes. (For another one based on clams and chorizo, see page 315.) Here you must use ripe summer tomatoes (even overripe are fine; they mostly break down anyway). In the winter, try the egg variation—completely different and super.

Salt

1 cup short-grain brown rice

2½ cups vegetable stock (for homemade, see pages 135 to 138) or water

1½ pounds ripe tomatoes, cored and cut into thick wedges

Black pepper

4 tablespoons olive oil

1 onion, chopped

1 tablespoon minced garlic

1 tablespoon tomato paste

Pinch of saffron threads, optional

2 teaspoons pimentón (smoked paprika)

1 cup cooked or canned red beans, drained

Chopped fresh parsley, for garnish

1. Heat the oven to 450°F. Bring a medium pot of water to a boil and salt it. Stir in the rice, adjust the heat so that the water bubbles steadily, and cook, without stirring, for about 12 minutes. Drain. Use the pot to warm the stock over medium-low heat. Put the tomatoes in a medium bowl, sprinkle with salt and pepper, and drizzle with 1 tablespoon of the oil. Toss gently to coat.

2. Put the remaining 3 tablespoons oil in a 10- or 12-inch ovenproof skillet over medium-high heat. When it's hot, add the onion and garlic, sprinkle with salt and pepper, and cook, stirring occasionally, until the vegetables soften, 3 to 5 minutes. Stir in the tomato paste, saffron if you're using it, and paprika and cook for a minute more. Add the rice and beans and cook,

(F) Fast   (M) Make-Ahead   (P) Pantry Staple

stirring occasionally, until everything is coated with oil, another minute or 2. Carefully add the warm stock and stir until just combined.

3. Put the tomato wedges in a single layer on top of the rice and beans and drizzle with the juices that accumulated in the bottom of the bowl. Put the pan in the oven and roast, undisturbed, for 15 minutes. Check to see if the rice is dry and just tender. If not, return the pan to the oven for another 5 minutes. If the rice looks too dry at this point but still isn't quite done, add a small amount of stock or water. When the rice is ready, turn off the oven and let the paella sit for at least 5 minutes and up to 15 minutes.

4. Remove the pan from the oven and sprinkle with parsley. If you like, put the pan over high heat for a few minutes to develop a bit of a bottom crust (called *soccarat* in Spain) before serving either hot or at room temperature.

Simple Paella with Eggs. Omit the tomatoes. In Step 3, when the rice is out of the oven the first time to check for doneness, make 4 indentations in the top of the paella with a large spoon and carefully crack an egg into each. Proceed with the recipe, cooking the eggs just until the whites set up (on no account should the yolks overcook), anywhere from 5 to 10 minutes. To serve, scoop up a whole egg and some of the rice.

Lemony Zucchini Risotto

Makes: 4 servings   Time: 45 to 60 minutes

Risotto can be almost meager or incredibly luxurious; this one manages to be both, as the grated zucchini mostly melts away, leaving behind a creamy richness that doesn't depend on tons of rice or mounds of cheese. Parboiling the brown rice as directed in Step 1 (a little trick you can read more about on page 296) helps the rice absorb water quickly and evenly.

Salt

1 cup short-grain brown rice

2 tablespoons olive oil

1 onion, chopped

Black pepper

1/2 cup dry white wine or water

3 to 5 cups vegetable or chicken stock (for homemade, see pages 135 to 140) or water

4 small or 2 large zucchini (about 1 1/2 pounds), grated

Grated zest and juice of 1 lemon

1/2 cup grated Parmesan cheese, optional

1 tablespoon butter or additional olive oil, optional

1/2 cup chopped fresh basil, plus more for garnish, optional

1. Bring a medium pot of water to a boil and salt it. Stir in the brown rice, adjust the heat so that the water bubbles steadily, and cook, without stirring, for 10 to 15 minutes. Drain well.

2. Put the oil in a large, deep skillet over medium heat. When it's hot, add the onion and cook, stirring occasionally, until it softens, about 5 minutes. Add the rice and cook, stirring occasionally, until it is glossy and coated with oil, just a couple of minutes. Sprinkle with salt and pepper, then add the wine. Stir and let the liquid bubble away.

3. Begin to add the stock, about 1/2 cup at a time, stirring after each addition and every minute or so. When the stock is just about evaporated, add more.

(F) Fast   (M) Make-Ahead   (P) Pantry Staple

The mixture should be neither soupy nor dry. Keep the heat medium to medium-high and stir frequently.

4. After about 15 minutes of adding stock, stir in the zucchini and cook, stirring, until it releases its liquid and the mixture again becomes dry. Begin tasting the rice about 5 minutes later; you want it to be tender but with still a tiny bit of crunch. It could take as long as 45 minutes to reach this stage. When it does, stir in the lemon zest and juice, and the Parmesan, butter, and basil if you're using them. Taste and adjust the seasoning. Serve immediately, garnished with additional basil if you like.

Lemony Zucchini Risotto with Fried Eggs. When the risotto is almost done, put a medium skillet over medium heat for about a minute. Add 1 tablespoon olive oil or butter and swirl it around the pan. When the oil is hot, crack 4 eggs into the skillet. When the whites become opaque, a minute later, turn the heat to low and sprinkle the eggs with salt and pepper. Cook until the yolks are set as you like them and the whites are completely firm; cut through the uncooked parts, if necessary, to encourage the still-liquid white to spread over the surface of the pan. Put 1 fried egg on top of each serving of risotto.

Risi, Bisi, e Carote
(Rice, Peas, and Carrots)

Makes: 4 servings   Time: 40 minutes

The classic version of this dish (*risi e bisi*) is creamy with cheese and the rice's starch, but it's firmer than risotto. To make it with brown rice, let the grains cook until they just start to burst—you'll get much the same effect. The carrots are all-American, and they add both gorgeous color and a note of sweetness.

> 2 or 4 tablespoons olive oil
>
> 2 bacon slices or 1 ounce pancetta, chopped, optional
>
> ¾ cup short-grain brown rice
>
> 1 onion, chopped
>
> 4 carrots, chopped
>
> Salt and black pepper
>
> 3 cups fresh or frozen peas
>
> ¼ cup grated Parmesan cheese
>
> ¼ cup chopped fresh parsley

1. If you're using bacon, put 2 tablespoons oil in a large pot over medium heat. A minute later, add the bacon and cook until it is crisp and has rendered most of its fat, 5 to 10 minutes. If you're not using the bacon, put 4 tablespoons oil in the pot, heat, and proceed to Step 2.

2. Add the rice and cook, stirring constantly, until it is shiny and a little translucent, just a couple of minutes. Add the onion and carrots, sprinkle with salt and pepper, and continue to cook, stirring occasionally, for another minute or 2.

3. Add enough water to cover by about 1 inch, bring to a boil, and adjust the heat so that the mixture bubbles gently. Cook, stirring occasionally and adding water if needed to keep the mixture a little wet but not swimming, until the rice is fully tender, 20 to 30 minutes.

4. Stir in the peas and continue to cook, stirring occasionally, until the mixture is no longer soupy but not bone dry. Stir in the Parmesan and parsley and taste and adjust the seasoning. Serve hot or warm.

(F) Fast   (M) Make-Ahead   (P) Pantry Staple

Crisp Brown Rice Cake

Makes: 6 to 8 servings   Time: 2 hours, largely unattended

Cooking brown rice until the grains burst and release all of their starch allows you to make a perfectly crisp cake without adding any binder. You can slice it into wedges and garnish simply with soy sauce and chopped scallions, or use the whole cake as a bed for any stir-fry or Asian-style braised dish. Be sure to synchronize the flavor of the oil here with whatever you're serving it with.

> 2 cups brown basmati rice
>
> Salt
>
> Boiling water as needed
>
> 4 tablespoons vegetable or olive oil

1. Put the rice in a large pot along with a big pinch of salt. Add enough water to cover by 1½ inches. Bring to a boil, then adjust the heat so the mixture bubbles gently.

2. Cook, stirring occasionally and adding more boiling water if the rice begins to stick to the bottom, until the grains are very tender and burst, about an hour. When the rice is starchy and very thick, transfer it to a bowl and put it in the fridge to cool, at least 30 minutes and up to a few hours.

3. When the rice is cool enough that it will easily hold its shape, add 2 tablespoons of the oil to a large skillet over medium-high heat and swirl it around. When hot, add the rice to the skillet, smooth out the top, and cook until the bottom is golden brown and crisp, about 15 minutes.

4. Carefully put a large plate over the skillet and flip it to turn out the cake. Add the remaining 2 tablespoons of oil to the pan, swirl it around, and gently slide the cake off the plate and back into the skillet, uncooked side down, all in one piece. Cook until this side is also golden brown, then cut into wedges if you like, and serve hot, warm, or at room temperature.

Polenta "Pizza" with Stewed Green Olives and Tomatoes

Makes: 4 servings   Time: About 45 minutes, plus 1 hour for chilling

Both the "pizza"—firm-cooked polenta pressed into a pan—and the sauce can be made up to a day before serving, so this impressive and unusual dish is ideal for entertaining. If you prefer soft polenta (or if you're in a hurry), start the vegetables first and then make the polenta just through the end of Step 1. To turn this into a vegan dish, substitute nondairy milk (or water) for the whole cow's milk.

> 3 tablespoons olive oil, plus more as needed
>
> 1 cup coarse cornmeal
>
> Salt
>
> ½ cup milk, preferably whole
>
> Black pepper
>
> 2 onions, chopped
>
> 1 tablespoon minced garlic
>
> ¾ cup green olives, pitted and roughly chopped
>
> 3 cups chopped tomatoes (canned are fine; include their juice)
>
> ½ cup chopped fresh basil, plus more for garnish
>
> ½ cup grated Parmesan cheese, optional

1. Brush a layer of oil on a pizza pan or baking sheet. Put the cornmeal and a large pinch of salt in a medium saucepan; slowly whisk in 2½ cups water and the milk to make a lump-free slurry. Set the pot over medium-high heat and bring almost to a boil, then reduce the heat to low. Cook, whisking frequently, until thick, 10 to 15 minutes. If the mixture becomes too thick, whisk in a bit more water; you want the consistency to be like thick oatmeal.

2. Stir 1 tablespoon of the oil into the polenta. Spoon it onto the prepared pan, working quickly so the polenta doesn't harden; spread it evenly ½ inch thick all over. (It doesn't have to be a perfect circle.) Sprinkle with salt and pepper, cover the polenta with plastic wrap, and refrigerate until firm, 1 hour or more (you can refrigerate it for up to 24 hours if you prefer).

Ⓕ Fast   Ⓜ Make-Ahead   Ⓟ Pantry Staple

3. Heat the oven to 450°F. Bake the polenta until it begins to brown and crisp on the edges, 25 to 30 minutes. Meanwhile, put 2 tablespoons oil in a large skillet over medium heat. Add the onions and garlic and cook, stirring occasionally, until the onions begin to soften, about 5 minutes. Add the olives and tomatoes, sprinkle with salt and pepper, and cook, stirring occasionally, until the tomatoes break down and thicken a bit, about 15 minutes. (You can make the stewed olives ahead to this point and refrigerate for up to a day; gently reheat before proceeding.) Stir in the basil, taste and adjust the seasoning, and keep warm.

4. When the polenta cake is ready, cut it into wedges. Serve the stewed olives and tomatoes over the pieces of polenta cake; drizzle with more olive oil and garnish with more basil and the cheese if you like.

Polenta "Pizza" with Stewed Green Olives, Tomatoes, and Squid. Use black olives here if you prefer. Omit the Parmesan. Clean 12 ounces squid and cut it into bite-size pieces. Add it to the skillet after the tomatoes are done in Step 3. Cook, stirring once or twice, until the squid is opaque but not tough, 2 to 3 minutes. Remove from the heat, stir in the basil, and proceed with the recipe.

Creamed Corn and Millet

Makes: 4 servings   Time: 45 minutes

A very yellow dish, and lovely. (I sometimes add a little parsley at the end for more color contrast, but that's entirely optional.) Millet becomes quite creamy when you cook it until the grains burst, and a splash of cream adds a bit of richness. Change up the flavors by substituting other seasonings for the herbs (nutmeg is traditional, jalapeño is awesome). Try using this as a bed for grilled vegetables, meat, seafood, or chicken.

> 2 tablespoons olive oil
>
> 1 onion, chopped
>
> 1 tablespoon minced garlic
>
> 1 cup millet
>
> 2 cups corn kernels (frozen are fine)
>
> Salt and black pepper
>
> ½ cup cream or half-and-half, optional
>
> 1 tablespoon chopped fresh tarragon, or 2 tablespoons chopped fresh chives

1. Put the oil in a pot over medium heat. When the oil is hot, add the onion and garlic and cook, stirring occasionally, until soft, about 5 minutes.

2. Add the millet, half the corn, 3 cups water, and a sprinkling of salt and pepper. Bring to a boil, then lower the heat so the mixture bubbles gently. Cover and cook, stirring occasionally, until the millet bursts and the corn has fallen apart, about 30 minutes; add a little more water if the mixture becomes too dry.

3. Add the remaining 1 cup corn and the cream if you're using it. Cook, stirring occasionally, until the corn is tender, 5 to 10 minutes, adding more water if you want a thinner consistency. Stir in the tarragon or chives and taste and adjust the seasoning. Serve warm. (You can refrigerate the finished dish up to 3 days.)

Coconut Creamed Corn and Millet. Use one 14-ounce can coconut milk in place of 1½ cups of the water in Step 2. Omit the cream. Instead of tarragon or chives, stir in ½ cup chopped mint or cilantro.

Farro or Wheat Berries
with Grapes and Rosemary

Makes: 4 servings   Time: 30 minutes

The nutty flavor and slightly chewy texture of farro—a traditional Tuscan grain—is extraordinary here, but if you can't find it, use wheat berries, Kamut, barley, or short-grain brown rice. (All will take somewhat longer to cook, the wheat berries the longest.) For even more fruitiness—and a gorgeous color—use red wine for the liquid.

3 tablespoons olive oil

1 large red onion, halved and sliced

1 tablespoon minced garlic

1 cup farro

Salt

2 cups any stock (for homemade, see pages 135 to 140), red wine, or
    water

2 cups red or green grapes (seedless or seeded)

1 tablespoon chopped fresh rosemary, or 1 teaspoon dried

Black pepper

1. Put the oil in a large, deep skillet over medium-high heat. When it's hot, add the onion and garlic and cook, stirring occasionally, until softened, 3 to 5 minutes.

2. Add the farro and cook, stirring, until it is completely coated in oil and beginning to toast, a minute or 2. Sprinkle with salt, then stir in the stock and bring to a boil. Reduce the heat so the mixture bubbles gently and cover.

3. Cook until the grains are just getting tender and the liquid is almost entirely absorbed, 15 to 20 minutes. Stir in the grapes, rosemary, and a good amount of black pepper. Cover and cook for another 5 minutes or so. Fluff the farro with a fork and taste and adjust the seasoning. Serve hot or at room temperature.

Farro with Grapes and Sausage. In Step 1, begin by frying 8 ounces crumbled sausage in the olive oil until it's browned a bit, 5 to 10 minutes. Stir in the onion and garlic and proceed with the recipe.

Farro with Grapes and White Beans. Add 1 cup cooked, drained cannellini beans along with the grapes in Step 3.

Chipotle Quinoa with Corn and Black Beans

Makes: 4 servings   Time: About 40 minutes

Quinoa originally comes from Peru, so it's the natural choice to complement the other Latin American ingredients and flavors in this dish. If you're feeling adventurous, toss some chopped mango into the pot when the quinoa is just about tender. And remember that the adobo sauce in which chipotles are canned is very hot, so use it judiciously.

3 tablespoons olive oil

1 onion, chopped

1 tablespoon minced garlic

2 (or more) canned chipotle chiles, minced, with some of their adobo sauce

1 tablespoon chopped fresh oregano, or 1 teaspoon dried

¾ cup quinoa, rinsed and drained

Salt and black pepper

1 cup cooked or canned black beans, drained

½ cup corn kernels (frozen are fine)

1½ cups vegetable stock (for homemade, see pages 135 to 138), beer, or water

Lime wedges

Ⓕ Fast   Ⓜ Make-Ahead   Ⓟ Pantry Staple

1. Put the oil in a large skillet over medium heat. When it's hot, add the onion and garlic and cook, stirring, until the onion is soft, about 5 minutes. Add the chipotles and adobo (use almost none to a lot, depending on how hot you want the finished dish) and oregano and continue stirring for about 1 minute.

2. Turn the heat up to medium-high, add the quinoa, and sprinkle with salt and pepper. Continue to cook, stirring frequently, for 3 to 5 minutes. Add the beans, corn, stock, and some salt and pepper and bring to a boil. Stir, cover, and reduce the heat to low. Cook, undisturbed, for 15 minutes.

3. Uncover and test the quinoa for doneness. If the kernels are still crunchy, make sure there's enough liquid to keep the bottom of the pan moist; cover and cook for another 5 minutes or so. When they're tender, taste and adjust the seasoning. Serve warm or at room temperature with lime wedges.

Chipotle Quinoa with Corn, Black Beans, and Shrimp. When the quinoa is almost tender, uncover it, add 8 ounces chopped peeled shrimp and stir well. Cover and cook over low heat for about 5 minutes before serving.

Giant Quinoa "Tamale" with Tomatillo Salsa

Makes: 6 to 8 servings   Time: About 2 hours, largely unattended

Don't let the time and number of steps here put you off: This loaf is a fraction of the work of traditional tamales, and all of the components can be made ahead for last-minute assembly. I like the tamale a little soft, with a center that oozes a bit, but if you want a firmer tamale-like texture, bake the loaf uncovered for another 15 or 20 minutes.

Use the tomatillo salsa recipe on its own for a quick sauce that keeps well and comes in handy for serving with steamed vegetables, beans, fish, or tortilla chips (for homemade, see page 47).

1 pound tomatillos (about 5 or 6 large), husked and rinsed (canned are fine; drain and reserve their juice)

1 large poblano or other fresh mild green chile

1 large onion, roughly chopped

4 garlic cloves, smashed

2 tablespoons olive oil, plus more for greasing the loaf pan

2 cups quinoa, rinsed and drained

Salt

1 tablespoon chopped fresh oregano, or 1 teaspoon dried

2 tablespons lime juice

Black pepper

½ teaspoon baking powder

1 cup crumbled queso fresco or grated Monterey Jack, plus more for garnish

1 tablespoon chili powder

½ cup chopped fresh cilantro, for garnish

1. Heat the oven to 400°F. Put the tomatillos, chile, onion, and garlic on a rimmed baking sheet and drizzle with 2 tablespoons of oil. Roast, turning once or twice, until the chile skin is blistered and everything is browned,

(F) Fast   (M) Make-Ahead   (P) Pantry Staple

40 to 45 minutes. Remove the pan but leave the oven at 400°F if you're making the tamale right away.

2. Meanwhile, put the quinoa in a large pot along with a big pinch of salt. Add water to cover by about 1½ inches. Bring to a boil, then adjust the heat so the mixture bubbles gently. Cover and cook, stirring occasionally, until the grains are very tender and begin to burst, 25 to 30 minutes. If the grains get too dry, add just enough water to keep them submerged. When the grains are starchy and thick, remove from the heat. (You can cook the quinoa up to a day ahead and refrigerate; return to room temperature before proceeding.)

3. Remove the skin, seeds, and stem from the chile and put the flesh in a blender or food processor along with the tomatillos, onion, garlic, and any pan juices. Add the oregano, lime juice, ½ cup water (or the reserved canned tomatillo liquid), and a large pinch of salt and pepper. Blend or process until smooth, adding enough water to thin the mixture into a pourable sauce; taste and adjust the seasoning. (The salsa can be made ahead to this point and covered and refrigerated for up to a day; return to room temperature or gently warm right before serving.)

4. When you're ready to make the tamale, generously grease a 9 × 5-inch loaf pan with some oil. Mix the baking powder and a pinch of salt into the quinoa with a fork. The consistency should be thick but spreadable; if it's too stiff, add a few drops of water. Spread half of the quinoa mixture in the bottom of the pan and sprinkle with the queso fresco and chili powder. Add the remaining quinoa, smooth it out evenly, and press down a bit to seal the loaf. Cover the pan tightly with foil. (At this point the quinoa loaf can be covered and refrigerated for up to several hours.)

5. Bake the loaf for 30 minutes, then remove the foil and bake until the top is golden brown, another 30 minutes or so. Remove the pan from the oven and let the tamale sit for 10 minutes before turning it out onto a platter. Garnish with the cilantro and a little more cheese, cut the tamale into slices, and serve, passing the salsa at the table.

Fish Kebabs over Warm Olive Tabbouleh

Makes: 4 servings   Time: 45 minutes

The hypnotic fragrance of warm olives, garlic, and olive oil soaks all the way into the cooked bulgur and even flavors the kebabs once you lay them on top.

½ cup bulgur

Salt

2 tablespoons olive oil, plus more as needed

½ cup black olives, pitted and chopped

1 tablespoon minced garlic

1 cucumber, peeled, seeded, and chopped

1 cup chopped fresh parsley

1 cup chopped fresh mint

3 lemons: 1 juiced and 2 cut into wedges

Black pepper

12 ounces firm white fish (see page 22), cut into 4 chunks

2 cups cherry tomatoes

2 red onions, cut into wedges

1. If you're using wooden skewers, soak them in water for 20 to 30 minutes (see page 69). Prepare a grill to medium-high heat and put the rack about 4 inches from the fire. Put the bulgur in a small pot with a pinch of salt and water to cover by about 1 inch (no more). Bring to a gentle boil and cook, without stirring, until the water boils off and the bulgur is tender, 5 to 10 minutes, depending on the grind. Fluff the grains with a fork and transfer them to a large bowl to cool.

2. Put 2 tablespoons oil in a large, deep skillet over medium heat. A minute later, add the olives and garlic and cook, stirring occasionally, until the garlic begins to color, 3 to 5 minutes. Pour the mixture over the bulgur and add the cucumber, parsley, mint, and lemon juice. Toss with a fork to combine, adding lots of pepper and enough oil to moisten everything. Taste and adjust the seasoning. (You can make the tabbouleh to this point and refrigerate it for up to a day.)

(F) Fast   (M) Make-Ahead   (P) Pantry Staple

3. Thread the fish, tomatoes, and red onions onto the skewers to make 4 kebabs (the kebabs will be easier to turn if you use 2 skewers per kebab). Brush them with oil and sprinkle with salt and pepper. Grill, turning as each side browns, until the fish is tender but not dry and the tomatoes and onions are a little charred, about 2 minutes per side or 5 minutes total. Serve the kebabs on top of the tabbouleh with the lemon wedges.

Pared-Down Paella with Peas, Clams, and Chorizo

Makes: 4 servings   Time: About 45 minutes

This easy paella is perfect when you don't want to use the oven. If you can't find Spanish-style smoked chorizo, or if you'd rather skip the meat, cook the onion, pepper, and garlic with a good sprinkling of pimentón (smoked paprika) or a pinch of saffron. Shrimp, scallops, and mussels are all potential replacements for the clams.

1 tablespoon olive oil

8 ounces Spanish chorizo or other smoked sausage, cubed

1 onion, chopped

1 red bell pepper, chopped

1 tablespoon minced garlic

1 cup long-grain brown rice

Salt and black pepper

1 ripe tomato, chopped

1 cup fresh or frozen peas

2 pounds littleneck or other hard-shell clams, well scrubbed, those with broken shells discarded

½ cup chopped fresh parsley, for garnish

Lemon wedges

1. Put the oil in a large, deep skillet over medium-high heat. When it's hot, add the chorizo and cook, stirring occasionally, until lightly browned, 3 to 5 minutes. Add the onion, bell pepper, and garlic and cook, stirring occasionally, until the onion turns translucent, 3 to 5 minutes more.

2. Stir in the rice, sprinkle with salt and pepper, and cook, stirring, until the rice is glossy and completely coated with oil, just a minute or 2. Add the tomato and 2 cups water. Stir, adjust the heat so that the liquid boils steadily but not violently, and cover.

3. Cook for 30 minutes before checking for doneness; add a little water if the rice is dry but not yet tender. Cover and cook until the rice is just done and the liquid is absorbed, another 5 to 10 minutes. Stir in the peas and the clams, replace the lid, and continue cooking until the clams are open, 3 to 5 minutes (if any don't, you can open them with a butter knife). If you want a crunchy crust of toasted rice to form at the bottom of the pan (*soccarat*), uncover the pot and turn the heat up so the rice sizzles. Cook, without stirring, until you can smell the rice toasting (but not burning), then turn off the heat. Remove the clams from the shells and return them to the pot if you like. Taste and adjust the seasoning and toss. Serve, garnished with parsley and lemon wedges.

Ⓕ Fast   Ⓜ Make-Ahead   Ⓟ Pantry Staple

Bouillabaisse with Fennel over Grits

This recipe requires two pots going at the same time—one for the grits and one for the fish and vegetable stew—but it's worth it: The result is an unusual but perfectly sensible combination, a kind of legitimate Creole French-Southern thing that also smacks of the Mediterranean. If you're feeling harried, try the variation, which replaces the grits with low-maintenance rice.

> 1 cup grits or coarse cornmeal
>
> Salt
>
> 3 tablespoons olive oil
>
> 3 fennel bulbs, cored and thinly sliced, fronds roughly chopped and reserved
>
> 2 leeks, trimmed, well rinsed, and cut into coins, white and tender green parts only (or use onions)
>
> 1 tablespoon minced garlic
>
> Grated zest from 1 orange
>
> Big pinch of saffron, optional
>
> 1 dried hot chile, or pinch of cayenne, or to taste
>
> 2 cups chopped tomatoes (canned are fine; drain their juice)
>
> About 1 pound almost any seafood (like monkfish, cod, scallops, squid, or shrimp), peeled, skinned, boned, and cut into chunks as needed (see page 22)
>
> 2 carrots or parsnips, cut into coins
>
> 2 cups vegetable, shrimp, or fish stock (for homemade, see pages 135 to 138); dry white wine; or water; plus more as needed
>
> Black pepper

1. Put the grits and a large pinch of salt in a medium saucepan; slowly whisk in 3 cups water to make a lump-free slurry. Set the pot over medium-high heat and bring almost to a boil. Reduce the heat to low and cook, whisking frequently, until thick, 10 to 15 minutes. If the mixture becomes too thick, whisk in a bit more water; you want the consistency to be like oatmeal.

2. Meanwhile, put 2 tablespoons of the oil in a large pot or Dutch oven over medium heat. Add the sliced fennel, leeks, garlic, and orange zest and cook, stirring occasionally, until softened, about 5 minutes. Add the saffron if you're using it and the chile or cayenne and cook for about a minute.

3. Add the tomatoes, seafood, carrots, and stock, adding enough extra stock to just cover the fish and vegetables. Bring to a boil, cover, and turn off the heat. Let the pot rest for about 5 minutes. The carrots you just added should be crisp-tender and the seafood should be opaque and cooked through; if not, return the pot to medium heat for a couple of minutes. Keep the lid on the pot until the stew is ready.

4. By now the grits should be thickened and cooked; remove the pot from the heat and whisk in the remaining 1 tablespoon oil and a lot of black pepper. Then taste and adjust the stew's seasoning. Serve the stew over the grits, garnished with the reserved fennel fronds.

Bouillabaisse with Fennel over Rice. You can use just about any other grain as a base here. About 20 minutes before making the bouillabaisse, put 1 cup brown rice in a medium pot with a pinch of salt. Add enough water to cover by about 1 inch, cover, and bring to a boil. Adjust the heat so that the mixture bubbles gently and cook, stirring occasionally, until the rice is tender, about 40 minutes. Serve the bouillabaisse over the rice instead of grits.

(F) Fast (M) Make-Ahead (P) Pantry Staple

Wild Rice with Celery and Steamed Salmon

Makes: 4 servings   Time: About 1 hour

Common as it is, celery is underappreciated, but it has a wonderful herbaceous flavor when cooked. The hearts are tender and mild and the leaves make a terrific garnish. The idea here is to cook the dish long enough for the celery to melt and the rice to become thick and soft, but if you prefer firmer rice, use a little less liquid and cook for 5 to 10 fewer minutes before adding the salmon.

To gild the lily, stir in some dried cranberries or fresh blueberries or blackberries before adding the fish. (Fruit is also nice if you omit the salmon and serve this as a side dish.)

    1 head celery (about 1 pound)

    2 tablespoons olive oil

    1 onion, chopped

    1 tablespoon minced garlic

    1 cup wild rice

    3½ cups vegetable or fish stock (for homemade, see pages 135 to 138) or
        water

    1 bay leaf

    Salt and black pepper

    2 thick salmon steaks (about 8 ounces), preferably wild (see page 22)

    Lemon wedges

1. Remove the outer stalks from the celery and chop them. Reserve the tender celery heart and its leaves from the center of the head.

2. Put the oil in a deep skillet over medium heat. When it's hot, add the onion and garlic and cook, stirring, until the onion begins to soften, about 5 minutes. Add the chopped celery and wild rice and continue to cook, stirring frequently, until the rice is fragrant and glossy, just a couple minutes. Stir in the stock, bay leaf, and some salt and pepper and bring to a boil.

3. Adjust the heat so that the mixture bubbles gently, cover, and cook, undisturbed, until the rice is very tender and just beginning to burst, 30 to 40 minutes (or more). At this point there should still be a little liquid at the bottom of the pan (no more than about ¼ inch); if not, add a little water.

4. Put the salmon on top of the rice, sprinkle with a little salt and pepper, and replace the lid. Steam until the fish is done (a thin knife can be inserted with little resistance), 5 to 10 minutes. Meanwhile, chop the reserved celery heart and leaves. Remove the salmon and cut each steak in half. Fluff the rice with a fork, discard the bay leaf, and taste and adjust the seasoning. Serve the fish on top of the rice, topped with the chopped celery leaves and heart and the lemon wedges.

Wild Rice with Celery and Grilled or Broiled Salmon. Ten minutes before the rice is done, prepare a grill or turn on the broiler; the heat should be medium-high and the rack about 4 inches from the fire. Brush the salmon with plenty of olive oil, sprinkle with salt and pepper, and grill, turning once, for a total of 5 to 10 minutes. Serve as described in the main recipe.

Wild Rice with Celery and Pan-Cooked Salmon. Ten minutes before the rice is done, put a heavy skillet over medium heat for about a minute, then add 2 tablespoons olive oil. Add the salmon to the pan, sprinkle with salt and pepper, and raise the heat to medium-high. Turn the salmon over after 4 minutes, then continue cooking until cooked through, another 3 to 5 minutes (or a minute or 2 less for medium-rare if you prefer). Serve as described in the main recipe.

 Ⓕ Fast Ⓜ Make-Ahead Ⓟ Pantry Staple

Vegetable and Shrimp Fried Rice

Makes: 4 servings   Time: 30 minutes

Think of this as a stir-fry with a little added rice, rather than a ton of rice with a few vegetables. But don't feel you must use the exact ingredients in the proportions listed here. Take whatever you have on hand and toss it in the skillet. (If you use harder vegetables, like broccoli, cauliflower, or asparagus, cut them into very small pieces or parboil them before adding.) And if you don't have leftover rice in the fridge, use whatever grain you do.

3 tablespoons vegetable oil

½ cup sliced scallions, plus more for garnish

1 cup bean sprouts

1 cup snow or snap peas

1 red bell pepper, roughly chopped

1 celery stalk, sliced

1 carrot, cut into coins

4 to 8 ounces shrimp, peeled and roughly chopped (see page 22)

1 tablespoon minced garlic

1 tablespoon minced ginger

1 cup cooked long-grain brown rice, preferably leftover and chilled

¼ cup rice wine, sherry, dry white wine, or water

2 tablespoons soy sauce

1 tablespoon sesame oil

Salt and black pepper

1. Put 1 tablespoon of the oil in a large skillet over high heat. When it's hot, add the scallions, bean sprouts, snow peas, bell pepper, celery, and carrot and cook, stirring occasionally, until they soften and begin to brown, 5 to 10 minutes. Lower the heat if the mixture threatens to scorch. Transfer the vegetables to a bowl with a slotted spoon.

2. Add another tablespoon oil to the pan, followed by the shrimp. Cook and stir until the pieces are uniformly pink, 2 to 3 minutes. Add them to the bowl with the vegetables. Put the remaining 1 tablespoon oil in the skillet, followed by the garlic and ginger. About 15 seconds later, begin to add the rice, a bit at a time, breaking up any clumps with your fingers and stirring it into the oil.

3. When all the rice is added, return the shrimp and vegetables to the pan and stir to combine. Add the rice wine and cook, stirring, for about a minute. Add the soy sauce and sesame oil, then taste and season with salt and pepper. Serve, garnished with the extra scallions.

Scallop or Squid Vegetable Fried Rice. Use sea scallops (sliced in half crosswise) or cleaned squid (cut into bite-size pieces) instead of the shrimp.

Spicy Fried Rice with Bean Sprouts, Chicken, and Peanuts

Makes: 4 servings   Time: 30 minutes

Toss typical pad Thai ingredients—bean sprouts, fish sauce, and peanuts—with a little cooked brown rice for a quick stir-fry. To vary, use shrimp or tofu instead of chicken or omit it altogether and just add one or two more eggs. This dish is also wonderful with leftover quinoa or barley.

3 tablespoons vegetable oil

½ cup sliced scallions

1 carrot, chopped

3 cups bean sprouts

8 ounces boneless, skinless chicken breast or thighs, cut into pieces of the same size

1 tablespoon minced garlic, or to taste

2 cups cooked long-grain brown rice, preferably chilled

1 egg

½ cup coconut milk

2 tablespoons nam pla (fish sauce)

Salt and black pepper

        Fast   Ⓜ Make-Ahead   Ⓟ Pantry Staple

¼ cup chopped peanuts

½ cup chopped fresh basil, preferably Thai

1 or more small fresh hot green chiles (preferably Thai), seeded and sliced

Lime wedges

1. Put 1 tablespoon of the oil in a large skillet over high heat. When it's hot, add the scallions, carrot, and bean sprouts and cook, stirring occasionally, until they soften and begin to brown, 3 to 5 minutes. Lower the heat if the mixture threatens to scorch. Transfer the vegetables to a bowl with a slotted spoon.

2. Add another tablespoon of the oil to the pan, followed by the chicken pieces; cook, stirring occasionally, over high heat until the chicken is no longer pink, 3 to 5 minutes. Add to the bowl with the vegetables, leaving as much oil in the pan as possible.

3. Put the remaining 1 tablespoon oil in the skillet, followed by the garlic. About 15 seconds later, begin to add the rice, a bit at a time, breaking up any clumps with your fingers and stirring it into the oil. When all the rice is added, make a well in its center and break the egg into it; scramble it a bit, then incorporate it into the rice.

4. Return the chicken and vegetables to the pan and stir to integrate. Add the coconut milk and cook, stirring, until most of the liquid has boiled off, just a minute or so. Add the fish sauce, then taste and season with salt and pepper. Turn off the heat and stir in the peanuts, basil, and chiles. Serve with the lime wedges.

Spicy Fried Rice with Carrots, Pork, and Peanuts. Use 2 grated carrots and pork (preferably sliced pork shoulder) instead of the carrot, bean sprouts, and chicken.

Crisp Rice Cakes
with Stir-Fried Vegetables and Chicken

Makes: 4 servings   Time: 45 minutes with precooked rice   Ⓜ Ⓟ

Made from seasoned soft-cooked brown basmati rice, these crisp rice cakes are a real treat—and an amazing alternative to plain rice—when topped with stir-fries. You can even make a large batch, wrap tightly, and freeze for up to several months; they reheat well in a hot oven (or even a microwave in a pinch). Or form them into mini cakes to serve for appetizers.

3 cups soft-cooked brown basmati rice (see page 273)

Salt and black pepper

1 tablespoon sesame oil

3 tablespoons vegetable oil, or more as needed

12 ounces boneless, skinless chicken thighs or breasts, chopped into small pieces

1 onion, chopped

2 tablespoons minced garlic

2 large carrots, chopped

3 celery stalks, chopped

2 cups snow peas

1 tablespoon nam pla (fish sauce)

Juice of 1 lime

Chopped fresh cilantro, for garnish

1. Heat the oven to 200°F. Sprinkle the rice with salt and pepper if necessary, then stir in the sesame oil with a fork. Use your hands to form the rice into four 1-inch-thick cakes.

2. Put 2 tablespoons of the vegetable oil in a large skillet over medium heat. When it's hot, add the cakes to the skillet, working in batches if necessary, and cook, turning once and until golden brown, 3 to 5 minutes per side. Transfer the cakes to the oven to keep them warm.

Ⓕ Fast   Ⓜ Make-Ahead   Ⓟ Pantry Staple

3. Put the remaining 1 tablespoon vegetable oil in the same skillet over medium-high heat. After a minute, add the chicken and sprinkle with salt and pepper. Let it sizzle for a couple minutes before stirring for the first time, then cook and stir until the chicken is browned and just cooked through, 3 to 5 minutes for breast meat, or a couple minutes longer for thighs.

4. Remove the chicken from the pan and pour in a little more oil if it looks dry. Add the onion and garlic; cook and stir for 30 seconds or so. Add the carrots and celery; cook, stirring occasionally, until they just begin to soften, 3 to 5 minutes. Add the snow peas; cook and stir until the vegetables are tender but still have a little crunch, another minute or 2. Stir in the fish sauce, a few tablespoons water, the lime juice, and the chicken; cook, stirring, until the sauce thickens a bit, about a minute. Taste and adjust the seasoning. Serve the stir-fry on top of the cakes, garnished with cilantro.

Arroz con Pollo—and Then Some

Makes: 4 servings   Time: About 1 hour, largely unattended

There are all forms of arroz con pollo, but they all have in common chicken, rice, and onions. Stock is optional (the chicken turns water into "stock" anyway), as is saffron, and peas and beans are frequent visitors. To take the classic dish even further, add minced garlic, a chopped red bell pepper, or some chopped tomato along with the rice. Or take the dish out of Latin America by varying the seasonings: cardamom, cloves, and cinnamon for an Indian-style biryani; or use sesame oil, scallions, fresh ginger, and cilantro for a Chinese-style spin. It's no longer arroz con pollo at that point, but it's really good.

3 tablespoons olive oil

1 large or 2 medium onions, halved and sliced

Salt and black pepper

1 cup short-grain brown rice

1 bay leaf

Pinch of saffron threads, optional

4 bone-in chicken thighs

3 cups chicken or vegetable stock (for homemade, see pages 135 to 140)
    or water

1 cup cooked or canned pinto or cranberry beans, drained

1 cup fresh or frozen peas

Chopped fresh parsley, for garnish

Lemon or lime wedges, for serving

1. Put the oil in a large, deep skillet over medium-high heat. A minute later, add the onion and a sprinkling of salt and pepper. Cook, stirring occasionally, until the onion softens and becomes translucent, 3 to 5 minutes.

2. Add the rice and stir until it's coated with oil, a minute or 2; add the bay leaf, sprinkle with the saffron if you're using it, and stir again. Nestle the chicken pieces in the rice, add a little more salt and pepper, and pour in the stock. Bring the mixture to a boil, then adjust the heat so that the mixture bubbles gently but steadily.

3. Cover and cook until all the liquid is absorbed, the rice is tender, and the chicken is cooked through, 30 to 40 minutes; the bird is done when an instant-read thermometer inserted into the thickest part of the thigh reads 155° to 165°F. Stir in the beans and peas. Cover, turn the heat down very low, and heat the dish through for a few minutes. (At this point, you may keep the dish warm for another 15 minutes off heat.) Remove the bay leaf, taste and adjust the seasoning, and fluff the rice with a fork. Garnish with parsley and serve with lemon or lime wedges.

Chile-Chicken Chilaquiles

Makes: 4 servings   Time: 45 minutes

Everywhere bread is traditional, people developed the means to use it stale—think of Italy's crostini, or *fattoush*, the pita salads of the Middle East. Chilaquiles—scrambled tortilla strips—are Mexico's contribution. Traditional versions often include eggs and/or salsa to soften and flavor the tortillas, with meat stirred in as almost an afterthought. To make this vegetarian, skip the chicken and add a couple of eggs scrambled during the last few minutes of cooking; to make it vegan, add a handful of cooked or canned pinto beans instead.

One technical note: Charring and peeling poblanos is the classic method, but if you cut them up small or thin enough, you can skip this step.

8 small corn tortillas (stale are fine)

½ cup olive or vegetable oil

2 boneless, skinless chicken breasts or thighs

2 poblano or other fresh mild chiles, seeded and thinly sliced

1 red bell pepper, cut into strips

1 onion, halved and sliced

1 tablespoon minced garlic

8 Roma (plum) tomatoes, seeded if you like, chopped (canned are fine; drain their juice)

½ cup chopped fresh cilantro

Lime wedges

1. Cut the tortillas in half and then crosswise into strips about 1 inch wide. Put the oil in a deep skillet over medium-high heat. When it's hot but not smoking, fry the tortilla strips, turning frequently, until golden brown and crisp on both sides, about 3 minutes. Work in 2 or 3 batches to avoid crowding. Use a slotted spoon to transfer them to towels to drain.

2. Pour off all but 2 tablespoons of the oil. Add the chicken and brown well, turning as necessary, until no longer pink inside but not dry, 10 to 15 minutes depending on the cut. Remove the chicken from the skillet and add the poblanos, bell pepper, onion, and garlic. Cook, stirring frequently, until the vegetables soften and begin to turn golden, 5 to 10 minutes. Add the tomatoes and cook, stirring, until their liquid has boiled off.

3. When the chicken is cool enough to handle, slice or chop it and return the pieces to the pan along with the tortillas. Cook, stirring, just long enough to warm the chicken and tortilla strips, about 2 minutes. Taste and adjust the seasoning. Sprinkle with the cilantro and serve with the lime wedges.

Braised Chard and Chicken with Steel-Cut Oats

Makes: **4 servings**   Time: **30 minutes**

Hearty stews are usually tricky to pull off on weeknights, when you want something on the table quickly. But here's a delicious braised grain dish with that odd acidic sweetness of chard (substitute other greens if you prefer) and the crisp juiciness of chicken thighs. Bulgur also works well.

About 1½ pounds chard

2 tablespoons olive oil

4 bone-in chicken thighs

Salt and black pepper

1 red onion, halved and sliced

3 garlic cloves, sliced

¾ cup steel-cut oats

Ⓕ Fast   Ⓜ Make-Ahead   Ⓟ Pantry Staple

½ cup white wine or water

2 cups vegetable or chicken stock (for homemade, see pages 135 to 140)
   or water, or more as needed

2 tablespoons balsamic vinegar

1. Cut the stems out of the chard leaves. Cut the leaves into wide ribbons and slice the stems; keep the leaves and stems separate.

2. Put the oil in a large skillet over medium-high heat. When it's hot, add the chicken thighs, skin side down, and sprinkle with salt and pepper; cook, rotating and turning as necessary, until browned on all sides, 10 to 15 minutes. Remove the chicken. Add the onion and garlic to the skillet and cook, stirring, until softened, 3 to 5 minutes.

3. Add the chard stems and oats along with another sprinkling of salt and pepper; cook, stirring occasionally, until the oats are glossy and coated with oil, 2 to 3 minutes. Add the wine, stir, and let the liquid bubble away. Add the 2 cups stock all at once and return the chicken thighs to the skillet (skin side up). Reduce the heat to medium-low, cover, and cook. Check to see if the oats are tender after 15 minutes; if they're not quite done, cook for another 5 minutes, then test again. If the oats become dry, add a little more stock or water.

4. When the oats are almost done, add the chard leaves and the vinegar. Replace the lid, remove the skillet from the heat, and let rest for 5 minutes. Fluff with a fork and taste and adjust the seasoning. Serve.

Drumsticks, Cabbage, and Rice, Stuck-Pot Style

Makes: 4 servings   Time: About 1½ hours, largely unattended

This is a terrific, venerable, and underappreciated technique known world-wide but not much used here; you intentionally overcook the bottom of a pot of rice (there has to be some fat in there) until it's crisp. (This is how to create the famous *soccarat* that is the soul of classic paella.) That crust on the bottom of the pot—which will become the top of the dish after you invert it onto a platter—is as crunchy as it is gorgeous. All you have to do is ignore the pot for 45 minutes. Don't worry if it doesn't come out in one piece; it's all good.

Salt

1 cup brown basmati rice

¼ cup olive oil, or more as needed

4 chicken drumsticks

Black pepper

1 small head cabbage, cored and thinly sliced

2 tablespoons minced garlic

½ cup stock (for homemade, see pages 135 to 140) or water, or more as needed

Chopped fresh dill, for garnish

Lemon wedges, for serving

1. Fill a large pot or Dutch oven with water, bring it to a boil, and salt it. Stir in the rice, adjust the heat so that the water bubbles steadily, and cook without stirring for about 12 minutes. Drain. Transfer the rice to a bowl and wipe out the pot.

2. Put the oil in the same pot over medium-high heat. A minute later, add the drumsticks and sprinkle with salt and pepper. Cook the drumsticks, turning and rotating as necessary, until they're browned all over but not cooked through, 5 to 10 minutes; remove. Add the cabbage and garlic to the pot, sprinkle with salt and pepper, and cook, stirring occasionally, until they begin to soften, 5 to 10 minutes. Remove the vegetables. There should be about ⅛ inch fat left in the bottom of the pot; if not, add a little more oil.

Ⓕ Fast Ⓜ Make-Ahead Ⓟ Pantry Staple

3. Add half of the rice to the bottom of the pot, nestle the drumsticks into the rice, add the cabbage and garlic mixture, then put the rest of the rice on top. Pour in the stock, cover the pot, and cook over medium-high heat for 5 minutes. After 5 minutes, turn the heat down very low and cook, completely undisturbed, for about 45 minutes. (If the rice starts to smell like it might be toasting too quickly, turn the heat down even more.) The rice should be tender and fragrant; if not, add another ½ cup liquid, cover, and cook for 5 minutes or so. When it's ready, remove the pot from the heat and let it sit, covered, for at least 5 minutes or up to 15 minutes.

4. To serve, put a plate over the top of the pot and carefully turn the rice out. If some of the rice sticks to the bottom of the pot, scrape it out and put it on top. Garnish with dill and serve with lemon wedges.

Rolled Cabbage

Makes: 4 servings   Time: 1½ hours, largely unattended

Stuffed anything usually demands a lot of preparation. Still, once you get the rolled cabbage into the pot, you can walk away for a long time. You can replace the sausage with any kind of ground meat you like; just be sure to season it well with fresh or dried herbs and maybe some anise or caraway seeds.

Salt

1 large head cabbage (about 2 pounds), cored

1 cup brown rice

8 ounces fresh sausage, casings removed

½ cup chopped scallions

Black pepper

Two 28-ounce cans diced tomatoes, with their juice

1 bay leaf

1 cinnamon stick

4 or 5 whole cloves

1. Bring a large pot of water to a boil and salt it. Add the cabbage and cook, turning it in the pot once or twice, until it begins to get tender, 15 to 20 minutes. Remove the cabbage (do not pour out the water) and rinse the leaves with cool water to stop the cooking. Pull off 10 of the largest, most intact leaves, then chop the remaining leaves and put them in a large bowl. Return the pot to a boil and stir in the rice. Cook, stirring occasionally, for 15 minutes, then drain.

2. Add the cooked rice, raw sausage, scallions, and a good sprinkling of salt and pepper to the bowl of chopped cabbage and mix just enough to combine. Put a large spoonful of the rice mixture into a cabbage leaf, taking care not to overfill it, and roll loosely. You're shooting for 8 cabbage rolls, but if you have extra filling, use all of the leaves. Put the rolls seam side down in the bottom of a large pot or Dutch oven; it's okay to stack them on top of each other in the pot.

3. Add the tomatoes and their juice to the Dutch oven along with 1 cup water, the bay leaf, cinnamon stick, cloves, and some salt and pepper. Cover and bring to a boil. Reduce the heat so that the mixture barely bubbles and cook, undisturbed, for 30 minutes. Check to see if there's still liquid in the pot. The cabbage should be just submerged; if not, add a little water. Cover and cook for another 30 minutes before checking again.

4. When the rolls have plumped up and absorbed most of the liquid, and are firm, turn off the heat and let rest, still covered, for at least 10 minutes (or up to 20). Put the rolled cabbage in shallow bowls, removing the whole spices as you come across them. Taste the pot juices and adjust the seasoning if necessary. Pour a big ladleful over the cabbage rolls and serve.

Ⓕ Fast Ⓜ Make-Ahead Ⓟ Pantry Staple

Meat-and-Grain Loaf, Burgers, or Balls

Makes: 6 to 8 servings, or more for appetizers   Time: About 1 hour, or less if you start with ground meat and pre-cooked grains

The best of both worlds: the moisture and flavor of ground meat combined with the chewiness of grains. Any leftovers are good cold from the fridge for a few days (like any meat loaf, they make terrific sandwiches), or freeze them for up to a few months.

Use the same mixture to form burgers or balls of any size. You can cook them in a skillet on the stove in some olive oil, but baking them as described in the recipe requires less attention.

2 tablespoons olive oil

Salt

1 pound spinach or other tender greens

1 pound boneless, skinless chicken or turkey thighs, beef chuck or sirloin, or pork or lamb shoulder, excess fat removed; or use ground meat

1 small onion or 2 shallots, chopped

2 teaspoons minced garlic

Pinch of cayenne

1 teaspoon cumin or 1 tablespoon chili powder

Black pepper

1 egg

2 cups cooked, drained bulgur or any other grain

1. Heat the oven to 400°F. Grease a loaf pan, rimmed baking sheet, or large roasting pan with 2 tablespoons oil. Bring a large pot of water to a boil and salt it; fill a large bowl with ice water. Wilt the spinach in the boiling water for about 30 seconds. Drain and immediately plunge into the ice water. Drain, squeeze tightly to dry thoroughly, and roughly chop. Put the spinach in a bowl. If you're using ground meat, add it to the spinach and skip to Step 3.

2. If you're using whole pieces of meat, cut them into large chunks and put in a food processor. Pulse several times to process until ground but not puréed, stopping the machine and scraping down the sides if necessary. Transfer to the bowl with the spinach.

3. Add the onion, garlic, and spices, sprinkle with salt and pepper, and stir. Add the egg and bulgur and mix until thoroughly combined using a rubber spatula or your hands. Transfer the mixture to the loaf pan or shape into a free-form loaf, burgers, or balls, and put on the baking sheet or in the roasting pan. Transfer to the oven and roast until firm and browned all over. A loaf will take about 50 minutes; burgers and balls with take 20 to 30, depending on their size (carefully turn them once or twice for even cooking).

Fish or Shrimp Loaf, Burgers, and Balls. You might try 1 tablespoon curry powder instead of the chili powder. Replace the meat with 1 pound raw firm fish or shrimp (see page 23); clean, bone, and shell it as needed. Proceed with the recipe.

Bean-and-Grain Loaf, Burgers, and Balls. Instead of the meat, use 2 cups cooked or canned beans, mashed with enough of their liquid to keep them moist. Proceed with the recipe.

Ⓕ Fast   Ⓜ Make-Ahead   Ⓟ Pantry Staple

Rice Casserole with Escarole and Little Meatballs

Makes: 4 servings   Time: About 1 hour

This garlicky baked rice dish features *polpetti*, those light, cheesy Italian meatballs. Traditionally, they're made with a mixture of pork, beef, and veal, and you can do that, though I'm using only beef here. The escarole almost melts away into the casserole, but to make the rice even creamier, add ½ cup to 1 cup more stock, uncover, and stir a couple of times while it's baking.

1 thin slice good bread, preferably whole wheat

¼ cup milk

8 ounces ground sirloin

¼ cup chopped onion

¼ cup grated Parmesan cheese

2 tablespoons chopped fresh parsley

Salt and black pepper

1 tablespoon olive oil

2 tablespoons minced garlic

1 cup short-grain brown rice

½ cup white wine

2 cups chicken or vegetable stock (for homemade, see pages 135 to 140) or water, or more as needed

1 pound escarole, cut into ribbons

1. Heat the oven to 350°F. Soak the bread in the milk until soggy, about 5 minutes. Squeeze the liquid from the bread and combine the bread gently with the meat, onion, Parmesan, parsley, and some salt and pepper. Shape into ½-inch meatballs, pressing no more than is necessary.

2. Put the oil in a large pot or Dutch oven over medium heat for 1 minute. Add the meatballs and cook, turning once or twice, until well browned and firm, 5 to 10 minutes total; as they finish cooking, remove them with a slotted spoon.

3. Add the garlic to the pot and cook, stirring, until soft, about 5 minutes. Add the rice and stir until glossy and coated with oil, about 1 minute more. Add the white wine and let the liquid bubble away. Add the stock, escarole, meatballs, and a sprinkling of salt and pepper. Bring to a boil.

4. Cover and bake, undisturbed, for 30 minutes. Remove the cover and test a grain of rice. It should be almost tender but not quite ready; if it's still too tough, check to make sure there's some water left in the bottom of the pot, cover again, and bake for another 10 minutes. When the rice is done, remove the pot from the oven and let it rest for at least 5 minutes or up to 15 minutes. Taste and adjust the seasoning. Serve.

Brown Rice and Lamb Burgers with Spinach

Makes: 4 servings   Time: 1 hour

The rice gives these burgers an amazingly crisp crust and moist interior. Use ground turkey or beef instead of lamb if you like, and try topping the burgers with a little yogurt and lemon juice—it's a nice touch.

> 1 cup brown rice
>
> Salt
>
> 5 tablespoons olive oil
>
> 3 teaspoons minced garlic
>
> 1 pound spinach, roughly chopped
>
> Black pepper
>
> 8 ounces ground lamb
>
> 1 small red onion, chopped
>
> 1 tablespoon chopped fresh oregano, or 1 teaspoon dried
>
> 1 teaspoon cumin
>
> ¼ cup crumbled feta cheese

     Fast   Make-Ahead Ⓟ Pantry Staple

1. Put the rice in a saucepan with a pinch of salt and add water to cover by about 1 inch. Bring to a boil, then adjust the heat so that the mixture bubbles gently. Cover and cook until the rice is nearly done (it should be a little chewy and a little wet but not swimming), 30 to 35 minutes. Transfer the rice to a mixing bowl.

2. Meanwhile, put 2 tablespoons of the oil in a large, deep skillet over medium heat. When it's hot, add 2 teaspoons of the garlic and cook, stirring occasionally, until it begins to soften, just a minute or 2. Add the chopped spinach and cook, stirring occasionally, until all the leaves are just wilted and cooked almost dry, 5 to 10 minutes. Sprinkle with salt and pepper and remove it from the pan. Wipe out the skillet.

3. Add the lamb, onion, oregano, cumin, feta, and the remaining 1 teaspoon garlic to the mixing bowl with the rice; stir just enough to combine all the ingredients but don't overwork it. Form the mixture into 4 patties. (The dish can be made ahead to this point; cover the spinach and the patties and refrigerate for up to a few hours. Bring the spinach to room temperature before proceeding.)

4. Put the remaining 3 tablespoons oil in the same skillet over medium-high heat. When it's hot, add the patties and cook, turning once and working in batches if necessary, until they are golden brown on both sides and the meat is just cooked through, about 5 minutes per side. To serve, put a burger on a mound of spinach and drizzle with the pan juices.

Quickly Stewed Tomatoes and Sausage with Bulgur

Makes: 4 servings   Time: 30 minutes

Considering how delicious this is, it's way too easy—a kind of bulgur-fortified tomato sauce that you can eat any time of day. Though Italian sausage naturally goes well with fresh oregano, you can use any combo of fresh sausage and herbs you like. Or try bacon, pancetta, or guanciale instead of sausage, or omit the meat entirely (chopped zucchini or eggplant replaces it nicely).

2 tablespoons olive oil

4 to 8 ounces fresh sausage in casings

1 tablespoon minced garlic

1 cup bulgur

4 cups chopped tomatoes (canned are fine; drain their juice)

1 tablespoon chopped fresh oregano, or 1 teaspoon dried

2 cups chicken or vegetable stock (for homemade, see pages 135 to 140)
   or water

Salt and black pepper

½ cup chopped fresh parsley, for garnish

1. Put the oil in a deep skillet over medium heat. When it's hot, add the sausage and cook, turning occasionally and pricking with a fork a few times to release its fat. When the sausage is nicely browned and just cooked through, after 10 minutes or so, remove it and turn the heat to low. (When it's cool enough to handle, cut it into bite-size pieces.)

2. Add the garlic to the skillet and cook until fragrant, about 1 minute. Add the bulgur and stir until it's glossy. Raise the heat a bit and return the sausage to the pan along with the tomatoes, oregano, and stock. Sprinkle with salt and pepper. Turn the heat to low, stir, and cover. Cook until the bulgur is tender, 10 to 15 minutes. Let rest off the heat for 5 minutes. Taste and adjust the seasoning and fluff with a fork. Serve garnished with the parsley.

Ⓕ Fast   Ⓜ Make-Ahead   Ⓟ Pantry Staple

Skillet Tamales

Makes: 4 servings   Time: 45 minutes

Tamale casseroles were popular back in the 1970s and are perfectly positioned for a comeback. They're much less labor-intensive than real tamales and just as comforting. Plus they're fun: The cornmeal puffs up in the oven, forming a nice layer over the meat and vegetables. For a more authentic tortilla flavor, use masa harina instead of cornmeal.

1 cup cornmeal (fine or medium grind)

1½ cups hot water, or more as needed

Salt

2 tablespoons olive oil, or more as needed

8 ounces ground beef, pork, or lamb

Black pepper

1 onion, chopped

1 tablespoon minced garlic

1 tablespoon chili powder

8 Roma (plum) tomatoes, chopped (canned are fine; drain their juice)

3 cups corn kernels (frozen are fine)

½ teaspoon baking powder

¼ cup chopped fresh cilantro, for garnish

1. Heat the oven to 400°F. Combine the cornmeal, hot water, and a large pinch of salt; stir with a fork until smooth. Let it sit while you prepare the filling.

2. Put the oil in a deep, ovenproof skillet (cast iron is ideal) over medium-high heat. When it's hot, add the meat, sprinkle with salt and pepper, and cook, stirring occasionally, until nicely browned, 5 to 10 minutes. Lower the heat a bit, add the onion and garlic, and cook, stirring occasionally, until the vegetables soften, about 5 minutes more; add more oil if the mixture starts to look too dry. Stir in the chili powder, tomatoes, and corn and turn off the heat.

3. Stir the baking powder into the cornmeal mixture until it's completely incorporated. The mixture should be the consistency of thick pancake batter;

if not, add a little more water. Spoon the batter into the skillet on top of the filling and spread it around a bit. Bake until the cornbread has cracked and turned golden and is cooked all the way through (a toothpick inserted into the cornbread should come out clean), 20 to 25 minutes. Garnish with the cilantro and serve hot or at room temperature.

Quick Posole (Pork and Hominy Stew)

Makes: 4 servings   Time: 30 minutes with cooked or canned hominy

If you've never cooked with hominy (from which grits are ground), posole—the pork and corn stew of central Mexico—is a good place to start. The flavor is amazing. Because posole is lime-treated corn (the first step in making tortillas), it has a character unlike other dried corn products. (For a vegetarian version, omit the pork and add 2 cups pinto or black beans in Step 2.) Soft corn tortillas are the classic accompaniment for scooping up the posole and soaking in its delicious broth, but a batch of Mostly Whole Wheat Tortillas (page 526) would not be amiss.

    2 tablespoons olive oil

    2 center-cut loin pork chops, about 1 inch thick

    Salt and black pepper

    1 large onion, chopped

    1 tablespoon minced garlic

    1 tablespoon chili powder

    1 pound kale, collards, or other sturdy greens (stems are fine), chopped

    3 cups cooked or canned hominy, liquid reserved

    1 bunch radishes, chopped or grated, for garnish

    ½ cup chopped fresh cilantro, for garnish

1. Put the oil in a large pot or Dutch oven over medium-high heat. When it's hot, add the pork chops, sprinkle with salt and pepper, and cook, turning once or twice, until browned on both sides, 5 to 10 minutes. Remove them from the skillet. Add the onion and garlic and cook, stirring, until softened,

Ⓕ Fast   Ⓜ Make-Ahead   Ⓟ Pantry Staple

3 to 5 minutes. Add the chili powder and another sprinkling of salt and pepper and continue cooking and stirring for about a minute.

2. Return the pork chops to the skillet along with the greens, hominy, and 2 cups of its liquid; add water to make up the difference if you don't have enough. Stir and bring to a boil. Adjust the heat so the mixture bubbles gently, then cover and cook until the greens and the pork are tender, 5 to 10 minutes. (If the mixture becomes too dry, add a little water.)

3. Fish the pork chops out of the pot, remove the meat from the bones, chop it up a bit, and stir it back into the stew. (The posole can be made ahead to this point and refrigerated for up to 3 days; gently reheat before proceeding.) Taste and adjust the seasoning. Serve garnished with the radishes and cilantro.

Posole from Scratch. Start with 1½ cups uncooked hominy. Put the hominy in a large pot with water to cover. Bring to a boil, then reduce the heat so the hominy bubbles gently. Cover and cook, stirring occasionally and adding water as necessary to keep the mixture covered, until the kernels have burst and are tender, 3 to 4 hours. Drain and reserve the liquid, then proceed with the recipe.

Picaditas with Potatoes and Chorizo

Makes: 4 servings   Time: 45 minutes

Strictly speaking, these are not *picaditas*—the thick pancakes from Veracruz in Mexico—because I cheat a bit and use masa harina instead of the traditional tamale dough known simply as *masa*. But if you have access to good masa (or *nixtamal*, the partially cooked and limed whole hominy used to make it), then by all means use it as the foundation here instead of the harina-water combination.

In any case, *picaditas* themselves are fast and easy to make. You may find yourself making them often and topping them with whatever you have handy, or eating them plain like bread.

1 cup masa harina

½ teaspoon baking powder

Salt and black pepper

2 tablespoons olive oil, plus more for frying

8 ounces Mexican (fresh) chorizo

2 large baking potatoes, peeled if you like

½ cup chopped scallions

Lime wedges, for serving

1. Combine the masa harina, baking powder, ½ teaspoon salt, and a little pepper in a medium bowl. Add 1 tablespoon of the oil and stir with a fork until the mixture looks like coarse meal. Stir in 1 cup water to make a thick batter and let sit.

2. Heat the oven to 200°F. Put another tablespoon oil in a large skillet over medium-high heat. Add the chorizo and cook, stirring occasionally and adjusting the heat as necessary, until it breaks up, darkens, and releases some of its fat, 10 to 15 minutes. Meanwhile, grate the potatoes and squeeze them dry. Remove the chorizo from the pan with a slotted spoon and add the potatoes.

3. Cook the potatoes, stirring once or twice, until they brown in places and become a little tender but are still crisp, 5 to 10 minutes. Return the chorizo to the pan along with the scallions and stir. Taste and adjust the seasoning and lower the heat to keep warm.

Ⓕ Fast   Ⓜ Make-Ahead   Ⓟ Pantry Staple

4. Put a thin film of oil in another large skillet over medium-high heat. When it's hot, drop half of the masa batter in spoonfuls into the skillet to form 4 thick cakes, each about 4 inches in diameter. Cover and adjust the heat so the batter steams but the oil doesn't smoke; cook until the *picaditas* are crisp on the bottom, a little puffed, and firm on top, 5 to 7 minutes. Transfer to the warm oven and repeat with the remaining batter to make 8 cakes. Top the *picaditas* with some of the potato mixture and serve with the lime wedges.

Kimchi Rice with Beef

Makes: 4 servings   Time: About 4 hours, almost entirely unattended

Even though store-bought kimchi is acceptable, I encourage you to try a homemade batch because it's unbelievably good. It needs to cure for at least a couple of hours, but you can make it up to a week in advance. You might even double the recipe; it's that good. Just be aware that the longer it sits, the stronger it will be, so over the course of a week it becomes pretty potent. (Not that it's weak to begin with.)

    1 small head (about 12 ounces) green, Savoy, or Napa cabbage, cored and
        shredded

    Salt

    6 scallions, chopped

    2 tablespoons minced garlic, or to taste

    1 tablespoon minced ginger

    1 tablespoon red chile flakes

    1 tablespoon sugar

    2 tablespoons soy sauce

    3 tablespoons vegetable oil

    8 ounces beef flank or skirt steak, very thinly sliced

    2 cups cooked short- or long-grain brown rice

1. Put the shredded cabbage in a colander and toss it well with 2 tablespoons salt. Let it sit over a bowl until it wilts, at least 2 hours. Rinse the cabbage and pat it dry.

2. Combine the scallions, garlic, ginger, red chile flakes, sugar, and soy sauce in a bowl or large jar. Toss the mixture with the cabbage. (You should make the kimchi at least 2 hours in advance; see the headnote.)

3. When the kimchi is ready, put a large, deep skillet over high heat until it begins to smoke, 3 to 4 minutes. Swirl in 2 tablespoons of the oil, add the beef, and cook, stirring occasionally, until it is seared but still pink inside, 2 to 3 minutes. Remove the beef from the skillet.

4. Add the remaining 1 tablespoon oil to the skillet, swirl it around, and begin to add the rice, a bit at a time, breaking up any clumps with your fingers and stirring it into the oil. When all the rice is added, cook, stirring frequently, until the rice becomes nice and crisp, 3 to 5 minutes. Return the beef to the pan and stir in the kimchi. Serve hot or at room temperature.

Ⓕ Fast Ⓜ Make-Ahead Ⓟ Pantry Staple

Wheat Berries
with Braised Beef and Parsnips

Makes: 4 servings   Time: 1½ to 2 hours, largely unattended

A rich, substantial wintertime stew that benefits from fresh vegetables added late enough that they don't turn to mush. To turn this into a delicious twist on the Belgian classic, beef carbonnade, omit the wine and use your favorite dark beer in place of half of the stock.

2 tablespoons olive oil

12 ounces boneless beef chuck or round, cut into large cubes

Salt and black pepper

2 onions, cut into wedges

4 garlic cloves, sliced

½ cup red wine

4 cups beef or vegetable stock (for homemade, see pages 135 to 140) or water, or more as needed

¾ cup wheat berries

1 bay leaf

1 sprig fresh thyme, or several pinches dried

1 pound parsnips, cut into ½-inch slices

¼ cup chopped fresh parsley, for garnish

1. Put the oil in a large pot or Dutch oven over medium-high heat. When it's hot, add the beef a few pieces at a time, turning as they cook and sprinkling with salt and pepper. (Don't crowd or the cubes will not brown properly; cook in batches if necessary.) Brown the meat well on all sides, 5 to 10 minutes total.

2. As the pieces brown, remove them with a slotted spoon. Pour off all but 3 tablespoons of the fat from the pan and turn the heat down to medium. Add the onions and garlic and cook, stirring, until softened and beginning to color, 5 to 10 minutes. Add the wine and cook, stirring to scrape up any brown bits from the bottom of the pan, for a minute or 2. Add the stock, wheat berries, bay leaf, thyme, and meat and bring to a boil. Turn the heat down so the liquid bubbles gently. Cover and cook, undisturbed, for 1 hour.

3. Uncover the pot; the mixture should still be wet and the wheat berries almost fully tender. If not, add a little more liquid, cover, and cook for another 15 minutes, then check again; the grains should be tender and the mixture soupy but not swimming in liquid. If not, repeat this step until they're ready.

4. Add the parsnips, turn the heat up for a minute or so to bring the liquid back to a boil, then lower the heat and cover again. Cook, stirring once or twice, until the parsnips are tender but not too soft, 10 to 15 minutes. Remove the bay leaf and thyme sprig, then taste and adjust the seasoning. (The stew can be made ahead to this point and refrigerated for up to 3 days; reheat gently before proceeding.) Garnish with parsley and serve.

Braised Broccoli Rabe and Pork with Wheat Berries. Substitute pork shoulder for the beef and chopped broccoli rabe for the parsnips. Deglaze with white wine instead of red in Step 2 and proceed with the recipe.

Ⓕ Fast   Ⓜ Make-Ahead   Ⓟ Pantry Staple

Beans

The rumor that bean cooking is time consuming or difficult is false. In fact, in recent years eating beans has become a part of my daily life; I always liked them and cooked them occasionally, but now they're a staple.

Beans—also known by their umbrella term, legumes—are among the most convenient, versatile, economical, and health-giving ingredients you can stock in your pantry. Many taste good enough on their own to eat nearly unadorned, with maybe olive oil, lemon juice, and pepper—or hot sauce. But they also act as a mirror for flavors that are cooked with them. This is exactly what makes them so perfect for Food Matters recipes: A little meat, poultry, or even fish goes a long way in a pot of beans; a slew of vegetables is almost always welcome; and in many dishes whole grains can play a fantastic supporting role.

Recently I've begun to use canned beans more often. (More than half of the dishes in this chapter offer the choice of using your own cooked beans or canned.) But I still don't use them a lot, because I try to follow my own advice, which I cannot say loudly enough: Make a pot of beans (easier than ever; see page 350), and you'll eat well for several meals. They keep in the refrigerator for days and freeze beautifully.

Here's how this chapter is organized: A basic recipe, followed by simply seasoned bean dishes; beans with cheese or eggs; and, later, beans with fish, poultry, or meat. Recipes that feature tofu—which is made from soybeans—are included in this chapter if it is a featured ingredient and elsewhere when it plays a lesser role. The cooking times and icons will give you, at a glance, an indication as to which start with cooked (or canned) legumes and which are based on slowly cooked dried beans. None is difficult, and most require very little attention.

The majority of recipes here serve four as a main dish; the ones that might be considered "pantry staples" are calibrated to serve four with leftovers. Shopping information, tips, and more encouragement are sprinkled throughout the chapter.

Beans at a Glance

Here's a short rundown of the most common types of beans and their key characteristics. There are literally hundreds of varieties of beans available (see Specialty Beans on page 401 for a few examples), but please remember: Beans are virtually interchangeable, especially once they're cooked or if they come from a can. When cooking from scratch—the smaller the bean, the faster they become tender.

Small Beans

Black-eyed peas: Ivory or grayish, with a black spot, black-eyed peas (also known as cowpeas) are quick-cooking and popular in the American South.
Lentils: These are the smallest legumes and among the fastest cooking—you never soak them. Brown, green, and red—which actually look orange when raw and cook up yellow—are the most widely available varieties.
Navy beans: White, almost round, mild, and creamy, they are traditionally used in baked bean recipes.
Dried peas: Most dried peas are split and available in green and yellow; they tend to fall apart when cooked, which makes them good for thickening soups.
Pigeon peas: Beige, round, and slightly flattened, pigeons are mild and sweet with a slightly grainy texture.
Pink beans: These are much like pinto beans (see below), only smaller and pinker.
Soybeans: Almost round and nutty tasting, they are either pale yellow or black when dried. Young green soybeans are called edamame and are sold fresh and frozen.

 Fast  Make-Ahead (P) Pantry Staple

Medium Beans

Black beans (turtle beans): Dried, they look almost black; cooked, they're dark gray. Black beans have a deep, earthy flavor and slightly gritty texture. (They're not the same as fermented black beans, which are actually soybeans.)

Chickpeas (garbanzo beans): These are acorn-shaped, golden, and nutty tasting, with a slightly grainy texture. Cooked from scratch, they yield an extremely flavorful broth.

Pinto beans: These earthy, creamy beans are brown and speckled and are the basis for traditional refried beans.

Large Beans

Cannellini beans: Shaped like kidney beans but ivory colored, they are supercreamy and great for puréeing.

Fava beans: Favas are green and fragrant when fresh, but they require first shelling, then peeling. They're light brown (and podless) when dried.

Great Northern beans: Like cannellini, only oval—like big navy beans—they're easy to find and versatile.

Kidney beans: Kidneys are reddish brown and tend to hold their shape when cooked.

Lima beans: Available both large and small, limas are green when fresh, white when dried, and almost always buttery and robust, with a dense texture.

Pot of Beans

Makes: 6 to 8 servings   Time: 30 minutes to 2 hours, depending on bean and soaking option; largely unattended   Ⓜ Ⓟ

I'm on a mission to make sure every fridge or freezer in America is stocked with a container of home-cooked beans, and this recipe is my ammunition. The process requires no advance soaking (though it's certainly an option) and very little attention. Yet each batch provides the backbone for several meals.

What you get here is a basic pot of beans with lots of flavorful liquid. Scoop out the beans with a slotted spoon (or drain them), and you've got the equivalent of rinsed canned beans, only way better. (Or save their broth for delicious soups and stews.) Meat undeniably adds richness, and it doesn't take much to do the trick. (See Adding Flavor to a Pot of Beans, page 352, for some flavoring and serving suggestions.)

The bean-cooking process is full of variables. How much time beans need to become tender and how much water they absorb depends on their age, type, growing conditions, the hardness of your water, and even the humidity of where they've been stored. In the end, though, none of that matters much because with a little patience it's virtually impossible to go wrong. For more nuanced tips—including different ways to soak beans—see Spontaneity and Cooking Beans, page 353.

> 1 pound dried beans (any kind but lentils, split peas, or peeled and split beans), rinsed, picked over, and soaked if you like
>
> Salt and black pepper

1. Put the beans in a large pot and cover them with cold water by at least 3 inches. Bring the pot to a boil, then reduce the heat so the mixture barely bubbles. Cover tightly and let the beans cook, undisturbed, for 30 minutes.

2. Taste a bean. If it's at all tender (unlikely), add a large pinch of salt and several grinds of black pepper. Make sure the beans are covered with about 1 inch water; add a little more if necessary. If the beans are still hard, don't add salt yet and keep covered with 2 to 3 inches water.

3. Again make sure the liquid is just barely bubbling and cover. Check the beans for doneness every 10 to 15 minutes and add more water if necessary, a little at a time. Small beans will take as little as 15 minutes more; older large beans can take up to an hour or more. If you haven't added salt and pepper yet, add them when the beans are just turning tender. Stop cooking when the beans are done the way you like them. Taste and adjust the seasoning.

4. Here you have a few options. Drain the beans (reserving the liquid separately) to use them as an ingredient in salads or other dishes where they need to be dry, or finish them with one of the ideas from the list on page 352. (Or store the beans and use with or without their liquid as needed. They'll keep in the fridge for days and in the freezer for months.)

Pot of Lentils or Split Peas. No need to soak, since they cook fast—usually in less than 30 minutes. Put them in a large pot and cover with cold water by at least 3 inches. Bring the pot to a boil, then reduce the heat so that the liquid bubbles gently. Cover tightly and cook, stirring infrequently and checking for doneness every 10 to 15 minutes; add a little more water if necessary. When they start to get tender, add a large pinch of salt and several grinds of black pepper; stop cooking when they're done the way you like them. Taste and adjust the seasoning. Use immediately or store.

Pot of Fresh (or Frozen) Shell Beans. For limas, favas, edamame (in or out of the pod), and the like: Cook like vegetables. Bring a pot of water to a boil and salt it. Add the beans and cook until just tender, testing one every now and then. This can be as quick as a few minutes for frozen beans, or up to 30 minutes for freshly shelled beans. Drain, reserving the liquid if you like, and serve or refrigerate for later.

Adding Flavor to a Pot of Beans

Here are some ingredients that are good to add (alone or in combination) when you start cooking the beans.

Herbs or spices: a bay leaf, a couple cloves, some peppercorns, thyme sprigs, parsley leaves and/or stems, chili powder, or other herbs and spices. (Remember that you'll want to remove some of these before eating.)

Aromatics: Chopped onion, carrot, celery, and/or garlic.

Chopped canned tomatoes, with or without their liquid.

Any stock, (for homemade, see pages 135 to 140) in place of all or part of the water.

Other liquids: A cup or so of beer, wine, coffee, tea, or juice.

Smoked meat: Ham hock, pork chop, beef bone, or sausage. Fish it out after cooking, chop the meat, and stir it back into the beans.

Add any of these ingredients after you cook and drain the beans; the quantities listed work for about 3 cups cooked beans, or 4 servings. You might reheat the beans gently to blend flavors, adding the reserved cooking liquid if needed to keep them moist.

Olive oil or sesame oil to taste: a couple tablespoons or so.

Chopped fresh parsley, cilantro, mint, or any basil: 1/2 cup.

Chopped fresh rosemary, tarragon, oregano, epazote, thyme, marjoram, or sage: more or less depending on the strength of the herb.

Chopped scallions, garlic, ginger, or lemongrass: to taste.

1 cup any cooked sauce: like All-Purpose Tomato Sauce, page 194.

1 tablespoon or so dried herb or spice blend: like curry powder, garam masala, or herbes de Provence.

Soy, Worcestershire, or hot sauce: to taste.

Miso: a couple tablespoons thinned with hot bean-cooking liquid.

Chopped leafy greens: like spinach, kale, or collards.

Chopped fresh tomato: at least one cup.

Cubed bacon or pancetta: 1 or 2 slices.

Crumbled fresh sausage: cooked until crisp, with some of the fat if you like.

Ⓕ Fast Ⓜ Make-Ahead Ⓟ Pantry Staple

Spontaneity and Cooking Beans

To soak or not to soak? I have wavered: I've done my fair share of soaking—both for long periods of time in tepid water, and using the quick-soak method where you boil the beans for a couple of minutes, then cover them and let them sit for an hour. The problem with the whole idea of soaking is that it makes beans seem like a hassle, something for which you either have to plan ahead or not do at all.

So now I don't sweat soaking. In reality it often saves only a little time, and if the beans are oversoaked, they tend to have a very small window of tenderness before they burst. Instead I cook beans in a tightly covered pot, very slowly, in abundant water. I don't mess with stirring (which can break the skins anyway), and I'm left with plenty of flavorful liquid for cooking or for refrigerating or freezing with any leftover beans.

Beans are done cooking when they're good and ready. You have no way of knowing how old they are or how much moisture is in them. With this method, even the longest-cooking beans—like chickpeas or big limas—rarely take longer than an hour to become tender and creamy, with their skins still intact. Without soaking.

To salt or not to salt? In my experience, salting does not affect the rate at which beans cook, but it does, as always, act as a flavor enhancer. So I always salt beans as they're cooking, but I wait until they just start to get tender. Acid—like lemon juice or vinegar—will help beans retain their skins (which shouldn't be much of a problem if you use my lots-of-water, gentle-simmer cooking method), but it will also affect the flavor. If you want your beans to taste like lemon juice or vinegar, add lemon juice or vinegar; if you don't, don't.

Refried Black Beans

Makes: 4 servings   Time: 20 minutes with cooked or canned beans

Lard is traditional in refried beans, and if you eat butter without fear, you shouldn't be worried about a little pig fat. (Hydrogenated vegetable shortening has been proven to be much worse for you than either lard *or* butter.) But if you can't get behind the idea, just use olive oil.

If you want lard, you can get it from a butcher, buy it in a supermarket, or render your own. To do so, cook fresh pork fat (or salt pork or even bacon) over medium-low heat in a skillet for about 10 minutes, remove the solids with a slotted spoon, and you're all set. As a bonus, any leftover cooked bits of meat make a delicious garnish for refried beans (as do queso fresco, sour cream, and cilantro).

Red or pinto beans are the classics for frijoles refritos.

> ⅓ cup lard or drippings from bacon, fresh pork belly, or salt pork; or olive oil
>
> 4 cups cooked or canned black beans, drained, liquid reserved
>
> 1 onion, chopped
>
> 1 tablespoon cumin, or to taste
>
> ¼ teaspoon cayenne, or to taste
>
> Salt and black pepper

1. Put the fat in a large skillet over medium heat. When it's hot, add the beans and mash with a large fork or potato masher until they're as smooth as you like.

2. Add the onion, cumin, and cayenne and sprinkle with salt and pepper. Continue to cook, mashing and stirring, until the beans are more or less broken up (some remaining chunks are fine) and the onion is lightly cooked, about 5 minutes more. As you stir, add a little bean liquid as necessary to get the texture you want. Taste and adjust the seasoning. Serve immediately (or refrigerate for up to 3 days or freeze for months).

Refried Beans with Hominy. Like eating beans and tortillas. Substitute 1 cup cooked or canned hominy for 1 cup of the black beans.

Puréed White Beans with Tons of Fresh Herbs

Makes: 4 servings   Time: 10 minutes with cooked or canned beans

This purée has a stunning green color from all of the fresh herbs and is the perfect dip—warm, cold, or at room temperature—for toasted bread or crudités. Or serve it as a main dish under bits of crumbled bacon, sausage, or prosciutto, or a small piece of simply cooked chicken or fish.

> 1 tablespoon butter
>
> 1 tablespoon olive oil, plus more for garnish
>
> 1 leek, white part and some of the green, trimmed, well rinsed, and chopped; or 1 onion, chopped
>
> 1 cup chopped mixed mild herbs, like parsley, cilantro, mint, basil, or chervil
>
> 1 tablespoon chopped fresh oregano, tarragon, or thyme
>
> 3 cups cooked or canned cannellini, navy, or other white beans, drained, liquid reserved
>
> About 1 cup bean-cooking liquid, stock (for homemade, see pages 135 to 140), or water, or more as needed
>
> Salt and black pepper

1. Put the butter and oil in a large skillet over medium heat. When the butter is melted, add the leek and cook, stirring occasionally, until it is soft, about 5 minutes. Add the chopped herbs and cook a minute or 2 more.

2. If you want the mixture super-smooth, transfer it—along with the beans—to a blender, food processor, or food mill and process, adding as much liquid as you need to make a smooth but not watery purée. If you want a lumpier texture, mash the beans right in the pan with a fork or potato masher, adding liquid slowly to get them as soupy as you like.

3. Sprinkle with salt and pepper; taste and add more if necessary. Heat and serve immediately or keep warm over low heat for up to an hour or so. Garnish with a drizzle of olive oil if you like.

Hummus Served Hot

Makes: 6 to 8 servings   Time: 20 minutes with cooked or canned chickpeas

The first time I ate this was in Turkey, and it stunned me. But why? Of course, hummus, a Middle Eastern staple, has uses beyond sandwich spread or meze platter. Served warm, it makes an elegant, fondue-like dip, sauce, or side dish. Offer this as an appetizer in a large bowl alongside crudités of all sorts: cubes of cooked potato, eggplant, or crusty bread, or strips of pita for dipping. You can also serve this mixture on grains, with pasta, or straight up as an alternative to mashed potatoes.

3 cups cooked or canned chickpeas, drained, liquid reserved

1 or 2 garlic cloves

¼ cup olive oil, or to taste

¼ cup tahini, or to taste

Salt and black pepper

3 tablespoons lemon juice, or to taste

Chopped fresh parsley, for garnish

1. Put the chickpeas with ½ cup of their cooking liquid (or water) in a blender, add the garlic, oil, and tahini, and sprinkle with salt and pepper. Purée for a minute or 2 until the mixture is very smooth. Add more cooking liquid, oil, or tahini as you like until the consistency is like a smooth dip or thick soup. (Refrigerate for up to a couple days or freeze for months.)

2. Transfer the purée to a medium saucepan over medium heat (or use the microwave); heat through while stirring constantly. Add the lemon juice, then taste and adjust the seasoning, adding more salt, pepper, or lemon juice as needed. Serve warm, garnished with parsley.

Ⓕ Fast   Ⓜ Make-Ahead   Ⓟ Pantry Staple

Ways to Flavor Hummus Served Hot

Stir in any of these just before serving, either alone or in combination; taste and add more if you like.

½ cup chopped roasted bell peppers (for homemade, see page 417)

½ cup mashed roasted garlic (for homemade, see page 421) in place of
  the raw garlic

½ cup grated Parmesan, Gruyère, or fontina cheese

¼ cup pesto (for homemade, see page 197) or herb paste

¼ cup chopped nuts, like walnuts, almonds, or pistachios

¼ cup chopped black or green olives

1 tablespoon cumin

1 tablespoon pimentón (smoked paprika)

1 tablespoon curry powder

1 tablespoon chile paste

Quick Lima Bean and Pea Stew

Makes: 4 servings   Time: About 20 minutes with frozen beans

With fresh beans and peas, this is a springtime revelation, but even in mid-winter, with frozen limas and peas, it's a real treat. The secret ingredient? Shredded romaine lettuce, which melts into the mixture, adding body and unexpected flavor. Serve with toasted whole grain bread, although it's also nice with Whole Grain Bread Salad with Dried Fruit (page 156).

1 tablespoon butter

2 tablespoons olive oil

3 shallots, chopped

2 to 4 anchovy fillets, chopped, optional

½ cup dry white wine

1 cup vegetable stock (for homemade, see pages 135 to 138) or water, or more as needed

3 cups fresh or frozen lima beans

2 cups shredded romaine lettuce

1 cup fresh or frozen peas

½ cup chopped fresh mint or parsley, plus more for garnish

Salt and black pepper

½ cup grated Parmesan cheese, for garnish

1. Put the butter and oil in a large pot or Dutch oven over medium heat. When the butter is melted, add the shallots and anchovies if you're using them, and cook, stirring occasionally, until the shallots are soft, about 5 minutes.

2. Add the wine, raise the heat a bit, and cook for a minute, stirring to loosen the bits on the bottom of the pot, until some of the liquid bubbles away. Add the stock and lima beans. Bring to a boil and lower the heat. Cover and bubble gently until they begin to get soft, anywhere from 10 minutes for frozen to 15 minutes or more for fresh. Add more liquid if the mixture seems too dry.

(F) Fast   (M) Make-Ahead   (P) Pantry Staple

3. Remove 1 cup of the limas, mash them roughly with a fork or potato masher, and return to the pot along with the lettuce, peas, mint, and a sprinkling of salt and pepper. Cook, stirring occasionally, until the lettuce is disintegrating and the mixture has thickened, about another 2 minutes. Taste and adjust the seasoning. Serve, garnished with more mint and the grated Parmesan.

Quick Lima Bean and Olive Stew. Use ½ cup chopped black olives, preferably oil-packed, instead of the peas, and use chopped spinach instead of the lettuce. Serve with lemon wedges.

Lentil Stir-Fry with Mushrooms and Caramelized Onions

Makes: **4 servings**   Time: About 30 minutes with cooked lentils

Precooked lentils are so useful that it makes total sense to cook extra. Once you do that, it's a snap to make this one-skillet dish, which you can serve with good bread or rice; or make the variation, an approximation of *mujaddarah*, a dish popular throughout the Middle East that adds rice to the skillet. Lentil cooking water and porcini soaking water are both invaluable liquids; you can use either (or a little of both) to moisten the stir-fry and save the rest to flavor other dishes.

½ cup dried porcini mushrooms, optional

Boiling water as needed

2 tablespoons olive oil, or more as needed

2 onions, halved and thinly sliced

1 pound mushrooms, preferably an assortment, sliced

3 cups cooked lentils, drained, liquid reserved

1 tablespoon fresh thyme, or 1 teaspoon dried

Salt and black pepper

1. If you're using the porcini, put them in a small bowl, cover with boiling water, and let soak for about 20 minutes. Drain, reserving the soaking liquid, and roughly chop.

2. Meanwhile, put 2 tablespoons oil in a medium skillet over medium heat. When it's hot, add the onions and cook, stirring frequently, until they are dark brown but not burned, about 15 minutes; then remove them from the skillet.

3. Add a little more oil to the pan if it's very dry and add the fresh mushrooms and the porcini if you're using them. Cover the skillet, reduce the heat to medium-low, and let the mushrooms cook, undisturbed, for about 5 minutes to release their liquid. Remove the cover and continue to cook, stirring occasionally, until the mushrooms are dry, shrunken, and slightly crisp, about 5 minutes more.

4. Stir in the lentils, ¼ cup or so of the lentil cooking water (or porcini soaking water), and the thyme; sprinkle with salt and pepper. Cook, stirring occasionally, over medium heat until everything is heated through, about 5 minutes. Serve garnished with the caramelized onions.

Lentil and Rice Stir-Fry with Mushrooms and Caramelized Onions. Substitute 1 cup cooked brown rice for 1 cup of the lentils; add more water if needed to keep the mixture moist as it cooks.

Easiest Dal

Makes: 4 servings   Time: 40 minutes, largely unattended

Dal is the Indian word for beans and also describes any dish made with them. Here is the basic rendition, most often made with lentils but sometimes with yellow split peas, pigeon peas, or mung beans. (In other words, you can use any small bean, pea, split pea, or lentil you have.)

Dal presents the perfect opportunity to try other Indian seasonings, like chaat masala or garam masala; if you have either, use it instead of the curry powder. Using coconut milk for some or all of the water will make the dal rich and slightly sweet. Or vary the recipe by adding even more vegetables or by stirring in a *tarka*-spiced butter at the end. See the variations and the recipe on page 362 for some ideas.

Ⓕ Fast   Ⓜ Make-Ahead   Ⓟ Pantry Staple

1 cup dried red lentils, rinsed and picked over

1 small cauliflower (or ½ large), cored and cut into chunks, optional

2 tablespoons minced ginger

1 tablespoon minced garlic

2 tablespoons curry powder

1 dried mild chile (like ancho), optional

Salt and black pepper

2 tablespoons butter or vegetable oil, optional

¼ cup chopped fresh cilantro, for garnish

1. Combine all the ingredients except the salt, pepper, butter or oil, and cilantro in a saucepan. Add water to cover by about 1 inch and bring to a boil. Adjust the heat so the mixture bubbles gently, cover, and cook, stirring occasionally and adding water if necessary (the mixture should be saucy but not soupy), until the lentils and cauliflower are tender, 25 to 35 minutes.

2. Fish out the chile if you used it, sprinkle with salt and pepper, and stir in the butter or oil if you're using it. (The recipe can be made ahead to this point. Refrigerate for up to a couple days or freeze for months; gently reheat before proceeding.) Taste and adjust the seasoning, garnish with the cilantro, and serve.

Easiest Dal with Extra Flavor. Seasoning the butter or oil before stirring it in (a technique known as adding a *tarka*) gives the dal an incredible flavor boost. Reserve the curry powder instead of using it in Step 1. Increase the butter or oil to 3 tablespoons and put it in a small pot over medium heat. Add the curry powder and cook until the spices are toasted and very fragrant but not burning, just a minute or 2. Proceed with the recipe.

Easiest Dal with Peanut Sauce. Follow the directions in the first variation but add 1 tablespoon peanut butter to the tarka along with the butter.

Dal with Lots of Vegetables

Makes: 4 servings   Time: 40 minutes, largely unattended

In India, dal is often a thin lentil stew, but whenever vegetables or meat are available, they're added. In any case, the stew is cooked a long time, so the vegetables melt into the lentils and absorb all the seasonings from the cooking liquid. No need to be finicky about the variety of vegetables you use—leafy greens, root vegetables, squash, and tomatoes all work.

This recipe isn't difficult by any means, though browning the vegetables in batches (unless you have an extremely large skillet) helps to develop deep flavors. To streamline the process, try the first variation; it's also good.

1 tablespoon vegetable oil, plus more as needed

1 tablespoon butter

1 cup chopped onion

2 tablespoons minced ginger

1 tablespoon minced garlic

2 cups cauliflower florets and stems cut into bite-size pieces

1 cup cubed eggplant (salted, rinsed, and dried if you like)

1 cup cubed zucchini

4 cardamom pods

1 tablespoon mustard seeds

2 whole cloves

Black pepper

1 dried mild chile (like ancho), optional

1 cup dried brown or red lentils, washed and picked over

Salt

½ cup chopped fresh cilantro, for garnish

1. Put the oil and butter in a large pot or Dutch oven over medium heat. When the butter is melted, add the onion, ginger, and garlic and cook, stirring, until softened, about 5 minutes; remove from the pot.

Ⓕ Fast   Ⓜ Make-Ahead   Ⓟ Pantry Staple

2. Turn the heat up to medium-high, add the cauliflower, and cook, stirring, until browned, 5 to 10 minutes. Remove the cauliflower and add a little more oil to the pan to prevent sticking. Add the eggplant and zucchini and cook, stirring, until browned, another 5 to 10 minutes. Add the cardamom, mustard seeds, cloves, a lot of black pepper, and the chile if you're using it. Stir until the spices are fragrant but not burning, just a minute or 2.

3. Return the onion mixture and the cauliflower to the pot along with the lentils and water to cover by about 1 inch. Bring to a boil, then adjust the heat so the mixture bubbles gently. Cover and cook, stirring occasionally and adding water if necessary (the mixture should be saucy but not soupy), until the lentils are tender, 25 to 35 minutes. (The recipe can be made ahead to this point. Refrigerate for up to a couple days or freeze for months; gently reheat before proceeding.) Remove the cardamom pods, cloves, and chile. Sprinkle with salt, then taste and adjust the seasoning. Garnish with the cilantro and serve.

Quickest Dal with Lots of Vegetables. Omit the cardamom, mustard seeds, and cloves and substitute 2 tablespoons curry powder, chaat masala, or garam masala (see the headnote on page 360). In Step 1, put the oil, butter, vegetables, lentils, and seasonings all in the pot at the same time and cover with water by about 2 inches. Cook until the lentils and vegetables are tender, 25 to 35 minutes. Season with salt and pepper to taste. Garnish and serve.

Dal with Lots of Vegetables and Chicken. After putting the oil and butter in the pot in Step 1, turn the heat to medium-high. When it's hot, add 8 ounces boneless, skinless chicken breast or thighs, cut into chunks. Cook, turning as needed, until browned on all sides, 5 to 10 minutes. Add the onion, ginger, and garlic and cook and stir for about 5 minutes more. Proceed with the recipe.

Super-Lemony Kidney Beans

Makes: 6 to 8 servings   Time: About 3 hours, largely unattended

Based on an Afghan dish called *lubia chalow*, this soupy bean stew begins with quick preserved lemons, a staple of Middle Eastern cooking. Usually the lemons are left whole or halved, heavily salted, and set aside to cure in a mixture of spices and their own juice. Chopping the fruit helps speed the process considerably with delicious (if not entirely authentic) results. Six lemons are enough so that you can use some of the mixture for the beans and store the rest in a jar in the fridge for later. (They get better and better with age.) These beans are good served over basmati or jasmine rice with a dollop of yogurt.

6 lemons

Salt

⅓ cup olive oil

2 onions, chopped

2 tablespoons minced garlic

1 tablespoon cumin seeds

1 tablespoon mustard seeds

4 cardamom pods

1 cinnamon stick

1 dried mild chile (like ancho)

¼ cup tomato paste

1 pound dried kidney beans, rinsed and picked over; don't bother to soak them

Black pepper

½ cup chopped fresh mint, for garnish

1. Heat the oven to 325°F. Trim the ends from 4 of the lemons; quarter them, remove the seeds, and put them (rind included) in a food processor. Add the juice of the remaining 2 lemons to the food processor (again, without the seeds) along with 2 teaspoons salt. Pulse several times to chop the lemons into bits but don't purée. Put the mixture in a jar and leave it on the counter while you cook the beans; shake it every once in a while.

    Ⓕ Fast   Ⓜ Make-Ahead   Ⓟ Pantry Staple

2. Put the oil in a large ovenproof pot or Dutch oven over medium-high heat. When the oil is hot, add the onions and cook, stirring occasionally, until soft, 3 to 5 minutes. Add the garlic and cook for about a minute more. Stir in the cumin, mustard seeds, cardamom pods, cinnamon stick, and dried chile; cook, stirring, for 30 seconds or so. Stir in the tomato paste.

3. Add the kidney beans and water to cover by about 3 inches. Bring to a boil, cover the pot, and bake for 90 minutes (you can ignore the beans this whole time). After 90 minutes, stir the beans and check to see if they are tender. If they are, add water if necessary to keep the beans covered by about 1 inch and stir in ½ cup of the pickled lemons. Cover and continue baking for another 30 minutes. If the beans are not yet tender, make sure they are covered by about 2 inches water and don't add the lemons yet. Cover the pot and check again in 30 minutes; repeat this step as necessary until the beans are tender enough to add the lemons.

4. When the beans are completely tender and the liquid has thickened, fish out the cinnamon stick and chile if you like (and the cardamom pods if you can find them easily). Then taste and adjust the seasonings, adding pepper and some more of the lemons if you like. Serve, garnished with the mint. (You can make the beans ahead and refrigerate them for up to several days; gently reheat before serving.)

Super-Lemony Baked Kidney Beans with Chicken. Start by browning 4 bone-in chicken thighs on both sides in the oil and remove them before adding the onions. Return the chicken to the pot along with the beans in Step 3. When the beans are done, remove the chicken, pull or cut the meat off the bones, and stir it back into the pot.

Edamame Cakes
with Soy Drizzling Sauce

Makes: 4 servings   Time: About 30 minutes

Edamame generally stay firmer than other beans with smooth interiors, so they add a pleasant texture to these green-tinted griddle cakes. Make them silver-dollar size for an addictive appetizer (serve a bowl of the sauce alongside for dipping) or make larger patties for a main course—they're great with plain rice or millet and some simply cooked greens.

¼ cup soy sauce

1 tablespoon rice vinegar or sake

2 tablespoons sesame oil

1 teaspoon sugar

1 teaspoon minced garlic, optional

1 teaspoon minced ginger, optional

2 cups fresh or frozen edamame

1 egg

½ cup sliced scallions

Whole wheat, brown rice, or all-purpose flour as needed

Salt and black pepper

Vegetable oil, for frying

1. Heat the oven to 200°F. Bring a pot of water to a boil. Combine the soy sauce, rice vinegar, half the sesame oil, sugar, and garlic and ginger if you're using them, in a small bowl.

2. Add the edamame to the boiling water and cook until tender, 5 to 10 minutes. Drain, reserving 1 cup of the cooking liquid.

3. Transfer the beans to a food processor and pulse a couple of times to break them down, then add the remaining 1 tablespoon sesame oil, egg, and scallions. Process until combined but not finely puréed; you want a thick batter with some texture that drops from a spoon. If the mixture is too stiff, stir in a little of the reserved cooking liquid; if too wet, add a little flour.

Ⓕ Fast   Ⓜ Make-Ahead   Ⓟ Pantry Staple

Sprinkle with salt and pepper and stir until the mixture is thoroughly combined.

4. Put a large skillet or griddle over medium heat. When a few drops of water dance on its surface, add a thin film of oil. Working in batches, spoon on the batter, making any size pancakes you like. Cook until the top sets and the bottom is browned, about 4 minutes. Turn and cook the other side for a couple minutes more. Keep the finished griddle cakes in the warm oven while you finish the others. Serve hot or at room temperature with the soy drizzling sauce.

Edamame Pancakes with Sesame-Chile Sauce. Before making the pancakes, toast 1 or 2 dried hot red chiles (like red Thai, chipotle, or pequín) in a dry skillet over medium heat for a minute or 2 on each side, then soak them in boiling water until soft, 15 to 30 minutes. Drain the chiles and remove and discard the seeds and veins if you like. Purée in a food processor or blender with 2 tablespoons sesame seeds and the remaining drizzling sauce ingredients, adding a few drops of water if necessary, until smooth. Proceed with the recipe from Step 2.

Edamame Pancakes with Miso Drizzling Sauce. Whisk together 2 tablespoons any miso paste, ¼ cup warm water or sake, 1 teaspoon mirin or honey, 1 teaspoon rice vinegar, and a little salt. Serve the pancakes with this instead of the soy drizzling sauce.

Tofu Chili with Soy Sauce

Makes: 4 servings   Time: About 2 hours, largely unattended

Soy sauce and tomatoes are a wonderful combination, and along with the tofu, they contribute to making this unconventional chili a real winner. The tofu takes on a tremendous amount of flavor by the time the beans are done cooking, and the texture becomes surprisingly meaty. On the flip side, if you want the tofu to lend a little of its own flavor to the chili, try starting with smoked tofu.

2 tablespoons vegetable oil

1 block firm or extra-firm tofu (about 1 pound), blotted dry

1 bunch scallions, chopped

1 tablespoon minced garlic

1 tablespoon minced ginger

2 teaspoons five-spice powder, or ½ teaspoon ground cloves

1 dried hot chile (like Thai), or to taste

One 28-ounce can tomatoes, chopped; include their juice

2 cups dried black, pinto, or soy beans, rinsed, picked over, and soaked if you like

2 tablespoons soy sauce, plus more for serving

Salt and black pepper

¼ cup chopped peanuts, for garnish

½ cup chopped fresh cilantro, for garnish

1. Put the oil in a large pot or Dutch oven over medium-high heat. When it's hot, crumble in the tofu and cook, stirring occasionally, until well browned, 5 to 10 minutes. Add all but a handful of the scallions, the garlic, and ginger and cook, stirring and scraping frequently, until the vegetables soften, 3 to 5 minutes.

2. Stir in the five-spice powder, dried chile, tomatoes, and beans. Add water to cover, bring the pot to a boil, and adjust the heat so that the beans bubble gently. Cover and cook, stirring every now and then; check the beans for doneness every 15 minutes or so and add more water if necessary a little at a time.

Ⓕ Fast   Ⓜ Make-Ahead   Ⓟ Pantry Staple

3. When the beans begin to soften (30 to 60 minutes, depending on the type of bean and whether or not you soaked them), add the soy sauce. Cook, stirring and checking, until the beans are completely tender, another 15 to 30 minutes. (The chili can be made ahead to this point and refrigerated for up to a few days or frozen for months; gently reheat before proceeding.) Fish out the chile if you like; taste and add lots of pepper, and salt if necessary. Serve, garnished with the remaining scallions, the peanuts, and cilantro. Pass soy sauce at the table.

Tempeh Chili with Soy Sauce. Substitute tempeh for the tofu. Make sure it's well browned in Step 1, which might take another 5 minutes. Proceed with the recipe.

Adding Flavor to Vegetarian Beans

You can skip the meat, fish, or poultry in any of these dishes. Here are some ways to make up for the missing flavor:

Increase the quantities of the seasoning ingredients that are already called for, careful to add seasonings a little at a time and tasting after each addition.

A squeeze of fresh lemon, lime, or orange juice or a drizzle of balsamic or rice vinegar will add bright top notes.

For more complexity, try adding ingredients that are smoked, fermented, or otherwise highly flavored—like soy sauce, cubed smoked tofu, soaked and chopped sea greens, toasted nuts or seeds, cooked or dried mushrooms, or tomato paste (especially when caramelized in a little oil first).

Use something other than water for cooking the beans; beer, wine, stock (for homemade, see pages 135 to 140), and juice are all good choices.

Drizzle the finished dish with a few drops of flavorful olive, sesame, or nut oil (depending on the dish's flavor profile).

Include a little bit of intensely flavored cheese.

Bean Fritters

Makes: 6 to 8 servings   Time: 1 hour, plus 24 hours to soak the beans   Ⓜ

You can use this same method with any bean or lentil—falafel is made this way, with a combination of chickpeas and favas, or one alone—but you must start with dried beans. Instead of cooking them, you just soak them for a long time until tender enough to grind. Some will soften sooner than others, but they can only absorb so much water, so better too long a soak than too short. As long as you drain them thoroughly and don't add too much liquid to the batter, they'll fry up just fine.

If you're tentative about deep-frying, flatten the fritters a bit and bake them on a well-greased sheet pan in a 400°F oven until they're browned on both sides (flip them if necessary), which will take anywhere from 15 to 25 minutes total, depending on their size. They'll be good but not as crisp or juicy as fritters fried in oil.

1¾ cups dried beans (any kind), lentils, or split peas, rinsed and picked over

2 garlic cloves, lightly crushed

1 small onion, quartered

1 cup chopped fresh parsley or cilantro

1 teaspoon salt

½ teaspoon black pepper, or to taste

½ teaspoon baking soda

1 tablespoon lemon or lime juice, or to taste

Vegetable oil, for deep-frying

1. Put the beans in a large bowl and cover with water by 3 to 4 inches. Soak for 24 hours or longer for larger beans or 12 hours for lentils or split peas; add more water if necessary to keep the beans submerged.

2. Drain the beans well and transfer them to a food processor with all the remaining ingredients except the oil; pulse until puréed, scraping down the sides of the bowl as necessary. Add water a tablespoon at a time if necessary to allow the machine to do its work but keep the mixture as dry as possible. Taste and adjust the seasoning, adding more salt, pepper, herb, or lemon juice as needed.

3. Put at least 2 inches of oil in a large, deep saucepan. The narrower the saucepan, the less oil you need, but the bigger the pan, the more fritters you can cook at the same time. Turn the heat to medium-high and heat the oil to about 350°F (a pinch of batter will sizzle immediately). Carefully drop heaping tablespoons of the bean mixture into the hot fat. Fry in batches, without crowding, until nicely browned, turning as necessary; total cooking time will be less than 5 minutes. As they finish cooking, drain them on towels. Serve immediately.

Bean-and-Carrot Fritters. Reduce the quantity of dried beans to 1¼ cups and add 1½ cups shredded carrots to the food processor in Step 2.

Some Ways to Vary Bean Fritters

Add ½ cup nuts to the mixture before processing.

Reduce the quantity of dried beans to 1¼ cups and add ½ cup rolled oats.

Add the grated zest of a lemon, lime, or orange.

Add 1 tablespoon any seasoning blend, like chili or curry powder.

Add up to ½ cup any grated or crumbled cheese.

For an approximation of falafel, use chickpeas and add 1 teaspoon coriander, 1 tablespoon cumin, and 1 teaspoon cayenne.

Substitute 1 cup cooked, squeezed dry, and chopped spinach for the parsley or cilantro.

Substitute 1 small bunch scallions for the onion.

Add 1 fresh hot chile, such as jalapeño or Thai, seeded if you like.

Add a 1-inch piece ginger, peeled and roughly chopped.

Follow proportions for Bean-and-Carrot Fritters but use any root vegetable (parsnip, potato, turnip, sweet potato, celery root) or squash instead of the carrots.

Braised Chickpea Fritters and Vegetables

Makes: 6 to 8 servings   Time: 1½ hours, plus 24 hours to soak the beans

Bean fritters, which are much like falafel, are common throughout the Mediterranean, Middle East, Africa, and India. In this Ethiopian-inspired recipe, they're braised in a spicy tomato sauce with potatoes and collard greens. (For a totally different flavor profile, see the variation.) Since this recipe is a little labor-intensive, I like to make a big batch and build a party around it. Serve with brown rice or Easy Whole Grain Flatbread (page 512).

1¾ cups dried chickpeas

Double recipe of All-Purpose Tomato Sauce (page 194), made without the 3 optional ingredients (see Step 1)

2 tablespoons minced ginger

2 tablespoons minced garlic

½ teaspoon each allspice, cardamom, cinnamon, and turmeric

Pinch of cayenne, optional

1 pound all-purpose potatoes, peeled and cut into small chunks

1 bunch collard greens (about 1 pound), cut into ribbons

2 garlic cloves

1 small onion, quartered

1 cup chopped fresh parsley or cilantro

Salt and black pepper

½ teaspoon baking soda

1 tablespoon lemon juice, or to taste

Vegetable oil, for deep-frying

1. Put the beans in a large bowl and add water to cover by 3 to 4 inches. Soak for 24 hours (add more water if necessary to keep the beans submerged). Meanwhile, make the tomato sauce (see page 194) in a large pot or Dutch oven. Instead of using the optional ingredients, add the ginger, garlic, and the spices to the onions as they cook in Step 1. (You can make the sauce up to this point several days ahead of time and refrigerate; gently reheat before proceeding.)

Ⓕ Fast   Ⓜ Make-Ahead   Ⓟ Pantry Staple

2. When you're ready to finish the dish, add the potatoes to the sauce and adjust the heat so the mixture bubbles steadily. Cover and cook until almost tender, 10 to 15 minutes. Stir in the collards and turn off the heat.

3. Drain the beans well and transfer them to a food processor with all the remaining ingredients except the oil; pulse until minced, scraping down the sides of the bowl as necessary. Add water a tablespoon at a time if necessary to allow the machine to do its work but keep the mixture as dry as possible. Taste and adjust the seasoning, adding more salt, pepper, or lemon juice as needed.

4. Put at least 2 inches of oil in a large, deep saucepan; the narrower the saucepan, the less oil you need, but the bigger the pan, the more fritters you can cook at the same time. Turn the heat to medium-high and heat the oil to about 350°F (a pinch of batter will sizzle immediately). Carefully drop heaping tablespoons of the bean mixture into the hot fat. Fry in batches, without crowding, until nicely browned, turning as necessary; total cooking time will be less than 5 minutes. As they finish cooking, add them to the tomato sauce.

5. When all the fritters are done, bring the tomato sauce back to a boil, then lower the heat so the mixture gently bubbles. Cook, adding more water as necessary to keep it from sticking, until the fritters soak up some sauce and the greens and potatoes are tender, 5 to 10 minutes. Taste and adjust the seasoning and serve.

Braised White Bean Fritters and Vegetables. Substitute dried white beans for the chickpeas, a large eggplant for the potatoes, and escarole for the collards. Omit the ginger, allspice, cardamom, cinnamon, and turmeric from the tomato sauce in Step 1; instead make the sauce with the optional basil and cheese called for in the sauce recipe (page 194) and proceed.

Braised Bean Dumplings and Vegetables. Follow either the main recipe or the first variation. Instead of frying the fritters in vegetable oil in Step 4, drop the batter into the simmering sauce with a spoon after adding the collards. Cover the pot and cook until the dumplings are firm and cooked through, 10 to 20 minutes, depending on their size.

Black Beans Cooked Purple

Cooked grated beets and red cabbage add a hint of sweetness and terrific earthiness to these black beans, as their flavors contribute mightily to the cooking liquid. Serve this (or the equally colorful variation) over baked potatoes or whole wheat egg noodles.

2 tablespoons olive oil

8 ounces crumbled smoked or cooked sausage, or chopped smoked ham

1 large red onion, chopped

2 tablespoons minced garlic

1 tablespoon chopped fresh sage, or 1 teaspoon dried, or to taste

1 pound beets (about 2 large), peeled and grated

½ head red cabbage, grated

1½ cups dried black beans, rinsed, picked over, and soaked if you like

Salt and black pepper

Dijon mustard, for serving

1. Put the oil in a large pot or Dutch oven over medium-high heat. When it's hot, add the sausage and cook, stirring frequently, until nicely browned, 5 to 10 minutes. Reduce the heat to medium, add the onion, garlic, and sage, and cook, stirring, until the mixture is soft and golden, 5 to 10 minutes more.

2. Add the beets and cabbage and cook, stirring occasionally, until they are soft and deeply colored, 15 to 20 minutes. Add the beans and enough water to cover by about 2 inches. Bring the mixture to a boil, then reduce the heat so it bubbles gently. Cover and cook, stirring once in a while and adding water if necessary, until the beans are tender, 45 minutes to 2 hours.

3. When the beans are tender and the stew has thickened, season with salt and pepper. Serve, passing the mustard at the table.

Pinto Beans Cooked Orange. Substitute dried pinto beans for the black beans and 1½ pounds grated pumpkin or winter squash for the beets and cabbage. Omit the mustard. Garnish with chopped hazelnuts or almonds if you like.

Beans Rancheros

Makes: 4 servings   Time: 45 minutes with cooked or canned beans

Smoky, spicy, roughly mashed beans are a wonderful bed for baked eggs. Double the recipe for a crowd (and use a 9 × 13-inch baking dish). You can even add more eggs without changing the cooking time, and you only have to use one pan. The presentation is gorgeous, too. Serve the beans with warm corn tortillas, chips, or rice or potatoes on the side.

> 1 tablespoon olive oil
>
> 3 cups cooked or canned pinto or black beans, drained
>
> 1 or 2 canned chipotle chiles, minced, with some of their adobo sauce
>
> 1 teaspoon cumin
>
> Salt and black pepper
>
> 2 or 3 ripe tomatoes, chopped
>
> 4 eggs
>
> ¼ cup chopped scallions, for garnish
>
> Lime wedges, for serving

1. Heat the oven to 350°F. Coat a 9-inch square baking dish or ovenproof skillet with the oil. Add the beans, chipotles and adobo, cumin, and a sprinkling of salt and pepper and roughly mash the mixture with a potato masher or fork. Stir in the tomatoes and transfer the pan to the oven.

2. Bake until the mixture is hot, bubbly, and some of the liquid has evaporated, 15 to 20 minutes. (The dish can be prepared ahead to this point and refrigerated for up to a day; bring to room temperature before proceeding.)

3. Make 4 indentations in the beans with the back of a spoon. Crack 1 egg into each hole, sprinkle the eggs with salt and pepper, and return the pan to the oven. Bake until the yolks are still jiggly and the whites have turned opaque (or longer if you want the eggs cooked firm), 10 to 20 minutes. Garnish with the scallions and serve with lime wedges.

Cheesy Beans Rancheros With or Without Eggs. Top each egg with 1 tablespoon grated cheddar or Jack cheese or crumbled queso fresco, or simply substitute the cheese for the eggs if you like.

Mashed Favas
with Warm Tomatoes and Feta

Makes: 4 servings   Time: 20 minutes with fresh, frozen, or cooked dried beans   Ⓕ

Fava beans come in many forms (see page 349), and you can use any of them in this recipe. If you have the time to cook a batch, dried favas (the most traditional) will give you a nuttier flavor and a deep, coffee-colored dish with complex flavors. (Buy split dried favas instead of whole, or you'll have to squeeze them out of their skins after you cook them.) Fresh or frozen shelled favas—the green ones that look like neon lima beans—have a brighter taste and are by far the most convenient.

3 cups fresh, frozen, or cooked dried fava beans

1 cup stock (for homemade, see pages 135 to 140), water, or bean-cooking liquid

Juice of 1 lemon

Salt and black pepper

¼ cup olive oil

1 red onion, chopped

2 teaspoons minced garlic

4 ripe tomatoes, chopped

½ cup crumbled feta cheese

¼ cup chopped fresh parsley or mint, for garnish

Lemon wedges

1. Put the favas, ½ cup of the liquid, the lemon juice, and a sprinkling of salt and pepper in a large, deep skillet over medium heat. As the beans begin to heat, roughly mash and stir them with a potato masher or fork. If they begin to stick to the skillet, add more liquid—a little at a time—to loosen them to the consistency you like. Transfer the beans to a shallow serving bowl or platter.

2. Wipe out the pan, add the oil, and return it to medium heat. When the oil is hot, add the onion and garlic and cook, stirring occasionally, until they begin to soften, 3 to 5 minutes. Add the tomatoes, feta, and a sprinkle of salt and pepper and cook, stirring, only until the tomatoes are warmed

Ⓕ Fast   Ⓜ Make-Ahead   Ⓟ Pantry Staple

through and the cheese softens, just another minute or 2. Spoon the tomato and feta mixture over the mashed favas, making sure to drizzle the pan juices over everything. Garnish with the herb and serve with lemon wedges.

Mashed Cannellinis and Potatoes with Gorgonzola

Makes: 4 servings   Time: 30 minutes with cooked or canned beans

With soothing potatoes, pungent Gorgonzola, and creamy cannellinis, this is comfort food, modernized. And it's perfect for any time you've got a leftover baked potato in the fridge. Cannellinis are ideal for rough mashing because they almost perfectly mimic potatoes. This dish is even better if you use roasted garlic (for homemade, see page 421)—a full head, or even more—instead of fresh.

1 large all-purpose or baking potato, cooked or raw

1 tablespoon olive oil

1 tablespoon minced garlic

1 tablespoon chopped fresh rosemary or lavender, or 1 teaspoon dried

2 cups cooked or canned cannellini beans, drained, liquid reserved

¼ cup half-and-half or whole milk

½ cup crumbled Gorgonzola or other blue cheese

¼ cup chopped fresh parsley

Salt and black pepper

1. If you haven't cooked the potato yet, cook it whole in the microwave until tender, or cut it into chunks and cook it in boiling water until tender, 15 to 20 minutes. Once cooked (or if already cooked), peel the potato.

2. Put the oil in a large, deep skillet over medium heat. When it's hot, add the garlic and rosemary and cook, stirring, until fragrant, just a minute or 2. Add the cannellinis, potato, half-and-half, Gorgonzola, and a splash of bean-cooking liquid or water.

3. Mash and stir the beans and potato with a fork or potato masher, adding a little more bean liquid or water if the mixture begins to stick to the pan. Once it's hot and the consistency you like, stir in the parsley. Taste and add some salt and pepper. Serve.

Ultrasmooth Mashed Cannellinis and Potatoes with Gorgonzola. Put the beans and potato through a potato ricer or food mill before adding them to the pan in Step 2.

Twice-Baked Mashed Cannellinis and Potatoes with Gorgonzola. This works with either the main recipe or the above variation. Heat the oven to 450°F. Toss 1 cup bread crumbs (preferably whole grain and homemade) with 2 tablespoons olive oil and ¼ cup parsley if you like. Put the bean mixture in a 9-inch baking dish or ovenproof skillet and spread the bread crumbs out on the top. Bake until hot, bubbly, and browned, 10 to 15 minutes.

White Bean and Shrimp Burgers

Makes: 4 servings   Time: 30 minutes with cooked or canned beans

You can give these the hamburger treatment, and either serve them on buns with the usual condiments or eat them as unadorned patties with a couple of side dishes. For an appetizer, roll them into bite-size fritters. Or double the recipe and bake the mixture in a loaf pan (see page 333).

Change the flavorings just as easily: Try stirring in ginger, garlic, chiles, soy sauce, fresh herbs, citrus zest, or a blend like curry or chili powder—alone or in combination.

> 1 large garlic clove
>
> 8 ounces shrimp, peeled (see page 22)
>
> 2 cups cooked or canned white beans, well drained
>
> ¼ cup roughly chopped chives or scallions
>
> ¼ cup chopped fresh parsley
>
> Salt and black pepper
>
> ¼ cup olive oil, or more as needed

    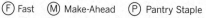 Ⓕ Fast   Ⓜ Make-Ahead   Ⓟ Pantry Staple

1. Combine the garlic, a couple of the shrimp, and ½ cup of the white beans in a food processor and pulse until blended but not quite puréed, stopping the machine to scrape down the sides of the container as necessary. Add the remaining shrimp and beans, the chives, parsley, and a sprinkle of salt and pepper and pulse until the mixture is roughly chopped and just combined.

2. Shape the mixture into whatever size patties you like and refrigerate them for at least 10 minutes or up to several hours. When you're ready to cook, put a film of oil in a large skillet over medium heat (or on an electric griddle set to 350°F). Cook the burgers until nicely browned on one side, 5 to 10 minutes, depending on the thickness of the burgers; turn carefully and cook on the other side, adding more oil if the pan looks dry, until it is also browned and the center is firm and cooked through, about another 5 minutes. Serve hot or at room temperature.

White Bean and Salmon Burgers. Substitute salmon for the shrimp, and dill for the chives if you like.

Broiled White Bean and Shrimp or Salmon Burgers. After shaping the patties in Step 2, turn on the broiler and put the rack about 4 inches from the heat source. Put the patties on a well-greased rimmed baking sheet, brush the tops with olive oil, and broil, turning once, until cooked through and browned on both sides, 10 to 15 minutes total.

New Orleans–Style BBQ Shrimp with Vinegary Black-Eyed Peas

Makes: 4 servings   Time: About 30 minutes with cooked or canned beans

Traditional New Orleans BBQ shrimp are served in their shells in a pool of bright red sauce, making for fun if messy eating. If you don't want to deal with peeling saucy shrimp at the table, use peeled shrimp with the tails left on, if possible. Or skip the shrimp altogether and try this recipe with soft-shell crabs (see the variation), hard-shell crabs (cook them exactly as you would the shrimp, only longer), or lump crab meat (just warm it in the sauce for a couple minutes in Step 3).

Use already cooked, frozen, fresh, dried, or canned black-eyed peas here. If you are making the beans from scratch for this dish, cook them until they are tender but not falling apart.

2 tablespoons olive oil

1 onion, chopped

2 celery stalks, chopped, any leaves chopped for garnish

1 red bell pepper, chopped

3 cups cooked or canned black-eyed peas, drained

2 tablespoons sherry or apple cider vinegar

2 tablespoons butter

12 large, shell-on shrimp or peeled shrimp with the tails left on (see page 22)

2 tablespoons paprika

1 teaspoon cayenne

Salt and black pepper

1 tablespoon Worcestershire sauce

¼ cup dry white wine

¼ cup chopped fresh parsley, for garnish

Hot sauce, for serving

1. Put the oil in a large skillet over medium heat. When it's hot, add the onion, celery, and bell pepper and cook, stirring occasionally, until the vegetables soften and turn golden, 5 to 10 minutes.

2. Add the black-eyed peas and cook until they are heated through, a few minutes more. Add the vinegar, scraping up any brown bits from the bottom of the pan, and transfer the mixture to a serving platter.

3. Wipe out the pan, return it to medium-high heat, and add the butter. When it foams, add the shrimp, paprika, cayenne, a sprinkle of salt and pepper, and the Worcestershire. Cook, stirring occasionally for a minute or 2, then add the wine. Cook until the shrimp are pink all over (but not rubbery) and the sauce has reduced a bit, 5 to 10 minutes. (The sauce should be the consistency of thin barbeque sauce; if it looks like it is getting too thick, add a few drops of water.)

4. Pour the shrimp and sauce over the black-eyed peas, garnish with the parsley and celery leaves, and serve with hot sauce passed at the table.

BBQ Soft-Shell Crabs with Vinegary Black-Eyed Peas. Substitute 4 small, cleaned soft-shell crabs for the shrimp. Before Step 3, dredge them in flour if you like and cook them in the butter for a minute or 2 on each side before adding the remaining ingredients. Proceed with the recipe.

Steamed Lima Beans with White Fish

Makes: 4 servings   Time: 30 minutes

Steaming on a bed of beans and tomatoes yields a thick, creamy, almost stewlike sauce that pairs beautifully with a perfectly cooked piece of fish. You can substitute any just-cooked beans for the limas, and the type of fish is totally up to you as well, as long as it is sturdy enough to hold together during cooking.

  2 tablespoons olive oil, plus more for serving

  1 onion, chopped

  1 tablespoon minced garlic

  2 cups chopped tomatoes (canned are fine; include their juice)

  1 bay leaf

  3 cups fresh, frozen, or cooked dried lima beans

  Salt and black pepper

  12 ounces sturdy white fish (see page 22), cut into 4 equal portions

  Chopped fresh basil, for garnish

1. Put the oil in a large, deep skillet over medium-high heat. When it's hot, add the onion and garlic and cook, stirring occasionally, until they begin to soften, 3 to 5 minutes. Add the tomatoes and bay leaf and cook, stirring occasionally, until they just start to release some juice, about 5 minutes. Stir in the lima beans and sprinkle with salt and pepper.

2. Lay the pieces of fish on top of the tomatoes and beans and sprinkle with salt and pepper. Make sure the mixture is bubbling steadily, then cover the pan and cook until the fish is just done, 5 to 10 minutes, depending on the thickness of the fish (a thin-bladed knife inserted into the center will meet little resistance). Taste and adjust the seasoning if necessary. Serve each piece of fish with some of the tomatoes and limas, garnished with the basil and a little more olive oil if you like.

Steamed Lima Beans with Whole Small Fish. Substitute 4 small, whole fish, like mackerel or large sardines, for the fish fillets. They will take a few minutes longer to cook.

(F) Fast   (M) Make-Ahead   (P) Pantry Staple

Steamed Clams with Double Black Beans

Makes: 4 servings   Time: 30 minutes with cooked or canned beans

An updated twist on a Chinese dim sum classic. The first kind of black beans are salted fermented black soybeans, which keep in the fridge indefinitely. They're small and slightly shriveled with a strong fermented soy flavor and aroma. The second are familiar black turtle beans. The resulting dish is a little saucy and fabulous spooned over short-grain brown rice, millet, or buckwheat noodles.

  2 tablespoons vegetable oil

  1 teaspoon sesame oil

  1 bunch scallions, white and green parts separated, all chopped

  1 tablespoon minced garlic

  1 tablespoon minced ginger

  1 fresh hot chile (like jalapeño or Thai), minced

  2 tablespoons fermented black beans

  ½ cup sake or dry white wine

  1 tablespoon soy sauce

  2 cups cooked or canned black beans, drained, liquid reserved

  2 pounds littleneck or other hard-shell clams, well scrubbed, those with broken shells discarded

Salt and black pepper

Chopped fresh cilantro, for garnish

Toasted sesame seeds, for garnish, optional

1. Put the vegetable and sesame oils in a large skillet over medium-high heat for 1 minute. Add the white parts of the scallions along with the garlic, ginger, and chile and cook, stirring occasionally, until soft, 3 to 5 minutes. Add the fermented black beans, sake, and soy sauce and cook for another minute, stirring and scraping up the brown bits from the bottom of the pan.

2. Add the cooked black beans with ½ cup of their liquid and the clams. Cover, bring to a boil, and reduce the heat to maintain a gentle bubble. Cook, undisturbed, for 5 minutes, then lift the lid to check the clams' progress. If the majority of their shells haven't opened, cover again and give them a couple more minutes. When they're all open (if any don't, you can open them with a butter knife), remove from the heat. Taste and add a little salt and pepper if you like. Serve the clams and beans in bowls, garnished with the scallion greens, cilantro, and sesame seeds.

White Bean Gratin with Sliced Salmon and Dill

Makes: **4 servings**   Time: **1 hour with cooked or canned beans, largely unattended**   Ⓜ

Just the thing for easy entertaining. Salmon is terrific here—broil it so it's just barely cooked through—or use thin slices of any other fish instead, or shrimp or scallops (which you'll need to turn halfway through cooking). Or use nothing at all: The gratin is that good. Flageolets are an excellent substitute for cannellinis here, if you can get your hands on them.

> 3 tablespoons olive oil
>
> 3 cups cooked or canned cannellini beans, drained, liquid reserved
>
> 2 zucchini, grated
>
> Grated zest and juice of 1 lemon
>
> Salt and black pepper
>
> 8 ounces salmon fillet, preferably wild (see page 22), cut into thin slices
>
> ¼ cup chopped dill, for garnish
>
> Lemon wedges, for serving

1. Heat the oven to 400°F. Grease a 2-quart baking dish or a 9 × 13-inch baking pan with 1 tablespoon of the oil. Combine the beans, zucchini, and lemon zest in the prepared dish; sprinkle with salt and pepper and drizzle with the lemon juice and a little of the reserved bean liquid. Cover with foil and bake until the zucchini is tender and releasing its juice, about 20 minutes.

2. Uncover the gratin and continue baking until it is nearly dry, 25 to 30 minutes more. Remove the dish from the oven. (The dish can be made ahead to this point and refrigerated for up to a day; bring it to room temperature

     Ⓕ Fast Ⓜ Make-Ahead Ⓟ Pantry Staple

before proceeding.) Turn on the broiler; the heat should be medium-high and the rack as close to the heat source as possible.

3. Put the salmon slices on top of the bean mixture (they won't cover the whole thing but that's fine). Sprinkle with salt and pepper and drizzle with the remaining 2 tablespoons oil. Broil until the salmon is just done, only a couple minutes. Garnish with the dill. Serve hot or at room temperature with lemon wedges.

White Bean Gratin with Squid and Tomatoes. Substitute 1 cup chopped tomatoes, fresh or drained canned, for the zucchini. Substitute 8 ounces squid for the salmon. Garnish with chopped fresh basil instead of dill.

Using Canned, Cooked, Frozen, and Fresh Beans in These Recipes

I remain a strong advocate of cooking a pot of beans from scratch every week. But I no longer totally avoid canned beans. They've gotten better for one thing, and the convenience is undeniable.

So here are some tips for converting recipes back and forth between canned beans and dried. In recipes that call for 1 pound dried beans, figure 5 to 6 cups cooked beans (thawed if they've been frozen); add them in the last step. If the recipe calls for water or stock, hold it back until you incorporate the beans into the dish and then add only what it takes to keep everything moist.

If you're using canned beans instead of home-cooked beans, drain and rinse them, then use water or stock for the liquid in the recipe. Use the liquid from the can if you like, but remember that it can be very salty (and, unfortunately, a little metallic-tasting).

You can also use fresh or frozen beans in these recipes. The most common are limas, favas, and edamame, but sometimes you can find black-eyed peas and chickpeas, too. (Whenever you see them fresh, grab 'em, even if they require shelling; they're worth the work.) Bring a large pot of water to a boil, salt it, add the shelled fresh or frozen beans, then lower the heat and simmer. Check them frequently. Some frozen beans can become tender in just a few minutes; fresh beans can take 20 to 30 minutes or more. Once they're tender, use them just as you would precooked or canned beans, only save their flavorful cooking liquid, which will almost always come in handy.

Fava Gratin with Scallops and Pesto Bread Crumbs

Makes: 4 servings   Time: 30 minutes with shelled or frozen beans

There is no denying that shucking and peeling fresh fava beans is a pain, but you might consider this supereasy, extremely flavorful gratin the reward. Alternatively (and fortunately) you can use convenient frozen favas, which are available in many supermarkets and specialty stores. To use fresh, you'll need about 3 pounds in the pod; shell them and remove the skins, then blanch them in boiling water for a few minutes until they're just tender.

8 ounces bread (about 4 thick slices), preferably whole grain and day old, torn into pieces

1 packed cup fresh basil

1 garlic clove

4 tablespoons olive oil

⅓ cup grated Parmesan cheese

Salt and black pepper

3 cups frozen fava beans

2 tablespoons lemon juice

¼ cup dry white wine or water

4 large or 8 small sea scallops

1. Heat the oven to 450°F. Put the bread in a food processor. Pulse a few times, then let the machine run for a few seconds until coarsely chopped. Transfer the bread crumbs to a small bowl.

2. Add the basil, garlic, and 3 tablespoons of the oil to the food processor and pulse, stopping to scrape down the sides of the container if necessary. Add the basil mixture to the bread crumbs, sprinkle with the Parmesan and some salt and pepper, and toss to combine.

3. Put the beans in a 9-inch baking dish or ovenproof skillet and toss with the remaining 1 tablespoon oil, the lemon juice, wine, and a sprinkle of salt and pepper. Cover and bake until hot and bubbly, about 10 minutes.

     Fast   Ⓜ Make-Ahead   Ⓟ Pantry Staple

4. Nestle the scallops into the beans and sprinkle the bread crumb mixture over all. Bake, uncovered, until the scallops are opaque halfway through, 5 to 10 minutes (peek with a sharp knife). Serve hot or at room temperature.

Curried Chickpeas and Cauliflower with Chicken

Makes: 4 servings   Time: 40 minutes with cooked or canned beans

Chicken, cauliflower, and chickpeas all take well to strong seasonings, and they taste great together. In this one-pan Indian-tinged stir-fry, two other *c*'s— curry and coconut milk—round out the dish into a light stew that's perfect to serve with brown basmati rice or Whole Wheat Chapatis (page 522).

   3 tablespoons vegetable oil

   8 ounces boneless, skinless chicken breast or thighs, cut into chunks or
      slices and blotted dry

   Salt and black pepper

   1 tablespoon minced ginger

   $\frac{1}{2}$ cup chopped scallions, white parts only

   2 cups cooked or canned chickpeas, drained

   1 tablespoon curry powder

   1 cup coconut milk

   1 small cauliflower, cored and roughly chopped

   1 or 2 small dried hot red chiles (like Thai), or a pinch of red chile flakes

   1 teaspoon sugar, optional

   $\frac{1}{2}$ cup chopped fresh cilantro, for garnish

1. Put a large, deep skillet over high heat. Add 2 tablespoons of the oil, swirl it around, and immediately add the chicken. Stir once, sprinkle with salt and pepper, and let it sit for 1 minute before stirring again. Cook, stirring occasionally, until the chicken has lost its pink color, 3 to 5 minutes. Add the ginger and scallions and cook for a half minute or so. Remove everything from the pan.

2. Add the remaining 1 tablespoon oil to the skillet. When it's hot, add the chickpeas and sprinkle with salt and pepper. Cook, shaking the pan occasionally, until the chickpeas are lightly browned, 5 to 10 minutes. Sprinkle with the curry powder, stir again, and remove from the pan.

3. Put the coconut milk, cauliflower, and chiles into the hot pan and reduce the heat so it bubbles gently. Cook, stirring occasionally, until the cauliflower is tender and the mixture thickens, 10 minutes or longer.

4. Return the chicken and chickpeas to the pan and toss once or twice. Stir in the sugar if you like, then garnish with cilantro and serve.

Curried Chickpeas with Okra with Chicken. Instead of the cauliflower, trim the stems from 1 pound okra but leave the pods whole. Proceed with the recipe, cooking the okra with the coconut milk mixture in Step 3 until it's just tender, which could be less than 5 minutes, depending on its size.

Chickpea Tagine with Chicken and Bulgur

Makes: 4 servings   Time: About 1½ hours with cooked or canned beans, largely unattended

Braise precooked (or canned) chickpeas and chicken in a North African spice mixture and the chickpeas disintegrate, the chicken becomes fork-tender, and everything is intensely flavored. It's an extraordinary dish and made even more so by the bulgur, which is cooked right in the stewing liquid.

2 cups cooked or canned chickpeas, drained, with liquid reserved

2 cups bean-cooking liquid, stock (for homemade, see pages 135 to 140), or water, or more as needed

Salt and black pepper

2 tablespoons olive oil

4 bone-in chicken thighs

1 large onion, chopped

1 tablespoon minced garlic

1 teaspoon minced ginger

      Fast   Make-Ahead   Ⓟ Pantry Staple

1 tablespoon cumin

1½ teaspoons coriander

1½ teaspoons cinnamon

½ cup raisins, chopped dates, or currants

1 cup chopped tomatoes (canned are fine; include their juice)

½ cup bulgur

½ cup chopped fresh parsley, for garnish

1. Heat the oven to 400°F. Put the beans and the liquid in a large pot or Dutch oven over medium heat; sprinkle with salt and pepper. Adjust the heat so the mixture barely bubbles.

2. Meanwhile, put the oil in a large, deep skillet over medium-high heat. Season the chicken with salt and pepper and add it to the skillet. Cook, turning and rotating as necessary, until it's brown on both sides, 10 to 15 minutes. Add the chicken to the pot of beans.

3. Pour off all but 3 tablespoons fat from the skillet. Turn the heat down to medium and add the onion. Cook, stirring occasionally, until the onion is soft, 5 to 10 minutes. Add the garlic, ginger, cumin, coriander, cinnamon, raisins, and tomato; cook and stir just long enough to loosen any brown bits from the bottom of the pan. Transfer the mixture to the beans and adjust the heat so the mixture returns to a gentle bubble.

4. Cover the pot and cook, checking occasionally to make sure the mixture is bubbling gently, for 20 to 30 minutes. Stir the bulgur into the bottom of the pot; it should be covered with about 1 inch of liquid. If not, add more water. Cover and cook until the chicken is tender and the bulgur is done, another 10 to 15 minutes. Serve each chicken thigh with a big spoonful of the chickpea mixture and garnish with parsley.

Chickpea Tagine with Lamb Shank and Bulgur. Even more authentic. Substitute 2 lamb shanks for the chicken. Brown them as you would the chicken and proceed with the recipe, allowing an extra 30 to 40 minutes to cook the lamb in Step 4. When the stew is done, the meat should be nearly falling off the bone. Remove it from the pot, shred the lamb with a fork, and return the meat to the pot. Serve and garnish as described above.

White Chili with Chicken and White Root Vegetables

Makes: 6 to 8 servings   Time: 2 to 2½ hours, largely unattended

More refined than Chili con Poco Carne (page 397) but no less substantial. There's no reason to go the canned bean route here; dried beans don't take much longer and the results are exponentially better.

2 tablespoons olive oil

4 bone-in chicken thighs

Salt and black pepper

2 leeks, trimmed, well rinsed, and chopped, or 2 onions, chopped

4 parsnips, chopped

1 celery root, chopped

1 large or 2 medium turnips, chopped

2 all-purpose potatoes, chopped

1 tablespoon chopped fresh sage, or 1 teaspoon dried

1 bay leaf

1 dried mild chile (like ancho), or 1 tablespoon chili powder

1 tablespoon cumin

Grated zest and juice of 1 lime

2 cups any dried white beans, rinsed, picked over, and soaked if you like

½ cup chopped fresh cilantro, plus more for garnish

½ cup chopped scallions, for garnish

1. Put the oil in a large pot or Dutch oven over medium-high heat. When it's hot, add the chicken thighs, skin side down, and sprinkle with salt and pepper. Brown them well, rotating and turning the pieces as necessary, 10 to 15 minutes. Remove the chicken and pour off all but 2 tablespoons of the fat.

2. Add the leeks to the pot and cook, stirring and lowering the heat if necessary, until softened, 3 to 5 minutes. Add the parsnips, celery root, turnip, potatoes, sage, bay leaf, chile, cumin, and lime zest and toss to coat with the

Ⓕ Fast   Ⓜ Make-Ahead   Ⓟ Pantry Staple

oil. Add the beans, chicken, and enough water to cover by about 2 inches. Bring to a boil, then adjust the heat so the chili bubbles steadily.

3. Partially cover and cook until the beans begin to soften (30 to 90 minutes, depending on the beans and whether or not you soaked them). Sprinkle with salt and pepper. Continue to cook, stirring occasionally and adding water if necessary, until the beans are quite tender and the root vegetables are nearly disintegrated, another 30 to 60 minutes.

4. Remove the chicken thighs, chile, and bay leaf. Pull the chicken meat from the bones, chop if necessary, and return the meat to the pot along with the lime juice and cilantro. Stir, taste, and adjust the seasoning. Serve, garnished with more cilantro and the scallions (or store, covered, in the refrigerator for up to 2 days).

White Chili with Ground Chicken or Turkey. Instead of the chicken thighs, use 8 ounces ground chicken or turkey and cook in Step 1 until it has lost its color, 5 to 10 minutes. Remove the meat to cook the leeks and return to the pot in Step 2.

Cassoulet with Lots of Vegetables

Makes: 4 to 8 servings   Time: 40 minutes with cooked or canned beans

This is one of my favorite recipes from *Food Matters*, and not only the dish I demonstrate most frequently but also the one I cook for any gathering of ten or more people. (I've done it for sixty; no problem.) It has nearly all of the richness of a traditional, slow-simmered cassoulet but is easier, faster, and better for you. The main recipe starts with already cooked or canned beans and is ready relatively fast. To begin with dried beans, see the variation; it takes more time, but the results are even better.

> 2 tablespoons olive oil
>
> 1 pound Italian sausages in casings, bone-in pork chops, confit duck legs, or fresh duck breasts, or a combination
>
> 1 tablespoon minced garlic
>
> 2 leeks, trimmed, well rinsed, and sliced, or 2 onions, sliced
>
> 2 carrots, cut into 1-inch lengths
>
> 3 celery stalks, cut into ½-inch pieces
>
> 2 zucchini or 1 small head green cabbage, cut into ½-inch pieces
>
> Salt and black pepper
>
> 4 cups chopped tomatoes (canned are fine; include their juice)
>
> ¼ cup chopped fresh parsley
>
> 1 tablespoon chopped fresh thyme, or 1 teaspoon dried
>
> 2 bay leaves
>
> 4 cups cooked or canned white beans, drained, liquid reserved
>
> 2 cups stock (for homemade, see pages 135 to 140), dry red wine, bean-cooking liquid, or water, or more as needed
>
> Pinch of cayenne, or to taste

1. Put the oil in a large pot over medium-high heat. A minute later, add the meat and cook, turning as needed, until the pieces are deeply browned on all sides, 10 to 15 minutes. Remove from the pan and drain off all but 2 tablespoons of the fat.

Ⓕ Fast   Ⓜ Make-Ahead   Ⓟ Pantry Staple

2. Reduce the heat to medium and add the garlic, leeks, carrots, celery, and zucchini; sprinkle with salt and pepper. Cook until softened, about 5 minutes. Add the tomatoes with their liquid, the reserved meat, and the herbs and bring to a boil. Add the beans and bring to a boil again, stirring occasionally. Reduce the heat so the mixture bubbles gently but continuously. Cook for about 20 minutes, adding the stock when the mixture gets thick and the vegetables are melting away, about halfway through cooking.

3. Fish out the meat, remove the bones and skin as needed, and discard the bay leaves. Chop the meat into chunks and return to the pot along with the cayenne. Cook for another minute or 2 to warm through, then taste and adjust the seasoning. Serve.

Slow-Cooked Cassoulet. Start with dried beans. After browning the meat in Step 1, leave it in the pan and add 8 ounces dried white beans (they'll cook faster if you soak them first; see page 353) and enough water or stock to cover by 2 inches. Bring to a boil, then reduce the heat to a gentle bubble. Cover tightly and cook, stirring occasionally, for about 1 hour. Meanwhile, in a separate pan with another 2 tablespoons olive oil, cook the vegetables as directed in Step 2. When the beans are beginning to get tender, add the vegetables to the pot of beans along with the tomatoes and herbs. Bring to a boil, then reduce the heat to a gentle bubble. Cover and cook, stirring occasionally, until the beans are fully tender, adding more liquid as necessary to keep them covered by about 1 inch. This will take anywhere from another 15 to 60 minutes, depending on the age of your dried beans.

Cannellini with Shredded Brussels Sprouts and Sausage

Makes: 4 servings   Time: 20 minutes with cooked or canned beans

Cannellini beans with garlic and sausage are admittedly hard to beat (there's a reason you see it everywhere). But shredded Brussels sprouts are a welcome addition to this classic combination; if there are still Brussels sprout haters out there, this will convert them. Serve this dish, with its beautifully flavored pan juices, over cooked grains like farro, bulgur, or cracked wheat, or a couple of thick slices of toasted bread.

3 tablespoons olive oil

8 ounces Italian sausage, casings removed

2 tablespoons minced garlic

Red chile flakes, to taste

Salt and black pepper

1 pound Brussels sprouts, shredded in a food processor or roughly chopped

½ cup white wine or water

2 cups cooked or canned cannellini beans, drained

1. Put the oil in a large skillet over medium heat. When it's hot, crumble the sausage into the pan and cook, stirring occasionally to break the meat into relatively small bits, until browned, 5 to 10 minutes. Add the garlic and chile flakes and sprinkle with salt and pepper. Cook and stir for another minute or so.

2. Add the Brussels sprouts and wine to the skillet and cook, stirring frequently, until the sprouts are tender but still a bit crunchy, 5 to 10 minutes.

3. Add the beans and cook, stirring occasionally, until they are heated through, just a minute or 2. Taste and adjust the seasoning. Serve.

Ⓕ Fast   Ⓜ Make-Ahead   Ⓟ Pantry Staple

Creamy Navy Bean and Squash Gratin with Bits of Sausage

Makes: 4 servings   Time: 1½ hours with cooked or canned beans, largely
unattended

The small amounts of sausage, half-and-half, and Parmesan make a big contribution to the flavor of this gorgeous gratin, whose texture benefits from slow baking. If you're looking for a quicker-cooking casserole, use zucchini or summer squash in place of the butternut.

4 ounces Italian sausage, casings removed, optional

¼ cup half-and-half or cream

1 tablespoon chopped fresh rosemary, or 1 teaspoon dried

3 cups cooked or canned navy beans, drained, liquid reserved

Salt and black pepper

1 small butternut squash, peeled and seeded

½ cup vegetable stock (for homemade, see pages 135 to 138) or water, or
   more as needed

3 tablespoons olive oil

¼ cup grated Parmesan cheese, optional

1. Heat the oven to 325°F. If you're using the sausage, put a small skillet over medium-high heat. When it's hot, add the sausage and cook, stirring to break it into small pieces, for 5 to 10 minutes; don't brown it too much. (If you're not using the sausage, skip to Step 2.)

2. Combine the half-and-half, rosemary, and beans in a 2-quart baking dish; sprinkle with salt and pepper. Tuck the crumbled sausage (if you're using it) into the beans.

3. Cut the butternut squash halves into thin slices. Spread the slices out on top of the beans, overlapping a bit; press down gently. Pour the stock over the top, drizzle with the oil, and sprinkle with more salt and pepper.

4. Cover with foil and bake for 45 minutes. Remove the foil and continue baking until the top is browned and glazed, another 45 minutes or so. Add a little more stock if the mixture seems too dry. And sprinkle the top with the Parmesan if you're using it for the last 10 minutes of cooking. Serve immediately or at room temperature.

Beans on Toast, Updated

Throughout the United Kingdom, beans on toast means canned white beans in tomato sauce on crisp buttered white bread (HP Sauce optional). It's an idea—and a quick, light meal—that easily translates across the pond. Slice fresh or slightly stale whole grain bread as thickly or thinly as you like, brush it with a little olive oil, and run it under a broiler or toast it on a grill.

Almost all of the bean recipes in this chapter will work on top of toast. You want them moist but not soupy, so drain them if necessary. A smear of mashed beans (like Puréed White Beans with Tons of Fresh Herbs, page 355) is a tidy option; whole beans, like Better Boston Baked Beans (page 406) become a knife-and-fork affair. There's really no need to garnish, but a slice of ripe tomato between the beans and the bread never hurts. If you don't have any leftovers handy, open a can and mash some beans in a skillet over medium heat with minced garlic, olive oil, and maybe some tomato paste, a handful of fresh herbs, or a pinch of chili powder.

For even more ideas, see Bruschetta, Rethought (page 51) or go utterly untraditional and serve a spoonful of beans over a savory pancake (like Loaded Cornpone, page 519).

  Ⓕ Fast Ⓜ Make-Ahead Ⓟ Pantry Staple

Beer-Glazed Black Beans
with Chorizo and Orange

The ratio of flavor to effort in this recipe is high. If you can't get your hands on smoked Spanish-style chorizo, a little cubed bacon or cooked and crumbled Mexican chorizo will do fine. You will taste the beer you use here, so make sure it's one you like. Serve these with long-grain brown rice, Loaded Cornpone (page 519), or Mostly Whole Wheat Tortillas (page 526).

1 orange

8 ounces Spanish chorizo, thinly sliced

1 red onion, chopped

1 red bell pepper, chopped

1 tablespoon minced garlic

One 12-ounce bottle beer

3 cups cooked or canned black beans, drained, liquid reserved

1 tablespoon chili powder

1 tablespoon honey

Salt and black pepper

½ cup chopped fresh cilantro, for garnish

1. Halve the orange and seed it if necessary. Peel one half, divide the segments, and save the rind; squeeze the juice from the other half.

2. Put the chorizo in a large skillet over medium heat. Cook, stirring and turning to brown the slices, for 5 to 10 minutes. Add the onion and bell pepper and cook, stirring occasionally, until soft, 5 to 10 minutes. Add the garlic and cook, stirring, for about a minute. Add the orange rind and juice, beer, beans, chili powder, honey, and a good sprinkling of salt and pepper.

3. Adjust the heat so the mixture bubbles steadily and cook until the liquid is slightly reduced and thickened, about 15 minutes. Taste and adjust the seasoning. Fish out the orange rind, garnish with the reserved orange segments and cilantro, and serve hot (or refrigerate for up to 3 days or freeze for months).

Chili con Poco Carne

Makes: 6 to 8 servings   Time: About 1 hour with cooked or canned beans

A perfect example of how a little bit of meat can go a long way. For a vegetarian version, just leave out the meat—better yet, try the variation. Either way, this recipe, which reheats beautifully, makes extra for your fridge or freezer.

3 tablespoons olive oil

1 pound beef chuck, pork shoulder, or lamb shoulder, cut into small cubes

Salt and black pepper

1 large onion, chopped

2 tablespoons minced garlic

1 large or 2 small eggplants, cubed

1 zucchini, chopped

2 carrots, chopped

1 cup quartered mushrooms or a handful of rinsed dried porcini

1 (or more) fresh or dried hot chile (like jalapeño or Thai), minced

1 tablespoon cumin, or to taste

1 tablespoon chopped fresh oregano, or 1 teaspoon dried

2 cups chopped tomatoes (canned are fine; include their juice)

4 cups cooked or canned kidney, pinto, or black beans, drained, liquid reserved

2 cups vegetable stock (for homemade, see pages 135 to 138) or water, or more as needed

½ cup chopped fresh cilantro or parsley, for garnish

1. Put the oil in a large pot or Dutch oven over medium-high heat. A minute later, add the meat, sprinkle with salt and pepper, and cook, stirring occasionally, until it is well browned all over, about 10 minutes. Remove the meat from the pan and pour off all but 3 tablespoons of the fat.

2. Put the pot over medium heat. Add the onion and garlic and cook, stirring, until just softened, about 3 minutes. Add the vegetables, sprinkle with salt and pepper, and cook, stirring frequently, until they begin to soften and

Ⓕ Fast   Ⓜ Make-Ahead   Ⓟ Pantry Staple

become fragrant, adjusting the heat so that nothing scorches. After 10 to 15 minutes, the vegetables should start to brown a bit and dry out.

3. Add the chile, cumin, and oregano and stir. Add the tomatoes with their juice and enough of the bean-cooking liquid to submerge everything (use some stock or water if you don't have enough) and return the meat to the pan. Bring the mixture to a boil, then lower the heat so it bubbles steadily. Cover and cook, stirring occasionally and adding more liquid if necessary, until the meat is fork-tender and the flavors have mellowed, 30 to 40 minutes. Add the beans and more liquid if necessary, and cook just long enough to heat the beans through, only a couple minutes. Taste and adjust the seasoning. Garnish with the cilantro and serve.

Chili non Carne. Omit the meat from Step 1. At the beginning of Step 2, add 2 chopped red bell peppers and 2 tablespoons tomato paste along with the garlic and onion. Let the mixture brown a bit, stirring frequently so the tomato paste doesn't burn, and proceed with the recipe.

Skillet Carnitas with Pinto Beans

Makes: **4 servings**   Time: **About 1 hour with cooked or canned beans**

Producing carnitas—crisp and chewy pieces of braised-then-sizzled pork—is usually a long-term commitment, but cooking them in a skillet is easy. Add beans and lots of crunchy raw cabbage and radishes, and you have the perfect filling for whole wheat tortillas, whether store-bought or your own (see page 526).

2 tablespoons olive oil

12 ounces pork shoulder or butt, sliced into thin 2-inch strips

Salt and black pepper

One 12-ounce bottle beer, optional

4 or more garlic cloves, smashed whole

1 tablespoon cumin

3 cups cooked pinto beans, drained, liquid reserved

2 cups shredded cabbage, for serving

1 cup chopped radishes, for serving, optional

Cilantro sprigs, for garnish

Lime wedges, for serving

Whole wheat tortillas (for homemade, see page 526), for serving

1. Put the oil in a large skillet over medium-high heat. When it's hot, add the pork, working in batches if necessary to avoid crowding, and sprinkle with salt and pepper. Cook the strips until they are nicely browned on all sides, 5 to 10 minutes.

2. Add the beer or enough water (or a combination) to nearly submerge the pork. Bring the mixture to a boil, then partially cover and adjust the heat so that it bubbles steadily. Cook until the pork is quite tender, 30 to 40 minutes.

3. Uncover the skillet and add the garlic. Turn the heat up so that the liquid begins to bubble away. Cook, stirring occasionally, until the pork is nicely browned and crisp, another 5 minutes or so. Add the cumin and stir until fragrant, just a few seconds.

4. Add the pinto beans with some of their liquid and cook, stirring occasionally and scraping up any brown bits from the bottom of the pan, until the beans are warmed through, just a couple minutes. Taste and adjust the seasoning. Serve with the cabbage, radishes, cilantro, lime, and tortillas.

Ⓕ Fast Ⓜ Make-Ahead Ⓟ Pantry Staple

Specialty Beans

Here's a (small) sampling of the heirloom, Asian, and European legumes that you can find these days without much trouble. If you can't find these or others you're looking for nearby, look into mail-order suppliers that sell specialty ingredients. Remember almost all beans are interchangeable.

Adzuki beans: Dark red with a thin white stripe down one side; traditionally sweetened and used in East Asian desserts, though they can also stand in for soybeans in savory recipes.

Anasazi beans: Mottled white and deep red, native to the American Southwest; they work well as a replacement for pinto beans.

Cranberry beans: Also called borlotti beans, these lovely, purple-flecked white beans are good substitutes for pintos, favas, or pink beans.

Flageolet beans: Immature kidney beans with a mild, grassy flavor, traditionally used in cassoulet. Use flageolet instead of navy beans, cannellini beans, or any other white bean.

Gigante beans: So big you can serve them like crudités with dip; starchy and very Mediterranean. Use in place of limas, favas, cannellinis, or other white beans.

Le Puy lentils: The only legume to receive France's *appellation d'origine contrôlée*, the same geography-based distinction given to regional wines. Green Le Puys can (obviously) replace any other kind of lentil, though they stay firm longer than most.

Mung beans: These come in many hues (usually green, tan, or yellow) and can be used like red or yellow lentils or dried peas in dals and curries; they just take a little longer to cook.

Tarbais beans: Grown in France near the Spanish border, these are white and can be used in lieu of cannellini, Great Northern, or navy beans.

Tepary beans: Teparies, which range in color from white to brown, are small and slightly flat, like big lentils. They're native American beans, from the Southwest, and a nice alternative to black-eyed peas, pintos, pink beans, black beans, and kidney beans.

Ma-Po Tofu with Tomatoes

Makes: 4 servings   Time: 20 minutes

Ma-po tofu, the classic Sichuan dish of simmered tofu and ground pork, is intensely flavorful and very quick to make. Serve it over brown rice or toss it with brown rice noodles or whole wheat spaghetti. Just remember that the dish takes only 20 minutes to prepare and cook, so start your rice or noodles first thing.

    1 tablespoon peanut or vegetable oil

    1 tablespoon minced garlic

    1 tablespoon minced ginger

    ¼ teaspoon red chile flakes, or to taste

    4 ounces ground pork

    ½ cup chopped scallions

    2 cups chopped tomatoes (canned are fine; drain their juice)

    ½ cup stock (for homemade, see pages 135 to 140) or water

    12 ounces firm silken tofu, cut into small cubes

    2 tablespoons soy sauce

    Salt

    Chopped fresh cilantro, for garnish

1. Put the oil in a large, deep skillet over medium-high heat. When it's hot, add the garlic, ginger, and chile flakes and cook just until they begin to sizzle, less than a minute. Add the pork and stir to break it up; cook, stirring occasionally, until it loses most of its pink color and begins to crisp, 3 to 5 minutes.

2. Add the scallions, tomatoes, and stock. Cook for a minute or 2, scraping the bottom of pan with a wooden spoon to loosen any brown bits of meat. Add the tofu and cook, stirring once or twice, until the tofu is heated through, about 2 minutes.

3. Stir in the soy sauce; taste and season with salt and more red chile flakes if you like. Garnish with cilantro and serve.

Ma-Po Edamame. Substitute 3 cups fresh or frozen shelled edamame for the tofu. It will take 5 to 7 minutes of cooking at a gentle simmer for fresh edamame to become tender.

Skillet Hoppin' John

Makes: 4 servings   Time: 30 minutes with cooked or canned beans   Ⓕ

A stir-fried version of the Southern black-eyed-pea-and-rice staple that makes good use of leftovers and gets a ton of flavor from bits of bacon or ham. Use this formula for any combination of cooked grains and rice, using whatever seasonings and vegetables you have handy. To round out the meal, serve it with Ten-Minute Green Salad (page 143) or stewed collard greens.

    2 tablespoons olive oil

    4 ounces slab bacon or smoked ham, cubed

    2 onions, chopped

    2 red bell peppers, chopped

    1 tablespoon minced garlic

    1 tablespoon chopped fresh rosemary or thyme, or 1 teaspoon dried

    Salt and black pepper

    2 cups cooked brown rice, preferably chilled

    2 cups cooked or canned black-eyed peas, drained, liquid reserved

    Chopped fresh parsley, for garnish

1. Put the oil in a large skillet over medium-high heat. A minute later, add the bacon and cook, stirring occasionally and adjusting the heat so the meat doesn't burn, until the pieces are crisp and browned, 5 to 10 minutes. Pour off all but 2 tablespoons of the fat from the pan and lower the heat to medium.

2. Add the onions, peppers, and garlic to the pan and cook, stirring occasionally, until soft and browned, 5 to 10 minutes. Add the rosemary and a good sprinkling of salt and pepper. Begin to add the rice, a bit at a time, breaking up any clumps and stirring it into the oil. When all the rice has been added and is glossy, add the peas with ½ cup of their liquid. Cook and stir until heated through, 1 to 2 minutes. Taste and adjust the seasoning. Serve, garnished with parsley.

Red Beans, Almost the Classic Way

Makes: 4 servings   Time: About 2 hours, largely unattended

Cubes of sweet potato add another dimension to a dish that is already smoky, faintly spicy, and rich. Serve a heaping spoonful over a mound of brown rice, and add a couple shakes of hot sauce if you like.

1½ cups dried kidney, pinto, or other red beans, rinsed, picked over, and soaked if you like

1 meaty smoked ham hock or ham bone or a 4-ounce chunk of bacon or pancetta

2 tablespoons olive oil

1 andouille or hot Italian sausage in casings

1 large onion, chopped

1 green and 1 red bell pepper, chopped

1 tablespoon minced garlic

2 or 3 sprigs fresh thyme, or 1 teaspoon dried

2 bay leaves

¼ teaspoon allspice

Pinch of cayenne

1½ cups chopped tomatoes (canned are fine; include their juice)

2 large sweet potatoes, cubed

Salt and black pepper

Chopped fresh parsley, for garnish

Hot sauce, optional

1. Put the beans and the ham hock in a large pot with water to cover by about 2 inches. Bring to a boil, skimming foam from the top if necessary. Turn the heat down so the beans barely bubble. Cover and cook, stirring infrequently and adding water if necessary to keep the beans always covered by about 2 inches.

2. Put the oil in a large skillet over medium heat. Add the sausage and cook, turning occasionally and pricking the sausage a few times to release its fat, until nicely browned, 5 to 10 minutes. Transfer it to the pot of beans (don't worry about whether it is done). Pour off some of the fat from the skillet if you like.

3. Add the onion, bell peppers, and garlic to the skillet and cook, stirring frequently, until the peppers are softened, 5 to 10 minutes. Transfer the vegetables to the pot of beans with a slotted spoon. Add the thyme, bay leaves, allspice, cayenne, and tomatoes. Adjust the heat so the mixture bubbles gently and make sure there's enough water to submerge everything. Cover and cook, stirring once in a while, until the beans begin to get tender. (This could take anywhere from 30 minutes to almost 2 hours, depending on the beans and whether you soaked them.)

4. Fish out the meat and sausage and stir in the sweet potatoes and a sprinkle of salt and pepper. Cook until the beans and sweet potatoes are very tender, 15 to 30 minutes more. Meanwhile, chop up the meat, slice the sausage, and return everything to the pot. (You can make the stew up to this point and refrigerate for up to several days or freeze for months; gently reheat it before proceeding.) When you're ready to serve, remove the bay leaves and season to taste with salt and pepper. Garnish with parsley and serve.

Better Boston Baked Beans

Makes: 6 to 8 servings   Time: 3 to 4 hours, largely unattended

Most recipes for Boston baked beans—including some of my older ones—are exercises in excess, especially sweetness. With a few tweaks to the technique and a little tomato paste, you can cut the amount of bacon and sweetener in half without missing them one bit. As an added bonus, the dish requires virtually no work once you pop it in the oven. For a vegan or vegetarian version, use 2 tablespoons olive oil or butter instead of the bacon, and if you like add a large piece of kombu seaweed to the pot before baking.

8 ounces slab bacon, cubed or thickly sliced

2 onions, chopped

¼ cup tomato paste

¼ cup molasses

2 tablespoons Dijon mustard, or to taste

1 pound dried navy or other white beans, rinsed, picked over, and soaked if you like

Salt and black pepper

1. Heat the oven to 300°F. Put the bacon in a large ovenproof pot or Dutch oven over medium heat. Cook, stirring, until the pieces are crisp and some fat is rendered, 5 to 10 minutes. Scoop out the bacon with a slotted spoon. Add the onions to the fat and cook, stirring, until very soft and browned, 15 to 20 minutes.

2. Stir in the tomato paste and keep cooking and stirring until it darkens and dries a bit, another minute or 2. Return the bacon to the pot and stir in the molasses and mustard. Add the beans and enough water to cover by 3 inches. Bring the mixture to a boil, stirring and scraping up any brown bits from the bottom of the pot. Cover the pot and transfer it to the oven.

3. Bake, undisturbed, for the first hour, then stir. The beans should still be submerged by at least 2 inches of water; if not, add a little more. Cover and bake for another hour, then check and stir again. By now the beans should be getting tender; keep checking every 30 minutes.

(F) Fast   (M) Make-Ahead   (P) Pantry Staple

4. When the beans are tender, remove the lid and make sure they are covered by about 1 inch of liquid. Raise the oven heat to 400°F. Bake until the mixture thickens and bubbles and the top and sides brown a bit, anywhere from 15 minutes to 1 hour. Season to taste with salt and pepper and add more mustard if you like. Serve immediately (or cool and refrigerate for up to a few days or freeze for months).

Beans and Ribs. Omit the bacon. In Step 1, put 1 tablespoon olive oil in the pot over medium-high heat for 1 minute. Add 2 meaty country-style pork ribs or 4 spareribs to the pot and sprinkle with salt and black pepper or cayenne. Cook, more or less undisturbed but adjusting the heat so the meat browns without burning, for 5 to 10 minutes; turn the ribs and brown on the other side for a few minutes more. Remove the ribs from the pot, add the onions, and proceed with the recipe, returning the meat to the pot along with the beans in Step 2.

Beans "Bolognese"

Makes: 4 servings   Time: About 2 hours, largely unattended

Beans and ragu—the hearty Italian tomato sauce that doesn't come from a jar—are a match made in heaven. The combo (think homemade sloppy joes with beans) is incredibly versatile: You can toss it with pasta, spoon it over thick toasted bread or a mound of rice, or serve it with nothing other than a spoon. You can use fresh tomatoes as long as they're really ripe; figure ten to fifteen. I don't bother to peel and seed them, though you certainly can if you're feeling ambitious.

2 tablespoons olive oil

1 onion, chopped

2 carrots, chopped

2 celery stalks, chopped

¼ cup chopped bacon or pancetta, optional

8 ounces lean ground beef, or (ideally) 4 ounces lean ground beef plus 4 ounces lean ground pork or veal

¾ cup red wine

One 28- or 35-ounce can whole Roma (plum) tomatoes, drained, liquid reserved

1½ cups dried pinto, cranberry, or other pink or red beans, rinsed, picked over, and soaked if you like

Salt and black pepper

¼ cup cream, half-and-half, or milk, optional

1. Put the oil in a large, deep skillet or saucepan over medium heat. When it's hot, add the onion, carrots, celery, and bacon if you're using it. Cook, stirring occasionally, until the vegetables are tender and the bacon begins to render some fat, 5 to 10 minutes.

2. Add the ground meat and cook, stirring and breaking up any clumps, until no longer pink, 5 to 10 minutes. Add the wine, raise the heat a bit, and cook, stirring occasionally, until most of the liquid bubbles away, just a minute or 2.

3. Core the tomatoes if you like, crush them a little with a fork or your hands; then add them and the reserved liquid to the pot, and stir. Add the beans and enough water to cover them by 2 inches. Bring to a boil, then adjust the heat so the mixture bubbles gently. Cover and cook, stirring once in a while to break up the tomatoes and any clumps of meat that remain. The beans will begin to get tender in 30 to 60 minutes or more, depending on the beans and whether or not you soaked them. Once they do, sprinkle with salt and pepper. Continue to cook, stirring occasionally and adding water if necessary, until the beans are quite tender, another 15 to 30 minutes. (At this point, you can refrigerate it for a day or 2 or freeze for several weeks. Reheat before proceeding.)

4. Add the cream if you're using it and cook for another 5 to 10 minutes, stirring occasionally. Taste and adjust the seasoning. Serve.

Crisp and Spicy Roasted Chickpeas with Lamb

Makes: 4 servings   Time: 45 to 60 minutes with cooked or canned chickpeas

Using a hot oven and a pan with a lot of surface area guarantees that the chickpeas and spiced meat will get so crisp that they almost crunch. Feel free to use ground beef instead of lamb. Serve this with Sesame Pita Pockets (page 544) and sliced ripe tomatoes and cucumbers.

> 2 cups cooked or canned chickpeas, drained
>
> 3 tablespoons olive oil
>
> Salt and black pepper
>
> 8 ounces ground lamb
>
> 1 red onion, chopped
>
> 8 ounces green beans, roughly chopped
>
> 1 tablespoon minced garlic
>
> Grated zest of 1 orange
>
> 1 tablespoon cumin
>
> Cayenne to taste
>
> Juice of 2 oranges
>
> $1/2$ cup chopped fresh parsley, for garnish

1. Heat the oven to 400°F. Combine the chickpeas and 2 tablespoons of the oil in a large roasting pan and bake, shaking the pan once or twice, until they're crisp and browned, 15 to 20 minutes. Sprinkle with salt and pepper, toss, and remove the chickpeas from the pan with a slotted spoon.

2. Add the remaining 1 tablespoon oil to the pan along with the lamb. Break it up a bit and roast until it is no longer pink and has cooked dry, 5 to 10 minutes. Stir, breaking it up more, and continue baking until it begins to crisp, another 5 minutes or so.

3. Stir the onion, green beans, garlic, orange zest, cumin, and cayenne into the lamb; sprinkle with salt and pepper. Return the roasting pan to the oven and continue roasting until the vegetables are tender and browned, the lamb

Ⓕ Fast   Ⓜ Make-Ahead   Ⓟ Pantry Staple

is very crisp, and the spices are fragrant, 10 to 15 minutes. Remove the pan from the oven, stir in the chickpeas, and transfer everything to a serving dish.

4. Put the roasting pan on the stovetop over medium heat. Add the orange juice and cook, stirring and scraping up any brown bits on the bottom of the pan, until warm and slightly thickened, 5 to 10 minutes. Drizzle the orange reduction over the lamb and chickpeas and taste and adjust the seasoning. Garnish with the parsley and serve.

Vegetables

The title of this chapter is perhaps a little misleading because this isn't a collection of basic vegetable recipes. In fact, there are plenty of recipes that include meat, poultry, fish, cheese, and eggs in quantities ranging from "here's a little taste" to quite substantial. But in every case, it's the vegetable(s)—and in some cases, fruit—that dominates.

In other words, these are, for the most part, what might be called "mains." Some are quick stir-fries or otherwise come together in one skillet; some are braised on the stove or in the oven; and others are roasted, grilled, or broiled. But nowhere will you find meat, fish, chicken, or eggs at the center of the plate with a spoonful each of starch and vegetable.

In every case, you'll need little else—some bread, cooked grains or beans, or a salad—to make these a light and satisfying meal. A lot of the recipes play with multiple and sometimes unexpected textures, using simple techniques to produce soft, tender, and crunchy sensations with the same ingredient. This brings new interest to many dishes.

The chapter begins with recipes and techniques for cooking basic vegetables, then builds to add more ingredients: first eggs and cheese, then fish and poultry, and finally beef, pork, and lamb.

Boiled or Steamed Vegetables, As You Like 'Em

Makes: 4 servings   **Time:** 10 to 30 minutes

When I say "as you like 'em," I mean tender or crisp, whichever you want, whenever you want. Just parboiled (that is, dunked into boiling water or steamed) for a minute or two, still-crisp vegetables are perfect for salads or used as an ingredient in another dish, like a stir-fry. Crisp-tender vegetables offer little resistance when you bite into them but aren't outright crunchy; they are delicious dressed simply in olive oil and lemon juice or vinegar and served immediately. Truly tender vegetables can be luxurious in a variety of circumstances, and even what we might consider overcooked vegetables are useful for purées, sauces, and spreads.

I recommend special treatment for thick-stemmed greens like chard, bok choy, kale, collards, and broccoli: Separate the stems (sometimes called "ribs") from the leaves (or florets in the case of broccoli) and begin cooking the stems two or three minutes before you start cooking the leaves (or florets)—this way everything will become tender at about the same time. And another tip: Try bending or breaking whatever it is you're planning to cook; the more pliable the pieces are, the more quickly they will become tender.

Salt

About 2 pounds virtually any vegetable (including greens), peeled, stemmed, seeded, and/or chopped as needed

Lemon juice, as you like

Olive oil or butter, as you like

Black pepper

Chopped fresh herbs or ground seasonings, optional

1. Bring a pot of water to a boil and salt it or fit a steaming basket into a large pot with water below. (If you don't have a basket, use 2 ovenproof plates: put the first one facedown in the pot and the second faceup. Fill the pot with enough water to submerge the plate on the bottom; use the top plate to hold the vegetables.) If you want to "shock" the vegetables to capture doneness at a precise moment, fill a large bowl (or a clean sink) with ice water.

Ⓕ Fast   Ⓜ Make-Ahead   Ⓟ Pantry Staple

2. When the water boils, add the vegetable to the pot or steamer. Check tender greens in less than a minute; root vegetables (which are usually but not always best completely tender) will take 10 minutes or more. Everything else is somewhere in between. Every so often while the vegetables are cooking, use tongs to grab a piece out and test it. (With experience, you'll do this less frequently.) Remember that unless you shock them in ice water, the vegetables will continue to cook after they're off the heat.

3. When the vegetables are cooked as you like them, drain well. Serve, drizzled with lemon juice and oil, with more salt and pepper, herbs or seasonings, or whatever. Or plunge the drained vegetables immediately into the ice water, drain again, and keep to use later. (You can refrigerate cooked vegetables in a covered container for up to a few days or freeze them for up to a month.)

Sautéed Vegetables. You can boil or steam the vegetables first, then sauté them; or cook them, starting raw, directly in the oil. I often add 1 to 2 tablespoons of water to the pan, which helps the vegetables cook faster and stay moist. Put a film of olive oil in a large skillet and turn the heat to medium-high. When it's hot, add the vegetables, sprinkle with salt and pepper, and cook, stirring occasionally and checking for doneness as described in Step 2. (The only difference is that you'll be fishing test pieces out of a skillet, not out of a pot of boiling water.) Precooked vegetables are ready as soon as they're warmed; tender greens will take 5 to 10 minutes; and cubed root vegetables up to 30 minutes. When they're ready, taste and adjust the seasoning (add fresh herbs or spices and lemon juice if you want), stir, and serve hot, warm, or at room temperature.

Roasted Vegetables. Heat the oven to 425°F. Put the vegetables, alone or in combination (hearty greens work well here too), in a large roasting pan or on a rimmed baking sheet and toss them with at least 3 tablespoons olive oil. Sprinkle with salt and pepper and start roasting. Check tender vegetables in 10 minutes, sturdier ones in 15. Whenever you check, turn or stir as necessary to promote even cooking. Total time will be between 15 and 45 minutes, depending on the size and type of vegetable. When the vegetables are ready, taste and adjust the seasoning (add fresh herbs or spices and lemon juice if you want), toss, and serve hot or at room temperature.

Grilled or Broiled Vegetables. Sturdy greens like radicchio and romaine work here; just quarter or halve them, leaving the root ends intact. Prepare a grill or turn on the broiler; the heat should be medium-high and the rack about 4 inches from the fire. Put the vegetables in a large bowl, toss them with at least 2 tablespoons olive oil, and sprinkle with salt and pepper. When the fire is hot, put them on the grill or in a pan under the broiler. Start checking tender vegetables in a minute or 2, sturdier vegetables in 10. Turn and move them around as necessary to promote even cooking. Total time will be between 5 and 20 minutes, depending on the size and type of vegetable. When the vegetables are ready, sprinkle with more salt and pepper, a squeeze of lemon, herbs, or spices.

Dressing Up Plainly Cooked Vegetables

It's impossible to go wrong when you finish cooked vegetables with a simple dressing of olive oil—or butter—and lemon juice, but there are many ways to make it a little more exciting, starting with My Favorite Vinaigrette (page 186) or any of the other dressings beginning on page 187. To tap the flavors of Asia, try lime juice or wine vinegar and sesame oil; lemon juice, ginger, and soy sauce are also good.

If you want a no-fat topping, just lemon juice or vinegar (especially balsamic or sherry vinegar) are great options; use them by drops or small splashes, not the spoonful. And don't underestimate the power of salt and pepper. Coarse salt is particularly nice because you get a little crunch in the first bites before it melts away into the vegetables.

Herbs are a natural with vegetables—use a lot of parsley, mint, basil, and cilantro. But go easy with the stronger herbs like rosemary, marjoram, oregano, thyme, and dill; a pinch will usually do. Spice blends, like curry or chili powders, Chinese five-spice powder, and garam masala are especially handy in winter.

For serious crunch—better when the vegetables are cooked soft and silky, not crisp-tender—scatter a handful of toasted nuts, seeds, or bread crumbs over the vegetables; or toss them with croutons (for homemade, see page 47). For color and a little sharpness, grate citrus zest or a little Parmesan cheese on top just before serving, then give a final toss so the heat releases and disperses the flavor.

(F) Fast   (M) Make-Ahead   (P) Pantry Staple

Roasted Bell Peppers

Makes: 4 to 8 servings   Time: 20 to 60 minutes, depending on the method

An open flame delivers the best flavor and is the most efficient way to soften peppers and char their skins so they peel off easily, but roasting and broiling are also good methods. Roasted peppers dressed with oil keep well in the fridge for several days, so you may as well do up a big batch. But keep in mind that roasting intensifies the flavor and green peppers can be a little bitter. My favorite ways to eat these are in salads, omelets, and frittatas, or on thick slices of good bread, sometimes with an anchovy and/or capers. Try, too, a little garlic, balsamic vinegar, olives, Parmesan, goat cheese, toasted almonds, or virtually any fresh herb.

> 8 red, yellow, orange, or green bell peppers, rinsed but left whole
>
> Salt
>
> Olive oil as needed

1. Heat the oven to 450°F or prepare a grill or turn on the broiler; the heat should be medium-high and the rack about 4 inches from the fire. To roast or broil, put the peppers in a foil-lined roasting pan, then cook, turning the peppers as each side browns, until they have darkened and collapsed. The process will take 15 or 20 minutes under the broiler or up to 1 hour in the oven. To grill, put the peppers directly over the heat. Grill, turning as each side blackens, until they collapse, about 15 minutes.

2. Wrap the cooked peppers in foil (if you roasted the peppers, use the same foil that lined the pan) and let them sit until cool enough to handle. Remove the skin, seeds, and stems; this process is sometimes easier under running water, though you also wash away some flavor. Don't worry if the peppers fall apart. (If not using them within an hour or so, refrigerate them for up to several days.) Serve at room temperature, sprinkled with a little salt and a little (or a lot) of olive oil.

Roasted Bell Pepper Sauce. Best with red, orange, or yellow peppers. Put the peeled roasted bell peppers in a food processor or blender with a few drops of olive oil, stock, white wine, or water—just enough to get the machine working. Sprinkle with salt and pepper or add other ingredients (see the headnote) as you like.

Simplest Cooked Mushrooms

Makes: 4 servings · **Time:** About 20 minutes

Mushrooms are absolutely indispensable for adding flavor and chew to everything from salads and pasta to grain and bean dishes. But let's not forget how great they are on their own.

To clean mushrooms, first remove hard and dry spots with a knife (and stems, too, if they're shiitakes), then rinse them quickly, removing all traces of dirt.

¼ cup olive oil

1 pound assorted mushrooms, sliced

Salt and black pepper

¼ cup dry white wine or water

1 teaspoon to 1 tablespoon minced garlic, optional

¼ cup chopped fresh parsley, for garnish

1. Put the oil in a large skillet over medium heat. When it's hot, add the mushrooms and sprinkle with salt and pepper. Cook, stirring occasionally, until tender, 10 to 15 minutes.

2. Add the wine, let it bubble away for a minute, and turn the heat down to medium-low. Add the garlic if you're using it, stir, and cook for 1 minute. Taste and adjust the seasoning. Garnish with the parsley and serve hot, warm, or at room temperature.

Cooked Mushrooms, Dry-Pan Style. Crisp and chewy, with intense flavor. Reduce the amount of oil to 2 tablespoons, and put it in a large skillet over medium-high heat. Add the mushrooms, salt, and pepper and stir. Cover, turn the heat down to medium-low, and cook, undisturbed, for 5 minutes; the mushrooms will have released a fair amount of liquid. Remove the lid, turn up the heat until the liquid bubbles steadily, and cook, undisturbed, until the liquid boils off, 3 to 5 minutes. Add the garlic if you're using it and continue to cook, stirring often, until the mushrooms are dry, shrunken, and nearly crisp, about 5 minutes more. Remove from the heat and taste and adjust the seasoning. Serve hot, warm, or at room temperature, garnished with the parsley, or use in other dishes.

Ⓕ Fast   Ⓜ Make-Ahead   Ⓟ Pantry Staple

Cooked Fresh and Dried Mushrooms. Works well with both the main recipe and the variation. Put a handful of dried porcini mushrooms in a bowl and add hot water to cover. Soak until the mushrooms are tender, usually 10 to 15 minutes. Lift the mushrooms out of the soaking water with your fingers or a slotted spoon; reserve the liquid. Chop the porcini and add them to the pan with the fresh mushrooms. If you're making the main recipe, consider using some of the soaking liquid in place of the wine for extra mushroom flavor (or save it for another use); when you pour it, be careful to leave any sediment in the bottom of the bowl.

Braised Broccoli or Cauliflower with Lemony Tahini Sauce

Makes: 4 servings   Time: 30 minutes

Tahini—ground sesame seeds, a cousin of peanut butter—produces a sauce so rich it can turn vegetables into the centerpiece of any meal. In the main recipe everything cooks in one skillet, but for cauliflower that's more hands-off (and well browned), try the variation. Remember to undersalt if you're using olives as a garnish.

> 3 tablespoons olive oil
>
> 1 large head (about 1½ pounds) broccoli or cauliflower, cut into large florets
>
> ½ onion, chopped
>
> 1 tablespoon minced garlic
>
> Grated zest and juice of 1 lemon
>
> ⅓ cup tahini
>
> Salt and black pepper
>
> ½ cup chopped fresh parsley, for garnish
>
> ¼ cup oil-cured black olives, pitted and chopped, for garnish, optional

1. Put 2 tablespoons of the oil in a large deep skillet over medium-high heat. Add the broccoli florets and cook, stirring occasionally, until they begin to brown and get tender, 5 to 10 minutes. Remove the florets with a slotted spoon or tongs.

2. Lower the heat to medium. Add the remaining 1 tablespoon oil to the pan along with the onion and garlic; cook, stirring, until they soften, 3 to 5 minutes. Add the lemon zest and juice, tahini, a good sprinkling of salt and pepper, and ½ cup water. Stir until a relatively smooth sauce forms and begins to bubble and thicken, 3 to 5 minutes. Return the broccoli to the pan, stir to coat, and cook, stirring occasionally, until the broccoli is fully tender, 10 to 15 minutes. Taste and adjust the seasoning. Serve hot or at room temperature, garnished with the parsley and black olives if you're using them.

Roasted Broccoli or Cauliflower with Lemony Tahini Sauce. Heat the oven to 400°F. Put the cauliflower or broccoli in a roasting pan, drizzle with 2 tablespoons oil, sprinkle with salt and pepper, and toss. Roast, stirring occasionally, until the cauliflower is tender, about 30 minutes. Meanwhile, heat another tablespoon oil in a medium skillet. Cook the onion and garlic and make the tahini sauce as described in Step 2. Drizzle the tahini sauce over the roasted cauliflower and garnish as described in the main recipe.

Ⓕ Fast　Ⓜ Make-Ahead　Ⓟ Pantry Staple

Fast Roasted Garlic

Makes: 3 heads   Time: About 25 minutes

Sweet and creamy roasted garlic is insanely useful. Super on bread, it's also great as a replacement for raw or cooked garlic in soups, sauces, stir-fries, sandwiches, and vegetable purées. You can double or triple the quantity of oil and use the extra for pan-frying, sauces, and stir-fries. Just make sure to refrigerate both the garlic and the oil; they keep for a few days but not longer.

To make roasted garlic the traditional, whole-head way, put the ingredients in a small baking dish, cover with foil, and bake, undisturbed, until soft, at least 40 minutes.

3 whole garlic heads, unpeeled

3 tablespoons or more olive oil

Salt

1. Heat the oven to 375°F. Break the garlic heads into individual cloves but don't peel them. Spread them out in a pan, drizzle with oil, and sprinkle with salt. Bake, shaking the pan occasionally, until tender, 15 to 20 minutes.

2. To use, squeeze the garlic from the skins or carefully remove the skins with a knife.

Fast Braised Garlic. Peel the garlic. Increase the olive oil to ½ cup and put it in a skillet large enough to hold the garlic in one layer over medium-low heat. When the oil is warm, add the garlic, sprinkle with salt, and adjust the heat so the garlic barely sizzles (low heat should do it). Cook, turning occasionally so the garlic browns evenly, until it gradually turns golden, then begins to brown. The garlic is done when perfectly tender; it should take about 15 to 20 minutes. Store as above.

Oven-Dried Tomatoes or Fruit

Makes: 4 to 8 servings   Time: 2 to 12 hours, largely unattended

Nothing is wrong with store-bought dried fruit and tomatoes, but fruit you dry yourself in a low oven is guaranteed to be fresh and tastes a whole lot better. Peaches, plums, nectarines, grapes, cherries, berries, apples, papayas, pineapple, and coconut work particularly well. And it's almost impossible to mess this up—you can keep the oven going anywhere from 2 to 12 hours, and whatever went in will come out delicious.

Before doing this, make sure your oven is well calibrated. If that 225°F becomes 300°F due to oven error, the tomatoes or fruit will bake, not dry.

To prepare, remove any tough skins, seeds, and pits. Leave smaller fruits whole or halve them lengthwise; slice larger fruits.

3 pounds ripe Roma (plum) tomatoes, cored, cut in half lengthwise, and seeded; or fruit, prepared as described in the headnote

1. Heat the oven to 225°F. Set 2 wire racks on top of 2 (preferably rimmed) baking sheets. Put the tomatoes or fruit on the racks, cut side down. Put the pans in the oven and forget about them for 2 hours.

2. Turn the sheets around and check on the tomatoes or fruit. After 2 to 3 hours, the flesh will still be moist. The longer they stay in the oven, the drier and smaller they'll get; the flavors will concentrate too.

3. Check them every couple of hours until you get the hang of the process; after a couple batches you'll know how long it takes to get them as you like. (To store the finished tomatoes or fruit: If still soft and moist, wrap and refrigerate the pieces for several days or freeze for months. If they're totally dry, dark, and leathery, you can store them in a jar in the pantry for up to several months.)

Oven-Dried Kale or Collards. Worth a special mention because it's faster than drying tomatoes or fruit and makes an ideal side dish or snack. Heat the oven to 275°F. Clean, trim, and roughly chop 2 pounds kale. Toss the leaves with 2 tablespoons olive oil and a sprinkling of salt and pepper. Arrange the kale in a single layer on the wire racks and bake for 30 minutes. The kale will be crisp around the edges and slightly chewy in the middle. Serve immediately or cover and store in the refrigerator for up to 2 days.

Ⓕ Fast   Ⓜ Make-Ahead   Ⓟ Pantry Staple

Savory Tomato Crisp

Makes: 6 to 8 servings   Time: About 1½ hours, largely unattended

Of course, great summer tomatoes are ideal here, but since baking intensifies their flavor and masks their flaws, they don't need to be perfect, or even fully ripe. In fact, in the dead of winter, you can drain two 28-ounce cans whole tomatoes, season them with a little dried oregano or red chile flakes, and use them instead.

> 3 tablespoons olive oil, plus more for greasing
>
> 3 pounds ripe tomatoes (8 to 10 medium), cored and cut into wedges
>
> 1 tablespoon cornstarch
>
> Salt and black pepper
>
> 1 cup bread crumbs, preferably whole grain and homemade
>
> 1 cup rolled oats
>
> ½ cup chopped pecans or walnuts
>
> 1 tablespoon minced garlic
>
> ½ cup grated Parmesan or crumbled feta or blue cheese
>
> 1 tablespoon melted butter

1. Grease an 8- or 9-inch square or round baking dish or a deep pie plate with oil; heat the oven to 375°F.

2. Put the tomato wedges in a large bowl and sprinkle with the cornstarch and some salt and pepper. Toss gently and let the mixture sit. In another bowl, combine the bread crumbs, oats, pecans, garlic, cheese, 3 tablespoons oil, and butter, sprinkle with salt and pepper, and stir until thoroughly mixed.

3. Toss the tomato mixture again and transfer it to the prepared baking dish. Sprinkle with the bread crumb topping. Bake until the crisp is as dark as you like on top and bubbly underneath, 45 to 55 minutes. Let cool to warm or room temperature before serving. To serve, scoop portions out with a large spoon.

Potato-Leek Gratin
with Buttery Bread Crumbs

Makes: 4 servings   Time: About 1 hour

Cream works wonders in gratins, but so does this two-tiered technique, which renders leeks so tender and potatoes so fluffy, you'll forget about the absent dairy. (And you can actually taste the vegetables.) The topping is a bonus but too good to resist, especially if you've got good bread to use for the crumbs.

1½ pounds waxy potatoes, thinly sliced

1 pound leeks, trimmed, rinsed well, and thinly sliced

¼ cup olive oil

Salt and black pepper

4 sprigs fresh thyme, or several pinches dried

1 cup bread crumbs, preferably whole grain and homemade

2 tablespoons butter, melted

1. Heat the oven to 375°F. Put the potatoes and leeks in a large (9 × 13 or 3-quart) baking dish and toss them well with the oil. Sprinkle with salt and pepper and nestle the thyme sprigs among them (or sprinkle with dried thyme). Cover the baking dish with foil and bake until the vegetables are just tender, 30 to 40 minutes. Remove the dish from the oven, uncover, and raise the oven temperature to 425°F. (You can make the gratin ahead to this point. Leave covered and refrigerate for up to a day; bring to room temperature before proceeding.)

2. Toss the bread crumbs with the melted butter, sprinkle them over the vegetables, press down a bit, and return the pan to the oven. Bake until the bread crumbs and vegetables are nicely browned, 15 to 20 minutes more. Serve hot or at room temperature.

Ⓕ Fast   Ⓜ Make-Ahead   Ⓟ Pantry Staple

Garlicky Chard with Olives and Pine Nuts

Makes: 4 servings   Time: 40 minutes

Olives play a starring role in this dish, so quality really matters. Buy bulk olives if at all possible and see if you can find the glossy, deep black, shriveled oil-cured ones (taste one to make sure they're good). You can use spinach, kale, cabbage, or even bok choy instead of the chard and, for extra richness, crumble a little feta cheese on top right before serving.

- 1½ pounds chard
- ¼ cup pine nuts
- 2 tablespoons olive oil
- 6 garlic cloves, sliced, or to taste
- ⅓ cup good-quality black or green olives, pitted and chopped
- ½ cup red wine or water
- Salt and black pepper

1. Cut the leaves from the stems of the chard. Cut the leaves into wide ribbons and slice the stems (on the diagonal if you like); keep the leaves and stems separate.

2. Put the pine nuts in a large skillet over medium-low heat. Toast the nuts, shaking the pan and stirring often, until just starting to turn golden brown, 5 to 10 minutes. Remove the nuts from the pan. Put the oil in the skillet and heat for 1 minute. Add the garlic and cook, stirring, until soft, golden, and fragrant, about 10 minutes.

3. Turn the heat to medium and stir in the chard stems and olives. Cook, stirring occasionally, until the stems soften a bit, just a minute or 2. Add the chard leaves, wine, and a sprinkling of salt and pepper. Raise the heat to medium-high and cook, stirring, until the chard leaves are wilted and most of the liquid has evaporated, about 5 minutes. Stir in the pine nuts and taste and adjust the seasoning. Serve hot or at room temperature.

Garlicky Chard with Anchovies and Almonds. Substitute slivered almonds for the pine nuts and 4 or 5 (or more) lightly mashed anchovies for the olives.

Stir-Fried Bok Choy and Daikon with Crisp Tofu

Makes: 4 servings   Time: 30 minutes

This has everything you want in a stir-fry: delicious bok choy, with its wonderfully creamy stems; sharp daikon radish; crusty pan-fried tofu; and a load of spice.

Tempeh, the nutty fermented soybean cake, also goes beautifully with bok choy. If you want to use it in place of the tofu, crumble it into the hot oil and stir until it's crisp, 5 to 7 minutes.

1 head bok choy (about 1½ pounds)

4 tablespoons vegetable oil

1 block firm tofu (about 1 pound), cut into ¼-inch slices and patted dry

1 onion, chopped

1 tablespoon minced garlic

1 tablespoon minced ginger

1 or 2 fresh hot chiles (like jalapeño or Thai), seeded and minced

8 ounces daikon radish, cut into ¼-inch coins

2 tablespoons soy sauce, or to taste

Black pepper

1. Cut the leaves from the stems of the bok choy. Trim the stems as necessary, then cut them into 1-inch pieces. Cut the leaves into wide ribbons and keep them separate from the stems.

2. Put 2 tablespoons of the oil in a large skillet over medium heat. When it's hot, slide in the tofu, working in batches if necessary to avoid overcrowding the pan. Cook until the bottoms are crisp and golden, 3 to 5 minutes; carefully flip and cook for another 3 to 5 minutes on the other side. When the tofu slices are done, transfer them to paper towels to drain.

3. Add the remaining 2 tablespoons oil to the pan and raise the heat to medium-high. When it's hot, add the onion, garlic, ginger, and chile and cook, stirring, for just 1 minute. Add the bok choy stems and daikon and cook, stirring occasionally, until they just lose their crunch, about 3 minutes.

Ⓕ Fast Ⓜ Make-Ahead Ⓟ Pantry Staple

4. Add the bok choy leaves and about ½ cup water. Cook, stirring occasionally, until the liquid evaporates and the stems and radish are fully tender, 5 to 10 minutes; add a little more water if necessary. Return the tofu to the pan, stir in the soy sauce, and sprinkle with black pepper. Taste and adjust the seasoning. Serve hot or at room temperature.

Stir-Fried Celery and Daikon with Chicken. Same drill, totally different ingredients. You could use any meat or seafood here, really. Use 8 ounces boneless, skinless chicken breast or thighs instead of the tofu; cut it into chunks or slices of about the same size. Substitute 1 head celery for the bok choy. Cut it on the diagonal into chunks and add it when you would the bok choy stems.

Japanese-Spiced Roasted Beets

Makes: 4 servings   Time: About 1 hour, partially unattended

A peppery, smoky blend of spices and seeds tossed with roasted beets produces a sublimely earthy combo—the honey-glazed variation adds sweetness to the mix—that works equally well with parsnips, turnips, potatoes, and winter squash. You'll have extra spice mixture; refrigerate it for up to a week and use it to season rice, noodles, soups, salads, and other vegetables.

1 tablespoon vegetable oil, plus more for greasing the pan

2 pounds beets (about 4 large), peeled and cut into wedges

1 tablespoon sesame oil

1 tablespoon Sichuan or black peppercorns

2 teaspoons white sesame seeds

1 tablespoon grated orange zest

1 tablespoon chili powder

½ teaspoon poppy seeds

Salt

½ cup sliced scallions

1. Heat the oven to 400°F. Smear a large roasting pan or rimmed baking sheet with a little of the oil. Put the beets in the pan, drizzle with the 1 tablespoon vegetable oil and the sesame oil, and toss to coat.

2. Roast, undisturbed, for 20 minutes before checking. If the beets release easily from the pan, stir them up a bit or turn the pieces over with tongs. If they look dry and are sticking, drizzle with a little more oil and toss. Continue roasting, turning every 10 minutes or so, until crisp on the outside and just tender inside, another 20 to 30 minutes.

3. Meanwhile, put the peppercorns and white sesame seeds in a spice or coffee grinder and pulverize to a coarse powder. Transfer to a small bowl and stir in the orange zest, chili powder, and poppy seeds. When the beets are done—a skewer or sharp knife inserted into one will meet almost no resistance—toss them with the spice mixture, a sprinkling of salt, and the scallions. Return to the oven for a minute or 2, just long enough to toast the spices. Taste and adjust the seasoning. Serve hot or at room temperature.

Japanese-Spiced Beets with Honeyed Walnuts. While the beets are roasting, mix ⅓ cup chopped walnuts with 2 tablespoons honey in a medium bowl. Add the honeyed walnuts to the beets along with the spice mixture and scallions in Step 3.

Peach and Mango Curry

Makes: 4 servings   Time: 30 minutes

Fruit in a savory stew is nothing new (especially since tomatoes are a fruit), and believe me, it's impossible to resist a dish that tastes this spicy, fresh, and bright—and comes together so fast. Use whatever fruit you've got, especially if it's over- or underripe. Serve this colorful curry over rice or on Brown Rice Scallion Pancakes (page 520).

2 tablespoons vegetable oil

1 large onion, chopped

2 tablespoons minced ginger

Salt and black pepper

Ⓕ Fast   Ⓜ Make-Ahead   Ⓟ Pantry Staple

2 tablespoons curry powder

3 peaches, peeled if you like, pitted, and chopped

1 mango, peeled, pitted, and chopped

4 large ripe tomatoes, chopped

½ cup coconut milk

Chopped fresh cilantro, for garnish

Chopped pistachios, for garnish, optional

1. Put the oil in a large, deep skillet over medium heat for 1 minute. Add the onion and ginger and sprinkle with salt and pepper. Cook, stirring occasionally, until soft, about 5 minutes. Add the curry powder and cook, stirring, until fragrant, 30 seconds or so.

2. Stir in the fruit (including the tomatoes) and coconut milk and raise the heat so the mixture bubbles a bit. Cook, stirring occasionally, until the fruit is soft and the mixture thickens, 5 to 10 minutes. Taste and adjust the seasoning, garnish with the cilantro and nuts if you're using them, and serve.

Peach and Mango Curry with Chicken. In Step 1, before you add the vegetables to the skillet, sear about 12 ounces boneless, skinless chicken breast or thighs in the oil over medium-high heat. Turn and rotate as needed until the pieces are nicely browned and almost cooked through, 5 to 10 minutes. Remove the meat from the pan and proceed with the recipe. After adding the fruit in Step 2, return the chicken to the pan to finish cooking. Fish it out and taste the fruit and adjust the seasoning. Slice the chicken on the diagonal and serve alongside the curry.

Spinach-Tofu Burgers

Makes: 4 servings   Time: 40 minutes

Puréeing half of the tofu and leaving the other half crumbly helps these burgers hold together and gives them a nice contrast of textures. The Asian flavors are expected, but other directions are equally good; see the sidebar about flavoring vegetables on page 416 for some tips.

> 1 pound spinach (frozen is fine)
>
> 2 scallions, cut into 2-inch pieces
>
> 2 garlic cloves
>
> 1 block firm tofu (about 1 pound), patted dry
>
> ½ cup bread crumbs, preferably whole grain and homemade, or panko
>
> ¼ cup sesame seeds
>
> 1 tablespoon soy sauce
>
> 2 teaspoons sesame oil
>
> Salt and black pepper
>
> 2 tablespoons vegetable oil, or more as needed

1. Bring a pot of water to a boil and salt it; fill a large bowl with ice water. Add the spinach to the pot, stir, and let cook for no more than a minute, then drain and plunge it into the ice water. (If you're using frozen spinach, just let it thaw before proceeding.) When the spinach is cold, drain it again, use your hands to squeeze out as much water as you can, and chop it finely by hand or in a food processor. Transfer the spinach to a large bowl.

2. Put the scallions and garlic in a food processor and pulse a few times until minced. Transfer them to the bowl, then crumble half the tofu into the bowl with your hands. Put the remaining tofu into the food processor and let it run until the tofu is smooth. Add it to the bowl along with the bread crumbs, sesame seeds, soy sauce, sesame oil, and a sprinkling of salt and lots of pepper.

3. Combine the mixture until all of the ingredients are evenly distributed, then form into 4 patties. (You can prepare the patties up to a day ahead. Cover them tightly and refrigerate; bring them to room temperature before proceeding.)

4. Put the oil in a large skillet over medium heat. When the oil is hot, slide the patties into the skillet with a spatula. Cook, undisturbed, until they are nicely browned and easy to move, about 5 minutes. Carefully flip the patties and cook on the second side for 3 to 4 minutes more. Serve on buns or over rice.

Spinach-Tofu-Fish Burgers. Replace half of the tofu with boneless white fish fillets (see page 22). Roughly chop half of the fish and crumble half of the tofu and put them in the bowl. Then proceed as in the main recipe, processing the other half of the tofu and fish with the remaining ingredients in Step 2 until they are smooth.

More-Vegetable Less-Egg Frittata

Makes: 2 to 4 servings   Time: 30 minutes

Frittata is one of those rare any-time-of-day dishes. You can eat it when you make it, or at room temperature, or even cold, straight from the refrigerator. The revelation here is that one egg easily binds two cups of cooked vegetables, and they're all good: chopped spinach or chard, chopped fresh or dried tomatoes, potato or sweet potato slices, asparagus cut into 1-inch segments, roughly chopped broccoli rabe, cooked mushrooms, zucchini slices, or cubed, chopped, or grated winter squash, grated carrots or parsnips, or chopped eggplant.

If you're starting with raw vegetables, use the main recipe; for already cooked vegetables, go to the variation. For more heft and deeper flavor, substitute a half cup or so cooked beans or grains for some of the vegetables, or add cooked crumbled sausage, bacon, ham, or even shrimp just before adding the eggs.

2 tablespoons olive oil

½ onion or 1 large shallot, halved and sliced

Salt and black pepper

6 cups any sliced, chopped, or grated raw vegetables (see the headnote)

¼ cup chopped fresh basil, cilantro, or chives, or 1 teaspoon chopped
    fresh rosemary, tarragon or mint, optional

2 or 3 eggs

½ cup grated Parmesan cheese, optional

1. Put the oil in a large skillet over medium heat. When it's hot, add the onion and cook, sprinkling with salt and pepper, until soft, 3 to 5 minutes. Add the vegetables, raise the heat, and cook, stirring occasionally, until they soften, anywhere from a couple of minutes for greens to 15 to 20 minutes for sliced potatoes or winter squash. Adjust the heat so the vegetables brown a little without scorching, adding a few drops of water to the pan if they start to stick.

2. When the vegetables are nearly done, turn the heat to low and add the herb. Cook, stirring occasionally, until the pan is almost dry, up to another 5 minutes for wetter ingredients like tomatoes or mushrooms.

3. Meanwhile, beat the eggs with some salt and pepper, along with the cheese if you're using it. Pour the eggs over the vegetables and tilt the pan or use a spoon to distribute them evenly. Cook, undisturbed, until the eggs are barely set, 10 minutes or longer. (You can set them further by putting the pan in a 350°F oven for a few minutes or running it under the broiler for a minute or 2.) Cut into wedges and serve hot, warm, or at room temperature.

More-Vegetable Less-Egg Frittata, Starting with Cooked Vegetables. A perfect use for leftovers, especially grilled or roasted vegetables. In Step 1, after cooking the onion, stir in about 4 cups cooked vegetables (chopped or sliced as you like). Stir and cook just a minute or 2 to warm them up, then proceed with the recipe.

Better Poached Eggs. Soupy—in a really good way—and works the same for either the main recipe or the variation. In Step 2, instead of cooking the vegetables until dry, when they're still moist and on the raw side, add 2 cups (or more) vegetable stock or water. Bring to a gentle boil and carefully crack the eggs into the bubbling mixture. Cook, uncovered, until the eggs are set and done as you like them, anywhere from 3 to 7 minutes. Scoop the eggs, the vegetables, and some of the cooking liquid into bowls and serve.

(F) Fast (M) Make-Ahead (P) Pantry Staple

Scrambled Tomatoes and Herbs

Makes: 4 servings · Time: 20 minutes

In general, when you're trying to adjust the ratio of vegetables to eggs, the trick is to choose ingredients that replace the volume of eggs without obscuring the eggs' flavor and texture. Tomatoes do just that by virtually melting into the curds with sweetness and acidity that balance the richness of eggs perfectly.

From the main recipe there are several ways to go, starting with the soy-and-scallion variation. Or start by frying a little chopped bacon or a sausage in the pan before adding the shallots, or adding some chopped shrimp or lump crab meat along with the eggs.

2 tablespoons olive oil

2 shallots or 1 small red onion, chopped

8 ripe tomatoes, cored and cut into wedges

Salt and black pepper

2 eggs, beaten

¼ cup chopped fresh parsley, basil, mint, cilantro, or dill, or 1 teaspoon
 chopped fresh tarragon

1. Put the oil in a large skillet over medium-high heat. Add the shallots and cook, stirring, until soft, 3 to 5 minutes. Add the tomatoes, sprinkle with salt and pepper, and continue to cook, stirring, until the tomatoes are soft and their liquid has evaporated, 10 to 15 minutes.

2. Reduce the heat to medium-low. Add the eggs. Cook and stir for a minute or so, then turn the heat down very low (or off entirely) and stir occasionally until the mixture forms soft curds, no more than 5 minutes. Stir in the herb and taste and adjust the seasoning. Serve.

Scrambled Tomatoes, Scallions, and Soy. Substitute 1 tablespoon sesame oil and 1 tablespoon vegetable oil for the olive oil. Use ½ cup sliced scallions in place of the shallots, and stir in 2 tablespoons soy sauce instead of the herb. Garnish with more sliced scallions.

Reverse Fondue

Makes: 4 servings   Time: About 1 hour

When it comes to fondue, you can not only mess with the type of cheese—Gruyère or Emmental are traditional, though good aged cheddar or Gorgonzola are fine as well—but also the quantity. Here, I literally turn the concept upside down, creating a fondue-like cheese sauce to grace bread and vegetables. It's much less fussy too.

It's okay if all the vegetables don't roast to exactly the same stage of doneness; that's what gives this dish a nice variety of textures.

1 large head broccoli or cauliflower, cut into florets

2 large carrots, cut into chunks

1 large turnip or small celery root, cut into wedges

1 large onion, sliced into thick rings

Salt and black pepper

3 tablespoons olive oil

4 thick slices bread, preferably whole grain, cut into large cubes

1 cup dry white wine

1 teaspoon cornstarch

8 ounces any cheese (see the headnote)

1. Heat the oven to 450°F. Put the vegetables on a large rimmed baking sheet, sprinkle with salt and pepper, drizzle with the oil, and toss until well coated. Put the bread on a separate baking sheet. Roast both the bread and the vegetables, shaking the pans once or twice, until everything begins to brown, 15 to 25 minutes. Keep an eye on the bread; it may finish toasting before the vegetables are done. You want the vegetables mostly crisp-tender and the bread still a little soft inside.

2. Meanwhile, put the wine and cornstarch in a saucepan over medium heat and bring to a slow bubble. Gradually stir in the cheese and cook, stirring almost constantly, until it melts and the sauce becomes creamy, about 5 minutes; adjust the heat so the mixture does not boil.

3. Put the vegetables and bread on a serving platter or in individual bowls, drizzle with the fondue, and serve immediately.

Charred Stuffed Poblanos

Makes: 4 servings   Time: 30 minutes

Most often poblanos are roasted and peeled before further cooking—a nice technique that is a real pain. But as long as you remove the seeds and cook the peppers thoroughly, as you will here, you get skin that's easy enough to remove at the table. (Some people like its charred flavor; others find it a little bitter.) The stuffing is crunchy, sweet, and creamy, a nice counterpoint to the slightly spicy poblanos.

8 poblano chiles

½ cup chopped pumpkin seeds, almonds, or walnuts

½ cup chopped scallions

½ cup raisins

½ cup crumbled queso fresco

½ cup chopped fresh cilantro or parsley

Salt and black pepper

2 tablespoons olive oil, plus more for cooking

Lime wedges, for serving

1. Prepare a grill or turn on the broiler; the heat should be medium-high and the rack about 4 inches from the fire. Cut a slit down the length of each poblano, large enough to be able to stuff the peppers without tearing them apart. Remove as many of the seeds as you can, leaving the stems intact.

2. Put the chopped pumpkin seeds in a dry skillet over medium heat. Toast, stirring or tossing frequently, until they are lightly browned and fragrant, 3 to 4 minutes. Turn off the heat and stir in the scallions, raisins, queso fresco, cilantro, and a sprinkling of salt and pepper. Add the 2 tablespoons oil and stir again.

3. Carefully stuff the nut mixture into the poblanos; there should be a little more than ¼ cup filling for each one. Brush each poblano with a little more oil and grill or broil, turning as needed to cook them evenly, until they are soft and charred on all sides, 5 to 10 minutes total. Serve hot or at room temperature with the lime wedges.

Charred Poblanos Stuffed with Fish. Substitute ½ cup cooked salmon, sturdy white fish, mackerel, or cooked or canned tuna for the queso fresco (see page 22). Gently flake the fish as you mix it with the rest of the stuffing ingredients in Step 2.

Parmesan-Breaded Squash

Makes: 4 servings   Time: 1 hour, partially unattended

Breading and baking robust vegetables like winter squash (or celery root, eggplant, or anything else that can take this treatment) makes a kind of vegetarian "schnitzel"—not as meaty, of course, but just as satisfying. The bread crumbs need to be finely ground, so if you don't have a blender that pulverizes them that well, use store-bought instead. For a complete main course, top the slices with All-Purpose Tomato Sauce (page 194), which you can prepare while the squash rests, or serve them on a bed of quickly cooked garlicky broccoli rabe, chard, or other greens.

½ cup whole wheat flour

2 eggs

3 tablespoons milk or water

Salt and black pepper

1½ cups bread crumbs, preferably whole grain and homemade

¾ cup grated Parmesan cheese

2 pounds any winter squash, peeled, seeded, and cut into ½-inch thick slices

6 tablespoons olive oil

½ cup chopped fresh parsley, for garnish

Lemon wedges, for serving

1. Heat the oven to 400°F. Set out the flour in a shallow bowl or on a plate on your counter. Beat the eggs with the milk in another shallow bowl and sprinkle generously with salt and pepper. Combine the bread crumbs, Parmesan, and more salt and pepper in a third shallow bowl or on a plate. Have a stack of parchment or wax paper ready.

2. Dredge the squash slices, one at a time, in the flour, then dip in the egg mixture, then dredge in the bread crumb mixture. Stack the breaded cutlets between layers of wax paper and then chill the stack in the refrigerator for at least 10 minutes and up to 3 hours.

3. Put the oil in a large, deep skillet over medium-high heat; the oil is ready when a pinch of flour sizzles in it, about 350°F. Add a few of the squash

Ⓕ Fast   Ⓜ Make-Ahead   Ⓟ Pantry Staple

slices and cook until they're browned. Turn and cook the other side. The total cooking time should be about 10 minutes. As each piece is done, transfer it first to paper towels to drain briefly. Put half the oil in a roasting pan or on a baking sheet and arrange the squash slices in one layer on top. Drizzle on the remaining 3 tablespoons oil and bake, turning halfway through, until the squash is tender, 35 to 40 minutes. Serve, garnished with the parsley and with lemon wedges on the side.

Nut-Breaded Squash. Easy with a food processor. Substitute finely chopped pecans, walnuts, or almonds for the Parmesan.

Steamed Artichokes with Portobello "Pesto"

Makes: 4 servings   Time: About 1½ hours, largely unattended

Artichokes seem to have been built to hold stuff among their leaves, and this stuffing turns them into a main dish or excellent appetizer for sharing. Without the stuffing, this is your go-to recipe for preparing and steaming 'chokes. The portobello pesto is also terrific on its own, tossed with pasta, spread on toast, or used as a dip.

1 pound portobello mushrooms, cut into chunks

6 tablespoons olive oil, or more as needed

Salt and black pepper

Juice of 1 lemon

4 large artichokes

1 packed cup fresh basil

1 garlic clove, or to taste

2 tablespoons pine nuts or chopped walnuts

¼ cup grated Parmesan, Pecorino Romano, or other hard cheese, optional

1. Heat the oven to 400°F. Toss the mushrooms with 2 tablespoons of the oil in a roasting pan and sprinkle with salt and pepper. Roast, stirring occasionally, until the mushrooms are tender and almost dry, 20 to 30 minutes.

2. Meanwhile, fill a bowl with ice water and squeeze the lemon juice into it. Cut off the artichoke stems to create a flat surface on the bottom. Remove the toughest exterior leaves and trim the remaining leaves by about ½ inch. Open up the leaves as much as possible and dig out the spiny choke and its sharp leaves with a spoon. After you trim each artichoke, put it in the bowl to keep it from discoloring.

3. Put the mushrooms in a food processor. Add the basil, garlic, nuts, Parmesan, and 2 tablespoons oil and pulse several times to purée. Drizzle in another 2 tablespoons oil gradually while the machine is running. (You may need to add more oil to get a smooth, fairly thick paste.) Taste and adjust the seasoning if necessary. (At this point, you can refrigerate the pesto in a covered container for up to a day.) Fill the artichoke cavities and the spaces between the leaves with the mushroom pesto.

4. Rig a steamer (see page 414) and put the artichokes in it, stem side down. Cover and cook for 20 to 40 minutes. (When an outer leaf pulls away easily and its meat is tender, they're done.) Serve hot or at room temperature.

Grilled Artichokes with Portobello "Pesto." This method of cooking artichokes intensifies their flavor and adds a pleasant smoky contrast. Prepare a grill to medium-high heat and put the rack about 4 inches from the fire. Follow the recipe through Step 3. After trimming the artichokes in Step 2, bring a large pot of water to a boil and salt it. Boil the artichokes for 15 minutes, then remove them to cool and dry for a few minutes (or up to several hours) before stuffing with the mushroom pesto. Brush the artichokes lightly with some more olive oil and grill or broil, rotating once or twice, until tender, deeply colored, and charred in some spots, 10 to 15 minutes total.

Ⓕ Fast   Ⓜ Make-Ahead   Ⓟ Pantry Staple

Mexican-Style Fruit Salad with Grilled or Broiled Fish

Makes: 4 servings   Time: 30 minutes

Another recipe that doubles as a general guideline, since you can change the choice of fruit and fish at will. Some suggestions: peaches, plums, pineapple, mango, papaya, grapes, strawberries, or a combination of citrus. For the fish, first check out the sidebar on page 441. You can use thin or thick fish fillets (though thin fillets are too delicate to grill), steaks, or even shrimp, scallops, or squid.

   1½ pounds assorted fruit, peeled and pitted as necessary, and chopped

   1 or 2 small hot chiles (like jalapeño or serrano), minced

   ½ cup chopped fresh cilantro, mint, or basil, or a combination

   Salt and black pepper

   2 tablespoons olive oil, plus more for drizzling

   12 ounces fish fillets or steaks (see page 22), cut into 4 equal pieces

   Lemon or lime wedges, for serving

1. Prepare a grill or turn on the broiler; the heat should be medium-high and the rack about 4 inches from the fire. Toss the chopped fruit with the chile, herb, and a little salt and pepper; refrigerate if you want the fruit salad cold.

2. Use 2 tablespoons oil to brush the broiler pan or grill grates and the fish. Sprinkle the fish with salt and pepper and grill or broil, turning once if the pieces are thick and not at all if they are thin, until just done. Thin fish fillets will take less than 5 minutes, while thick fillets or steaks will take 8 to 10 minutes. When you can pass a thin-bladed knife through the fish with little resistance, it's done. (If you want the fish less well done, adjust accordingly.)

3. Put the fruit on a serving platter or individual plates, top with the fish and a drizzle of oil, and serve with the lemon or lime wedges.

Pan-Cooked Vegetables
with Crunchy Fish

Makes: 4 servings   Time: 30 minutes

Grated potatoes, winter squash, and root vegetables cook in 10 minutes, so even if you don't have a food processor and must grate by hand you still save time. Here the vegetables are heavily spiced with ginger (and/or garlic) and curry powder and then topped with crunchy fish. The list that follows gives some direction for using different types of seafood in this recipe.

> 4 tablespoons vegetable oil, or more as needed
>
> 1 small red onion or 4 scallions, chopped
>
> About 2 pounds winter squash, sweet potatoes, daikon radishes, turnips, carrots, parsnips, or celery root, peeled and grated
>
> 1 tablespoon minced ginger and/or garlic
>
> 1 tablespoon curry powder, or to taste
>
> Salt and black pepper
>
> ¼ cup cornmeal (fine or medium grind)
>
> ¼ cup all-purpose or whole wheat flour
>
> About 12 ounces sturdy white fish fillets (see page 22), cut into 4 pieces
>
> ¼ cup chopped fresh parsley or cilantro
>
> Lemon, lime, or orange wedges, for serving, optional

1. Put 2 tablespoons of the oil in a large skillet (preferably cast iron) over medium-high heat. When it's hot, add half the onion and the vegetables. Add the ginger and/or garlic and the curry powder and sprinkle with salt and pepper. Cook, stirring and adding a little more oil if the mixture is sticking, until the onion has caramelized and the vegetables are lightly browned, about 10 minutes; the vegetables need not be fully tender. Taste and adjust the seasoning. Transfer to a large serving platter (or divide among individual plates).

2. While the vegetables are cooking, combine the cornmeal and flour on a plate along with some salt and pepper. Dredge the fish in the cornmeal mixture, pressing to make some of it stick, then shake to remove the excess.

Ⓕ Fast   Ⓜ Make-Ahead   Ⓟ Pantry Staple

3. Return the skillet to high heat; don't bother to wipe it out. Add the remaining 2 tablespoons oil. When it's hot, add the fish to the pan and cook, turning only once, until nicely browned on both sides and cooked through—a thin-bladed knife will meet little or no resistance when the fish is done. Put the fish on top of the vegetables; garnish with the remaining onion and the herb. Serve with citrus wedges if you like.

Pan-Cooked Grated Vegetables with Sesame Fish. Instead of the cornmeal-flour mixture, use ½ cup sesame seeds to dredge the fish, pressing to make them stick to the sides. Proceed with the recipe, garnishing with cilantro and lime wedges.

Other Seafood to Use for This Dish and How Long to Cook It

Peeled shrimp (large ones will take about 2 minutes per side to cook; medium will take 3 minutes total)

Sea scallops (cook 3 to 4 minutes per side)

Sturdy fish fillets or steaks (5 to 10 minutes total cooking time, depending on the thickness)

Squid (cook and stir for just a couple of minutes)

Trout (whole fish are sturdier than fillets: cook 2 small whole fish or 1 large one; 5 minutes a side should do the trick)

Crab Cakes, My (New) Way

Makes: 4 servings   Time: 45 minutes

I've made crab cakes out of nearly 100 percent crab for most of my life, and I love them that way. But this alternative, which uses mild and creamy celery root as a not-so-secret ingredient, is really amazing. If you don't have time to make the tartar sauce–like mustard relish here, just serve them with cucumber or pickle spears or thick tomato slices.

8 ounces fresh lump crab meat (see page 22), picked over for cartilage and shell

1 small celery root (8 to 12 ounces), peeled and grated

1 egg

Salt and black pepper

2 tablespoons bread crumbs, preferably whole grain and homemade, or more as needed

2 tablespoons mayonnaise (for homemade, see page 188)

⅓ cup Dijon mustard

1 small cucumber, peeled, seeded, and chopped

1 red bell pepper, chopped

½ cup chopped scallions

About 1 cup whole wheat flour

2 teaspoons curry powder, optional

¼ cup vegetable oil

Lemon wedges, for serving

1. Mix together the crab meat, celery root, egg, and some salt and pepper. Add enough bread crumbs to bind the mixture just enough to form into cakes that don't crack too easily; start with 2 tablespoons and use more if you need it.

2. If you have time, refrigerate the mixture for at least 30 minutes or up to several hours; it will be easier to shape. Meanwhile, combine the mayonnaise, mustard, cucumber, bell pepper, and scallions in a small bowl. Sprinkle with salt and pepper and stir until well mixed; refrigerate the sauce until you're ready to eat.

Ⓕ Fast   Ⓜ Make-Ahead   Ⓟ Pantry Staple

3. Season the flour with salt and pepper, and stir in the curry powder if you're using it. Heat a large skillet (preferably cast iron) over medium-high heat for 2 to 3 minutes. Add the oil and heat until it shimmers. Shape the crab meat mixture into 1-inch-thick cakes, dredge each in the flour, and cook, adjusting the heat as necessary and turning once (very gently), until golden brown on both sides, about 5 minutes per side. (Work in batches if you're making small cakes; you don't want to crowd the pan.) Serve with lemon wedges and the mustard relish.

Not-So-Classic Seafood Pan Roast

Makes: 4 servings   Time: About 45 minutes

You don't need all that much seafood to capture the briny flavor of summertime at the shore, as long as it's good. Use a combination of your favorites and what looks best, though I must say that the juices of clams and mussels truly lend the taste of the ocean to this dish. For special occasions, roast a couple of small split lobsters over the vegetables (they'll take a little longer to cook).

1 pound small red or white potatoes, halved

3 tablespoons olive oil

Salt and black pepper

1 large fennel bulb or several celery stalks, cut into chunks

4 carrots, cut into chunks

4 ears fresh corn, shucked and cut into 2-inch pieces

¼ cup chopped fresh dill, or 1 tablespoon dill seeds

Pinch of cayenne

1 tablespoon mustard seeds, lightly crushed, or 1 teaspoon dry mustard

1 cup chicken or fish stock (for homemade, see pages 138 to 140), white wine, or water

About 1 pound clams, mussels, squid, shrimp, scallops, or a combination (see page 22)

Lemon wedges, for serving

1. Heat the oven to 400°F. Put the potatoes in a large roasting pan, toss with 1 tablespoon of the oil, sprinkle with (not too much) salt and (plenty of) pepper, and spread them out a bit, placing them cut side down. Roast until they begin to brown but are not yet tender, 10 to 15 minutes.

2. Add the fennel and carrots to the pan, drizzle with the remaining 2 tablespoons oil, and sprinkle with a little more salt and pepper. Toss the vegetables with the potatoes and roast for another 10 minutes. Add the corn, dill, cayenne, mustard, and stock to the pan. Stir to combine and scrape up any brown bits from the bottom of the pan. Spread the seafood on top of the vegetables. Roast until the potatoes and carrots are tender and all of the seafood has opened or is cooked through and is opaque, 10 to 15 minutes.

3. To serve, put the vegetables and seafood onto a big platter or divide among individual bowls. Spoon any liquid that remains in the pan over the top and sprinkle with a little salt if you like. Serve with lemon wedges.

Peruvian-Style *Causa* Filled with Herbs and Smoked Fish

Makes: 4 servings   Time: 1½ hours, largely unattended

Causa is one of Peru's best-loved dishes, in which layers of mashed potatoes are alternated with a seafood salad, often tuna based. This version includes fresh herbs and smoked fish and is popped into a muffin tin to be baked, resulting in warm, crusty mini-casseroles. All you need on the side is a big salad or some lightly dressed steamed vegetables.

You can even make little *causas* for hors d'oeuvres—just use mini-muffin tins. Either layer the potatoes and fish into bite-size cakes (which requires some patience) or take the lazy route and combine all the ingredients together and spoon them into the muffin cups.

2 tablespoons olive oil, plus more for greasing and brushing

2 pounds baking potatoes, like russet

Salt

8 ounces smoked salmon, trout, or whitefish flaked into pieces

¼ cup chopped fresh dill

¼ cup chopped fresh chives

½ cup milk

Salt and black pepper

Lemon wedges, for serving

1. Heat the oven to 400°F. Generously grease a 12-cup muffin tin. Put the potatoes on a baking sheet and roast, turning once halfway through, until the potatoes are tender (a skewer or sharp knife will pierce one fairly easily), anywhere from 45 to 60 minutes. Let the potatoes cool a bit, then peel them. (You can make the dish ahead to this point; just wait to peel the potatoes before proceeding.)

2. Meanwhile, combine the fish and herbs in a small bowl with a fork.

3. Run the potatoes through a potato ricer or food mill over a large bowl, or smash them with a fork or potato masher in a bowl. Add the milk, 2 tablespoons oil, and lots of salt and pepper and stir until smooth.

4. Divide about two-thirds of the potato mixture among the muffin cups. Press down and use a small spoon to make a well in each. Fill each well with some of the fish mixture and use the remaining potato mixture to enclose the filling. Brush the tops with some oil, sprinkle with a little more salt, and bake until golden brown, 25 to 30 minutes. (You can also cover the muffin tin and refrigerate it for up to several hours before baking.) Let cool for 5 minutes in the pan, then remove. Serve hot, warm, or at room temperature with lemon wedges.

Roasted Okra and Shrimp
with Tomato Chutney

Makes: 4 servings   Time: 40 minutes

Here is gumbo, deconstructed: okra, shrimp, and tomato, with some surprises thrown in, including filé, a seasoning made from sassafras. If you don't have (or don't like) okra, use whole green beans or zucchini sticks instead. This is good with long-grain brown rice or roasted potato wedges; cook the potatoes on a separate pan in the oven along with the okra.

5 tablespoons olive oil

1 small red onion, chopped

1 green bell pepper, chopped

2 celery stalks, chopped

1 tablespoon minced garlic

Salt and black pepper

Pinch of cayenne

2 teaspoons filé powder or cumin

1 tablespoon tomato paste

2 cups chopped tomatoes (canned are fine; include their juice)

1 tablespoon brown sugar or honey

1½ pounds okra

8 ounces shrimp, peeled (see page 22)

½ cup chopped fresh parsley, for garnish

1. Heat the oven to 425°F. Put 3 tablespoons of the oil in a medium skillet over medium-high heat. A minute later, add the onion, pepper, celery, and garlic, sprinkle with salt and pepper, and cook, stirring, until the vegetables soften, 5 to 7 minutes. Add the cayenne, filé, and tomato paste and cook, stirring, until fragrant but not burning, just a minute or 2. Stir in the tomatoes and sugar and bring to a boil. Lower the heat so the mixture bubbles gently and cook, stirring occasionally, until it thickens, 15 to 20 minutes. (You can make the chutney up to 3 days ahead and refrigerate; bring to room temperature before proceeding.)

Ⓕ Fast   Ⓜ Make-Ahead   Ⓟ Pantry Staple

2. Meanwhile, put the okra in a roasting pan or on a rimmed baking sheet; drizzle with the remaining 2 tablespoons oil and sprinkle with lots of salt and pepper. Toss until well coated. Roast, stirring once or twice, until browned and crisp on the outside but not mushy, 10 to 15 minutes.

3. Stir the shrimp into the okra and continue roasting until they're opaque inside but not dried out, 3 to 5 minutes. Taste and adjust the seasoning. Garnish with the parsley and serve, hot or warm, with the tomato chutney.

Minted Peas and Lettuce with Mackerel or Sardines

Makes: 4 servings   Time: 30 minutes

Romaine lettuce turns a quick pea sauce silky and sweet; grill it (see the variation), and it becomes a smoky and tender base for fish and sauce. Either way, it's the perfect match for oily mackerel or sardines, both among the most sustainable finfish. For more assertive flavor, try radicchio, escarole, or endive instead of the romaine. Serve this with plain rice or lots of bread to soak up the juices.

2 tablespoons olive oil

1 onion, chopped

1 tablespoon minced garlic

Salt and black pepper

1 cup chopped tomatoes (canned are fine; include their juice)

½ cup white wine or water

3 cups fresh or frozen peas

1 large head romaine lettuce, cored and shredded

1 medium mackerel fillet or 6 to 8 cleaned sardines (see page 22), about
    12 ounces total

½ cup chopped fresh mint, for garnish

1. Put the oil in a large skillet over medium heat. A minute later, add the onion and garlic and cook, stirring, until soft and golden, about 5 minutes. Sprinkle with salt and pepper, turn the heat to high, and add the tomatoes and wine.

2. When the liquid comes to a boil, lower the heat to medium-low, and stir in the peas and lettuce. Top the vegetables with the fish, cover, and cook until the fish is done (a thin knife will pierce the thickest part of the fish with little resistance), 5 to 10 minutes for sardines, 10 to 15 minutes for mackerel. Serve hot, garnished with the mint.

Minted Peas and Mackerel over Grilled or Broiled Romaine. Prepare a grill or turn on the broiler; the heat should be medium-high and the rack about 4 inches from the fire. Instead of shredding the lettuce and cooking it with the peas, trim the end of the romaine but leave the core intact; cut it into quarters. Brush the lettuce with 1 tablespoon olive oil. While the fish is cooking, put the romaine on the grill or on a broiler pan, cut sides toward the heat source. Grill or broil, turning once, until it softens a bit and begins to char, 3 to 5 minutes total. Transfer the wedges to plates, top with the peas and mackerel, garnish with mint, and serve.

(F) Fast   (M) Make-Ahead   (P) Pantry Staple

Stir-Fried Fennel and Pink Grapefruit with Shrimp

Makes: 4 servings   Time: 30 minutes

I love grapefruit and fennel; I love grapefruit and shrimp; I love shrimp and fennel. So here you go—a fast, juicy, ultra-flavorful dish that is as good cold as hot.

If you know how to cut grapefruit into "supremes"—where the segments are sliced free of the thick membranes that divide them—go for it. But peeling the grapefruit (removing as much of the bitter white pith as possible), separating it into regular segments, and roughly chopping it is just fine. If grapefruit is too bitter for you, substitute oranges for some or all of it. Serve this dish over rice or other grains.

   3 tablespoons vegetable or olive oil

   1 bunch scallions, cut into 1-inch pieces

   1 tablespoon minced garlic

   1 tablespoon minced ginger

   1 fresh hot chile (like jalapeño or Thai), minced

   2 large fennel bulbs, cored and thinly sliced

   2 grapefruit, peeled, segmented, and chopped (see the headnote)

   8 ounces shrimp, peeled (see page 22)

   1 tablespoon soy sauce, or to taste

   ¼ cup chopped fresh mint, cilantro, or a combination

   Salt and black pepper

1. Put the oil in a large skillet over high heat. When it's hot, add the scallions, garlic, ginger, and chile and cook, stirring, for a minute or 2. Stir in the fennel and cook for another minute or 2. Add the grapefruit segments along with the shrimp and soy sauce. Cook, stirring occasionally, until the shrimp are uniformly pink, 3 to 5 minutes.

2. Turn off the heat and stir in the herb. Taste and sprinkle with salt and pepper if necessary. Serve hot or at room temperature, or chill for up to several hours and serve cold.

Pan-Fried Celery Root and Fish with Mustard Seeds

Makes: 4 servings   Time: 1¼ hours

Fish fries are not forbidden fruit, but they benefit from a little reinvention. Here, celery root is breaded and pan-fried along with the fish (trout is classic, but use what you like), and the drizzle beats tartar sauce by a mile.

1½ pounds celery root

Two 6-ounce trout or other sturdy white fish fillets (see page 22)

2 cups cornmeal (fine or medium grind)

½ teaspoon cayenne, or to taste

Salt and black pepper

¾ cup buttermilk or yogurt

Vegetable oil, for frying

2 tablespoons olive oil

1 red onion, chopped

1 tablespoon mustard seeds

1 cup white wine

½ cup chopped fresh parsley

1. Heat the oven to 200°F. Cut the celery root into sticks about 3 inches long and ½ inch wide; cut the fish into strips of about the same size. Combine the cornmeal, cayenne, and a good sprinkling of salt and pepper in a shallow bowl or plate. Put the buttermilk in another big bowl set out next to the cornmeal mixture. Have a baking sheet and a stack of parchment or wax paper ready.

2. Put the celery root in the buttermilk and toss to coat, then dredge each piece in the cornmeal mixture, stacking them on the baking sheet between layers of wax paper as you finish. Dip the fish pieces first in the buttermilk, then in the cornmeal mixture, and layer them on the baking sheet, again separated by wax paper. Chill the stacks in the refrigerator for at least 10 minutes and up to 3 hours.

3. Put about ½ inch vegetable oil in a deep pan on the stove and turn the heat to medium-high; the oil is ready when a pinch of cornmeal sizzles in it. Put in a few of the celery root slices; cook in batches to avoid crowding the pan and add more oil as necessary. Turn the celery root slices as soon as they're browned, then cook the other side. The total cooking time should be between 5 and 10 minutes. As each piece is done, transfer it first to paper towels to drain briefly, then to the oven. Cook the fish strips in the same way (they will need a few minutes less to cook) and transfer them to the oven.

4. Put the 2 tablespoons olive oil in a small skillet over medium-high heat. Add the onion, sprinkle with salt and pepper, and cook, stirring frequently, until the onion softens and browns a bit, 3 to 5 minutes. Add the mustard seeds and cook until fragrant, about 30 seconds. Add the wine, bring to a boil, and let bubble until reduced and slightly thickened, just a couple minutes more. Stir in the parsley and taste and adjust the seasoning. Serve the fish and celery root together, passing the sauce at the table.

Seared Fish and Watermelon with Wasabi Drizzle

Makes: 4 servings   Time: 40 minutes

Watermelon makes a surprisingly good "steak" and a refreshing companion for fatty, rich fish. To grill this dish, put the sesame seeds in the sauce and just brush the melon and fish with the oil.

1 tablespoon wasabi powder

1 tablespoon soy sauce

Juice of 1 lemon

1/2 small watermelon, about 2 1/2 pounds

2 tablespoons sesame seeds

Salt and black pepper

2 sturdy fish steaks or fillets (see page 22), about 12 ounces total, cut into
    4 pieces

1 teaspoon sesame oil

3 tablespoons vegetable oil, or more as needed

1/2 cup sliced scallions, for garnish

1. Whisk together the wasabi, soy sauce, and lemon juice in a small bowl.

2. Cut the watermelon into 8 slices, each between 1 and 2 inches thick (you can leave the rind on if you like). Use a fork to remove as many seeds from the heart as you can without beating the flesh up too much. Put the sesame seeds on a plate with some salt and pepper and stir to combine. Dredge the fish in the mixture and press to make it stick.

3. Put a large skillet over medium-high heat and add the sesame oil and 1 tablespoon of the vegetable oil. When hot, add the watermelon; work in batches to avoid overcrowding the pan and add more vegetable oil as needed. Cook the pieces, adjusting the heat as necessary and turning once, until the slices begin to release some water, brown, and shrivel a bit, 3 to 5 minutes; turn and cook for another 3 to 5 minutes. Transfer the melon along with any pan juices to a serving plate.

(F) Fast   (M) Make-Ahead   (P) Pantry Staple

4. Wipe out the pan with a paper towel, add the remaining 2 tablespoons vegetable oil, and return to the heat. When it's hot, add the fish. Cook, turning once, until the crust is well browned and the inside is cooked as you like it (rare for tuna, cooked through or nearly through for other fish), 5 to 10 minutes total. Put the fish on top of the watermelon, drizzle with the wasabi sauce, garnish with scallions, and serve.

Caramelized Leeks with Gently Cooked Scallops

Makes: 4 servings   Time: 30 minutes

Drizzling very hot oil over thinly sliced scallops cooks them ever so slightly and firms them perfectly. In this case, the oil is flavored with the leeks that you serve alongside, so the seafood takes on that pleasant onion-grass flavor. Just make sure the scallops are of good quality and look and smell superfresh. Beyond that, all you need here is good bread for a light one-dish meal.

> ⅓ cup olive oil
>
> 1½ pounds leeks, trimmed, well rinsed, and sliced
>
> Salt and black pepper
>
> 8 ounces large scallops, each cut crosswise into several very thin rounds
>
> Grated zest and juice of 1 lemon
>
> Lemon wedges, for serving

1. Put the oil in a large skillet over medium heat. A minute later, add the leeks, sprinkle with salt and pepper, and cook, stirring occasionally, until tender and nicely browned, 10 to 15 minutes. Transfer the leeks to a bowl with tongs or a slotted spoon, leaving as much oil as possible behind in the pan. Toss the leeks with the lemon zest and juice and a little more salt and pepper if necessary.

2. Meanwhile, use some of the oil in the pan to lightly grease a serving plate and put the scallops on it in a single layer.

3. Heat the oil that's left in the pan until it is very hot and shimmers but doesn't smoke. Drizzle the hot oil over the scallops and sprinkle them with a little salt. Serve, passing them at the table along with the leeks and lemon wedges.

Fish Nuggets Braised in Rhubarb Sauce

Makes: 4 servings   Time: 30 minutes

Cooking fish—and other things—in caramelized sugar is a classic Vietnamese technique, one that may sound oddly sweet. It isn't, though, because the sugar (of which there is a lot less here than in traditional versions) becomes bitter, and the black pepper, lime juice, and rhubarb pull this together into an incredible sauce. You can give pork, chicken, beef, or even tofu the same treatment (see the variation). When fresh rhubarb isn't in season, use frozen. Serve with plain rice or noodles.

> ¼ cup sugar
>
> 1½ pounds rhubarb, roughly chopped
>
> 1 large onion, chopped
>
> 1 fresh hot chile (like Thai or jalapeño), minced, optional
>
> Salt
>
> 1 teaspoon black pepper
>
> Juice of 2 limes
>
> About 12 ounces sturdy white fish fillets (see page 22), cut into chunks
>
> Chopped fresh cilantro, for garnish
>
> Chopped scallions, for garnish

1. Put a large, deep skillet over medium heat and add the sugar and ¼ cup water. Cook, occasionally shaking the pan gently, until the sugar dissolves, then bubbles and darkens, 5 to 10 minutes. Turn off the heat and carefully stir in ¼ cup water. Turn the heat to medium-high and cook, stirring constantly, until the caramel dissolves in the water and thickens slightly, a minute or 2.

2. Add the rhubarb, onion, and chile if you're using it to the caramel and sprinkle with salt; adjust the heat so the mixture bubbles a little but doesn't boil. Cook, stirring occasionally, until the vegetables soften and begin to melt into the sauce, about 10 minutes.

3. Stir in the black pepper and lime juice, then add the chunks of fish. Cover and cook, undisturbed, until the fish is done (a thin-bladed knife inserted into the center will meet little resistance), about 5 minutes. Taste and adjust the seasoning. Serve, garnished with the cilantro and scallions.

Pork Braised with Escarole in Caramel Sauce. Use the juice of 1 orange instead of the lime juice. Substitute escarole for the rhubarb and thinly sliced pork shoulder for the fish. Increase the cooking time in Step 3 to about 10 minutes, so that the pork is thoroughly cooked but not tough.

Vegetable and Oyster Pancakes, Korean Style

Makes: 4 servings   Time: 45 minutes

Crisp on the outside, chewy on the inside, these classic savory pancakes are among my favorite foods from Korea. Try substituting corn or chopped or shredded daikon (or other) radishes for the bean sprouts, or using other seafood in place of the oysters (check out the variation; besides shrimp I've seen—and used—octopus, scallops, squid, finfish, clams, and a combination of seafood). And definitely try them as appetizers: Make them silver-dollar size and serve soy sauce mixed with lime juice for a dipping sauce.

> 1 cup whole wheat or brown rice flour
>
> ½ cup all-purpose flour
>
> 1 egg
>
> 1 tablespoon vegetable oil, plus more for frying
>
> 2 cups bean sprouts
>
> 4 scallions, green parts only, sliced
>
> 1 large carrot, grated
>
> 12 shucked raw oysters (see page 22), rinsed and drained
>
> Lime wedges, for serving
>
> Soy sauce, for serving

1. Heat the oven to 200°F. Fit a baking sheet with a wire rack and put it in the oven. Whisk together the flours, egg, 1 tablespoon oil, and 1 cup water to make a smooth batter. Let it rest while you prepare the vegetables. When you're ready to cook, stir the bean sprouts, scallions, and carrot into the batter.

2. Put a thin film of oil in a large skillet over medium-high heat. When it's hot, ladle in a quarter of the batter and spread it out evenly into a large circle. Tuck 3 oysters into the pancake, as close to the center as you can. Turn the heat to medium and cook until the bottom is browned, about 5 minutes; flip and cook for another 5 minutes. Transfer the pancake to the oven. Repeat with the remaining batter.

3. To serve, cut the pancakes into wedges and pass the lime wedges and soy sauce at the table.

Kimchi Pancakes. Omit the bean sprouts, scallions, and carrot; keep the oysters (or other seafood) if you like. Drain 2 cups kimchi (for homemade, see page 343, or use high-quality store-bought). In Step 1 add the kimchi to the batter instead of the vegetables and proceed with the recipe.

Vegetable and Shrimp Pancakes, Thai Style. Substitute chopped raw shrimp for the oysters. Add 1 tablespoon nam pla (fish sauce) to the batter. Serve with lime wedges.

Ⓕ Fast Ⓜ Make-Ahead Ⓟ Pantry Staple

Kohlrabi Stir-Fry with Chicken or Pork

Makes: **4 servings**   Time: **20 minutes**

Kohlrabi is an underrated vegetable, largely because it's weird looking. The small, Sputnik-like bulbs, which are a member of the cabbage family, come in white, green, and purple. They may be eaten raw—they're radish-like in texture but sweet in flavor—or cooked, which makes them perfect for a quick stir-fry. If you can't find kohlrabi, jícama, Jerusalem artichokes, daikon radishes, or even big chunks of cabbage are fine stand-ins. Serve this with plain rice or tossed with noodles, or if you're in a hurry, wrap it up in a large flour tortilla with some lettuce and call it a meal.

2 tablespoons vegetable oil

12 ounces boneless, skinless chicken thighs or pork shoulder, thinly sliced or cut into small chunks

Salt and black pepper

1 tablespoon minced ginger

1 pound kohlrabi, peeled and chopped

2 tablespoons soy sauce

Juice of 1 lemon

½ cup sliced scallions

1. Put the oil in a large skillet over medium-high heat. A minute later, add the chicken or pork, sprinkle with salt and pepper, and cook, stirring constantly, until it starts to brown, 3 to 5 minutes. Add the ginger and keep stir-frying until fragrant, just 30 seconds or so.

2. Add the kohlrabi and ¼ cup water; cook and stir until it softens a bit and the water evaporates, about 3 minutes. Turn off the heat and stir in the soy sauce, lemon juice, and scallions. Taste and adjust the seasoning. Serve hot or at room temperature.

Loaded Guacamole with Chicken Kebabs

Makes: 4 servings   Time: About 45 minutes, plus time to marinate

Guacamole, of course, can stand on its own—but it can also act as a support for plenty of other ingredients. Here the avocado is combined with corn kernels and lettuce, but you can use frozen peas, grilled or roasted asparagus, or ripe tomatoes. If you marinate the chicken ahead of time and mix the guacamole a little before serving, the meal comes together in a heartbeat.

12 ounces boneless, skinless chicken thighs or legs, cut into 12 or 16 large chunks

1 large onion, cut into large chunks

8 ounces cherry tomatoes

1 bell pepper, any color, cut into large chunks

2 tablespoons olive oil

4 teaspoons minced garlic

1 tablespoon chili powder

Salt and black pepper

3 avocados, skin and pits removed

Grated zest and juice of 1 lime

1 cup corn kernels (thawed frozen are fine)

2 cups shredded romaine or iceberg lettuce

1 fresh hot chile (like serrano or jalapeño), seeded and minced

2 tablespoons chopped fresh cilantro, plus more for garnish

Lime wedges, for serving

1. If you're using wooden skewers (you'll need at least 8), soak them in water for 20 to 30 minutes (see page 69) while you prepare the chicken. Thread the chicken, onion, cherry tomatoes, and bell pepper alternately onto the skewers, leaving a little space between the pieces.

2. Combine the oil, 3 teaspoons of the garlic, the chili powder, and some salt and pepper; taste and adjust the seasoning. Brush the chicken and vegetables with the oil mixture and let marinate for at least a few minutes or up to 1 hour at room temperature. When you're ready to cook, prepare a grill or

Ⓕ Fast   Ⓜ Make-Ahead   Ⓟ Pantry Staple

turn on the broiler; the heat should be medium-high and the rack about 4 inches from the fire.

3. Meanwhile, make the guacamole: Mash the avocados in a large bowl until they're as smooth or chunky as you like. Stir in the remaining 1 teaspoon garlic, the lime zest and juice, corn, lettuce, chile, and cilantro. Sprinkle with salt and pepper, stir, and taste and adjust the seasoning. Cover and refrigerate until you're ready to eat, but no longer than an hour or so.

4. Broil or grill the chicken kebabs, turning once or twice, until the chicken is cooked through, 12 to 15 minutes (to check for doneness, cut into a piece with a thin-bladed knife; the center should be white or slightly pink). Spoon guacamole onto serving plates, top with the kebabs, garnish with cilantro, and serve with lime wedges.

Mixed Grill with Chimichurri

Makes: 4 servings   Time: 45 minutes

Chimichurri, the incredibly flavorful, super-simple Argentine herb sauce is one of the world's best condiments for grilled *anything*. It's most often made with parsley, but you can add or substitute cilantro and/or basil if you like. Though chimichurri doesn't keep more than a day or so in the fridge, in the course of that day you'll find yourself using it on plain rice, beans, cooked vegetables, raw carrots, chips—pretty much whatever you can grab.

A mixed grill like this requires a lot of surface area for cooking, so you'll probably have to work in batches to avoid overcrowding. But that's fine: Everything tastes just as good at room temperature, so cook leisurely. The recipe will help you get the hang of the timing.

> 1 or 2 eggplants, cut into thick slices
>
> 2 cups fresh parsley (mostly leaves, but thin stems are okay)
>
> Salt and black pepper
>
> 3 garlic cloves
>
> ½ cup olive oil, plus more for grilling
>
> 2 tablespoons sherry vinegar or lemon juice
>
> 1 teaspoon red chile flakes
>
> 2 portobello mushrooms
>
> 2 summer squash, cut lengthwise into thick slices
>
> 4 ripe tomatoes, cored but left whole
>
> 12 ounces boneless, skinless chicken breast or pork tenderloin, cut in half crosswise and pounded to about ½ inch thick
>
> 1 bunch scallions

1. Prepare a grill or turn on the broiler; the heat should be medium-high and the rack about 4 inches from the fire. If time allows, sprinkle the eggplant liberally with salt, let rest in a colander for at least 20 minutes or up to an hour, rinse, and pat dry.

2. Combine the parsley with a sprinkle of salt and pepper, the garlic, and about ¼ cup of the oil in a food processor or blender. Process, stopping to

Ⓕ Fast   Ⓜ Make-Ahead   Ⓟ Pantry Staple

scrape down the sides of the container once or twice. With the machine running, add the remaining ¼ cup oil gradually, then add the vinegar and chile flakes. Add a little bit of water if you want a thinner mixture. Taste and adjust the seasoning.

3. Brush the eggplant, portobellos, and squash with oil and sprinkle with salt and pepper. Working in batches, grill or broil the pieces, turning occasionally, until browned and tender, 15 to 20 minutes. When the mushrooms are done, slice them. As all the vegetables finish, transfer them to a large serving platter.

4. Brush the tomatoes and chicken with oil and sprinkle with salt and pepper. Again working in batches, grill or broil the pieces, turning just once, until the tomatoes are charred and collapsed and the chicken or pork is white or very slightly pink on the inside, 5 to 10 minutes total. Transfer to the serving platter and cut the meat up a bit if you like. Finally, cook the scallions (no need to brush them with oil), turning once or twice, until they are lightly charred, just a minute or 2. Drizzle some of the chimichurri over the meat and vegetables and pass the rest at the table.

Sesame-Glazed Brussels Sprouts with Chicken

Makes: 4 servings   Time: 40 minutes

I love Brussels sprouts braised and glazed like this—they retain some crunch but become a little creamy in places, mostly tender, and not at all raw. Season them with ginger and sesame seeds, add a bit of seared chicken, and you've got a satisfying main dish. Serve it with plain potatoes, rice, or—the best— soba noodles.

> 3 tablespoons sesame seeds
>
> 2 tablespoons vegetable oil
>
> 8 ounces boneless, skinless chicken breast or thighs, cut into small chunks
>
> 2 tablespoons minced ginger
>
> 1 tablespoon sesame oil
>
> 1 pound Brussels sprouts
>
> ½ cup stock (for homemade, see pages 135 to 140), white wine, or water, or more as needed
>
> Salt and black pepper
>
> Soy sauce, for serving
>
> Lemon wedges, for serving

1. Put the sesame seeds in a large, deep skillet over medium-low heat and toast, shaking the pan often, until they begin to brown but don't burn, 5 to 10 minutes. Remove the seeds from the skillet.

2. Add the oil to the skillet and raise the heat to medium-high. When it's hot, add the chicken and cook, stirring occasionally, until it browns a bit on the outside, 3 to 5 minutes. Add the ginger and stir until fragrant and beginning to soften, just a minute or so, then remove.

3. Add the sesame oil, Brussels sprouts, and ½ cup stock to the pan (no need to wipe it out first), sprinkle with salt and pepper, and bring to a boil. Cover and adjust the heat so the mixture bubbles gently; cook until the sprouts are just tender, 5 to 10 minutes, checking once or twice and adding more liquid if needed.

Ⓕ Fast   Ⓜ Make-Ahead   Ⓟ Pantry Staple

4. Uncover and return the chicken and ginger to the pan. Raise the heat to boil off all the liquid so that the Brussels sprouts and chicken become glazed and eventually browned. Resist the urge to stir frequently; just let it sizzle until golden and crisp, then shake the pan and loosen the sprouts and chicken pieces to roll them over. Stir in the sesame seeds and taste and adjust the seasoning. Serve hot or at room temperature, passing the soy sauce and lemon wedges at the table.

Sesame-Glazed Carrots with Chicken. Use carrots, cut into coins or sticks, in place of the Brussels sprouts.

Roast Potatoes and Chicken with Romesco

Makes: 4 servings   Time: 1 hour, largely unattended

There are many ways to make romesco, the nutty, sharp Catalan sauce: with tomatoes or bell peppers, with chiles or without, with almonds or hazelnuts, raw or cooked. This fresh vinegar-spiked version brightens up classic roast potatoes and chicken. If you have roasted red bell peppers (for homemade, see page 417) on hand, by all means use one in place of the raw bell pepper; it will add an extra dimension of smokiness.

6 tablespoons olive oil, or more as needed

1½ pounds new potatoes or other small potatoes, halved

Salt and black pepper

2 sprigs fresh rosemary

4 bone-in chicken thighs; or 2 bone-in chicken breasts, each cut in half

½ cup almonds

1 large red bell pepper, roughly chopped

1 large or 2 medium ripe tomatoes, cored and roughly chopped

1 garlic clove, or to taste

1 packed cup fresh parsley

2 tablespoons sherry or white wine vinegar

1. Heat the oven to 400°F. Drizzle the bottom of a shallow roasting pan or a rimmed baking sheet with 2 tablespoons of the oil. Add the potatoes, toss to coat with the oil, spread in a single layer, and sprinkle with salt and pepper. Roast, undisturbed, until they're just beginning to sizzle, about 10 minutes.

2. Top the potatoes first with the rosemary, then the chicken pieces, all skin side up. Sprinkle with salt and pepper, and drizzle with 2 more tablespoons of the oil. Roast for about 15 minutes, then baste the chicken with the pan drippings and rotate the pan. If necessary, adjust the oven temperature so the chicken and potatoes brown but do not burn. Chicken breasts will be done in 15 to 20 more minutes, thighs in 25 to 30.

3. Meanwhile, combine the almonds, bell pepper, tomato, garlic, parsley, and vinegar in a food processor or blender. With the machine running, slowly add the remaining 2 tablespoons oil; purée into a thick paste, adding more oil if necessary to keep the machine running and scraping down the sides of the bowl as needed. Season with salt and pepper.

4. The chicken and potatoes are done when the potatoes are tender and release easily from the pan and the chicken is opaque and the juices run clear. Serve each piece of chicken with a spoonful of the potatoes, a little of the pan juices, and a dollop of romesco.

Provençal Vegetables and Chicken in Packages

Makes: 4 servings   Time: About 1 hour, largely unattended

Take the components of ratatouille—eggplant, zucchini, and tomatoes—combine them with sliced potatoes and chicken, and cook everything in packages for an appealing one-dish meal. Since the contents of the packages steam in their own juices, the results are like a quick braise. The vegetables become super silky and the meat juicy and tender. These are especially convenient since you can assemble them ahead of time and do virtually nothing while they bake. If you want the vegetables to retain a firmer texture, just slice them a bit thicker.

(F) Fast   (M) Make-Ahead   (P) Pantry Staple

1 small eggplant, cut lengthwise into equal ¼-inch slices

Salt

8 ounces all-purpose potatoes, like Yukon Gold, sliced ¼ inch thick

2 small zucchini, sliced ¼ inch thick

2 large ripe tomatoes, cored and sliced ¼ inch thick

½ cup black or green olives, pitted

Black pepper

4 sprigs fresh thyme

4 boneless, skinless chicken thighs

4 tablespoons olive oil

½ cup dry white wine or water

1. Heat the oven to 375°F. If time allows, sprinkle the eggplant liberally with salt, let rest in a colander for at least 20 minutes or up to an hour, rinse, and pat dry.

2. Cut parchment paper or foil into 4 rectangles of about 16 by 12 inches, fold in half crosswise to crease, then open again like a book. On one half of each rectangle, layer a portion of the potatoes, eggplant, zucchini, tomatoes, and olives, keeping the vegetables close to the center. Sprinkle with salt and pepper and top with a sprig of thyme. Add a piece of chicken and sprinkle again. Drizzle each serving with 1 tablespoon oil and 2 tablespoons wine. Seal the packages by enclosing the filling and rolling the open edges together tightly. Transfer the packages to a rimmed baking sheet.

3. Bake the packages undisturbed until the chicken is no longer pink inside and the vegetables are silky and tender, about 40 minutes. (You won't know for sure until you open one, but it is unlikely that the dish won't be done in that time.) Be careful of the steam when you open the packages. Serve immediately or at room temperature, in the packages, or transferred to plates, with the juices poured over all.

Vegetables au Vin with Coq

Makes: **4 servings**   Time: **About 40 minutes**

You're probably familiar with coq au vin, chicken braised in a rich red wine-mushroom sauce. Replace some of the chicken with eggplant and green beans, and the dish is, in fact, more interesting, yet still luxurious, since the eggplant literally melts into the sauce, thickening and flavoring it, while the green beans become tender. If you don't feel like using bacon, just use 2 tablespoons more olive oil to brown the chicken, mushrooms, and eggplant. Serve the stew with crusty bread, boiled or roasted potatoes, and more red wine.

1 eggplant, cut into large cubes

Salt

2 ounces slab bacon, cut into ¼-inch cubes

4 bone-in chicken thighs or 2 bone-in chicken breasts, split in half cross-wise

Black pepper

2 tablespoons olive oil

20 pearl onions, peeled, or 1 large onion, halved and sliced

1 pound mushrooms, preferably an assortment, roughly chopped

6 garlic cloves (or more)

2 cups chicken or vegetable stock (for homemade, see pages 135 to 140)

2 cups Burgundy (pinot noir) or other fruity red wine

2 bay leaves

Several sprigs fresh thyme

Several sprigs fresh parsley

8 ounces green beans, left whole

1 tablespoon butter

Chopped fresh parsley, for garnish

1. If time allows, sprinkle the eggplant liberally with salt, let rest in a colander for 20 minutes, rinse, and pat dry. Put the bacon in a large, deep skillet or Dutch oven that will hold all the chicken, eggplant, and mushrooms. Cook over medium-high heat, stirring occasionally, until the bacon gives up

Ⓕ Fast   Ⓜ Make-Ahead   Ⓟ Pantry Staple

its fat and becomes brown and crisp, 5 to 10 minutes. Remove the bacon. Add the chicken, skin side down, to the hot fat, sprinkle with salt and pepper, and cook, turning and rotating as necessary, until well browned, 10 to 15 minutes.

2. Remove the chicken from the pan. Add the oil, onions, mushrooms, and eggplant. Cook, stirring occasionally, until the vegetables give up their liquid and begin to dry out and brown, 10 to 15 minutes; after about 5 minutes of cooking, add the garlic.

3. Spoon off any excess fat from the pan. Add the stock, wine, bay leaves, herb sprigs, and green beans. Return the chicken to the pot along with the bacon. Bring to a boil, then adjust the heat so that the mixture bubbles gently but steadily. Cover and cook until the chicken is tender and cooked through, 15 to 20 minutes; an instant-read thermometer should register about 155°F for the breast and 165°F for the thigh. Remove the chicken from the pan and turn the heat up a bit.

4. Let the liquid boil until it is reduced by about half and becomes thick and saucy. Lower the heat again, stir in the butter, and return the chicken to the pan. Turn just long enough to warm it through and coat with the sauce. (You can make the dish ahead to this point and refrigerate for up to a day; reheat gently.) Remove the bay leaves. Taste and adjust the seasoning. Garnish with parsley and serve.

Anise-Scented Poached Chicken with Squash

Makes: 4 servings   Time: About 1 hour, largely unattended

I've long been a fan of a classic Chinese dish called "white cut chicken," where whole chicken is simply poached in seasoned water. But recently I began adding sweet, creamy winter squash. Kabocha is perfect here, but it's not always easy to find, in which case switch to butternut or any other orange-fleshed winter squash. Serve this at room temperature over soba noodles or short-grain brown rice, or chill it to serve cold over salad greens. If you don't have star anise, use a teaspoon of anise seeds, or change things up by using several whole bay leaves.

> 5 or 6 slices unpeeled ginger
>
> 1 bunch scallions, chopped
>
> 2 star anise
>
> 2 tablespoons salt
>
> 1 tablespoon honey or sugar
>
> 1 pound any winter squash, peeled, seeded, and sliced ½ inch thick
>
> 1 half small chicken, or about 1½ pounds bone-in chicken pieces
>
> Soy sauce, for serving

1. Combine the ginger, most of the scallions (reserve some for garnish), anise, salt, and honey in a large pot with 6 cups water. Bring to a boil. Add the squash and chicken and bring the water back to a boil. Turn the heat to low, cover, and bubble gently for 20 minutes.

2. Remove the pot from the heat and let the chicken and squash sit in the water, covered, for another 15 minutes or so; the chicken is done when an instant-read thermometer inserted into the thickest part of a thigh reads 155°F to 165°F.

3. Remove the chicken from the pot, cool to room temperature, and pull the meat from the bones. Serve the squash and the chicken together with soy sauce and scallions passed at the table (or cover and refrigerate for up to 2 days).

Ⓕ Fast   Ⓜ Make-Ahead   Ⓟ Pantry Staple

Braised Red Cabbage and Cherries with Broiled Chicken

Makes: 4 servings   Time: About 45 minutes

Apples and cabbage are a common combination, but cherries provide an interesting sweet-to-tart balance. If you buy them frozen and already pitted, this dish is a snap. If you'd rather use apples, you'll need just two. Either way, the dish is perfect with simply cooked potatoes or white beans, or just hearty bread—especially the Black Rolls with Caraway on page 547.

4 boneless, skinless chicken thighs, pounded to uniform thickness

4 tablespoons olive oil

2 tablespoons lemon juice

Salt and black pepper

1 red onion, halved and sliced

2 pounds red cabbage, cored and shredded

1 tablespoon caraway seeds, optional

½ cup chicken stock (for homemade, see page 139), not-too-dry white wine, apple cider, or water, or more as needed

1 cup pitted and halved cherries, preferably sour (frozen are fine)

Chopped fresh dill, for garnish

1. Put the chicken on a broiler pan or a rimmed baking sheet and toss with 2 tablespoons of the oil and the lemon juice. Sprinkle with salt and pepper. Cover with plastic wrap or foil and let sit while you proceed (or marinate in the refrigerator for up to a few hours).

2. Put the remaining 2 tablespoons oil in a large, deep skillet or saucepan over medium heat. When it's hot, add the onion and cook, stirring occasionally, until it softens, about 5 minutes. Add the cabbage and caraway seeds if you're using them, and stir to coat everything with the oil. Add the stock and cherries and cook, stirring occasionally, until everything becomes quite soft, 20 to 25 minutes; add more liquid if the mixture becomes dry.

3. Turn on the broiler; the heat should be medium-high and the rack about 4 inches from the fire. When the cabbage is almost ready, broil the chicken, turning once, until nicely browned and just cooked through, 6 to 8 minutes. (To check for doneness, cut into a piece with a thin-bladed knife; the center should be white or slightly pink.) Serve each piece of chicken on a mound of cabbage and cherries, garnished with dill.

Braised Parsnips and Chicken with Pumpkin Seed Sauce

Makes: 4 servings   Time: 45 minutes

Ground nuts and seeds are excellent options for thickening sauces, in many ways better than flour. They're more flavorful, nutritious, and (in this case at least) colorful. Almonds, hazelnuts, pecans, and pine nuts are all good here, but pumpkin seeds are my favorite. Chopped nuts can work well, too; try to get them as fine as possible.

You can substitute carrots (see the variation), rutabagas, turnips, or new potatoes for some or all of the parsnips if you like.

> 3 tablespoons olive oil
>
> 4 bone-in chicken thighs
>
> Salt and black pepper
>
> 1 onion, chopped
>
> 1 tablespoon minced garlic
>
> 1 tablespoon chopped fresh oregano leaves, or 1 teaspoon dried
>
> 1½ pounds parsnips, cut into large chunks
>
> ½ cup ground or finely chopped pumpkin seeds, plus more for garnish
>
> 1 cup dry white wine or water
>
> 1 cup chicken or vegetable stock (for homemade, see pages 135 to 140) or water, or more as needed
>
> Chopped fresh parsley, for garnish

1. Put 2 tablespoons of the oil in a large skillet over medium-high heat. When it's hot, add the chicken thighs, sprinkle with salt and pepper, and cook, turning once or twice, until golden brown, about 10 minutes. Remove the chicken from the pan.

2. Add the remaining 1 tablespoon oil and the onion. Cook, stirring, until soft, 3 to 5 minutes. Add the garlic, oregano, parsnips, and pumpkin seeds and cook, stirring frequently so that the pumpkin seeds don't burn, until the parsnip chunks are coated with oil and beginning to turn golden, about 10 minutes.

3. Stir in the wine and stock and return the chicken to the pan. Bring to a boil, then turn the heat down to medium-low. Cover and bubble gently until the parsnips are tender, 15 to 20 minutes. Add more stock if they start to stick. Taste and adjust the seasoning. Serve hot or at room temperature, garnished with more pumpkin seeds and the parsley.

Braised Carrots and Chicken with Sesame Seed Sauce. Add some chopped fresh red chile at the last minute if you like a little heat. Instead of the olive oil, use 2 tablespoons peanut oil in Step 1 and 1 tablespoon sesame oil in Step 2. Substitute carrots for the parsnips, scallions for the onion, and ¼ cup sesame seeds for the pumpkin seeds. Instead of salting for the final seasoning, add a drizzle of soy sauce.

Grilled Turkey Hash with Red Wine Glaze

Makes: 4 servings   Time: About 1 hour

Potatoes and turkey are a good classic combo any time of the year, and this rich hash is a *lot* easier to prepare than Thanksgiving dinner. With the quick and full-flavored red wine glaze, it's more interesting too. And if it's not grilling season, you can always broil the turkey or use leftovers instead.

    1 cup red wine

    2 garlic cloves, crushed

    3 sprigs fresh thyme, or 1 teaspoon dried

    4 large all-purpose potatoes (like Yukon Gold), peeled and cut lengthwise
        into ½-inch slices

    1 turkey thigh (about 1 pound)

    1 red onion, halved

    Olive oil as needed

    Salt and black pepper

    ¼ cup chopped fresh parsley, for garnish

1. Put the wine, garlic, and thyme in a saucepan over medium-high heat. Bring the mixture to a boil, then adjust the heat so that it bubbles gently. Cook until the wine is reduced to a syrup, 15 to 20 minutes.

2. Meanwhile, prepare a grill to medium-high heat and put the rack about 4 inches from the fire; keep one part of the grill fairly cool for indirect cooking.

3. Drizzle the potatoes, turkey, and onion with oil and sprinkle with salt and pepper. Put everything on the cool side of the grill with the turkey skin side up. Cover the grill and cook, turning the pieces once or twice, until the potatoes are tender and the turkey is no longer pink, 25 to 30 minutes. Uncover the grill and move the potatoes and onion so they stay warm but don't burn. Put the turkey over the hotter part of the fire and grill, turning occasionally, until it is browned on both sides and cooked through, 10 to 15 minutes more. (You can prepare everything up to this point a day ahead of time; just gently reheat the vegetables, turkey, and red wine glaze before assembling.)

Ⓕ Fast   Ⓜ Make-Ahead   Ⓟ Pantry Staple

4. Pull the turkey meat off the bone and roughly chop the potatoes and onion. Toss everything with the red wine syrup and chopped parsley. Serve hot or at room temperature.

Roasted Turkey Hash with Red Wine Glaze. Use sweet potatoes instead of Yukon Gold, and instead of preparing a grill, heat the oven to 375°F. Cut the potatoes and onion into cubes. Follow the recipe through Step 1. In Step 3 put the vegetables and turkey in a large roasting pan, drizzle with the oil, and season with salt and pepper. Roast, turning occasionally, until the turkey and vegetables are browned and cooked through, 45 to 50 minutes. Pick up the recipe again at Step 4.

Thanksgiving Roast Root Vegetables and Turkey with Pan Juices

Makes: 8 servings   Time: About 2½ hours, largely unattended

No one in their right mind would suggest that Americans forgo one of our most beloved rituals. But root vegetables are closer to what the Pilgrims ate than sweet potato casserole and cranberry sauce, so why not move them into the foreground of the celebration? In addition to the vegetables listed below, you might consider waxy potatoes, winter squash, radishes, rutabagas, or Jerusalem artichokes, all in season midfall.

The idea is to leisurely roast the turkey and vegetables while you prepare other dishes and set the table. The results are deeply golden, tender vegetables and moist meat that's easy to slice. Even though you're not cooking a whole bird, you'll still need a pretty big roasting pan to hold all the vegetables.

A word about preparing the turkey: Sometimes you can find a half turkey breast—meaning one side of a double-breast—at the grocery store or at the butcher's, but more often than not turkey breasts are sold whole. The easiest way to get around this is to ask your butcher to split the breast for you. If you choose to do it yourself, use a very sharp chef's knife to cut it lengthwise, through the breastbone; don't be afraid to apply a little force to break the bone apart.

3 to 4 pounds turnips, parsnips, carrots, or celery root, or a combination, cut into large cubes

2 large onions, sliced into thick rings

4 tablespoons olive oil

Salt and black pepper

1 half bone-in turkey breast, 2 to 3 pounds

8 or more garlic cloves, lightly crushed

1 cup dry white or fruity red wine

2 cups chicken or turkey stock (for homemade, see page 139) or water

1 tablespoon chopped fresh sage, or 1 teaspoon dried

1 tablespoon cornstarch

2 tablespoons butter

Chopped fresh parsley, for garnish

1. Heat the oven to 325°F. Put the root vegetables and onions in a large roasting pan, toss with 3 tablespoons of the oil, and sprinkle with salt and pepper. Using your fingers, loosen the skin of the turkey breast and tuck the garlic cloves between the skin and the meat. (If they won't all fit, that's okay; just toss the remaining cloves with the root vegetables.) Put the turkey on top of the root vegetables, rub with the remaining 1 tablespoon oil, and sprinkle with salt and pepper.

2. Roast, stirring the vegetables occasionally, until they are soft and browned and the turkey is done, 1½ to 2 hours (an instant-read thermometer inserted into the thickest part of the breast should read 165°F). Transfer the turkey to a cutting board and the vegetables to a serving bowl.

3. Put the roasting pan on a burner over medium-high heat. Add the wine, stock, and sage and bring to a boil. Mix the cornstarch with a ladleful of the pan liquid in a small bowl until smooth, then stir the mixture back into the pan. Cook, stirring to loosen any bits of turkey or vegetable from the bottom of the pan, until the juices are slightly thickened, about 5 minutes. Stir in the butter, taste, and adjust the seasoning. Pry the turkey breast away from the bone and thinly slice crosswise (against the grain). Serve a few slices of turkey with lots of vegetables, all drizzled with pan juices and garnished with parsley.

Ⓕ Fast   Ⓜ Make-Ahead   Ⓟ Pantry Staple

Roast Turnips and Duck with Pear Jus

Makes: 4 servings   Time: About 1 hour

Even though duck is no more difficult to prepare than chicken, it always feels much more elegant. Braise it with turnips, and it's a classic; with the addition of a pear-brandy sauce, it becomes sweeter, more complex, and downright luxurious. Simply cooked leafy vegetables or Ten-Minute Green Salad (page 143) are all you need on the side.

    1 or 2 boneless duck breasts (about 1 pound), with the skin

    Salt and black pepper

    1 pound turnips or rutabagas, cut into large chunks

    8 fresh sage leaves

    1 bay leaf

    2 garlic cloves, smashed

    2 pears, peeled and chopped

    ½ cup vegetable or chicken stock (for homemade, see pages 135 to 140)
        or water

    ¼ cup brandy

    Chopped fresh parsley, for garnish

1. Heat the oven to 400°F. Score the skin of the duck breasts, sprinkle with salt and pepper, and place them skin side down in a large, ovenproof skillet or Dutch oven over medium-high heat. Brown thoroughly on both sides, rotating and turning as necessary, 10 to 15 minutes total. Remove the duck from the pan and pour off all but 2 tablespoons of the fat.

2. Add the turnips, sprinkle with salt and pepper, and roast until they are nicely browned on the bottom and just getting tender, 15 to 20 minutes. Stir in the sage, bay leaf, and garlic and return the duck to the pan. Roast until the turnips are tender and the duck is cooked to your liking, about 15 minutes for medium-rare. Put the duck on a plate or cutting board to rest, and transfer the turnips to a serving platter.

3. Put the pan on a burner over medium-high heat. Add the pears, stock, and brandy and bring to a boil. Cook, stirring to loosen any browned bits from the bottom of the pan, until the pears are soft and the pan juice is slightly thickened, 5 to 10 minutes. Remove the bay leaf. Thinly slice the duck. Serve a few slices on top of a pile of the turnips and spoon the pear sauce over the top. Garnish with parsley and serve.

Stir-Fried Sweet Potatoes and Beef with Vietnamese Flavors

Makes: 4 servings   Time: 30 minutes

Firm vegetables work fine in stir-fries as long as you grate them first. The quick treatment changes the ratio of surface area to interior so that they cook in a flash, which is exactly what you want.

Instead of beef, you can use chicken, tofu, or tempeh here, or even firm white fish (see page 22). Or leave out the concentrated protein altogether and serve this as an unconventional but delicious Thanksgiving side dish. In any case, serve on top of brown rice or another grain.

3 tablespoons vegetable oil

8 ounces beef chuck, flank, or sirloin steak, cut into bite-size pieces

2 pounds sweet potatoes, peeled and grated, about 4 cups

1 cup sliced scallions

1 or 2 fresh hot chiles (like jalapeño or Thai), seeded and chopped, optional

1 tablespoon minced garlic

Salt and black pepper

¼ cup nam pla (fish sauce)

Juice of 1 lime

½ cup chopped fresh cilantro, basil (preferably Thai), or mint

1. Put a large skillet over high heat for 3 to 4 minutes. Add 1 tablespoon of the oil and the beef. Stir immediately, then stir every 20 seconds or so until the meat is no longer pink, just a minute or 2. Transfer the beef to a plate.

Ⓕ Fast   Ⓜ Make-Ahead   Ⓟ Pantry Staple

2. Reduce the heat to medium-high and add the remaining 2 tablespoons oil. When it's hot, add the sweet potatoes, scallions, chiles if you're using them, and garlic and sprinkle with salt and pepper. Cook, stirring only occasionally, until the potatoes change color and begin to brown; then stir more frequently until they are tender but not at all mushy, 10 to 15 minutes.

3. Return the beef to the pan along with the fish sauce and lime juice. Cook, stirring and scraping the bottom of the pan, until the liquid is reduced slightly and you've scraped up all the bits of meat and vegetable. Toss in the herb and serve.

The New "New Joe's Special"

Makes: 4 servings   Time: About 45 minutes, or faster with frozen spinach

Nearly every restaurant in San Francisco with Joe in its name serves a hearty ground beef and spinach hash and calls it either "Joe's Special" or "New Joe's Special." With my "new" seesaw ratio (see page 7), the name changes, but with the vegetables gaining prominence it's even better. Serve on top of whole wheat garlic toast, or toss with cooked grains or pasta, a little olive oil, and a dusting of Parmesan.

3 tablespoons olive oil

1 onion, chopped

2 tablespoons minced garlic

8 ounces ground beef sirloin or chuck

Salt and black pepper

2 pounds spinach (frozen is fine)

1 pound fresh button or cremini mushrooms, sliced

Pinch of nutmeg

1 tablespoon chopped fresh oregano or marjoram, or 1 teaspoon dried

1 egg

¼ cup grated Parmesan cheese, plus more for serving

1. Put 2 tablespoons of the oil in a large skillet over medium-high heat. When it's hot, add the onion, garlic, and beef; sprinkle with salt and pepper and cook, stirring often to break up the meat, until the beef is well browned, 5 to 10 minutes. If you're using fresh spinach, rinse it well, remove any thick stems, and roughly chop.

2. Remove the beef mixture from the pan with a slotted spoon and turn the heat to medium. Add the remaining 1 tablespoon oil with the mushrooms and another sprinkling of salt and pepper; cook, stirring occasionally to scrape up any brown bits from the bottom of the pan, until almost all the liquid has evaporated, about 10 minutes. Stir in the nutmeg and oregano and transfer the mushrooms to the bowl with the beef mixture.

3. Add the spinach to the pan and cook, stirring occasionally and chopping it up with a spatula, until the greens are wilted and almost dry again, 3 to 5 minutes. Return the meat mixture to the pan. Stir in the egg and cheese and cook until set, just a minute or 2 more. Taste and adjust the seasoning and serve with more cheese at the table if you like.

(F) Fast (M) Make-Ahead (P) Pantry Staple

Seared Bean Sprouts
with Beef and Sesame Orange Sauce

Makes: 4 servings   Time: 20 minutes

Bean sprouts are light, crisp, and incredibly fast to prepare: The freshest ones require only rinsing. Plus they cook in the wink of an eye, which makes them perfect for stir-fries, especially this classic with orange- and sesame-flavored beef. Toss this with soba noodles (or make the Crisp Noodle Cake on page 236) or serve over short-grain rice or quinoa.

2 tablespoons sesame seeds

3 tablespoons vegetable oil

8 ounces beef sirloin or chuck, very thinly sliced

Salt and black pepper

1 pound bean sprouts

1 bunch scallions, white and green parts separated, all chopped

3 tablespoons soy sauce

Grated zest and juice of 2 oranges

1 tablespoon honey, or more to taste

1. Put the sesame seeds in a large dry skillet over medium-low heat and toast, shaking the pan often, until they begin to brown but don't burn, 3 to 5 minutes. Remove them from the skillet.

2. Put 1 tablespoon of the oil in the skillet and turn the heat to high. When the oil is hot, add the beef, sprinkle with salt and pepper, and cook, stirring just once or twice, until it sears and loses its red color, just a minute or 2. Remove the beef from the skillet.

3. Add the remaining 2 tablespoons oil. When the oil is hot, add the bean sprouts and the white parts of the scallions. Cook, stirring frequently, until browned in places and starting to wilt, 2 or 3 minutes. Add the beef, soy sauce, orange zest and juice, and honey. Cook and stir until the bean sprouts are just tender and everything is warmed through, a final 2 to 3 minutes more. Taste and adjust the seasoning, adding more honey if you like. Garnish with the sesame seeds and scallion greens and serve.

Not Your Usual Steak Fajitas

Makes: 4 servings   Time: 40 minutes

These fajitas aren't just meaty and smoky—they sizzle with crunchy jícama, a touch of sweet pineapple, and an eye-opening tequila-lime glaze. Though soft corn tortillas are traditional, you can think of this as a Mexican stir-fry and spoon it over brown rice. But serving it with Loaded Guacamole (page 458) is (nearly) a must.

 3 tablespoons vegetable oil

 8 to 12 ounces beef skirt, rib-eye, tenderloin, or sirloin steak, thinly sliced

 Salt and black pepper

 1 large onion, halved and thinly sliced

 2 red or green bell peppers, cut into strips

 1 or 2 fresh hot chiles (like jalapeño or Thai), seeded and minced

 1 tablespoon minced garlic

 8 ounces jícama, peeled and cut into sticks

 2 large carrots, cut into sticks

 1 cup cubed fresh pineapple

 ¼ cup lime juice

 ½ cup tequila or water, or a combination

 Chopped fresh cilantro, for garnish

 Warm corn or whole wheat tortillas, for serving, optional

1. Put a large skillet over high heat until it smokes, 3 to 4 minutes. Add 1 tablespoon of the oil and, a few seconds later, the steak. Sprinkle with salt and pepper and stir immediately. Cook, stirring every 20 seconds or so, until it loses its color, just a minute or 2. Transfer to a plate.

2. Add 1 tablespoon of the remaining oil to the skillet and reduce the heat to medium-high. Add the onion, bell peppers, chile, and garlic and cook, stirring, until soft and golden brown, about 5 minutes. Transfer to the plate with the steak.

3. Raise the heat to high again and add the remaining 1 tablespoon oil, the jícama, and carrots. Stir immediately, then cook, stirring every 30 seconds

Ⓕ Fast   Ⓜ Make-Ahead   Ⓟ Pantry Staple

or so, until the vegetables soften and begin to char slightly, 3 to 5 minutes. Transfer everything to the plate with the steak.

4. Add the pineapple, lime juice, and tequila to the skillet. Bring to a boil and cook, stirring to scrape any brown bits stuck to the bottom of the pan, until the glaze thickens a little. Return all the vegetables and meat to the pan and toss to coat with the lime and tequila mixture. Garnish with cilantro and serve with warm tortillas.

Not Your Usual Chicken Fajitas. Use boneless, skinless chicken breast or thighs, cut into ½- to ¾-inch chunks, instead of the steak.

Whole Cauliflower with Sausage

Makes: 4 servings   Time: About 30 minutes

You get the best texture out of cauliflower when you steam it whole, and the presentation of this dish—the sausage and bread crumbs are the "sauce"—is quite striking. (If you're looking for easier serving at the table, break the cauliflower into florets before topping with the sausage mixture.) Bulk sausage will make your life easier, but if all you can find are links, remove the meat from the casings before beginning.

    1 cauliflower (about 1½ pounds), cored

    Salt

    8 ounces sweet or hot pork sausage, casings removed if necessary

    2 tablespoons olive oil

    1 onion, chopped

    1 or 2 fresh hot chiles (like jalapeño or Thai), seeded and chopped

    Black pepper

    1 cup bread crumbs, preferably whole grain and homemade

    ½ cup chopped fresh parsley

1. Put the cauliflower in a steamer (see page 414) above 1 to 2 inches of salted water. Bring the water to a boil, cover, and reduce the heat so it bubbles steadily. Cook until the cauliflower is just tender enough to be pierced to the core with a thin-bladed knife (no longer). Because it's large, the cauliflower will retain quite a bit of heat after cooking, so it should still be ever-so-slightly crunchy when you remove it from the steamer. Total cooking time will be 12 to 25 minutes, depending on the size of the head. Drain the cooked cauliflower well.

2. Meanwhile, put the sausage and oil in a large skillet over medium-high heat. Cook, stirring to break the meat into small pieces, until no longer pink, 5 to 10 minutes. Pour off all but 2 to 3 tablespoons of the fat. Add the onion, chile, and a sprinkling of salt and pepper and cook until the onion is softened, 3 to 5 minutes. Remove the mixture from the pan with a slotted spoon.

3. Add the bread crumbs and parsley to the skillet and cook, stirring, until the bread crumbs are crisp and golden brown, about 5 minutes. Return the meat to the pan, stir, and taste and adjust the seasoning.

4. Break up the cauliflower head a bit with 2 forks, scatter the sausage mixture over all, and serve.

Whole Cauliflower with Sausage and Tomatoes. What you lose in bread crumb crunchiness, you make up for with bright flavor. In Step 2, after you cook the sausage mixture, add 2 cups chopped tomatoes (canned are fine; drain them first). Cook and stir for another 5 minutes or so, until they become slightly thickened and saucy. Proceed with the recipe.

(F) Fast   (M) Make-Ahead   (P) Pantry Staple

Asparagus Gratin with Bacon Bread Crumbs

Makes: 4 servings   Time: 30 minutes

Roast asparagus with nothing more than olive oil, salt, and pepper, and it's pretty outstanding. Adding a crisp mixture of bacon, garlic, and bread crumbs makes the dish sensational. The variations with tomato and cheese toppings are equally good and just as easy.

About 1½ pounds asparagus, peeled if thick

3 tablespoons olive oil

Salt and black pepper

2 thick bacon slices, chopped

1 tablespoon minced garlic

¾ cup bread crumbs, preferably whole grain and homemade

1. Heat the oven to 400°F. Put the asparagus in a baking dish and toss with 2 tablespoons of the oil so that both the asparagus and the bottom of the dish are coated. Sprinkle with salt and pepper. Roast, turning once or twice, just until the thick part of the stalks can be pierced with a knife, 10 to 15 minutes. (You can roast the asparagus up to an hour or so ahead of time.)

2. Meanwhile, put the bacon and remaining 1 tablespoon oil in a skillet over medium-high heat. Cook, stirring occasionally, until the bacon begins to crisp, about 10 minutes. Stir in the garlic and bread crumbs and cook for another minute or 2. Remove the asparagus from the oven. Turn on the broiler; the heat should be medium-high and the rack about 4 inches from the fire.

3. Top the asparagus with the bacon and bread crumb mixture and broil until the topping is golden brown, 3 to 5 minutes. Serve hot or at room temperature.

Asparagus Gratin with Tomatoes. Substitute 2 chopped tomatoes and a few chopped basil leaves for the bread crumbs. In Step 2, add them to the pan after the bacon has crisped, cook for a minute or 2, and proceed with the recipe.

Asparagus Gratin with Feta Bread Crumbs. Good with blue cheese, too. Omit the bacon. In Step 2, toast the bread crumbs and garlic with the oil until golden. Remove from the heat, toss in ½ cup crumbled feta cheese, and proceed with the recipe.

Braised Cabbage and Sauerkraut with Sausages

Makes: 4 servings   Time: About 1 hour

This leisurely but easy braise is a dish for those people who don't like sauerkraut, or think they don't, because the sweetness of fresh cabbage beautifully offsets its fermented cousin, mellowing it without robbing it of its character. Since this reheats well, you can even cook the dish up to a day or so ahead; serve it with Black Rolls with Caraway (page 547), or baked potatoes, and good beer.

> 2 tablespoons olive oil
>
> 8 ounces kielbasa or other smoked sausage, cut diagonally into 8 chunks
>
> 2 onions, halved and sliced
>
> 1 tablespoon minced garlic
>
> 1 pound Savoy or other green cabbage, cored and shredded
>
> 1 pound sauerkraut, preferably fresh or bagged, drained
>
> 1½ cups beer, vegetable stock (for homemade, see pages 135 to 138), or water
>
> 1 tablespoon caraway seeds
>
> Salt and black pepper
>
> Coarse mustard, for serving

1. Put the oil in a large, deep skillet or Dutch oven over medium-high heat. A minute later, add the sausage and cook, turning the pieces as necessary, until browned but not cooked through, about 5 minutes. Remove the sausage from the pan.

2. Add the onions and garlic to the pan and cook, stirring, until softened, 3 to 5 minutes. Add the cabbage, sauerkraut, beer, and caraway seeds and nestle in the sausages. Sprinkle with a little salt and pepper and stir. Cover and reduce the heat to medium. Cook, stirring occasionally, until the cabbage is tender but not mushy, about 30 minutes. Serve hot or warm with mustard.

Ⓕ Fast   Ⓜ Make-Ahead   Ⓟ Pantry Staple

Braised Vegetables
with Prosciutto, Bacon, or Ham

Makes: 4 servings   Time: 45 minutes

Stovetop braising is a method that gives you tender, succulent vegetables with very little work. And when you add a little really good smoked or cured meat, these become a main event. (To lighten things up a bit, try skipping the meat entirely and tossing the vegetables with a generous grating of Parmesan about a minute before removing them from the heat.)

You can use any vegetable here, but to get a lot of different textures going on, try a mix of sturdy root vegetables and hearty greens. Choose from Brussels sprouts, eggplant, carrots or parsnips, turnips or rutabagas, beets, kale or collards, green beans, fennel, kohlrabi, or celery. Serve over grains, pasta, or toast, with a side of Easiest Bean Salad on the Planet (page 153) if you're really hungry.

> 2 pounds any vegetable (see the headnote)
>
> 3 tablespoons olive oil
>
> 1 large onion or several shallots, halved and sliced
>
> 4 ounces prosciutto, cured or smoked ham, pancetta, or bacon, chopped
>
> 1 or 2 small dried hot chiles, optional
>
> Salt and black pepper
>
> 2 or 3 sprigs fresh thyme, oregano, or marjoram, or 1 sprig fresh rosemary
>
> 2 cups vegetable stock (for homemade, see pages 135 to 138), white or red wine, beer, or water, or more as needed
>
> ½ cup chopped fresh parsley, for garnish

1. Trim and peel the vegetables as needed and cut them into large (at least 2-inch) chunks or wide ribbons, or leave them whole if they're any smaller than that.

2. Put 2 tablespoons of the oil in a large pot or Dutch oven over medium heat. When it's hot, add the onion, meat, and chiles if you're using them and sprinkle with salt and pepper. Cook, stirring occasionally, until the onion begins to color, about 5 minutes. Add the herb sprigs, turn the heat down a bit, and keep cooking, stirring once in a while, until the color deepens, another 5 minutes or so. Remove everything with a slotted spoon.

3. Return the pot to medium-high heat and add the remaining 1 tablespoon oil. When it's hot, add the vegetables and sprinkle with salt and pepper. Cook, stirring occasionally, until they start to brown a bit. Return the onion mixture to the pot, add the liquid, and bring to a boil. Lower the heat so that the mixture bubbles gently. Cover and cook, stirring occasionally, until the vegetables are tender (or softer if you like), anywhere from 5 to 30 minutes. Poke them with a fork or knife every once in a while to check, and add more liquid if the vegetables become too dry. (At this point, you can make the dish up to 2 days ahead and refrigerate; gently reheat before proceeding.) Taste and adjust the seasoning. Garnish with parsley and serve.

Roasted Pork Shoulder with Potatoes, Apples, and Onions

Makes: 4 servings   Time: About 1½ hours, largely unattended

Pork, potatoes, and apples are a wonderful warming fall or winter combination, especially roasted. Let the potatoes and apples get as brown as you like, but be careful not to overcook the pork, or it'll dry out.

Serve with Garlicky Chard with Olives and Pine Nuts (page 425) or another strongly flavored greens preparation.

> One 12-ounce boneless pork shoulder roast
>
> 5 or 6 garlic cloves, cut in half lengthwise
>
> 1 tablespoon chopped fresh sage, or 1 teaspoon dried
>
> Salt and black pepper
>
> 2 tablespoons olive oil
>
> 1 pound waxy or all-purpose potatoes, unpeeled, cut into 1-inch chunks
>
> 1 pound apples, peeled, cored, and cut into 1-inch chunks
>
> 2 onions, cut into 1-inch chunks
>
> ½ cup white wine

 (F) Fast   (M) Make-Ahead   (P) Pantry Staple

1 tablespoon Dijon mustard

Chopped fresh parsley, for garnish

1. Heat the oven to 325°F. Put the pork in a large roasting pan. Use a thin-bladed knife and your fingers to make slits all over the meat and insert the garlic and most of the sage. Spread the rest of the sage all over the outside of the roast, sprinkle with salt and pepper, and rub with 1 tablespoon of the oil. Roast, undisturbed, until a lot of the fat is rendered and the outside is beginning to form a crust, about 45 minutes.

2. Remove the pan from the oven and increase the heat to 425°F. Turn the roast over and scatter the potatoes, apples, and onions all around. Drizzle with the remaining 1 tablespoon oil, sprinkle with salt and pepper, and stir to coat the vegetables with the pan drippings. Return the roasting pan to the oven and cook, undisturbed, until the potatoes begin to brown a little on the edges, 15 to 20 minutes.

3. Stir the vegetables and continue roasting, undisturbed, until the pork and the vegetables are fork-tender and well browned, another 15 to 20 minutes. (An instant-read thermometer inserted into the center of the roast should read between 140°F and 155°F, depending on how well done you like the pork.) Transfer the meat to a cutting board and the vegetables and apples to a serving platter.

4. Add the wine, mustard, and ½ cup water to the roasting pan and put it on a burner over medium-high heat. Cook, stirring and scraping, until the liquid thickens into a sauce, 3 to 5 minutes. Taste and adjust the seasoning. Cut the pork into thin slices, return it to the pan, and toss with the pan sauce. Put the pork slices on top of the vegetables and drizzle with any remaining pan sauce. Garnish with parsley and serve.

Pork Stew with Green Beans and Oregano

Makes: 4 servings   Time: About 2 hours, largely unattended   Ⓜ

The delicious juices of pork shoulder combine with strong flavorings and white wine—use a semisweet, fruity one for most complex flavor—to give green beans a character unlike any other: tender, rich, really delicious. This is one of those stews that is just as good (if not better) the next day, so feel free to make it in advance. Mashed potatoes are an obvious and wonderful side dish, but to keep this a little lighter, serve it with whole wheat couscous or bulgur, or just a salad.

> 2 tablespoons olive oil
>
> 8 ounces boneless pork shoulder, cut into large chunks
>
> Salt and black pepper
>
> 3 shallots or 1 large onion, chopped
>
> 1 tablespoon minced garlic
>
> 1 tablespoon chopped fresh oregano, or 1 teaspoon dried
>
> 2 cups white wine (see the headnote)
>
> 2 pounds green beans, roughly chopped

1. Put the oil in a large, deep skillet or Dutch oven over medium-high heat. When it's hot, add the pork to the pan and sprinkle with salt and pepper. Cook, turning as needed, until the pork is deeply browned all over, 10 to 15 minutes total. Pour off some of the fat (or not) and turn the heat down to medium.

2. Add the shallots and garlic and cook, stirring occasionally, until nicely browned, 10 to 15 minutes. Stir in half of the oregano and return the pork to the skillet. Add the wine and enough water to half cover the meat in liquid (you might not need any water). Bring the mixture to a boil, stirring to scrape up any brown bits from the bottom of the pan. Adjust the heat so that the mixture bubbles steadily but not vigorously. Cover and cook, stirring once in while, until the pork is nearly falling apart and the liquid has become saucy, about 1 hour.

3. Add the green beans to the skillet, raise the heat to medium-high, and cook, uncovered and stirring occasionally, until they are crisp-tender, 5 to 10 minutes. Stir in the remaining oregano, taste and adjust the seasoning, and serve.

Chili-Rubbed Pork
with Warm Pickled Vegetables

Makes: 4 servings   Time: About 45 minutes

Pork, roasted with spices and served with fresh, quickly made pickled vegetables—a nice combo. I usually go with classic pickling vegetables here, but broccoli, fennel, celery, and cabbage would all work too.

The pickling technique gives you crunchy, tangy veggies, delicious enough to justify making a batch on their own. To do so, use only Step 1 of the recipe. Let the vegetables cool a bit, then store them in the fridge, submerged in their brine. They'll keep for at least a week.

½ cup red wine vinegar

1 bay leaf

2 sprigs fresh oregano, or 1 teaspoon dried

Salt

3 tablespoons olive oil

1 small cauliflower, cut into florets

2 zucchini or summer squash, sliced crosswise

2 carrots, cut into coins or sticks

1 red bell pepper, sliced

1 large onion, halved and sliced

1 tablespoon minced garlic

1 bone-in pork loin chop, 2 inches thick (about 1 pound)

1 teaspoon chili powder

1 teaspoon paprika

2 teaspoons cumin

Black pepper

1. Heat the oven to 325°F. Put the vinegar, bay leaf, oregano, 1 teaspoon salt, 2 tablespoons of the oil, and 2 cups water in a large pot and bring the mixture to a boil. Add the cauliflower and cook for 1 minute. Add the zucchini, carrots, bell pepper, onion, and garlic; cover the pot and turn off the heat. (You can make the pickled vegetables up to several days ahead of serving.)

2. Smear the pork with the remaining 1 tablespoon oil, then rub it with the chili powder, paprika, cumin, and a sprinkling of salt and pepper. Put it in an ovenproof skillet and roast the chop until it is firm but still pink in the middle, 20 to 30 minutes (the internal temperature should be about 140°F when you remove it from the oven).

3. When the pork is ready, remove the pan from the oven and put it on the stove over medium-high heat. Brown the pork on both sides until it is cooked to your liking, 3 to 5 minutes total. Remove the pork from the pan. Add 1 cup of the brine from the pickles to the pan and stir to scrape up any browned bits from the bottom. Cut the bone from the pork and put it in the pan too. Lower the heat so the mixture bubbles steadily and cook, stirring occasionally, while you carve the pork. You want the liquid to reduce to a sauce.

4. Cut the pork against the grain into thin slices. Taste the pan sauce and adjust the seasoning. Drain the vegetables (reserving the brine if you like) and serve a spoonful with the pork, drizzled with the pan sauce.

Plantain Planks with Pork Picadillo

Makes: 4 servings   Time: About 1 hour

A quick, flavorful pork-and-raisin braise makes an almost-classic Latin American topping for roasted plantains, which is served like an open-face sandwich. For plantains with a softer interior, try to find some that are slightly riper and a little yellow in color, but not yet soft. If you're using beer as a braising liquid (highly recommended), try experimenting with different types, from lager to stout.

> 3 tablespoons olive oil, plus more for greasing the pan
>
> 12 ounces boneless pork shoulder, thinly sliced
>
> Salt and black pepper
>
> 2 medium onions, chopped
>
> 1 tablespoon minced garlic
>
> 2 tablespoons minced canned chipotle chiles with some of their adobo sauce, or to taste

Ⓕ Fast   Ⓜ Make-Ahead   Ⓟ Pantry Staple

2 carrots, chopped

3 celery stalks, chopped

½ cup raisins

2 cups beer or stock (for homemade, see pages 135 to 140)

2 large green plantains, peeled

Chopped fresh cilantro, for garnish

Lime wedges, for serving

1. Put 2 tablespoons of the oil in a large, deep skillet over medium-high heat. When it's hot, sprinkle the pork with salt and pepper and add it to the skillet. Cook, stirring occasionally, until the pork slices are nicely browned all over, 5 to 10 minutes. Remove the pork from the skillet.

2. Add the onions, garlic, chipotles, carrots, and celery to the skillet and cook, stirring occasionally, until they begin to brown, 5 to 10 minutes. Return the pork to the skillet along with the raisins, beer, and enough water to almost cover the pork and vegetables. Stir to scrape up any brown bits from the bottom of the pan. Bring the mixture to a boil, then adjust the heat so it bubbles steadily but not vigorously. Cook, stirring once or twice, until the pork is tender and the liquid has reduced to a sauce, 30 to 40 minutes. Taste and adjust the seasoning. (The dish can be made ahead to this point and refrigerated for up to 2 days; gently reheat before proceeding.)

3. Heat the oven to 400°F. Grease a baking sheet generously with oil. Cut each plantain lengthwise into 4 thin planks. Lay the plantain slices in a single layer on the prepared baking sheet, smear them with the remaining 1 tablespoon oil, and sprinkle with salt and pepper. Roast, turning once, until they are nicely browned and just tender, about 20 minutes. Turn off the oven and keep the plantains inside to stay warm.

4. When the pork is ready, lay the plantain planks on a serving platter or individual plates and spoon the pork mixture over the top. Garnish with cilantro and serve with lime wedges.

Kale with Pork Picadillo. Just pour the pork mixture over the greens. Instead of the plantains, substitute 1 large bunch kale, cut into ribbons, and steam it instead of roasting. When the pork is about halfway done in Step 2, rig a steamer over an inch or 2 of water in a large pot (see page 414). Cover, bring to a boil, and cook until the kale is bright green and tender but still a bit crisp, 5 to 7 minutes; drain well. Sprinkle the kale with salt and pepper and serve.

Eggplant Mash with Seared Lamb Chops

Makes: 4 servings   Time: About 45 minutes   Ⓜ Ⓟ

Steaming eggplant gives you incredibly tender flesh that you don't have to add any fat to while cooking. Mashed with scallions, garlic, and chile, it makes a nice pillow for seared lamb. You can make the mashed eggplant up to a day ahead. You can also use it on its own as a sandwich spread, dip, or side dish.

1½ pounds large or small eggplants, halved lengthwise

Salt

4 tablespoons olive oil, or more as needed

1 bunch scallions, chopped

2 tablespoons minced garlic

1 or 2 fresh hot chiles (like Thai or serrano), seeded and minced

1 tablespoon chopped fresh oregano, or 1 teaspoon dried

Black pepper

4 lamb rib or loin chops (about 12 ounces)

½ cup red wine or chicken stock (for homemade, see page 139)

Chopped fresh parsley, for garnish

1. Put the eggplants in a steamer (see page 414) above about 1 inch of salted water. Bring the water to a boil and cook the eggplants until very tender, anywhere from 15 to 30 minutes depending on their size. Let the eggplants cool until you can handle them.

2. Meanwhile, put 2 tablespoons of the oil in a large skillet over medium heat. When the oil is hot, add the scallions, garlic, and chiles and cook, stirring occasionally, until they soften a bit, 3 to 5 minutes.

3. Cut the eggplant into pieces and put them in a large bowl with the scallion mixture. Add the oregano, sprinkle with salt and pepper, and roughly mash the mixture, adding more oil if you like. Taste and adjust the seasoning. (The mashed eggplant can be made ahead to this point and refrigerated for up to day; gently reheat before proceeding.)

4. Wipe out the skillet, add the remaining 2 tablespoons oil, and put it over medium-high heat. When it's hot, add the lamb chops and sprinkle with salt

Ⓕ Fast   Ⓜ Make-Ahead   Ⓟ Pantry Staple

and pepper. Cook until they are well browned and release easily from the pan, 2 to 3 minutes; turn and cook the other side until they are done how you like them, just another 2 to 3 minutes for rare or medium-rare. Remove the lamb from the skillet. Add the red wine and stir to scrape up all of the brown bits from the bottom of the pan. When the wine gets syrupy, turn off the heat. Serve a lamb chop on a spoonful of the mashed eggplant with the pan juices drizzled over all. Garnish with chopped parsley.

Eggplant Mash with Grilled Lamb Chops and Zucchini. A whole meal. After making the eggplant mash, prepare a grill to medium-high heat and put the rack about 4 inches from the fire. Cut 2 zucchini lengthwise into slices. Brush the lamb and the zucchini with a little of the oil, sprinkle with salt and pepper, and grill, turning once, until the meat is done as you like it and the zucchini is tender and well browned, 2 to 5 minutes per side.

Braised Lamb Shanks
with Tomatoes and Tomatillos

Makes: 4 servings   Time: About 3 hours or more, largely unattended

If you make this for friends and don't tell them what's in it, they'll never guess—but they'll love it. Use canned tomatoes and tomatillos when you can't find fresh. Serve the chili (which is essentially what this is) with a pot of brown rice or millet or scoop it up with Easy Whole Grain Flatbread (page 512) or soft corn tortillas.

> 2 tablespoons vegetable oil
>
> 2 lamb shanks (about 1 pound)
>
> Salt and black pepper
>
> 1 onion, chopped
>
> 2 tablespoons minced garlic
>
> 1 tablespoon chili powder
>
> ½ cup coconut milk
>
> 2 cups chopped tomatoes (canned are fine; include their juice)
>
> 2 cups chopped tomatillos (canned are fine; include their juice)
>
> ¼ cup chopped fresh cilantro, plus more for garnish

1. Heat the oven to 325°F. Put the oil in a large pot or Dutch oven over medium-high heat. When it's hot, add the lamb, sprinkle with salt and pepper, and cook, turning and rotating as necessary, until brown on all sides, 10 to 15 minutes. Remove the lamb and pour off all but 2 tablespoons of the fat from the pan. Add the onion and garlic and cook, stirring occasionally, until softened and golden, 3 to 5 minutes.

2. Add the chili powder and cook for another minute. Add the coconut milk, tomatoes, tomatillos, and ½ cup water and season with salt and pepper, and stir to combine. Bring to a boil, then return the lamb shanks to the pan, turn them once or twice, cover the pot, and put it in the oven.

3. Cook until the shanks are very tender (a toothpick inserted should meet little resistance) and the meat is nearly falling from the bone, about 2½ hours. (You can make the stew ahead to this point and refrigerate it for a day or 2;

gently reheat before proceeding.) Remove the shanks from the pot and let cool for a few minutes; then chop the meat or just pull it off the bone and return it to the pot. Stir in the cilantro, taste and adjust the seasoning, and serve garnished with more cilantro.

Miso-Glazed Carrots and Lamb

Makes: 4 servings   Time: 40 minutes

Carrots and lamb each have a surprising, wonderful affinity with miso—there are so many flavors in this mixture it's amazing. Tofu, pork, beef, and chicken are all good alternatives to the lamb, but they're not quite the same. What *is* as good is goat, but that can be hard to find. Even finding small quantities of boneless lamb can be tricky, so either buy a whole leg and freeze portions for other meals, or just use ground lamb.

Large carrots should be peeled, but if you can find true slender baby carrots (not the machine-formed ones), just trim and cook them whole. Serve this quick little braise over brown rice or tossed with soba noodles.

2 tablespoons vegetable oil

8 ounces boneless lamb, preferably from the leg, cut into thin slices

Salt and black pepper

1 pound carrots, cut into coins or sticks

½ cup sake, white wine, or water

1 tablespoon soy sauce

2 tablespoons any miso

1 tablespoon minced fresh hot chile (like jalapeño or Thai)

Sliced scallions, for garnish

1. Put the oil in a deep skillet or Dutch oven over medium-high heat. When it's hot, add the lamb, sprinkle with salt and pepper, and cook, turning as needed, until browned well on both sides, 5 to 10 minutes total. Pour off all but 2 tablespoons of the fat.

2. Add the carrots and sake to the pan. Bring to a boil, then cover and adjust the heat so the mixture bubbles gently. Cook, more or less undisturbed, until the carrots are tender and beginning to stick to the bottom of the pan, and the liquid is gone, 10 to 20 minutes.

3. Whisk together the soy sauce, miso, minced chile, and 2 tablespoons water in a small bowl. When the carrots are tender, uncover them, turn off the heat, and stir in the miso mixture. Taste and adjust the seasoning. Serve hot, or within an hour or 2, garnished with scallions.

Ⓕ Fast Ⓜ Make-Ahead Ⓟ Pantry Staple

Bread, Pizza, Sandwiches, and Wraps

Since most of us grew up eating deli-style sandwiches (where the main feature is an inch-thick layer of meat) and pizzas piled with mozzarella and pepperoni, the recipes in this chapter will not seem traditional. And they're not, by twentieth-century American standards. But these pizzas, wraps, and sandwiches will expand your thinking, helping you to move beyond (or continue to move beyond, if you've already changed direction) lunch meats and cheeses into a different kind of tradition, the realm of vegetable-oriented—or at least vegetable-enhanced—fillings and toppings.

As with the other recipes in this book, the ratio of meat to plants is more in tune with the way people used to eat than the way we have in the last sixty years or so. That is to say I've offered some suggestions about when and where to add cheese, meat, fish, or poultry, but they're used as flavorings, not as bulk. And trust me: You won't be stuck eating shredded lettuce between two pieces of bread.

This chapter also includes a bunch of fantastic from-scratch savory baked goods: quick whole grain breads—including skillet-made flatbreads and griddle cakes—as well as a few easily made yeasted breads and a killer pizza dough, almost all of which are entirely whole grain, or nearly so.

TLB: Tomato, Lettuce, and Bacon Sandwiches

Makes: 2 sandwiches   Time: 20 minutes

A model sandwich: Just flip the usual ratio of "B" to that of "LT" and take it from there, making this a formula you can use to spin many of the classics without losing their essence. Here, after cooking the bacon, let the tomato slices warm in the residual heat for a minute or two before assembling the sandwich. Right before you bring the bread slices together, drizzle the remaining pan juices over all; you'll get terrific flavor that way.

> 2 to 4 bacon slices
>
> 2 large ripe tomatoes (about 12 ounces total), sliced crosswise
>
> Mayonnaise to taste (for homemade, see page 188)
>
> 4 slices bread, preferably whole grain, toasted
>
> Salt and black pepper
>
> 6 to 8 leaves romaine, iceberg, or butter lettuce, torn into large pieces

1. Put the bacon in a cold skillet and set it over medium heat. Cook the bacon, turning as needed, until as crisp or chewy as you like it, anywhere from 5 to 10 minutes. Drain on towels for a bit, then break each strip into several pieces. If you like, after turning off the heat, warm the tomato slices in the pan as described in the headnote.

2. Spread a bit of mayonnaise on each slice of toasted bread. Top with the tomato slices (and their juices if warmed in the pan) and sprinkle with salt and pepper. Distribute the bacon pieces over the tomatoes on one side and pile the lettuce up on the other. Bring the bread together to finish the sandwich. Cut in half if you like and serve.

FAP: Fig, Arugula, and Prosciutto. In Step 1, cook a couple thin slices prosciutto in the skillet on both sides for a few minutes. Proceed with making the sandwich, using olive oil for the mayo, sliced fresh figs for the tomatoes, and a couple handfuls of arugula instead of the lettuce.

CSS: Cucumber, Sprouts, and Smoked Fish. Skip Step 1. Break a couple ounces smoked salmon or other smoked fish into large flakes. Proceed with

Ⓕ Fast   Ⓜ Make-Ahead   Ⓟ Pantry Staple

making the sandwich, using coarse mustard for the mayo; sliced, peeled, and seeded cucumber for the tomatoes; and a couple handfuls of alfalfa sprouts and thinly sliced red onion instead of the lettuce.

Easy as Sliced Bread

Making sandwiches with the kinds of bread I suggest buying and making is easier said than done because slicing can be a challenge. It's important to use a relatively long, sharp serrated knife, then cut with a slow but firm back-and-forth motion to slice straight vertically or horizontally. Mishaps are usually the result of rushing or a dull knife, or both. (But really how bad can it be? After all, the worst-case scenario is an open-face sandwich.)

Some Specific Tips

For loaves where a thick crust surrounds a tender interior full of gaping holes: It's often best to cut the loaf into large chunks, then split the pieces in half horizontally like crusty rolls.

If the loaf is tall, leaving too much tender bread inside: Pull out some of the interior and use it for bread crumbs or stuffing so that you're using two crusts with an inch or so of crumb attached to sandwich your fillings.

Slice wedges or squares of flatbreads in half horizontally: Hold the knife parallel to the counter and carefully saw your way through. This way, it's possible to make a sandwich with even very thin flatbreads.

Dense whole grain breads: Sliced thinly, they often benefit from toasting.

Whenever you're slicing homemade bread: Resist the urge to do so when it's hot from the oven; it'll never slice right.

And for wraps: Make sure the bread is soft and pliable, so you can roll it without breaking; warming it helps. Once you enclose the filling, cut the sandwich straight across or at a diagonal into manageable pieces.

Mediterranean Club Sandwich

Makes: 2 to 4 servings   Time: About 25 minutes with cooked chickpeas   **F**

Mashed chickpeas, tahini-yogurt sauce, fresh veggies, and briny olives tucked among layers of pita makes an immensely appealing club-style sandwich. If you're in a hurry (or have pocketless pita), don't bother splitting the rounds; just smear, layer, and stack the ingredients among three pieces of bread, then cut like a pie. Or abandon the layering altogether and use the filling ingredients to make three simple taco-style wraps.

For more filling ideas, see the list of ingredients, or use your favorite fresh or cooked veggies and condiments. But resist the urge to overstuff.

3 whole wheat pitas with pockets (or without; see the headnote)

1 cup cooked or canned chickpeas, drained, some liquid reserved

1 tablespoon olive oil, or more as needed

1 teaspoon cumin or pimentón (smoked paprika)

Salt and black pepper

¼ cup tahini

¼ cup plain yogurt, preferably whole milk

Juice of 1 lemon

1 small cucumber, peeled, seeded, and thinly sliced

2 cups bite-size pieces lettuce or assorted salad greens

2 ripe tomatoes, thinly sliced

⅓ cup oil-cured black olives, pitted and chopped

1. If you'd like the pitas toasted, heat the oven to 450°F. Split the breads in half like English muffins to create 6 thin rounds. Put them on a baking sheet and cook, flipping once, until just barely crunchy, 5 to 10 minutes total.

2. Meanwhile, mash the chickpeas (by hand or in a food processor) with the oil, cumin, and some salt and pepper. Add a few drops of bean liquid as necessary to make a thick but spreadable mixture. In a separate small bowl, whisk together the tahini, yogurt, and lemon juice. Season with a little salt and pepper.

Ⓕ Fast   Ⓜ Make-Ahead   Ⓟ Pantry Staple

3. Whether you have 3 pita rounds or 6, spread some of the mashed chickpeas on one of the pita layers and top with some cucumber and lettuce. Top with another pita layer, spread with the tahini mixture, and add some tomato and black olives. Repeat until all the ingredients are gone and drizzle with more oil if you like. You'll end up with a tall sandwich that looks a little like a layer cake. Secure each quarter of the sandwich with a toothpick, then cut the circle in half and in half again. Serve immediately.

Other Potential Fillings for a Mediterranean Club Sandwich

Cooked chopped greens like spinach or escarole (squeezed dry)

Roasted bell peppers (for homemade, see page 417)

Mashed fava beans

Preserved lemons (for homemade, see page 175; go easy on these, they're intense)

Roasted Red Pepper and Walnut "Pesto" (page 50)

Canned or leftover cooked sardines

Sliced hard-boiled eggs

Oil-packed tuna or Olives, Cucumbers, and Tuna, Mediterranean Style (page 66)

Feta Drizzle (see page 75)

Upside-Down Tuna Salad Sandwich

Makes: 4 sandwiches   Time: 20 minutes

When you finely chop vegetables—which is quickly accomplished in a food processor—and bind them with tuna, olive oil, and a little mayonnaise, the results are more like a true salad than the typical tuna-and-mayo. The variations extend the same idea to egg, chicken, shrimp, and crab salads, using other fruits and vegetables.

  2 carrots, cut into chunks

  2 celery stalks, cut into chunks

  2 scallions, cut into chunks

  ½ cup cooked or canned cannellini or other white beans, drained

  Grated zest and juice of 1 lemon

  2 tablespoons olive oil

  2 tablespoons mayonnaise (for homemade, see page 188)

  One 6-ounce can tuna, preferably packed in olive oil, drained

  Salt and black pepper

  8 slices bread, preferably whole wheat, toasted or not

  2 cups shredded lettuce

1. In a food processor (or by hand if you prefer), pulse (or chop) the carrots, celery, and scallions until they are in small bits but have not yet become mush. Add the white beans, lemon zest and juice, oil, and mayonnaise and pulse 3 or 4 times (or mash with a fork if you're working by hand).

2. Fold the tuna into the vegetable mixture. Sprinkle with salt and pepper and taste and adjust the seasoning if necessary. Divide the salad among 4 slices of bread and top with shredded lettuce and another slice of bread. Press and gently, cut in half if you like, and serve immediately.

Upside-Down Egg Salad Sandwich. Substitute several radishes for the carrots, ¼ cup pitted black olives for one 1 of the scallions, and chickpeas for the white beans. Instead of the tuna, fold in 3 chopped hard-boiled eggs; use alfalfa sprouts instead of lettuce if you like.

(F) Fast   (M) Make-Ahead   (P) Pantry Staple

Upside-Down Chicken Salad Sandwich. Use a cored green apple instead of the carrots and a small wedge of cabbage instead of the celery. Add a little Dijon mustard if you like. Instead of the tuna, fold in about 6 ounces chopped cooked chicken.

Upside-Down Shrimp Salad Sandwich. Use a red bell pepper for the carrots, a mango for the celery, black beans for the white beans, and lime for the lemon. Season with a pinch of chili powder. Instead of the tuna, fold in about 6 ounces chopped cooked shrimp.

Upside-Down Crab Salad Sandwich. Substitute 1 cup fresh corn kernels for the carrots, ½ cup fresh cilantro for the celery, a cubed avocado for the beans, and a lime for the lemon. Instead of the tuna, fold in about 6 ounces cooked crab meat.

Grilled Tomato Sandwich,
With or Without Cheese

Makes: 1 sandwich   Time: 10 minutes

When tomatoes are in season, you *need* them on sandwiches. (When they aren't, see the variation.) The idea here is to grill the bread just long enough so the outside is crisp and the tomatoes barely warm and juicy. A little cheese helps hold everything together and adds richness, but you can also try this with a smear of mayo (for homemade, see page 188) or Any-Herb Pesto (page 197) on the inside. (Plums or peaches also work well instead of tomatoes, especially with blue cheese.) To make more than one sandwich at a time, assemble as many as you want on a baking sheet and broil them instead.

> 1 tablespoon olive oil
>
> 1 tomato, thickly sliced
>
> 2 thick slices bread, preferably whole grain
>
> Salt and black pepper
>
> 4 or more fresh basil leaves
>
> Sprinkling of grated mozzarella or Parmesan, optional

1. Put the oil in a small skillet over medium heat. Lay the tomato slices on one slice of bread. Sprinkle with salt and pepper, then top with the basil leaves, cheese if you're using it, and the second slice of bread.

2. When the oil is hot, add the sandwich to the pan and cook until the bottom is golden brown and crisp. Carefully flip and continue cooking until the second side is browned and the insides are warm, pressing down gently with a spatula to meld the slices together. Cut in half if you like and serve immediately.

Grilled Avocado and Black Bean Sandwich. Omit the tomatoes, basil, and cheese. Roughly mash up cooked black beans with a fork and spread on one slice of bread. Sprinkle with chili powder, salt, and pepper. Top with half an avocado, sliced, and chopped pickles and close the sandwich. Proceed with the recipe. Serve with Homemade Salsa (page 195) on the side.

More-or-Less Muffuletta

Makes: 4 servings   Time: 45 minutes

New Orleans–style muffuletta is one of the truly classic American creations, and though cold cuts and cheeses are typical, it's really the salad-like relish that makes the sandwich memorable. This interpretation combines quickly marinated chopped olives and vegetables with eggplant for a more manageable sandwich.

1 medium or 2 small eggplants, cut into ½-inch slices

Salt

4 tablespoons olive oil, or more as needed

Black pepper

½ cup brine-cured black olives, pitted and chopped

½ cup green olives, pitted and chopped

2 tablespoons capers

¼ cup chopped red onion

2 celery stalks, chopped

1 small red bell pepper, preferably roasted (page 417), chopped

1 tablespoon chopped fresh oregano, or 1 teaspoon dried

1 teaspoon minced garlic

1 tablespoon sherry or wine vinegar

4 crusty sandwich rolls or buns, preferably whole grain

2 ripe tomatoes, sliced

1. If time allows, sprinkle the eggplant liberally with salt, let rest in a colander for at least 20 minutes or up to an hour, rinse, and pat dry. Turn on the broiler; the heat should be medium-high and the rack about 4 inches from the fire. Brush both sides of the eggplant slices with some of the oil, put it on a baking sheet, and sprinkle with salt and pepper. Broil until tender and browned on both sides, turning once or twice, 10 minutes or less total. Let cool slightly before handling.

2. Meanwhile, combine the black and green olives, capers, onion, celery, bell pepper, oregano, garlic, vinegar, 2 tablespoons of the oil, and a sprinkle of pepper in a medium bowl.

3. Slice the rolls in half horizontally and use your fingers to remove some of their doughy insides to make room for the fillings. Spread the olive salad evenly on all of the pieces of bread and drizzle with any leftover juices. Top half of them with the eggplant and tomato slices. Close the sandwiches and serve immediately.

More-or-Less Pan Bagnat. The Provençal specialty. Omit the olives, capers, and celery. While the eggplant is broiling, cook the bell pepper and onion with 2 cups sliced mushrooms in 2 tablespoons olive oil in a medium skillet; when softened, toss with the remaining salad ingredients. Layer romaine lettuce leaves between the vegetables and the eggplant, and add a little shredded cooked chicken or a couple anchovies to each sandwich if you like. After closing the sandwiches, wrap them well in foil, put them between 2 large plates, and weigh down the top plate with something heavy, like a cast-iron skillet or some cans of tomatoes. Refrigerate for at least 2 hours before serving.

Tofu-Peanut or Tofu-Sesame Wrap

Makes: 4 wraps   Time: 30 minutes

When thinly sliced, brushed with a sweet and spicy glaze, and broiled or grilled, tofu—especially when pressed or frozen first—develops a meaty texture and more intense flavor. Pair it with peanut butter and bright fresh veggies, and you've got a sandwich reminiscent of pad Thai.

Cook the full amount of tofu even if you're making only one wrap; it keeps well in the fridge for up to a week.

¼ cup soy sauce

2 tablespoons sesame oil

2 teaspoons honey

1 fresh hot chile (like Thai or jalapeño), seeded and minced, optional

1 block firm tofu (about 1 pound), frozen or squeezed dry (see page 177),
   cut into ½-inch slices

Salt

     Fast   Ⓜ Make-Ahead   Ⓟ Pantry Staple

4 whole wheat lavash or large whole wheat tortillas

4 tablespoons peanut butter or tahini

2 carrots, grated or julienned

2 ripe tomatoes, chopped

2 scallions, chopped

2 cups shredded lettuce or bean sprouts

½ cup chopped fresh cilantro

1 lime, halved

1. Prepare a grill or turn on the broiler; the heat should be medium-high and the rack about 4 inches from the fire. Combine the soy sauce, sesame oil, honey, and chile in a small bowl. Pat the tofu dry if necessary, sprinkle lightly with salt, and brush with some of the soy glaze on all sides, reserving the rest. Grill or broil the tofu until nicely browned (watch it so it doesn't burn), then turn the pieces and do the same on the second side. The total cooking time will be less than 10 minutes. (The tofu can be cooled and stored in an airtight container for up to a week at this point.)

2. To warm the wrappers, stack the lavash or tortillas and roll them up in a piece of foil; set them on a rack under the tofu in the oven or over indirect heat if you're using the grill. While the tofu cooks, let them heat enough to become just pliable.

3. To assemble the sandwiches, spread 1 tablespoon peanut butter on each of the flatbreads and evenly distribute the carrots, tomatoes, scallions, lettuce, cilantro, and tofu on top. Drizzle with the reserved sauce and squeeze lime juice over all. Roll up the wraps, cut in half if you like, and serve.

Shrimp-Cashew Wrap. Use cashew butter instead of peanut butter and shredded Napa cabbage for the lettuce. Instead of tofu, use 8 medium shrimp, peeled and split in half lengthwise. Toss the shrimp in 2 tablespoons of the glaze, keeping the rest separate for drizzling. Proceed with the recipe. The shrimp halves will take only a minute or 2 to cook, so watch them closely; they're ready when they just turn opaque.

The World of Wraps

Here are some dishes that work especially well in wraps—alone or in combination. Drain the filling of any excess liquid and start with some big lettuce leaves to help make the sandwich even sturdier.

Olives, Cucumbers, and Tuna, Mediterranean Style (page 66)

Quick-Pickled Lima Beans with Parmesan (page 58)

Lentil "Caviar" with All the Trimmings (page 64)

Beet Tartare (page 45)

Sweet Potato, Ginger, and Chicken Teriyaki Skewers (page 71)

Black Kale and Black Olive Salad (page 150)

Mediterranean Cobb Salad (page 149)

Chopped Salad with Thai Flavors (page 152)

Classic (or Not) Caesar Salad (page 146)

Chickpea Salad with Cashew Chutney (page 174)

Fava Bean, Asparagus, and Lemon Salad (page 175)

Chopped Cauliflower Salad, North African Style (page 167)

Plum Chicken Salad (page 178)

Italian-American Antipasto Salad with Tomato Vinaigrette (page 180)

Gingered Tomato Salad with Shrimp (page 179)

Ma-Po Tofu with Tomatoes (page 402)

Dal with Lots of Vegetables (page 362)

Garlicky Chard with Olives and Pine Nuts (page 425)

Scrambled Tomatoes and Herbs (page 433)

Roasted Okra and Shrimp with Tomato Chutney (page 446)

 Ⓕ Fast Ⓜ Make-Ahead Ⓟ Pantry Staple

Beans 'n Greens Burritos

Makes: 4 servings   Time: 30 minutes

Terrific basic burritos that freeze well: Just wrap them individually in foil or wax paper and freeze in a tightly sealed container. Then you always have them handy to reheat in the microwave or oven. Check the list that follows for a variety of other combos.

> 4 large or 8 small whole wheat flour tortillas
>
> 2 tablespoons olive oil
>
> 1 onion, chopped
>
> 1 tablespoon minced garlic
>
> 1 tablespoon chili powder
>
> Salt and black pepper
>
> 1 bunch kale (about 1 pound), roughly chopped
>
> 2 cups cooked or canned black beans, drained, liquid reserved
>
> ½ cup crumbled queso fresco or feta cheese, optional
>
> *Pico de gallo* (page 46)

1. Heat the oven to 300°F. Stack the tortillas and roll them up in a sheet of foil. Put them in the oven to warm while you cook the filling.

2. Put the oil in a large skillet over medium heat. When it's hot, add the onion and garlic and cook, stirring occasionally, until soft and beginning to color, 5 to 10 minutes. Sprinkle with the chili powder and salt and pepper. Add the kale and cook, stirring occasionally, until it wilts and releases its liquid, about 5 minutes. Stir in the black beans; mash them up a bit with a fork or potato masher and add a spoonful of the reserved liquid if the mixture seems dry.

3. To roll each burrito, lay a tortilla on a flat surface and put ¼ of the filling (or ⅛ if you're using small tortillas) on the third closest to you. Sprinkle with some of the cheese if you're using it. Fold the tortilla over from the bottom to cover the beans and greens, then fold in the 2 sides to fully enclose them; finish rolling and put the burrito seam side down on a plate. Serve with *pico de gallo* on the side.

Beans 'n Greens 'n Meat Burritos. Begin by browning 8 ounces of chorizo, chopped ham, sausage, or ground meat in the oil until warm or cooked through in Step 2. Then add the onion and garlic and continue with the recipe.

5 More Beans 'n Greens Combos for Burritos

Cannellini beans, escarole, and Parmesan

Chickpeas, chard, and pimentón (smoked paprika)

Pinto beans, cabbage, and chipotle

Green lentils, spinach, and tarragon

Edamame, bok choy, and soy sauce

Fish Tacos with Wilted Cabbage

Makes: 4 servings   Time: 30 minutes

Fish tacos in soft corn tortillas, a Cal-Mex standard, are usually served with shredded raw cabbage as a garnish. But if you stir-fry the cabbage with a little fish (or shrimp if you prefer), the flavors blend together nicely and the vegetables gain a silky-yet-crunchy texture that folds perfectly into the tortilla. This quick cooking technique works on all sorts of combos; just make sure you cut the fish, meat, or whatever into bite-size pieces and grate, shred, or finely chop the vegetable.

3 tablespoons olive oil

1 fresh hot chile (like jalapeño), seeded and minced, optional

About 8 ounces firm white fish (see page 22), cut into 1-inch chunks

Salt and black pepper

1 large head cabbage, (about 1½ pounds), cored and shredded

½ cup chopped fresh cilantro

Ⓕ Fast   Ⓜ Make-Ahead   Ⓟ Pantry Staple

Juice of 1 lime

1 tablespoon chili powder

12 corn tortillas

1 cup chopped ripe tomato or tomatillos

1 avocado, skin and pit removed, cubed, optional

1. Put 2 tablespoons of the oil in a large skillet over medium-high heat. When it's hot, add the chile if you're using it, along with the fish; sprinkle with salt and pepper. Cook, stirring once or twice, until the fish is opaque and just cooked through, about 2 minutes. Remove from the skillet and raise the heat to high.

2. Add the remaining 1 tablespoon oil to the pan along with the cabbage, 1 to 2 tablespoons water, and another sprinkling of salt and pepper. Cook, stirring almost constantly, until the cabbage just begins to soften, about 5 minutes. Turn off the heat and stir in the cilantro, lime juice, chili powder, and fish. Taste and adjust the seasoning.

3. Warm the tortillas one at a time in a dry skillet over medium heat (they take just a few seconds on each side), or wrap the pile in a damp kitchen towel and pop it in the microwave for 30 to 60 seconds on high. Put 3 tortillas on each individual plate. Distribute the fish and cabbage mixture evenly over the tortillas, garnish each with tomato and avocado if you're using it, and serve.

Spicy Sweet Potato and Pork Tacos. Substitute bite-size pieces of boneless pork loin or shoulder for the fish and use peeled and grated sweet potatoes instead of the cabbage. Garnish with 1 cup chopped radishes instead of the tomato or tomatillos and avocado.

Easy Whole Grain Flatbread

Makes: **4 to 8 servings**   Time: **About 1 hour, largely unattended (longer for resting if time allows)**

The batter for this flatbread requires less than a minute to put together and takes perfectly to all sorts of flavorings, mostly savory but sweet as well. (See the list that follows for some potential add-ins.)

With a batter this simple, controlling some of the other variables will make the bread come out exactly as you want it every time. So bear with me here for a little detail:

If you let the batter rest for up to 12 hours, the bread will have a creamier, less gritty texture and a more complex flavor. These are subtle distinctions, though; the bread is fantastic even if you only let the batter rest while the oven heats. Really.

You can make this bread in a 10-inch pan or skillet too. It will be thicker and take another 5 to 10 minutes to cook. That's all.

The amount of oil you need will vary depending on the surface of your pan. With a well-seasoned cast-iron (or nonstick) skillet, use just 2 tablespoons oil; with seasoned steel, try 3 tablespoons; for stainless steel, you'll be safest with all 4. Don't worry about the bread getting greasy. It will only absorb what it needs to release from the pan's surface—excess oil will stay in the pan.

You can increase the oven temperature to 450°F to create a faster, crisper bread, but watch the time and check the bottom after about 20 minutes. With this method, you will need to flip the flatbread once it sets up to ensure even browning.

If you cut the quantity of water down to 1 cup, you'll get a slightly more dense, cracker-like bread; add a full 1½ cups water and the bread is still sliceable but a little custardy inside. I like it both ways.

> 1 cup whole wheat flour, cornmeal (fine or medium grind), or chickpea flour (besan), or a combination
>
> 1 teaspoon salt
>
> 2 to 4 tablespoons olive oil (see the headnote)
>
> ½ large onion, halved and thinly sliced, optional
>
> 1 tablespoon fresh rosemary leaves, optional

Ⓕ Fast   Ⓜ Make-Ahead   Ⓟ Pantry Staple

1. Put the flour in a bowl and add the salt. Slowly add 1¼ cups water, whisking to eliminate lumps. The batter should be the consistency of thin pancake batter. If it's not, whisk up to another ¼ cup water into the mixture, 1 tablespoon at a time. Cover with a towel and let sit while the oven heats, or as long as 12 hours.

2. When ready to bake, heat the oven to 400°F. Put the oil in a 12-inch rimmed pizza pan or skillet and put in the heated oven. Wait a couple minutes for the oil to get hot but not smoking; the oil is ready when you just start to smell it. Carefully remove the pan. Add the onion and rosemary if you're using them and give them a little stir. Pour in the batter, gently swirl the pan to distribute the oil, and return the skillet to the oven.

3. Bake until the flatbread is well browned, firm, and crisp around the edges, about 45 minutes. (It will release easily from the pan when it's done.) Let it rest for a couple minutes before cutting it into wedges or squares.

Additional Ingredients for Easy Whole Grain Flatbread (with how and when to add them)

Cumin, garam masala, or curry powder, up to 2 teaspoons, in Step 2 after the oil is hot.

Chopped scallions, up to 1 cup, in Step 2 after the oil is hot.

Grated or minced ginger (or try crystallized ginger), up to 2 tablespoons, in Step 2 after the oil is hot.

Minced garlic or chopped fresh chiles, as much as you like, in Step 2 after the oil is hot.

Grated citrus zest, up to 2 tablespoons, mixed directly into the batter in Step 1.

Honey or maple syrup, up to ¼ cup, mixed directly into the batter in Step 1.

Seeds; shredded, unsweetened coconut; or chopped nuts, up to ½ cup, in Step 2 after the oil is hot.

Soy sauce, in place of up to ¼ cup of the water, mixed directly into the batter in Step 1.

Easy Skillet Pizza

Makes: 4 to 8 servings   Time: About 1 hour, including time to make the flatbread   Ⓜ

Easy Whole Grain Flatbread (page 512) is the basic dough for this simple skillet pizza, which you can make up to a few hours ahead or freeze for even longer. This topping is like a deconstructed pesto, but you can top it with almost anything, including a smear of tomato sauce and a sprinkling of mozzarella.

> 1 recipe Easy Whole Grain Flatbread, fully baked (page 512)
>
> ¼ cup chopped fresh basil
>
> 2 tablespoons pine nuts
>
> 1 tablespoon olive oil
>
> ½ cup grated Parmesan cheese
>
> Black pepper or red chile flakes

1. Turn on the broiler; the heat should be medium-high and the rack about 4 inches from the fire. When the flatbread is done and out of the oven, top with the basil and pine nuts, drizzle with the oil, and sprinkle with the cheese and pepper.

2. Broil the flatbread until the Parmesan is bubbling, 3 to 5 minutes. Remove the pan from the broiler and let the pizza rest for a few minutes. Slide the pizza out of the pan, cut into wedges or squares, and serve hot or at room temperature.

Chile-Cornbread Skillet Pizza. Use all cornmeal in the Easy Whole Grain Flatbread recipe. Top with a little fresh tomato salsa (for homemade, see page 46) or a thinly sliced tomato with some chopped fresh chiles and onions. Use cheddar or Jack cheese instead of the Parmesan.

Fennel and Goat Cheese Skillet Pizza. Instead of the herb and pine nuts, top with about ½ cup thinly sliced fennel, and use crumbled goat cheese instead of the Parmesan.

Olive and Garlic Skillet Pizza. Omit the basil and Parmesan. Top with ½ cup pitted, chopped olives, pine nuts, 1 tablespoon minced garlic, and 2 teaspoons chopped fresh rosemary. Drizzle with another tablespoon oil before broiling.

Ⓕ Fast   Ⓜ Make-Ahead   Ⓟ Pantry Staple

Roasted Mushroom Quesadillas

Makes: 2 servings   Time: About 1 hour, largely unattended

Because whole wheat tortillas bake up flakier than their white flour counterparts, these quesadillas are almost like savory pastries, with just enough cheese to hold everything together. The sage adds a nice touch (especially if the filling also contains a little crumbled bacon, chopped chorizo, or flaked smoked trout or whitefish). Serve with a spoonful of Loaded Guacamole (page 458) or Apple Slaw (page 154) on the side.

    2 tablespoons olive oil, plus more for greasing the pan

    About 1 pound button or cremini mushrooms, thinly sliced

    Salt and black pepper

    1 tablespoon minced garlic

    1 fresh hot chile (like jalapeño), minced, or pinch of red chile flakes, or to
        taste

    1 tablespoon chopped fresh sage, or 1 teaspoon dried

    2 large whole wheat tortillas

    ¼ cup grated Mexican-style melting cheese (like cotija or Monterey Jack)

1. Heat the oven to 400°F. Put the 2 tablespoons oil in a large ovenproof skillet and put it in the oven for a few minutes. When it's hot—fragrant, but not smoking—add the mushrooms, sprinkle with salt and pepper, and stir. Return to the oven and check after 20 minutes or so; the mushrooms should be releasing their water.

2. Stir in the garlic, chile, and sage. Continue to roast, stirring every 10 minutes, until the mushrooms are fairly dry and deeply colored; total time will be about 40 minutes. (You can make the mushrooms ahead up to this point; cover and refrigerate for up to a day and bring to room temperature before proceeding.)

3. Meanwhile, generously grease a large baking sheet and spread the tortillas on it. (It's okay if they overlap a bit.) Sprinkle the cheese over both. When the mushrooms are done, taste and adjust the seasoning and scatter them over the top.

4. Bake the tortillas until the cheese begins to melt, about 10 minutes. Fold each tortilla in half and press down gently. Bake for another 5 minutes, then flip them over and swirl them around the pan to coat in the oil. Bake for another 5 minutes until well toasted and crisp. Cut into wedges and serve.

Flatbread with Vegetables

Makes: 4 to 8 servings   Time: About 1½ hours, largely unattended

The basic flatbread batter on page 512 is also an excellent springboard for a heartier side dish, light meal, or snack. (Be sure to check out the guidelines in the headnote on that page; they apply here too.) A few possibilities are listed here in the main recipe, but also try grated sweet potatoes or zucchini, chopped eggplant or carrots, or other vegetables.

In fact, the basic batter will hold up to 4 cups of any cooked vegetable, meat, or a combination, so you can also experiment with leftovers; cooked chopped greens or plain-cooked beans and grains are all good. To vary the flavorings, use water instead of the coconut milk and whatever seasonings you like.

> About 2 pounds broccoli, broccoli rabe, or cauliflower, roughly chopped
>
> 3 to 4 tablespoons vegetable oil (see the headnote on page 512)
>
> Salt and black pepper
>
> 1 cup whole wheat flour
>
> One 14-ounce can coconut milk (light is best here) or water
>
> 2 teaspoons cumin

1. Heat the oven to 400°F. Put the vegetables in a roasting pan or on a rimmed baking sheet, drizzle with 1 tablespoon of the oil, sprinkle with salt and pepper, and toss. Spread out into a single layer and roast until the pieces are just tender and browned in spots, tossing with a spatula halfway through, for a total of 15 to 20 minutes.

2. While the vegetables are roasting, put the flour into a bowl; add a pinch of salt and the coconut milk, whisking to eliminate lumps. The batter should be about the consistency of pancake batter. Cover with a towel and let sit while the vegetables roast.

Ⓕ Fast   Ⓜ Make-Ahead   Ⓟ Pantry Staple

3. When the vegetables are finished roasting, sprinkle them with the cumin and toss. You should have about 4 cups of this mixture; fold it into the batter.

4. Pour the remaining oil in a 12-inch rimmed pizza pan or skillet and put in the heated oven. (Use just 2 tablespoons if your skillet is well-seasoned cast iron or nonstick). Wait a couple of minutes for the oil to get hot but not smoking; the oil is ready when you just start to smell it. Carefully remove the pan, pour in the batter, spread it around evenly, and return the skillet to the oven. Bake for about 1 hour, until the flatbread is well browned, firm, and crisp around the edges. (It will release easily from the pan when it's done.) Let it rest for a couple minutes (or up to an hour or 2) before cutting it into wedges or squares.

Lentil (or Other Bean) Flatbread

Makes: 4 to 8 servings   Time: About 1 hour with precooked lentils

Here's yet another spin on Easy Whole Grain Flatbread (page 512; be sure to check out the basic instructions there before making this). If you don't have leftover cooked lentils handy (or other beans for that matter), make a fresh batch and save the rest. You can even use drained canned beans in a pinch.

  1 cup whole wheat flour

  Salt

  3 to 4 tablespoons olive oil (see the headnote on page 512)

  1 shallot, chopped

  1½ cups cooked or canned lentils or beans, drained

  1 tablespoon chopped fresh tarragon, sage, or thyme, or 1 teaspoon dried sage or thyme, or ½ teaspoon dried tarragon

  Black pepper

1. Put the flour in a bowl and add 1 teaspoon salt. Slowly add 1¼ cups water, whisking to eliminate lumps. The batter should be the consistency of thin pancake batter. If it's not, whisk up to another ¼ cup water into the mixture, 1 tablespoon at a time. Cover with a towel and let sit while the oven heats, or as long as 12 hours.

2. Heat the oven to 400°F. Heat 1 tablespoon of the oil in a 12-inch skillet over medium heat. Add the shallot and cook, stirring occasionally, until it becomes translucent, about 2 minutes. Add the lentils, herb, a sprinkle of salt, and lots of black pepper and cook for 1 minute. Stir the lentil mixture into the batter.

3. Wipe out the skillet, add the remaining oil, and put it in the heated oven. (Use just 2 tablespoons if your skillet is well-seasoned cast iron or nonstick.) Wait a couple of minutes for the oil to get hot but not smoking; the oil is ready when you just start to smell it. Carefully remove the pan, pour in the batter, spread it around evenly, and return the skillet to the oven. Bake until the flatbread is well browned, firm, and crisp around the edges, about 1 hour. (It will release easily from the pan when it's done.) Let it rest for a couple minutes (or up to an hour or 2) before cutting it into wedges or squares.

Flatbread with Beans and Sausage or Ham. Before adding the shallot to the skillet in Step 2, fry about 4 ounces crumbled sausage or chopped ham in the olive oil.

A Quick Word About Flours

Most of the recipes in this book call for regular whole wheat flour, whole wheat pastry flour (which has less protein and is good for using in cakes), or all-purpose flour (meaning all-purpose unbleached white flour). I also use cornmeal (preferably stone ground), often in combination with wheat flours. These are all available in most supermarkets, though sometimes you might have to hunt a little bit for whole wheat pastry flour.

What about specialty flours? Since you can grind any grain—or bean for that matter—into flour, you can find flours made from most anything, even in supermarkets. You can't substitute them directly for traditional wheat flour, but they do make terrific additions to things like griddle cakes and many international foods. Some of my favorites: masa harina (ground from the same corn used to make tortillas, it tastes like it; the key ingredient in tamales); chickpea flour (also called *besan*; used for breading, in simple water-based batters, or for authentic *socca*); and buckwheat flour (for delicate pancakes known as blinis and as a nice addition—in small doses—to yeast bread).

Ⓕ Fast Ⓜ Make-Ahead Ⓟ Pantry Staple

Loaded Cornpone

Makes: **4 servings**   Time: 30 minutes

This spin on Southern-style cornbread (or New England johnnycakes) is made like pancakes in a skillet instead of bread in the oven. The simplicity of the batter makes it the perfect vehicle for any number of added ingredients and seasonings; have at it with some ideas for stir-ins from the list that follows on page 520. I wouldn't make these more than a couple hours in advance, but they do reheat well wrapped in foil and warmed in a 300°F oven for 15 minutes or so.

> 1½ cups cornmeal (fine or medium grind)
>
> 1 teaspoon salt
>
> ¼ teaspoon black pepper, optional
>
> 1½ cups boiling water
>
> ½ cup buttermilk or whole milk, or more as needed, optional
>
> 2 tablespoons olive oil, plus more for frying
>
> 1 cup corn kernels (frozen are fine)

1. Heat the oven to 200°F. In a bowl, combine the cornmeal, salt, pepper if you're using it, and boiling water and let it sit until the cornmeal absorbs the water and softens, 5 to 10 minutes.

2. Stir in the buttermilk (or just use more water), a little at a time, until the batter is spreadable but still thick. Stir in 2 tablespoons oil and the corn and sprinkle with salt and pepper.

3. Put a large skillet or griddle (cast iron if you have it) over medium heat. When a few drops of water dance on its surface, add a thin film of oil and let it get hot. Working in batches, spoon the batter onto the griddle or skillet, making any size pancakes you like. Cook until bubbles appear and burst on the top and the underside is golden brown, 3 to 5 minutes; turn and cook on the other side until golden. Transfer the cooked cakes to the warm oven and continue with the next batch. Serve warm.

More Ways to Load Up Your Cornpone

½ cup chopped fresh mild herbs, like parsley, mint, basil, or cilantro

1 tablespoon chopped fresh intense herbs, like rosemary, thyme, or
  oregano, or 1 teaspoon dried

½ cup chopped scallions

1 tablespoon chili powder

1 jalapeño, seeded and minced

1 or 2 bacon slices, cooked and crumbled

½ cup grated cheddar, Gruyère, or Parmesan, or crumbled goat cheese

½ cup chopped nuts

½ cup fresh or dried fruit (blueberries, apricots, raisins, dried cranberries,
  or the like)

2 tablespoons maple syrup or honey

a few cloves roasted garlic (for homemade, see page 421)

1 cup chopped cooked greens, squeezed dry

Brown Rice Scallion Pancakes

Makes: 4 servings   Time: 20 minutes

Brown rice gives these a nuttier flavor and heartier texture than scallion pancakes made entirely with all-purpose flour, but they're just as pliable. If you
can't find brown rice flour—it's usually available in natural food stores and
even some supermarkets—it's easy to make with a food processor or blender
(see Step 1). If you're planning on serving these as finger food, rather than
along with a larger meal, be sure to make the quick dipping sauce.

    ¾ cup brown rice flour or short-grain brown rice

    ¼ cup all-purpose flour

    1½ cups boiling water

    1 teaspoon sesame oil

    1 tablespoon vegetable oil, plus more for frying

Ⓕ Fast   Ⓜ Make-Ahead   Ⓟ Pantry Staple

Salt and black pepper

4 scallions, green parts only (save the bottoms for another use), or 1 small bunch fresh chives

1 egg

½ cup soy sauce, optional

1 tablespoon minced ginger, optional

1. Heat the oven to 200°F. If you don't have brown rice flour, grind the rice in a food processor or blender for several minutes until it becomes the consistency of cornmeal. Whisk together the flours, boiling water, sesame oil, 1 tablespoon vegetable oil, and a generous sprinkling of salt and pepper. Let the batter rest while you heat the pan or griddle or up to 1 hour or so.

2. Put a large skillet or griddle over medium heat. Cut the scallion tops into several long pieces, then slice thinly into slivers. Stir them into the batter along with the egg. The batter should be thinner than pancake batter but thickly coat the back of a spoon; add more all-purpose flour or boiling water, a little at a time, to get it the right consistency. If you're making the dipping sauce, stir together the soy sauce and ginger.

3. When a few drops of water dance on the surface of the skillet or griddle, add a thin film of oil and let it get hot. Ladle the batter onto the griddle or skillet, making any size pancakes you like; be careful not to crowd them. Cook the pancakes until crisp and golden on the bottom, about 5 minutes; flip them and brown the other side for 2 to 3 minutes. Transfer the finished pancakes to the oven to stay warm while you cook the remaining batter. Serve warm, with the dipping sauce if you like.

Brown Rice Black Bean Pancakes. Substitute 2 tablespoons fermented black beans for the scallions and add ½ cup chopped fresh cilantro to the batter. Serve with rice vinegar for dipping.

Brown Rice Chile Pancakes. Substitute 1 (or more) chopped fresh chiles (like jalapeño, serrano, or poblano) for the scallions; ½ cup chopped cilantro is optional but nice.

Whole Wheat Chapatis

Makes: 8 to 12 chapatis   Time: At least 1 hour

Few recipes are as impressive or simple as chapati, the puckered flatbread from India. This version is 100 percent whole wheat, which means it is just a tad stiff to roll out, but also full of flavor.

Sometimes I sift the flour first, because the wheat germ can burn and get a little bitter, but if you want all the fiber (and don't mind the mildly charred taste), skip this step. You can also adjust the flavor of the chapatis by substituting up to ½ cup of the flour with cornmeal or chickpea flour.

Chapati dough comes together quickly in a food processor, but it's easy enough to use a bowl and wooden spoon (and eventually your hands). Just be sure to keep working until the dough loses its stickiness.

> 3 cups whole wheat flour
>
> 1 teaspoon salt
>
> 1½ cups warm water
>
> All-purpose flour, for rolling the dough

1. If you want to remove the bran (see the headnote), set a fine-mesh strainer or a flour sifter over a food processor, add the flour, and sift. Discard the bran or save for another use. If you're not sifting, put the flour in the processor and skip to Step 2.

2. Add the salt to the flour and, with the machine running, pour in the water. Process for about 30 seconds; the dough should form a barely sticky, easy-to-handle ball. If it's too dry, add more water 1 tablespoon at a time and process for 5 to 10 seconds after each addition. If too wet, which is unlikely, add 1 to 2 tablespoons flour and process briefly. Put the dough on a lightly floured surface, cover, and let rest for at least 30 minutes or up to 2 hours. (The dough can be made ahead to this point. Wrap tightly in plastic and refrigerate for up to a day; bring to room temperature before proceeding.)

3. Pinch off pieces of the dough; the recipe will make 8 to 12 chapatis. Using all-purpose flour as necessary on your hands and your work surface, pat each piece into a 4-inch disk. Dust lightly with flour to keep them from sticking and cover them with plastic or a damp cloth while you pat out the others. (It's okay to overlap them a bit, but don't stack them.)

(F) Fast   (M) Make-Ahead   (P) Pantry Staple

4. Put a large skillet or griddle over medium heat. When a few drops of water dance on its surface, roll out a disk until it's fairly thin, about ⅛ inch, dusting as necessary with flour; it doesn't have to be perfectly round. Pat off the excess flour and put the chapati on the griddle or in the pan, count to 15 or so, and use a spatula to flip the bread over. Cook the other side until it starts to blister, char, and puff up a bit, about 1 minute (enough time to roll out the next disk). Turn and cook the first side again until dark and toasty smelling. Transfer to a cloth-lined basket and repeat until all are cooked. Serve immediately.

Mostly Whole Wheat Chapatis. Instead of all whole wheat flour, use 2¼ cups whole wheat flour and 1 cup all-purpose flour. Reduce the warm water to 1 cup to start, then add more as needed.

Grilled Chapatis. Works for either the main recipe or the variation. Prepare a grill to medium-high heat and put the rack about 4 inches from the fire. Oil the grates well. Roll all the chapatis out, flour them well, and stack between layers of wax or parchment paper. Cook the chapatis, several at a time, as described in Step 4, only directly on the grill grates. When they start to bubble, char, and puff up, turn.

Onion Chapati Turnovers

Makes: 18 turnovers   Time: About 1½ hours

These are somewhere between samosas and empanadas, but they're easier to make than either. After adding the oil to the onions, cook them as long as you want—shorter and they'll be light and mild; longer and they'll be dark and jamlike.

Adding flavors only complements the onions' sweetness: The first variation includes chutney spices. Or you might try some fresh herbs, a splash of soy sauce or coconut milk, or some chopped nuts. You can cut this recipe in half, but leftovers freeze beautifully and make great snacks, so I wouldn't bother.

> 3 cups whole wheat flour
>
> Salt
>
> 1 cup warm water
>
> 4 large onions, halved and sliced
>
> ¼ cup olive or vegetable oil, plus more for greasing the pans
>
> All-purpose flour, for rolling the dough

1. If you want to remove the bran (see the headnote on page 522), set a fine-mesh strainer or a flour sifter over a food processor, add the flour, and sift. Discard the bran or save for another use. If you're not sifting, put the flour in the processor and skip to Step 2.

2. Add 1 teaspoon salt to the flour and, with the machine running, pour in the warm water. Process for about 30 seconds; the dough should form a barely sticky, easy-to-handle ball. If it's too dry, add more water 1 tablespoon at a time and process for 5 to 10 seconds after each addition. If too wet, which is unlikely, add 1 to 2 tablespoons flour and process briefly. Put the dough on a lightly floured surface, cover, and let rest for at least 30 minutes or up to 2 hours. (The dough may be made ahead to this point. Wrap tightly in plastic and refrigerate for up to a day; bring to room temperature before proceeding.)

3. Put the onions in a large skillet over medium heat. Cover and cook, stirring occasionally, until the onions are dry and almost sticking to the pan, 20 to 25 minutes. Stir in the oil and a large pinch of salt and turn the heat

Ⓕ Fast   Ⓜ Make-Ahead   Ⓟ Pantry Staple

down to medium-low. Cook, stirring occasionally, for 15 minutes or longer, depending on how caramelized you want the onions to be.

4. Once the dough has rested, divide it into 18 pieces. Heat the oven to 450°F and grease a couple baking sheets. Using all-purpose flour as necessary for your hands and the board, pat or roll each piece into a thin 4½-inch circle. Top each circle with a heaping tablespoon of the onions and moisten the edges of the dough with a little water. Fold one edge over onto the other and press with the tines of a fork to close. Put the turnovers on the prepared baking sheets. Bake until the dough is golden brown and hot, flipping over once, 20 to 30 minutes total. Serve warm or at room temperature. (The turnovers will keep for a couple days wrapped or in a sealed container at room temperature or in the refrigerator and for months in the freezer; gently reheat before serving.)

Spiced Onion Chapati Turnovers. Stir 1 or 2 minced fresh hot chiles, 1 teaspoon mustard seeds, 1 teaspoon cumin, 1 teaspoon coriander, and 1 teaspoon brown sugar into the onions along with the oil and salt in Step 3.

Spiced Carrot Chapati Turnovers. Substitute 2 pounds chopped or grated carrots for the onions and use the same spice combination as in the first variation. The carrots will need at least 30 minutes additional cooking time once the spices have been added before they get tender—but they're worth it.

Mostly Whole Wheat Tortillas

Makes: 8 tortillas   Time: About 1½ hours, partially unattended   Ⓜ Ⓟ

They're more than a little work, but fresh tortillas are a special treat, a good activity for kids, and a not-difficult process (especially with a food processor), similar to chapatis (page 512). A little white flour in the dough makes them flaky and easy to roll out. Note the corn tortilla variation.

> 1 cup whole wheat flour, plus more as needed
>
> ½ cup all-purpose or bread flour
>
> ¼ teaspoon salt
>
> 2 tablespoons vegetable oil, olive oil, softened butter, or lard
>
> About ½ cup boiling water, or more as needed

1. In a bowl or food processor, mix together the flours and salt. Stir or pulse in the oil. Add the water slowly—a tablespoon or 2 at a time if you are mixing by hand or in a thin stream with the food processor running—until the dough holds together in a ball.

2. Turn the dough out onto a lightly floured surface and knead until it becomes smooth and elastic (this will take about 4 to 5 minutes if you mixed the dough by hand, and about 1 minute if you used a food processor). Wrap the dough in plastic and let it rest at room temperature for at least 30 minutes or up to a couple hours (or in the fridge for up to a few days).

3. If you refrigerated the dough, bring it back to room temperature. Divide the dough into 8 pieces. On a lightly floured surface (or between floured hands), flatten each piece into a disk, then cover and rest again, this time for just a few minutes. When you're ready to cook the tortillas, roll each disk out as thin as possible to a circle 8 inches or more in diameter, stacking them between sheets of plastic or wax paper as you work.

4. Put a large skillet—cast iron if you have one—over medium-high heat for 4 to 5 minutes. Cook the tortillas one at a time until brown spots begin to appear on the bottom, less than a minute; turn and cook the other side. Total cooking time will be just a couple of minutes per tortilla. Wrap the finished tortillas in a towel to keep warm while you cook the rest. Serve imme-

Ⓕ Fast   Ⓜ Make-Ahead   Ⓟ Pantry Staple

diately (or let them cool, wrap tightly, and store in the fridge for a few days or the freezer for up to a few months).

Corn Tortillas. Substitute masa harina (available in most supermarkets) for the flours. Proceed with the recipe above, adding 1 cup or more boiling water to bring the dough together. Since the dough will be stiffer and a bit stickier, divide it into 12 to 16 pieces in Step 3 and roll out each piece between sheets of plastic wrap dusted with flour to a diameter of 4 to 6 inches. Cook as described in Step 4.

Grinding Your Own Nuts, Seeds, and Grains for Flour

If you want flours that are fresh, nutritious, and free of additives, grinding your own is the best option. But after grinding, use the flour as soon as possible; home-milled flour turns rancid much more quickly than store-bought. (This isn't usually a problem, since you'll be grinding in small batches.)

Some homemade flours don't require special equipment: You can make oat and brown rice meal (it won't get quite as fine as commercially ground flours) by running the whole grains in a blender or food processor, or for small amounts in a mortar with a pestle or in a clean coffee grinder. You can also use a food processor for nut and seed flours as long as your ingredients are not too oily (it helps if you freeze them ahead of time). Raw nuts and seeds taste totally different from those that have been toasted and tend to have more moisture. Don't grind either too long or they turn to paste.

If you're serious about grinding your own, consider investing in a home flour mill. Flour mills range in price from about $50 for a basic, hand-operated model to hundreds of dollars for a fancy electric version.

Mostly Whole Wheat Crackers

Makes: About 4 servings   Time: 30 minutes   Ⓟ

The small amount of white flour helps the dough roll out more easily and gives the crackers some flakiness. I like to stir some poppy or sesame seeds in with the dry ingredients, or sometimes even a little Parmesan cheese.

> ¼ cup all-purpose flour, plus more as needed
>
> ¾ cup whole wheat flour
>
> ½ teaspoon salt
>
> 2 tablespoons butter
>
> 2 tablespoons olive oil
>
> Coarse salt, pepper, sesame or poppy seeds, minced garlic, or whatever you like for sprinkling, optional

1. Heat the oven to 400°F. Line a baking sheet with parchment paper or lightly dust with all-purpose flour. Put the flours, salt, butter, and oil in a food processor and pulse until combined. (Or use a bowl and 2 forks or your fingers.) Add ¼ cup water and let the machine run for a bit; continue to add more water 1 teaspoon at a time until the mixture holds together but is not sticky.

2. Dust a work surface with a little all-purpose flour and roll out the dough ¼ inch thick or even thinner, adding flour as needed. Drape the sheet of dough over the rolling pin to transfer it to the prepared baking sheet. Score the top lightly with a sharp knife, pizza cutter, or pastry wheel if you want to break the crackers into squares or rectangles later on. Sprinkle with salt or other toppings if you like.

3. Bake until lightly browned, 10 to 15 minutes. Cool on a wire rack. Serve warm or at room temperature or store in a tin for a few days.

Almost Whole Wheat Quick Bread

Makes: 4 to 6 servings   Time: About 1 hour, largely unattended

This bread, made with a combo of whole wheat and white flour (for lightness), is easy to make and a joy to vary. Fold in fresh herbs, grated cheeses, olives, dried tomatoes, ground spices, whole seeds, dried fruits, or chopped nuts after mixing the dough and removing it from the food processor. See the variations for some good combinations, or mix and match from the list below.

> 5 tablespoons olive oil
>
> 2 cups whole wheat flour, or more as needed
>
> 1 cup all-purpose flour
>
> $\frac{1}{2}$ teaspoon baking powder
>
> 1 teaspoon baking soda
>
> 1$\frac{1}{2}$ teaspoons salt, preferably coarse or sea salt, plus more for sprinkling
>
> $\frac{3}{4}$ cup yogurt or buttermilk
>
> $\frac{3}{4}$ cup warm water
>
> 2 tablespoons honey, optional

1. Heat the oven to 375°F. Grease a baking sheet or 8-inch square baking pan with 1 tablespoon of the oil. Put the flours, baking powder, soda, and salt in a food processor and turn the machine on. Into the feed tube, pour first the remaining 4 tablespoons oil, then the yogurt or buttermilk, most of the water, and the honey if you're using it.

2. Process for a few seconds until the dough is a well-defined, barely sticky, easy-to-handle ball. If it's too dry, add the remaining water 1 tablespoon at a time and process for 5 to 10 seconds after each addition. If it is too wet (this is unlikely), add 1 to 2 tablespoons whole wheat flour and process briefly.

3. Form the dough into a round and put it on the baking sheet or press into the prepared pan, all the way to the edges. Bake for 20 minutes. Sprinkle the top with a little coarse salt and continue baking for another 35 to 40 minutes, until the loaf is firm and a toothpick inserted in the center comes out clean. Let cool completely. Cut the bread into slices or squares and serve or store for up to a day.

Jalapeño-Cheddar Almost Whole Wheat Quick Bread. After processing the dough in Step 2, remove the dough from the machine and fold in ½ cup grated cheddar cheese and 1 seeded and minced jalapeño.

Dried Tomato and Roasted Garlic Almost Whole Wheat Quick Bread. After processing the dough in Step 2, remove it from the machine and fold in ½ cup chopped dried tomatoes, 3 mashed roasted garlic cloves (for homemade, see page 421), and 1 tablespoon chopped fresh parsley.

Caramelized Onion, Olive, and Goat Cheese Almost Whole Wheat Quick Bread. After processing the dough in Step 2, remove it from the machine and fold in ½ cup caramelized onions (about 2 onions), ¼ cup pitted, chopped kalamata or oil-cured olives, and ¼ cup creamy goat cheese.

More Additions to Almost Whole Wheat Quick Bread Dough

After processing in Step 2, remove the dough from the machine and fold or stir in the following ingredients, alone or in combination.

Chopped fresh herbs (just a pinch of the strong ones like rosemary)

Roasted garlic (for homemade, see page 421; a whole head is nice)

Capers (a tablespoon or two)

Any seasoning blend, dried ground spices, or whole spice seeds (just a pinch or two)

Rolled oats (½ cup or so)

Grated orange, lemon, or lime zest (from 1 whole fruit)

Chopped dried fruit (no more than ½ cup; rehydrated if you like in warm brandy, rum, or water and drained)

Chopped nuts or whole seeds (no more than ½ cup)

 F Fast M Make-Ahead P Pantry Staple

Black Pepper Hardtack

Makes: About 50 small biscuits   Time: About 1¼ hours

Hardtack—a thick crunchy cracker with a long shelf life—got a bad rap in the eighteenth and nineteenth centuries as a meager ration on long voyages or in the battlefield. Though in fairness I wouldn't touch the original stuff—which was essentially flour and water, baked hard—with a modern treatment it makes a tremendously handy snack to dunk in coffee, tea, beer, or wine.

Though these will survive an ocean voyage in an airtight container, at my house they usually don't survive more than a few days.

   ¼ cup olive oil, plus more for greasing the pans

   2 cups rye flour

   2 cups whole wheat flour

   2 teaspoons salt

   2 teaspoons black peppercorns, freshly crushed or coarsely ground

   All-purpose flour, for rolling the dough

1. Heat the oven to 325°F. Lightly grease 2 baking sheets with a little oil. Combine the rye and whole wheat flours, salt, and pepper in a medium bowl. Add 1⅓ cups water and the ¼ cup oil and stir until a thick dough forms.

2. With floured hands, divide the dough into 4 pieces and roll each into a rope about 1 inch thick. Cut each rope into 1-inch pieces. Use the palm of your hand or a floured glass to press each piece into a thick round; it's okay if they're shaped unevenly but you want them to be between ¼ and ½ inch thick. Prick the surface of each cracker with the tines of a fork a few times.

3. Transfer the crackers to the baking sheets. Bake until beginning to brown, about 30 minutes; turn them over and bake until the other side is browned, another 30 minutes or so. Cool and store in a tightly covered container for up to a couple of weeks.

Prosciutto-Black Pepper Hardtack. Before starting the recipe, heat the oil in a skillet and crisp ½ cup chopped prosciutto and sprinkle with the black pepper. Add this mixture to the dough along with the water. (Store these in the fridge or freezer and let come to room temperature before serving.)

Sweet Potato Muffins

Makes: 12 to 15 muffins, depending on their size   Time: 35 to 45 minutes

AKA: The lightest, fluffiest, easiest whole grain muffin ever. And I know of no better way to use leftover sweet potatoes (in fact, you will find yourself intentionally creating leftovers to have an excuse to make these). To vary the spices, try adding a teaspoon cinnamon, or a pinch of nutmeg, allspice, or chili powder instead of the ground ginger.

$2\frac{1}{2}$ cups whole wheat flour, preferably pastry flour

$\frac{3}{4}$ cup sugar

2 teaspoons baking powder

1 teaspoon ground ginger

$\frac{1}{4}$ teaspoon baking soda

$\frac{1}{4}$ teaspoon salt

$\frac{1}{4}$ cup melted unsalted butter, plus more for greasing the pans

$\frac{1}{4}$ cup vegetable oil

1 cup puréed or mashed cooked sweet potato

1 egg, beaten

$\frac{1}{2}$ cup buttermilk

1. Heat the oven to 375°F. Grease 12 muffin cups or add paper liners. In a large bowl, mix together the flour, sugar, baking powder, ginger, soda, and salt. In another bowl, whisk together the butter, oil, sweet potato, egg, and buttermilk. Fold the wet mixture into the dry mixture and stir until just combined.

2. Fill the muffin cups at least three-quarters full. Bake until the muffins are puffed and turning golden brown on top, 20 to 25 minutes. Serve warm if possible.

Banana Nut Muffins. Reduce the sugar to ½ cup. Replace the sweet potato with 1 cup mashed bananas (really ripe bananas work best here) and add ½ cup chopped walnuts or almonds to the batter.

Pumpkin Coconut Muffins. Replace the sweet potato with 1 cup pumpkin (canned is fine) and add ½ cup shredded, unsweetened coconut to the batter.

No-Work Mostly Whole Wheat Pizza Dough

Makes: 1 large or 2 or more small pizzas Time: 8 to 14 hours, almost entirely unattended

Add some white flour to a mostly whole wheat pizza crust, and you get the best of both worlds: the crisp, chewy texture from the gluten in white flour, with the nutty wholesomeness of whole grains—without overwhelming the toppings the way 100 percent whole wheat sometimes does.

This technique is based on my friend Jim Lahey's no-knead method, which I have written extensively about in the *New York Times*. The idea is to slowly ferment a relatively wet, soft dough, which develops both complex flavors and a lovely chew. As an added bonus, it's the easiest pizza dough to make: You start it in the morning, then shape and top it right before baking. All without mixers, processors, or hand kneading. Note that pizza dough freezes really well; after dividing it, just wrap it tightly and use it within a couple months (see Step 3).

whole wheat flour

all-purpose or bread flour, plus more as needed

aspoon instant yeast

aspoon salt

tablespoons olive oil, plus more for greasing

1. Combine the flours, yeast, and salt in a large bowl. Stir in 1½ cups water. The dough should be relatively sticky and wet, like biscuit batter. If not, add a little more water.

2. Scrape down the sides of the bowl, cover, and put it in a warm spot. Let the dough sit for at least 6 or up to 12 hours. (The longer it ferments, the more complex the flavor.)

3. When you're ready, heat the oven as described in the pizza recipes that follow. Generously oil a baking sheet or large ovenproof skillet. Dust your hands with a little white flour and fold the dough over in the bowl a few times. It will be sticky, but resist the urge to use too much flour; dust your hands again only when absolutely necessary and use a light, gentle touch. If you're making small pizzas, divide the dough in half or quarters. Gently press the dough into the skillet or onto the baking sheet; it's not important that the pizzas be perfectly round, but you do want to be careful not to tear the dough.

4. Brush or drizzle the top of the pizza or pizzas with 2 tablespoons oil, cover, and let sit while you get the toppings together, but no more than 60 minutes or so.

Crunchy No-Work Mostly Whole Wheat Pizza Dough. Substitute ½ cup cornmeal (fine or medium grind) for ½ cup of the whole wheat flour.

Herbed No-Work Mostly Whole Wheat Pizza Dough. This works for the main recipe or the variation above. Add 1 tablespoon chopped fresh rosemary, thyme, oregano, or tarragon, or 1 teaspoon dried, to the dry ingredients at the beginning of Step 1.

Ⓕ Fast Ⓜ Make-Ahead Ⓟ Pantry Staple

Topping Pizza, the Food Matters Way

Go easy: Overloading your pizza makes the crust doughy and often underdone.

Ingredients to Put On Before Baking

All-Purpose Tomato Sauce (page 194)

Any-Herb Pesto (page 197)

Simplest Cooked Mushrooms (page 418)

Caramelized onions with fresh thyme or rosemary

Roasted garlic (for homemade, see page 421)

Roasted bell peppers (for homemade, see page 417)

Dried tomatoes, soaked in hot water and drained

Chopped, pitted oil-packed black olives

Chopped marinated artichoke hearts or baby artichokes

Spoonful of capers

Chopped anchovies or sardines

Sliced fresh tomatoes

Thinly sliced fennel

Parboiled broccoli, broccoli rabe, cauliflower, or Brussels sprouts, drained

Sautéed spinach, chard, or kale

Sliced cooked waxy potatoes or sweet potatoes

Grilled or broiled eggplant or zucchini

Lightly mashed beans: black beans with chopped chipotle chiles or salsa (for homemade, see page 46), white beans with walnut oil and lemon juice, chickpeas with tahini . . .

Smear of fresh ricotta or crème fraîche

Crumbled goat cheese

Sliced fresh mozzarella

Ingredients to Put On After Baking

A drizzle of extra virgin olive oil, flavored olive oil, nut oil, or sesame oil

Chopped fresh basil, mint, or cilantro

Shaved Parmesan, grated ricotta salata, or crumbled feta

Freshly ground black pepper

Baby spinach, arugula, or mâche, tossed with a little olive oil

Sliced hard-boiled eggs (or raw eggs, broken over the pizza and broiled for the last 2 minutes of baking time)

Toasted pine nuts, almonds, walnuts, cashews, sesame seeds . . .

Fresh Tomato and Cheese Pizza

Makes: 1 large or 2 or more small pies   Time: About 45 minutes with premade
dough

Pizza at its most basic, but since every ingredient counts, use ripe in-season to-matoes, fresh whole milk mozzarella, and real Parmigiano-Reggiano. In win-ter, when tomatoes taste like wet wood (and come from who knows where), use the canned tomato variation, which is just as easy and nearly as good.

Cooking the tomatoes first just takes a couple minutes and dries them out a bit so the crust doesn't get soggy. I like to toss this quick sauce with the cheeses so the flavors mingle more than they do in most pizzas.

> 1 recipe No-Work Mostly Whole Wheat Pizza Dough (page 533), mixed and risen
>
> About 3 tablespoons olive oil
>
> 2 garlic cloves, thinly sliced
>
> 3 ripe tomatoes, cored and chopped
>
> ¾ cup (about 3 ounces) grated mozzarella cheese
>
> ½ cup grated Parmesan cheese
>
> 1 tablespoon chopped fresh oregano, thyme, or rosemary, or 1 teaspoon dried
>
> Salt and black pepper

1. Shape the dough and brush with olive oil as described in Step 4 on page 534. Heat the oven to 500°F. Put 1 tablespoon of the oil in a skillet over medium-low heat; when it's hot, add the garlic and cook, stirring frequently, until it softens, about 1 minute. Raise the heat a bit and add the tomatoes; cook, stirring frequently, just until most of their liquid has evaporated, about 5 minutes. Let the tomatoes cool.

2. Toss the tomatoes with the mozzarella, Parmesan, and herb. Spread this mixture on the pizza dough and sprinkle with salt and pepper. Put the baking sheet or skillet in the oven and bake until the crust is crisp and the cheese melted, usually 8 to 12 minutes. Let stand for several minutes before slicing so the cheese sets.

Canned Tomato and Cheese Pizza. Substitute one 14.5-ounce can whole tomatoes, drained and roughly chopped, for the fresh tomatoes.

Ⓕ Fast   Ⓜ Make-Ahead   Ⓟ Pantry Staple

Stuffed Pizza with Broccoli, White Beans, and Sausage

Makes: 1 calzone, enough for 4 to 8 servings

Time: About 1 hour with premade dough

Somewhere between a rolled stromboli and a folded giant calzone, this large filled free-form pie is an all-American spin on pizza. You cut and serve it like a sub—warm or at room temperature—so it makes excellent party food.

Serve some All-Purpose Tomato Sauce (page 194) on the side, and you're more than set. Here I start with a quick filling of beans, broccoli, and—if you like—cheese, but you have all sorts of other options; see the list below for some ideas. But really, you could use 5 to 6 cups of almost any leftover dish you like; make sure to cook or drain off any excess liquid before filling the pizza.

> 1 recipe No-Work Mostly Whole Wheat Pizza Dough (page 533), mixed and
> risen
>
> 3 tablespoons olive oil, plus more for greasing the pan
>
> Salt
>
> 2 cups chopped broccoli or broccoli rabe
>
> 4 ounces Italian sausage, cut into ½-inch pieces, optional
>
> 1 tablespoon minced garlic, or to taste
>
> 2 cups cooked or canned cannellini or other white beans, drained
>
> Black pepper
>
> 1 teaspoon red pepper flakes, optional
>
> ½ cup ricotta cheese, optional
>
> ½ cup grated Parmesan cheese, optional

1. Roll or pat out the dough on a greased baking sheet so that it forms a 10 × 14-inch rectangle, with the longest side running in front of you, left to right. Brush with a little olive oil. Heat the oven to 350°F.

2. Bring a large pot of water to a boil over high heat and salt it. Add the broccoli, cook until just tender, about 3 minutes, and drain.

3. Put 2 tablespoons of the remaining oil in a large skillet over medium heat and, a minute later, add the sausage if you're using it and cook, stirring occasionally, until it's cooked through and browned in places, 5 to 7 minutes. Pour off all but 2 tablespoons of the fat in the pan. Add the garlic and cook, stirring constantly, for 1 minute. Add the drained broccoli, beans, and a sprinkle of salt and pepper. Cook just until everything is warmed and well combined, a minute or 2. Turn off the heat and stir in the red pepper flakes and cheeses if you're using them.

4. Spread the filling on the dough to within about 4 inches from the ends and 1 inch from the sides. Carefully pull one end of the dough up over half of the filling, then repeat with the other end so that the dough forms a seam in the middle and the filling is completely enclosed. Pinch the seam and the outer edges together. Drizzle the remaining 1 tablespoon oil over the top and sprinkle with salt. Use a sharp knife to make 3 or 4 slashes, each about ¼ inch deep, in the top of the dough to allow steam to escape. Bake the stuffed pizza until it's nicely browned and bubbly and easily releases from the pan, 40 to 50 minutes. If you want an extra-crisp top crust, broil it for a minute or 2. Let stand for 10 minutes before slicing and serving.

More Delicious Fillings for Stuffed Pizza

Roasted Chickpeas (page 63) and artichoke hearts

The sauce from Pasta with Smashed Peas, Prosciutto, and Scallions (page 202)

Mashed Cannellinis and Potatoes with Gorgonzola (page 377)

Garlicky Chard with Olives and Pine Nuts (page 425) with roasted bell peppers
  (for homemade, see page 417)

Cannellini with Shredded Brussels Sprouts and Sausage (page 394)

Ⓕ Fast   Ⓜ Make-Ahead   Ⓟ Pantry Staple

Real Whole Wheat Bread

Makes: One 9-inch loaf   Time: 4 to 28 hours, almost completely unattended   Ⓜ Ⓟ

Poofy, soft supermarket "whole wheat" bread isn't; this is. And it's one of the easiest yeast loaves imaginable, intensely flavored and dense, with a concise ingredient list and a quick stir-wait-pour-bake method.

The heft is an asset: This bread makes a sturdy, flavorful base for sandwiches, a robust partner for strong cheese, jam, or spreads, and an ideal starting point for croutons (page 47) or Bruschetta, Rethought (page 51). It's also one of the most versatile and valuable breads I know; see the variations and try them.

To hurry things along, increase the yeast to 1½ teaspoons and reduce the first rise to 2 hours and the second rise to 1 hour. And since there's no white flour, expect the loaf to rise almost to the top of the pan but not beyond that.

> 3 cups whole wheat flour
>
> ½ teaspoon instant yeast
>
> 2 teaspoons salt
>
> 2 tablespoons olive oil or vegetable oil

1. Combine the flour, yeast, and salt in a large bowl. Add 1½ cups water and stir until blended; the dough should be quite wet, almost like a batter (add more water if it seems dry). Cover the bowl with plastic wrap and let it rest in a warm place for at least 12 (or up to 24) hours. The dough is ready when its surface is dotted with bubbles. Rising time will be shorter at warmer temperatures, a bit longer if your kitchen is chilly.

2. Use some of the oil to grease a 9 × 5-inch loaf pan. Scoop the dough into the loaf pan and use a rubber spatula to gently settle it in evenly. Brush or drizzle the top with the remaining oil. Cover with a towel and let rise until doubled, an hour or 2 depending on the warmth of your kitchen. (It won't reach the top of the pan, or will just barely.) When it's almost ready, heat the oven to 350°F.

3. Bake the bread until deeply brown and hollow-sounding when tapped, about 45 minutes. (An instant-read thermometer should register 200°F when inserted into the center of the loaf.) Immediately turn the loaf out of the pan onto a wire rack and let cool before slicing.

Easy Variations on Real Whole Wheat Bread

Substitute buckwheat, rye, oat, cornmeal, or other whole grain flour for up to 1
cup of the whole wheat flour.

Add 1 teaspoon (or to taste) chopped fresh thyme, tarragon, rosemary, marjoram, or other strong herb (or ½ teaspoon dried) at the beginning of Step 1.

Fold in up to 1 cup chopped walnuts, almonds, pecans, sunflower seeds, or other
nuts or seeds just before putting the dough in the pan in Step 2. (Or half nuts,
half raisins; see below.)

Fold in up to 1 cup pitted and chopped olives (any kind) just before putting the
dough in the pan in Step 2.

Fold in up to 1 cup raisins, dried cranberries, chopped dried apricots, or other
dried fruit just before putting the dough in the pan in Step 2.

Fold in up to 1 cup cooked oatmeal, quinoa, brown rice, millet, wheat berries or
another whole grain just before putting the dough in the pan in Step 2.

Sprinkle the top of the loaf with cornmeal or wheat bran after brushing with oil
in Step 2.

 Fast  Make-Ahead Ⓟ Pantry Staple

Whole Wheat Bread with Pumpkin

Makes: One 9-inch loaf   Time: About 4 hours, almost completely unattended

Vegetables and fruit are common in sweet breads and cakes, but here's a yeasty whole grain loaf that takes these additions in a different and delicious direction. The main recipe and the variations represent different techniques you can try with other grated, chopped, or puréed fruits, berries, and vegetables. Don't knock it until you try it: These are dense, rich, full-flavored loaves that can form the centerpiece of a real meal.

> 3 cups whole wheat flour
>
> 1½ teaspoons instant yeast
>
> 2 teaspoons salt
>
> Pinch of nutmeg, optional
>
> 1 cup puréed cooked pumpkin, butternut, or other winter squash (canned is fine)
>
> 2 tablespoons vegetable oil

1. Combine the flour, yeast, salt, and nutmeg if you're using it in a large bowl. Add the pumpkin and about ½ cup water and stir until blended; the dough should be quite wet, almost like a batter (add more water if it seems dry). Cover the bowl with plastic wrap and let it rest in a warm place for about 2 hours. The dough is ready when its surface is dotted with bubbles. Rising time will be shorter at warmer temperatures, a bit longer if your kitchen is chilly.

2. Use some of the oil to grease a 9 × 5-inch pan. Scoop the dough into the loaf pan and use a rubber spatula to gently settle it in evenly. Brush or drizzle the top with the remaining oil. Cover with a towel or plastic wrap and let rise until doubled, an hour or 2 depending on the warmth of your kitchen. (It won't reach the top of the pan.) When it's almost ready, heat the oven to 350°F.

3. Bake the bread until deeply golden and hollow-sounding when tapped, about 45 minutes. (An instant-read thermometer should register 200°F when inserted into the center of the loaf.) If the loaf releases easily from the pan, turn it out immediately and let cool on a wire rack before slicing; if it sticks a little, let cool in the pan before turning it out.

Zucchini Bread. Omit the nutmeg. Instead of the pumpkin, use 1 packed cup grated zucchini; you'll probably need more than ½ cup water to get the dough to come together. If you like, right before transferring the dough to the pan in Step 2, fold in 2 tablespoons fresh chopped dill or 1 teaspoon dried.

Blueberry Bread. Omit the pumpkin. Substitute cornmeal (fine or medium grind) for 1 cup of the flour if you like. Just before transferring the dough to the pan in Step 2, gently fold in up to 1½ cups blueberries. (Frozen are fine; just make sure they're thawed and drained.)

Banana Bread. Use cinnamon instead of the nutmeg. Instead of the pumpkin, use mashed ripe bananas. For a sweeter bread add a tablespoon or 2 of sugar to the dough in Step 1.

Mostly Whole Wheat Baguettes

Makes: 2 large or 4 small baguettes   Time: About 2 hours, largely unattended

There are a few special steps in making baguettes, but none is that difficult or time consuming. And nearly whole wheat baguettes (*pain complet*) are just as traditionally French (and nearly as popular) as the white version. A bit of sugar in the dough helps retain the crackling crust of an all-white loaf, but for even more crunch, try sprinkling with sesame or poppy seeds before baking, or stir bulgur into the dough (see the variation).

  2 cups whole wheat flour

  1½ cups all-purpose flour, plus more for shaping

  2 teaspoons salt

  1 teaspoon brown sugar

  1½ teaspoons instant yeast

  Vegetable oil, for greasing the pan, optional

  ¼ cup sesame or poppy seeds, optional

Ⓕ Fast   Ⓜ Make-Ahead   Ⓟ Pantry Staple

1. In a food processor, combine the flours, salt, sugar, and yeast. (You can mix the dough by hand, but it will take longer; use a big bowl and a wooden spoon or sturdy rubber spatula.) With the machine running, pour about 1½ cups water through the feed tube. Process until the dough forms a ball, adding 1 tablespoon more water at a time until it becomes smooth. You want a pretty wet but well-defined ball. The whole process should take 30 to 60 seconds. If the dough is too dry, add water 1 tablespoon at a time and process for 5 to 10 seconds after each addition. If it becomes too wet, add 1 to 2 tablespoons flour and process briefly. Put the dough in a large bowl, cover with plastic wrap, and let rise at room temperature until doubled in size, at least 1 hour.

2. Lightly flour your work surface and hands and knead the dough a few times. For small baguettes, divide the dough into 4 pieces; for larger ones, make 2. Roll each piece of dough into a log of any length that will fit in your oven. If you plan to bake the loaves on a sheet pan, lightly grease it with oil and transfer the loaves to the pan. Cover with a towel and let rise until the loaves are puffed to almost twice their original size, 30 minutes or so. Heat the oven (with a pizza stone if you have one) to 400°F while you let the baguettes rise.

3. When you're ready to bake, slash the top of each loaf a few times with a razor blade or sharp knife. If you are topping the baguettes with seeds, brush each loaf with a little water and sprinkle them on. If you are using a pizza stone, gently transfer the loaves to the stone with a floured rimless baking sheet, lightly floured peel, plank of wood, or flexible cutting board. Turn the heat down to 375°F and bake until the crust is golden brown and the internal temperature of the bread is at least 210°F (it can be a little lower if you plan to reheat the bread later) or the loaves sound hollow when tapped. Remove, spray with a bit of water if you would like a shinier crust, and cool completely on a wire rack before slicing.

Mostly Whole Wheat Baguettes with Bulgur. In Step 1, add 1 cup rinsed (unsoaked) bulgur before adding the water. Proceed with the recipe, adding more water as necessary.

Sesame Pita Pockets

Authentic pita—the kind you get at Middle Eastern markets—is dimpled, chewy, and flavorful. But it only rarely has pockets. So if you want to make filled sandwiches you're left with the oddly stiff and incredibly bland disks sold in grocery stores.

But making delicious pita *with* pockets is pretty easy at home, and you can vary it any number of ways: Substitute rye flour for half of the whole wheat, or omit the sesame seeds and add a pinch of dried thyme instead. You can also make these smaller or larger; just divide the dough into more or fewer pieces in Step 2.

> 1½ cups all-purpose flour, plus more as needed
>
> 1½ cups whole wheat flour
>
> 3 tablespoons olive oil, plus more for greasing the pan and brushing the finished loaves
>
> 2 teaspoons instant yeast
>
> 2 teaspoons salt
>
> ½ teaspoon honey or molasses
>
> 2 tablespoons sesame seeds

1. Combine the flours, 3 tablespoons oil, yeast, and salt in a food processor. Turn the machine on and add 1 cup water through the feed tube along with the honey and sesame seeds. Process for about 30 seconds, adding more water a little at a time, until the mixture forms a ball and is slightly sticky to the touch. If it's dry, add 1 to 2 tablespoons water and process for another 10 seconds. (In the unlikely event that the mixture is too sticky, add more all-purpose flour, 1 tablespoon at a time.) Put the dough in a bowl, cover with plastic wrap, and let rise until doubled in size, 1 to 2 hours.

2. When the dough is ready, lightly flour your hands and the work surface. Form the dough into a ball and divide it into 12 equal pieces; roll each piece into a small ball. Put each ball on a lightly floured surface, sprinkle with a little flour, and cover with plastic wrap or a towel. Let rest until they puff slightly, about 20 minutes.

3. Roll each ball less than ¼ inch thick, using flour to prevent sticking as necessary. As you work, spread the flat disks on a floured surface and keep them covered. When all the disks are rolled out, heat the oven to 350°F (the disks should rest for at least 20 minutes after rolling). If you have a pizza stone, use it on a rack set low in the oven; if not, lightly oil a baking sheet and put it in the oven on a rack set in the middle.

4. To bake on a stone, slide the individual disks—as many as will fit comfortably—directly into the oven, using a peel or a large spatula. Or bake 4 to 6 disks at a time on a baking sheet. For either method, bake the pita until lightly browned on the first side, then flip and brown on the other side. They should puff up a bit when they are ready. Total baking time will be between 5 and 10 minutes, generally only 5 to 6.

5. As the breads finish baking, remove them from the oven and brush them with a little extra oil if you like. These can be eaten right away or cooled, stored in wax paper or plastic bags, and gently reheated before using. (You can freeze them, too.)

Skillet Pita Pockets. Instead of preheating the oven, lightly oil and wipe out a heavy skillet and heat it over medium heat. Cook the pitas individually (or 2 at a time, depending on how big your skillet is) for 2 to 4 minutes on each side.

Olive Oil Breadsticks

Makes: 50 to 100 breadsticks   Time: 1 day or so, largely unattended

Made with mostly whole wheat flour, these breadsticks have an earthy flavor and crisp texture. And because you roll them out on the counter, they have a wonderfully rustic and authentic look—understandable, since they're rustic and authentic. For quick flavor boosters, try sprinkling the breadsticks just before baking with chopped fresh herbs, nuts or seeds, grated Parmesan, any dried spice blend, or sea salt.

These are best when fresh but keep quite well in a covered container (like a tin) for a week or so.

 2 teaspoons instant yeast

 1 teaspoon sugar

 2¼ cups whole wheat flour

 ¾ cup all-purpose flour, plus more for rolling the dough

 2 teaspoons salt

 2 tablespoons olive oil, plus more as needed

 ½ cup coarse cornmeal

1. Combine the yeast, sugar, flours, and salt in a food processor; pulse once or twice. Add the 2 tablespoons oil and pulse a couple more times. With the machine running, add 1 cup water through the feed tube. Continue to add water, 1 tablespoon at a time, until the mixture forms a ball. The dough should be a little shaggy and quite sticky.

2. Put a little oil in a bowl, transfer the dough ball to it, and turn to coat well. Cover with plastic wrap and let rise for 1 hour in a warm place. Re-shape the ball, put it back in the bowl, cover again, and let rise in the refrigerator for several hours, or preferably overnight.

3. When you're ready to bake, heat the oven to 400°F. Lightly grease 2 baking sheets with oil and sprinkle them very lightly with cornmeal. Cut the dough into 3 pieces; keep the other 2 covered while you work with the first. Use all-purpose flour to dust the work surface well and roll a piece of dough out as thinly as possible into a large rectangle, about a foot long. Use a sharp knife or pastry wheel to cut the dough into roughly 1¼-inch-thick

Ⓕ Fast   Ⓜ Make-Ahead   Ⓟ Pantry Staple

strips (slightly smaller is better than slightly bigger). Flour your hands and roll the strips a bit to make them round, transferring the finished breadsticks to the prepared pans as you work.

4. Brush the breadsticks with more oil. Bake until crisp and golden, 10 to 20 minutes. Cool completely on wire racks. Serve immediately or store in an airtight container for up to 1 week.

Black Rolls with Caraway

Makes: 12 sandwich rolls   Time: About 4 hours, largely unattended

These are mini versions of black bread, the classic Russian loaf made with unexpected ingredients. These deeply flavored rolls easily turn soup into a meal, and they also make a great ploughman's lunch with pickles, mustard, an apple, and a little sharp cheese. For an unorthodox twist, you can use stout (chocolate stout, which is not good for much else, is perfect here) in place of the coffee.

½ cup 100-percent bran cereal (not bran cereal flakes) or ground bran

2 cups all-purpose flour, plus more for dusting and kneading

1 cup rye flour

1 cup whole wheat flour

2 tablespoons cocoa powder

1 tablespoon instant yeast

2 teaspoons salt

1 tablespoon caraway seeds

¼ cup vegetable oil, plus more for greasing the bowl and pan

6 tablespoons molasses

2 tablespoons cider vinegar or lemon juice

1¼ cups strong black coffee

1. If you're using cereal, put it in a food processor and let it run for about 10 seconds, until it's finely ground; if you're using already ground bran, just put it in the food processor. Add the flours, cocoa, yeast, salt, and caraway seeds and pulse. Add the ¼ cup oil and molasses and pulse a few more times. With the machine running, pour the vinegar and most of the coffee through the feed tube. Process for about 30 seconds. The dough should be a barely sticky, easy-to-handle ball. If it's too dry, add coffee 1 tablespoon at a time and process for 5 to 10 seconds after each addition. If too wet, which is unlikely, add 1 to 2 tablespoons all-purpose flour and process briefly.

2. Use a little more oil to grease a large bowl. Shape the dough into a rough ball, put it in the bowl, and cover with plastic wrap or a damp towel. Let rise until nearly doubled in bulk, at least 2 hours. Deflate the dough and shape it once again into a ball; let it rest, covered, on a lightly floured surface for about 15 minutes. (You can make the dough ahead to this point, cover it well, and refrigerate for several hours or overnight; return it to room temperature before proceeding.)

3. Lightly dust your hands and the work surface with all-purpose flour (just enough to keep the dough from sticking). Knead the dough a few times, divide it into 12 equal pieces, and use your hands to roll each piece into a ball. Use the remaining oil to grease a baking sheet. Put the rolls on the sheet. Cover again and let rise until the dough has plumped up again considerably, about 1 hour.

4. Heat the oven to 325°F. Make a shallow slash in the top of each roll using a sharp knife or razor blade. Bake until the bottom of a roll sounds hollow when you tap it or the internal temperature reaches about 210°F, 35 to 40 minutes. Cool on a wire rack before serving.

Black Bread with Caraway. In Step 3, shape the dough into a large oval loaf or divide it in half and shape each half into a round loaf. A large loaf will need 55 to 60 minutes in the oven, while 2 smaller loaves will need 40 to 45 minutes.

Ⓕ Fast Ⓜ Make-Ahead Ⓟ Pantry Staple

Desserts and Sweet Snacks

Desserts are treats, but that doesn't mean you have to throw all of the Food Matters principles out of the window in order to indulge. On the other hand, most of us don't want constant offerings of super-"healthy" or vegan desserts. So what you have here is a meeting on middle ground: satisfying desserts made from real food, but completely different from their traditional counterparts in that fruits, whole grains, and nuts are the primary focus. To the extent that butter (and other dairy) and sugar are included, they're in supporting roles. (And all you chocolate lovers should find plenty here to make you happy.)

A word about some specific ingredients. I don't believe in forbidden or so-called evil foods. I use granulated and brown sugars, honey, and maple syrup because they're easy to find and perform reliably. (For more about sweeteners and potential substitutions, see page 554.) In some places, I suggest whole wheat pastry flour instead of whole wheat all-purpose flour because it makes more tender baked goodies. It's now available in most supermarkets and all natural food stores. If you bake a lot, buy it in bulk and freeze half of it so you always have it on hand.

The chapter starts out with cookies (and one candy), fast and universally loved. Next come cakes, crisps, and other pastries like turnovers. Puddings and custards, frozen desserts, and finally a bundle of especially fruity treats like soups—all easy to make and impressive to serve—round out the repertoire.

Chocolate Chunk Oatmeal Cookies

Makes: About 3 dozen   Time: About 30 minutes, plus time to cool

Almost, but not quite, classic. You can follow three distinct paths here: vegan, "regular," or somewhere in between. Any route you take will give you a rich-tasting, chewy, not-too-sweet treat. If you prefer a sweeter cookie, increase the brown sugar to ¾ cup.

> ½ cup vegetable oil, or 8 tablespoons (1 stick) unsalted butter, softened, or a combination
>
> ½ cup sugar
>
> ½ cup brown sugar
>
> ¼ cup applesauce, or 2 eggs
>
> ¾ cup whole wheat flour
>
> ¾ cup all-purpose flour
>
> 2 cups rolled oats
>
> ½ cup chopped walnuts or pecans
>
> Pinch of salt
>
> 2 teaspoons baking powder
>
> ½ cup almond milk, rice milk, oat milk, or cow's milk
>
> ½ teaspoon vanilla extract
>
> 4 ounces bittersweet chocolate, broken into small chunks

1. Heat the oven to 375°F. Use an electric mixer to cream the oil or butter and the sugars together; add the applesauce or eggs and beat until well blended.

2. Combine the flours, oats, nuts, salt, and baking powder in a bowl. Alternating with the milk, add the dry ingredients to the sugar mixture by hand, a little at a time, stirring to blend. Stir in the vanilla, then the chocolate chunks.

3. Put teaspoon-size mounds of dough about 3 inches apart on ungreased baking sheets. Bake until lightly browned, 10 to 12 minutes. Cool for about 2 minutes on the sheets, then use a spatula to transfer the cookies to a wire rack to finish cooling. Store in a tightly covered container at room temperature for no more than a day or 2.

Ⓕ Fast   Ⓜ Make-Ahead   Ⓟ Pantry Staple

Lemon-Almond Florentines

Makes: About 3 dozen · Time: About 40 minutes, plus time to cool

Many Florentine recipes call for coating the cookies in melted chocolate, which I think is overkill. I really prefer the touch of lemon.

>   Unsalted butter for greasing the pans
>
>   2 cups whole almonds
>
>   ½ cup powdered sugar
>
>   1 egg white
>
>   ¼ teaspoon salt
>
>   Grated zest and juice of 2 lemons

1. Heat the oven to 300°F. Grease 2 baking sheets with a generous smear of butter.

2. Grind the nuts in a food processor until they are just beginning to form a paste; this takes less than a minute. Transfer the nuts to a bowl and add the sugar, egg white, salt, and lemon zest. Stir, adding some lemon juice, a few drops at a time, until the mixture drops easily from a teaspoon. Save the leftover lemon juice.

3. Use the teaspoon to put dollops of the batter about 3 inches apart on the prepared sheets. Dip a fork in the reserved lemon juice and spread the batter into thin (about ⅛ inch) circles, roughly 1½ inches in diameter. Bake, rotating the pans once or twice, until firm, golden brown on top, and slightly darkened around the edges, 15 to 20 minutes. Let the cookies cool on the baking sheets, then transfer them to wire racks to let them become crisp. Store in a tightly covered container at room temperature for no more than a day or 2.

Orange-Hazelnut Florentines. Use hazelnuts instead of almonds, and orange zest and juice instead of lemon.

Tropical Oatstacks

Makes: 2 to 3 dozen   Time: About 30 minutes, plus time to cool

Different and amazingly good cookies that fall somewhere between banana bread and macaroons. The not-too-sweet oatstacks contain no sugar except for the natural sugars in the bananas, but if you have a real sweet tooth, you can roll the mounds of dough in sugar before you bake them. These are good vegan too: Just substitute vegetable oil for the butter.

> 4 tablespoons (½ stick) unsalted butter, melted, plus more for greasing the pans
>
> 3 large ripe bananas
>
> 1 teaspoon vanilla extract
>
> ⅔ cup rolled oats
>
> ½ cup chopped cashews or macadamia nuts
>
> 1 cup shredded, unsweetened coconut
>
> 1 teaspoon baking powder
>
> ¼ teaspoon salt

1. Heat the oven to 350°F. Grease 2 baking sheets with a little butter.

2. Put the bananas in a large bowl and mash them well with a fork or potato masher. Stir in the melted butter and vanilla. In a separate bowl, mix together the oats, nuts, shredded coconut, baking powder, and salt. Add the dry ingredients to the banana mixture and stir just until combined.

3. Drop tablespoon-size mounds of dough about 3 inches apart on the baking sheets. Bake, rotating the pans as necessary, until golden brown, 12 to 15 minutes. Cool for about 2 minutes on the sheets before using a spatula to transfer the cookies to a wire rack to finish cooling. Store in a tightly covered container at room temperature for no more than a day or 2.

    Ⓕ Fast Ⓜ Make-Ahead Ⓟ Pantry Staple

Walnut Biscotti

Makes: 2 to 3 dozen   Time: About 1¼ hours, partially unattended

Even without eggs and butter, these biscotti aren't too dry, and they maintain their pleasant texture for days. Serve with coffee—or make either of the variations and serve with tea.

    1⅓ cups walnut halves

    1 cup all-purpose flour, plus more for dusting

    1¼ cups whole wheat flour

    ⅔ cup brown sugar

    1 teaspoon baking powder

    ½ teaspoon baking soda

    ½ teaspoon cinnamon

    Pinch of salt

    ¼ cup honey

    Vegetable oil for greasing the pans

1. Heat the oven to 350°F. Put half the walnuts in a food processor and pulse until finely ground. Transfer to a large bowl and add the remaining walnuts along with the flours, sugar, baking powder, baking soda, cinnamon, and salt; mix well. Add the honey and ¾ cup water and mix until just incorporated, adding a little extra water if needed to bring the dough together.

2. Lightly grease 2 baking sheets with a little oil and dust them with flour; invert the sheets and tap them to remove excess flour. Divide the dough in half and shape each half into a 2-inch-wide log. Put each log on a baking sheet. Bake until the loaves are golden and beginning to crack on top, 30 to 40 minutes; cool the logs on the sheets for a few minutes. Lower the oven temperature to 250°F.

3. When the loaves are cool enough to handle, use a serrated knife to cut each on a diagonal into ½-inch-thick slices. Put the slices on the sheets, return them to the oven, and leave them there, turning once, until they dry out, 25 to 30 minutes. Cool completely on wire racks. Store in an airtight container for up to several days.

Almond-Lavender Biscotti. Much more subtle. Use almonds instead of walnuts and white sugar instead of brown. Substitute 1 tablespoon minced fresh lavender for the cinnamon.

Pistachio-Ginger Biscotti. Use pistachios instead of the walnuts, and 1 to 2 tablespoons chopped crystallized ginger in place of the cinnamon.

Refined Sugars and Other Sweeteners

Eat—or drink—too much sugar and you can wind up with serious health issues like obesity or diabetes. But I would never eliminate granulated white sugar from my diet. Instead I use it judiciously: in my morning coffee, once in a while on a bowl of oatmeal, and in desserts. However, I do advocate ditching anything that contains high-fructose corn syrup; you'll never miss it. Really.

The beauty of eating (and cooking) sanely is that you control how much sweetener goes into desserts and other dishes, and you'll be surprised how little it takes to do the trick, especially if you depend on fruits, nuts, and whole grains and flours.

Most of the recipes here use common sweeteners, like white and brown sugars, honey, maple syrup, and sometimes turbinado or "raw" sugar, which is delicious but doesn't always dissolve thoroughly in some desserts. It's getting easier to find less-refined options that were once considered esoteric, like agave or brown rice syrups, so feel free to experiment with them as you like.

Just be aware that your results might not be quite what you expected. Aside from white and brown sugar—only marginally less refined than ordinary granulated cane sugar—these sweeteners are not necessarily interchangeable and often add their own distinctive flavor. For example, honey is sweeter than sugar and behaves differently since it actually traps moisture when heated. This is the main reason why I simply use a little white sugar: It's predictable, familiar, and has a neutral taste that lets the other dessert ingredients shine through.

 Ⓕ Fast Ⓜ Make-Ahead Ⓟ Pantry Staple

Chocolate-Cherry Panini

Makes: 4 sandwiches   Time: 30 minutes

Based very loosely on a classic Turkish dessert, this delicious little gem is incredibly simple and easily varied. You can use thin slices of bread from a hearty sandwich loaf or choose something lighter, like a rustic French or Italian country bread. Fresh cherries are the best filling (the absolute best are fresh sour cherries), though frozen are acceptable (thaw and drain them first). You can also use ½ cup dried cherries.

4 tablespoons (½ stick) unsalted butter, softened

8 slices bread, preferably whole wheat

1 cup halved pitted dark or sour cherries (see the headnote)

4 ounces bittersweet chocolate, chopped

1. Heat the oven to 400°F. Butter 4 slices of the bread on one side with half the butter and lay them, butter side down, on a baking sheet. Spread the cherries evenly over the bread and sprinkle with the chopped chocolate. Close each sandwich with a second slice of bread and butter the top sides. Cover the sandwiches with a second baking sheet, weigh down the sheet with something heavy, like a cast-iron skillet or some cans of tomatoes, and let sit for 5 minutes.

2. Remove the weight and top baking sheet. Bake the sandwiches until the bottom of the bread is browned lightly, about 5 minutes, then turn and cook for 5 minutes on the other side. Cut each sandwich in half and serve warm.

Chocolate-Cherry Panino. Dessert—or breakfast—for one. Assemble one sandwich by filling 2 slices whole wheat bread with ¼ cup cherries and ½ ounce chopped chocolate. Put 2 teaspoons butter in a skillet set over medium heat. When the butter melts, put the sandwich in the skillet, cover it with a plate, and weigh down the plate as described above (or simply press down on it gently). Cook until the bottom of the bread is browned lightly, 2 to 3 minutes, lift the sandwich from the pan, add another teaspoon butter, let it melt, then return the sandwich and repeat on the other side. Eat immediately.

Cherry Truffles

Makes: 10 truffles   Time: About 30 minutes   **F** **M**

This fun spin on truffles combines no more than dried fruit, booze (or water), and a dusting of cocoa powder. They're nice and gooey without being too sweet and have enough chocolate to satisfy any craving. To vary the fruit, substitute something dry—like raisins or pineapple—for the cherries, and a fruit that's more moist and chewy—like dates or pears—for the figs; you need the contrast to help hold everything together. For the outside, roll some around in powdered sugar, shredded coconut, or finely chopped nuts. Before you know it, you'll have an assortment.

> 1 cup bourbon, brandy, cherry liqueur, or water
>
> 1½ cups dried cherries
>
> ½ cup dried figs or apricots
>
> ¼ cup cocoa powder

1. Put the liquor or water in a medium saucepan over high heat. When it's steaming but not boiling, stir in the cherries, turn off the heat, and cover. Let sit until soft, 10 to 15 minutes. Drain the cherries well, reserving the liquid.

2. Transfer the cherries to a food processor and add the figs. Pulse until the mixture is puréed and comes together, adding a few drops of the reserved liquid if necessary to keep the machine running. (You can prepare the recipe to this point and refrigerate for up to a day.)

3. Put the cocoa in a shallow bowl. Take about 1 tablespoon of the mixture and roll it into a ball with your hands, then roll it around in the cocoa. Put on wax or parchment paper. Repeat until you have used up all of the mixture. Serve immediately or store the truffles at room temperature in a tightly sealed container for up to a week.

Brownie Cake

Makes: About 8 servings   Time: 1½ hours, plus time to cool

Using puréed prunes instead of butter in baking recipes was a big trend during the low-fat-crazed 1990s. That's not exactly my style, but prunes are a great idea, especially when you build back in a little butter. The fruit makes the cake moist, dense, and fudgelike, and its taste is mysterious (and mild). I actually could have called this recipe triple-chocolate cake: The batter has melted chocolate, cocoa powder, and chocolate chunks.

> 4 tablespoons (½ stick) unsalted butter, softened, plus more for greasing the pan
>
> 1½ cups pitted prunes (dried plums)
>
> 1 cup whole wheat pastry flour
>
> ½ cup unsweetened cocoa powder
>
> ¼ cup sugar
>
> 2 teaspoons baking powder
>
> ½ teaspoon baking soda
>
> ¼ teaspoon salt
>
> 4 ounces bittersweet chocolate, chopped
>
> 2 eggs
>
> 1 teaspoon vanilla extract

1. Heat the oven to 350°F. Grease an 8- or 9-inch square or round baking pan with a little butter. Put the prunes and 2 cups water in a medium saucepan over medium-high heat. Bring to a boil, then reduce the heat so the mixture bubbles gently. Cover and cook, stirring once in a while, until the prunes are very soft, about 15 minutes. Meanwhile, combine the flour, cocoa, sugar, baking powder, baking soda, and salt in a large bowl.

2. When the prunes are ready, add half the chocolate to the fruit and stir off the heat until the chocolate has melted. Transfer the prune mixture to a food processor and purée. Add 4 tablespoons butter along with the eggs and vanilla and process until smooth and creamy. Add the prune mixture to the flour mixture and stir just to combine. Stir in the remaining chocolate.

3. Turn the batter into the prepared pan and bake until the middle is set, 35 to 45 minutes. Let the cake cool in the pan for 10 minutes, then invert onto a wire rack to cool for at least another hour before serving. Store at room temperature, covered with wax paper, for up to a day or 2; use plastic wrap and it will keep for an extra day or so.

Spicy Carrot Cake

Makes: About 8 servings　　Time: About 1 hour, plus time to cool　

Most carrot cake recipes call for raw carrots but this one treats them differently. First you cook the carrots with butter, brown sugar, and some sliced apples to intensify the flavors and create a tender crumb without too much butter. Once that's done, the batter comes together quickly.

You can grate the vegetables and fruit by hand, but if you have a food processor, you will minimize both the effort and cleanup.

  4 tablespoons (½ stick) unsalted butter, softened, plus more for greasing
    the pan

  12 ounces carrots (about 4 medium)

  1 tart apple (about 4 ounces), peeled, cored, and cut into chunks

  ½ cup brown sugar

  ½ cup sugar

  2 tablespoons vegetable oil

  2 eggs

  1 cup whole wheat pastry flour

  ½ cup all-purpose flour

  1½ teaspoons baking powder

  ¼ teaspoon salt

  1 teaspoon cinnamon

  ½ teaspoon nutmeg

  ½ teaspoon cloves

  ¼ cup milk

　　　Ⓕ Fast　Ⓜ Make-Ahead　Ⓟ Pantry Staple

1. Heat the oven to 350°F. Grease an 8- or 9-inch square or round baking pan with a little butter. Grate the carrots and apples in a food processor or by hand. Put 2 tablespoons of the butter in a large skillet over medium heat. When the butter is melted, add the carrots, apple, and brown sugar and cook, stirring, until soft, colored, and fairly dry, 5 to 10 minutes. Let the carrots and apples cool for a few minutes, then transfer them to a blender or food processor (no need to wash it out if you used it for grating) and purée.

2. Add the remaining 2 tablespoons butter, sugar, and oil to the food processor and pulse until combined. (Or from this point mix everything together in a large bowl.) With the machine running, add the eggs one at a time.

3. Combine the flours, baking powder, salt, cinnamon, nutmeg, and cloves in a separate bowl. Add about a third of the flour mixture to the carrot mixture. With the machine running, add about half the milk; add another third of the flour, followed by the rest of the milk, then finally the last of the flour. Process until the batter just evens out.

4. Turn the batter into the prepared pan. Bake until the middle is set (your fingers should leave only a small indentation when you gently press the cake), 45 to 50 minutes. Cool in the pan for at least an hour before serving. Store at room temperature, covered with wax paper, for up to a day or 2; use plastic wrap and it will keep for an extra day or so.

Apricot Polenta Cake

Makes: About 8 servings   Time: About 1 hour, plus time to cool

Cornmeal combines nicely with the orange juice here, and using it allows you to reduce both flour and eggs. The subtle flavor of olive oil is a nice surprise, as is the slight sponginess. For a larger cake, double the recipe and bake either two layers or use a 9 × 13-inch pan. And if you like, use dried cherries, currants, blueberries, or chopped dates instead of the apricots.

> ⅓ cup olive oil, plus more for greasing the pan
>
> ½ cup coarse cornmeal
>
> ¼ teaspoon salt
>
> ½ cup all-purpose flour
>
> 1½ teaspoons baking powder
>
> ½ cup sugar
>
> 2 eggs, separated
>
> 3 tablespoons orange juice
>
> 1 cup chopped dried apricots
>
> Powdered sugar, for dusting

1. Heat the oven to 350°F. Grease an 8- or 9-inch square or round baking pan with a little oil. Put the cornmeal and salt in a medium saucepan; slowly whisk in 1¼ cups water to make a lump-free slurry. Set the pot over medium-high heat and bring almost to a boil. Reduce the heat to low and bubble gently, whisking frequently, until thick, 10 to 15 minutes. Remove from the heat and let cool slightly.

2. Combine the flour and baking powder in a bowl. With an electric mixer (or a whisk) to beat ⅓ cup oil with the sugar until creamy; add the egg yolks and beat until thick, scraping down the sides of the mixing bowl as necessary (this will take 5 to 7 minutes). Mix in the polenta until smooth, then mix in the dry ingredients until smooth. Add the orange juice and apricots and stir until blended.

3. In a separate bowl, beat the egg whites until they form soft peaks. (When you remove the beaters or whisk, a soft peak should fold over onto itself.)

Ⓕ Fast   Ⓜ Make-Ahead   Ⓟ Pantry Staple

Stir them thoroughly but as gently as possible into the batter (the base batter is fairly thick and it's okay if the whites aren't fully incorporated).

4. Turn the batter into the prepared pan. Bake until a toothpick inserted in the center comes out clean, about 35 minutes. Let the cake cool in the pan. Invert it out onto a plate if you like and sprinkle with powdered sugar just before serving. Store at room temperature, covered with wax paper, for a day or 2; use plastic wrap and it will keep for an extra day or so. (Dust again with powdered sugar after storing.)

Some Food Matters Ideas for Frosting Lovers

I like a good buttercream as much as the next person (I think), but only on occasion. Most of the time, I turn to one of these alternatives for topping or serving with cake:

A single type of cooked fresh fruit (like peaches, mangoes, or berries), puréed if you like

Fresh or dried fruit soaked in wine, liquor, or a little honey mixed with water

A few drops of good booze, port, or liqueur

Ground nuts or shredded coconut (toasted, lightly sugared, and spiced nuts are excellent)

A sprinkle of brown sugar or a drizzle of honey while the cake is still warm

A dusting of powdered sugar or a dollop of whipped cream (classic but always good, especially spiked with a little citrus zest)

Fresh fruit salad or berries on the top or on the side

Fruitcake You Actually Want to Eat

Makes: 8 to 10 servings   Time: About 2 hours, largely unattended

I could never stand fruitcake, but then I realized what I really hated were those awful neon-colored candied fruits. Why not (I thought) use good dried fruit, bound together with just enough batter to make the loaf sliceable?

With this recipe, the rum or brandy is used for macerating the fruit rather than saturating the cake after baking. For a good balance, try a combination of sweet and sour fruits, taking into consideration different textures and colors. But don't get too fussy; use what you like and it'll be fine.

2 tablespoons unsalted butter, plus more for greasing

4 loosely packed cups mixed dried fruit (like cherries, citron, pineapple, apricots, raisins, dates, apples, etc.), chopped as needed

½ cup chopped crystallized ginger, optional (or use more fruit)

1 cup dark rum, brandy, or orange juice

1 tablespoon grated orange zest

1¼ cups whole wheat flour

¾ cup chopped nuts (any kind)

½ teaspoon baking soda

½ teaspoon cinnamon

Pinch of salt

Pinch of either allspice, nutmeg, or cloves

2 eggs

¼ cup molasses

1. Heat the oven to 300°F. Generously grease a 9 × 5-inch loaf pan with butter. Put the fruit, ginger if you're using it, rum, zest, and 1 cup water in a saucepan over medium-high heat. Bring to a boil, then remove the pan from the heat. Cover and let cool for 15 to 20 minutes.

2. Combine the flour, nuts, baking soda, cinnamon, salt, and spice in a small bowl. In a large bowl, beat the 2 tablespoons butter, eggs, and molasses together until the mixture is thick, 3 to 5 minutes.

Ⓕ Fast   Ⓜ Make-Ahead   Ⓟ Pantry Staple

3. Drain the fruit over a third bowl, pressing down on the fruit to capture as much liquid as possible. Stir the fruit into the egg mixture (save the fruit liquid for another use). Add the dry ingredients by hand, stirring just to combine; do not beat. Pour the batter into the prepared loaf pan, smooth the top, and put the pan on a baking sheet.

4. Bake until the sides of the cake pull away from the pan and a toothpick inserted in the center of the loaf comes out clean, 1 to 1¼ hours. Let the cake cool in the pan before inverting it onto a wire rack. Remove the pan, then turn the cake right side up. Slice and serve, or store at room temperature, wrapped in wax paper or foil for up to 2 weeks.

Mango (or Other Fruit) Crisp

Makes: 6 to 8 servings   Time: 40 minutes

Mangoes aren't always available, but when they are, this is a stunning (and stunningly easy) way to prepare them. (When they aren't, use peaches, apples, pears, or plums in this crisp.) The only tricky part is pitting the mango: Hold the fruit vertically on the cutting board, so that it couldn't stand up without your help. Then use a sharp knife to cut down right along the pit; repeat on the other side of the pit. Now peel and slice both pieces. Try to get as much flesh as you can off the pit and chop that too.

> 4 tablespoons (½ stick) unsalted butter, softened, plus more for greasing the pan
>
> 2 tablespoons vegetable oil
>
> 1 cup brown sugar
>
> ½ cup shredded, unsweetened coconut
>
> 1 tablespoon lemon or lime juice
>
> ½ teaspoon cinnamon, or to taste
>
> ½ cup whole wheat flour
>
> ½ cup rolled oats
>
> Pinch of salt
>
> 3 pounds mangoes, peeled, pitted, and chopped (see the headnote)

1. Heat the oven to 400°F. Grease an 8- or 9-inch square or round baking dish with a little butter. Cream the 4 tablespoons butter, oil, and brown sugar with an electric mixer or fork. Stir in the coconut, lemon juice, cinnamon, flour, oats, and salt until combined and crumbly. (You can make the topping ahead to this point, tightly wrap, and refrigerate for up to a day or freeze for up to several weeks; thaw before proceeding.)

2. Spread the mangoes in the bottom of the prepared dish and crumble on the topping. Bake until golden and just starting to brown, 25 to 35 minutes. Serve immediately, or at least while still warm.

(F) Fast   (M) Make-Ahead   (P) Pantry Staple

Pear Turnovers

Makes: 8 servings   Time: 45 minutes

These turnovers have a lot going for them. They're easy, juicy, and perfectly sweet, *and* you don't have to roll out any dough, because they're made with phyllo instead of the more traditional puff pastry. They're also portable; just wrap them in foil or wax paper or slip them into a container.

Some other fruits to try: apricots and cherries (which make a cheerful color combination), apples, or any mixture of stone fruit. (But berries are just too juicy to use here.)

> 8 ripe pears, peeled, cored, and roughly chopped
>
> ¼ to ⅓ cup sugar
>
> 1 tablespoon cornstarch
>
> 8 to 10 sheets (about 4 ounces) whole wheat phyllo dough, thawed
>
> 4 tablespoons (½ stick) unsalted butter, melted, plus more for greasing
>
> Powdered sugar, for dusting

1. Heat the oven to 350°F. Line a baking sheet with parchment paper. Combine the pears, ¼ cup sugar, and cornstarch in a large bowl. Taste and add another tablespoon or 2 sugar if you like.

2. Set the phyllo dough on your work surface and cover with a piece of plastic and a damp towel to keep it from drying out. Remove one sheet, put it in front of you, brush it with some butter, and fold it in half lengthwise. Put about one-eighth of the pear mixture at one end of the phyllo strip and fold it over to enclose the filling and make a triangle, like folding a flag. Next fold the strip the other way so that the open seam is enclosed; brush the top of the turnover with a little more butter. Keep folding the triangle back and forth until you reach the end of the sheet. Transfer the turnover to the prepared baking sheet and brush it with a little more melted butter. Repeat with the remaining phyllo sheets and pear mixture. You should have 8 turnovers. If there's any phyllo left over, save it for another use; you can even refreeze it.

3. Bake the turnovers until golden brown, 20 to 30 minutes. Serve warm or at room temperature, dusted with powdered sugar.

Lemon-Blueberry Crisp
with Pine Nut Topping

Makes: 6 to 8 servings   Time: 40 to 50 minutes

You can hardly go wrong with blueberries and lemon, the basis for this rich, summery, and fragrant dessert. The topping is special too: Ground pine nuts with butter and brown sugar deliver marzipan-like intensity, while whole pine nuts provide crunch. A tablespoonful of good ricotta or mascarpone cheese makes a lovely garnish (as, of course, does ice cream or whipped cream).

Sour cherries, raspberries, or other berries are all good alternatives to the blueberries.

    4 tablespoons (½ stick) unsalted butter, softened, plus more for greasing
        the pan

    4 to 6 cups fresh or frozen blueberries

    1 cup pine nuts

    ½ cup sugar

    ½ cup whole wheat flour

    ½ teaspoon nutmeg

    Pinch of salt

    Grated zest of 1 lemon

1. Heat the oven to 375°F. Grease an 8- or 9-inch square or round baking dish with a little butter. If you're using frozen berries, set them in a colander to thaw for a bit while you prepare the crust. Put ¾ cup of the pine nuts in a food processor along with the 4 tablespoons butter and sugar; let the machine run until the nuts are finely ground and the mixture is creamy and fluffy.

2. Transfer the mixture to a bowl and add the whole pine nuts, flour, nutmeg, and salt and stir with a fork until crumbly. (You can make the topping ahead to this point, tightly wrap, and refrigerate for up to a day or freeze for up to several weeks; thaw before proceeding.)

3. Spread the blueberries in the prepared baking dish and sprinkle the top with the lemon zest. Crumble the topping over all and press down gently.

Ⓕ Fast   Ⓜ Make-Ahead   Ⓟ Pantry Staple

Bake until the filling is bubbling and the crust is just starting to brown, 30 to 40 minutes. Serve immediately, or at least while still warm.

Coconut Tart with Chocolate Smear

Makes: 6 to 8 servings   Time: About 30 minutes, plus time to cool

If you like Mounds bars, you will like this tart, which is sort of an inside-out version in the form of a great big cookie. The chocolate filling is enriched with eggs and coconut milk, which makes it a little custardy and quite yummy. If you want to gild the lily, top the whole thing with a layer of fresh raspberries or cut-up strawberries.

> 2 cups shredded, unsweetened coconut
>
> ½ cup sugar
>
> 2 eggs, separated
>
> 1 teaspoon vanilla extract
>
> ¼ teaspoon salt
>
> 6 ounces bittersweet chocolate, roughly chopped
>
> 1 cup coconut milk (light is fine)

1. Heat the oven to 350°F. Combine the shredded coconut, sugar, egg whites, vanilla, and salt in a bowl. Press the mixture into the bottom and up the sides of a 9-inch tart pan. Bake until the tart shell is firm and lightly toasted, 10 to 15 minutes.

2. Meanwhile, combine the chocolate, egg yolks, and coconut milk in a saucepan over low heat. Cook, whisking almost constantly, until the chocolate is completely melted and steaming, but don't let the mixture boil and separate.

3. When the tart shell comes out of the oven, spread the chocolate mixture in it. Let the tart cool and become firm before cutting into wedges and serving. The tart will keep, covered and refrigerated, for a day or two.

Pistachio Tart with Chocolate Smear. Substitute 2 cups ground pistachios for the shredded coconut.

Cardamom-Scented Pear Crisp

Makes: 6 to 8 servings   Time: 40 to 50 minutes

Even imperfect, not-quite-ripe pears will become tender and richly flavored when baked in a crisp (apples, of course, are another good way to go). What makes this crisp especially lovely is cardamom, an assertive, warm spice, traditional in baking (especially in Sweden) with a wonderfully home-filling aroma.

4 tablespoons (½ stick) unsalted butter, plus more for greasing the pan

2 tablespoons vegetable oil

¾ cup brown sugar

½ cup chopped walnuts or pecans

1 tablespoon lemon juice

1 cup rolled oats

½ cup whole wheat flour

Pinch of salt

3 pounds pears, cored and sliced

1 teaspoon cardamom

1. Heat the oven to 400°F. Grease an 8- or 9-inch square or round baking dish with a little butter. Cream the 4 tablespoons butter, oil, and sugar together using an electric mixer or fork. Stir in the nuts, lemon juice, oats, flour, and salt until combined and crumbly. (You can make the topping ahead to this point; tightly wrap, and refrigerate for up to a day or freeze for up to several weeks; thaw before proceeding.)

2. Put the pears in the prepared dish, sprinkle with the cardamom, and toss. Crumble the topping over all. Bake until the filling is bubbly and the crust is just starting to brown, 30 to 40 minutes. Serve immediately, or at least while still warm.

Ⓕ Fast   Ⓜ Make-Ahead   Ⓟ Pantry Staple

Strawberry-Rhubarb Gratin "Brûlée"

Makes: 6 to 8 servings   Time: About 1 hour

This dessert is a cross between a gratin, a crisp, and a clafoutis, the French dessert of fruit baked in pancake-like batter. Here, I go for the fresh taste of fruit and whipped custard made with heavy cream, along with a lightly sweet and crunchy nut topping. As long as you have 1½ pounds fruit total, substitute whatever you like: Plums, peaches, sour cherries, or blueberries are particularly nice.

Unsalted butter for greasing the pan

2 eggs

½ cup sugar

Pinch of salt

½ cup cream

2 pints strawberries (about 1 pound), hulled and halved

8 ounces rhubarb, tough strings removed, sliced 1 inch thick

½ cup roughly chopped hazelnuts

1. Heat the oven to 350°F. Grease a medium gratin dish (about 9 × 5 × 2 inches) or an 8- or 9-inch square or round baking dish with butter.

2. Whisk the eggs in a large bowl until frothy. Add half the sugar and the salt and whisk until combined. Add the cream and whisk until smooth and slightly foamy.

3. Put the strawberries and rhubarb in the prepared dish and pour the custard over the fruit. Bake until the top of the gratin is golden brown and bubbly, 40 to 45 minutes. Remove it from the oven. Heat the broiler and move the rack about 4 inches from the fire. Sprinkle the top of the gratin with the hazelnuts and the remaining ¼ cup sugar. Broil until the sugar bubbles, only a minute or 2. Let cool for at least 5 minutes. Serve within a couple hours of making it.

Apple-Cranberry Brown Betty

Makes: 6 to 8 servings   Time: 45 minutes

A brown betty is a simple, old-fashioned dessert made with day-old bread, fruit, butter, and sugar. It's moist, sweet, and not as heavy as bread pudding (better, really, which makes it all the more surprising that it fell out of favor). And this version has an added twist: a hint of rosemary, one of the few herbs that complement sweet flavors as well as savory. If you can get your hands on lavender, that's another good choice.

3 cups cubed day-old bread, preferably whole wheat

3 cups peeled, cored, and sliced apples (3 to 4 medium-to-large apples)

2 cups fresh cranberries

Juice of ½ lemon

1 teaspoon chopped fresh rosemary, or ¼ teaspoon dried

4 tablespoons (½ stick) unsalted butter

½ cup apple juice

¼ cup brown sugar

¼ cup sugar

1. Heat the oven to 300°F. Spread the bread out on a baking sheet and bake, shaking the pan once or twice, until very lightly browned, about 10 minutes. Meanwhile, toss the apples and cranberries with the lemon juice and rosemary. Melt the butter with the apple juice in a small saucepan over low heat.

2. When the bread is done, turn the oven heat to 375°F. Toss the bread with the sugars and half the butter mixture. Spread 1 cup of the bread mixture in a medium gratin dish (about 9 × 5 × 2 inches) or an 8- or 9-inch square or round baking dish. Top with half the apple-cranberry mixture. Repeat and finish with a layer of bread. Drizzle the remaining butter mixture over all.

3. Bake until the liquid in the dish is bubbly and the top is nicely browned, at least 30 minutes. Serve hot or warm, or let sit at room temperature for up to several hours and then reheat at 300°F for about 15 minutes.

    (F) Fast (M) Make-Ahead (P) Pantry Staple

Coconut Flan

Makes: 4 servings   Time: About 30 minutes, plus at least 4 hours to chill

The classic caramel-sauced custard of Spain and Latin America is usually made with milk or cream and plenty of egg yolks. This version is creamy, rich, and sweet but dairy-free, thanks to coconut milk, tofu, and gelatin. For best results, use full-fat (not light) coconut milk. You can also add ½ cup shredded coconut to the custard, which will sacrifice the flan's smoothness but does add some chew and intensifies the flavor.

> ½ cup plus 2 tablespoons sugar
>
> One 14-ounce can coconut milk
>
> 1 tablespoon unflavored gelatin
>
> ½ cup soft silken tofu
>
> 1 tablespoon vanilla extract
>
> Pinch of salt

1. Put ½ cup sugar and ½ cup water in a small, heavy saucepan. Turn the heat to medium-low and cook, shaking the pan occasionally (it's best not to stir), until the sugar liquefies, turns clear, then turns golden brown, about 20 minutes. Immediately pour the caramel into the bottom of a medium glass bowl or gratin dish, or four 6-ounce ramekins.

2. Put the coconut milk in a medium saucepan and sprinkle the gelatin over it; let sit for 5 minutes. Turn the heat to low and cook, stirring, until the gelatin dissolves completely.

3. Put the tofu, vanilla, salt, and remaining 2 tablespoons sugar in a blender or food processor and purée. Add the coconut milk mixture and blend until smooth. Pour the custard into the prepared bowl or ramekins and transfer to the refrigerator.

4. Chill until set, at least 4 hours or up to 24 hours. Serve the flan from the bowl (with a big spoon for scooping out the caramel) or ramekins; or dip the bottom of the vessel(s) in hot water for about 10 seconds, run a thin knife all the way around the edge, then invert onto plates, scraping the sauce over all.

Coconut and Brown Rice Pudding

Makes: 4 servings   Time: About 2½ hours, largely unattended

To make a really luscious brown rice pudding you have to break the grains up a bit in the food processor so they'll release their thickening starches; it works. I use coconut milk here, but you can substitute cow's milk for some or all of the liquid. See the sidebar for some ideas about stir-ins and garnishes. If you want a thicker pudding, veer toward the high end of the rice quantities listed below.

⅓ to ½ cup long-grain brown rice

Two 14-ounce cans coconut milk

½ cup brown sugar

Pinch of salt

A cinnamon stick, a few cardamom pods, a split vanilla bean, a pinch of saffron, or other flavoring (see the sidebar), optional

1. Heat the oven to 300°F. Put the rice in a food processor and pulse a few times to break the grains up a bit and scratch their hulls; don't overdo it, or you'll pulverize them.

2. Put all the ingredients in a 2-quart ovenproof pot or Dutch oven. Stir a couple of times and put the pan in the oven, uncovered. Cook for 45 minutes, then stir. Cook for 45 minutes more, and stir again. At this point the milk will have darkened a bit and should be bubbling, and the rice will have begun to swell.

3. Cook for 30 minutes more. The milk will be even darker, and the pudding will start to look more like rice than milk. It's almost done. Return the mixture to the oven and check every 10 minutes, stirring gently each time you check.

4. It might (but probably won't) take as long as 30 minutes more for the pudding to be ready. Just trust your instincts and remove the pudding from the oven when it is still soupy; it will thicken a lot as it cools. (If you overcook the pudding, it will become fairly hard though still quite good to eat.) Remove the whole spices if you used them. Serve the pudding warm, at room temperature, or cold, alone or with your favorite topping.

Ⓕ Fast   Ⓜ Make-Ahead   Ⓟ Pantry Staple

How and When to Embellish Brown Rice Pudding

At the beginning you could add:

1 cup shredded, unsweetened coconut
1 teaspoon grated lemon or orange zest

About halfway through cooking add ¼ cup or more:

Raisins
Dried berries
Chopped dates
Fresh or dried chopped figs
Chopped mango or papaya
Sliced plums
Small chunks of pineapple

Just before serving, garnish with:

Toasted coconut
Chopped nuts
Grated chocolate
Chopped fresh mint or basil

Baked Pumpkin-Orange Custard

Take the crust off pumpkin pie—and make it even more pumpkiny—and you have an easy and beautiful fall dessert without all that white flour. The recipe calls for canned pumpkin; be sure to get the kind that isn't seasoned or sweetened. If you're feeling ambitious, cook pumpkin or other squash (or sweet potatoes for that matter) and purée them yourself, or use leftovers. For a really tasty garnish, sprinkle the top with chopped candied ginger and/or crushed gingersnaps. And if you like your desserts on the sweet side, increase the sugar to 1 cup.

 2 tablespoons unsalted butter, melted, plus more for greasing the pan

 2 eggs

 ¾ cup brown sugar

 12 ounces soft silken tofu

 3 cups (two 14-ounce cans) puréed pumpkin (see the headnote)

 ½ teaspoon cinnamon, or more to taste

 ¼ teaspoon nutmeg

 ¼ teaspoon allspice

 Grated zest and juice of 1 orange

 Pinch of salt

1. Heat the oven to 350°F. Grease an 8- or 9-inch square pan or pie plate with a little butter. Use an electric mixer or a whisk to beat the eggs and sugar in a large bowl until light. Add the tofu and beat until smooth, a minute or 2 longer.

2. Add the 2 tablespoons melted butter and remaining ingredients and beat until everything is thoroughly combined. Pour the mixture into the prepared pan and bake until set around the edges but still a little jiggly at the center, about 1 hour. Let cool completely before serving, or refrigerate for up to a day and serve cold.

Chocolate-Banana Pudding Parfaits

Makes: 4 to 6 servings   Time: 30 minutes, plus time to chill

Pudding without milk? Yes. The "secret" is silken tofu, which has a surprisingly non-beany flavor and smooth texture. To make either all chocolate or all banana pudding, omit one from the ingredient list and double the other.

½ cup sugar

1 pound soft silken tofu

4 ounces bittersweet or semisweet chocolate, melted

½ teaspoon vanilla extract

2 ripe bananas

⅛ teaspoon salt

1. Put the sugar and ½ cup water in a small saucepan; bring to a boil and cook until the sugar dissolves, stirring occasionally. Cool for at least 10 minutes.

2. Put half the sugar syrup, half the tofu, all of the chocolate, and the vanilla in a food processor or blender and purée until completely smooth. Transfer to a bowl and rinse out the machine.

3. Put the remaining sugar syrup, remaining ½ pound tofu, the bananas, and salt in the food processor or blender and purée until completely smooth.

4. Cover the bowls of pudding with plastic wrap and chill for at least 30 minutes or up to several hours. Before serving, stir each until smooth. Layer alternate spoonfuls of the puddings in tall glasses or champagne flutes.

Raspberry Cabernet Sorbet

Makes: At least 4 servings   Time: 10 minutes   F M

All you need is a food processor to make this supereasy frozen dessert. If you can find good fresh raspberries and freeze them yourself, so much the better. The small amount of alcohol in the mix makes the texture a little less icy than in a typical sorbet, and leaves you and your guests with nearly a full bottle of wine to polish off.

1 pound frozen raspberries

½ cup silken tofu, yogurt, or crème fraîche

3 to 4 tablespoons sugar

2 to 4 tablespoons cabernet or other full-bodied, flavorful red wine

1. Put the raspberries, tofu, sugar, and 2 tablespoons wine in a food processor. Process until just puréed and creamy, stopping to scrape down the sides of the bowl as needed and adding more wine 1 tablespoon at a time if the fruit does not break down completely. Be careful not to overprocess or the sorbet will liquefy.

2. Serve immediately or freeze for up to a day or two; if serving later, allow 10 to 15 minutes for the sorbet to soften at room temperature.

Minty Green Tea Granita

Makes: 4 servings   Time: About 2 hours, largely unattended

It's not too often you get a dessert that's both refreshing and invigorating, and it doesn't hurt that this requires only about 15 minutes of work, total (though it's spread over a couple of hours). Use good-quality green tea, since the complexity will benefit the overall flavor. For a different, even brighter twist, use about a tablespoon of sliced fresh ginger in place of the mint.

> 3 green tea bags, or 2 tablespoons loose green tea
>
> ¼ cup fresh mint
>
> ¼ cup honey, or more as needed
>
> Juice of 1 lemon

1. Bring 3 cups water almost to a boil. Add the tea and mint, cover, and turn off the heat. Let steep for 10 minutes, then strain to remove the solids. Stir in the honey and lemon juice. Taste and add more honey if necessary to make a nicely sweet blend.

2. Pour the mixture into a shallow glass or ceramic pan and freeze for at least 2 hours, stirring to break up the crystals every 30 minutes or so. It should be slushy and crunchy with ice crystals. If the granita becomes too hard, pulse it (do not purée) in a food processor before serving, or set it in the fridge for a bit and stir once in a while to bring back the desired texture.

Spiked Pink Grapefruit Granita

Makes: 4 servings   Time: At least 3 hours, largely unattended

You can serve this either as an icy apéritif or a dessert that doubles as a night-cap. Use whatever citrus or other juice that strikes your fancy (you might think Bloody Mary mix is fun, for example), but be careful adding the sugar syrup—some juices require almost no extra sugar. The alcohol in this granita ensures the texture remains icy-slushy and not too firm.

½ cup sugar

2½ cups grapefruit juice

½ cup vodka

Grated grapefruit zest to taste, optional

1. Combine the sugar with ½ cup water in a small saucepan. Bring to a boil and cook until the sugar dissolves, stirring occasionally. Remove from the heat and cool.

2. Combine the juice, vodka, and a pinch of the zest. Add some of the sugar syrup to sweeten the blend as you like (you probably will not need all of it; reserve the rest). Stir, taste, and add more zest or syrup as needed.

3. Pour the mixture into a shallow glass or ceramic pan and freeze for at least 3 hours, stirring to break up the crystals every 30 minutes or so. It should be slushy and crunchy with ice crystals. (You can make the granita up to a day or 2 ahead.) If the granita becomes too hard, pulse it (do not purée) in a food processor before serving, or set it in the fridge for a bit and stir once in a while to bring back the desired texture.

Chocolate Tofu Ice Cream

Makes: At least 4 servings   Time: 20 minutes, plus time to chill and freeze

If you think vegan ice cream is too extreme, stick to real ice cream, but be aware that silken tofu produces a surprisingly creamy and delicious alternative. Once the mixture is made, you have some options. If you don't have an ice cream machine, simply put the mixture in the freezer; four hours is ideal, but if you leave it in too long, just break it up a bit, and then whip it up in a food processor right before serving; or freeze it, then let it thaw a bit, and eat it like frozen pudding, without doing anything else. If you're looking for last-minute stir-ins, try chopped toasted walnuts or pistachios, or a handful of cherries or raspberries.

  ¾ cup sugar

  1 pound soft silken tofu

  8 ounces bittersweet chocolate, melted

  1 teaspoon vanilla extract

1. Combine the sugar with ¾ cup water in a small saucepan. Bring the mixture to a boil and cook, stirring occasionally, until the sugar dissolves. Let it cool a bit.

2. Put all of the ingredients (including the sugar syrup) in a blender and purée until it is completely smooth, stopping to scrape down the sides if necessary. Freeze in an ice cream machine according to the manufacturer's instructions. Or transfer the mixture to an airtight container and freeze until it is firm, at least 4 hours; then break into chunks and purée in the food processor. Or simply let thaw a bit and eat as soon as it's scoopable.

Almond Ice Milk

Makes: At least 4 servings   Time: 20 minutes, plus time to chill and freeze

You don't need an ice cream machine to enjoy this icy combination of dairy and nondairy milks with big almond flavor and crunch. If you want a more luxurious texture, use a little cream in place of some of the cow's milk. Other potential additions: chopped dark chocolate, raisins, chopped dried apricots or dates, toasted coconut, crumbled cookies, crystallized ginger—you get the idea.

2 cups almond milk

1 cup whole milk

2 tablespoons cornstarch

¾ cup sugar

½ cup chopped almonds

1. Put the almond milk and cow's milk in a saucepan over medium-high heat and bring just to a boil, stirring. Meanwhile, mix the cornstarch with 2 tablespoons or so cold water to make a slurry.

2. Whisk the slurry and sugar into the milk mixture. Lower the heat so the mixture doesn't quite boil and cook, stirring constantly, until thick. The mixture is ready when it coats the back of a spoon and a line drawn with your finger on the back of the spoon remains intact, 10 to 15 minutes. Strain the mixture if you think there might be any lumps of cornstarch.

3. Cool, then stir in the almonds. Freeze in an ice cream machine according to the manufacturer's directions. Or transfer the mixture to an airtight container and freeze until it is firm, at least 4 hours; then break into chunks and purée in the food processor. Or let thaw a bit and eat as soon as it's scoopable.

Hazelnut Ice Milk. Use hazelnut milk and chopped hazelnuts instead of almond milk and chopped almonds.

       F Fast   M Make-Ahead   P Pantry Staple

Apple Fritters

Makes: 4 servings   Time: 30 minutes

These are close enough to apple fritters to use the name, but since they're more like apple pancakes, you don't need to deep-fry. Leave out the yogurt and serve with Hazelnut Ice Milk (page 580) for a really terrific combo.

5 apples, peeled, cored, and grated (about 3 packed cups)

1 egg, lightly beaten

2 tablespoons sugar

1 teaspoon cinnamon

Pinch of salt

¼ cup whole wheat flour

Vegetable oil, for frying

Plain yogurt, for serving, optional

1. Heat the oven to 275°F. Squeeze the apples dry with your hands or a towel and put them in a large bowl. Add the egg, sugar, cinnamon, salt, and flour; mix well. (You can prepare the batter ahead of time to this point and refrigerate for up to a couple of hours before cooking.)

2. Put about ¼ inch oil in a large skillet over medium-high heat. When it's hot, drop spoonfuls of the apple mixture in the oil and spread them out a bit. Work in batches to prevent overcrowding. Cook, turning once, until golden on both sides and cooked through, about 5 minutes. Drain the finished fritters on paper towels and transfer them to the warm oven until all are finished. Serve hot or at room temperature with yogurt if you like.

Baked Apricots with Phyllo Topping

Makes: **4 servings**   Time: About 1 hour, largely unattended

Here's an impressive but simple dessert based on a classic Turkish dish called *tel kadayif*. If you can't serve it warm from the oven, make it up to a few hours ahead and gently reheat it. Topping the apricots with a little scoop of vanilla ice cream or dollop of whipped cream isn't necessary but sure doesn't hurt.

2 tablespoons unsalted butter, melted, plus more for greasing the pan

12 apricots, halved and pitted

Juice of 1 lemon

8 sheets phyllo dough, whole wheat, preferably

¼ cup brown sugar

½ cup chopped pistachios

¼ cup whole wheat flour

Pinch of salt

1. Heat the oven to 375°F. Grease an 8- or 9-inch square or round baking dish with a little butter. Put the apricots cut side up in the dish and drizzle with the lemon juice.

2. Shred the phyllo by hand or by pulsing it in a food processor. Toss it with the 2 tablespoons butter, sugar, pistachios, flour, and salt. The mixture is supposed to be crumbly and not hold together like a dough.

3. Scatter the topping over the apricots. Bake until the apricots are soft and the topping is golden brown, 20 to 30 minutes. Serve warm from the oven if you can.

Ⓕ Fast   Ⓜ Make-Ahead   Ⓟ Pantry Staple

Grilled (or Broiled) Peaches with Maple-Brandy Cream

Makes: 4 servings   Time: 20 minutes or less

Stone fruit is lovely when grilled or broiled just long enough to deepen its color and flavor and is even better paired with spiked, lightly sweetened whipped cream. Use your judgment about adding brown sugar to the peaches; perfectly juicy peaches probably won't need it, but less-than-ripe peaches might. To make this a little fancier, top with julienned mint leaves and/or toasted slivered almonds.

> 4 peaches, halved and pitted
>
> 2 tablespoons unsalted butter, melted
>
> 2 tablespoons brown sugar, optional
>
> ¾ cup cream
>
> 3 tablespoons maple syrup
>
> 2 tablespoons brandy

1. Prepare a grill or turn on the broiler; the heat should be medium-high and the rack about 4 inches from the fire. Brush the peaches on both sides with the butter. Starting with the cut side facing the fire, grill or broil until as softened and marked as you like, anywhere from 3 to 5 minutes. Turn, sprinkle with brown sugar if you like, and grill the skin side the same way.

2. When the peaches are done, beat the cream in a glass or metal bowl until it's doubled in volume and medium peaks form. (When you remove the beaters or whisk, a solid but soft peak will fold over but not onto itself.) Beat in the maple syrup and brandy. Serve the peaches hot or warm, topped with the whipped cream.

Grilled Peaches with Grappa Mascarpone. Omit the maple syrup. Use softened mascarpone cheese in place of the heavy cream (it will not double in volume, but it's quite rich, so you won't need much) and grappa in place of the brandy.

Frozen Chocolate Bananas

Makes: 4 servings   Time: 20 minutes

Your first instinct might be to make these for kids, but adults love them too. Bananas—especially slightly overripe ones—freeze into hard but creamy sticks with the texture of Creamsicles. If you're serving a crowd, make several chocolate bananas and several chocolate pineapples (see the variation) and set out assorted nuts, coconut, and crushed cookies so that your guests can dress their own.

> 4 ripe (but not brown) bananas, bottoms trimmed, but unpeeled
>
> 6 ounces bittersweet chocolate, chopped
>
> ¼ cup cream
>
> ½ cup chopped peanuts or cashews, optional

1. Impale each banana lengthwise with a wooden skewer; freeze for at least 15 minutes or wrap tightly in plastic or foil and freeze for up to a week.

2. Melt the chocolate in a double boiler, a small saucepan over very low heat, or the microwave. Whisk in the cream and transfer the chocolate mixture to a shallow bowl. If you're using nuts, put them on a plate next to the melted chocolate.

3. Peel the bananas, dip them first in the chocolate, then in the nuts. Eat immediately or put them in a wax-paper-lined airtight container and freeze them for up to a day or so.

Frozen Chocolate Pineapple. Shredded, unsweetened coconut is a nice topping here. Instead of the bananas, trim, peel, and core a small pineapple, then cut it lengthwise into 8 spears. Proceed with the recipe from Step 1.

Ⓕ Fast   Ⓜ Make-Ahead   Ⓟ Pantry Staple

Honey-Melon Soup

Makes: 4 servings   Time: About 1 hour, largely unattended

When the weather is too hot to bake but you want dessert, this soup is one terrific way to go. Though the mixture keeps in the refrigerator for a couple of days, it's best within a couple of hours of making it. And since everything comes together so quickly, it's never much of a hassle to prepare right before dinner, which leaves it plenty of time to cool before you're ready to eat.

¼ cup honey

1 sprig fresh rosemary or lavender

1 cantaloupe or honeydew melon, about 2 pounds, flesh seeded, removed
    from the rind, and cut into large chunks

Grated zest and juice of 1 lemon or lime

¼ cup rum, optional

1. Combine the honey and herb with ½ cup water in a small pot; bring to a boil and cook until the honey dissolves, stirring occasionally. Turn off the heat and let steep for about 10 minutes. Discard the herb and let the syrup cool to room temperature. (You can make the syrup a few days ahead of time and store it in the refrigerator.)

2. Put the melon in a blender; add the lemon or lime zest and juice, the rum if you're using it, and the honey syrup. Purée until liquefied. Pour through a fine-mesh strainer set over a large bowl; press down on the pulp to squeeze as much juice out as you can. Chill the soup for at least 30 minutes before serving.

PART IV: RECIPE LISTS, SOURCES, AND INDEX

WHERE TO FIND: FAST RECIPES

WHERE TO FIND: MAKE-AHEAD RECIPES

WHERE TO FIND: RECIPES FOR PANTRY STAPLES

Common Measurements

VOLUME TO VOLUME

3 teaspoons = 1 tablespoon
4 tablespoons = ¼ cup
5⅓ tablespoons = ⅓ cup
4 ounces = ½ cup
8 ounces = 1 cup
1 cup = ½ pint

VOLUME TO WEIGHT

¼ cup liquid or fat = 2 ounces
½ cup liquid or fat = 4 ounces
1 cup liquid or fat = 8 ounces
2 cups liquid or fat = 1 pound
1 cup sugar = 7 ounces
1 cup flour = 5 ounces

Metric Equivalencies

LIQUID AND DRY MEASURES

CUSTOMARY	METRIC
¼ teaspoon	1.25 milliliters
½ teaspoon	2.5 milliliters
1 teaspoon	5 milliliters
1 tablespoon	15 milliliters
1 fluid ounce	30 milliliters
¼ cup	60 milliliters
⅓ cup	80 milliliters
½ cup	120 milliliters
1 cup	240 milliliters
1 pint (2 cups)	480 milliliters
1 quart (4 cups)	960 milliliters (0.96 liters)
1 gallon (4 quarts)	3.84 liters
1 ounce (by weight)	28 grams
¼ pound (4 ounces)	114 grams
1 pound (16 ounces)	454 grams
2.2 pounds	1 kilogram (1,000 grams)

OVEN TEMPERATURES

DESCRIPTION	°FAHRENHEIT	°CELSIUS
Cool	200	90
Very slow	250	120
Slow	300–325	150–160
Moderately slow	325–350	160–180
Moderate	350–375	180–190
Moderately hot	375–400	190–200
Hot	400–450	200–230
Very hot	450–500	230–260

SOURCES: BOOKS, JOURNALS, MAGAZINES, ONLINE RESOURCES, AND DATABASES

Barilla Center for Food and Nutrition. *Climate Change, Agriculture, and Food*, 2009. http://www.barillacfn.com/uploads/file/62/1244800029_ClimateChangeEN_BarillaCFN_0609.pdf.

Block, Gladys. "Foods Contributing to Energy Intake in the US: Data from NHANES III and NHANES 1999–2000." *Journal of Food Composition and Analysis*, 17 (2004): 439–447.

Burros, Marian. "Obamas to Plant Vegetable Garden at White House." *The New York Times*, March 19, 2009. http://www.nytimes.com/2009/03/20/dining/20garden.html.

Cascio, Jamais. "The Cheeseburger Footprint." *Open the Future*. http://openthefuture.com/cheeseburger_CF.html.

Centers for Disease Control and Prevention. "Chronic Disease Prevention and Health Promotion." http://www.cdc.gov/nccdphp/press/#3.

Compassion in World Farming. *Global Warming: Climate Change and Farm Animal Welfare*, 2008. http://www.ciwf.org.uk/includes/documents/cm_docs/2008/g/global_warning_summary.pdf.

Environmental Working Group. "Shopper's Guide to Pesticides." http://www.foodnews.org/fulllist.php.

FAOSTAT. Food and Agriculture Organization of the United Nations (FAO). Animal production online database FAOSTAT, 2006. http://faostat.fao.org/default.aspx.

Goodland, Robert, and Jeff Anhang. "Livestock and Climate Change." *World Watch*, November/December, 2009. http://www.worldwatch.org/files/pdf/Livestock%20and%20Climate%20Change.pdf.

Huffman, Mark. "Organic Milk: Are You Getting What You Pay For?" ConsumerAffairs.com, May 13, 2008. http://www.consumeraffairs.com/news04/2008/05/organic_milk.html.

Humane Society of the United States. *An HSUS Report: The Welfare of Animals in the Meat, Egg, and Dairy Industries*, 2006. http://www.hsus.org/web-files/PDF/farm/welfare_overview.pdf.

McDonald's website. http://www.aboutmcdonalds.com/mcd/our_company.html and http://www.aboutmcdonalds.com/mcd/select_your_country_market.html.

National Gardening Association. *The Impact of Home and Community Gardening in America*, 2009. http://www.gardenresearch.com/files/2009-Impact-of-Gardening-in-America-White-Paper.pdf.

Pimentel, David, and Marcia Pimentel. *Food, Energy, and Society: Third Edition*. Florida: CRC Press, 2008.

Pimentel, David, and Marcia Pimentel. "Sustainability of Meat-based and Plant-based Diets and the Environment." *American Journal of Clinical Nutrition*, 78 (2003): 660S-663S. http://www.ajcn.org/cgi/content/full/78/3/660S?ck=nck.

ProCon.org. "Is drinking non-homogenized milk healthier than drinking homogenized milk?" http://milk.procon.org/viewanswers.asp?questionID=808.

Steinfeld, Henning, et al. *Livestock's Long Shadow: Environmental Issues and Options*. FAO, Rome, 2006. http://www.fao.org/docrep/010/a0701e/a0701e00.htm.

United States Department of Labor Occupational Safety & Health Administration. *Safety and Health Guide for the Meatpacking Industry*, 1988. http://www.osha.gov/Publications/OSHA3108/osha3108.html.

USDA Agricultural Research Service, Nutrient Data Laboratory. http://www.nal.usda.gov/fnic/foodcomp/search/.

USDA Economic Research Service. http://www.ers.usda.gov/Data/FoodConsumption/.

USDA Food Safety and Inspection Service. "Meat and Poultry Labeling Terms." http://www.fsis.usda.gov/FactSheets/Meat_&_Poultry_Labeling_Terms/index.asp.

Weise, Elizabeth. "'Natural' Chickens Take Flight." *USA Today*, January 23, 2006. http://www.usatoday.com/news/health/2006-01-23-natural-chickens_x.htm.

ACKNOWLEDGMENTS

The Food Matters Cookbook was probably the most challenging of my books to put together, and the one that relies least on classic recipes; we are trying to create a new American style of cooking, and to change the way most Americans eat in the process—no small task. That the book exists is thanks in large part to the incredibly hard work of a band of true believers—Suzanne Lenzer, Laura Anderson, and Daniel Meyer—led by my colleague and friend Kerri Conan. Kerri inspired both by example and a near-religious fervor, and the results are in your hands.

There have been significant efforts by others as well: Sydny Miner was the book's editor in its earlier stages; when she moved on, my friend Beth Wareham gave the manuscript a boost, and then Priscilla Painton took over; all of them (and us) were capably aided by Michelle Rorke. (Similarly, David Rosenthal was the publisher, and his departure brought the arrival of Jonathan Karp.) Simon and Schuster's design, marketing, and sales departments have all been fabulous, and as you read this I'm probably on the phone with the wonderful publicist Alexis Welby. (Her erstwhile assistant, Jessica Alba, has moved on, happily for her and sadly for Alexis and me.) It should be noted that the book's design and cover were based on work originally done by Kelly Doe.

Once again I'd like to mention Sid Baker, my doctor, mentor, and friend, who started all of this, at least from a personal perspective. And, gratitude to my heroes in this field, chief among them Marion Nestle and Michael Pollan, both of whom I'm glad to count among my friends.

Thanks, too, to David, Pamela, Shari and Harry, Chuck, Drs. Ringwald and Tsalbins, Mitch, MAR, Fred, Chris, Trish, Rick, Scott, Sam, Pete, and other friends, relatives, and co-workers. Special ultra-uber-thanks to Angela, Doc, my fabulous wife, Kelly, and my incredible women-children, Kate and Emma.

Mark Bittman
July 2010
New York

roasted:
    and Meat Sauce, Pasta with, 252–53
    and Scallions with Miso Rice, 292
    Vegetables au Vin with Coq, 466–67
escarole, 144
    Braised, Shells with White Beans, Sausage and, 253–54
    Braised White Bean Fritters and Vegetables, 373
    Pasta and Beans with, 114
    Pork Braised with, in Caramel Sauce, 455
    Rice Casserole with Little Meatballs and, 335–36
    Smashed Potato Salad with, 157
    with Hard-Boiled Eggs, 157
    with Parmesan and Frizzled Meat, 157
Ethiopian-Style Braised Chickpea Fritters and Vegetables, 372–73

fajitas, not your usual:
    Chicken, 481
    Steak, 480–81
FAP: Fig, Arugula, and Prosciutto Sandwiches, 498
farro, 270
    Batch of, 271–72
    Baked, Without Measuring, 272
    Softer, 273
    terrific additions to, 272
    with Grapes and Rosemary, 309–10
    and Sausage or White Beans, 310
    Tomato Soup with Seafood, Tuscan, 103
fats, 29
fava bean(s), 19, 349
    Asparagus, and Lemon Salad, 175
    fresh, preparing, 386
    Fresh (or Frozen), Pot of, 351
    adding flavor to, 352
    Gratin with Scallops and Pesto Bread Crumbs, 386–87
    Mashed, with Warm Tomatoes and Feta, 376–77
    Succotash Salad, 171
fennel, 18
    bouillabaisse with:
        over Grits, 317–18
        over Rice, 318
    and Goat Cheese Skillet Pizza, 514
    and Orange Salad with Green Olive Tapenade, 151
    Pasta with Caramelized Onion and, 200–201
    Creamy, 200
    with Sausage, 201
    Pasta with Chicken and, Risotto Style, 246–47
    Stir-Fried Pink Grapefruit and, with Shrimp, 449
    Tomato and Bread Soup with Fish and, 105–6
feta (cheese):
    Bread Crumbs, Asparagus Gratin with, 483
    Cheesy Roasted Red Pepper and Walnut "Pesto," 50
    Drizzle, Greek "Nachos" with, 75
    Mashed Favas with Warm Tomatoes and, 376–77
    Quick-Pickled Watermelon with, 58
    Savory Tomato Crisp, 423
    Watermelon and Tomato Gazpacho with, 106
fideos, 229
fig(s):
    Baked Rigatoni with Brussels Sprouts, Blue Cheese and, 221
    Chicken Salad, 178
    "Crostini," 56
    dried, in Cherry Truffles, 556
    FAP: Fig, Arugula, and Prosciutto Sandwiches, 498
fish, 20, 21–22, 27
    Broiled, Miso Soup with Bok Choy, Soba and, 127–28
    Charred Stuffed Poblanos with, 435
    Crunchy, Pan-Cooked Vegetables with, 440–41
    CSS: Cucumber, Sprouts, and Smoked Fish Sandwiches, 498–99
    Grilled or Broiled, Mexican-Style Fruit Salad with, 439
    Kebabs over Warm Olive Tabbouleh, 314–15
    Loaf, Burgers, and Balls, 334
    Nuggets Braised in Rhubarb Sauce, 454–55
    Pan-Fried Celery Root and, with Mustard Seeds, 450–51
    Seared Watermelon and, with Wasabi Drizzle, 452–53
    Sesame, Pan-Cooked Grated Vegetables with, 441
    smoked:
        Peruvian-Style *Causa* Filled with Herbs and, 444–45
        Wild Rice Salad with Smoked Anything, 170
    Spinach-Tofu-, Burgers, 430–31
    Stock, Quick, 136
    substituting, 23
    Tacos with Wilted Cabbage, 510–11
    Tomato and Bread Soup with Fennel and, 105–6
    White, Steamed Lima Beans with, 382
    Whole Small, Steamed Lima Beans with, 382
    see also anchovy(ies); mackerel; salmon; sardines; seafood; tuna
flageolet beans, 401
Flan, Coconut, 571
Flapjacks, Coconut, 285
flatbreads:
    with Beans and Sausage or Ham, 518
    chapatis:
        Grilled, 523
        Mostly Whole Wheat, 523
        Whole Wheat, 522–23
    Lentil (or Other Bean), 517–18
    slicing, 499
    with Vegetables, 516–17
    Whole Grain, Easy, 512–13
    additional ingredients for, 513
    as base for Easy Skillet Pizza, 514